Focus on the Past
One Volume Edition

FOCUS ON THE PAST

One Volume Edition

Gerard Brockie
and
Raymond Walsh

Gill & Macmillan

Published in Ireland by
Gill & Macmillan Ltd
Goldenbridge
Dublin 8
with associated companies throughout the world

Design and print origination: O'K Graphic Design, Dublin
Illustrations: Joanne Hugo
Additional maps: Denis Baker
Printed in Ireland by ColourBooks Ltd, Dublin

0 7171 2207 7

Contents

Political Developments in Ireland in the Twentieth Century

Ireland and the USA—Social Change in the Twentieth Century

Acknowledgments

The reconstruction of Glendalough (Ch. 12) and the illustrations of crowds cheering the Solemn League and Covenant (Ch. 66) and of riots in Belfast (Ch. 73) are by Stephen Conlin and are reproduced with his kind permission

The painting of the scene 'GPO—1916' is by Thomas Ryan RHA and is reproduced with his kind permission

For permission to reproduce colour transparencies and photographs, grateful acknowledgment is made to the following:

Agence Giraudon; Ancient Art and Architecture Collection; J. Allan Cash; Ann Ronan Picture Library; Archiv für Kunst und Geschichte; Barnaby's Picture Library; Alan Betson; Bettmann Archive; Bord Fáilte; Bridgeman Art Library; Camera Press; Department of the Environment for Northern Ireland—Historic Monuments and Buildings Branch; Don Sutton Photo Library; George A. Duncan; E.T. Archive; Dr Garret FitzGerald; Gamma; Hulton Picture Company; Kobal Collection; Lensmen; Mansell Collection; Mary Evans Picture Library; George Morrison; National Gallery of Ireland; National Library of Ireland; National Museum; National Portrait Gallery, London; Noel Mitchell; Novosti; Brian O'Halloran; Office of Public Works; Pacemaker; Peter Newark's American Pictures; Photographie Bulloz; Popperfoto; Public Record Office, Belfast; Rod Tuach; RTE/Cashman Collection; RTE; Michael Scully; Topham Picture Library; Trinity College, Dublin; Ulster Museum.

Learning about the Past

1. Into the Past

2. Evidence from the Past

3. Digging up the Past

Into the Past

Looking back

We all remember events and experiences from our past. Most of us recall special, happy occasions such as our first day at school, an enjoyable holiday or an exciting Christmas. Sometimes our memories of the past are sad and may include events such as an accident or a death in the family.

In addition to looking back at events which took place in our own lives, we may also remember important happenings in our local area, our country or in distant places around the world.

Today's Complete Stocks 5 Star Final LATE SPORTS

10¢ Honolulu Star-Bulletin KGMB-TV

KENNEDY KILLED; EX-TURNCOAT HELD

Sniper's Bullet Fells President

The assassination of President John F. Kennedy on 22 November 1963 made newspaper headlines all over the world.

If your parents were asked to draw up lists of important events, they would have much more to tell. Most of them would probably have included the murder of President John F. Kennedy in November 1963 and the first moon landing in July 1969.

Your grandparents could look back much further into the past. They could probably remember the day when World War II began in September 1939 and the dropping of the first atomic bomb on Hiroshima, Japan, in August 1945.

When we look back into the past in this way, we study history. History not only shows us what life was like when our parents and grandparents were growing up; it also tells us how people lived hundreds of years ago.

One of the most exciting events in the history of mankind: man walks on the surface of the moon for the first time.

The burned out ruins of Hiroshima after the dropping of the Atomic bomb on 6 August 1945.

History is about time past

We use the term the past when talking about events that happened yesterday as well as about something which took place as long ago as the Battle of Clontarf (1014).

When studying the past, it is important to be able to tell when events happened and whether one event came before or after another. To do this properly we need to measure time. The main unit of time is the year. For example, we tell how old we are by the number of years which have passed since we were born.

Let us now take a closer look at why the past is so important in all our lives.

Test your knowledge

1 What do we do when we study history?

2 What is a century?

3 In what centuries after the birth of Christ are the following dates: 550, 830, 1850?

4 Explain the letters BC and AD.

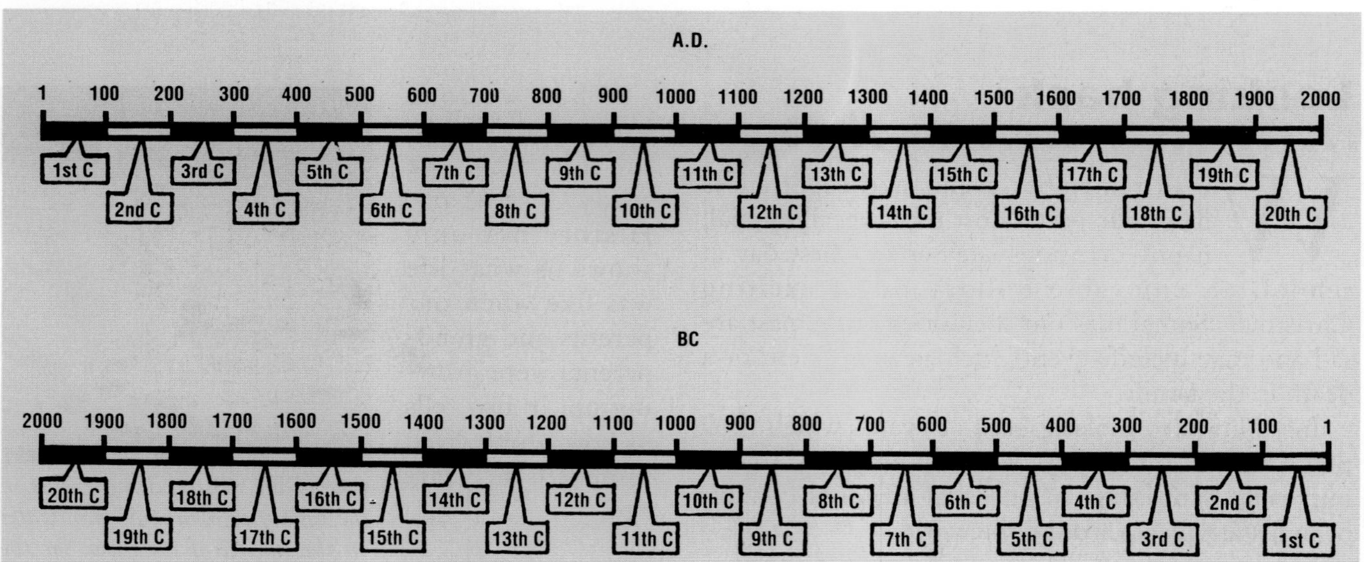

The period of time most often used in studying history is the century—a period of a hundred years.

We are now approaching the end of the twentieth century which covers the years 1901–2000.

We record all events in history from the birth of Jesus Christ. The years before the birth of Christ are followed by the letters BC (before Christ). The years after the birth of Christ use the letters AD (*Anno Domini*—the Year of Our Lord).

Study the time chart to see how this works. You will see that the year 90 AD is in the first century, the year 190 AD is in the second century and the year 1990 AD is in the twentieth century.

The time chart shows that history stretches into the past to include recent events which we ourselves can recall, as well as happenings that date back hundreds or even thousands of years.

Learning from the past

History is part of all our lives. Signs of the past are everywhere. In each local area there are fields, houses, churches, streets, monuments and ruins which remind us of how people lived in earlier times. History, of course, does not only help us to understand our own local area. It also helps us to learn about the wider world in which we live.

Fast-moving cars and aeroplanes, television and videos, big factories and sprawling cities, computers and space travel are all part of today's world. These did not suddenly appear, of course, but were developed over many years. When we study the past we learn how these things came about.

History can also help us to understand many of the problems which trouble us today. Wars throughout the world, starvation in the Third World and violence in Northern Ireland can all be tracked back to the past.

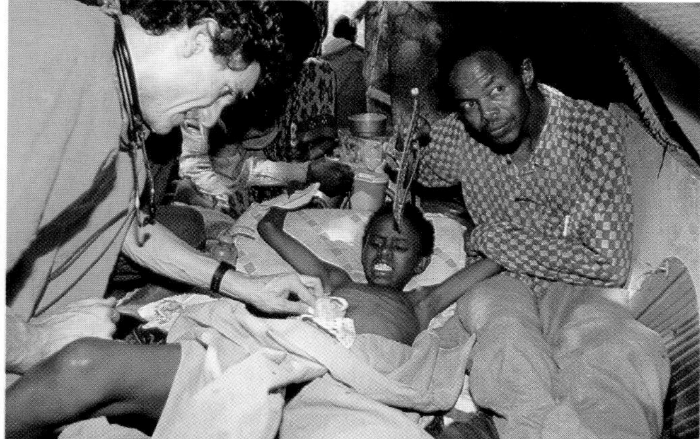

A victim of famine and war in Africa.

The reasons for violence in Northern Ireland today, as seen here, can be traced back to the past.

We often think that history is only about great people and events. But it is important to remember that history also concerns the lives and times of ordinary people. In this book you will learn about great leaders and world events. But you will also read about how ordinary men, women and children have lived, worked and enjoyed themselves.

Above all, looking into the past is exciting and enjoyable. No matter what your interests are, history touches them in some way.

Whether you are a sports enthusiast, a music fan, a follower of fashion or interested in politics and government, knowing about your hobby's past deepens your knowledge and understanding of it.

When we look back into the past we cannot enter a time tunnel, travelling back to experience life in earlier times at first hand. In order to relive and understand the past, we need to stretch our imagination and try to see what life was like for people living in another age.

To do this, of course, we cannot depend on imagination alone. Like detectives, we need *evidence* and *information* to build up an accurate account of the past. In the next chapter, we will investigate the use of this evidence, and see how it is pieced together to form a picture of life in days gone by.

Success in sport can bring excitement into the lives of ordinary people. Shown here is the arrival home to Dublin of the Irish soccer team following the World Cup competition. Around a quarter of a million people turned out to give them a huge welcome. In later years this will be remembered by ordinary people as a great sporting occasion.

Test your knowledge

1. What signs of the past can we see around us?
2. How does history help us to understand the world in which we live?
3. Name some of the problems in today's world which can be traced back to the past.
4. Is history only about important people and events?
5. How does history affect everybody's interests?
6. Why are people who want to find out about the past like detectives?

Chapter 1: Review

• Our memories of the past include not only events from our own lives but also happenings of local, national and worldwide importance.

• Our parents and grandparents can remember many interesting and important events which took place during their lifetimes.

• History is the study of the past. It deals with recent events as well as with the lives of people who lived hundreds or even thousands of years ago.

• We date events in history from the birth of Jesus Christ. The years before this are followed by the letters BC (before Christ). Dates after the birth of Christ use the letters AD (*Anno Domini*—the Year of Our Lord).

• History shows us how today's world developed and helps us to understand the causes of many of its problems.

• History is not only about important people and events. It also tells us about the lives of ordinary people down through the ages.

CHAPTER 2 Evidence from the Past

Historians and their sources

People who find out about the past by gathering evidence are known as historians. Anything which provides this evidence is called a source. Sources are many and varied. They include ruins, buildings, books, letters, diaries, newspapers and even interviews with people about their past lives. Two main types of sources—*primary* and *secondary*—are used by historians.

Primary sources

Primary sources include any evidence surviving from the past which is later examined by historians. Such clues from the past might be the remains of buildings, or objects once used by people living in earlier times. Other examples of primary sources might be a letter, diary or government report written at the time when the event being described took place.

Secondary sources

We often get our information on the past from books or films produced by people who did not witness the events in question. They are called *secondary sources*. They rely on primary sources to produce their materials, often many years after an event took place.

Like detectives, historians sift through the evidence they have collected. They weigh up the importance of this evidence and must decide whether some of it is unreliable or unsafe. They then use only the reliable evidence to piece together a clear picture of the past.

Let us now take a closer look at the different types of evidence which historians use to build up a picture of what life was like in earlier times.

Test your knowledge

1 Describe the work of historians.
2 What is a source?
3 Explain the difference between a primary and a secondary source.
4 How do historians deal with the evidence they have collected?

Asking people about the past

One of the most enjoyable ways of finding out more about the recent past is to ask people who lived at the time. We have already seen how our parents and grandparents can recall changes and events when they were growing up. We often hear older people say, 'Things were different in my young days' as they contrast the life of young people today with life when they themselves were growing up.

However, people's memories are not always reliable. They sometimes forget important details and often give their own version of events. We must therefore be careful not to rely too much on memories to provide us with accurate accounts of the past. We can see how unreliable our own memories are from the way a story may change in certain details when passed from person to person.

Examine the evidence

Read the following account of one man's memories of life in Ireland at the time of World War II.

'Youngsters today don't know how well off they are. When I was a boy times were very tough. Because of the war, food was in short supply and had to be strictly rationed. Sugar, tea and fruit were hard to get. Cars were hardly to be seen on the roads as there was no petrol—'twas bicycles everywhere. My mother lived in dread of the Glimmer Man who would cut off the gas on her if he caught her using it at the wrong time. But we made the best of things. Unlike people today, we were honest and hard-working folks who helped our neighbours out ... '

1 What do we learn about life in Ireland at the time of World War II from the memories of this man?
2 Pick out an example of exaggeration in this account.
3 The old man has given us his views on life then compared with life now. How reliable do you think his views are?

Through the eye of the camera

Photographs from the past provide the historian with another good primary source. The camera was invented by an Englishman named William Fox Talbot in 1841. Photography is therefore extremely important in studying people's lives for the past 150 years.

Examine the evidence

Look at the following photographs showing various scenes from the past. Then answer the questions about each one

1 How do we know that the family pictured here is well off?
2 This family has obviously posed for the camera. Do you think that this photograph gives a totally true impression of what they were really like?

A well-off family posing for the camera around the year 1900.

A scene from the Dublin tenements around 1900.

1 What does this photograph tell us about the living conditions of the poor in the tenements?

Spreading the news

A hundred years from now, people who want to find out about how we live our lives today might turn to our newspapers as sources of information. These newspapers will report the dramatic news of the day as well as telling about the sports and entertainment which we enjoy. In the same way, we can also use old newspapers to explore life in the past.

We have already seen how photographs can take us back in time. Newspapers take us back further still, telling us about events both before and after the invention of the camera.

Let us now take a look at some newspapers from the past and see what they tell us.

Examine the evidence

The following two newspaper accounts take different views of a strike among Dublin workers in 1913.

Paper 1
The Irish Worker—a union newspaper
What view does this paper take of the strike?

The Irish Worker
Edited by Jim Larkin
Wednesday 27 August 1913

Manifesto to the Citizens of Dublin and Visitors

We appeal with confidence to citizens and lovers of fair play for sympathy and active resistance in this struggle for freedom.

Don't Use the Trams!

The 'Independent' and 'Herald' Newspapers Company **Dismissed** 60 Odd Men and Boys For **No Cause**

Paper 2
The Irish Independent
What side does this paper support in the strike?

Irish Independent
Wednesday 27 August 1913

'On The Run'
The Strike Fiasco

A 'Malign influence'

'Feeblest Attempt in History of Tram Strikes'

Duty of Employers

'I think I have broken the malign influence of Mr Larkin,' said Mr W. M. Murphy in an interview last night, 'and set him on the run. It is now up to the employers to keep him going.'

As you can see we cannot always depend on newspapers to give us a complete and unbiased account of events. Newspapers are often one-sided in their views and sometimes leave out important facts. Despite their drawbacks, however, newspapers do provide a lively and exciting record of life in the past.

Letters and diaries

Letters and diaries provide valuable information about the past because they were written by all sorts of people—from kings and queens to ordinary workers. As primary sources, letters provide two main types of evidence. Some letters tell us about the everyday lives of ordinary people, rich and poor, through the centuries. Other letters, written by rulers and politicians, describe how different countries were governed and how they got on with one another. Like other sources, letters do not always tell the full truth. They often contain the personal views of the writer and may not be always reliable.

Many people today keep diaries to record happenings in their daily lives. People in the past also kept diaries which tell us a lot about themselves and the times in which they lived.

We can read many famous diaries when studying history. One of the greatest was a diary kept by an Englishman called Samuel Pepys from 1600 to 1669. In his diary, Pepys gives an honest and vivid account of life in the middle of the seventeenth century. It includes a famous description of the Great Fire which destroyed London in September 1666.

The Great Fire of London, 1666, as shown in a picture made shortly after the event.

Anne Frank writing her diary.

One of the most moving diaries of all time was kept by a young Jewish girl during World War II. Her name was Anne Frank. When Hitler came to power in Germany, Anne and her family fled to Amsterdam in Holland. After the Germans conquered Holland in 1940, the Frank family, along with some Jewish friends, went into hiding in a secret room above Mr Frank's Amsterdam office. On 12 June 1942, her thirteenth birthday, Anne was given a diary which she kept for over two years. This provides a startling account of her fears and hopes during those years.

Examine the evidence

Read the following extracts from *The Diary of Anne Frank*. This famous book was made known to the world in 1947, two years after Anne had died in a German concentration camp.

Extract 1

'Saturday, 20 June 1942

After May 1940 good times rapidly fled ... That is when the sufferings of us Jews really began. Anti-Jewish decrees (orders) followed each other in quick succession. Jews must wear a yellow star. Jews must hand in their bicycles, Jews are banned from trams and are forbidden to drive. Jews are only allowed to do their shopping between three and five o'clock and then only in shops which bear the placard, 'Jewish shop'. Jews must be indoors by eight o'clock and cannot even sit in their own gardens after that hour. Jews are forbidden to visit theatres, cinemas and other places of entertainment. Jews may not take part in public sports. Swimming baths, tennis courts, hockey fields and other sports grounds are all prohibited to them. Jews may not visit Christians. Jews must go to Jewish schools, and many more restrictions of a similar kind ...'

Extract 2

'Friday, 26 May 1944

Again and again I ask myself, would it not have been better for us all had we not gone into hiding, and if we were dead now and not going through all this misery, especially as we should be no longer dragging our protectors into danger. But we recoil from these thoughts too, for we still love life; we haven't yet forgotten the voice of nature, we still hope, hope about everything. I hope something will happen soon now, shooting if need be—nothing can crush us more than this restlessness. Let the end come, even if it is hard; then at least we shall know whether we are finally going to win through or go under.'

1 What do you learn from the first extract about how Jews were treated after May 1940?
2 The second extract is full of both hope and despair. Give one example of each feeling.
3 Give an example from Extract 2 which shows that Anne was an unselfish girl.
4 Is *The Diary of Anne Frank* a primary or secondary source? Explain your answer.

Government records

As governments play a vital role in the making of history, the records which they leave behind are very good sources of information for the historian.

Government documents include laws, treaties, speeches in parliament and enquiries into problems such as housing conditions and unemployment. The census reports produced by governments also give very useful information because they deal with population, housing conditions, jobs and the education of the entire population of a country.

Examine the evidence

A special Committee of Enquiry was set up by the government to report on housing conditions among the poor in Dublin around 1914. Read the following extract from the Committee's report.

'There are many tenement houses with seven or eight rooms that house a family in each room and contain a population of between forty and fifty souls. We have visited one house that we found to be occupied by 98 persons, another by 74 and a third by 73. The entrance to all tenement houses is by a common door off either a street, lane or alley, and in most cases the door is never shut day or night ... Generally the only water supply of the house is furnished by a single tap which is in the yard ... The roofs of the tenement houses are as a rule bad ... Having visited a large number of these houses in all parts of the city ... it is no uncommon thing to find halls and landings, yards and closets of the houses in a filthy condition.'

1 From this description, what do you think tenement houses were?
2 How do we know from this report that tenement houses were overcrowded?
3 What was life like for those living in these houses? Explain your answer by providing evidence from the extract.

Manuscripts

Until the invention of printing around 1450, books were produced very slowly by hand. These were known as *manuscripts* from the Latin words for hand (*manus*) and writings (*scriptum*).

Most manuscripts were written by monks in monasteries and they are our principal sources of information before the invention of printing.

Not only history but poetry, stories and religious works like the Bible were written in manuscripts. One of Ireland's most famous manuscripts is the

Book of Kells, a copy of the four Gospels written by monks around 750 AD.

This illustrated manuscript shows knights setting out on a journey. Describe the activities you can see.

The search for truth

In this chapter you have learned about the different types of evidence which historians use to build up a picture of the past. You have seen how some sources of information are more reliable than others. It is not only the sources which may be one-sided. We, the people using them, can also be biased or one-sided in our judgements. In studying the past we must be careful to tell all sides of the story and give a fair hearing to all concerned. History should teach us to be tolerant of other people's beliefs and opinions.

However, historians often change their accounts of the past when new evidence becomes available. At one time in Ireland, the Vikings were only remembered for attacking monasteries. Because of further evidence we now realise that they also brought many of their traditions and skills to Ireland. For example, the Vikings were responsible for setting up our first towns and introducing money to Ireland.

Much of the new evidence on the Vikings has not come from written sources but from digging up the remains of their towns and burial sites. Digging up the past in this way is known as archaeology. It provides us with a great source of information on earlier times.

In the next chapter we will see how archaeology can help us to piece together a picture of the distant past.

Chapter 2: Review

- People who find out about the past by gathering and studying evidence are known as historians.

- Anything which provides evidence on the past is called a source. Two types of sources are used by historians: primary and secondary sources.

- Primary sources consist of evidence surviving from the past such as ruins, letters, diaries or government reports.

- Secondary sources include books or films produced after the events they describe are over.

- Before writing their accounts of the past, historians weigh up the evidence carefully and reject any information which turns out to be false.

- An interesting way to find out about life in the recent past is to ask people who lived at the time. However, we must be careful not to rely too much on memories to provide us with an accurate account of the past.

- Newspapers, letters, diaries and government papers are also good primary sources for the historian.

- For the past 150 years, photographs have provided us with excellent information.

- For studying the period before 1450, handwritten books called manuscripts are important primary sources.

- In studying the past we must be careful not to be one-sided or biased in our views.

- History should teach us to be tolerant of other people's beliefs and opinions.

CHAPTER 3

Digging up the Past

Great discoveries at Wood Quay in Dublin

In 1850 workmen laying railway lines in Dublin made some unusual discoveries. When digging up the ground they kept coming across iron tools, weapons and human skeletons. They did not realise that they had in fact stumbled upon one of the largest Viking burial grounds in Europe.

When experts called archaeologists examined the area, they found weapons such as spears and swords, and tools such as hammers and knives alongside the bones of the Viking warriors which had lain undisturbed for around a thousand years. Since these discoveries, many archaeologists have dug up or excavated parts of Dublin to find clues about life in the distant past.

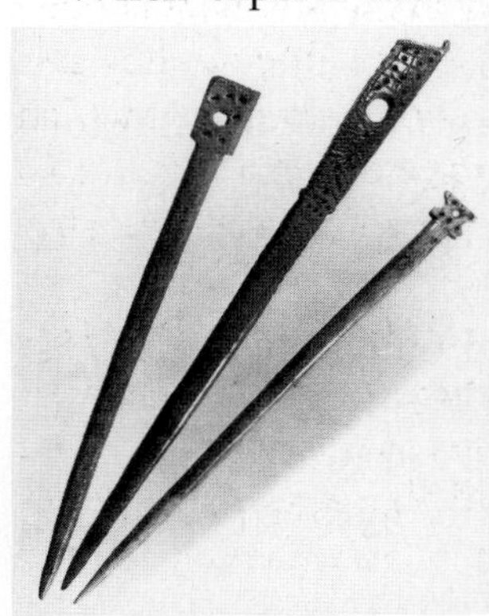

Long pins such as these were used to fasten garments. While the ones shown here were made from bone, many bronze pins were also found on the Wood Quay site.

The most famous Viking excavations took place between 1974 and 1981 in an area of the city centre known as Wood Quay. The archaeologists were amazed by the wealth of material which was uncovered. Parts of the walls of the old city of Dublin were discovered, together with the remains of Viking houses and workshops. Over 100,000 objects or artefacts, including weapons, tools and household utensils, were carefully removed from the ground. The Vikings always buried their rubbish in holes known as cesspits. By examining these, the archaeologists could tell how the Vikings had lived and worked and what they ate.

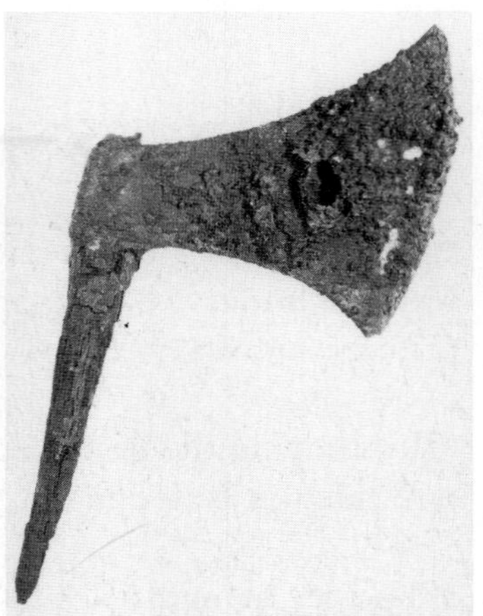

A great number of tools and weapons were excavated at Wood Quay. Here we see a Viking axe made from iron.

Finds such as this chess piece made from antler can teach us a lot about the pastimes enjoyed by the Viking settlers.

A leather boot dating from Viking times.

We now know much more about the life of the Vikings in Ireland because of discoveries like these made by archaeologists. Let us now take a closer look at how the archaeologist carries out his or her work.

Test your knowledge

1 What unusual discoveries were made by workmen in Dublin in 1850?
2 What experts were called in to examine the finds?
3 What is an excavation? Where did the most famous excavations take place in Dublin?
4 What name is given to the objects found by archaeologists in an excavation?
5 List some of the finds made by archaeologists at Wood Quay.

Clues from the past

You should now realise that archaeology involves building up a picture of the past by digging up or excavating the remains left by people in earlier times. These remains include everything made by human beings—from simple tools and wooden houses to magnificent tombs, temples and palaces.

In Chapter 2 we examined various types of written evidence used by historians. However, human beings had lived on earth for thousands of years before writing was developed. This period before the development of writing is called *prehistoric times.* In studying prehistoric times, we must rely on the discoveries of archaeologists to tell us how people lived then. Even for those periods when written records do exist, the findings of archaeologists can greatly increase our knowledge and understanding.

Mounds such as this one can be seen easily above the surface and may mark the site of an ancient burial chamber.

Millions of objects end up in or on the ground. Some objects were simply lost or thrown away. Some were buried or hidden for safekeeping. Others were placed alongside the dead in burial sites. Sometimes the remains of houses and other buildings became buried in the ground as new buildings were placed on top of them.

A ruined church . Ruins such as this are clearly visible and are examined by archaeologists to learn about the past.

Most objects and buildings from the past do not survive. They either rot in the ground or are destroyed over the years by people or by wind, rain and other natural forces.

Some objects, however, are very well preserved because of the special conditions in which they are found. Particularly when the conditions are either very dry or very wet, objects from the distant past may survive to the present day. For this reason, archaeologists have made many valuable finds in marshes or peat bogs and in desert areas.

Archaeologists use aerial photographs such as this one to identify features on the ground. What do you think is shown here?

Some remains from the past are easily located by archaeologists. These include buildings and mounds of earth which can still be seen above the surface of the ground. The photographs illustrate a few examples of such objects.

Other remains are more difficult to locate because they are below the surface. Aerial photographs are often used by archaeologists to find traces of ancient fields, towns, roads and monuments. Underwater remains such as the wrecks of ships are often found by using sonar equipment.

Written records, when they are available, can also be a great help. By looking at old documents and maps, archaeologists might uncover evidence which would help them in their work. Records written 350 years ago helped to locate a Spanish treasure ship which had been wrecked off the coast of Florida.

Sometimes archaeologists can be inspired by legends and stories which lead them to make spectacular discoveries. The German archaeologist, Heinrich Schliemann, went in search of the legendary city of Troy after reading the work of a Greek writer named Homer!

Archaeologists use many different methods to locate clues from the past. The next stage in their work involves studying these clues and using them to build up a picture of life in earlier times.

Test your knowledge

1 What is archaeology?

2 Why do we rely on the work of archaeologists to tell us about prehistoric times?

3 How do millions of objects end up in the ground?

4 In what conditions do some of these objects survive?

5 Why are some remains from the past easy to locate?

6 Explain why archaeologists use aerial photographs.

7 What other methods do archaeologists use to find clues from the past?

Digging up the past

A dig is a carefully organised and planned investigation of an archaeological site. Even before an excavation begins, archaeologists do a lot of preparation and groundwork. A survey of the site area is first carried out to find out its size, shape and type of soil and rock.

The main tools used during the dig are shovels, pickaxes, spades, trowels, brushes and sieves. The trowels and brushes are used with great care to uncover small and fragile artefacts. The sieves are used to filter the tiniest objects from the surrounding soil.

As archaeologists excavate a site and carefully remove objects, they have a number of questions in mind. They are not treasure hunters digging for gold or other valuable objects. Instead, they want to find out how old the objects are and what they were used for.

The objects removed from the ground have often been lying there for hundreds or even thousands of years. They are therefore very fragile and easily broken. This explains why small trowels and brushes must be used. Each find is then carefully cleaned and listed or catalogued according to type, place and time of discovery.

Archaeologists use two main methods for dating their finds.

Here we see archaeologists carrying out a 'dig'. Can you pick out three activities from this photograph?

Stratigraphy

When people have lived in the same place for a very long time, layers of remains will be found, one on top of the other. The oldest remains are at the bottom and the newest on the top. By measuring the depth at which an object is found, archaeologists can work out how old it is. This method is called stratigraphy.

Carbon 14 dating

All living things contain a substance called Carbon 14. When creatures or plants die, the Carbon 14 in them begins to decline. By measuring the amount of Carbon 14 left in the remains, archaeologists can tell roughly how old they are.

Archaeologists are seen here examining a human skeleton found in London. They showed by Carbon 14 dating that the person buried in the grave had lived around 1500 years ago.

Test your knowledge

1 Why do archaeologists carry out a survey before excavating a site?

2 What tools do archaeologists use during a dig?

3 How do they treat the objects they remove from the ground?

4 Why are different layers of remains sometimes found?

5 What is stratigraphy?

6 What is Carbon 14 dating?

The past around us

Through the work of archaeologists many sites in Ireland and around the world have been excavated to provide a wealth of information on the past.

In our towns, villages and countryside, features of the landscape such as ruins, mounds, stones and burial sites often provide us with a glimpse of the past.

In the next chapters we will see how artefacts and ruins can show us how people lived and worked thousands of years ago. By sifting through the evidence from the past, we will try to unravel the fascinating story of the ancient Romans and Celts.

Chapter 3: Review

- Workmen laying down railway lines in Dublin around 1850 accidentally discovered a huge burial ground.

- Since then, experts called archaeologists have excavated or dug up parts of Dublin in search of evidence from the past. The most famous excavations took place at Wood Quay in the centre of the city where Viking tools, weapons and other objects or artefacts were found.

- Archaeology is about the study of the past by digging up or excavating the remains left by people in earlier times. We depend almost totally on archaeology to tell us about prehistoric times.

- Most objects buried in the ground do not survive. However, those found in very wet, dry or cold conditions are often well preserved. Some remains from the past are easily located because they are visible above the surface. Others are more difficult to find because they are below the level of the ground.

- The archaeologist does a lot of preparation and groundwork before excavating a site. He or she carries out a survey, studies old maps and takes aerial photographs. As the site is excavated, objects are carefully removed with the aid of trowels, brushes and sieves.

- The archaeologist uses two main methods to date an object: Carbon 14 dating (measuring the amount of carbon left in an object) and stratigraphy (measuring the depth of an object in the ground).

Ancient Rome

A Walk around Ancient Rome

Travelling through time

Imagine travelling back in time and walking around one of the greatest cities the world has ever known. About 2,000 years ago, Rome was the largest and most magnificent city in the world. Visitors from distant lands were amazed at its wealth, beauty and excitement. Huge splendid buildings were everywhere to be seen. Crowds passed through the busy streets as rich and poor bought goods and sold their wares in the noisy marketplaces, and excited onlookers flocked to see bloody and violent fights and games.

A model of Rome in ancient times. Notice the large and magnificent public buildings together with the narrow streets.

From this great city the Romans ruled over many lands both near and far. Around two thousand years ago they were the most powerful people in the world. In this chapter we will go back in time and wander through the busy and exciting streets of ancient Rome.

Buying and selling in the Roman Forum

We begin our walk around ancient Rome in the city's lively marketplace. This is the Roman Forum, a large, flat area where people gather from early morning onwards to buy and sell goods.

An artist's reconstruction of the Roman Forum.

A victorious general parading through the Via Sacra in triumph.

On ordinary working days the Roman Forum is a hive of activity. Here people buy wine, bread, meat, fish, and other types of food. Men buy swords, knives, shields and saddles for their horses. Children really enjoy a visit to the Forum where they can buy many toys such as footballs, hoops and marbles.

The Forum is at its busiest every eight days when markets are held. Schools are closed on market days because many of them are located near marketplaces and the noise would prevent the students from concentrating on their studies.

In our visit to the Forum we do not only see people buying and selling goods. Many people are discussing politics and business, while others are exchanging the latest news and gossip.

The long, straight road which runs through the middle of the Forum is called the *Via Sacra* or Sacred Way. Along this road, thousands of people stand to watch the generals and armies as they march in triumph after victory in battle. What a thrill it must be to see the colourful banners, row upon row of marching soldiers and the proud generals on their horses parading through the Forum!

The ruins of the Via Sacra or Sacred Way through the Forum.

Test your knowledge

1 Name the main marketplace in ancient Rome.

2 What goods were bought and sold there?

3 Why were schools closed on market days?

4 Name the road through the middle of the Forum.

5 Why did thousands of people sometimes line this road?

The Roman aqueducts

On our walking tour of ancient Rome we can see huge stone arches high above us. These are the *aqueducts*. They contain cement-lined pipes which carry water from the hills into the city. When this water reaches Rome it is gathered into huge cisterns.

Building an Aqueduct. This was a very skilful and difficult task involving engineers, surveyors, stonemasons and labourers.

From these it flows into public fountains where the people come to draw water. Rich people sometimes have their water piped into their homes for a special fee. Water from the aqueducts is also used in Rome's public toilets. When the toilets are flushed, the water then passes through a system of underground sewers into the River Tiber.

Aqueducts like this one carried water from the hills into the City of Rome.

Despite this advanced water supply system, walking around ancient Rome can have its unpleasant side. All types of rubbish, including the contents of chamber pots, are emptied from the upper storeys of flats onto the streets, much to the danger and surprise of the unsuspecting passer-by!

A visit to the baths

Reconstruction of a Roman bath, using the ruins of the Baths of Caracalla in Rome as a model.

The aqueducts also supply water to the public baths. We can see hundreds of these on our tour of ancient Rome. The baths open their doors to the public at around half past ten in the morning and usually close before dinner in the late afternoon.

The baths contain a number of special rooms. On entering, people change in the dressing room and from there go to a fairly warm hall called the *tepidarium*. They then enter a cold room, the *frigidarium*, which contains a swimming pool. There is also a hot room called the *caldarium* where people can have a sauna or Turkish bath. Bathers are rubbed down by masseurs who spread oil and perfume on their bodies and scrape away the dirt with a special instrument called a *strigil*.

Though most of the baths are small, those built by the emperors are both large and extravagant. The one built by the Emperor Nero contains 1,600 marble bath seats. The greatest of all, however, are the Baths of Diocletian and the Baths of Caracalla. The Baths of Diocletian cover thirty-two acres and can accommodate more than three thousand bathers at a time.

The baths are not only places where people came to bathe. Some of them are like small cities containing rooms for exercising, shops, libraries, gardens, museums and restaurants. The Roman baths are noisy, bustling places where rich and poor came to bathe and exchange the latest gossip. When the baths close their doors in the late afternoon, the refreshed and relaxed Romans return to their homes for dinner.

Test your knowledge

1 How was water supplied in ancient Rome?

2 Why was walking around ancient Rome sometimes unpleasant?

3 Name three special rooms in the baths and describe how each was used.

4 What were the two most famous baths in ancient Rome?

5 In what ways were the baths like small cities?

A day at the races

An artist's reconstruction of an exciting chariot race in the Circus Maximus.

As we travel through ancient Rome you cannot miss a huge open-air stadium called the *Circus Maximus*. This is a type of racecourse called a *hippodrome* where the Romans came to watch chariot races. It is 200 metres wide, 600 metres long, and can hold 250,000 spectators.

The chariots are usually pulled by four horses and are driven seven times around the centre of the ring at great speed. Immense

A marble carving of a charioteer dating from Roman times.

skill is required to control the chariots, especially when rounding bends. Many spectacular crashes take place and chariot drivers can be trampled to death, much to the excitement of the crowd.

The chariots and their drivers are divided into four teams, and named according to the colours they wear: the Whites, Greens, Blues and Reds. Each team has its own followers and huge bets are placed on the outcome of the races. People are always talking about the chariot races. Little boys play in toy chariots pulled by goats and dogs, and great charioteers are heroes throughout Rome.

A visit to the games

One of the most exciting places to visit in ancient Rome is the *Colosseum*. This vast round open-air stadium is called an *amphitheatre*. There are many amphitheatres in Rome but the Colosseum is the largest; it can hold 50,000 people.

The ruins of the Colosseum as seen today. This was the largest amphitheatre in Rome and could hold over 50,000 people. It had several underground passages and even lifts to bring wild animals to the arena. The main area was sometimes flooded for the staging of mock naval battles.

Popular games involving wild beasts and fighters known as *gladiators* are held in the Colosseum. Many of the gladiators have been captured in war. Others are criminals who are sent into the arena to fight one another or dangerous wild animals. Some of the gladiators are professionals and are trained in special schools at Rome and other cities.

A Roman in combat with a wild animal.

'Thumbs Down!' The onlookers call for the death of a defeated gladiator.

Gladiators are armed with swords, daggers, forks and nets. Wild animals such as lions, tigers, elephants and even giraffes are brought from distant lands. Most fights end in the brutal deaths of animals and gladiators. When two gladiators are about to fight they cry out to the Emperor, 'Hail Caesar. Those who are about to die salute you.' When one of the gladiators falls, the crowd has the power of life and death over him. If they want him spared, they give a thumbs-up sign; but a thumbs-down sign calls for his death.

The gladiatorial games are very popular in ancient Rome and most Romans really enjoy spending a day's holiday at the amphitheatre.

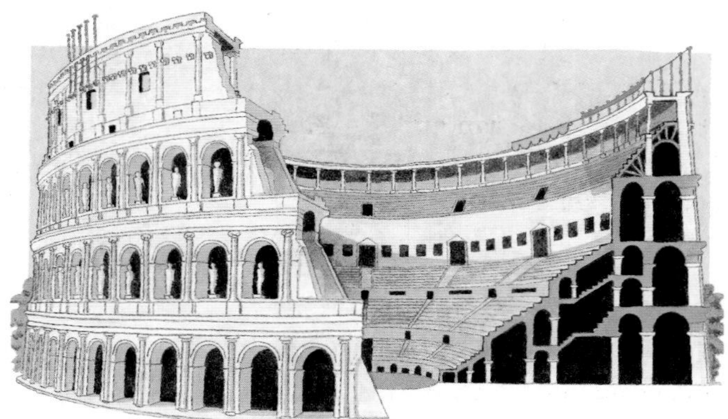

A reconstruction of the Colosseum, based on the ruins that are still visible in Rome today.

Test your knowledge

1 Where were chariot races held?

2 Name the most famous hippodrome in ancient Rome.

3 Why do you think watching chariot racing was one of the Romans' most exciting pastimes?

4 How do we know that chariot racing was so popular in ancient Rome?

5 What was the bloodiest form of entertainment enjoyed by the Romans?

6 Where were the gladiatorial fights held?

7 Name the most famous amphitheatre in ancient Rome.

The Theatre of Marcellus in Rome. Like the Greeks, the Romans enjoyed plays. Many Roman plays were comedies in which foolish people were mocked. The Theatre of Marcellus is the only ancient theatre building still standing in Rome. In ancient times it could accommodate 15,000 people.

Roman actors rehearsing for a play.

Back to the present

In our tour of ancient Rome we saw some of the great sights of the city. Visiting places such as the Forum, the Colosseum and the baths has helped us to see how the people of ancient Rome lived and enjoyed themselves.

The pictures in this chapter show that the ruins of many great Roman buildings still survive. Visitors to Rome today can walk around the ruins of the Forum, the Colosseum and the Baths of Caracalla. From these ruins we can try to imagine what life was like two thousand years ago when Rome was a rich and powerful city.

In the next chapter we travel southwards to the Roman town of Pompeii. We will read how archaeologists have excavated the city, providing us with fascinating details of what life was like in Roman times.

Chapter 4: Review

• About 2,000 years ago Rome was the largest and most magnificent city in the world. The Romans were a powerful people who ruled over many lands both near and far.

• The busiest place in ancient Rome was the Roman Forum. This was the city's lively marketplace to which thousands of people came every day to buy and sell goods.

• Huge stone arches called aqueducts carried water from the hills to the city.

• The ancient Romans loved to relax in the baths. The greatest of all the public baths were the Baths of Diocletian and the Baths of Caracalla. They were like small cities containing libraries, restaurants and even shops.

• The Romans enjoyed spending a day at the Circus Maximus where they watched the exciting and dangerous chariot races. These races were very popular in ancient Rome. People placed large bets on them and the best charioteers were heroes throughout the land.

• The most exciting place in ancient Rome was the Colosseum. This was the city's largest amphitheatre where games took place involving wild beasts and fighters known as gladiators.

The Story of Pompeii

Disaster strikes Pompeii

On 24 August in the year 79 AD, the Roman city of Pompeii was bustling with activity. Bakers and shopkeepers were selling their goods. Many people had gathered in the Forum to exchange the latest news and gossip. Others were eating and drinking in the taverns.

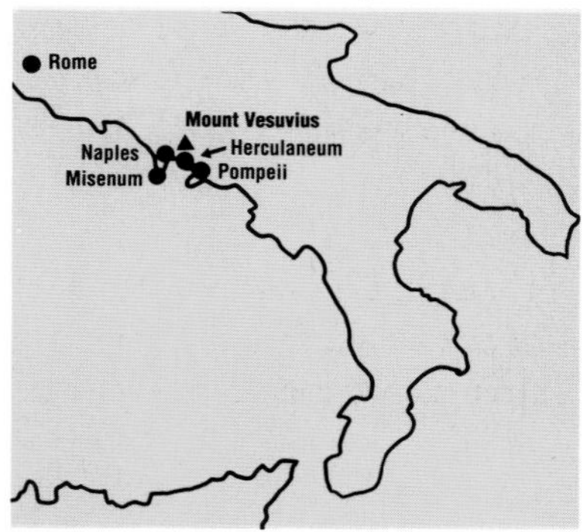

Rome and Pompeii.

Suddenly a huge crash shook the ground. As people rushed outside, they could see smoke and flames belching from the top of Vesuvius, a volcanic mountain overlooking the city of Pompeii. Lava and ashes began to rain down and the sky became dark and gloomy. Many people fled in panic.

Within hours Pompeii was buried under layers of lava, ashes and stones. The 2,000 people who had been trapped in the city, indeed the city itself, disappeared without trace beneath the ashes. Where a few hours earlier thousands of people had hurried about their daily business, all that now remained of Pompeii was a grey and empty wilderness.

An artist's impression of Mount Vesuvius during a volcanic eruption.

The much smaller town of Herculaneum also vanished from sight. Unlike Pompeii, Herculaneum was buried under a sea of boiling mud. This completely filled the buildings and preserved everything within them, including furniture and even food.

Pompeii rediscovered

For over a thousand years after the disastrous eruption of Vesuvius, the towns of Pompeii and Herculaneum remained buried and forgotten. When workmen accidentally discovered some ruins, people began to search for the towns. Herculaneum was the first to be excavated and for many years treasure hunters came in search of valuables.

When the excavation of Herculaneum proved difficult, people turned to Pompeii. We owe its discovery to a brilliant Italian archaeologist named Giuseppe Fiorelli. His interest was not in seeking treasure but in finding out about the past.

In 1860, Fiorelli and a group of archaeologists began work on Pompeii. They cleared away mounds of earth which covered the site. For the first time since the day of the disaster in 79 AD, the streets of Pompeii could be seen once more.

Fiorelli drew up a plan of the city and divided it into different regions. Each region was given a number. Every doorway was also numbered so that each house and shop in the city could be identified. Fiorelli also made a note of every object found and recorded its place of discovery and its depth in the ground.

A plaster cast of a victim from Pompeii.

Fiorelli's most fascinating achievement was the plaster casts which he made of the dead. When people died in the disaster, ash and stones settled around their bodies. Although flesh and clothes had rotted away over the years, the skeletons and the imprints of bodies remained in the ashes. Fiorelli pumped a type of plaster into the detailed shapes left by the bodies. In this way he created plaster casts of the people who had been killed at Pompeii.

Excavations continue at Pompeii today.

These plaster casts help us to relive the last horrific moments of the citizens of Pompeii as they fled in terror from the eruption of Vesuvius.

Test your knowledge

1 What disaster struck the city of Pompeii on 24 August in the year 79 AD?

2 Describe how the town of Herculaneum vanished from sight.

3 Name the archaeologist who excavated Pompeii.

4 Why did he divide the city into regions and number each doorway?

5 How was Fiorelli able to make plaster casts of the dead?

The ruins of the Temple of Apollo at Pompeii.

The ruins of the Forum at Pompeii as seen today, with Mount Vesuvius in the background.

Walking around Pompeii

Ever since the time of Fiorelli, archaeologists have continued excavations at the site of Pompeii. Nearly all of the ancient city has been rediscovered. Today visitors to Pompeii can walk along its streets, wander through the Forum and even enter houses, shops and bars. By looking at the ruins of Pompeii we can imagine what life was like in Roman times.

Pompeii was a harbour town and people came from far and wide to buy and sell goods. As in Rome, the busiest place in the town was the Forum, Pompeii's marketplace and business centre. Today we can see the remains of a line of columns which once ran along three sides of the Forum. In ancient times, merchants set up their stalls beneath these columns.

A reconstruction of the Temple of Augustus in Pompeii.

Many great buildings once stood around the Forum. The ruins of the basilica and temples can still be seen. The basilica was a kind of law court as well as a place where people came to do business.

Most of Pompeii's streets were narrow. They were paved with blocks of stone with a raised footpath on either side. The road itself was also raised slightly in the centre to allow water to run into gutters. Unlike Rome, the city of Pompeii had no proper sewerage system. People threw out their

A street in Pompeii. Notice the paved surface and the stepping stones.

The ruins of a tavern excavated at Pompeii. What do you believe was the purpose of the holes in the counter?

rubbish into the gutters and the streets must have been very dirty indeed. Large stepping stones have been found along the roads. These allowed people to cross without getting dirty.

Stone pots in the ruins of a kitchen at the back of a house at Pompeii.

Pompeii's streets were lined with shops, bars and taverns. Many food shops have been excavated. These contained masonry counters with large earthenware pots set into them. At one time, the pots were filled with grain, fruit and liquids. The shopkeepers carefully weighed the food for their customers and many bronze scales have been found.

Bars and taverns were everywhere in Pompeii. These were often tiny rooms which served food and drink. Like the food shops they contained counters in which large earthenware pots were set.

A fresco or wall-painting from the house of a rich family at Pompeii. Describe the scene which it shows.

'The House of the Faun', Pompeii. Can you say how it got its name? Do you think a rich or a poor family once lived here? Explain your answer.

Many craftsmen and traders lived in Pompeii. The house of bronzesmiths, goldsmiths, bakers, clothmakers and launderers have all been excavated.

The people of Pompeii enjoyed many forms of entertainment. Like the citizens of Rome, they loved to relax in the public baths. Ruins of these baths have been excavated and some of them have even been restored. During excavations, ointment jars and strigils were found in the area of the baths.

The ruins of two theatres have been discovered: a large open-air building which could hold 5,000 people and a smaller, roofed theatre which could seat 1,000. Many musical instruments such as pipes, cymbals and rattles have been discovered.

A gladiator's dagger made from iron, bone and ivory found during excavations at Pompeii.

As in Rome, gladiatorial fights in the amphitheatre were by far the most popular form of entertainment. An ancient amphitheatre and gladiators' barracks have both been excavated at Pompeii. Many pieces of armour, together with the bodies of four gladiators, were found in the barracks. Notices announcing gladiatorial fights were also discovered.

Learning about the past

By studying the ruins of ancient Rome and Pompeii, we can see how remains from the past can teach us what life was like in earlier times. By looking at the fascinating discoveries made by archaeologists at Pompeii and Herculaneum, we can imagine how people lived, worked and enjoyed themselves in the hours before disaster struck.

In the next chapter we will use archaeological discoveries to look more closely at the everyday life and times of ancient Romans.

Test your knowledge

1 What was the busiest place in Pompeii?

2 Describe what we can see of the Forum in Pompeii today.

3 What were the streets of Pompeii like?

4 Name some of the craftsmen who lived in Pompeii.

5 What do the ruins tell us about the forms of entertainment enjoyed by the people of Pompeii?

Chapter 5: Review

- On 24 August in 79 AD, disaster struck the Roman city of Pompeii. The volcanic mountain of Vesuvius erupted and within hours the town was buried under layers of lava, ashes and stones.

- The much smaller town of Herculaneum also vanished from sight, buried under a sea of mud. This mud preserved furniture and even food.

- For over a thousand years the lost cities of Pompeii and Herculaneum were almost forgotten. Herculaneum was the first to be excavated but work there proved to be slow and difficult.

- People then turned their attention to the site of Pompeii. The archaeologist who rediscovered this lost city was an Italian named Fiorelli. He divided the city into different regions and numbered each doorway.

- Fiorelli made plaster casts of the dead. By pouring plaster into the imprints made by bodies in the ashes, he was able to recreate the last dying moments of the people of Pompeii.

- The streets of Pompeii were narrow and dirty. They were lined with shops, bars and taverns. These contained counters with huge earthenware pots set into them.

- Many craftsmen and traders lived in Pompeii. The houses of bakers, bronzesmiths and clothmakers have been excavated.

- The citizens of Pompeii enjoyed many forms of entertainment. Public baths, two theatres and an amphitheatre have been excavated.

CHAPTER 6

The Roman Way of Life

Rich and poor

In our walks around ancient Rome and Pompeii, we saw that most Romans enjoyed a visit to the baths, the theatre and the games. In the baths, rich people were always helped by their slaves. At the theatre, the best seats were specially reserved for the wealthy.

The way people dressed in Roman times.

It was easy to recognise the difference between rich and poor from the clothes they wore. Poor people wore a single short garment in both summer and winter. The rich wore a tunic made from wool or linen. The tunic had short sleeves and reached down to the knees. Over this rich men wore a *toga*, while women wore a garment called a *stola*.

The richest people in ancient Rome were also very powerful. Some of them helped to rule the empire. Others were generals in the army. Wealthy Romans also looked after their huge estates in the countryside where they lived in great luxury.

While a few Romans were very wealthy, most were poor. Many of them were not able to earn a living and were given free grain by the government. This was called the dole. Although life for the poor was very hard, another group was even worse off. They were the slaves.

A slave's life

Slaves were found everywhere in ancient Rome. Most of them were prisoners who had been captured during wars. A slave in Rome was regarded as a piece of property that could be bought and sold. Rich people usually owned one or two slaves but some very wealthy people owned hundreds or even thousands. In the emperor's palace, there were more than 20,000 slaves.

The treatment of slaves varied greatly. Some were treated very well by their masters and given important work to do, such as managing farms and teaching the master's children. These slaves were often given money with which they could buy their freedom over a number of years.

Other slaves, however, were savagely treated by their masters. Slaves working in the mines were treated worst of all. They were chained together and forced to work long hours in dark and damp tunnels. It is not surprising that many slaves ran away. If caught they would be brutally punished: they could be crucified or branded with a hot iron.

Test your knowledge

1 Describe the clothes worn by poor people in ancient Rome.

2 How were rich people dressed?

3 What was the dole?

4 How did people become slaves?

5 How were they treated by their masters?

Inside a Roman house

The world of the rich

A rich Roman family at home. Describe the different people shown and their activities. Name the two parts of a Roman house shown in the picture.

Rich people lived in beautiful houses in the towns and in large villas in the countryside. We know a great deal about these houses from the excavations at Pompeii and Herculaneum.

The passser-by was faced by a blank wall on the street side of the house. In Pompeii, advertisements and graffiti were often found on this outside wall. From the street a small entrance led into a central room called the *atrium*. Rainwater fell through a square hole in the middle of the roof and was gathered in an ornamental pond.

Each house had a garden courtyard called a *peristyle*. This was surrounded by a covered passage in which Roman families sat to relax and chat. The bedrooms overlooked the peristyle, and the dining-room and kitchen also opened on to it.

Many houses of the rich had running water which flowed in through lead pipes. Some even had a system of central heating: hot air from a furnace passed through a space under the floor.

'Cave Canem' or 'Beware of the Dog': a mosaic found inside the door of a house at Pompeii.

The houses of wealthy Romans were beautifully decorated. Many of the houses excavated at Pompeii contained colourful wall paintings called murals. Some of the floors were covered in pictures known as mosaics. A mosaic found inside the door of one house in Pompeii showed a vicious-looking dog baring its teeth. The words '*Cave Canem*' (Beware of the Dog) were written underneath it.

Rich Romans did not have as much furniture as we do today. The main items of furniture were tables, chairs, couches and beds. Many tables and benches made from stone and bronze have been found at Pompeii. Unlike Pompeii, many pieces of wooden furniture have been found at Herculaneum. This was because Herculaneum was buried under a sea of mud rather than hot ashes.

Inside a rich Roman's house.

The world of the poor

Most Romans did not live in luxury houses, however. Instead, a poor family rented a single room in a five- or six-storey block of flats. In this small, uncomfortable room the entire family cooked, ate and slept. Access to these flats was usually by means of a wooden ladder. The flats were often made from very poor materials and fires could spread easily throughout them.

Many landlords built taller and taller blocks of flats. The cheapest and most overcrowded accommodation was always on the top storeys. Eventually the Emperor Augustus limited the height of flats to about six storeys.

The greatest problem faced by those living in high-rise flats was carrying jugs of water from the ground level. Because of poor heating and insula-

We can see from this reconstruction, the dirty and overcrowded conditions of a typical Roman slum.

tion, the flats were cold and damp in winter and hot and stuffy in summer. The streets were usually muddy and dirty as people threw their rubbish out the window. Around Pompeii many of the little rooms occupied by the poor have been excavated.

Wining and dining

The Romans loved to eat and drink. In one house at Herculaneum, food was laid out on a table ready for lunch. Bread, salads, eggs and fruit have been preserved in the mud which buried the town. Even the shells of the eggs were unbroken.

Roman food and kitchen utensils discovered at Herculaneum.

Rich people loved to hold lavish dinner parties and invite many friends. As the guests reclined on couches, they enjoyed banquets of fruit, vegetables, meat and fish, all served up to them by slaves. The slaves also washed the feet of the guests while they ate.

The wine flowed freely and dinner parties could sometimes get out of hand. In one house in Pompeii the following warning to guests was written on the wall of the dining-room: '*Restrain yourself from getting angry or using offensive language. If you can't then get back to your own house.*'

The Portland Vase, a magnificent example of Roman pottery.

The guests at these dinner parties sometimes had a special way of dealing with indigestion. When they could eat no more they went to a room called the *vomitorium*. Here a slave put a feather down their throats, causing them to vomit their food. With empty stomachs, they returned once more to the banquet table.

The food eaten by the poor was very different from that of the rich. The poor rarely ate meat and lived mostly on the free grain which they made into bread or porridge. Indeed, the slaves in a rich person's house were very often better fed than the poorer, free citizens of Rome.

A mosaic of a banquet from the ruins of Pompeii.

Test your knowledge

1 In what types of houses did rich people live?
2 What was the atrium?
3 What was the garden courtyard called?
4 How were the houses of wealthy Romans decorated?
5 Describe the housing conditions of the poor.
6 Name the main types of food eaten by wealthy Romans.
7 Describe the diet of the poor.

The remains of bakeries have been found at Pompeii. This reconstruction is based on those sources. Look at it and write down three activities connected with the work of a baker.

A child's world

Roman children were brought up very strictly. At the time, a father even had the power to sell or kill his children. While boys were always at their fathers' sides, girls stayed at home with their mothers where they learned spinning, weaving and painting.

A mosaic showing a Roman student carrying a stylus.

Both boys and girls attended an elementary school between the ages of seven and eleven. This school was called *ludus*, a Latin word meaning 'play'. Schools were held in any available space — in marketplaces, sheds or the peristyle of the teacher's house.

From the ages of twelve to sixteen, Roman boys attended a grammar school where they studied Greek and Latin grammar and the works of great writers such as Homer, Virgil, Cicero and Horace. Roman youths also learned how to make good speeches in public. This skill was called rhetoric or *oratory*.

Cicero (106–43 BC) the greatest of the Roman orators, whose speeches were widely admired and studied, is seen here addressing the Senate.

Discipline was very strict in Roman schools. Flogging was widely used. One picture found in Pompeii shows a boy being flogged on the back while being held by two other pupils.

A Roman boy wore a toga with a purple stripe. At about the age of sixteen he went to the temple where he was given the plain white toga. This meant that his childhood was over and he was now a man.

Although Roman children were reared strictly, a child's life also had its bright side. Just as they do today, children in ancient Rome played with many toys such as marbles, hoops and footballs. Little boys even tried to copy the great charioteers by riding around in boxes pulled by dogs and goats.

A Roman game board with counters.

Test your knowledge

1 How were Roman children brought up?
2 What was the first type of school attended by boys and girls?
3 Describe what Roman boys learnt at grammar school.
4 How do you think the education of boys and girls differed?
5 How do we know that discipline in Roman schools was very strict?
6 What kind of toys did Roman children have?

Chapter 6: Review

- While some of the people of ancient Rome and Pompeii were very rich, most were poor. Poor people wore a single short garment. The rich wore tunics. Over this, men wore the toga and rich women wore the stola.

- Most poor people were not able to earn their own living. They were given free grain from the government.

- The poorest people in ancient Rome were the slaves. Many of them had been captured in wars. They were regarded as pieces of property that could be bought and sold. While some slaves were treated very badly, others were treated very well by their masters and given important jobs to do like teaching the children of the house.

- The rich lived in large, beautiful houses which contained a central room called the atrium and a garden courtyard called the peristyle. The bedrooms overlooked the peristyle and the dining-room and kitchen also opened on to it.

- The houses of the rich were beautifully decorated. Paintings called murals covered the walls while colourful mosaics covered the floors.

- Poor people lived in high multi-storey flats. These were uncomfortable and overcrowded. They were cold and damp in winter and hot and stuffy in summer.

- Rich Romans greatly enjoyed dinner parties. They were served several courses consisting of fruit, vegetables, meat and fish. Wine also flowed freely.

- Poor people rarely ate meat. Instead, their main diet consisted of porridge and bread which they made from the free grain.

- Children were brought up very strictly in ancient Rome. Both boys and girls attended an elementary school between the ages of 7 and 11. While boys then went to grammar school, girls usually stayed at home with their mothers where they learned spinning, weaving and painting.

The Conquering Romans

The Roman Empire

We can still see evidence which proves that the Romans once ruled over most of Europe, North Africa and the Middle East. Whenever the Roman armies conquered new territories, they were followed by engineers and builders who designed and built splendid forts, walls, roads and bridges.

The illustrations in this chapter will demonstrate some of the Romans' magnificent work which can still be seen in many lands far away from Rome itself.

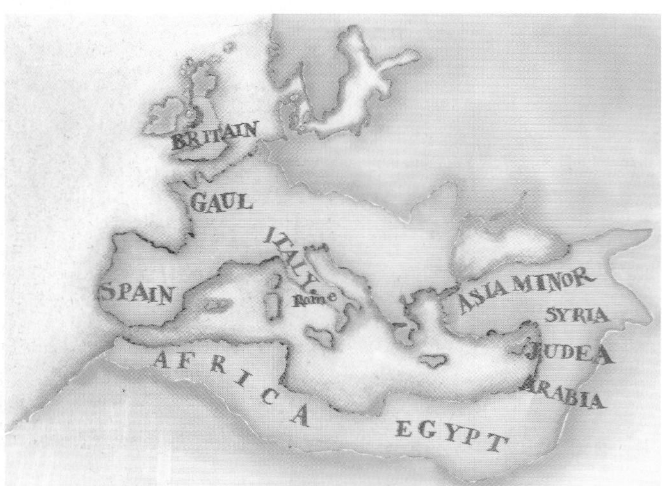

The Roman Empire.

The foreign lands ruled over by the Romans were known as an *empire*. The map shows that when the Roman Empire was at the height of its power around 100 AD, it stretched from the north of England right down to Egypt.

Roman remains in many lands

The Pont du Garde, a magnificent Roman aqueduct which passes through southern France.

Hadrian's Wall, England. This strong defensive wall was built by the Romans in the north of England to protect their English province from attack.

The ruins of a Roman town near Hadrian's Wall.

Roman baths at Bath in England can still be seen today.

Roman ruins at Carthage in North Africa.

The Roman amphitheatre in the town of Verona in northern Italy which is still used as an outdoor theatre for the performance of operas and plays.

A Roman triumphal arch at Orange in southern France.

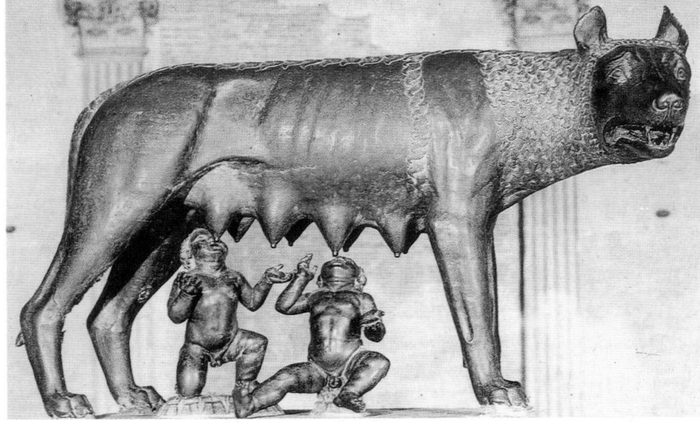

Romulus and Remus, the legendary founders of Rome being fed by the she-wolf. According to legends these twins founded Rome and later generations of Romans looked back with pride at the small beginnings of their city.

How the empire was ruled

Augustus Caesar (66 BC–14 AD) who became the first Roman Emperor in 27 BC. During his long reign he brought peace to the Roman Empire, carried out the first census of population and built splendid temples and other public buildings throughout Rome. It was said of him that he found a city of brick and left one made of marble.

One man ruled over this vast empire. He was called the *emperor* and usually lived in a magnificent palace in Rome itself. The emperor appointed governors to rule over distant provinces of the empire. One of the most famous of these governors was Pontius Pilate. He was in charge of the Roman province of Judea around 30 AD, the time of the crucifixion of Jesus Christ.

Because of high taxes, the Romans were often hated by the local people throughout the empire. There were frequent rebellions which were put down savagely by the Roman armies. The emperor himself sometimes took part in the wars which were fought in distant parts of the empire.

The Arch of Titus built to celebrate the capture of Jerusalem in 70 AD by the Emperor Titus.

We have many sources of information on these wars. We can read accounts of them in the writings of Roman historians such as Tacitus (55–117 AD).

A scene from the Arch of Titus showing Roman soldiers carrying off treasures from the Temple in Jerusalem.

We can learn about these exciting conquests by looking at some of the great monuments which survive to this day in Rome. For example, the Arch of Titus shows scenes of the Roman conquest of Jerusalem (70 AD). Trajan's Column gives us a detailed record of the victories of Emperor Trajan (98–117 AD).

Trajan's Column which celebrates the victories of the Emperor Trajan (98–117 AD).

A model showing a Roman fort and legionaries.

The Roman army

Without the strength and determination of its army, the Roman Empire could never have been so splendid or glorious. If you look at a map of the Roman Empire, you will begin to understand the army's great achievements. From a tiny settlement in the middle of Italy, Rome expanded as its armies conquered more and more lands, north, south, east and west.

A Roman army on the march.

A Roman legionary.

The main fighting unit in the army was called a legion. Each legion was made up of foot soldiers (the *infantry*), horse soldiers (the *cavalry*) and soldiers in charge of large weapons (the *artillery*).

A Roman legionary generally served for twenty years. He usually joined the army when he was eighteen. When his service came to an end, he was given some land in a distant corner of the empire.

Often Roman armies contained legions made up of foreigners who were not citizens of the empire. Such legions were called *auxiliaries*. Famous examples of these auxiliaries included special groups of *archers* from the island of Crete and *slingers* from the Balearic Islands off the coast of Spain.

Going into battle

A Roman soldier carried a pack weighing about 35 kg. It contained two weeks' rations and tools such as axes and spades. His dress consisted of a tunic covered with a metal breastplate. He wore a helmet made of bronze and iron, and on his feet he wore thick leather hob-nailed sandals.

A half-metre long two-edged sword was the Roman soldier's most useful weapon. He also carried 2-metre long javelins and a large shield.

Roman armies were commanded by many famous and brilliant generals. The most successful of them all was a politician and statesman of genius. His name was Julius Caesar.

Julius Caesar (100–44 BC) was a brilliant Roman statesman and general. He conquered Gaul (France) and wrote a book about his success, De Bello Gallico (The Gallic Wars)*. He also visited Britain and served as Roman governor of Spain. Caesar fought a civil war against another Roman general called Pompey. In 45 BC he was made dictator for life as well as chief priest and commander of the army. However on 15 March 44 BC, Julius Caesar was assassinated in Rome. As well as his great victories and his improvements in the government of Rome, he is also remembered for reforming the calendar—the month of July is called after him.*

Test your knowledge

1 Name three Roman remains which still exist in various lands.
2 What is meant by an empire?
3 How did the emperor rule distant lands?
4 Give one reason why local people often rebelled against the Romans.
5 What was the main fighting unit in the Roman army called?
6 Who were the auxiliaries?
7 List two weapons carried by Roman soldiers.
8 Name the most famous Roman general of all time.

The Roman roads

As they conquered more and more lands for Rome, Julius Caesar and other military leaders would have travelled along the great roads built by the Romans themselves. Many of these roads still survive in lands as far apart as England and Syria.

The Romans built their roads in long, straight lines which stretched from Rome itself to the most distant parts of the empire. Roman roads were built on a level base consisting of sand or lime mortar. Layers of stone and gravel were placed on top of this and blocks of stone were set in concrete to form the surface. Drainage channels at the side of the roads were used to carry rainwater away.

The Appian Way was one of the main roads out of ancient Rome to the south. It led to the port of Brindisi from which ships sailed to Greece and the East.

Milestones marked the distance from Rome along the path of these roads. The distances were measured from the golden milestone which stood in the Roman Forum.

One of the most famous Roman roads was the *Appian Way* (*Via Appia*) which stretched from Rome to Brindisi in southern Italy, the port which people used for travelling to Greece. The Appian Way was quite wide; two carriages could pass each other with ease. Extensive remains of the Appian Way exist around Rome, enabling us to see for ourselves what Roman roads looked like.

The main reason for the construction of these roads was to enable Roman armies to move quickly from place to place in the empire. A Roman soldier stationed at Hadrian's Wall in the north of England could reach Rome more quickly than travellers in later times could, until the invention of railways.

Travel by sea

As well as travelling by road, the ancient Romans also journeyed by sea. They usually sailed in small ships with one or two sails. Sea travel depended a great deal on the weather and the seasons of the year. Summer was usually the safest time to travel, spring and autumn were in between but winter sailing was generally dangerous. People only travelled by sea during the winter for the most urgent reasons.

An ancient carving of a Roman ship with soldiers on board.

Travel to Greece and the Middle East was usually by sea from the port of Brindisi. It took merchants around a hundred days to reach Palestine from

Rome, although army messengers in faster ships could cover the distance in about half that time.

Unlike people today, the Romans travelled by land or by sea not for pleasure or enjoyment, but only if they had some business to carry out.

Trade with distant lands

Apart from travelling in distant lands as soldiers or government officials, the Romans also travelled to carry out trade with foreign peoples. At the time of the Roman Empire a huge amount of trade was carried on between Rome itself and faraway places.

A Roman coin with the head of the Emperor Hadrian (117–138 AD).

Corn was imported from Egypt and other areas of North Africa, while wine was brought to Rome from Greece and Sicily. The richest trade, however, was with areas producing luxury goods—Arabia, India and China. Incense and a rich ointment called myrrh came from Arabia. From distant India the Romans imported parrots, pearls and spices such as cinnamon and pepper. The presence of the Romans in India has been proved by archaeologists who have discovered Roman coins and pieces of Roman glass there. The principal luxury item imported by the Romans from China was silk.

Although never conquered by Roman armies, ancient Ireland had trade links with the Roman Empire, and Roman coins and pieces of Roman pottery and jewellery have been found here.

Very little of the trade in the Roman Empire benefited the poorer people. However, the rich spent enormous sums of money on luxury goods from distant lands. Archaeologists are still unearthing ancient Roman coins found during excavations in these countries.

Test your knowledge

1 How did the Romans build their roads?
2 What was the Appian Way?
3 Why did the Romans construct such fine roads?
4 When did the Romans travel by ship?
5 With which countries did the Romans carry on their richest trade?
6 Name some of the luxury goods imported into Rome.
7 What proof do we have that the Romans traded with distant lands?
8 Did the Romans trade with ancient Ireland? Explain how you know.

Chapter 7: Review

- In many parts of Europe, North Africa and the Middle East, remains of Roman buildings and roads still exist to remind us that the Romans once ruled over these lands.

- The foreign lands ruled by the Romans made up the Roman Empire. It stretched from the north of England to Egypt and was at the height of its power around the year 100 AD.

- The emperor, who usually lived in Rome, was the ruler of the Roman Empire. He appointed governors to rule the distant provinces of the empire.

- Local peoples often rebelled against their Roman rulers. These rebellions were put down savagely by the Roman armies.

- We can learn about the wars of the Roman Empire from a number of sources, including the writings of historians like Tacitus. We can also learn about Roman victories from monuments like the Arch of Titus and Trajan's Column.

- The main fighting unit in the Roman army was called the legion. Each legion contained foot soldiers (infantry), horse soldiers (cavalry) and soldiers in charge of large weapons (artillery).

- A Roman legionary usually remained in the army for around twenty years. On leaving he was given some land in a distant corner of the empire.

• Roman armies were commanded by many famous and successful generals. The most brilliant of all was Julius Caesar (100–44 BC) who was also a great political leader and ruler of Rome.

• The Romans built splendid roads to enable their armies to reach distant parts of the empire quickly. The remains of many Roman roads can be seen in several countries stretching from England to Syria.

• Travel by sea only took place at certain times of the year. As the Romans sailed in small ships with one or two sails, they avoided making journeys during winter if at all possible.

• At the time of the Roman Empire, a large amount of trade was carried on between Rome itself and distant lands. Corn was imported from North Africa while wine was brought to Rome from Greece and Sicily.

• The richest trade was with areas producing luxury goods. Incense and myrrh came from Arabia, silk from China, and from India, parrots, pearls and spices were imported into Rome.

• Archaeologists have proved the existence of Roman trade with countries like India from findings such as Roman coins and pottery. Such finds have also been made in Ireland and they show that trade existed between Ireland and the Roman Empire.

CHAPTER 8

Pagans and Christians

Religion in Ancient Rome

Walking through the Roman Forum today, we notice that many of the ruins are those of pagan temples. This is not surprising because the Romans did not believe in one god but in several. The various Roman gods and goddesses each had temples built in their honour. The most important was the Temple of Jupiter on Capitol Hill. Jupiter was the Father of the Gods and it was to his temple that victorious generals marched in triumph along the Sacred Way (Via Sacra) of the Forum.

The Roman Forum today contains many ruins of ancient temples.

One of the best preserved and most splendid buildings to survive in Rome from ancient times is the Pantheon. This temple was built in 27 BC and dedicated to all of the gods. With its magnificent dome, it remains one of the greatest

The Pantheon.

An artist's impression of the inside of the Pantheon in ancient times. Describe the building and the activity taking place.

achievements of Roman architects. (Later in this book we shall learn how, 1,500 years later, the great Italian architect Michelangelo modelled buildings like St Peter's Basilica on the Roman Pantheon.)

Jupiter, the Father of the Gods.

Neptune, the God of the Seas.

A household shrine from Pompeii.

A pagan Roman funeral scene carved on a stone tomb.

As well as worshipping their gods and goddesses in temples, the Romans also built altars to the gods in their homes. They believed that the spirits of their ancestors were always close to them.

The Roman belief in some kind of life after death can be seen from their funeral ceremonies. A coin was often placed in the dead person's mouth as a payment for Charon, the legendary ferryman of the underworld who would carry the spirits of the dead across the River Styx into heaven. Although burial was common among poor people, rich Romans were usually cremated.

Charon bringing the dead across the River Styx in the afterlife.

We know from the ruins of temples and from written accounts that the Romans had a religious custom which reminds us of the people of ancient Egypt—emperor-worship. At first, Roman emperors were declared gods after they had died. Later on, however, living emperors named themselves gods and insisted that people worship them. The pagan Romans were willing to do this. However, members of a new religion from the Middle East refused to worship the Roman emperors. They were known as Christians and were to suffer terrible persecution for their beliefs in the Roman Empire.

Christianity comes to Rome

Christianity first arrived in Rome from Jerusalem through Asia Minor and Greece. Under the leadership of the apostle Peter, numbers of Jews had been converted to Christianity. The apostle Paul, a Roman citizen from Tarsus in Asia Minor, began life as a persecutor of Christians. After his conversion while on the road to Damascus, he became the leading missionary spreading Christianity among non-Jews or gentiles. During his missionary journeys Paul wrote epistles or letters to Christians in various cities which he had visited. These form part of the New Testament of the Christian Bible. Together with the Acts of the Apostles by St Luke, the epistles are an important source of knowledge on the spread of Christianity in the Roman Empire.

Test your knowledge

1 What evidence of Roman religion is to be found in the Forum?
2 Why was the Temple of Jupiter on Capitol Hill so important?
3 What was the Pantheon and when was it built?
4 How do we know that Romans believed in a life after death?
5 Who was Charon?
6 Explain 'emperor-worship'.

The Circus of Nero

Looking at the magnificent St Peter's Basilica at the Vatican today, it is hard to imagine that it stands on the site of the ancient Circus of Nero, an amphithe-

The Basilicas of Rome

Constantine the Great, the first Christian Emperor of Rome.

At this time, law courts or basilicas were turned into Christian churches. Inside the basilicas there was a central nave or hall with rows of pillars on each side. There were side aisles beyond these pillars. When basilicas became churches, the main altar was placed where the judge's chair used to stand.

A Roman law court or basilica which became a Christian church.

While Christianity was spreading throughout the Roman Empire, the empire itself was becoming weaker and weaker and open to attack from its enemies.

The end of the Roman Empire

We have already seen that many people in ancient Rome led lives of luxury. From around 300 AD onwards, the Romans faced attacks from warlike peoples outside the empire. Because they had grown accustomed to lazy living, the once mighty Romans were no longer a match for their ruthless attackers.

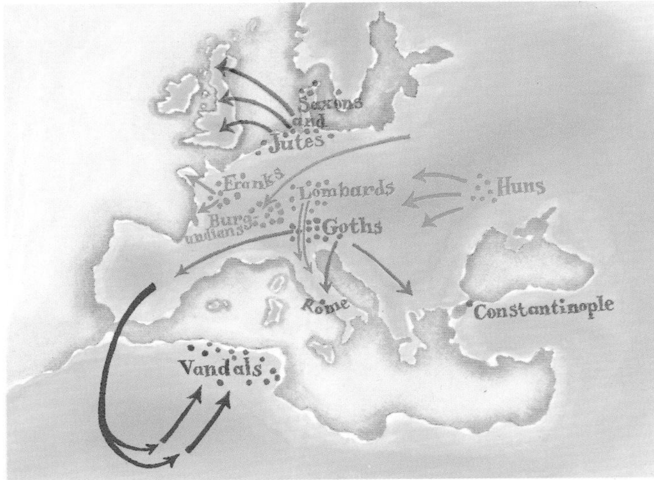

The destruction of the Roman Empire.

In northern and central Europe, outside the borders of the Roman Empire, there lived many fierce and warlike tribes. Most of these were of the Germanic race. Although the Romans had conquered the Celts by the time of Julius Caesar, they never succeeded in conquering the Germanic peoples.

The principal German tribes in central Europe were the Goths, the Vandals and the Franks, the Burgundians and the Lombards. Farther north there were the Angles, Saxons and Jutes, the Germanic tribes which eventually captured the Roman province of Britain. Along with these, casting envious eyes on the rich lands of the Roman Empire, were the fiercest of all—the Huns. These came from Central Asia around 400 AD and brought terror and destruction everywhere they went under the direction of their famous leader, Attilla.

All of these people were regarded as barbarians by the Romans because they lacked most of the signs of civilisation like reading, writing, towns, great buildings and art.

From around 250 AD onwards, various attacks were made on the borders of the Roman Empire by barbarian tribes. Eventually, in 410 AD, the city of Rome itself fell to an army of Goths who plundered and burned the city. It was the first time in eight hundred years that Rome had been conquered by a foreign enemy, and over the next two hundred years various barbarian tribes set up kingdoms in different parts of the former Roman Empire.

The former vast, glorious and magnificent Roman Empire which had covered most of the known world was no more.

Test your knowledge

1 What group of Romans were the first converts to Christianity?

2 What help did wealthy converts give to the local Christians?

3 Name the first Roman emperor to become a Christian.

4 What was a basilica in Rome before the coming of Christianity?

5 To what new use were basilicas put?

6 What race of people lived beyond the borders of the Roman Empire in northern Europe?

Chapter 8: Review

• There are many ruins of ancient temples still to be seen along the Roman Forum. This is not surprising as the ancient Romans worshipped several gods and goddesses.

• The most famous ancient temple was the Temple of Jupiter on Capitol Hill. Jupiter was the chief Roman god and victorious generals marched along the Sacred Way in triumph to this spot to give thanks to Jupiter.

• The Pantheon, a temple of all the gods, was built in 27 BC. It is one of the most splendid of all ancient buildings and can still be seen by visitors to Rome.

• The ancient Romans had some belief in a life after death and they showed great respect for the dead at their funerals and afterwards.

• Like the Egyptians, the Romans believed that dead emperors were gods. Later again, living emperors declared themselves gods and ordered their people to worship them.

• Christianity first arrived in Rome from Jerusalem through Asia Minor and Greece. After the fire of Rome in 64 AD, Emperor Nero carried out a savage persecution of Christians. Among the thousands put to death were the two leading apostles of Christianity, St Peter and St Paul.

• For nearly 300 years, Christians in the Roman Empire were tortured and killed because of their religion. Those who died in this way were called martyrs.

• Outside the walls of Rome there are many underground tunnels where the early Christians buried their dead. Known as catacombs, these places provide us with much valuable evidence on the life and times of the early Christians.

• After the Emperor Constantine became a Christian, the persecution of Christians in the Roman Empire ended. Christianity became the official religion of the state.

• Around the time of Constantine, several law courts or basilicas were changed into Christian churches. Many more churches were built on the model of the ancient basilicas.

• Because of laziness and easy living among the Romans themselves and attacks by fierce Germanic tribes from outside, the Roman Empire began to collapse around 400 AD.

• In 410 AD, the city of Rome was captured by foreign enemies for the first time in eight hundred years. The vast and glorious Roman Empire was now almost at an end.

Ancient and Early Christian Ireland

9 The Remains of Ancient Ireland
10 Tracing our Celtic Past
11 The Celtic Way of Life
12 Pagans and Christians in Early Ireland
13 Treasures from the Past

The Remains of Ancient Ireland

The first settlers

Archaeologists believe that the first people arrived in Ireland around 8,000 years ago (6000 BC). They came into Britain from Scandinavia and then crossed the narrow stretch of water from Scotland to Ireland.

The earliest settlers were a Stone Age people. Like their ancestors in Europe they lived by hunting, fishing and gathering. We know how these first people lived from the remains of their flint and stone weapons and tools which have been found by archaeologists during excavations.

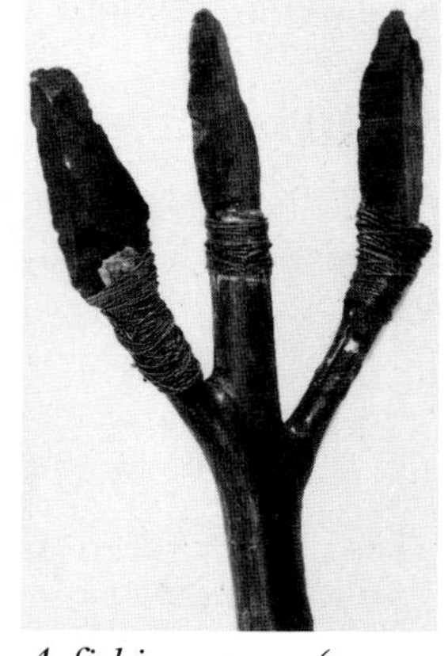
A fishing spear (reconstruction using original flint heads).

A flint axe head.

The Irish countryside in ancient times was very different from what it is today. Because Ireland was covered in thick forests, the earliest people settled near rivers and lakes and travelled in small boats made of animal hides. The forested countryside remained almost unchanged until the arrival of the first farmers around 3500 BC.

Neolithic times in Ireland

The first farmers

Farming first developed in the Fertile Crescent of the Middle East around 8000 BC. This period of time, when people farmed crops and reared animals but still used stone tools, has been called the Neolithic or New Stone Age. It was not until nearly 5,000 years later that the first farming settlers arrived in Ireland. They cleared the forest to grow crops and rear animals. They also brought with them the skills of pottery-making and weaving which, along with farming, had developed earlier in the Middle East. Early settlers in Ireland built comfortable dwellings made of a wooden frame covered in turf sods. Roofs were thatched with rushes.

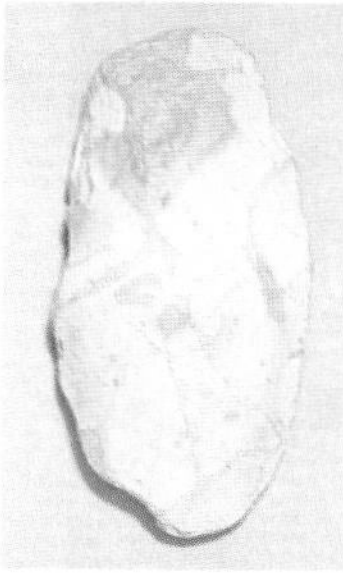
A flint knife.

Archaeologists have unearthed many remains which tell us about the way of life and skills of these Neolithic settlers. From impressions of grain found on pottery we learn that they grew crops such as wheat and barley. A great number of animal bones have been found which prove that they reared livestock such as cattle and sheep.

Lough Gur in Co. Limerick is famous for its remains of ancient settlements. The earliest finds date from Neolithic times and include circular houses built around 3000 BC. In the pictures you can see archaeologists at work together with a reconstruction of an ancient house. Visitors to Lough Gur today can see more than thirty ancient sites and monuments including dwellings, megalithic tombs, stone circles and standing stones.

Many stone and flint axe heads have also been excavated, and even the remains of axe factories have been discovered. In these, the stone was chipped to the rough shape of axe heads and then taken away elsewhere for polishing.

From finds such as these we learn that the early Neolithic settlers in Ireland were a skilful and organised people who cleared forests, grew crops, reared cattle, made pottery and cloth, and even carried out a type of industry and trade. Their skills are even more obvious when we look at the great stone burial chambers which they constructed for their dead.

Test your knowledge

1 When did the first people arrive in Ireland?

2 How did these people live?

3 From what materials were their weapons and tools made?

4 Why did these settlers live near rivers and lakes?

5 When did the first farmers arrive in Ireland?

6 Name three finds made by archaeologists which tell us about the lifestyle of these people.

7 How do we know that Ireland's Neolithic settlers were a skilful and organised people?

Burial customs in ancient Ireland

Many mounds may be seen throughout the Irish countryside. Very often they contain the remains of stone burial chambers which were built in ancient times.

Mounds such as this can be seen all around Ireland. They are usually the sign of an ancient burial site.

The custom of building great tombs of stone first developed around the Mediterranean and came to Ireland from western France, and particularly from Brittany. Because these tombs were made of large stones, they have been called megalithic—from the Greek words *mega* (great) and *lithos* (stone).

Three main types of megalithic tombs have been excavated by archaeologists in Ireland: court cairns, portal dolmens and passage tombs.

Court cairns

Look closely at this picture of a court cairn. Can you see the two rectangular burial chambers and the circular court at the entrance?

This is the earliest type of tomb built by the first farmers. It usually consists of one or two rectangular chambers covered by a stone mound. An open, unroofed circular court lies at the entrance to the chambers. In most of the court cairns found in Ireland, the cairn or mound of stones has been partially or totally removed so that only the upright stones of the chamber now remain.

Portal dolmens

Another type of stone tomb built in Ireland in Neolithic times was called the *portal dolmen*. This usually consists of a single burial

Portal dolmens such as this can be seen in many parts of Ireland.

chamber and gets its name from the two large upright stones at the entrance or portal of the chamber. A huge capstone called a dolmen was placed on top of the two upright stones. How the builders of the portal tombs lifted the huge capstone into place is something of a mystery—especially since a capstone could weigh 100 tonnes. We can only guess that they used wooden levers and props of wood or stone, together with timber rails laid on ramps.

Passage tombs

These were the most spectacular megalithic tombs of all and were built in Ireland around 2500 BC. A typical passage tomb consists of a circular mound with a passage leading from the edge to the burial chamber within. A number of them are usually found together in concentrations known as cemeteries.

The three main passage graves in the Boyne Valley cemetery:

(a) Newgrange.

(b) Dowth.

(c) Knowth.

The burnt and unburnt remains of the dead were found in stone basins such as this one from Knowth.

The most famous examples in Ireland can be seen in the Boyne Valley in Co. Meath where the three great passage graves of Newgrange, Knowth and Dowth were constructed. Excavations are at present being carried out at Knowth. In all, archaeologists have recognised the remains of about thirty passage tombs in the Boyne Valley cemetery, but they believe that many more might still be discovered.

We can learn a lot about the people who built these tombs from the artefacts unearthed in them. These include decorated round-bottom bowls, stone pins and pendants, and clay and chalk balls. We know that cremation was the most common form of burial, although unburnt bones have been found alongside the cremated remains. The stones around the tomb are often decorated with spiral patterns, indicating that the people had developed a form of art. The best example of this spiral pattern work can be seen in Newgrange and Knowth.

These large stones found at both Newgrange (above) and Knowth (below) are decorated with spiral patterns.

The stone roof of the burial chamber at Newgrange. It is known as a corbelled roof. It is made by placing closely-fitting slabs of rock on top of one another. As you will see from the picture, these were placed in such a way that the roof narrows until a single stone covers the top. No plaster was used: instead the dry stones were placed tightly together.

The burial chamber at Newgrange. On 21 December each year, the sun's rays shine through the passage and light up this burial chamber.

Test your knowledge

1 What were megalithic tombs?

2 What were the earliest tombs built by the first farmers?

3 Describe a portal dolmen.

4 Where can we find the most famous examples of passage graves in Ireland?

5 What do these chambers tell us about the life of the people who built them?

The use of metal

Metal was first used around 4000 BC. In 3000 BC, metalsmiths combined copper and tin to make bronze. This development marked the end of the Stone Age and the beginning of the Bronze Age.

About a thousand years later, the first metal-workers arrived in Ireland. These settlers were descendants of the Beaker People who were named after the special form of decorated pottery which they developed. They mined copper and made bronze weapons, tools and ornaments. They also discovered gold in Co. Wicklow and from this they made beautiful jewellery.

A wedge tomb found in Co. Clare.

In the early Bronze Age (after 2000 BC), the most commonly used type of burial chamber was called a wedge tomb. This consisted of a rectangular chamber which was narrower and lower towards the back, and was roofed with slabs. Many of these wedge tombs have been excavated throughout the country, especially in Munster where rich copper deposits occurred. Archaeologists have found many examples of Beaker pottery, together with some metal artefacts.

While Irish farming and trade flourished during the Bronze Age, another people were becoming powerful in Central Europe. They had discovered a stronger durable metal called iron. These people were called the Celts and were soon to arrive in Ireland.

Chapter 9: Review

- Archaeologists believe that the first people arrived in Ireland around 6000 BC. They came from Scandinavia, through Scotland, and then to Ireland.

- At that time Ireland was covered with dense forests. The earliest settlers were a Stone Age people who lived by hunting, fishing and gathering.

- The first farmers arrived in Ireland around 3500 BC. They cleared the forest to grow crops and rear animals. They were a Neolithic or New Stone Age people.

- The Neolithic settlers were also skilled at pottery-making and weaving. They used axes for clearing the forests and other weapons made from stone and flint.

- The Neolithic people built huge stone burial chambers called megalithic tombs. There were three main types of these: court cairns, portal dolmens and passage tombs.

- Court cairns were the earliest type of megalithic tomb. They consisted of one or two chambers covered by a mound.

- Portal dolmens usually consisted of a single stone burial chamber and they got that name from the two large upright stones at the entrance or portal of the chamber. Dolmens were the huge capstones placed flat across the upright stones in portal tombs.

- Passage tombs were the most splendid of all the megalithic tombs and they were built in Ireland around 2500 BC. They consist of a circular mound with a passage leading from the edge to the burial chamber within.

- The most famous example of passage tombs in Ireland are to be found in the Boyne Valley where Knowth and Dowth and Newgrange may be seen.

- Cremation was the most common form of burial, although unburnt bones have also been found in passage graves. The stones around these tombs are often decorated with spiral patterns.

- Around 2000 BC, the first metal workers arrived in Ireland. They mined copper and made bronze weapons, tools and jewellery. They also discovered gold in Co. Wicklow.

- During the early Bronze Age (after 2000 BC) the most common type of burial chamber used in Ireland was the wedge tomb, a rectangular chamber which was narrower and lower towards the back. Many wedge tombs have been excavated, especially in Munster.

CHAPTER 10 Tracing our Celtic Past

The Celts

The Celts were a farming and warlike people who came from Central Europe, an area covering part of present-day France and southern Germany. Between 450 BC and 250 AD, they were one of the most powerful groups in Europe and their influence was to spread to many lands. The power of the Celts was based on the use of a new metal—iron. this was stronger and more durable than bronze and gave the Celts a great advantage over their enemies in battle.

The Greeks and Romans referred to the Celts as barbarians because they had not developed reading and writing and had not built great towns or fine buildings. To the Greeks they were known as *Keltoi*, while the Romans referred to them as *Gauls*.

Much of our knowledge about the Celts is based on the writings of ancient Greeks and Romans. However, our most spectacular evidence on this remarkable people comes from the earth. Dramatic archaeological remains exist throughout Europe and Ireland which reveal for us the story of our Celtic past.

Discoveries at Hallstatt

High in the Austrian Alps, at a place called Hallstatt near the town of Salzburg, archaeologists have made some remarkable discoveries. They have found an ancient salt mine and a huge prehistoric cemetery, both of which have provided valuable information on the earliest Celts.

The Celtic community at Hallstatt depended on salt for its prosperity. Because of the preservative quality of the salt, many remains have survived in the mines and graves which tell us a great deal about the everyday life of the first Celts.

A jar found at Hallstatt by archaeologists.

In the mines, archaeologists have discovered items of clothing made of leather, wool or linen. They have unearthed the remains of food such as barley, millet, beans and a form of apple and cherry.

On the surface of the mines, traces of wooden huts have been repeatedly discovered. Many imported goods from Greece and Rome have also been found, showing that the earliest Celts had trading links with these ancient civilisations.

The Celtic community at Hallstatt was extremely prosperous. The huge cemetery, containing almost 2,500 graves, and the lavish burial customs are clear proof of this. The body, burnt or unburnt was laid under a four-wheeled wagon in a wooden chamber under a grave mound. Many personal possessions were buried with the dead person. These included vessels, iron tools and weapons, joints of meat, and jewellery such as buckles, armlets, rings and necklaces.

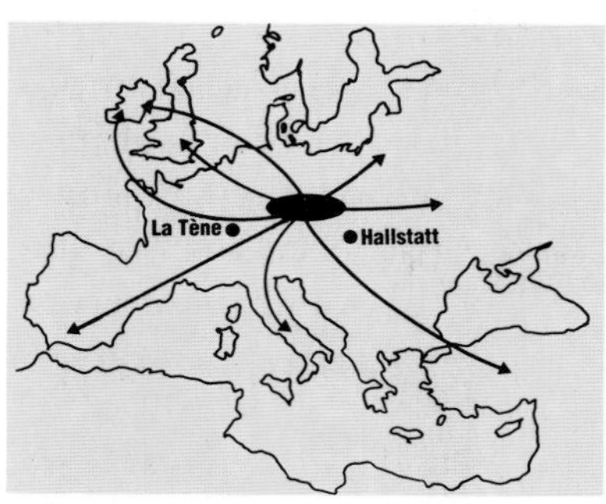

The movements of the Celts from their homeland outwards to conquer new lands.

The remarkable finds at Hallstatt are a great source of information on the first Celts. As a result of these discoveries, the earliest Celts (from 700–500 BC) have been called the Hallstatt Celts. Traces of this Hallstatt civilisation have been found in Austria, Germany and parts of France, Spain and the British Isles.

Further archaeological discoveries in Switzerland have identified a later group of Celts—the La Tène Celts.

Test your knowledge

1 Who were the Celts and where did they come from?

2 What new metal did the Celts use?

3 Why did the Greeks and Romans refer to the Celts as barbarians?

4 Where does much of our knowledge about the Celts come from?

5 What discoveries were made by archaeologists at Hallstatt?

6 Name three things which we learn about the first Celts from the discoveries at Hallstatt.

7 By what name are the earliest Celts now known?

Discoveries at La Tène

Around 1858 at a place called La Tène in Switzerland, the water level of Lake Neuchâtel began to drop and timbers were seen protruding from the mud. These proved to be the remains of types of bridges built by the Celtic settlers about 500 BC.

The remains of a Celtic chariot burial at La Tène. Describe what you can see.

In the lake, archaeologists found great quantities of metal and other objects which they believed had been thrown into the water as offerings to the gods. Many of these objects were decorated in a new form of art which involved the use of swirling patterns and elaborate floral designs.

Four Celtic death masks from La Tène.

The La Tène Celts not only differed from the Hallstatt Celts in their art form. They also had different burial customs. The body of the La Tène Celt was laid out under a light, two-wheeled war chariot along with decorated wine flagons, drinking vessels and joints of pork, all of which showed some belief in a life after death. These later Celts, from around 500 BC, have been called the La Tène Celts after the finds made in Switzerland.

A bronze shield found at Battersea in London. It dates from Celtic times and is decorated in the La Tène style.

The conquering Celts

This Celtic flagon dates from around 400 BC and was found in France.

The Celts were a warlike and adventurous people who spread out from their homelands to conquer many new lands. They moved eastwards to central Europe, west to France and Spain, south to Italy, Greece and Asia Minor, and northwards to Britain and Ireland.

Celtic graves, pottery, iron tools and weapons have been found in places as far apart as Ireland and Asia Minor. However, it was in Ireland that the Celts were to make their most lasting impression, since the rest of Europe was soon to be brought under Roman rule and influence.

The remains of a Celtic sanctuary or holy place found in France. Actual human skulls are in holes in the pillars.

The Celts arrive in Ireland

In the last chapter, we learned how different groups of settlers arrived in Ireland in prehistoric times. The most important of these groups was undoubtedly the Celts.

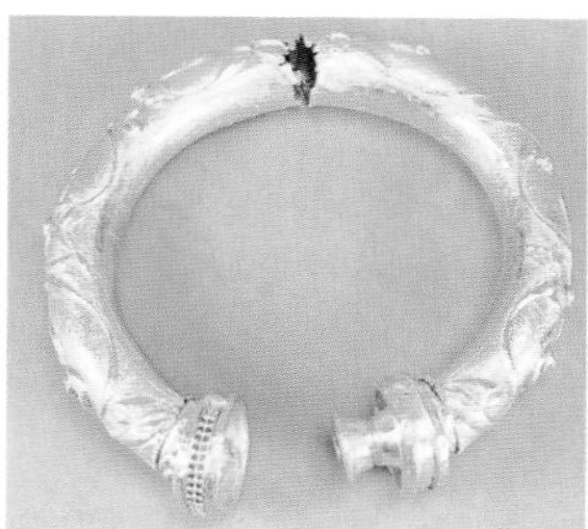

A gold collar from Broighter, Co. Derry, made around 100 BC and decorated in the La Tène style.

Archaeologists are not sure when the first Celts arrived in Ireland, but they believe that it was some time around 600 BC. They may have come from the Continent and probably entered by way of northeastern Scotland. The Celts brought many new customs and skills to Ireland, including their own language and iron weapons and tools.

We cannot depend on archaeology alone to tell us the story of the Celts in Ireland. No spectacular remains have been found like those at Hallstatt or La Tène. We must therefore also rely on two other sources to provide us with information on the Celts. These are the comments of the Greeks and Romans, and the Irish heroic tales and sagas written around the eighth century AD.

The Turoe Stone, a granite boulder situated in Co. Galway. It stands over 1 metre high and is decorated with patterns in the La Tène style.

Test your knowledge

1 What was discovered at La Tène around 1858?

2 Why did the Celts throw objects in the lake?

3 What new art form was found at La Tène?

4 How did the burials at La Tène differ from those found at Hallstatt?

5 By what name have the later Celts become known?

Chapter 10: Review

- The Celts were both a farming and warlike people who originally came from Central Europe. From there they spread out to control many lands. Their power was based on the use of a new and stronger metal—iron.
- Much of our knowledge of the Celts comes from the writings of Greeks and Romans who called the Celts 'barbarians' because they could not read or write.
- At Hallstatt in Austria, archaeologists have made some remarkable discoveries concerning the lifestyle of the earliest Celts. Remains of food, clothing and houses have been unearthed.
- From examining the huge cemetery at Hallstatt, archaeologists have discovered chariot-burials and other evidence which shows the Celts believed in a life after death.
- Because of the findings at Hallstatt, the earliest Celts (700–500 BC) have become known as the Hallstatt Celts. Traces of their civilisation have been found throughout Europe and the British Isles.
- Around 1858, remains of early Celtic settlements were discovered at La Tène in Switzerland. Many metal objects bearing different designs from those at Hallstatt were found.
- The La Tène Celts lived at a later period than the Hallstatt Celts. Like the earlier people they also had chariot-burials and believed in some form of afterlife.
- The Celts were a fierce and warlike people. They moved eastwards into Central Europe, west to France and Spain, south to Italy, Greece and Asia Minor and northwards to Britain and Ireland.
- Celtic graves, pottery, iron and tools and weapons have been found in places as far apart as Ireland and Asia Minor.
- Archaeologists believe that the Celts first arrived in Ireland around 600 BC. They brought new customs and skills to the country, including their own language and the use of iron weapons and tools.

The Celtic Way of Life

The past around us

In the chapter we will look around the Irish countryside for evidence of how the Celts of early Ireland lived and worked. From remains still visible throughout the land, we can piece together a picture of their houses, food, pastimes and warfare. Let us begin to explore life in ancient Ireland by looking at the sites of Celtic homes.

The houses of Celtic Ireland

The people of Celtic Ireland did not live in towns and cities like the Greeks and the Romans. Instead, they lived in isolated dwellings scattered throughout the countryside. These dwellings were called forts and the remains of many of them have been found and excavated.

The ringfort

Part of the stone bank at Dowth ringfort, Co. Meath.

This was the most common type of fort built in ancient Ireland. We can find examples of ringforts in almost every county in the land. Look carefully at the pictures, which show that a ringfort was shaped like a circle and surrounded by a bank or ditch of earth or stone.

As we enter the fort we can see houses and storage buildings. These were also circular and were built of wood and covered with a thatched roof.

The roofs were held up by wooden posts. Very often the postholes are the only remains of the houses found by archaeologists. Sometimes the buildings inside the ringfort were made from dry stone. The remains of these can still be seen at some sites.

The remains of a ringfort or rath, at Ballyconran in Co. Wexford. We can recognise the presence of an ancient ringfort from the raised circular shape of the earth.

This picture shows a stone passage called a souterrain, a feature which was often found under a ringfort. It was used to store goods or sometimes as a hiding place. Many souterrains have been found by workmen while they were quarrying rock or ploughing the land.

The hillfort

The remains of a stone fort on the clifftop at Dun Aengus, Inishmore, Co. Galway. This is known as a promontory fort.

A hillfort looked very like the ringfort. However, it was usually larger and was built on a cliff or hilltop. From these high positions, people had a great view of the surrounding countryside and could easily protect themselves from attack by their enemies.

The crannóg

The picture shows an island in the middle of a lake called a *crannóg*, a very common type of dwelling place in ancient Ireland. A crannóg was built up with layers of material such as lake mud, brushwood and stones and then surrounded by closely set wooden stakes.

Because of the moist conditions around crannógs, parts of wooden stakes and many other wooden and leather artefacts have survived down to the present day.

Sometimes causeways linked the crannóg to the shore. We know that boats were used, as hollowed tree trunks have been found during excavations. While the people of the crannóg farmed on the neighbouring shore, archaeological discoveries show that small industries such as metal-working were carried out within the crannóg.

Visitors to Craggaunowen in Co. Clare or Ferrycarrig in Co. Wexford can see for themselves what a crannóg really looked like. In these places, archaeologists have built models of ancient crannógs using the same methods and materials as the people of Celtic Ireland.

The reconstruction of a crannóg has been built at Craggaunowen in Co. Clare. The crannóg may be reached from the shore by means of a wooden gangway. It is surrounded by a post and wattle fence. Inside there are two circular houses built of wattle and daub (mud). The roofs of the houses are thatched with straw.

Test your knowledge

1 Describe a ringfort.

2 What kind of houses were built inside the ringfort?

3 Why were some forts built on the tops of hills?

4 What is a souterrain?

5 How would you recognise a crannóg?

6 Why have many artefacts found in crannógs been so well preserved?

Crops and cattle

Gathering food: hunting and farming in Celtic Ireland.

(a) An axe head.

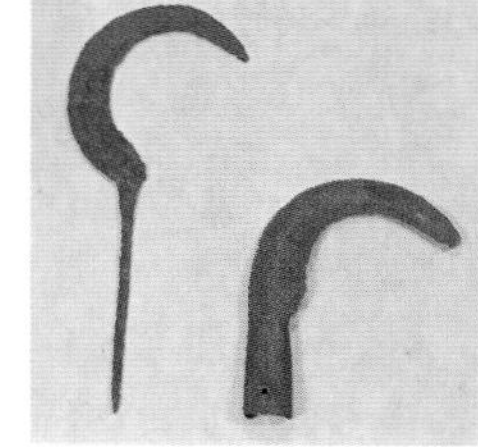

(b) Fish hooks.

Most of the people living in ringforts and crannógs were farmers who grew crops such as wheat, rye, barley and oats. They made a type of porridge from these grains. They also got food by hunting and fishing. We know this from the many bronze fish hooks, iron axes and spearheads found during excavations. Archaeologists have also found deers' antlers, fish and bird bones, together with limpet and periwinkle shells. Scientists can tell the age of these finds by means of Carbon 14 dating.

Cattle were greatly prized by the people of ancient Ireland. They were used to provide meat, cheese and milk. At night, farmers brought their cattle inside the ringfort as cattle raids were very common. Many of the stories enjoyed by the Celts were about such cattle raids. The most famous of these tales is the *Táin* or the *Cattle Raid of Cooley*. This tells about a terrible war between Ulster and Connacht which took place over a cattle raid.

The ancient method of cooking

The remains of ancient cooking sites can be found throughout Ireland. Today they look like mounds of burnt stones and charcoal. This type of cooking site was known as a *fulacht fiadh*.

A fulacht fiadh excavated by archaeologists at Drombeg in Co. Cork.

By digging out the mound of a *fulacht fiadh*, archaeologists have found a hollow space which marks the place of the hearth. Here a fire was lit and large stones were heated. Nearby a timber trough was filled with water. The heated stones were then places in the water, causing it to boil. Large joints of meat were then cooked in the boiling water.

Many of the hot stones shattered into pieces when they were dropped in the cold water. These broken stones were then taken from the trough and placed on a heap to one side. These heaps or mounds of broken or burnt stones are the main signs of an ancient cooking site.

Feasting

Feasting at lavish banquets was one of the great pleasures of the rich in Celtic Ireland. The Greek and Roman writers often commented on the Celts' great love of food and drink. In addition, Irish stories give us a vivid account of the merry-making enjoyed at a Celtic feast.

Preparing meals
A rotary stone quern for grinding corn into flour.

An early Irish metal ladle.

Pottery food vessels.

However, feasts were sometimes the scene of fighting and bloodshed. The greatest warrior present was given the best piece of meat known as 'The Hero's Portion'. There was often a fight to the death to decide who the best warrior was. One Irish story called *Bricriu's Feast* tells how three Ulstermen, including the legendary Cúchulainn, seized their weapons and fought fiercely over the 'The Hero's Portion'.

If we are to believe the Irish stories, war was never far from the minds of the ancient Celts.

Test your knowledge

1 What type of crops were grown by the Celts?
2 What evidence have archaeologists found to show the Celts also went hunting and fishing?
3 How do we know that cattle-rearing was important in the life of Celtic Ireland?
4 What do we learn from ancient cooking sites about the cooking of food in Celtic times?
5 What evidence do we have to show that feasting was a popular pastime among the richer Celts?
6 Why did feasts often end up in fighting and bloodshed? Have we any evidence to back this up?

Wars and warriors

From the weapons and war chariots found in their graves we know that the Celts were a warlike people. This archaeological evidence is again backed up by the Roman and Greek writers, and especially by the Irish sagas which are full of tales about warriors and wars. Many of these stories tell of the deeds and adventures of the legendary hero and warrior, Cúchulainn.

From archaeological discoveries and the Irish sagas, we know that iron swords and spears were the Celts' main weapons. Slings and javelins were also used, and round wooden shields or shields of leather were carried into battle.

The Celts often fought from light two-wheeled chariots which carried two men—the warrior and his charioteer. In the ancient Irish stories,

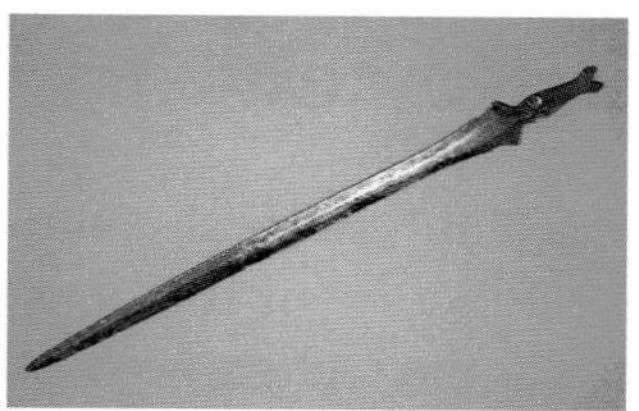

The remains of a leather shield and an iron sword, typical weapons used by the Celts in Ireland.

Cúchulainn is often seen going into battle on such a chariot, driven by his loyal and skilful charioteer, Laeg.

The favourite form of fighting carried out by the Celts was single combat. This involved the best warrior from one side fighting the best from the other side. Again, the Irish sagas provide us with evidence of this. In the greatest of these stories, the *Táin*, Cúchulainn fights his foster-brother, Ferdia, in single combat.

Headhunting was also a common custom among the Celts. They would cut off the heads of their enemies in battle and carry them home as trophies or as offerings to the gods.

Men were not only great warriors in Celtic Ireland. Many women were also skilled in the handling of weapons. Indeed, according to Celtic legend, the great Cúchulainn himself was trained by two women—Scatha and Aoife.

The Celts, however, did not spend all their time working and fighting. They also had plenty of opportunities for pastimes and amusements.

Pastimes and amusements

The Celts enjoyed many pastimes including hunting, storytelling, poetry and music. The poet or *file* was a very important person who was held in high regard. The most popular musical instrument seems to have been the harp and this is often seen in examples of stone carving and metal work from the time.

A wooden gaming-board dating from Celtic times which was found at Ballinderry, Co. Westmeath.

We learn from the ancient stories that outdoor games such as hunting and a form of hurling were enjoyed by the people.

A board-game called *fidchell* was also played. This was a type of chess and a gaming-board of carved yew-wood together with some bone dice have been discovered by archaeologists during excavations.

Test your knowledge

1 What evidence do we have that the Celts were a warlike people?

2 What were the main weapons used in Celtic Ireland?

3 On what did the Celts often ride into battle? What evidence do we have of this?

4 What was the favourite form of fighting carried out by the Celts?

5 What was headhunting?

6 Were men the only great warriors in Celtic Ireland?

7 What pastimes were enjoyed by those living in Celtic times?

8 What archaeological evidence do we have that the Celts played a form of chess?

How the Celts were governed

Having looked at the houses, food and pastimes of the Celts, we will now see how they were governed. In Celtic times, unlike today, Ireland was not ruled by a single government. Instead, the country was divided into around 150 small independent kingdoms called *tuatha*.

The stone seat at Tullahoge in Co. Tyrone where the O'Neills were crowned kings.

Each *tuath* was ruled over by its own king. There were great celebrations when a man became a king. The priests, or *druids*, performed religious ceremonies, a huge feast was held and the new king sat on a special throne or stood on a great flat stone. Some of the places where kings

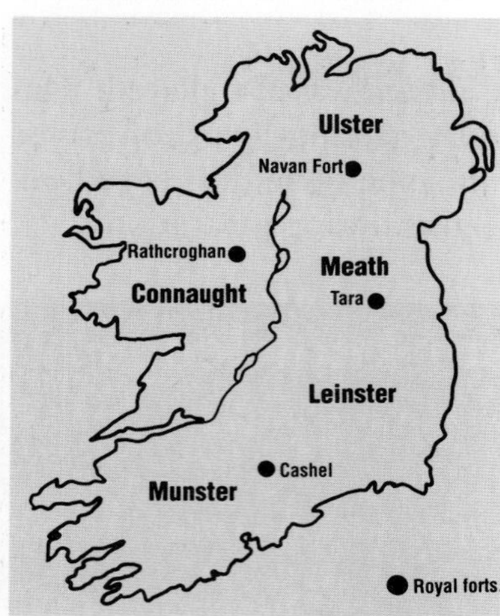

The provinces with their royal forts in Ireland around 400 AD.

were crowned still survive and have been investigated by archaeologists.

The people believed that a good king would win victories in battle and that the harvest would be plentiful during his rule. While many kings governed small areas of land, some ruled over large provinces. We can still see the sites of the palaces of the more powerful kings at places like the Hill of Tara in Co. Meath and Navan Fort in Co. Armagh.

The people of the *tuath* were divided into rich and poor. Next to the king came the nobles and the learned classes such as druids, poets and judges. The judges or *brehons* had their own type of Irish law called *Brehon Laws*—from the Irish word *breitheamh*, meaning judge. The Brehon Laws are an important source for historians investigating life in Ireland over a thousand years ago.

An aerial view of the ancient royal site of Tara in Co. Meath.

Next in importance to the learned classes came the freemen. These were farmers and craftsmen who owned their own land.

The rest of the people were unfree members of the *tuath*. They were little better than slaves and could not own property or carry weapons. Many of them were people who had been captured in war.

Having looked at the everyday lives of the ancient Celts, in the next chapter we will examine their religious beliefs. We will also learn how these beliefs changed completely when the Christian religion reached Ireland around 400 AD.

Chapter 11: Review

- From remains still visible around the Irish countryside we can piece together a picture of the houses, food, pastimes and warfare of the Celts who lived in ancient Ireland.

- The Celts of Ireland did not live in towns and cities like the Greeks and Romans. Instead they lived in isolated dwellings known as forts.

- Ringforts were the most common type of forts built in early Ireland. They were shaped like a circle and surrounded by a bank or ditch. Wooden houses and storage buildings were set up inside the ringforts.

- Souterrains were underground passages often found beneath ringforts. They were used as storage places or as hiding places.

- Hillforts were like ringforts except that they were usually larger and were built on the top of hills or cliffs as a protection from enemy attacks.

- Crannógs were a very common type of dwelling in ancient Ireland. They were houses built on islands in the middle of lakes. Sometimes causeways linked them to the shore.

- Visitors to Craggaunowen in Co. Clare or Ferrycarrig in Co. Wexford can see models of crannógs designed by archaeologists using the same methods and materials as the people of ancient Ireland.

- The Celtic people grew grain and crops from which they made a type of porridge. They also gathered food by hunting and fishing.

- Cattle were greatly prized by the Celts. They were used to provide meat, cheese and milk and were often brought inside the forts because cattle raids were quite common.

- Many of the stories enjoyed by the Celts involved cattle raids. The most famous of these, the *Táin* or the *Cattle Raid of Cooley*, featured the legendary hero, Cúchulainn.

• There are many ancient cooking sites to be found throughout Ireland. These were called *fulachta fiadh* and meat was cooked in them. Stones were first heated in a fire and then placed in a trough of water. When the water boiled the meat was placed in it and left to cook.

• Feasting was one of the favourite pleasures of the rich in ancient Ireland. Fighting often broke out at banquets concerning 'The Hero's Portion', a piece of meat set aside for the best warrior.

• Archaeologists have unearthed many ancient Celtic weapons used in Ireland such as swords, spears and shields. The Celtic heroes usually fought in chariots driven by an assistant.

• Single combat between the best warriors in different armies was very popular among the Celts. Headhunting was also practised. A victorious hero would return from battle with the heads of his enemies tied to the wheels of his chariot.

• The Celts enjoyed many pastimes such as hunting, storytelling, poetry and music. The poet or *file* was highly respected. A form of hurling was played and an ancient type of chess board has been discovered.

• In Celtic times, unlike today, Ireland was not ruled by a single government. Instead the country was divided into about 150 small independent kingdoms called *tuatha*, each ruled by its own king.

• Each *tuath* was strictly divided into rich and poor. After the king came the nobles and learned classes, followed by the freemen and craftsmen. Least of all were the unfree members of the *tuath* who were treated like slaves.

CHAPTER 12 Pagans and Christians in Early Ireland

The pagan Celts

From findings at Hallstatt and La Tène we know that the early Celts believed in some kind of life after death. The chariot-burials in these places contained objects which archaeologists believe were offerings for the gods.

Celtic graves excavated in Ireland show that personal possessions such as jewellery were placed alongside the cremated remains of the dead person. However, very little has survived from early times concerning the gods of the pagan Celts. We depend a lot on the writings of the Greeks and Romans and on early Irish stories for information about Celtic gods.

Like the Greeks and Romans, the Celts worshipped several gods. They were also very superstitious, believing that woods, lakes, rivers and wells were sacred places where gods dwelt.

The chief god of the pagan Celts was *An Dagda*, the good god and father of the people. They had many other gods including *Lug* who, according to legends, was the father of the hero, Cúchulainn. The Celtic people also worshipped goddesses such as *Morrigan*, *Badb* and *Nemain*.

The Celts offered animal sacrifices to their gods and even the occasional human sacrifice. All of these religious ceremonies were carried out by a very important group of pagan priests in ancient Ireland—the *druids*.

The druids

As the priests of the Celtic religion, the druids carried out sacrifices to the gods and organised festivals. They were also thought to have magical powers and to be able to foretell the future. In one famous story, a druid called Cathbad predicted that Cúchulainn would grow up to be a great hero.

The druids were not only pagan priests. They were also very learned men who often advised rulers and settled disputes between people. As there was no writing in Celtic times, the druids had to memorise all the customs and stories of the people. The training to become a druid was long and difficult and could take up to twenty years.

Many young men came to the schools of the druids in search of knowledge and wisdom.

Celtic festivals

Samhain	1 Nov	*The beginning of the Celtic year when animals were gathered in for winter and sacrifices were made to the god* Dagda.
Imbolc	1 Feb	*Dedicated to the goddess Brigid.*
Bealtaine	1 May	*Huge fires were lit and cattle were driven through them to be purified. The Celts believed that both crops and cattle would grow because of these rituals.*
Lughnasa	1 Aug	*Celebrated in honour of the* God Lug *in the hope of a good harvest.*

I E U O A R Z NG G M Q C T D H N S F L B

An ogham stone found in Co. Kerry. Ogham was the earliest form of writing in Celtic Ireland. It involved notches carved on the edges of stones to indicate the different letters. Ogham stones were used to mark boundaries or graves.

Test your knowledge

1 How do we know that the Celts believed in a life after death?

2 Name two Celtic gods.

3 Who were the druids?

4 What activities were carried out by the druids?

5 Which festival opened the Celtic year?

6 What happened on 1 May?

7 What festival was held in honour of the god *Lug*?

Changing times

From around 400 AD onwards, Ireland like the rest of Europe was to be converted to Christianity. This development brought about great changes in Ireland, including the introduction of reading and writing as we know them today. However, while Christianity brought changes to Irish life, many of the Celtic traditions and customs which you have read about continued into Christian times.

Ireland's first Christians

You have already learned how Christianity spread throughout the Roman Empire after the conversion of Constantine. Ireland alone of the West European countries was not brought under Roman control. However, many trading links existed between the Irish and the Romans, and archaeologists have uncovered many Roman artefacts in their excavations throughout the country.

A Roman coin found in Ireland and on display in the National Museum, Dublin. It is one of many Roman objects found by archaeologists in various parts of the country.

Roman merchants may have been the first to bring the Christian religion to Ireland. Although we do not know exactly when it arrived, there were probably some Christians in Ireland around 400 AD. In 431 AD, Pope Celestine sent a bishop called Palladius to visit the Christians in Ireland. However, he died soon after arriving in the country. In the following year the most famous Christian missionary of all arrived to preach the Gospel to the pagan Irish. His name was Patrick.

The arrival of St Patrick

St Patrick was born in Britain and spent some time in Ireland as a slave tending sheep. After escaping back to Britain he believed that he heard the voices of the Irish in his dreams calling him back to convert them to Christianity. He then studied to become a priest and returned to Ireland as a missionary in 432 AD.

We know about the life of St Patrick from two works which he himself wrote in Latin. One of these works is called *A Life of St Patrick*.

Patrick spent his time travelling around the country preaching and converting people. He liked to convert kings because, when that happened, their people often became Christians as well. St Patrick probably died in 461 AD. It is believed that he is buried at Downpatrick in Co. Down.

The Christian church founded by St Patrick in Ireland was organised into *dioceses* ruled by *bishops*. Many wooden churches were built throughout the country, but no remains of these have been found.

Test your knowledge

1 How did the Christian religion first arrive in Ireland?
2 Who was Palladius?
3 When did St Patrick return to Ireland as a missionary?
4 Why did he come back to Ireland?
5 What sources are there concerning St Patrick's life?
6 Where is St Patrick believed to be buried?

The first monasteries

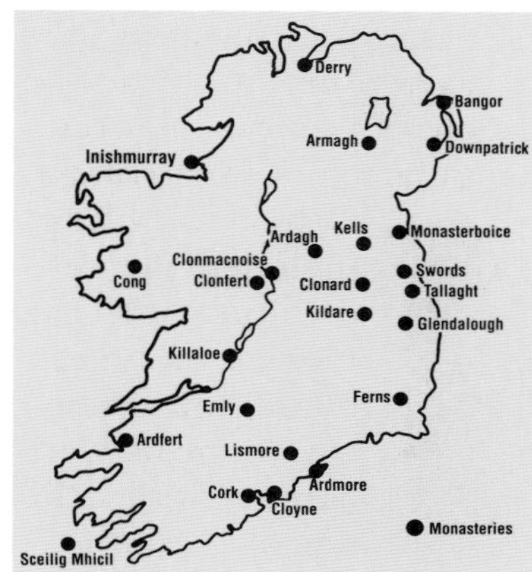

Early Christian Ireland.

By the year 500 AD, many important Christian monasteries had been founded in Britain to which Irishmen went to study. They then returned to Ireland to set up their own monasteries in remote places, living lives of work and prayer. In 490 AD St Enda returned from Britain to found a monastery on the Aran Islands. St Finian founded Clonard about 510 AD; St Ciarán founded Clonmacnoise about 500 AD, and the monasteries of Derry and Durrow were set up by St Columcille. The most famous of the women missionaries was St Brigid, who set up her community in Kildare.

The ruins at Clonmacnoise in Co. Offaly where St Ciarán first established a monastery on the banks of the River Shannon around the year 500 AD. Visitors to Clonmacnoise today can see a number of stone remains including several small churches, a cathedral, slabs and crosses and even a castle which was built to protect the area from attack. However, no remains survive of the earliest buildings which were all made of wood.

Soon the monasteries became more important than the dioceses, and the *abbot* or head of the monastery became a more powerful figure than the bishop.

Let us now take a close look at what an early Irish monastery looked like.

Archaeological remains

Archaeologists have found few remains of the first Irish monasteries. This is because the buildings were all made of timber. Using written sources, however, we can piece together what an early Irish monastery must have looked like.

In appearance an early monastery resembled a large ringfort. Within the stone or earthen bank, the buildings were made of oaken planks or wattle and daub, with roofs of thatch. The most important building was the rectangular church or *oratory*. Other buildings included the cells or huts of the monks, the guest-house, the *refectory* where meals were eaten, and the school.

Gallarus Oratory in Co. Kerry dates from early Christian times and was built without the use of mortar.

In looking for complete isolation, the monks sometimes chose remote islands off the west coast on which to build their monasteries. As timber was not available these buildings were made from stone. The remains of some of these island monasteries have survived, and they tell us a lot about the life and times of the first monks. Let us take a look at the two best preserved examples—Sceilg Mhicil off the coast of Kerry, and Inishmurray off the coast of Sligo.

Sceilg Mhicil—the remains of an island monastery

Sceilg Mhicil is a bare, towering rock rising some 200 metres above the stormy Atlantic. Built on a terrace just beneath the peak are the remains of an early Irish monastery which might have been founded by St Finian some time in the ninth century. The buildings consist of six dry-stone beehive cells in which the monks lived, and two small churches or oratories. The roof of both the cells and the oratories are *corbelled*. The waterproof cells are smoothly finished on the inside and contain stone cupboards.

There is also a tiny graveyard on Sceilg Mhicil with small rough slabs carved with crosses. Below a little garden there are steps that lead steeply down to three landing places.

The ruins at Sceilg Mhicil in Co.Kerry.

The remains of the beehive cells of the monks on Sceilg Mhicil.

Despite the fury of the Atlantic Ocean, the monastery itself was well situated in a sunny, sheltered location. The monks probably survived by rearing goats, hunting birds and fishing.

Ruins of Inishmurray

The remains of an early Irish monastery at Inishmurray in Co. Sligo.

The ruins of another stone monastery can be seen on the island of Inishmurray off the coast of Sligo. Here archaeologists have examined the remains of a massive wall, some five metres thick at the base, which enclosed the monastery. Within this enclosure the remains of beehive cells and a number of stone churches similar to those found on Sceilg Mhicil can be seen. About fifty slabs of rock carved with crosses are scattered both inside and outside the monastery walls. It is believed that this monastery was founded by St Molaise or Laisren in the early sixth century, and was plundered by the Vikings in the year 802 AD.

Although most of the early Irish monasteries were made of timber, the stone remains of the buildings at Sceilg Mhicil and Inishmurray give us a very good idea of what an Irish monastery looked like. Let us now take a closer look at the lives of the monks who lived in these places.

The life of the monks

From looking at the remains on Sceilg Mhicil and Inishmurray, it would appear that Irish monasteries were cold, bleak paces where the monks led lives of prayer and penance. Without doubt, life in an Irish monastery was very strict and disciplined. Under the rule of the abbot, the monks spent their days working, praying and studying.

The monastery was totally self sufficient, supplying all its own needs. While some monks grew crops and fished in the local river or the sea, others were busy in the forge and workshops producing tools.

The monasteries were also great centres of learning to which students flocked from far and wide. They were taught Latin by the monks and wrote their lessons on wax tablets with a *stylus*. Two such tablets containing verses of the *Psalms* can now be seen in the National Museum in Dublin.

The spread of the monasteries

By the year 700 AD many monasteries had been established throughout Ireland. By that time most of the Celtic rulers had become converted to Christianity and pagan festivals like those once held at Tara no longer took place.

Many monasteries grew in size and became much like small towns or villages. Usually when a monastery grew the monks did not build a larger church but instead built a number of smaller churches.

The monastic ruins at Glendalough in Co. Wicklow are spread along two miles of the valley. The picture shown here shows some of the buildings including a church and a round tower.

Glendalough in Co. Wicklow is a good example of a monastery which expanded greatly in size over the centuries. Among the ruins of this monastery today we find a small oratory and the remains of a beehive cell dating from the seventh century, together with later buildings nearly two kilometres away dating from the twelfth century.

An artist's reconstruction of the monastery at Glendalough, Co. Wicklow.

Test your knowledge

1 Why did Irishmen go to monasteries in Britain?
2 Name the saint who founded a monastery on the Aran Islands?
3 What was the most famous monastery founded by St Ciarán?
4 Where did St Brigid set up her religious community?
5 How did the early Irish monks spend their day?
6 Where can we find the remains of two island monasteries today?
7 What monastic remains can we see in Glendalough?

Irish Missionaries abroad

Many Irish monks founded monasteries not only in Ireland but throughout Britain and Europe as well. At first these founders went abroad as a penance, cutting themselves off from family and friends. Later the monks went to foreign lands as missionaries to convert pagan peoples to Christianity.

One of the first great Irish missionaries was St Columcille (or St Columba), the founder of monasteries at Durrow and Derry. He also set up a

The main monasteries founded by Irish monks abroad.

monastery on the tiny island of Iona off the west coast of Scotland in 563 AD. From Iona, St Columcille and his followers converted the pagan tribes of Scotland. Iona became a great centre for learning and many kings of Scotland were buried there. Since all the buildings in Columcille's original settlement were made of wood, none of them have survived. All the stone ruins to be seen there today date from a much later time.

However, archaeologists have excavated parts of Iona and have unearthed what is thought to be the foundations of St Columcille's hut, together with a flagstone for his bed and three stones which supported his writing table.

The monastery of Iona in Scotland as seen today.

After Columcille's death in 597 AD, missionaries from Iona spread the Christian faith into England. The most famous of these men was St Aidan, who founded the monastery of Lindisfarne off the coast of Northumbria in 635 AD. Later, missionaries from England joined Irish monks in the conversion of pagans in Europe.

One of the greatest Irish missionaries in Europe was St Columbanus, who founded many monasteries on the Continent, including Luxeuil in France (590 AD) and Bobbio in Italy (612 AD). As well as being the leading Irish missionary of his day, Columbanus was also a great writer and scholar. He was one of the most respected churchmen in Europe and both popes and kings looked for his advice.

Other great Irish missionaries in Europe included St Gall, who spread Christianity in Europe and saints Fergal and Killian who preached the Gospel in Germany.

The monasteries founded by Irish monks in Ireland, Britain and Europe became great centres of learning and art. Beautiful manuscripts and chalices remind us today of the wonderful skills and achievements of the early Irish monks. In the next chapter we will take a close look at some of the magnificent treasures which have earned this period its name: The Golden Age of Early Christian Art.

A picture of St John the Evangelist in a 7th century manuscript from the monastery of St Gallen in Switzerland. When early Irish monks went to Europe they brought their skills of writing and decorating manuscripts with them.

Test your knowledge

1 Why did Irish monks go abroad?

2 Who founded the monastery at Iona in Scotland?

3 Name the monastery set up by St Aidan.

4 Name two monasteries set up in Europe by St Columbanus.

5 In what country did St Killian preach the Gospel?

Chapter 12: Review

• Celtic graves excavated in Ireland show that personal possessions such as jewellery were placed alongside the cremated remains of the dead person, indicating perhaps some belief in a life after death.

• Like the Greeks and the Romans, the pagan Celts worshipped many gods. Their chief god was *An Dagda*. They also worshipped other gods such as *Lug* and goddesses like *Morrigan*, *Badb* and *Nemain*.

• The Celtic priests, or druids, offered animal sacrifices to the gods and even the occasional human sacrifice. As well as being pagan priests, the druids were also very learned men who were believed to have magical powers such as the ability to look into the future.

• There were four great pagan festivals each year in Celtic Ireland: *Samhain* (1 November), *Imbolc* (1 February), *Bealtaine* (1 May) and *Lughnasa* (1 August).

• Roman merchants may have been the first people to introduce the Christian religion into Ireland. In 431 AD Pope Celestine sent a bishop called Palladius to visit the Christians who lived in Ireland.

• St Patrick began his mission of converting Ireland to Christianity in 432 AD. He travelled around the country preaching the Gospel and baptising people. He wrote two accounts of his life which are important sources of information for historians.

• By the year 500 AD many important monasteries had been founded in Britain, where Irishmen went to study. They then returned to set up their own monasteries in Ireland.

• St Enda founded a monastery on the Aran Islands, St Finian founded Clonard, St Ciarán established Clonmacnoise and the monasteries at Durrow and Derry were set up by St Columcille.

• The earliest Irish monasteries resembled ringforts. They were clusters of wooden buildings including the most important—the church or oratory. The cells of the monks were grouped around this.

• Sceilg Mhicil in Kerry and Inishmurray in Sligo have splendid remains of early Irish stone monasteries. Situated as they were in remote and lonely places, their monks led strict lives of prayer, work and penance.

• Each monastery was self sufficient, that is its monks supplied all their own needs. They grew crops, fished, made tools and eating vessels, taught Latin and copied out manuscripts by hand.

• By 700 AD many monasteries had been founded throughout Ireland. Some grew into villages or small towns as houses and other buildings were placed around the monastery.

• One of the first of these missionaries was St Columcille, who founded a monastery on the island of Iona off the west coast of Scotland in 563 AD.

• One of the greatest Irish missionaries in Europe was St Columbanus, who founded many monasteries, including those at Luxeuil in France and Bobbio in Italy.

CHAPTER 13 Treasures from the Past

The wealth of monasteries

From around 700 AD onwards the monasteries in Ireland increased in size and wealth. Many larger monasteries owned vast amounts of land and huge herds of cattle. This wealth allowed the monks to create beautiful works of art such as gold and silver chalices, colourful manuscripts and ornamental stone crosses.

Many monks were wonderful craftsmen who were skilled in the use of precious metals and jewels. While some silver and gold were found locally in Ireland, some was probably imported as well. Tin and amber were also imported, while many decorative stones were found along local beaches.

Other monks were expert stone masons who carved and decorated crosses. The stones were all available locally and the crosses were decorated with scenes from the Bible.

Irish monks were famous all over Europe for decorating or illuminating manuscripts. These hand-written books were produced in a special room in the monastery called a *scriptorium*. Here monks wrote on *vellum*, a material made from calf skins. Since Ireland was a cattle-rearing country, vellum was always available. Most manuscripts were written in Latin and were copies of the Gospels and other parts of the Bible.

We will now take a closer look at some of the splendid works of art produced by the artists and craftsmen in early Christian Ireland.

Test your knowledge

1 Why do you think wealth was so important in producing beautiful works of art?
2 Where did the monks get their precious metals and jewels?
3 What was the *scriptorium*?
4 From what material were the manuscripts made?

The art of metalwork

The Derrynaflan Chalice found in Co. Tipperary in 1980 is a magnificent work of art dating from around 800 AD.

St Patrick's Bell Shrine, a wonderfully ornamented covering for the bell known as St Patrick's Bell. Notice the spiral-type Celtic designs.

Metalwork was a very ancient craft in Ireland. We have already seen many examples of Celtic metal ornaments such as brooches, torcs and weapons. The monks of the seventh and eighth centuries carried on this great tradition in metalwork and produced many beautiful objects in gold, silver and bronze. Most of these were for religious use and included chalices, book coverings, bells and *reliquaries* or containers which held the belongings or relics of the saints.

We will now take a look at some to the greatest works produced by the Christian metalsmiths.

The Ardagh Chalice

This is a large, two-handled silver cup made around 750 AD. It is beautifully decorated with gold, gilt bronze, enamel and glass. It was first discovered in 1868 in a

The Ardagh Chalice.

potato field in Ardagh, Co. Limerick. Four brooches and a small bronze cup were found along with the chalice. They probably belonged to some early Irish church or monastery and were hidden for safekeeping.

2 What types of metal objects were made by the monks?
3 Using the picture as a guide, describe the Ardagh Chalice.
4 Describe the Tara Brooch.

The Tara Brooch

The Tara Brooch.

A detail from the Tara Brooch.

This beautiful brooch is made of silver and is decorated with coloured stones and animal patterns. It was made at some time in the eighth century and was probably worn on the shoulder with the pin pointing upwards. The Tara Brooch was found on the seashore at Bettystown in Co. Meath.

The Moylough Belt Reliquary

The Moylough Belt Reliquary.

A detail from the Moylough Belt Reliquary.

The Moylough Belt Reliquary was discovered in a bog at Moylough, Co. Sligo. It was made around 750 AD from tinned bronze to hold the leather belt of a saint. It contains four sections. In the centre of each section there is a bronze medallion together with ornaments made from glass and enamel.

Test your knowledge

1 How do we know that metalwork was a very ancient craft in Ireland?

Stone crosses

An early type of stone cross found in Sceilg Mhicil.

In many monastic sites today we can see stone crosses dating from earlier times. The very earliest crosses in Ireland were simply slabs of rock with the crosses carved on the surface. Examples of this type of cross can be seen on Sceilg Mhicil in Co. Kerry.

Later, free-standing crosses were carved with the arms joined by a circle. The first true High Crosses of Ireland can be seen at Ahenny, Co. Tipperary and were built in the eighth century. The crosses were divided into panels which were decorated with carved figures of people, animals and processions. Still later, high crosses such as those seen today at Clonmacnoise and Monasterboice were decorated with carved scenes from the Bible such as the Crucifixion and Resurrection of Christ, Adam and Eve, and Daniel in the Lion's Den.

A High Cross at Ahenny in Co. Tipperary. Notice the circles joining the arms of the cross which make it a typical 'Celtic' cross. Notice also the spiral-type Celtic designs.

St Muireadach's High Cross at Monasterboice, Co. Louth. Notice its Celtic shape and the detailed scenes carved on its surface.

A panel from St Muireadach's Cross showing Adam and Eve (left) and their sons Cain and Abel (right).

Monks and manuscripts

The special ornamental cover or shrine made to house the Cathach, the earliest surviving Irish manuscript now in existence.

The earliest surviving Irish manuscript now in existence is a copy of the Psalms in Latin known as the *Cathach*. Supposedly written by St Columcille himself, it dates from the early sixth century and was kept in a special leather cover. It contains very little decoration or colourful illumination.

The first great decorated manuscript produced by Irish monks which has survived is the Book of Durrow. It dates from around 700 AD and was probably written in a monastery in northern England. It is a small manuscript of the Gospels which was preserved in the monastery at Durrow in Co. Laois. It was beautifully illuminated in four colours: brown, gold, yellow and green. At one time the Book of Durrow was owned by a local farmer who poured water on it as a cure for cattle!

A page from the Book of Durrow containing detailed and colourful Celtic designs.

One of the greatest illuminated manuscripts ever produced is the Book of Kells. This is a large manuscript of the four Gospels which was probably written around 800 AD at Iona in Scotland. When Vikings attacked Iona the precious manuscript was brought to the monastery of Kells in Co. Meath for safekeeping. The Book of Kells contains many full-page illustrations and includes pictures of animals and scenes from everyday life. This famous manuscript can now be seen in Trinity College, Dublin.

These pages from The Book of Kells show the high degree of skill in the craft of illumination achieved by the monks in early Ireland.

Test your knowledge

1 What were the earliest stone crosses like?

2 Describe the first true high crosses.

3 What type of carvings decorated the crosses?

4 What is the earliest surviving Irish manuscript?

5 Why is the Book of Durrow such an important manuscript?

6 Looking at the pictures, explain whether you think the Book of Kells is a great work.

The round towers

In this chapter we have seen some of the great treasures produced in Irish monasteries during the eighth century. In addition, the monasteries were given many valuables for safekeeping by kings and nobles. These riches made the monasteries very likely targets for attack by both Irish and foreign raiders in search of easy fortunes. While monasteries were often raided by bands of native Irish, from about 800 AD onwards a new and ruthless group of raiders arrived in Ireland from Scandinavia—the Vikings.

The monks now had to think of ways of defending themselves. They began to use stone instead of wood for their buildings and also constructed many round towers. These were first used as belfries to call the monks to prayer from the fields. They were also used as places of refuge in time of attack.

The Round Tower at Ardmore, Co. Waterford surrounded by the ruins of a monastery.

The round towers varied in height from 25 to 35 metres. The doorway was usually 3 to 5 metres above the ground and could be reached only by a removable ladder. Within the tower there were various wooden floors which were also connected to each other by removable ladders. Each floor had one narrow window. The windows faced in different directions, giving the monks a great view of the local countryside.

About eighty of these tall striking buildings survive around Ireland. Some of the best examples of round towers can be seen at Monasterboice in Co. Louth, Glendalough in Co. Wicklow, Clondalkin, Co. Dublin and at Ardmore in Co. Waterford.

The Round Tower at Glendalough, Co. Wicklow.

The Viking invaders not only caused havoc in Irish monasteries. They also had a great impact on nearly every aspect of Irish life. They were the first foreigners to invade the country since the arrival of the Celts over a thousand years before.

Test your knowledge

1 Why were the monasteries likely targets for attack?

2 Were the Vikings the only ones to attack Irish monasteries?

3 Why did the monks build round towers?

4 How can we tell that the round towers were useful to defend the monastery?

Chapter 13: Review

• The wealth built up in the larger Irish monasteries from around 700 AD onwards enabled the monks to create beautiful works of art such as gold and silver chalices, colourful manuscripts and ornamental stone crosses.

• The Irish monks were famous all over Europe for decorating or illuminating manuscripts, handwritten books made of *vellum*, or calf-skin. This work was done in a special room called a *scriptorium*.

• The monks carried on a great tradition of metalwork which already existed in Ireland and they used beautiful Celtic designs in their work. Famous examples of this work include the Ardagh Chalice, the Tara Brooch, the Moylough Belt Reliquary and the Derrynaflan Chalice.

• The earliest stone crosses in Ireland were simply slabs of rock with crosses carved on the surface. Later on, free-standing crosses were made with arms joined by a circle.

• The earliest surviving Irish manuscript is a copy of the Psalms in Latin called the *Cathach of St Columcille*. It contains very little decoration or colourful illumination.

• The Book of Durrow, dating from around 700 AD, was the first great decorated manuscript produced by Irish monks which has survived. It was probably written in northern England and is a small manuscript of the Gospels decorated with four colours: brown, gold, yellow and green.

• One of the greatest illuminated manuscripts ever produced was The Book of Kells. It is a large manuscript of the four Gospels and it was probably written at Iona around the year 800 AD. It contains many full-page illustrations and includes pictures of animals and scenes from everyday life.

• As well as their own riches, the monks took care of valuables placed in monasteries for safekeeping by kings and nobles. This left them open to attack from the armies of Irish kings and, after 800 AD, from new and dangerous enemies—the Vikings.

• To defend themselves from attack, the monks built round towers. These were tall stone structures with doorways 3 to 5 metres above the ground. They have windows facing in different directions from which enemies approaching could be seen.

The Middle Ages

14 A World of Knights and Castles
15 Living in Towns
16 Cathedrals, Monks and Pilgrims
17 A Look at Medieval Ireland

A World of Knights and Castles

Castles and towers

All around us—in towns, cities and throughout the Irish countryside—we can see castles and towers. Many are in ruins. The roofless remains are often covered with ivy and birds' nests. Some, however, like Bunratty Castle in Co. Clare or Kilkenny Castle are in good condition and are popular tourist attractions.

Castles were first built in a period known as the *Middle Ages* or medieval times, which lasted from around 500 to 1500 AD. It was a time of knights and battles, walled towns, lords who owned the land and poor people who worked for them.

In this section we will travel back in time to see what life was like for our ancestors who lived during the Middle Ages.

Bunratty Castle in Co. Clare is one of the best restored Irish medieval castles. By looking at it today we can well believe that it was built as a strong fortress to resist enemy attacks. It consists of a rectangular-shaped keep with four square towers, one at each corner. At one time it was almost completely surrounded by water. You can enter the castle today by means of a drawbridge which was built as part of the restoration work.

The remains of Lemeneagh Castle in Co. Clare, one of the many ruined castles scattered throughout Ireland.

Lords and vassals

For hundreds of years following the fall of the mighty Roman Empire, most of Europe was without any strong government. Law and order broke down, the skills of reading and writing almost disappeared and people were at the mercy of bands of armed men who robbed and plundered as they wished.

In these conditions, people began to look to the nearest powerful nobleman, or *lord*, for protection. In return for a piece of land and protection, a man promised to fight for the local lord whenever called on.

In this way a system of organising society spread throughout Europe. It led to a new way of life and became known as the *feudal system*.

The feudal system got its name from the Latin word *feudum*, which means the *fief*, or the plot of land given by the lord to those under his protection. The man who received the fief on this condition was known as a *vassal*. Vassals ranged from the holders of quite small farms right up to rich noblemen who held several fiefs from their own lord, the king.

Swearing loyalty to the lord

A vassal swearing an oath of fealty to his lord.

When a lord gave a fief to his vassal, an important ceremony took place. As most people during the Middle Ages could not read or write, they usually marked important agreements with public ceremonies. Then, if there was any doubt about an agreement in later years, people who were there could always remember what had happened.

During the ceremony at which he received a fief, the vassal swore an oath of *fealty* to his lord. He could now no longer fight for any other man but his lord.

A vassal served as a *knight*, or horse soldier, in his lord's army. Since warfare was frequent and neighbour fought against neighbour, a knight was often called upon to join his lord's army. During the Middle Ages the knight was a very powerful person. Let us now see how a young boy was trained to be a knight.

Test your knowledge

1 What was the condition of Europe following the destruction of the Roman Empire?
2 Where did people look for protection?
3 How did the feudal system work?
4 What is meant by the following words: (a) a fief; (b) vassal; (c) fealty?
5 Who was the most important person in the lord's army and the most powerful figure in each area?

Knights, squires and pages

The training of a future knight began at the age of seven when the young boy was sent to the castle of a neighbouring lord to work as a *page*. For the next seven years, in the company of other pages, the boy would serve at table, carry messages, learn his lessons and above all learn the proper manners for a future knight.

At the age of fourteen the boy became a *squire*. He now spent his time learning how to ride a horse in battle and how to use the various weapons carried by knights. As he grew older, he would often accompany the lord into battle, carrying the flag or helping with the horses.

At the age of twenty-one, if a squire had proved himself suitable he was made a *knight* at a special ceremony in his lord's castle. The young man spent the night before in a *vigil* of prayer and fasting. Kneeling in front of the alter in the chapel, he asked God to make him a good knight.

In the morning, the young man went to Confession and Mass. He then put on a white tunic and had his hair cut short. This was an imitation of monks and it was a sign that the new knight would honour God.

Look at this picture from a medieval manuscript showing a knight with his lady.

During the special ceremony known as *dubbing*, he wore a white tunic, a red robe and a black doublet, or jacket. These colours showed his purity (white), willingness to shed his blood for God's cause (red) and his acceptance of death (black). Wearing all the armour of a knight, the young man knelt before his lord. Tapping him on the shoulders with a sword, the lord said, 'Arise, Sir ...' The former squire was now a knight, and he spent the rest of the day feasting and celebrating with his family and friends.

Chivalry

Illustrations from medieval manuscripts such as this are important sources of information on the lifestyle of knights and their ladies.

Knights had to follow a very strict code of conduct called *chivalry*. This word came from *cheval*, the French for horse.

The laws of chivalry stated that knights must be brave in battle and have a very high sense of honour. They were bound to be especially kind and polite to noblewomen and to the poor. Even today if a man does a kind deed for a lady, we say he behaves in a chivalrous manner.

Wars and tournaments

Wars and battles were part of everyday life during the Middle Ages. Foot soldiers had been very important in the armies of Greece and Rome. But after the fall of the Roman Empire, armed knights on horseback were the mainstay of all armies.

The knight wore a suit of armour for protection. His main garment was a suit of *chainmail* consisting of small metal rings on a backing of leather or linen. Before 1300, knights charged the enemy on horseback and fought with lances. After that date they began to fight on foot with a variety of weapons including swords, hammers, maces and axes. Chainmail was also replaced by *plate-armour*. Covered from head to foot in armour, the knights travelled on splendid horses known as *steeds* or *chargers*.

There was no fighting during the winter months: spring and summer were the usual seasons for battles. The Church tried to limit the fighting further by insisting on a number of conditions for a *just war* and by starting a custom called the *Truce of God*. This banned warfare at certain times of the year, such as on Sundays and during Lent.

Tournaments, or jousting, *were very popular in medieval times. These were mock battles between knights held in special fields known as the* lists. *Here knights on horseback and in heavy armour fought against each other. The victorious knight not only received a generous prize but also won the favour of his lady.*

Activity

Describe this tournament scene from a medieval manuscript.

Test your knowledge

1 What was the first stage in the training of a future knight?

2 What was a squire?

3 What special ceremony took place when a squire became a knight?

4 What was chivalry?

5 How was a knight armed when going into battle?

6 What were tournaments?

Castles

Because the countryside was so wild and lawless during the Middle Ages, local lords were always on the alert, defending themselves and their followers from attack. All over Europe huge castles were built. These castles were not only homes for the rich but were also places

This medieval castle clearly stands out in the local countryside.

where lords, their families and followers could shelter in times of attack.

A restored castle hall.

A castle was usually built on top of a huge mound of earth called a *motte*. This was surrounded by a ditch. On top of this motte was built a square or circular stone tower called a *keep* or *donjon*. It was here that the lord and his family lived. The keep had a dining-hall, bedrooms, storerooms and a chapel.

Between the keep and the outer walls was an open yard called a *bailey*. This contained stables, workshops and soldiers' quarters.

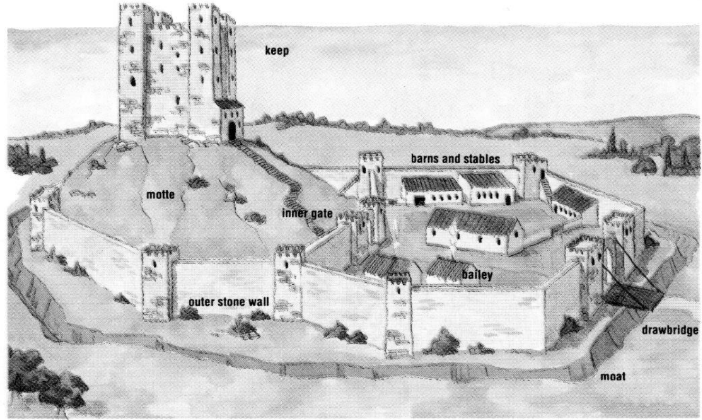

A motte and bailey castle.

The outer walls were defended by one or more *moats* which were crossed by drawbridges. In times of attack each drawbridge was raised and an iron grille called a *portcullis* was lowered to stop enemies coming in. The castle was also protected by an outer tower called a *barbican*.

The ruins of Trim Castle in Co. Meath. As in the rest of Europe rich people living in Ireland during the Middle Ages also built castles. Note the sturdy defensive walls of Trim Castle and the tall keep inside. You will read more about Irish castles in Chapter 17.

Small towers, or *turrets*, were often built along the outer walls or on the top corners of the keep. From these, defenders could throw stones or boiling water or oil on an enemy in time of attack.

Castles under attack

Castles were often attacked by enemy armies. By surrounding the thick stone walls, the attackers hoped that those inside would surrender due to hunger and thirst. However, a well-stocked castle with a good supply of fresh water could hold out against an enemy for a very long time.

A castle under attack.

A well-organised castle was always prepared for any attack. While the enemy forces were still a long way off, a watchman could spy them from the *battlements* on top of the castle. The neighbouring people and their livestock were quickly gathered inside the castle wall. The drawbridges were raised. Bows and arrows, rocks, stones and boiling oil were hurriedly prepared for use against the attackers.

A besieging army relied on a number of methods of attack. Some soldiers were sent to dig underneath the castle's outer walls, hoping that they would collapse. A *battering-ram* was used to break through gateways and walls, and huge stones were fired from a catapult-type machine called a *mangonel*. Once the attackers reached the walls, they used *scaling-ladders* to climb over them.

At home in the castle

Although built as a fortress, a castle was also the home of the lord and his wife and family—as well as a vast number of servants and armed followers. The principal living room was the great hall where meals were eaten and banquets held. While the lord and lady and their noble guests sat at the top table which

Scenes from castle life as shown in medieval manuscripts.

was raised on a *dais*, or platform, their followers were seated at tables which lined the hall.

Musicians called *minstrels* often entertained the company from a *gallery* high up on the wall. These minstrels' galleries can still be seen in many surviving medieval castles.

The only heating in the large room came from huge open fires which stood far apart from one another. Some of the most beautiful and skilled work of medieval stonemasons went into carving these huge fireplaces.

Each castle had its chapel where the lord and lady, their family and servants attended Mass. They had their private chaplain who usually taught Latin to the sons of the family, as well as performing religious ceremonies.

Ladies of the castle

While the lord and his sons spent much of their time defending their land and fighting battles, the ladies of the family led much quieter lives.

Although they were regarded as weaker than men and expected to stay at home, they were also held in high respect. The daughters of the rich were trained at home by their mothers to become good wives. Great stress was laid on needlework such as *embroidery*, the stitching of beautiful pictures with coloured thread on plain white cloth. Young women were also trained in spinning and weaving and in the use of herbs to cure illnesses.

While still in their teens, most young girls were given in marriage by their fathers to suitable men. The girls usually had no say in the matter. Marriage, once entered into, was for life. There was no divorce in the Middle Ages and the people of Europe accepted the Church's rules in the matter.

Activity

Examine these illustrations from medieval manuscripts and say what each tells us about the lives of those who lived in the castle.

Test your knowledge

1 How did local lords defend themselves during the Middle Ages?
2 Describe the appearance of a medieval castle.
3 What was a portcullis?
4 What methods were used by an army to attack a castle?
5 Where was the principal living room in the castle?
6 Who entertained the lord and lady and their guests?
7 How were the rooms of the castle heated?
8 What training did the daughters of the rich receive?

The medieval manor

Most people in the Middle Ages did not live like lords in castles. They earned their living by means of farming which was also organised according to the feudal system.

These illustrations from a medieval manuscript show us what life was like on the lord's manor throughout the year.

The land was divided into estates, or *manors* owned by local lords. The lord kept the best land for his own farm, or *demesne*, and rented the rest of it out to tenants who were called *serfs*.

Although serfs were not slaves who were owned by a master, they were still tied to their lord's land. They could not leave it without the lord's permission. They could not marry or become priests, monks or nuns without their lord's approval. Instead of paying for their rent with money, serfs had to work a number of days each week on the lord's demesne and give him some of their crops. Lords also forced their serfs to pay for the use of mills, wine-presses or sheep folds with the crops or livestock they reared.

Sometimes serfs could save up enough to buy their freedom from their lords. If a serf escaped from the manor to a town and managed to stay away for a year and a day, he was then a free man.

Work on the land

Most farm work was done by hand. The serfs had to labour in the fields from sunrise to sunset in order to grow enough food for their families and to pay their lord as well. The crops grown in each field were changed or rotated each year. Each field was rested, or left *fallow* for one year in three. Both of these practices helped to make the soil more fertile.

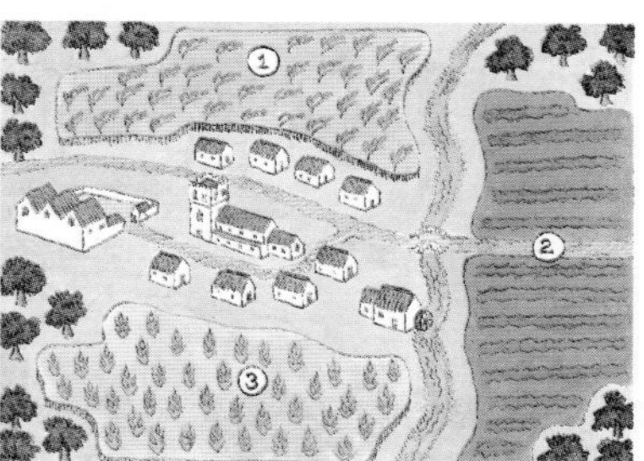

In this illustration Field 1 is planted with barley. Field 2 is left fallow and Field 3 is planted with wheat. The main buildings on the manor were the manor house, the church, the water mill and the houses of the tenants.

By around 1100 AD new improved ploughs were in use which greatly increased the yield of the harvest. Crop failures were frequent, however, and usually led to high prices and food shortages. Local famines were common throughout the Middle Ages.

Crime and punishment

The lord of the manor had the power to hold courts for the trial and punishment of his serfs and of other people in the local area. Serfs who quarrelled, stole or ran away were brought before the lord in his manor court. The lord was assisted by the *bailiff*, who managed his estates and reported any wrongdoings. While the lord dealt with minor crimes, travelling judges tried more serious offenders who were then punished by an official called a *sheriff*.

Punishments were much harsher in medieval times than they are today. Prisons were rarely used for criminals; prisoners of war were usually the only ones kept in *dungeons* deep below the castles. Murderers and those who stole large amounts were punished by death. Petty thieves might have a hand cut off, and people were whipped in public for lesser crimes.

During the Middle Ages, a practice known to us today developed: *trial by jury*. However, there were two other types of trial which might seem quite strange to us: *trial by combat* and *trial by ordeal*. In trial by combat, quarrelling knights engaged in hand-to-hand combat—the winner was believed to be the innocent person. In trial by ordeal, a person was thrown into a pond or forced to handle a red-hot iron. If he or she floated, or if the wound began to heal within three days, this was a proof of innocence.

A person wanted for a crime could take refuge in a church or monastery and remain for a certain period. This practice was called *sanctuary*, and it was also used by the wives and children of lords who went to war. Even kings and queens sometimes sought sanctuary in a monastery if they thought their lives were in danger.

Test your knowledge

1 What was the manor of the local lord?
2 What was the demesne?
3 In what ways were serfs tied to their lord's land?
4 What were the main kinds of punishment used in the Middle Ages?
5 What was sanctuary?

Chapter 14: Review

• The castles and towers throughout the country date from a period known as the Middle Ages or medieval times which lasted from around 500 to 1500 AD.

• Arising from the breakdown in law and order throughout Europe after the fall of the Roman Empire, a new way of life developed—the feudal system.

• Under the feudal system a man received a piece of land (fief) and protection from a powerful lord in return for fighting in the lord's army.

• The man who received the land was called a vassal. He had to swear an oath of fealty, or loyalty, to his lord and promise to be obedient.

• The most important type of soldier during the Middle Ages was the horse soldier, or knight. His training began at the age of seven when he went as a page to a neighbouring lord. From fourteen to twenty-one years of age he served as a squire, learning to fight in battle.

• At the age of twenty-one a young man became a knight in a special ceremony known as dubbing. He promised to serve God and to fight bravely for his lord.

• Knights were bound by a very strict code of chivalry. According to the rules of chivalry they had to fight bravely and be especially polite to noblewomen and to the poor.

• Wars were frequent in the Middle Ages and knights went into battle in heavy armour. The Church tried to limit fighting to certain times of the year under the Truce of God.

• Because the countryside was lawless and dangerous, local lords built huge castles to defend themselves, their families and followers.

• Castles were often attacked by enemies who laid siege to them and tried to force their owners to surrender by cutting off supplies of food and water. They also used scaling-ladders and battering-rams to attack castles.

• The principal living room in the castle was the great hall where the lord and lady entertained their guests with splendid banquets. Each castle also had its chapel where a private chaplain said Mass for the lord and his family.

• Most people, however, did not live in castles but earned their living by farming. These workers were known as serfs. They could not leave their lord's land or manor without his permission.

• Most farm work was done by hand and crops were rotated, with one field in three usually left fallow for a year. Local famines were common throughout the Middle Ages.

• Small crimes were punished by the local lord in his court, while travelling judges dealt with more serious offences. Punishments were very harsh compared to today. As well as hanging, whipping and cutting off of hands, the pillory and stocks were quite common.

Living in Towns

Life in the towns

In the Middle Ages towns were much smaller than they are today. They had populations of only a few thousand people who were huddled into crowded houses built in a maze of narrow streets.

The sturdy medieval gate of St Lawrence may still be seen in Drogheda today.

Some towns grew up on the sites of important churches or monasteries. Others were built at the crossroads of older trade routes, while many were built on sites near rivers or on hilltops where they could be more easily defended from attack.

Since warfare was widespread during the Middle Ages, towns were often attacked by armies in search of food and rich plunder. Because of this danger, towns were usually surrounded by high walls. Sentries stood guard on top of these walls to watch the approach of enemy armies. Sturdy gates in the walls allowed people and traffic to pass in and out. *Tolls*, or taxes, were charged on goods as they passed through the gates. The names of some of these gates still survive as placenames in many towns. In Dublin, the famous Guinness Brewery is at the site of St James's Gate and in London a famous prison once stood at the old site of Newgate. St Lawrence's Gate may still be seen in Drogheda. At night-time, the main gates along the town walls were closed. People wishing to leave or enter a town during the hours of darkness had to do so through a small opening called a *postern gate*.

Part of the medieval walls of Dublin seen at Cook Street.

Houses and streets

Most buildings in medieval towns were made of wood. Only churches and important buildings like town halls were made of stone. Wooden houses and shops faced each other across narrow, unpaved streets. The upper storeys of these buildings usually extended outwards, making the streets dark and narrow.

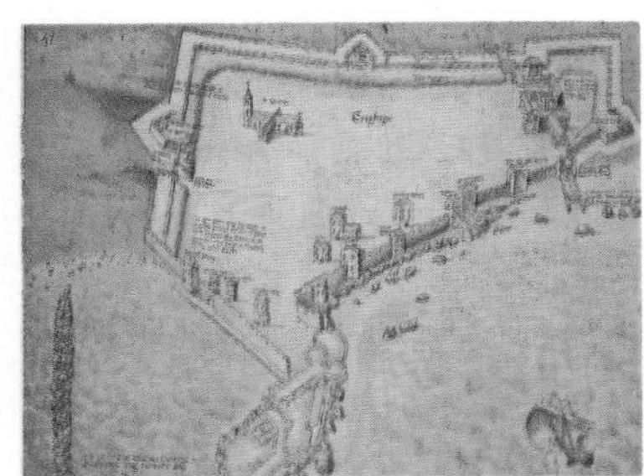
A view of the medieval town of Carrickfergus, Co. Antrim.

SRÁID SEANLAS AN ÉISC 8
FISHAMBLE STREET

Street signs like these two from Dublin can often tell how the streets originally got their names.

SRÁID AN gCÓCAIRE 8
COOK STREET

As cooking and heating were by means of open fires, there were strict rules about the use of fire. At sunset, church bells rang out to mark the arrival of the *curfew*, which means 'cover the fire'. At this time, all fires had to be put out. However, fires still broke out and spread rapidly through the crowded wooden buildings.

Disease was the other great danger facing people who lived in medieval towns. All sorts of rubbish was thrown on the streets which became a sea of mud during the winter months. Disease was also spread by contaminated water, and death among children in particular was common.

The worst disease which spread throughout medieval towns was known as the *Black Death*.

The Black Death

This dreaded killer plague first reached Europe from China in 1347 AD. Humans caught the disease when they were bitten by the infected fleas living on black rats. In the dirty conditions of medieval towns and cities, the Black Death spread rapidly. A monk in a French town left the following account of the Black Death:

A medieval manuscript showing a procession of people praying for an end to the Black Death.

'Whenever one or two people died in any house, at once or at least in a short space of time, the rest of the household were carried off. So much so, that very often in one home, ten or more ended their lives together, and in many houses, the dogs and even the cats died. Hence no one, whether rich or poor, was secure, but everyone from day to day, waited on the will of the Lord.'

This account shows that entire families often died from the plague. Panic spread throughout towns and cities. People refused to bury their own dead for fear of infection. Huge burial pits were dug outside town walls into which the bodies of the plague victims were thrown.

At the time, people had no understanding of the cause of the plague, and many believed that it was caused by the anger of God.

Within a few years the Black Death had run its course. However, for hundreds of years afterwards plague still came back to towns and cities every now and then.

About one-third of the population of Europe died as a result of the Black Death. Whole towns and villages were wiped out. Even today in parts of England, we can see the ruins of villages where people had died as a result of the Black Death.

Test your knowledge

1 Where did towns usually develop in the Middle Ages?

2 How were the towns protected from attack?

3 Why was fire a constant danger in these towns?

4 What was the curfew?

5 How did some streets get their names?

6 Why do you think disease spread so rapidly in medieval towns?

Craftsmen at work

Many skilled craftsmen and traders lived in medieval towns. Usually people of one trade had their shops in the same street. In this way Cook Street and Winetavern Street in Dublin got their names. Each trade and craft in a medieval town was also under the control of an organisation called a *guild*. The guild was made up of members of a particular trade who had been trained for many years before becoming *master craftsmen*.

Each guild had its own rules and regulations. The members of the guild decided on conditions of service for its *apprentices*—the young men learning the trade. Each apprentice was attached to the shop of a *master* and had to spend a certain number of years learning the trade. The term of apprenticeship could last as long as seven years. An apprentice had to work hard and be obedient to his master. A master had to feed and clothe his apprentice and to teach him all the skills of his trade.

Craftsmen at work during the Middle Ages.

When an apprentice had served his time and had passed a test set by the guild, he travelled from town to town working as a *journeyman*. When he wished to become a master himself, he made a special work, his *masterpiece*, and showed it to the guild. If the masterpiece was good enough, the guild welcomed its new member as a master craftsman.

Some guilds, like the goldsmiths and cloth merchants, were very rich and powerful. Their members had great influence in the running of the towns. Each guild had its patron saint on whose feast day they attended Mass at the local church. Guilds also had money for the decoration of churches. In church processions, the members of guilds walked behind their special banners.

How the towns were ruled

Unlike the countryside, which was ruled by the feudal lords from their manors, towns were governed by elected *corporations* or *councils*. Rich merchants and master craftsmen were chosen by their fellow citizens to serve on the town council. The councils had many of the powers which local lords had in the countryside. As well as making rules for trade and business and collecting taxes, the town councils also held courts which could punish criminals. While the *mayor* was head of the council, the man in charge of law and order was usually known as the *sheriff*.

Many townspeople were given the freedom to rule themselves by either the king or a local lord. A written document called a *charter* set out the rights of the townspeople, the rules for governing the town and the taxes due to the town council and to the king. Written in Latin, many of these medieval town charters survive to this day. They are important sources of information about life in towns at the time.

Guildhalls like this one in York, England, were built in many towns during the Middle Ages. Here members of a guild held their meetings.

Rich merchants were proud of their towns and many of them were willing to spend large sums of money on well-designed buildings. As a result many beautiful town halls and squares were built in the towns.

The best examples of splendid medieval buildings, however, are the magnificent cathedrals and churches which were built in Europe's cities and towns. In the next chapter we will take a look at these architectural wonders and at the religion and beliefs of the people who designed and built them.

Test your knowledge

1 What were guilds?

2 What was an apprentice?

3 What was a journeyman?

4 What celebrations did guilds organise?

5 Do you think guilds played an important part in medieval towns? Why?

6 Who ruled the medieval towns?

Chapter 15: Review

• Towns in the Middle Ages were much smaller than they are today. They usually contained only a few thousand people living in a maze of narrow streets.

• Because towns were often attacked, they were usually surrounded by high walls. Gates in the walls allowed traffic in and out by day and tolls were charged on goods entering the town. The gates were closed at night-time, however.

• Most buildings in medieval towns were made from wood. Only important buildings like churches or town halls were made of stone. Because of the wooden houses and narrow streets, fires were a constant threat.

• Medieval towns were very dirty places. There was no running water and all kinds of rubbish were thrown into the streets. Because of this, diseases spread quickly, causing widespread sickness and death.

• The worst disaster in Europe during the Middle Ages was a deadly plague known as the Black Death. It reached Europe from China in 1347 AD and was carried by fleas on black rats.

• Each trade and craft had its own guild, the organisation which controlled all of its activities. Guilds laid down rules for their members and decided how long an apprentice should spend learning his trade.

• To learn a trade, an apprentice had to spend a number of years in the workshops of a master craftsman who taught him the skills of the trade. When his time was up, he had to pass a test set by the guild.

• When an apprentice finished his training he became a journeyman, travelling from town to town practising his trade. If he wished to become a master craftsman, he first had to produce a masterpiece, an excellent piece of work, and show it to the guild.

• Some guilds were very rich and played an important part in the government of the towns. Guilds also organised processions, plays and religious festivals on special feastdays.

• Towns were ruled by corporations or councils chosen by the citizens. These councils were headed by mayors and they had many powers such as control over law and order and the right to raise taxes.

• The rights and duties of townspeople were usually set out in a written document called a charter. This contained the rules covering town government, markets and taxes. Charters were granted by the king or by a powerful local lord.

Cathedrals, Monks and Pilgrims

During the Middle Ages, most of the people of Europe belonged to one religion with the pope as its supreme ruler. Because Christians were united throughout the continent, Europe became known as *Christendom*, or Christ's land.

Religion played a very important part in people's lives during the Middle Ages. All schools and hospitals were run by priests, monks or nuns. As few people could read or write, the educated priests or monks were looked up to and their advice was greatly respected. From the vast number of great cathedrals and many ruins of churches and monasteries which survive throughout Europe, we can see how important the Christian religion was in the lives of our medieval ancestors.

Popes and bishops

The pope was the leader of the Christian Church. From his residence in Rome he ruled over Christians throughout Europe. As well as being head of the Church, the pope was also a prince who ruled over a kingdom in the centre of Italy known as the *Papal States*. During the Middle Ages, people had their own armies and often went to war against other princes.

Some popes expected kings and princes to obey them in all matters. Those who refused could be *excommunicated*—that is, put out of the Church. Excommunication was a very frightening ceremony. Bells were rung as at a funeral; candles were snuffed out and prayer books were closed. The person who was excommunicated was regarded as dead in the eyes of the Church. The most powerful medieval pope, Innocent III (1198–1216), often excommunicated his enemies, including King John of England.

Most popes did not neglect their religious duties, however. They kept strict watch over the lives of Christians through the *bishops* whom they appointed to local areas.

Medieval bishops were usually very powerful men. They were often rich local landowners as well, who helped kings and princes to rule their states. The area ruled by a bishop was called a *diocese*.

In each diocese the bishop usually owned one or more palaces. His own principal church was called a *cathedral* because the bishop's chair, or *cathedra*, stood near the altar. The most magnificent work of skilled medieval builders, artists and craftsmen went into building these cathedrals. We will now take a look at some of their achievements

Test your knowledge

1 By what name was Europe known during the Middle Ages? Why?

2 Who was the head of the Christian Church?

3 What was excommunication?

4 What area was ruled over by a bishop?

5 By what name was the bishop's principal church called? Why?

Medieval cathedrals

Our medieval ancestors often took hundreds of years to complete a cathedral. Only the best work was considered good enough for God's house.

Medieval cathedrals are easily recognisable, with their high slanted roofs, their arched doorways, and windows filled

The Cathedral at Rheims in France. During the Middle Ages splendid churches like this were built throughout Europe.

St Patrick's Cathedral, Dublin was the longest cathedral built in Ireland during the Middle Ages. It is still the longest church in the country.

with bright panes of stained glass. In Ireland there are some wonderful medieval cathedrals, including Christchurch and St Patrick's in Dublin and St Canice's in Kilkenny. The cathedral was the tallest building in the town and its spires could be seen for miles around by people in the surrounding countryside.

There were two main types of church architecture during the Middle Ages—*Romanesque* and *Gothic*. When you visit medieval churches or ruins, your trip will be more interesting and enjoyable if you can pick out each style for yourself.

Romanesque architecture

The Romanesque style nave of Durham Cathedral in northern England.

Cormac's Chapel on the Rock of Cashel, completed in 1134, was built in the Romanesque style. Look closely and see what features of the Romanesque style you can notice.

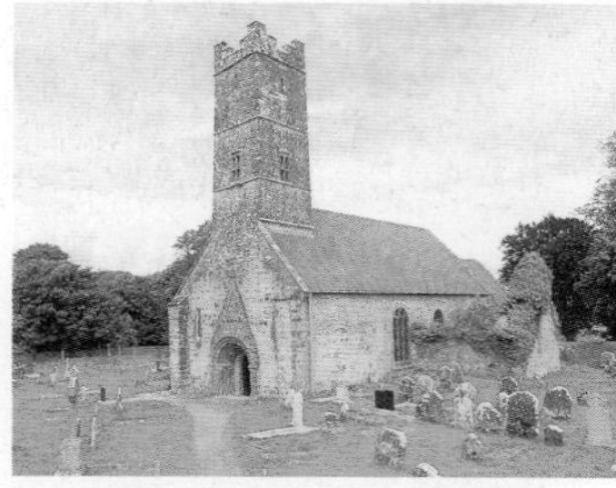
The Romanesque style of Clonfert Cathedral in Co. Galway.

A Romanesque doorway.

This was the earlier style which developed around the year 1000. We recognise it from the rounded arches at doorways and windows. Romanesque buildings often have stout, strong columns supporting the roof. In Ireland, surviving examples of this style include Cormac's Chapel on the Rock of Cashel and the Chancel Arch in St Mary's Cathedral, Tuam. Clonfert Cathedral in Co. Galway and the South Doorway in Christchurch Cathedral, Dublin, are also good examples of the Romanesque style.

A Romanesque window.

Gothic architecture

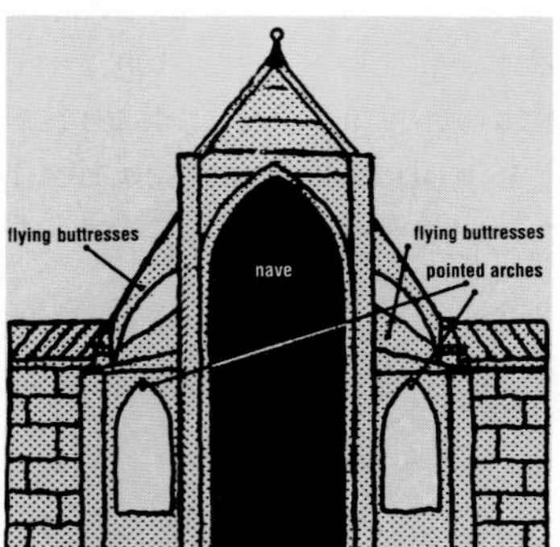

Cross-section of a Gothic Cathedral

The most splendid cathedrals of the Middle Ages were built in the Gothic style. It was first introduced in northern France around 1150 and spread from there to the rest of Europe.

We recognise Gothic churches by their doorways and windows which are crowned by pointed arches. Inside there are slender stone columns which support a number of arches on both sides of the central space, or *nave*, dividing it from the side aisles. Over these arches there are smaller arches called *triforia*. Above these are windows through which the light shines in.

A Gothic doorway (left) and (right) a Gothic window.

When architects began to put more windows along the side walls, there was a danger that the roofs might fall in. To overcome this, supporting arches called *flying buttresses* were built on the out-

The outside of the Gothic cathedral of Notre Dame in Paris. Notice the pointed arches of the doorways and windows, the twin towers and the carved statues of the saints. The round window in the centre is called the Rose Window.

Stained glass windows such as this one at Chartres were one of the glories of Gothic cathedrals.

The doorway at Chartres Cathedral in France is another good example of Gothic architecture. At a time when most people could not read or write, stone carvings like these helped to teach them about their religion.

The inside of Notre Dame Cathedral in Paris.

The Gothic style monastery church of Duiske Abbey at Graiguenamanagh, Co. Kilkenny.

A view of the flying buttresses at the Gothic Cathedral of Christchurch in Dublin.

side of the Gothic cathedrals. The famous cathedral of Notre Dame in Paris has splendid flying buttresses. We can also see flying buttresses at the two medieval cathedrals in Dublin, Christchurch and St Patrick's.

There are several medieval Gothic cathedrals in Ireland as well as some magnificent Gothic churches, like St Mary's in Youghal and St Nicholas's in Galway. There are also some beautifully restored Gothic monastery churches. These include Holy Cross Abbey in Tipperary, Duiske Abbey at Graiguenamanagh in Co. Kilkenny and Ballintubber Abbey in Co. Mayo. Besides these churches, which are still in use, the ruins of many medieval monasteries built in the Gothic style are scattered around the Irish countryside.

While medieval cathedrals remind us of the power and influence of the bishops, they also make us think about the faith of the ordinary people who practised their religion in their local parish under the guidance of a parish priest.

As well as local priests who were under the control of a bishop, many religious orders of monks were also formed during the Middle Ages. Let us now take a close look at the way of life of these monks

Test your knowledge

1 How would you recognise a Romanesque cathedral?

2 Give examples of cathedrals or churches built in this style.

3 How would you recognise a Gothic cathedral?

4 What are flying butresses?

5 How are windows decorated in Gothic cathedrals?

6 Give examples of some Irish cathedrals, churches and monasteries built in that style.

Monks and monasteries

It is hard for us to understand the important part which monks and monasteries played in the lives of medieval people. The monks provided education, hospital care and shelter for travellers. They also introduced great improvements in farming.

In Ireland, many monasteries were scattered throughout the country. One of the largest of these was St Mary's Abbey in Dublin. It stood near the site of the present day Capel Street. The head, or *abbot*, of St Mary's was one of the most powerful men in the country. For over four hundred years, the abbey owned large amounts of land around Dublin and provided food and shelter for the poor and sick in the surrounding area.

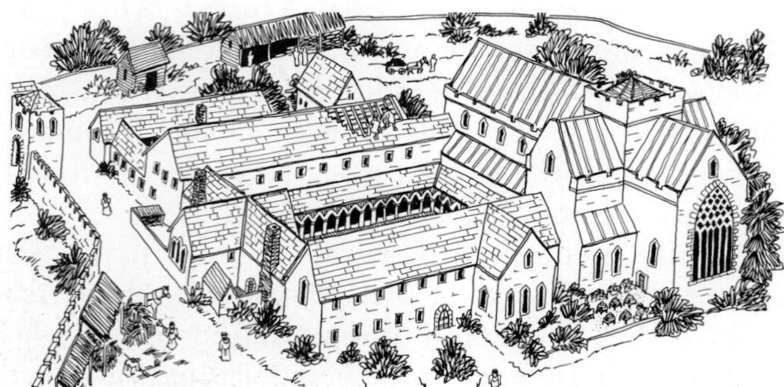

St Mary's Abbey, as it once was.

Most medieval monasteries followed rules drawn up by an Italian monk named St Benedict (480–543 AD). He laid great stress on the monks' duty to be obedient to the abbot or head of the monastery. Although his rules were strict, St Benedict made sure his monks ate healthy food and got enough sleep.

Although St Benedict's rule was followed in most medieval monasteries, some monks believed that a stricter form of monastic rule was needed. Two very strict orders were founded during the Middle Ages—the *Carthusians* and the *Cistercians*.

An illustration from a medieval manuscript showing St Bernard with other Cistercian monks at the Abbey of Clairvaux in France.

Carthusian monks lived in single cells. They ate alone and only met their fellow monks in church on special religious occasions.

The Cistercians were founded in 1098 by St Robert of Molesmes. The order is named after its first monastery, which was built in a wild, lonely place called Citeaux in eastern France. After St Bernard joined them in 1112, the Cistercian order spread rapidly throughout Europe. These monks laid great stress on prayer, fasting, silence and manual labour. There were several Cistercian abbeys in Ireland, including two which have been restored—Holy Cross in Tipperary and Duiske in Kilkenny.

Holy Cross Abbey, after its restoration in the 1970s.

Using Holy Cross Abbey in Tipperary as a guide, we will take a closer look at everyday life in a medieval monastery.

Life in a medieval monastery

The monk's day began very early indeed—at around three o'clock in the morning when they would leave their sleeping quarters, or *dormitory*, and go to the church to sing *Matins*, the first part of the Divine Office for the day. In Holy Cross Abbey, we can still see the stairway which led from the dormitory down to the church.

The Night Stairs, Holy Cross Abbey.

A day in the life of a medieval monk

3.00 A.M.	Rising and Office of Matins in the Church
4.00	Rest
6.00	Office of Prime, Meditation and Mass
7.00	Breakfast
8.00–9.30	Work

10.00	Solemn Mass in Church
11.00–2.00	Work
2.00 P.M.	Dinner
2.30	Reading
3.00	Work
5.00	Vespers
6.00	Supper
8.00	Compline and retire to bed

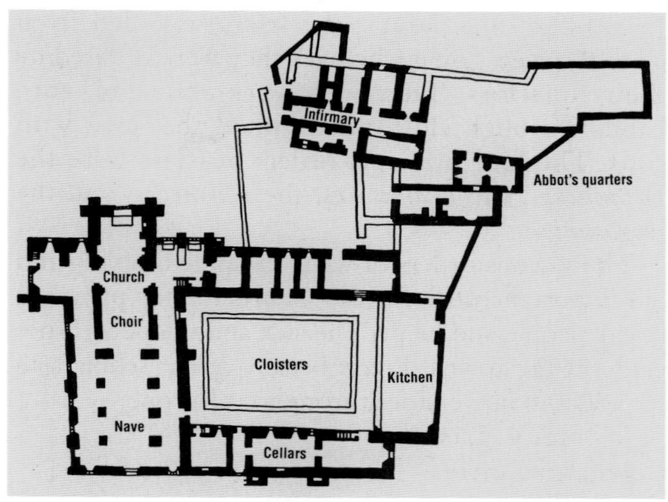

A ground plan of Holy Cross Abbey.

The day was divided between prayer, working and reading. Seven times a day, all the monks gathered in the church to sing parts of the Divine Office. Along with Matins, the evening service of *Vespers* was the most important. At around ten o'clock in the morning, a Mass was sung. Bells were rung before Mass and Offices, calling the monks to church from their work in the fields or in different parts of the monastery. The monk's day ended at around eight o'clock in the evening with more prayers in the church. After that, a strict silence was observed in the monastery until the following morning.

Work had a very important place in the lives of the monks. Each monastery was expected to grow its own food and provide clothes, furniture and other necessities. Because of this, different monks had their own special jobs. The *abbot* was head of the monastery and was elected by the monks. The *almoner* looked after visitors who stayed in the guesthouse attached to the monastery. Another important person in any monastery was the *infirmarian* who was in charge of the hospital. In the Middle Ages, the monasteries were the only places to which the sick and poor could go for help.

A monk copying a manuscript in the scriptorium of a monastery.

Test your knowledge

1 What rule was followed in most medieval monasteries?

2 Name two very strict orders of monks founded during the Middle Ages.

3 Name two Cistercian monasteries which have been restored in Ireland.

4 How did the monk's day begin?

5 What activities occupied the monk's day?

6 How did medieval monasteries assist the sick and the poor?

The coming of the friars

The monks belonging to older orders like the Cistercians rarely, if ever, left the monastery which they first entered. Around 1200, populations in towns throughout Europe grew rapidly. Priests and brothers were needed to travel from place to place, stopping where they were most required. To fill this need, new orders of wandering monks known as *friars* were founded.

The Pope giving approval to St Francis of Assisi to set up an order of friars — the Franciscans.

Unlike other monks, the friars travelled from place to place, going wherever they were ordered by their superiors. They were very poor and wore habits of rough cloth held around the waist with cord. The four principal orders of friars were the *Dominicans*, the *Franciscans*, the *Carmelites* and the *Augustinians*.

The various orders of friars expanded rapidly and did important work for the Church. They preached to the people and helped the sick and the poor, especially in the towns. Friars became great scholars in schools and universities throughout Europe.

In many Irish towns and cities, there are churches which are still run by one or more orders of friars. If you enquire, you may discover that friars still live on or near the site where their order first settled during the thirteenth century.

The Dominican church in Kilkenny known as the Black Abbey. The Dominicans were an order of friars founded by St Dominic. They had many churches in Ireland during the Middle Ages including this one in Kilkenny.

Pilgrims and pilgrimages

The Canterbury Pilgrims. An illustration from a medieval manuscript of Chaucer's Canterbury Tales showing the pilgrims on their way to Canterbury.

During the Middle Ages people of all ages and occupations used to make long journeys to holy places. Such journeys were called *pilgrimages* and the people making them were known as *pilgrims*.

People went on pilgrimages for various reasons. Some went in order to do penance for their sins. Others went to carry out a promise or vow which they had made to God—and many went simply to have a good time.

Pilgrims often visited the shrines of saints which were nearest their homes. In Ireland, Lough Derg and Croagh Patrick were the great centres of pilgrimage. In England, the most famous shrines were those of Our Lady at Walsingham in Norfolk and of St Thomas à Becket at Canterbury.

Many pilgrims, however, travelled to the three greatest medieval shrines of all. These were the tomb of St James at Compostella in Spain, the tombs of the Apostles Peter and Paul at Rome, and the scene of Christ's own life, death and resurrection—the Holy Land.

Pilgrims travelling to distant lands usually made their wills before leaving, as the journey took a long time and travel by land and sea was quite dangerous. As well as the risk of shipwreck, robbery or murder, pilgrims might be captured and sold into slavery by Muslim pirates.

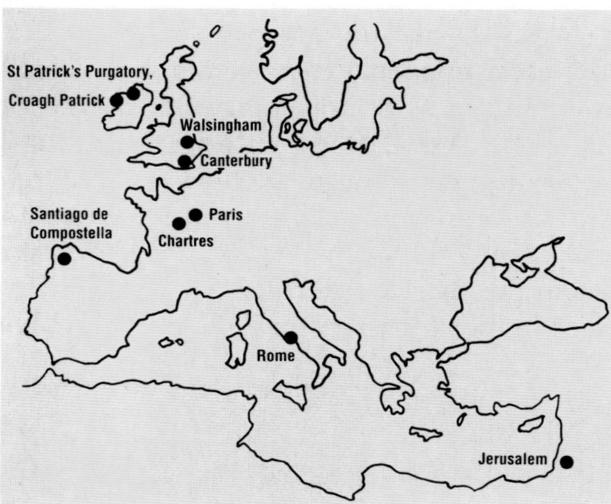

Important centres of pilgrimage during the Middle Ages.

Sometimes important people dressed as poor pilgrims and kept their identity secret while on pilgrimage. One such person was the Bishop of Cork and Cloyne, Thaddeus McCarthy. He died in 1494 in northern Italy on his way home from Rome. Bishop McCarthy was dressed as a humble pilgrim, and his identity was only discovered when his bishop's ring was found hidden in his luggage.

Not all pilgrimages were carried out for religious reasons. Some pilgrims just went along for the fun of it. They were more interested in eating and drinking too much than in saying their prayers. The English poet Geoffrey Chaucer mocked people like this in his famous poem, *The Canterbury Tales*.

Of all the centres of pilgrimage, the most dangerous to reach was the Holy Land itself. In 1076, Jerusalem was captured by fierce Turkish Muslims called *Saracens*. Christians were shocked and popes called for armies to travel to the Holy Land to free it from the Muslims. The expeditions which took place as a result were called the *Crusades*.

Test your knowledge

1 Why was there a need for new religious orders around 1200?
2 Who were the friars and what work did they do?
3 Name two orders of friars.
4 What were pilgrimages?
5 Name the three greatest medieval shrines.
6 Why did people go on pilgrimages?
7 What kind of dress was worn by pilgrims?
8 What was the most dangerous place of pilgrimage to reach ? Why?

Castles in the Holy Land

Modern visitors to the Middle East can see a great medieval castle perched on a hilltop. It is known as the *Krak des Chevaliers* or Castle of the Knights. It was built to guard a mountain pass, and inside its strong walls people had enough food and water to withstand a year's siege.

Castles such as this were built throughout the Holy Land by Crusaders during the Middle Ages.

Today many such castles are to be found throughout the Holy Land. These great castles were built by the knights who set out from Europe to win back the Holy Land from the Muslim Saracens.

The Crusades

The wars fought to win back the Holy Land were known as the *Crusades*, from the French word for 'cross'. A crusader setting out to do battle in the Holy Land wore a tunic embroidered on the front with a large cross. A crusader-knight also wore a suit of chainmail and was armed with a sword and a lance.

Crusading armies were slow moving. The heat of the sun and their heavy armour slowed them down. Both men and horses had to be rested often. When they reached the Holy Land, it often took many weeks of fighting before they captured a Muslim-held town.

An army of Crusaders.

Popes approved of the Crusades; in fact the First Crusade in 1096 was called together by Pope Urban III. In 1099, the crusading armies captured Jerusalem from the Saracens and took control of the Holy Land. Although the Crusaders built castles to defend their lands, their success was short-lived. The Saracens later recaptured the Christian-held areas, and more Crusades were then organised.

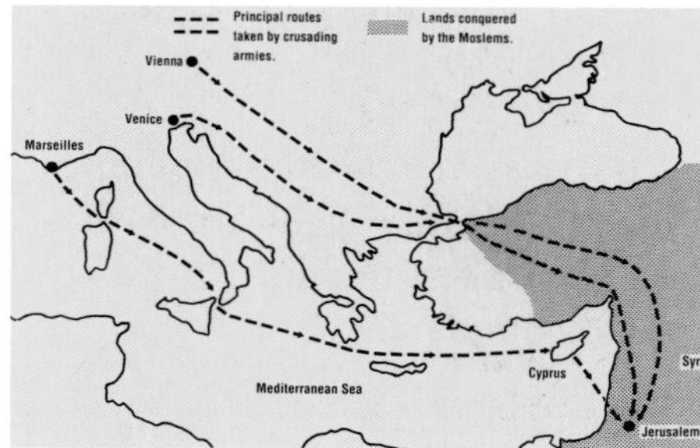

The Crusades.

Most knights who went on Crusade went to fight for their religion. They believed that if they died while on Crusade, their souls would go straight to heaven. However, some went only for adventure and plunder. Along the way they robbed and destroyed cities; in some cases they never even reached the Holy Land.

The Crusaders never succeeded in driving all the Saracens from the Holy Land. However, over the years the knights brought back many new types of food and cloth to Europe. Rice, melons, lemons, apricots, rugs, tapestries, and spices were carried home by returning Crusaders.

Test your knowledge

1 Where is the Castle of the Knights and why was it built?
2 What were the Crusades?
3 What reasons did knights have for going on the Crusades?
4 How were the crusading knights dressed and armed?
5 What new things did the Crusaders bring back from the Holy Land?

Chapter 16: Review

• During the Middle Ages most of the people of Europe belonged to one religion with the pope at its head. Because of this, Europe became known as Christendom or Christ's land.

• As well as ruling over the Christian Church, medieval popes also governed a kingdom in the centre of Italy known as the Papal States. Popes often tried to make kings and princes obey them. Those who refused could be excommunicated or put out of the Catholic Church.

• A bishop was usually a rich and powerful man. He ruled over an area called a diocese and lived in a palace. The bishop's main church was called a cathedral.

• As well as castles, the most magnificent buildings which survive from the Middle Ages are cathedrals. A cathedral was the tallest building in a town and took many years to complete.

• Medieval cathedrals and churches were built in two main styles of architecture: Romanesque and Gothic. Romanesque, which was based on round arches, began around 1000. The Gothic style which began around 1150 featured pointed arches.

• Each diocese was divided up into local areas known as parishes. These were under the care of parish priests. The parish priest was an important person in the local area as he was often the only person who could read and write.

• Monks and monasteries played a very important part in the lives of the medieval people. As well as being religious centres, monasteries also provided education, hospital care, shelter for travellers. They were also responsible for great improvements in farming.

• Most monasteries followed the rule of St Benedict, a famous Italian abbot. However other stricter orders were founded like the Carthusians and Cistercians. There were many Cistercian monasteries in Ireland including St Mary's Abbey (Dublin) and Holy Cross Abbey (Tipperary).

• The monk's day began at around three o'clock in the morning and lasted until eight o'clock at night. He spent his time in a strictly ordered routine of prayer, work and reading holy books.

• Each monastery had to provide for all the need of the monks, such as food, clothing and furniture. As well as the abbot or head of the monastery, other important people included his assistant, the prior, the almoner who looked after the guesthouse and the infirmarian who was in charge of the hospital.

• Around 1200 new types of religious orders, the friars, were founded for work in the towns. They were very poor and travelled from place to place preaching the Gospel. The main orders of friars were the Dominicans, the Franciscans, the Augustinians and the Carmelites.

• Many people during the Middle Ages went on pilgrimages to holy places such as Jerusalem, Rome, Canterbury or Lough Derg. While many people prayed and fasted on the way, others were more interested in enjoying themselves.

• The most dangerous of all the pilgrimages was a visit to the Holy Land. On the long journey by sea and land Christian pilgrims could be shipwrecked, robbed, sold into slavery or even murdered.

• During the Middle Ages a number of wars were fought by Christian knights to capture the Holy Land from the Muslims. These wars were known as the Crusades and castles built in the Middle East by the crusaders may still be seen

• Although kings and princes as well as ordinary knights went on crusade, the crusaders never succeeded in completely removing the Muslims from the Holy Land. Returning knights brought new types of food and cloth back to Europe. These included rice, melons, apricots, spices, rugs and tapestries.

Chapter 17 A Look at Medieval Ireland

The past around us

As in the rest of Europe, Ireland today has reminders of life during the Middle Ages. Castles, Gothic churches, parts of town walls and many ruins have survived from medieval times.

Archaeologists have added a great deal to our knowledge of the life in Ireland during the Middle Ages. In towns such as Dublin, Cork and Waterford, thousands of objects including the remains of medieval houses and churches have been excavated.

In this chapter we will take a close look at the people who left these remains behind. They first came to Ireland in 1169 and were called the Normans.

The Normans

The Normans were a strong and powerful people who conquered many lands during the eleventh and twelfth centuries. They were descendants of the Vikings and had settled in Normandy in the north of France. Wherever the Normans went, they brought their crafts, customs and traditions with them. They built great castles and monasteries and also introduced the feudal system. Under this system, knights fought for their lords in return for a grant of land.

The Normans spread out from their homeland in France to conquer other lands, including southern Italy and the Holy Land. Norman knights were famous for their skills in battle. Their most famous conquest took place when the Norman leader, William the Conqueror, defeated the English at the Battle of Hastings in 1066.

One of the best sources on the Norman conquest of England is a beautiful cloth wall-hanging called the Bayeux Tapestry.

The Bayeux Tapestry

The Bayeux Tapestry tells the story of the Norman conquest of England. It is a particularly good primary source because it was made by the Normans themselves soon after the events depicted. The tapestry can now be seen in the cathedral of Bayeux in Normandy. Thousands of visitors come to view it every year.

In this scene from the Bayeux Tapestry, Duke William of Normandy orders his men to build boats. This is the meaning of the Latin words on the top of the tapestry.

Can you see his followers beginning to carry out the Duke's orders?

The tapestry is a series of pictures sewn with coloured wool on linen cloth. It measures 70 metres (230 feet) in length, but is only 50 centimetres (20 inches) wide. This long, narrow tapestry is like a strip

The horses of the Normans leave the boats to land in England .

The death of the Saxon King Harold as pictured in the Bayeux Tapestry.

cartoon. The story of William and his conquest is told mainly through pictures, although there is some Latin writing.

This important historical source gives us detailed information on the conquest of England. But it is also one-sided, or biased. The Normans are always seen to be right, with the English in the wrong.

Look clearly at the pictures from the Bayeux Tapestry in this chapter. Write down what you learn about the Normans from this source.

Test your knowledge

1 Who were the Normans?
2 What skills, customs and traditions did the Normans bring to the lands they conquered?
3 What is the Bayeux Tapestry?
4 In what way is the tapestry a biased source?

The Normans arrive in Ireland

In time, the Normans who had settled in England began to think about taking over Ireland. In 1169, over a hundred years after the Battle of Hastings, they finally got their chance.

The Normans were given this opportunity by Dermot MacMurrough, king of Leinster. When Dermot was expelled from his own kingdom, he went to England and France, seeking the help of the Normans to defeat his enemies. The Norman king of England, Henry II, promised MacMurrough the help he needed. With Henry's permission, Dermot travelled about England, recruiting allies. In Bristol, he met Richard de Clare, better known as Strongbow, and other Norman lords including Maurice Fitzgerald and Maurice Fitzstephen.

Dermot and Strongbow made a bargain. In return for Strongbow's help against his enemies in Ireland, MacMurrough promised that Strongbow could marry his daughter, Aoife. When Dermot himself died, Strongbow was to inherit the kingdom of Leinster. Dermot then returned to Ireland and waited for the invading armies.

In May 1169, 600 Norman soldiers landed at Bannow Bay in Co. Wexford. Dermot MacMurrough came to meet them, and the town of Wexford was soon in Norman hands. In 1170 Strongbow himself arrived with a larger army and captured the town of Waterford. The Normans now marched on Dublin and with the help of MacMurrough they soon captured the city.

When MacMurrough died in 1171, Strongbow became king of Leinster. However, King Henry II of England was worried. He feared that Norman knights in Ireland might set up their own separate kingdom there and challenge his authority. In October 1171, Henry landed near Waterford with a fleet of 250 ships. The Norman knights, and many of the Irish kings as well, submitted to Henry and recognised him as lord of Ireland.

Henry II spent the winter of 1171–72 at Dublin. While there, he made plans for ruling his new lands in Ireland.

Dublin Castle

Wherever the Normans took over an area in Ireland, they built huge fortifications or castles to protect their new lands. At first these were built of wood on top of earthen mounds. Later, they built great stone castles to protect themselves from attack by the native Irish. Examples of these castles can be still seen throughout Ireland at places such as Carrickfergus, Maynooth and Kilkenny.

The ruins of the Norman castle at Carrickfergus in Co. Antrim. Notice the remains of the outer walls, the keep and the tower.

The most important Norman castle in Ireland was built in Dublin between 1204 and 1220 on the orders of King John of England. This great stone castle replaced an earlier wooden fortification which the Normans had built when they first took over the city.

Dublin Castle was rectangular in shape and guarded by a circular tower at each corner. The River Poddle ran beside the castle walls which were surrounded by a deep ditch. Entrance to the castle

This view of Dublin Castle shows the medieval Record Tower surrounded by later buildings such as the Chapel to the left and the State Apartments to the right.

was by means of a gateway and portcullis. Its many rooms included a great banqueting-hall, a chapel, offices, kitchens and a prison. Dublin Castle, the first building in Ireland to have piped water, was the most richly decorated castle of its time.

The English king's government in Ireland had its headquarters at Dublin Castle. The government's most important man was the *Lord Deputy* who was chosen by the king to rule his lands in Ireland. He was helped by a group of advisers called the *council*. The king's Lord Deputy and his council often travelled around the country keeping order, holding courts and collecting taxes.

Test your knowledge

1 Why did Dermot MacMurrough seek Norman help?
2 What agreement did he reach with Strongbow?
3 When and where did the first Norman army land in Ireland?
4 Why did Henry II come to Ireland in 1171?
5 What did the Normans do to protect their new lands in Ireland?
6 When was Dublin Castle built?
7 How was the castle protected?
8 What rooms were contained in the castle?
9 Who was appointed by the king to rule over his lands in Ireland?

Norman lords and manors

Although the Normans never succeeded in conquering all of Ireland and defeating the native Irish, by 1250 the most important towns and vast stretches of the countryside were under their control. Some of the most powerful Norman families in Ireland were the Fitzgeralds, the Burkes, the Butlers and the Powers. Norman lords such as these controlled huge areas of land in Ireland grouped around the manor house and the church.

Norman towns in Ireland

Many of our towns in Ireland were founded by the Normans. As well as taking over and expanding existing Viking settlements such as Dublin, Limerick and Waterford, they also set up many new towns of their own. The sites of these towns were carefully chosen so that they could be easily defended from attack.

Reginald's Tower in Waterford which was part of the medieval defensive walls around the town.

Many Norman settlements were situated on the coast or at a river crossing so they could also control the passing trade. These towns included Coleraine, Drogheda, Navan, Sligo, Galway, Athlone, Tralee, Youghal and Kinsale. Other Norman towns were situated on

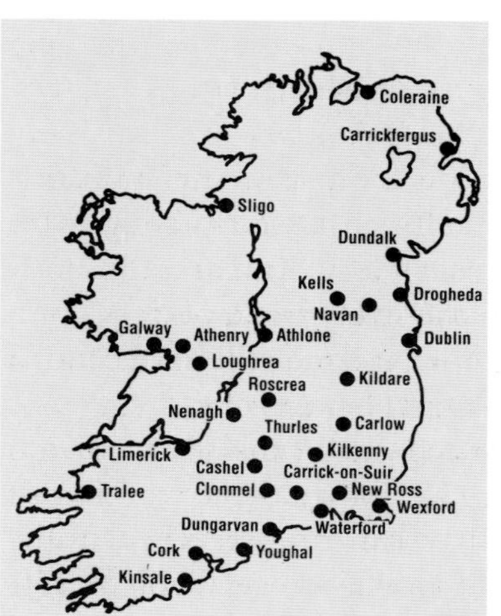

Irish towns built or developed by the Normans.

the sites of old monasteries such as Kilkenny, Kells, Kildare and Cashel.

Most Norman towns were founded in the south and east of Ireland. Little town-building took place in southwest Munster, Connaught and west Ulster.

While people in the countryside were not allowed leave the lord's manor, those living in the towns were free. Early Norman towns were populated by a great mixture of people. While many came from England and Europe, others were native Irish. Most of the port towns also had Viking quarters.

Medieval Irish towns were surrounded by walls and towers, just as they were in the rest of Europe. Archaeologists have excavated the original sites of many of the settlements. Waterford has the best-preserved medieval walls in the country, and in Dublin a part of the old wall has been reconstructed at St Audoen's Arch in Cook Street.

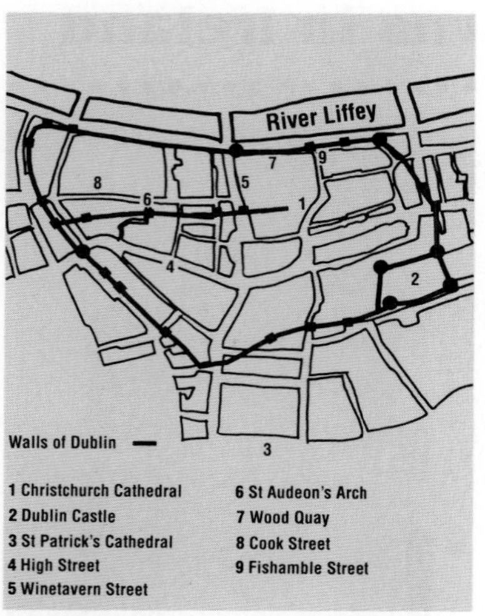

Dublin during the Middle Ages.

Medieval crafts

The towns in medieval Ireland were bustling centres of activity where people came to buy and sell their goods. Each town had its own marketplace where fairs and markets were held. As they brought their goods to market, people from the surrounding countryside paid tolls as they passed through the town gates. Placenames such as Cornmarket in both Dublin and Cork recall the lively trade of days gone by. Many towns throughout Ireland still have central squares where fairs and markets were once held.

Many crafts were carried out in the towns themselves. In Chapter 15 we saw how people working at the same trade often lived in one street. Dublin street names such as Fishamble Street, Cook Street, Winetavern Street and Skinner's Row are clear proof of this. Each group of craftsmen belonged to a guild which protected the rights of its members and looked after their welfare.

Archaeologists have excavated sites in Dublin, Cork and Waterford. The most common type of artefact found at these digs was pottery. At Dublin's Wood Quay, over half the pottery pieces found were made in Dublin. The rest came mainly from Ham Green near Bristol and from Saintonge near Bordeaux in France.

The manufacture of floor tiles was another important industry in medieval Ireland. Archaeologists have found far more of these in the east and south of the country than in the west.

The remains of a wattle screen found in Dublin. These screens were used in medieval times as partitions in houses. Also, notice the horse's skull. Many animal bones were found during excavations.

Leather boots found at High Street, Dublin. Shoemaking was an important trade in medieval Dublin.

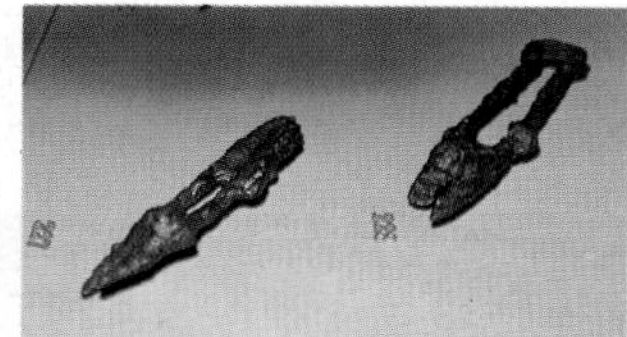

A shears dating from medieval times found during excavations in Dublin.

Our knowledge of cloth-making in medieval Ireland is quite limited. Since archaeologists have found very little evidence of cloth, we must depend on illustrations in manuscripts to see what kinds of clothes our medieval ancestors wore.

Unlike clothes and other cloth goods, excavations in Dublin and elsewhere have provided us with plenty of information on leather goods. Most leather was made from cattle hides, although some was made from goat skins. Leather shoes, knife-sheaths, wrist straps and belts have all been unearthed at Wood Quay, Dublin, and at Cork, Drogheda and Carrickfergus.

Metal-working was another important craft in Irish towns during the Middle Ages. Several bronze and iron tools and ornaments have been discovered in Dublin and in other towns.

As well as these crafts, carpenters and masons worked with wood and stone to produce houses, churches and other buildings. While the work of medieval carpenters has largely disappeared, we can still admire buildings put up by stonemasons, not only in towns but throughout the Irish countryside.

Merchants and trade

Irish traders had many markets for their goods. Merchants carried out a busy trade with local people as well as with many countries throughout Europe. Most of this trade passed through ports such as New Ross, Waterford, Youghal, Cork and Dublin.

Ireland's main exports were hides, wool, grain, linen and fish. Goods such as wine, salt, spices, cloth, metals and pottery were brought into Ireland from Europe. Archaeologists have found many examples of foreign pottery, such as wine jugs from France, in Irish towns.

While trade made some people extremely rich, most people in the towns continued to live in poverty.

Test your knowledge

1 Name some of the most powerful Norman families in Ireland.

2 Name five towns set up by the Normans.

3 What mixture of people lived in the towns?

4 Name the city in Ireland with the best-preserved medieval walls.

5 Explain briefly what placenames tell up about crafts and trade in Irish towns.

6 What is the most common type of artefact found by archaeologists in Irish towns?

7 What types of leather goods have been excavated?

Religion and the people

Trades, crafts and defence were not the only concerns of people living in medieval Ireland. The Christian Church was just as powerful in Ireland as it was in the rest of Europe. Religion played an important part in the everyday lives of the people.

Along with stone walls and castles, the other great buildings found in Norman towns were churches and cathedrals. In the city of Dublin, two great Gothic cathedrals were built by the Normans—Christchurch and St Patrick's.

Christchurch Cathedral in Dublin was built by the Normans on the site of an earlier Viking church. From looking at cathedrals in Chapter 16 you will be able to recognise its styles of architecture.

Cathedrals were also set up in many other dioceses throughout Ireland, each under the control of a bishop. Many of these medieval cathedrals are still in use today as Church of Ireland cathedrals. Some are small and in quiet country places like Clonfert in Co. Galway and Ross in Co. Cork. Others are large splendid buildings like St Mary's in Limerick or St Canice's in Kilkenny. All that remains on the site of some of the ancient cathedrals are ruins, with perhaps a round tower as at Kilmacduagh in Galway or Ardfert in Kerry.

Inside the medieval cathedral of St Canice in Kilkenny.

Norman lords made many grants of land to the church and also brought orders of monks from Europe. One of the most famous of these orders was the Cistercians. In 1142, they founded their first Irish monastery at Mellifont in Co. Louth.

The extensive remains of Mellifont Abbey in Co. Louth.

Dioceses and cathedrals founded during the Middle Ages.

Two Cistercian monasteries have been restored in recent times; at Holy Cross, Co. Tipperary and at Graiguenamanagh, Co. Kilkenny. In Dublin we can still see the Chapter House which is all that remains of St Mary's Abbey, a Cistercian House from 1147 onwards.

This room is all that remains today of the once great St Mary's Abbey.

As in the rest of Europe, people in Ireland still held on to some of the old superstitions. People fasted outside the houses of their enemies, hoping to bring a curse down on them. Some believed that relics and holy wells could bring magical cures for their sicknesses.

Pilgrimages were quite popular in medieval Ireland. The two most famous were to Croagh Patrick in Co. Mayo and Lough Derg in Co. Donegal. Pilgrims travelled from all over Europe to Lough Derg where they spent nine days praying while fasting on bread and water.

We get some idea of the importance of religion in medieval Ireland from the works of art which have survived. Objects like the Cross of Cong and buildings like St Patrick's Cathedral in Dublin show that people carried out some of their most skilled work for the glory of God.

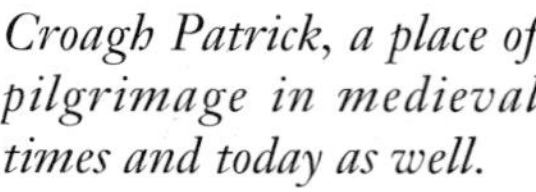

Croagh Patrick, a place of pilgrimage in medieval times and today as well.

The Cross of Cong is a good example of the beautiful work carried out by metalsmiths in Ireland during the Middle Ages.

Test your knowledge

1 Name the two cathedrals built by the Normans in Dublin.

2 Where is St Canice's Cathedral?

3 Name a famous order of monks that came to Ireland during the Middle Ages.

4 Name three abbeys founded by this order in Ireland.

5 What were the two most famous places of pilgrimage in medieval times?

6 List two superstitious habits of Irish people during the Middle Ages.

Chapter 17: Review

- The Normans were a strong and warlike people who conquered many lands in Europe during the eleventh and twelfth centuries. They were descended from Vikings who had settled in Normandy in the north of France.

- Norman knights were famous for their skills in battle. Wherever they went they introduced the feudal system. They were also great builders of castles and founders of monasteries.

- In 1066 the Norman leader, William the Conqueror, captured England after winning the

Battle of Hastings. These events are shown on the famous Bayeux Tapestry.

• The Normans arrived in Ireland in 1169 after they were invited in by Dermot MacMurrough, the king of Leinster, to help him in his wars against his enemies.

• Dermot MacMurrough made a bargain with the Norman leader, Richard de Clare, who was better known as Strongbow. In return for help against his enemies MacMurrough promised Strongbow his daughter, Aoife, in marriage and the kingdom of Leinster after his death.

• In 1169 the first Normans landed in Co. Wexford. In 1170 Strongbow arrived with a large army. He captured Waterford and went on to conquer Dublin.

• Fearing that the Norman lords might become too powerful, their leader, King Henry II of England, arrived himself in Ireland in 1171. The Norman knights and many of the Irish kings recognised Henry as lord of Ireland.

• The Normans built castles in many parts of the country. At first these were made of wood but were later replaced by strong stone buildings.

• The most important Norman stronghold in Ireland was Dublin Castle which was begun in 1204 on the orders of King John of England. It had many rooms including a banqueting-hall, a chapel, offices and a prison.

• Dublin Castle became the headquarters of the English government in Ireland. The Lord Deputy, the king's representative in Ireland, lived here when he was not travelling around the country keeping order and collecting taxes.

• Although the Normans never succeeded in capturing all of Ireland from the Irish chieftains, by 1250 the towns and vast stretches of the countryside were under their control. In these areas they introduced the feudal system.

• As well as taking over existing Viking towns in Ireland, the Normans also set up new towns of their own. Norman towns were mostly situated in the south and east.

• Many craftsmen worked at their trades in medieval Irish towns. Archaeologists have found a great amount of pottery pieces dating from the Middle Ages. They have also found many leather goods as well as bronze and iron ornaments and tools.

• Merchants in Irish towns carried on a great deal of trade in medieval times. The main exports from Ireland were hides, wool, grain, linen and fish. Goods such as wine, salt, spices, cloth, metals and pottery were imported from England and the continent of Europe.

• As in the rest of Europe, the Christian Church was very powerful in Ireland during the Middle Ages. The country was divided into different dioceses, each with its own bishop and cathedral.

• Many medieval Irish cathedrals like Christchurch and St Patrick's in Dublin and St Canice's in Kilkenny are still in use. Others like those at Kilmacduagh, Co. Galway and Ardfert, Co. Kerry are now in ruins.

• The Normans introduced orders of monks from Europe into Ireland. The most important of these was the Cistercians who founded their first Irish monastery at Mellifont in Co. Louth in 1142. Two Cistercian monasteries, Holy Cross Abbey in Co. Tipperary and Duiske Abbey at Graiguenamanagh, Co. Kilkenny were restored in recent times.

• As in other European countries, the people of Ireland had many superstitious habits during the Middle Ages. Some people fasted outside the houses of their enemies, while many people believed that relics and holy wells would provide magical cures.

• There were two great places of pilgrimage in medieval Ireland: Croagh Patrick and Lough Derg. People came from all over Europe to pray at these shrines.

The Renaissance

18 The Renaissance begins in Italy
19 Princes and Merchants
20 Painting, Sculpture and Architecture in Renaissance Italy
21 The Renaissance outside Italy
22 Science and Inventions during the Renaissance

The Renaissance begins in Italy

Exciting changes

Great and exciting changes took place in Europe between 1450 and 1650. During these two hundred years rulers became more powerful and towns increased in trade and wealth. The invention of printing made books available to more and more people. New lands were discovered and explored resulting in more accurate maps of the world.

People everywhere questioned the old beliefs of the Middle Ages, admiring instead the glories of ancient Greece and Rome. They hoped that by studying the writers and artists of ancient times they would bring about a rebirth of the learning and knowledge which had been lost to Europe after the fall of the Roman Empire around 400 AD.

This exciting and dazzling period of change, when many people tried to bring back the splendour and glory of ancient times, was called the *Renaissance*, a French word meaning rebirth.

400 BC →	400 AD →	1450 → 1650
Ancient Roman and Greek Civilisation.	*Middle Ages — much of Roman and Greek knowledge lost to the world.*	*Renaissance— rebirth of interest in Roman and Greek learning— a time of questioning and discovery.*

During the Renaissance, scholars throughout Europe searched for ancient writings. Artists were inspired by the ruins of ancient Rome to create great works. Rulers decorated their palaces with magnificent paintings and statues. Above all, human glories and achievements were praised as never before.

All these exciting changes were to begin in Italy around 1400 and spread from there to the rest of Europe.

Italy—Birthplace of the Renaissance

The states of Italy around 1450.

Today, Italy is a united country. The seat of government is in Rome, the capital city. In the fifteenth century (1401–1500), however, Italy was divided into a number of states. In the south was the kingdom of Naples, a fairly poor state. Central Italy was ruled by the pope from Rome and was known as the Papal States. The richest areas were in northern Italy where important states like Venice, Florence and Milan had grown wealthy through trade and commerce. It was in northern Italy that the Renaissance began.

Why did the Renaissance begin in Italy?

Here are the main reasons why the Renaissance began in Italy:

• The ruins scattered throughout Italy reminded Italians of the great achievements of the ancient Romans. They were anxious to learn about the Romans and to follow their example in literature, art and architecture.

The Forum in Rome. Ruins such as these reminded Italians of the glories of the ancient Roman Empire which you read about in Chapter 4.

• The Italian language was based on Latin, the language of the ancient Romans. Because of this, Renaissance Italians were interested in ancient Latin writings.

• Italy had larger and richer towns than other European states. There was a greater interest in art and learning in the towns than in the countryside.

• The wealthy Italian rulers and merchants were willing to spend their money on arts such as painting, sculpture, music and poetry.

• Italian states like Venice had trading links with the East. Contact with people like the Chinese and the Arabs provided new ideas and made them eager to explore and travel.

Merchant ships in the busy port of Venice. Italian ports like this prospered through trading with the East.

Turks storming the walls of Constantinople in May 1453.

• The Turks conquered the city of Constantinople in 1453 and put an end to the Christian Greek Empire. As a result many Greek scholars fled to Italy and brought with them precious Greek *manuscripts* (works written by hand) and a knowledge of ancient Greece.

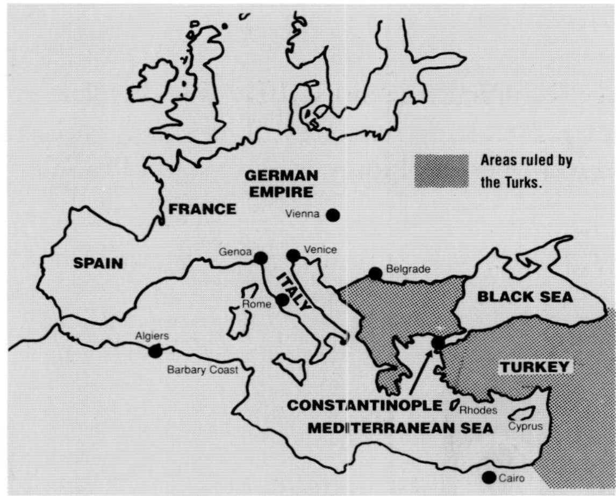

Turkish conquests including the city of Constantinople (1453), which became the capital of the Turkish Empire.

Test your knowledge

1 Why did many scholars begin to study the writings of ancient Greece and Rome?

2 What was the Renaissance?

3 Where did the Renaissance begin?

4 Name the main states into which Italy was divided in the fifteenth century.

5 How did the ancient ruins of the Roman Empire help to bring about the Renaissance in Italy?

6 What links had Italian states with the East? Why was this important for the Renaissance?

7 Why was the Turkish conquest of Constantinople so important?

The scene is set

Around 1400, the most important areas in Italy were those near the cities of Florence, Venice, Milan and Rome. These areas were called *city states*, since the city government also ruled the surrounding countryside.

The rulers and merchants in these rich city states were proud men. They enjoyed showing their glory to the world by paying for works of art like paintings or statues which would honour them. Rich men who paid artists were known as *patrons* of the arts. Without them, the Italian Renaissance would not have been possible.

In the next chapter we shall see how these rich patrons encouraged great artists to create the magnificent paintings, statues and buildings of the Italian Renaissance.

Chapter 18: Review

- Many changes took place in Europe between 1450 and 1650. People especially wanted to revive the glories of ancient Greece and Rome. This rebirth of ancient learning was called the Renaissance.
- In the fifteenth century, Italy was divided into a number of different states. The most important ones were Venice, Florence, Milan and Rome.
- The Renaissance began in Italy around 1350. The ruins of ancient Rome inspired many Italians to rediscover their past.
- In addition, the rich towns and wealthy merchants provided the money needed for the spread of art and learning.
- When the Turks conquered the city of Constantinople in 1453 many Greek scholars, familiar with the trading cities of the West, fled to Italy with their precious manuscripts.

CHAPTER 19 Princes and Merchants

During the Renaissance, each state in Italy had its own government which was usually controlled by a powerful family or prince.

Their courts were splendid buildings where they lived surrounded by hundreds of rich followers. The prince and his court enjoyed many pastimes such as chess, archery, tennis and especially hunting.

Some princes were also merchants and bankers who made their money from trade and commerce. Italian cities such as Venice, Florence and Genoa were bustling centres of trade. At ports such as Venice and Genoa, sailing ships brought in exotic goods from the East like spices and silks. Florence was famous for its luxury woollen goods and its banking.

Ludovico Sforza (1451–1508) was a famous Renaissance prince. He ruled Milan from 1476 until 1499. He is pictured here on one of his own coins. Ludovico was a strong and ruthless leader as well as a patron of artists such as Leonardo da Vinci.

Many rich princes and merchants used their enormous wealth to decorate their houses with works of art. They employed architects, painters and sculptors to design and decorate their palaces, churches and towns. They also invited poets and musicians into their palaces to entertain the court.

But their was another side to Renaissance life. These princes and rulers were often ruthless and violent men. Bitter feuds frequently broke out between rival families and Renaissance rulers did not hesitate to use violence to get rid of their enemies.

In this chapter we shall take a closer look at some of the great rulers of Renaissance Italy.

Florence: First city of the Renaissance

The city of Florence around 1450. Florence was the home of the Medici and the first city of the Renaissance.

Florence was the first city of the Renaissance. It was ruled by the Medici who had grown rich through trade and banking.

The first Medici ruler of Florence was Cosimo. He controlled the city from 1434 until his death in 1464. Under his rule Florence became the first great centre of the Renaissance in Italy.

Cosimo de Medici was a generous patron of the arts. He invited scholars and artists to his palace in Florence and sent agents abroad searching for rare manuscripts to fill his great library. For thirty years Cosimo brought peace and prosperity to Florence. When he died in 1464 the people of the city gave him the title 'Father of the Land' (*Pater Patriae*), which was written on his tomb.

Cosimo de Medici (1389–1464).

The next ruler of Florence was Cosimo's son, Piero. A weak ruler, Piero died after five years in power and was succeeded in 1469 by his son, Lorenzo. Lorenzo was to become the greatest of all Medici rulers.

Lorenzo the Magnificent (1449–92)

Lorenzo the Magnificent (1449–92), the Medici ruler of Florence and patron of the arts.

Lorenzo de Medici was only twenty years of age when he became head of the family and ruler of Florence in 1469. He was a man of many talents. Under his rule the Medici remained a great banking family and Florence continued to prosper.

Lorenzo was not only a good banker and ruler. He was also a poet, an athlete and, above all, a patron of the arts. He invited the great artists into his palace where he paid them to produce works of art. Great artists like Leonardo da Vinci, Michelangelo and Botticelli were helped by Lorenzo de Medici.

Like his grandfather, Cosimo, Lorenzo sent agents throughout Europe and the East in search of manuscripts. One scholar brought back two hundred Greek works, eighty of which were unknown in Europe. These works were stored in Lorenzo's library which became Europe's first public library since it was open to all.

Lorenzo de Medici was a great patron of art and literature. But he was also a clever and strong ruler. He had many enemies in Florence who were always looking for a chance to overthrow the Medici.

The Pazzi family were great rivals of the Medici. In 1478, they plotted to assassinate Lorenzo and his brother, Guiliano, while they both attended Mass on Easter Sunday. Two priests were chosen to kill the Medici brothers during the consecration.

Guiliano was stabbed to death, but Lorenzo managed to escape to the sacristy where he locked the door behind him. The people of Florence rallied behind the Medici, and the *Pazzi Conspiracy* ended in failure. An angry mob raced through the streets of Florence, killing anyone thought to be connected with the plot. Before the crisis ended over 200 people had been killed, including the Archbishop of Pisa, one of the leaders of the conspiracy.

After the attempt on his life, Lorenzo surrounded himself with an armed guard and tightened his grip on the government of Florence. Lorenzo believed strongly in peace between the different states of Italy and did his best to prevent war from breaking out between them

Lorenzo's death in 1492, at the age of forty-three, was a great blow both to Florence and to Italy. During his life he had been a great statesman and a brilliant patron of the arts. He had truly earned for himself the title of *Lorenzo the Magnificent*.

Test your knowledge

1 What family ruled Florence in the fifteenth century?

2 Who was the first Medici ruler of Florence?

3 Why did Florence become a centre of the Renaissance during the lifetime of Cosimo de Medici?

4 Who became ruler of Florence in 1469?

5 Why is it true to say that Lorenzo was a great patron of the arts?

6 What was the Pazzi Conspiracy?

7 Why do you think Lorenzo was called Lorenzo the Magnificent?

8 Why was the death of Lorenzo a turning point in the history of Florence?

The decline of Florence

The death of Lorenzo the Magnificent in 1492 was a turning point in the history of Florence. He was succeeded by his weak and stupid son, Piero. Under Piero, both Florence and the Medicis faced ruin. When the French invaded Florence in 1494, Piero fled from the city in panic.

The great days of Florence as the first city of the Renaissance were over. Artists such as Michelangelo left to search for work in Rome. This city, ruled by the popes, replaced Florence as the new centre of the Renaissance.

An assassination attempt. Violence such as this was common in Italy during the Renaissance.

The Renaissance in Rome

The Vatican Library, founded by Pope Nicholas V (1447–55).

Rome had once been the capital of the vast Roman Empire and the largest city in the world. The glories of Rome were long past with the coming of the Renaissance. But the many ancient monuments and ruins scattered throughout the city were constant reminders of Rome's ancient greatness.

In the fifteenth century, Rome was ruled by the popes. They were not only heads of the Church. They were also powerful princes who controlled the Papal States in central Italy. These Renaissance popes lived in great splendour and luxury. Many of them led their armies into war and were more concerned with politics and the affairs of the world than with religion. From around 1450 onwards, most popes were great patrons of the arts and invited the best scholars and artists to work in Rome.

Nicholas V (1447–55) was the first great

Renaissance pope. He founded the famous Vatican Library. When the Turks captured Constantinople in 1453, Nicholas sent messengers to Greece to buy as many of the manuscripts as they could. He drew up plans for the rebuilding of Rome, including the construction of the new St Peter's Basilica.

Sixtus IV (1471–84) was another great Renaissance pope. He greatly improved the city of Rome by widening streets, constructing bridges and building churches. He had the Sistine Chapel built and employed great artists such as Botticelli and Ghirlandaio to decorate it. Like all Renaissance popes, he was involved in politics and supported the Pazzi Conspiracy to overthrow Lorenzo de Medici.

The most scandalous of Renaissance popes was Roderigo Borgia who became Alexander VI (1492–1503). Like earlier popes he was a patron of the arts and improved the city of Rome. However, he did not live a very holy life. He had many mistresses and was the father of a number of children. Alexander VI also promoted members of his own family to high positions and made his son, Cesare Borgia, a cardinal.

Pope Julius II (1503–13) was a great patron of the arts. He also led his armies into war.

Julius II (1503–13), a nephew of Sixtus IV, was another typical Renaissance pope. He was a patron of great artists such as Michelangelo and Raphael. He was also very ambitious and often led the papal armies into battle.

Julius II was succeeded by Leo X (1513–21). The son of Lorenzo de Medici, he was made a cardinal in 1475 at the age of fourteen. Like his father, Lorenzo, Leo X was a magnificent patron of the arts. He organised lavish banquets and pageants in Rome to entertain members of the court and foreign visitors. Leo X's greatest project was the building of the new St Peter's Basilica.

Like Florence, Renaissance Rome was a city of contrasts. Under the rule of the popes, wonderful achievements in art existed side by side with violence and political corruption. Popes were patrons of the arts, but they were often ruthless rulers who were prepared to use war and violence to achieve their ambitions. As a result, these popes neglected their religious duties and by 1500 the Catholic Church was clearly in need of change and reform.

The Sistine Chapel, built during the reign of Pope Sixtus IV (1471–84).

Test your knowledge

1 Why did Rome replace Florence as the main centre of the Renaissance after 1492?

2 What pope founded the Vatican Library?

3 What pope had the Sistine Chapel built?

4 Why was Alexander VI the most scandalous of Renaissance popes?

5 In what sense was Julius II a typical Renaissance pope?

6 What pope was the son of Lorenzo the Magnificent?

7 In what way was Renaissance Rome a city of contrasts?

8 Why was the Church in need of change and reform by 1500?

Chapter 19: Review

• There were many rich princes and merchants in Renaissance Italy who lived in splendid surroundings and spent large sums of money on works of art. They employed architects, painters and sculptors to design and decorate their palaces, churches and towns.

• There was another side to Renaissance life, however. Many rulers were ruthless and violent men who did not hesitate to use violence against their enemies.

• The Medicis, a rich banking family, were the most powerful group in Florence between 1434 and 1492. Cosimo de Medici, who ruled the city from 1434 until his death in 1464, was a splendid patron of the arts as well as a wise ruler.

• Lorenzo the Magnificent, Cosimo's grandson, ruled between 1469 and 1492. As well as being a great businessman and ruler, he was a poet and athlete. Above all he was a most generous patron of the arts.

• In 1478, powerful enemies of Lorenzo de Medici tried to kill him during Mass on Easter Sunday. This was known as the Pazzi Conspiracy, and Lorenzo's brother, Guiliano, was killed but Lorenzo himself escaped.

• The death of Lorenzo the Magnificent in 1492 was a great blow to Florence and to Italy. He was succeeded by his weak son, Piero, who fled from the city when the French army invaded Florence in 1494. The great days of the Renaissance in Florence were now at an end.

• The city of Rome replaced Florence as the main centre of the Renaissance. At this time Rome was ruled by the popes. They lived lives of luxury and were deeply involved in politics and warfare.

• Nicholas V (1447–55) was the first great Renaissance pope. He founded the Vatican Library. He sent collectors all over Europe to gather ancient manuscripts.

• Sixtus IV (1471–84) was another great Renaissance pope. He improved the city of Rome and built the Sistine Chapel in the Vatican, employing artists like Botticelli and Ghirlandaio to decorate it.

• Alexander VI (1492–1503), a member of the Borgia family, was the most scandalous of all Renaissance popes. He was the father of a number of children, including Cesare Borgia, whom he made a cardinal.

• Julius II (1503–13) was continuously involved in wars in Italy. He was also a great patron of the arts and employed Michelangelo and Raphael in the Vatican.

• Leo X (1513–21) was a son of Lorenzo de Medici and had been made a cardinal at the age of fourteen. As pope he was a great patron of the arts and organised the rebuilding of St Peter's Basilica.

Painting, Sculpture and Architecture in Renaissance Italy

By 1400 many Italian cities had grown rich and famous through trade and banking. Italy had become a great centre of learning where rulers and merchants spent vast sums of money on works of art which would beautify their homes, towns and churches.

Painting

Before the Renaissance, painting was very different from what it is today. Then paintings were flat and lifeless and usually dealt with religious subjects. This changed greatly after 1400.

Before the Renaissance, paintings were flat, lifeless and lacking in detail.

The Tribute Money by Masaccio was one of the first paintings to show perspective. Notice that the figures in the foreground (front) appear closer to the viewer than those in the background.

- During the Renaissance artists learned how to give depth and background to their paintings. This is known as *perspective*. The Italian painter Masaccio (1401–28) was one of the first to use perspective in his work.

- There were also many changes in the materials used by artists. Five hundred years ago, artists could not buy ready-made colours in tubes and boxes. They had to prepare their own colours using plants and minerals. Using two stones, they would grind these materials into a fine powder. They then made a paste by mixing the powder with a liquid. During the Middle Ages, painters used egg whites to bind their paints. Renaissance painters began to use oils instead of eggs. This was a great improvement, since oils dried slowly, allowing artists to work with greater accuracy. They could also make changes in their work as they went along.

- A new painting technique was also used by Renaissance artists. It involved blurring the outlines in paintings by using soft shadows. This technique was known as *sfumato*. It can be clearly seen around the eyes and mouth of Leonardo da Vinci's masterpiece, the *Mona Lisa*. Art historians say that Leonardo himself invented *sfumato*.

The Mona Lisa, by Leonardo da Vinci. Notice the sfumato, *or soft shadows, around the eyes and mouth.*

- Many Renaissance artists painted pictures directly onto wet plaster walls. These wall paintings were known as *frescoes* because they were painted while the plaster was still 'fresh' and wet. Frescoes soon became popular for decorating the walls inside palaces, churches and monasteries.

- Like the artists of the Middle Ages, Renaissance painters were interested in religious subjects. But they also showed a new interest in painting ordinary people and scenes from nature. Many Renaissance artists studied the human body (*anatomy*) so that they could paint more life-like images.

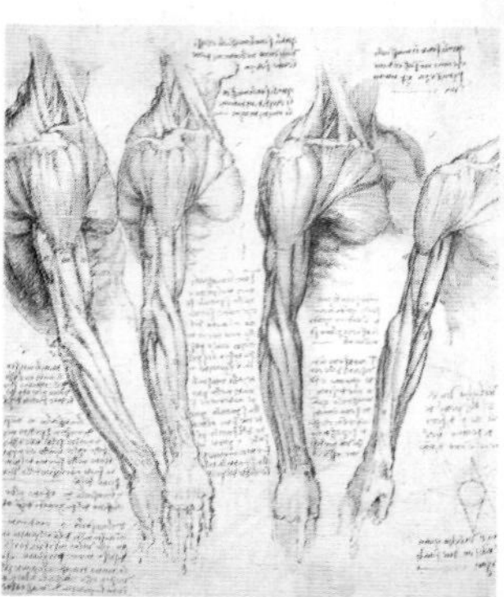

Drawings of the body by Leonardo da Vinci.

Chartres Cathedral, a typical Gothic church built during the Middle Ages.

Before the Renaissance, powerful rulers lived in castles and fortresses so they could defend themselves against attack. From around 1400 onwards, many rich people no longer lived in castles. They had beautifully decorated houses in the country known as *villas* and grand houses in the towns. These villas and *townhouses* were not built in Gothic style. Instead, Renaissance architects used the classical style based on the ancient buildings of Greece and Rome. Churches were also built in the classical style.

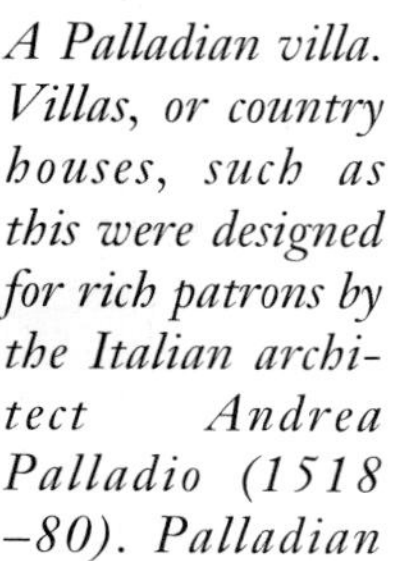

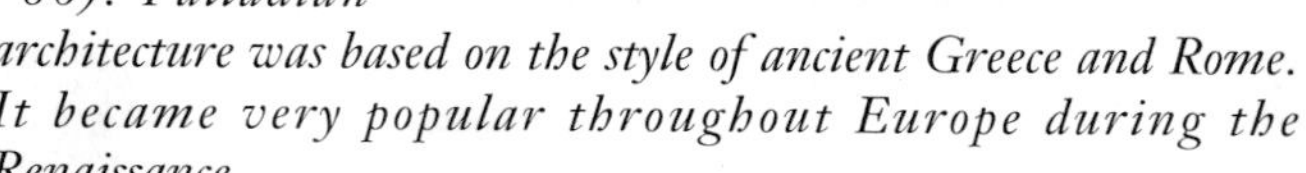

A Palladian villa. Villas, or country houses, such as this were designed for rich patrons by the Italian architect Andrea Palladio (1518–80). Palladian architecture was based on the style of ancient Greece and Rome. It became very popular throughout Europe during the Renaissance.

Sculpture

The statue of David by Donatello.

There was a rebirth in interest in sculpture during the Renaissance. Italian sculptors were inspired by ancient Greek and Roman statues and used them as models for their work.

One of the great Renaissance sculptors was a man from Florence called Donatello (1386–1466). People thought that his statue of *David* was the greatest piece of sculpture since Roman times. Like painters, Renaissance sculptors tried to produce realistic, life-like figures.

Architecture

Architecture, the study and planning of buildings, also changed greatly during the Renaissance. As we have learned, the most important medieval buildings were churches and castles. Most churches were built in the Gothic style. Gothic buildings had pointed rather than curved arches as well as many towers and spires.

Florence Cathedral with its magnificent dome designed by the architect Brunelleschi.

Renaissance architects got many ideas from the writings of Vitruvius Polio, one of the famous architects of ancient Rome.

The first great Renaissance architect was Filippo Brunelleschi (1377–1446). Brunelleschi was fascinated by ancient Roman buildings and ruins. He and the sculptor, Donatello, once went to Rome together where they studied Roman ruins, buildings and statues. Brunelleschi's greatest work is the dome of the cathedral in Florence. This huge structure, one of the great marvels of the time, was modelled on the Roman Pantheon.

Test your knowledge

1 What was painting like before the Renaissance?
2 What is meant by perspective? Which Renaissance painter was the first to use it?
3 How did materials used by painters in the Middle Ages differ from those used during the Renaissance?
4 What is a fresco?
5 Who was Donatello and what was his greatest work?
6 What style of architecture was common during the Middle Ages?
7 What inspired Renaissance sculptors and architects?
8 Who was Brunelleschi and what was his greatest work?

Leonardo da Vinci (1452–1519)

The early years

Leonardo was born in the town of Vinci near Florence on 15 April 1452. His father was a rich lawyer but he never knew his mother who was said to be a local servant girl.

Leonardo was an imaginative young boy who loved to daydream. He was full of curiosity and questioned everything around him. He showed a great talent for art and invention, and when he was fourteen years old he became an apprentice in the workshop of Andrea Verrocchio, one of Florence's best-known artists. Through Verrocchio, Leonardo met other young artists, including one named Botticelli who was also to become a famous painter.

As a young man, Leonardo was tall and handsome and had a good singing voice. He studied mathematics and physics and had a great interest in human anatomy. Leonardo was not only a brilliant painter. He was also an inventor and engineer of great genius.

The years in Milan

By 1482, Leonardo had tired of Florence so he decided to move to the larger city of Milan. He

The Birth of Venus *by Sandro Botticelli (1446–1510). This painting, showing the Roman goddess, Venus, rising from the sea, was painted in about 1485 for the country villa of a member of the Medici family.*

wrote a letter to the Duke of Milan, Ludovico Sforza, in which he boasted of his great inventions, including armoured cars and other new weapons of war. Ludovico could not resist Leonardo's claims. He invited the great artist to Milan where he was to work in the Duke's court for a number of years.

In Milan, Leonardo designed cannons and a system of central heating for the duke. He painted pictures of Ludovico's relations and created spectacular pageants and entertainments for the court. While in Milan Leonardo also painted two of his greatest pictures: *Virgin on the Rocks* and the great fresco of *The Last Supper* which was painted on a convent wall.

Virgin on the Rocks *by Leonardo da Vinci.*

The Last Supper *by Leonardo da Vinci was painted onto the wall of a monastery in Milan in 1493. This fresco of the Last Supper was different from earlier pictures of the same event. In earlier pictures the apostles were seen sitting quietly at the table. Leonardo's picture, however, is full of drama and excitement.*

Activity

Christ has just announced that one of the apostles is going to betray him. Look closely at the picture and describe their reaction to the news. Point out the figures of Christ and of Judas. [Hint — Judas is somewhat isolated from the rest of the apostles.]

From Florence to France

In 1499, when a French army conquered Milan, Duke Ludovico was taken prisoner. Leonardo returned to Florence, where he painted the portrait of a rich merchant's wife. This portrait is the famous *Mona Lisa*, one of the greatest paintings of the Renaissance.

In 1513, Leonardo went to Rome where his patron was the Medici pope, Leo X. Since he was not happy in Rome, he was pleased when King Francis I invited him to the French court in 1516. Leonardo spent the last three years of his life in the French chateau of Amboise, where he died in 1519.

The mark of genius

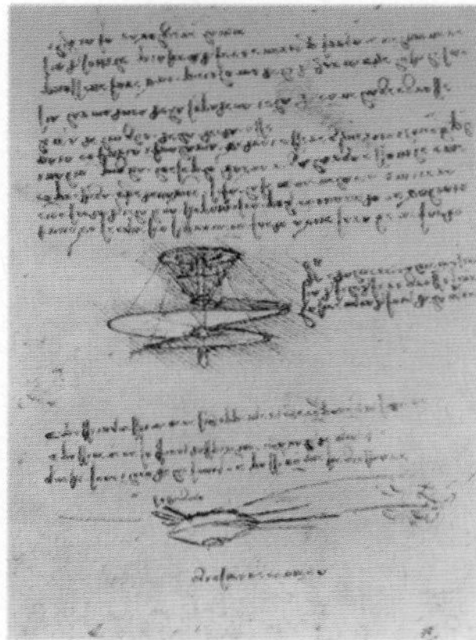

Leonardo's design for a flying machine.

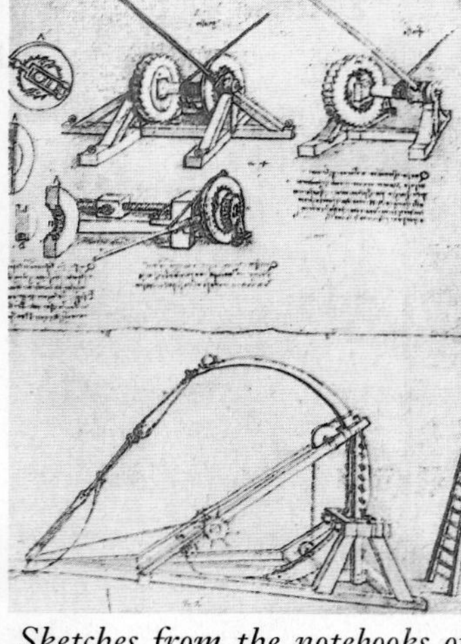

Sketches from the notebooks of Leonardo.

Leonardo da Vinci's Self Portrait..

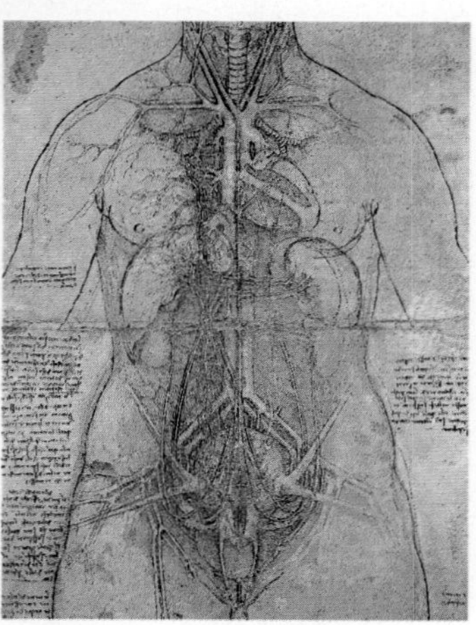

Leonardo da Vinci was a man who was ahead of his time—some of his inventions were not actually produced until the twentieth century. Over 5,000 pages of his notebooks have been preserved. They are written from right to left and can only be read by viewing them in a mirror. These pages are full of sketches which show birds in flight, a set of wings, a helicopter, a parachute, a submarine, a variety of weapons and an armoured car. Leonardo studied the human body, often visiting hospitals to observe the dying and even secretly dissecting corpses. His ideas, experiments, inventions and works of art show that he was truly a genius, one of the greatest men who ever lived.

Test your knowledge

1 Where and when was Leonardo born?

2 To whom was he apprenticed when he was fourteen years old?

3 Who became Leonardo's patron in Milan?

4 Who was his last patron?

5 Name two of Leonardo's famous paintings.

6 What sketches are contained in Leonardo's notebooks?

7 Why do you think Leonardo is regarded as one of the greatest men who ever lived?

Michelangelo Buonarroti (1475–1564)

Growing up in Florence

Michelangelo was born in the small village of Caprese near Florence in 1475. He was twenty-three years younger than his great rival, Leonardo da Vinci. Unlike Leonardo, Michelangelo's early life was very hard. His mother died when he was six and he lived with his hot-tempered father and selfish brothers. As a young boy he showed a great talent for drawing. Although his father did not want him to be an artist, he finally allowed his son to become an apprentice to a famous painter in Florence named Ghirlandaio.

In Ghirlandaio's workshop Michelangelo quickly

showed his great talent. On occasions he corrected his master's work. Michelangelo was as hot-tempered and touchy as his father and had his nose broken in a fight with an older apprentice.

Living in the Medici palace

When Michelangelo left Ghirlandaio's workshop, he worked in the gardens of the Medici Palace making statues. One day Lorenzo de Medici saw some of this work. He was so impressed that he invited Michelangelo to come to live in the Medici Palace.

In the palace, Michelangelo was treated like Lorenzo's own son. He dined with the family and took part in conversations with the many scholars and poets who flocked to the Medici home. After the death of Lorenzo in 1492, Michelangelo left Florence, going first to Bologna and then to Rome.

The master sculptor

The Pietà *by Michelangelo.*

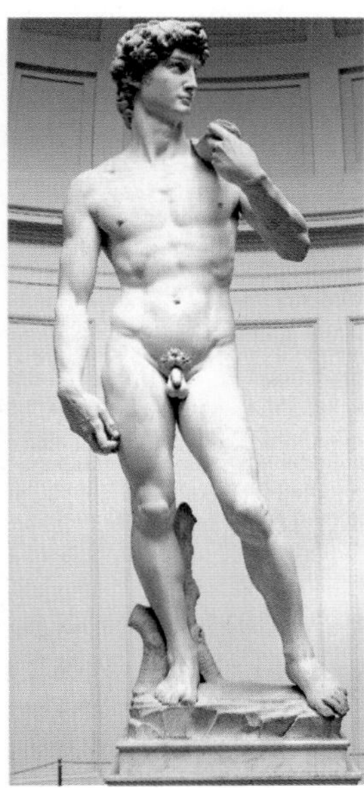

Michelangelo's David *was carved out of a single block of marble. It stands about five metres tall.*

Michelangelo was a brilliant painter, but sculpture was his first love. In Rome he created a statue of the dead Christ in his mother's arms. This was known as *The Pietà*, a work which made him famous throughout Italy. One day he overheard a passer-by giving another artist credit for the work. Angered by this, Michelangelo stole into St Peter's that night and carved his name on the statue. *The Pietà* is the only work in existence signed by Michelangelo.

When he returned to Florence in 1501, Michelangelo created his greatest statue from a massive block of marble. The result was the famous statue of *David*. Standing over five metres high, it took forty men four days to carry it to its chosen site in the central square of Florence. Ever since then, people have gazed in wonder at the powerful life-like figure of David. Like Leonardo, Michelangelo had dissected corpses so that he could understand the human body and make his figures more realistic. He was without doubt the greatest sculptor since ancient times.

Working in the Sistine Chapel

Michelangelo was soon to show his genius as a painter. In 1508 his great patron, Pope Julius II, hired him to paint the ceiling in the Sistine Chapel. This was a huge and difficult task. For four years Michelangelo had to lie on scaffolding and paint looking upwards. He became so involved in his work that he often forgot to sleep or eat. He dismissed assistant after assistant, and eventually would only allow an old servant and Pope Julius himself to watch him work.

While painting on to wet plaster, Michelangelo had at work at top speed. He became so used to his cramped position that when he received a letter, he held it over his head and bent backwards to read it! At last the scaffolding was removed. When the Sistine Chapel was opened to the public, people stared upwards in total amazement at what they saw. Before their eyes on the ceiling was the *Story of Creation*, containing 343 major figures. It is truly one of the greatest masterpieces of all time.

The Creation of Man, *a detail from Michelangelo's painting on the ceiling of the Sistine Chapel.*

The last years

Michelangelo spent his last years in Rome where he led a very strict life. He painted a fresco called *The Last Judgment* on the wall of the Sistine Chapel for Pope Paul III (1534–49). This pope also appointed him to design the dome of St Peter's Basilica. The magnificent dome, which towers over Rome to this day, shows that Michelangelo was also a brilliant architect. He also loved poetry and wrote some poems himself. Michelangelo—sculptor, painter, architect and poet—was, like Leonardo, a true genius.

The Last Judgment, *a huge fresco painted by Michelangelo on the altar wall of the Sistine Chapel.*

Self Portrait *of Michelangelo.*

The magnificent interior of St Peter's Basilica in Rome.

The giant dome of St Peter's in Rome was designed by Michelangelo.

Test your knowledge

1 When and where was Michelangelo born?
2 Who was Michelangelo's first master?
3 What famous Florentine leader was Michelangelo's patron?
4 Name two of Michelangelo's great pieces of sculpture.
5 What great work did Michelangelo begin in 1508?
6 What pope became Michelangelo's patron at this time?
7 What architectural work did Michelangelo create?

Raphael Sanzio (1483–1520)

While Michelangelo and Leonardo were working in Florence, another young artist arrived in 1504. His name was Raphael Sanzio.

Raphael was born in the Italian town of Urbino in 1483. His father, Giovanni, was a painter at the court of the Duke of Urbino. When his father died in 1495, Raphael went to Perugia where he was apprenticed to the great painter, Perugino. In 1504, Raphael travelled to Florence to study the work of Leonardo and Michelangelo. To earn money, he painted the portraits of many rich Florentines.

Raphael went to Rome in 1508 and was soon employed by Pope Julius II to paint frescoes in the Vatican's papal apartments. The most famous of these frescoes is *The School of Athens* which shows Plato, Aristotle and other ancient philosophers. He also became known for his paintings of beautiful Madonnas.

The School of Athens *by Raphael. The Greek philosophers, Plato and Aristotle, are debating in the centre of the painting. Notice the use of perspective.*

Michelangelo was also working in the Vatican at this time, and there was great rivalry between the two men. In 1514, Pope Leo X (1513–21) appointed Raphael the chief architect of the rebuilding of St Peter's Basilica.

When Raphael died in 1520, at the age of thirty-seven, he was one of Italy's most famous painters. His funeral in Rome was an occasion of great sadness and ceremony.

Raphael was famous for painting Madonnas such as this figure of the Blessed Virgin with the Christ Child and St John the Baptist.

The artists of Venice

After the death of Lorenzo the Magnificent, Rome had replaced Florence as the centre of the Renaissance. In 1527, seven years after the death of Raphael, Rome suffered terrible destruction when it was looted by German troops in the army of Emperor Charles V. Venice now became the centre of Renaissance activity.

Venice had a strong system of government. Its ruler, the *doge*, was assisted by the wealthy merchants. Venice had grown rich through trade and its merchants were also patrons of the arts. With its many canals, Venice was a damp place which did not suit frescoes, so oil paintings done on canvas were popular.

Portrait of Flora *by Titian.*

Venice's greatest painter was Titian (1480–1576). He was a famous portrait painter who was appointed the city's official painter in 1516. It was said that he died of the plague at the age of ninety-six.

Another famous Venetian was Tintoretto (1518–94). His work was full of life and vivid colours and he became Venice's official painter after the death of Titian.

Test your knowledge

1 When and where was Raphael born?

2 Who was Raphael's patron in Rome?

3 Name one of Raphael's most famous frescoes.

4 Name two Venetian painters of the Renaissance.

The end of an era

By 1600, the great days of the Italian Renaissance were nearly over. For 200 years, Italy had led the world in literature, painting, sculpture and architecture. Cities like Florence, Milan, Rome and Venice had become centres of art and learning, attracting scholars and artists from far and wide.

Soon new ideas began to spread beyond Italy to the rest of Europe. As towns and cities in France, Germany, the Netherlands and England grew in wealth, their rulers, like the Italian princes, became great patrons of the arts.

In the next chapter, we shall look at some of the great artists and writers who brought the glory of the Italian Renaissance to the rest of Europe.

Important figures in the Italian Renaissance and their achievements

Painting

MASACCIO (1401–28)
Tribute Money

BOTTICELLI (1446–1510)
Birth of Venus

LEONARDO DA VINCI (1452–1519)
Mona Lisa
Last Supper
Virgin on the Rocks

MICHELANGELO (1475–1564)
Ceiling of the Sistine Chapel
Last Judgment

RAPHAEL (1483–1520)
Madonnas
School of Athens

TITIAN (1480–1576)
Portrait of Flora

Sculpture

DONATELLO (1386–1466)
David

MICHELANGELO (1475–1564)
David
The Pietà

Architecture

BRUNELLESCHI (1377–1446)
Dome of Cathedral in Florence

MICHELANGELO (1475–1564)
Dome of St Peter's Basilica in Rome

Chapter 20: Review

• During the Renaissance artists introduced perspective into their paintings. They mixed their colours with oils instead of egg. They also developed the technique of painting on wet plaster known as fresco.

• Renaissance sculptures looked to ancient Greece and Rome for models. One of the first great Renaissance sculptors was Donatello (1386–1466) whose statue of *David* was considered the best piece of sculpture since ancient times.

• Renaissance architects rejected the Gothic style and went back to the classical style of the Greek and Roman models which they saw in ruins around them. They were also influenced by the writings of an ancient Roman, Vitruvius Polio.

• The first architect of Renaissance times was Filippo Brunelleschi (1377–1446) whose most brilliant work was the dome of the cathedral in Florence.

• Leonardo da Vinci (1452–1519) was one of the great geniuses of all time. His most famous paintings are *The Mona Lisa* and *The Last Supper*.

• As well as being a great painter, Leonardo was also an inventor. He invented weapons for Duke Ludovico Sforza of Milan and his notebooks contained sketches of spectacular inventions.

• In 1516, King Francis I of France offered Leonardo work and he spent the last three years of his life at the French castle of Amboise where he died in 1519.

• Michelangelo Buonarroti (1475–1564) was an artist of genius in both painting and sculpture. As a young man he studied art in the palace of Lorenzo the Magnificent in Florence.

• Michelangelo's greatest pieces of sculpture are the statue of *David* in Florence and *The Pietà* in St Peter's Basilica, Rome.

• In 1508 Pope Julius II asked Michelangelo to paint the ceiling of the Sistine Chapel in Rome. When the work was finished in 1512 all who saw it marvelled at its beauty. Later on, Michelangelo painted a fresco called *The Last Judgment* on a wall in the Sistine Chapel.

• Pope Paul III (1534–49) appointed Michelangelo to design the dome of the new St Peter's Basilica.

• Raphael Sanzio (1483–1520) the great Renaissance painter and rival of Michelangelo arrived in Rome in 1508. Pope Julius II gave him the job of decorating the papal apartments with paintings.

• Raphael was famous for his painting known as *The School of Athens* and for his beautiful Madonnas, or pictures of the Blessed Virgin. In 1514 Pope Leo X appointed him architect of St Peter's Basilica.

• After the destruction of Rome by German troops in 1527, the city of Venice became the main centre of the Renaissance. Venice was especially famous for great painters such as Titian (1480–1576) and Tintoretto (1518–1594).

The Renaissance outside Italy

While the Renaissance developed in Italy, the rest of Europe looked on and admired the brilliant work of Italian writers and artists. However, it was not long before the Renaissance spread to other parts of Europe.

From around 1500 onwards countries like France, Spain, the Netherlands and England produced their own Renaissance artists and writers. We shall learn about some of these people in this chapter.

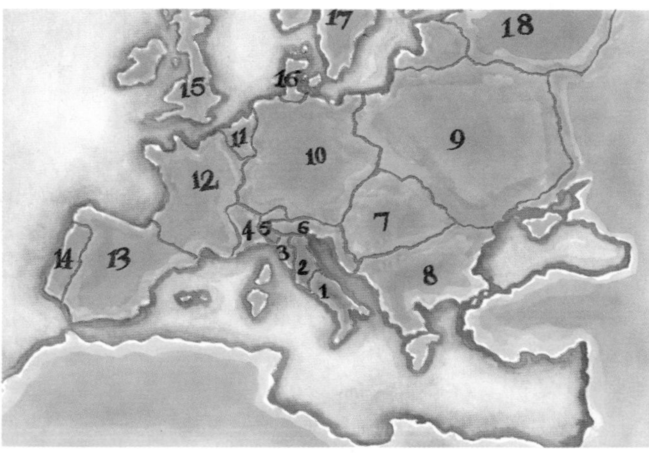

The main states of Europe at the time of the Renaissance.

1. Naples
2. Papal States
3. Florence
4. Savoy
5. Milan
6. Venice
7. Hungary
8. Turkish Empire
9. Poland
10. The German States of the Holy Roman Empire
11. Netherlands
12. France
13. Spain
14. Portugal
15. England
16. Denmark
17. Sweden
18. Russia

Vernacular writers

Before the Renaissance most European writers used the Latin language. Latin was understood by all educated people and it was the language used in the Church, in universities and in schools. During the Renaissance, writers began to use their own native languages. Languages such as Italian, French, Spanish and English are known as *vernacular languages*.

The Italians, Petrarch and Boccaccio, were among the first to write in their native language—Italian. Vernacular literature soon became popular in other countries as well. Before the Renaissance was over, great plays, poems and novels had been written in French, Spanish and English.

William Shakespeare: A great vernacular writer

William Shakespeare (1564–1616).

England's greatest Renaissance writer was William Shakespeare. He was born at Stratford-on-Avon on 23 April 1564 and attended the local grammar school. At the age of eighteen he married Anne Hathaway and soon afterwards moved to London.

In London Shakespeare became an actor and writer of plays. He opened his own theatre called the *Globe*. Here, Shakespeare's plays were performed in the open air. These plays appealed to people of all classes. They contained a wide variety of interesting characters, from kings and queens to fools and common rogues.

Shakespeare wrote tragedies such as *Hamlet*, *Macbeth*, *King Lear*, *Romeo and Juliet* and *Julius Caesar*. He wrote comedies such as *The Merchant of Venice*, *A Midsummer Night's Dream*, *As You Like It* and *Twelfth Night*, as well as plays like *Henry V* and *Richard II* which are called histories.

Shakespeare also wrote poems, including a

collection of sonnets. His plays made him rich and famous and he was greatly admired by Queen Elisabeth I. He died in 1616 and was buried under the altar of the church at Stratford-on-Avon.

A play being performed in the Globe Theatre, London.

Test your knowledge

1 What is meant by vernacular writing?
2 Where was William Shakespeare born?
3 What theatre did he open in London?
4 Name two tragedies and two comedies written by Shakespeare.
5 What collection of poems did he write?

Renaissance art outside Italy

By 1500, other European countries were beginning to follow Italy's lead, not only in literature, but in art and architecture as well. Artists and architects visited Italy to learn new styles and techniques. Many Italian artists and architects in turn worked in other European countries where they were assisted by kings and princes.

Albrecht Dürer (1471–1528)

The greatest German artist of this time was Albrecht Dürer who was born in Nuremberg in 1471. The son of a goldsmith, he became an apprentice in an artist's studio in Nuremberg. In 1494, Dürer travelled to Italy to learn from the works of the great Italian artists like Leonardo and Michelangelo.

Like Leonardo, Dürer was interested in nature and human anatomy. This is clearly seen in his detailed pictures of animals and landscapes. Although Dürer painted many fine pictures, he is best remembered as an *engraver*. He engraved patterns on wood and metal plates with a sharp instrument. These engravings were then covered with ink and printed on paper. Dürer's engravings were used as prints as well as to illustrate books.

Self Portrait *by Albrech Dürer.*

Like other Renaissance people, Dürer was a man of many talents. He was not only an artist and engraver. He also wrote on architecture, engineering and town planning.

The Hare *by Albrecht Dürer. Dürer loved nature and produced life-like and detailed etchings, sketches and paintings of animals and plants.*

Test your knowledge

1 Who was the greatest German artist of the Renaissance?
2 Why did he travel to Italy in 1494?
3 How do Dürer's paintings show his interest in nature?
4 For what kind of work is Dürer best remembered?
5 In what way was Dürer a man of many talents?

Artists of the Northern Renaissance

The Netherlands became one of the greatest centres of art outside Italy during the Renaissance. With many rich trading cities like Antwerp, Rotterdam and Amsterdam, the prosperous merchants lived in fine mansions and were generous patrons of the arts. From 1400 onwards great painters lived in the Netherlands. Their work became famous throughout Europe. This flowering of art and culture on the northwestern edge of Europe became known as *The Northern Renaissance*.

The Arnolfini Wedding Portrait *by Jan van Eyck (1390–1441). Note the scene reflected in the curved mirror at the back of the room. The two figures in the mirror are probably van Eyck himself and a witness to the marriage. The words above the mirror read:* 'Johannes de eyck fuit hic' —'*Jan van Eyck was present*'.

Jan van Eyck (1390–1441) was the first important artist of the Northern Renaissance. Van Eyck was one of the first to use oils in his painting. By using oils instead of egg to mix his paints, he could blend his colours better, work more slowly and achieve an accuracy of detail which astonished people at the time. Van Eyck was especially noted for his portraits. One of the most famous of these is *The Arnolfini Wedding Portrait* (1434).

Pieter Brueghel (1525–69) was another great artist of the Northern Renaissance. Like many northern artists, he visited Italy to study the works of the Italian painters. After his return from Italy he spent the rest of his life working in Antwerp and Brussels. Brueghel is best known for his scenes of peasant life. One of the most famous paintings is that of a country wedding in which Brueghel shows the merry-making of ordinary people.

Peter Paul Rubens (1577–1640) spent some time in Italy studying the works of the Italian artists before returning to Antwerp in 1608. Rubens liked to paint on huge canvases which were used to decorate churches and palaces. He was helped by kings and queens throughout Europe.

A County Wedding *by Pieter Brueghel (1525–69). Pick out three activities shown in this picture.*

Rembrandt van Rijn (1606–69) was the greatest painter of the Netherlands and one of the greatest painters of all time. The son of a wealthy miller in the university town of Leyden, he left home at the age of twenty-five to work as a painter in Amsterdam. He was soon to become a rich and famous portrait painter. In his paintings Rembrandt painted people and scenes as they really were. His most famous paintings are *The Anatomy Lesson* (1632) and *The Night Watch* (1642). Many of his paintings show scenes from the Bible. In order to paint these scenes accurately, Rembrandt lived in the Jewish area of Amsterdam where he studied the dress and way of life of the Jews.

Despite his fame, Rembrandt experienced real financial hardship. When he died in 1669, he left behind only some old clothes and his painting materials.

The Night Watch *by Rembrandt. This picture shows Rembrandt's masterful use of light and shade to highlight his figures.*

Test your knowledge

1 What was the Northern Renaissance?
2 How did oils improve the painting of Jan van Eyck?
3 What was his most famous painting?
4 Where did Pieter Brueghel work for most of his life?
5 What is his most famous painting?
6 Where and when was Rembrandt born?
7 Name his two most famous paintings.
8 Why did he live in the Jewish quarter of Amsterdam?

Chapter 21: Review

• Before the Renaissance most writers used the Latin language. From Renaissance times on, great works were written in the vernacular—the language of the people.

• The Renaissance in England produced one of the most brilliant writers of his time—William Shakespeare (1564–1616). He is famous for his sonnets and for plays like *Hamlet*, *Julius Caesar* and *Macbeth*.

• Albrecht Dürer (1471–1528) was the best German artist of the Renaissance. He is famous for his drawings of animals and landscapes and for his woodcuts which were used to illustrate books.

• Jan van Eyck (1390–1441) was the first great artist of the Northern Renaissance. He was one of the first to use oils in painting. His most famous painting is *The Arnolfini Wedding Portrait* (1434).

• Pieter Brueghel (1525–69), another great painter of the Northern Renaissance, was famous for his realistic paintings showing scenes from peasant life.

• Peter Paul Rubens (1577–1640) was famous for his large-scale portraits of people and his vast paintings of religious scenes for use in churches.

• The most brilliant painter from the Netherlands was Rembrandt (1606–69). He painted people and scenes as they really were. His most famous works are *The Anatomy Lesson* (1632) and *The Night Watch* (1642).

Chapter 22 Science and Inventions during the Renaissance

New discoveries

During the Renaissance educated people in Europe began to question and doubt many beliefs which had been accepted during the Middle Ages. This questioning spirit brought about exciting new discoveries and inventions in areas such as printing, astronomy and medicine. Because of these improvements people came to know more about themselves and the world around them.

The invention of printing

Before the Renaissance all books had to be written by hand. These manuscripts took a long time to produce and so they were very scarce. When Cosimo de Medici opened his library in Florence, he employed forty-five scribes to copy 200 books. It took them two years to complete their task. Rich men often left valuable manuscripts in their wills along with other property. Because manuscripts were rare and expensive, knowledge and new ideas spread slowly before the Renaissance.

The earliest form of printing is *block printing*. This involved carving letters on a wooden block to produce a single page. It took many hours to make a block, and then it could only be used for the one page for which it was carved. Before books could be printed in large quantities one vital invention was needed: moveable letters which could be quickly switched around to form different words. The man who made this tremendous breakthrough was a German named Johann Gutenberg (1398–1468).

Gutenberg and the first printing press

An early printing press in action. Can you list at least two different activities taking place?

Gutenberg worked as a goldsmith in the city of Mainz. He and his family were experts in cutting metals. The exact date of the invention of the *moveable metal type printing press* is uncertain, but in 1450 the new style of printing was widely known. The first great book printed by Gutenberg was the *Forty-Two-Line Bible*, so called from the number of lines on each page.

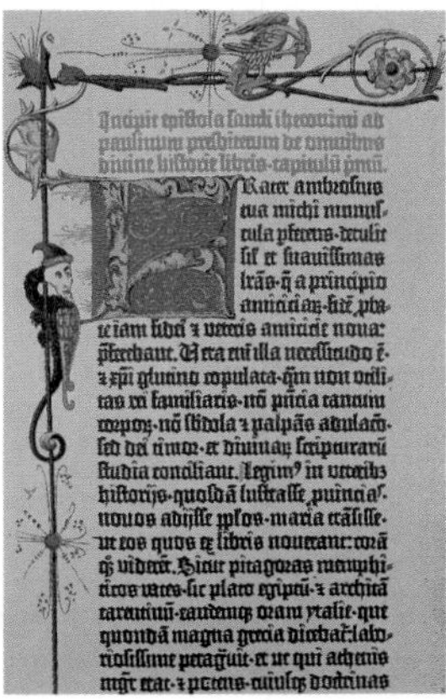

A page from Gutenberg's first printed edition of the Bible.

The invention of the new printing press encouraged the development of cheaper paper. Before the Renaissance manuscripts had been written on *parchment* or *vellum*. These writing materials were very expensive and it was common to scrape a manuscript clean and use it again for another work. Once cheaper methods of papermaking had been developed, this new material could be used in Gutenberg's printing press.

The paper was made from linen rags which were boiled into a pulp. A square wooden sieve was then dipped into the mixture. When this was lifted, the excess water was drained, leaving a thick white coating on the tray. This was then allowed to dry to make paper. The linen-based paper was of such good quality that books made from it 500 years ago still exist today.

The spread of printing

The skill of printing soon spread from Germany and within a short time, presses had been set up in Italy, France, the Netherlands and England. In the city of Bruges in the Netherlands, an Englishman named William Caxton learned these new methods of printing. When he returned to England, he set up a printing press near Westminster Abbey in London. During his career as a printer, Caxton published nearly a hundred books.

William Caxton reading the first page produced on his printing press near Westminster Abbey, London, in 1474.

The Italian city of Venice became the great printing centre of Europe during the Renaissance. The most famous Italian printer was Aldus Manutius (1450–1515). On his printing press he published editions of Greek and Latin works which became known as *The Aldine Classics*.

The invention of the moveable type printing press was one of the great breakthroughs of Renaissance times.

- It made large numbers of inexpensive books available throughout Europe.

- While many copies of the Bible and the ancient classics were printed, books also helped the spread of new ideas. This resulted in the rapid spread of learning.

- Without the invention of printing, the works of great Renaissance writers like Erasmus, Cervantes and Shakespeare would not have been as widely known.

- Martin Luther and others used the printing press to spread new ideas on religion (the Reformation).

Test your knowledge

1 How were books produced before the invention of printing?
2 What was the earliest form of printing called?
3 Who invented the first moveable type printing press?
4 What was the first book printed by Gutenberg?
5 What changes came about in papermaking during the Renaissance?
6 Who set up the first printing press in England?
7 Who was the most famous Italian printer during the Renaissance?
8 Why was the invention of the printing press such a great breakthrough?

The beginning of modern science

Printing was not the only great technical advance which was made during the Renaissance. This invention was widely known and appreciated because thousands of people bought books printed on the newly invented printing presses. Meanwhile, behind the scenes, learned people were experimenting in science and mathematics. Because of their work, the way in which people saw the world around them changed completely.

Two particular areas of science showed great developments during the Renaissance. These were *astronomy* (the study of the stars) and the age-old study of *medicine*.

The new science of astronomy

Before the Renaissance it was generally believed that the world was flat and motionless and that the sun and the planets moved around the earth. This belief was held by ancient scholars like the Greek, Aristotle, and the Egyptian, Ptolemy. Throughout the Middle Ages no one doubted this view of the universe. Around 1500 a Polish scholar named Nicholas Copernicus began to question the teaching of these ancient writers.

Nicholas Copernicus (1473–1543)

Nicholas Copernicus (1473–1543).

Copernicus was born in Poland in 1473, the son of a merchant. He was ordained a priest but combined his interest in astronomy with his duties in the church. Although he studied the sky from an observatory, Copernicus mostly used mathematics to develop his exciting new theories about the universe. He believed that the earth turned on its own axis and moved around the sun. He kept his ideas a secret for years in case people would think that he was mad. The book containing his stunning ideas—*On the Revolution of the Celestial Orbs*—was finally published in 1543, the year of his death. It was said that the first copy of this book was handed to Copernicus on his deathbed. It was now up to other scientists to carry on the revolutionary work begun by Copernicus.

Galileo Galilei (1564–1642)

Galileo was born in the Italian town of Pisa in 1564. He studied mathematics and medicine and at the early age of twenty-five became professor of mathematics at the University of Pisa. Galileo shocked many other scholars by the delight with which he disproved the ancient beliefs of Aristotle and other writers. His first great victory concerned the speed of falling objects.

One day while praying in Pisa Cathedral, Galileo noticed that the sanctuary lamp had just been filled and was swinging back and forth before coming to rest. It appeared that the swings, whether long or short, took the same time. This convinced Galileo that objects fell at the same speed, no matter what they weighed. To prove this, he climbed to the top of the Leaning Tower of Pisa and dropped a large, heavy cannon ball and a small bullet. To his delight, both reached the ground at almost the same time.

Galileo explaining his discoveries to an eager listener.

In 1609, Galileo heard of the invention of the telescope in Holland. Before waiting for the information to reach Italy he figured out how it was made. This new invention magnified objects nearly a thousand times. He started making telescopes for sale. He called his own telescope 'Old Discoverer' and with it he discovered the four moons of the planet Jupiter. This provided Galileo with the proof that Copernicus was right about the earth and other planets travelling around the sun.

Galileo designed telescopes like this one for observing the planets.

As a result of this work, Galileo became famous as Europe's greatest astronomer. However, in 1633, he suffered the worst defeat of his career when his work was condemned by the Catholic Church.

The Church disliked the new ideas in astronomy because they seemed to contradict the Bible. Galileo's friends warned him to stick to science and not to discuss the Bible. But he insisted that there was nothing in the Bible against his view that the earth moved around the sun. Galileo annoyed the Church further by writing in Italian. Books in Italian could reach more people than those written in Latin, the language used by scholars.

Galileo before the Inquisition in Rome.

In June 1633 Galileo was condemned by Pope Urban VIII (1622–44) and the Court of the Holy Office (the *Inquisition*). Galileo was now nearly seventy years old. He was threatened with torture unless he withdrew his views on the movement of the earth around the sun. After four months in prison, Galileo agreed to do this. He was forced to go down on his knees and state that Copernicus had been wrong. He was allowed to return to Florence where he remained a prisoner in his own home.

In his last years, Galileo turned to the study of physics in which he produced brilliant new work. He died in 1642, the year in which another great scientist, Isaac Newton, was born. Because of his great contribution to the development of astronomy and physics, Galileo has been called the *Father of Modern Science*.

Test your knowledge

1 What exciting new theories did Copernicus develop about the universe?

2 Where and when was Galileo born?

3 What experiment did Galileo carry out on the speed of falling objects?

4 Why did he shock many other scholars?

5 What new invention did Galileo use? What did he discover?

6 Why do you think Galileo has been called the Father of Modern Science?

Improvements in medicine

Medicine was another area of science which changed greatly during the Renaissance when the views of the ancient medical writers were challenged.

Renaissance doctors relied on experimentation to discover the truth about the workings of the human body. Accurate drawings were important to their understanding. Only then could they hope to treat illness properly. We have seen how artists like Leonardo and Michelangelo dissected bodies to understand how they worked.

The work of Vesalius

One of the most famous Renaissance doctors was Andreas Vesalius (1514– 64). He was born in Brussels and studied at the University of Paris. He later taught medicine at the University of Padua in Italy, one of Europe's greatest medical centres, and became private physician to the King of Spain.

Vesalius's great work, *On the Fabric of the Human Body*, was published in 1543. It contained many drawings of the human body based on dissection which he carried out himself. From then on, the study of anatomy was based on dissection alone, and not on the work of ancient writers like Galen. For his outstanding work, Vesalius became known as the *Father of Modern Anatomy*.

An operation carried out at the time of Vesalius.

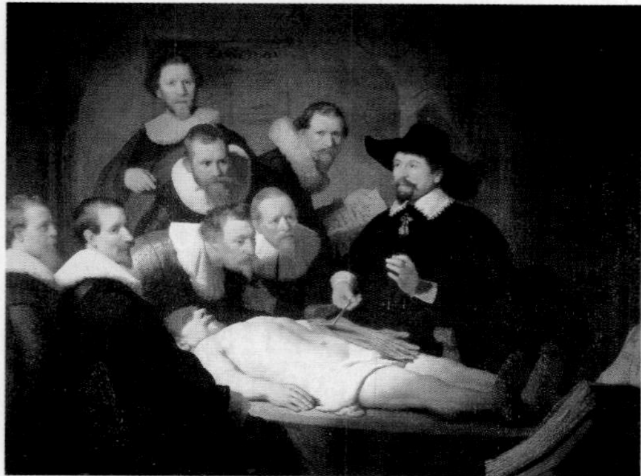

The science of anatomy is shown here in Rembrandt's famous painting, The Anatomy Lesson.

William Harvey—A great medical breakthrough

Another brilliant medical discovery made during the Renaissance concerned the circulation of the blood. In 1628, an English doctor named William Harvey (1578–1657) published a book called *On the Motion of the Heart and Blood.* In this work he proved that the heart was a type of pump which sent blood around the body. Harvey had been slow to publish his ideas because he thought people would mock him. In fact, the book harmed his career at first as many patients refused to be treated by him. It was many years before people recognised Harvey's discovery as a great breakthrough in medical knowledge.

Robert Boyle (1627–91), the Irish scientist who discovered the famous law about gases which became known as Boyle's Law.

A new age of science

Great changes in printing, astronomy and medicine took place during the Renaissance. These changes were so important and far-reaching that they became known as the *Scientific Revolution*. Renaissance scientists laid the foundation of even greater advances in the years ahead when scientists like Isaac Newton (1642–1727) finally brought science into the modern age.

Test your knowledge

1. Who was Vesalius and what was his great work?
2. Why do you think Vesalius became known as the Father of Modern Anatomy?
3. What great discovery was made by William Harvey?
4. What name has been given to the changes in science which took place during the Renaissance?

Scientific and medical advances during the Renaissance

Printing

GUTENBERG (1394–1468)
Inventor of the first moveable metal type printing press.

CAXTON (1422–91)
Set up the first printing press in England.

Astronomy

COPERNICUS (1473–1543)
Proved that the earth turned on its own axis and moved around the sun.

GALILEO (1564–1642)
Proved Copernicus to be right. Invented his own telescope. Proved that objects of different weight fall at the same speed.

Medicine

VESALIUS (1514–64)
Made detailed drawings of the human body. Founder of the science of anatomy.

HARVEY (1578–1657)
Discovered circulation of the blood.

Chapter 22: Review

• During the Renaissance educated people throughout Europe began to question old beliefs. This search for new ideas and ways of doing things led to exciting new developments in printing, astronomy and medicine.

• Around 1450, a goldsmith in the German town of Mainz, named Johann Gutenberg, is credited with the invention of printing by means of a moveable metal type press.

• The first book printed by Gutenberg was the *Forty-Two-Line Bible*, so called from the number of lines on each page.

• An Englishman, named William Caxton, went to the Netherlands to learn the craft of printing and returned home to set up a printing press in London.

• The city of Venice became a great centre of printing during the Renaissance. Its most famous printer was named Aldus Manutius (1450–1515) whose press produced *The Aldine Classics*.

• Nicholas Copernicus (1473–1543) was a Polish priest who developed the theory that the earth travelled around the sun in his book *On the Revolution of the Celestial Orbs* (1543).

• Galileo Galilei (1564–1642) proved that objects fall to the ground at the same speed, whatever their weight. He developed a telescope and used it to prove that the earth travels around the sun.

• In 1633, Galileo was condemned by the Court of the Inquisition of the Catholic Church for teaching beliefs that appeared to contradict the Bible. He was allowed to return to Florence where he died in 1642. Because of his great discoveries Galileo has been called the Father of Modern Science.

• During the Renaissance great advances were also made in medicine. Vesalius (1514–64), the Father of Modern Anatomy, published his brilliant work *On the Fabric of the Human Body* in 1543.

• In 1628, an English doctor, William Harvey (1578–1657), proved the circulation of the blood in his work, *On the Motion of the Heart and Blood.*

• The changes in science, astronomy and medicine during the Renaissance were so important and far-reaching that they have become known as the Scientific Revolution.

Exploration and Discovery

The Age of Discovery Begins

The world in 1450

Here is a modern map of the world showing the main continents and the oceans.

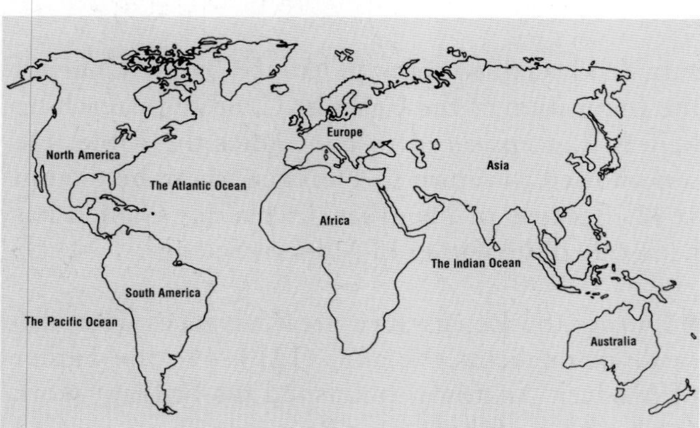

A map of the world known to Europeans in 1450.

In 1450, people's view of the shape and size of the world was very different from ours today. A map of the known world at that time showed the Mediterranean Sea at the centre, surrounded by Europe, North Africa and Asia. Ireland and Britain lay at the extreme west of the known world. Beyond this was a vast and terrifying ocean where sailors would not venture for fear of meeting sea monsters or falling off the edge of the earth.

Over the next 200 years, men set out on daring voyages of exploration and discovery which drastically changed people's knowledge of the world around them.

Three advances made possible this new age of discovery—more reliable maps, new navigational instruments and better ships.

New maps

About 1450, the work of an ancient Greek geographer named Ptolemy was rediscovered in Europe. In one of his books called *The New Geography*, Ptolemy had given a fairly accurate map of Europe and North Africa. Look closely at this map. Compare it with a modern map and state which parts are mainly correct and which are not.

Using Ptolemy's work as a guide, map-makers were now able to construct a more accurate map of the world. By this time, many educated people believed that the world was round, not flat. But they still underestimated the size of the world and did not yet realise that the vast continents of the Americas existed. Areas such as these would only be mapped when explorers returned from successful voyages of discovery.

Ptolemy's map of the world.

New instruments of navigation

Before 1450, most ships travelled along the coasts and rarely went out of sight of land. Seamen plotted these coastal areas on maps known as *portolan charts*. Ship's captains had few navigational instruments. They relied almost totally on their own traditional knowledge of the seas and the winds.

From around the thirteenth century, the *compass* was used to tell the direction in which a ship was travelling. A piece of magnetic iron called a *lodestone* was used to restore magnetism to the soft iron compass needle.

A sailor swinging the lead to measure the depth of the sea.

The depth of the water could be told by a method known as '*swinging the lead*'. A piece of lead was attached to a great coil of line which had a series of knots along it. A sailor would stand on the bow and cast the lead ahead of the ship. By the time the ship had caught up with the lead, the line was perpendicular. The sailor could then calculate the depth of the water which was indicated by the last knot above the water's surface.

A method of calculating a ship's speed was also developed around that time. This was known as the *log*. It involved throwing a piece of wood into the sea and timing it as it passed the known length of the ship. Later, a knotted rope was attached to the log and the knots were counted as they ran out. This gave rise to the method of measuring a ship's speed in *knots* or nautical miles which is still used today.

A knowledge of a ship's direction and speed was not enough, however. A captain also needed to know his ship's exact position or *latitude*. An instrument called the *astrolabe* helped sailors to calculate a ship's position by measuring the height of the noon sun or the pole star. They then checked tables listing known heights to find out the correct latitude for a particular date.

These great improvements in navigational instruments provided sailors with the tools they needed to discover and explore new lands.

Can you identify the various instruments and activities on board this ship?

Test your knowledge

1 What view did people have of the world around 1450?
2 Who was Ptolemy?
3 What were portolan charts?
4 What was meant by 'swinging the lead'?
5 What new method of calculating a ship's speed was developed at this time?
6 Name the instrument used to calculate a ship's exact position.

New and better ships

The new navigational instruments would have been of little use without improvements in ships themselves. Before 1400, there were two main types of ship in Europe. Countries on the Atlantic coast used *clinker-built ships.* Their sturdy hulls were built from overlapping timber planks and they used a single square sail. While these were strong vessels, they were very hard to steer in the wind.

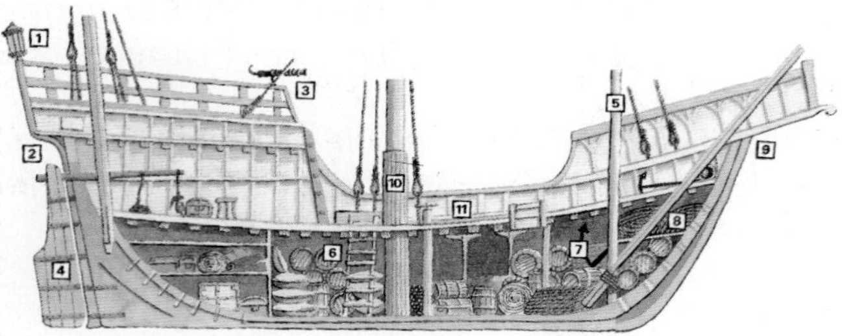

1 Stern Lantern 2 Stern 3 Swivel Gun 4 Rudder 5 Foremast 6 Storage for food and ammunition 7 Hold 8 Anchor cable 9 Bow 10 Main mast 11 Main deck

Mediterranean sailors used lighter ships with triangular sails known as *lateens.* Although these were weaker than the Atlantic-built ships, their lateen sails enabled them to sail more effectively against the wind.

Around 1400, a great advance was made when a ship known as the *caravel* was developed. This used a clinker-built hull with both square and lateen sails. From then on, ships became stronger, faster and safer.

In this picture of a Portuguese caravel, both square and lateen sails can be clearly seen.

Life on board ship

Each member of the crew had his own special task to do. The captain usually navigated the ship. The master was responsible for the safe handling of the ship, while the bosun was in charge of the crew. There were also many craftsmen aboard such as carpenters and coopers. The ship's boy did various jobs, including singing prayers at sunrise and sunset.

Cooking and eating on deck.

Sleeping conditions were cramped and overcrowded on board ship.

Cooking was always done on deck. Food was stored in wooden barrels which were often inspected by the cooper. During long-distance voyages, it was extremely hard to keep food and water fresh. Biscuits often became infested with worms which had to be tapped out before the food could be eaten.

Despite the great advances made in ship design around 1450, life on board remained difficult and dangerous. Death from disease was an ever-present threat. The most common disease was *scurvy*, caused by a lack of fresh vegetables and fruit, and *typhoid*, caught from foul drinking water. Rats, hunting desperately for food in the filthy holds, were also carriers of disease.

The men who ventured out on these long voyages of discovery did not just face death from disease. They were sailing into unknown waters where storms and shipwreck were constant threats. Unlike today, a ship in difficulty in the fifteenth century could not radio for help or hope that a friendly ship in the area might come to the rescue.

The men who sailed on these ocean-going ships

had to face great dangers and hardships which are unknown to modern travellers. Why, then, did they take such risks and set out on these long voyages of exploration and discovery?

The reasons why

The great improvements in maps, navigational instruments and ships took place at a time when many people were eager to explore new routes. Explorers set out on voyages of discovery for a variety of reasons.

- Merchants wanted to find new routes to the East where valuable spices were to be found. For hundreds of years traders had travelled over land to India and China. However, from around 1400 onwards the Turks captured land along this route and charged high taxes to merchants passing through. It became even harder for European traders after the Turks captured the city of Constantinople in 1453.
- European rulers hoped to build up powerful overseas empires. Many of them were prepared to sponsor voyages of exploration.
- Some explorers set out on their journeys to prove that the world was round. Others were driven by greed and the promise of riches.
- Rulers and explorers saw the chance of converting native peoples to Christianity.

Test your knowledge

1 How did the ships of the Atlantic differ from those of the Mediterranean?
2 What new type of ship was developed around 1400? How did it combine the best of the Atlantic and Mediterranean styles?
3 What role was played by the bosun on board ship?
4 Why do you think craftsmen travelled on the ship?
5 Name two dangers which constantly faced the crews.
6 Do you think the sailors needed to be tough? Why?
7 Why did merchants want to find new trade routes to the East?
8 Explain why some European rulers sponsored voyages of exploration.
9 Name the two countries that pioneered the great age of exploration and discovery.

Chapter 23: Review

- In 1450, many people still believed that the earth was flat. They thought that the world consisted of the Mediterranean Sea at the centre, surrounded by Europe, North Africa and Asia.

- Europeans knew more about the East because of the strong trading links which had long existed between East and West.

- Around 1450, new maps of the world were drawn. They were based on the work of an ancient Greek geographer named Ptolemy.

- New instruments of navigation were developed around this time. The compass told the ship's direction. The log measured its speed. The astrolabe was used to tell the ship's position.

- Improvements in ship design also took place. A new ship called the caravel was invented. It combined the clinker-built hull of the Atlantic ships with the triangular lateen sails of the Mediterranean ones. From then on, ships became faster, stronger and safer.

- Sailors of the time were at risk from disease and death because of the lack of fresh food and the filthy conditions in which they worked.

- After the invention of new navigational instruments and the development of better ships, merchants began to look for new trading routes.

- Some explorers were attracted by stories of great wealth, and European missionaries wished to convert the native people.

Explorers from Portugal

In this chapter we will look at some of the daring and adventurous men who led the way in the great voyages of discovery. The earliest explorers came from Portugal. These men sailed down the coast of Africa and eventually discovered a new sea route to Asia. The first great Portuguese explorer was *Prince Henry the Navigator*.

Prince Henry the Navigator (1394–1460)

Prince Henry the Navigator planning voyages from his castle near Cape St Vincent in Portugal.

Prince Henry was the son of the king of Portugal. When he was twenty-one years of age, he was made governor of Ceuta, a stronghold in North Africa which the Portuguese had captured from the Moors in 1415.

While in North Africa, Prince Henry heard stories of the great wealth in gold, ivory and slaves to be found along the west coast of Africa. He also heard of a legendary Christian king named Prester John who was supposed to live in East Africa. Prince Henry hoped that Prester John would help him defeat the Muslims and convert Africa to Christianity.

Prince Henry had a great interest in ships and navigation. In 1419, he set up home in an old fort on the rocky shores of Sagres Bay at the southern tip of Portugal. There he gathered together a group of sea captains, map-makers, mathematicians and ship-builders.

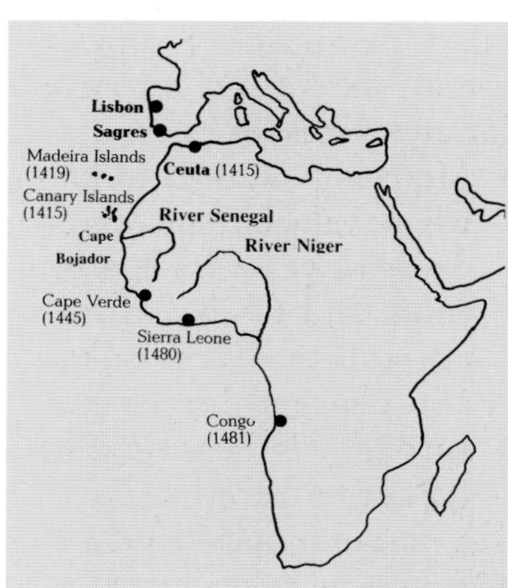

Portuguese exploration of the coast of Africa.

Under Prince Henry's direction, a constant stream of caravels set out from Sagres to explore the west coast of Africa. His ships visited the Canaries, Madeira and the Azores. Up to that time, no ship had gone beyond Cape Bojador, a long reef which was situated over 1,500 kilometres from Sagres. When sailors first saw the water swirling around the cape, they were sure that the sea was boiling and insisted that the captain return at once to Portugal. In 1434, Henry sent the same captain with a different crew back to Cape Bojador. This time they succeeded in sailing around the reef.

Although the tip of Africa had not been reached by the time of Prince Henry's death in 1460, his influence inspired Portuguese sailors to continue the search.

Diaz rounds the tip of Africa

In 1487, a Portuguese explorer named Bartholomew Diaz (1450-1500) became the first man to reach the southern tip of Africa and enter the Indian Ocean.

As a sign of thanksgiving to God, Diaz placed a huge cross on the headland. Because of the rough and stormy seas which he experienced Diaz named the tip of Africa the Cape of Storms. When King John II of Portugal heard this, he renamed it the Cape of Good Hope in the belief that Portugal would soon discover a new route to the East. The king's hopes were realised ten years later by another Portuguese explorer—Vasco da Gama.

The ships of Bartholomew Diaz on their voyage around the Cape of Good Hope in 1487.

Test your knowledge

1 Who was Prince Henry the Navigator?
2 What position did Henry hold when he was twenty-one years of age?
3 What stories did Henry hear when he was in North Africa?
4 Who was Prester John?
5 Who was the first Portuguese sailor to reach the southern tip of Africa?
6 What name did the king of Portugal give to the southern tip of Africa? Why?

Vasco da Gama

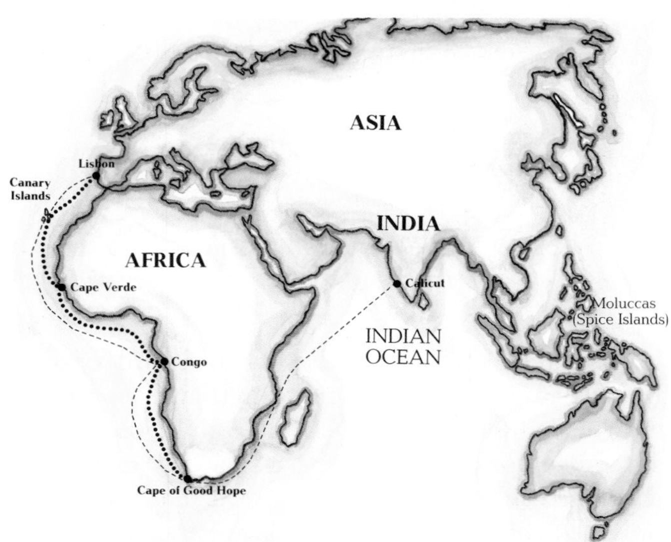

A new trade route to the East — the voyages of Diaz and da Gama.

On 8 July 1497, Vasco da Gama (1469-1524) set sail from Lisbon with three ships—*San Gabriel*, *San Raphael* and *Berrio*. After three unsuccessful attempts the expedition finally rounded the Cape of Good Hope in November. On Christmas morning, da Gama named the land they were passing Natal, in honour of the birth of Christ. An Arab pilot agreed to guide them up the east coast of Africa and across the Indian Ocean.

On 20 May 1498, history was made when the three ships landed at Calicut in southern Asia. The Portuguese had become the first to discover a new route to the East. Calicut was a great trading city. Da Gama filled his ships with jewels and spices and set sail for home.

Vasco da Gama arrives in Calicut.

Da Gama's journey proved to be a long and difficult one. Many of his men died along the way from scurvy—of the 148 men who had set out, only fifty-five returned. Although the cost was high, da Gama had shown Europeans that they could reach India by sea.

Portugal's achievement

The discoveries of Prince Henry, Diaz and Vasco da Gama made Portugal the world's leading country in exploration and discovery. During the fifteenth and sixteenth centuries, Portugal built up a huge trading empire, especially in Asia.

Portugal was soon to be challenged, however, by its powerful neighbour, Spain. Under the influence of Spanish rulers, expeditions set off from Spain which discovered new lands and gained massive wealth. In the next chapter we will look at the most famous of these expeditions led by a man called Christopher Columbus.

Test your knowledge

1 What Portuguese explorer was the first to round the Cape of Good Hope and reach Asia?
2 Where did the expedition land on 20 May 1498?
3 What mishaps did da Gama experience during the voyage?
4 Why do you think da Gama's achievement was so important?
5 What country soon challenged Portugal as the world's leader in exploration and discovery?

Chapter 24: Review

- Prince Henry the Navigator, the son of the king of Portugal, had a great interest in exploration and discovery.

- When he was governor of Ceuta in North Africa, Prince Henry heard stories of the great wealth to be found along the west coast of Africa and of the legendary king named Prester John who would help him fight the Muslims.

- Henry set up a navigational school at Sagres. Under his influence, Portuguese sailors discovered the Canary Islands, Madeira and the Azores.

- In 1487, Bartholomew Diaz became the first Portuguese sailor to reach the southern tip of Africa which he named the Cape of Storms. The king renamed it the Cape of Good Hope.

- In 1497, Vasco da Gama, another Portuguese sailor, was the first to round the Cape of Good Hope and sail on to land at Calicut in Asia in May 1498.

CHAPTER 25 Christopher Columbus

A man with a dream

Christopher Columbus was born in the Italian town of Genoa in 1451. He was the eldest son of a weaver and a tavern-keeper.

During Columbus' youth Genoa was an exciting seafaring town, and it was there that he got his first taste of travel and adventure. As a young man, Columbus travelled a great deal and became interested in exploration. Like many other explorers, he believed that the world was round. He was convinced that by sailing westwards from Europe he could reach Asia.

Christopher Columbus (1451–1506).

Columbus went to Portugal in search of a sponsor, but failed to persuade King John II to finance his western voyage.

Columbus explains his plans for a westward voyage to Queen Isabella of Spain.

He then went to King Ferdinand and Queen Isabella of Spain. For a long time they, too, refused to provide him with ships. In the end, however, they agreed to sponsor a western voyage of discovery. The Spanish king and queen hoped that this might provide Spain with great riches, land and converts to Christianity. For Columbus it was a dream come true.

The voyage westward

On 3 August 1492, Columbus and his sailors left Spain in three ships—the *Niña*, the *Pinta* and the *Santa Maria*. The three ships carried about ninety men altogether, including three doctors, an interpreter, and a man sent by Queen Isabella to keep track of gold and precious stones.

A model of Columbus' own ship, the Santa Maria. *Point out the lateen sails on this ship.*

Each ship contained a cabin for the master, while the crew slept on deck. Once a day, a fire was lit in an open box and a hot meal was cooked. Time was kept with sand-glasses which were turned every half hour by deck boys. At night the crew of each ship gathered to sing hymns.

Life was far from happy on board Columbus' three ships. Many of the sailors believed that the earth was flat and they feared that they would sail over its edge. The men soon began speaking of mutiny, and Columbus had to use all his powers of leadership to keep them from forcing him to turn back. One day, for example, the crew became very frightened when the wind died down and the ships entered a stretch of water which was almost solid with seaweed. They named the area *Sargasso*, which means 'sea plants'. Today, this stretch of water is still known as the Sargasso Sea.

Working with evidence

Columbus recorded the main events of the voyage every day. His logbook is the best primary source we have of the expedition. Look carefully at the information recorded in the following extracts from Columbus' own logbook.

- Sunday 9 September: Columbus sailed fifteen leagues [about 100 kilometres] that day, but decided to say it was less so that the crews would not take fright or lose courage if the voyage seemed too long. In the night, the ships travelled nearly 200 kilometres at 15 km an hour. The sailors steered badly, falling off to west by north, and even to west-north-west. The admiral rebuked them several times for this.
- Tuesday 25 September: Martin Alonso Pinzon, captain of the *Pinta*, shouted to the admiral that he had sighted land. The whole crew of the *Niña* climbed the mast and rigging, and agreed that it was land.
- Wednesday 26 September: Columbus followed a westward course until midday. They then discovered that what they thought was land was not land at all but cloud.
- Thursday 11 October: The ships sailed west-south-west. They saw reeds and seabirds called petrels. The men of the *Pinta* picked up a small stick, apparently shaped with an iron tool. At such signs, all breathed again and rejoiced. The *Pinta*, sailing ahead of the admiral, now sighted land and gave the signals which the admiral had commanded. The first man to sight land was a sailor called Rodrigo, who afterwards claimed the reward Columbus had promised.

1. Why did Columbus not tell his crew the correct distance travelled each day?
2. Write down one difficulty experienced by Columbus on his voyage.
3. What signs of land did the crew of the *Pinta* discover on 11 October?
4. Using the above source as a guide, state the kind of leader you think Columbus was.

Land is sighted

As Columbus himself wrote in his logbook, land was sighted on 11 October 1492, over two months after leaving Spain. Columbus landed on an island which he named San Salvador which means Holy Saviour. (Today, this place is known as Watling Island.) He claimed the land for Spain, and in thanksgiving to God for a successful voyage, he planted a cross in the ground.

Great excitement among Columbus' crew at the first glimpse of land.

Columbus approaching the island of San Salvador.

Columbus was convinced that he had reached the islands off Asia. However, he had totally miscalculated the distance involved and had in fact travelled less than halfway to Asia. Columbus had actually landed on one of the islands off the coast of a new, unknown continent which later became known as America.

Columbus is met by the native 'Indians'. Why is the cross being planted in the soil?

Columbus was well received by the native people whom he called Indians, since he believed he had reached India. Their gold necklaces convinced him that great riches were there for the taking. He spent two months exploring the area and discovered more islands, including Haiti and Cuba. But nowhere did Columbus find the great treasures of gold and spices which he had hoped to discover.

Working with evidence

Columbus' logbook gives us the following description of the native people.

> 'The men wore very few clothes. The women were the same, although we saw only one. All the people I saw were under thirty years of age. They were well built, with handsome bodies and very good faces. Their hair goes back to their eyebrows, except for a crop at the back which they never cut. They do not have weapons or know anything about them. When I showed them a sword, they got hold of it by the blade and cut themselves because they did not know what it was. They should be good servants because they soon repeated everything we said to them. I think it will be easy to turn them into Christians because they do not have any religion.'

1. Describe the appearance of the natives.
2. Do you think they were peaceful or warlike people? Why?
3. Why did Columbus think they would make good servants?
4. Apart from wealth, can you tell from this passage what other motive Columbus had in making his voyage of discovery?

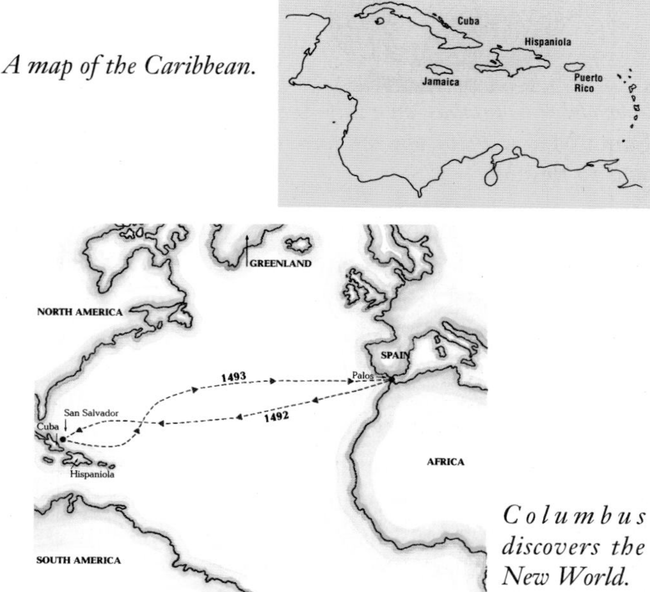

A map of the Caribbean.

Columbus discovers the New World.

Columbus returns to Spain

When the *Santa Maria* ran aground, Columbus returned home to Spain with his two other ships. Although he only brought with him six Indians, a parrot, some fish and a small amount of gold, he was given a hero's welcome. Everyone believed that he had found the islands in the East.

Columbus returns in triumph to the court of Ferdinand and Isabella.

Ferdinand and Isabella were so pleased that they financed another expedition westwards in 1493. This time, Columbus was given three galleons and four-

Columbus returns home in chains after being accused of cruelty to the natives.

teen smaller ships. During this and later voyages, he discovered Trinidad, Jamaica, Guadaloupe and the mouth of the Orinoco River in South America. However, he never reached Asia.

As a reward for his services, Ferdinand and Isabella made Columbus governor-general of the lands which he had discovered. However, his later years were full of disappointment. He was accused of treating the natives with great cruelty and was removed from his post as governor by the queen. Christopher Columbus died in 1506, convinced that his life as an explorer had been a failure.

The influence of Columbus

While Columbus had not reached Asia, he had stumbled on a whole new continent—America. He had been the first to sail westwards in the hope of reaching the East. While he failed to do so, he encouraged other explorers to take up the challenge. Columbus had discovered the 'New World' and will always be remembered as one of the greatest explorers of all time.

Test your knowledge

1 What did Columbus hope to achieve by sailing westwards?
2 Who sponsored Columbus' voyage?
3 When did Columbus set sail? What were the names of his three ships?
4 On what island did Columbus land on 11 October 1492? Where did he believe he was?
5 What kind of reception did Columbus get when he returned to Spain?
6 Why did he eventually return to Spain in disgrace?
7 What great influence did Columbus have on later explorers?

Christopher Columbus

- Born in Genoa, Italy in 1451.
- Interested in ships and travel from an early age.
- Convinced that he could reach Asia by sailing westward.
- Given money and ships for a voyage of discovery by Ferdinand and Isabella of Spain.
- On 3 August 1492, Columbus and his crew set sail from Spain in three ships—the *Niña*, the *Pinta* and the *Santa Maria.*
- Over two months after leaving Spain, land was sighted. Although Columbus thought he had reached Asia, he had in fact landed on an island off the coast of a continent unknown to Europeans—America.

- Columbus was given a hero's welcome when he returned to Spain. He later set out on other voyages of discovery, but never reached Asia.
- While governor-general of the new lands he had discovered, Columbus was accused of treating the natives cruelly. He was brought back to Spain in chains and died a disappointed man in 1506.

Chapter 25: Review

• Christopher Columbus was born in the Italian town of Genoa in 1451. As a boy, he got his first taste of travel and adventure in this seafaring town.

• Convinced that he could reach the East by sailing westwards, Columbus first went to Portugal in search of a sponsor. He was unsuccessful there, but eventually persuaded King Ferdinand and Queen Isabella of Spain to sponsor a voyage of discovery.

• On 3 August 1492, Columbus set sail with three ships—the *Niña*, the *Pinta* and the *Santa Maria*. After many weeks at sea, the sailors became uneasy as they feared that they might fall off the edge of the world.

• Land was finally sighted on 11 October 1492. Columbus and his crew landed on an island which they named San Salvador (Watling Island today).

• Although Columbus believed that he had reached the islands off Asia, he had in fact landed off the coast of a vast unknown continent which was later called America.

• Columbus returned to Spain to a hero's welcome. He was given a much larger expedition and made governor-general of the lands he had discovered.

• After further discoveries, Columbus was eventually removed from his post as governor-general after he was accused of cruelty to the natives. He returned to Spain in disgrace where he died in 1506, a disappointed and bitter man.

• Although Columbus never reached Asia, his discovery was a great one. He turned the eyes of later explorers westwards and paved the way for future voyages of exploration and discovery.

The Voyage of Ferdinand Magellan

Magellan sets sail

Ferdinand Magellan (1480–1521).

Ferdinand Magellan was the son of a Portuguese nobleman. As a young man, he travelled on many expeditions to Asia and the coast of Africa. By the time he set out on the greatest voyage of his life, he was already a skilled and experienced explorer and navigator.

As we learned in Chapter 24, the Portuguese were the first to find a new route to Asia. However, the Spanish were determined to find another westerly route to the Moluccas, the rich spice islands off the coast of Asia.

The Victorio, *one of Magellan's ships.*

In 1518, King Charles I of Spain gave Ferdinand Magellan the job of leading a Spanish expedition to the East. His task was to reach the Moluccas and return to Spain with cargoes of rich spices. Magellan was given five old and rickety ships—the *Trinidad* (his flagship), *San Antonio*, *Concepcion*, *Victorio* and *Santiago*. When the repairs were finally completed after about eighteen months, the fleet set sail from Seville on 20 September 1519, carrying around 270 men.

South America

Magellan believed that he could reach the East by sailing around the coast of South America. The voyage on which he was about to embark would be long, difficult and dangerous. As the fleet made its way down the coast of South America, Magellan explored many inlets and came across some unfriendly natives, including cannibals.

During the winter months, the fleet anchored at Port St Julian. It had already been six months since they had left Spain, and the officers especially were becoming restless. At midnight on Easter Day 1520, the Spanish captains rose in mutiny against their Portuguese commander. Magellan, acting with determination and ruthlessness, hanged one of the captains and abandoned another on the shore. However, his difficulties were far from over. He sent one of his ships, the *Santiago*, southwards to explore further along the coast. On 22 May 1520, the *Santiago* was wrecked about 100 kilometres from Port St Julian. Most of the survivors struggled back to the port after an exhausting overland march. On 18 October 1520, the expedition left the port and continued their southward journey.

Test your knowledge

1 Where were the Moluccas?

2 Who was king of Spain in 1518?

3 What was the aim of Magellan's expedition?

4 What was the name of Magellan's flagship?

5 State two difficulties experienced by Magellan and his crew.

Rounding the Straits

In the autumn of 1520, Magellan's fleet, now consisting of only three ships, faced the worst weather conditions they were ever to experience. As they rounded the tip of South America, through a passage which later became known as the Straits of Magellan, they met with dangerous currents and freezing gales which howled through the gaps in the mountains. One of the ships, the *San Antonio*, deserted and headed back to Spain with most of the supplies. It took the remaining two ships over a month to pass through the straits. When the ships eventually rounded the tip, they found themselves in a calm, still sea which they named the Pacific, meaning peaceful.

The fleet of Ferdinand Magellan rounding the tip of South America.

Problems in the Pacific

The Pacific Ocean soon presented problems of its own. Magellan and his men sailed in this ocean for four months. The crews were ravaged by starvation, thirst and scurvy. One of the survivors has given us the following description of these terrible conditions:

'We were three months and twenty days without getting any kind of fresh food. We ate biscuit which was no longer biscuit, but a powder of biscuit swarming with worms, for they had eaten the food. It stank strongly of the urine of rats. We drank yellow water that had been putrid for days. Had not God given us so good weather, we would have died of hunger in that exceeding vast sea. In truth, I believe no such voyage will ever be made again.'

By the time Magellan's ships had reached the islands off Asia, many men had died from starvation or disease.

Asia at last

In March 1521, Magellan reached the islands off the coast of Asia which later became known as the Philippines. He was the first European to cross the Pacific Ocean. He had also proved what Columbus had long believed—that the East could be reached by sailing westwards.

In the Philippines, Magellan was given supplies by a local chief. In return, he helped the chief in a tribal war. During this conflict Magellan himself was killed when a poisoned spear was thrown in his face.

The death of Magellan. Can you identify the explorer?

Test your knowledge

1 Using the account of the survivor, describe the problems faced by Magellan and his crew in the Pacific.
2 Where did the expedition land in March 1521?
3 What happened to Magellan in the Philippines?
4 Who led the expedition back to Spain? What route did he take?
5 Why was the achievement of Magellan's expedition so important?

The homeward voyage

It was up to the expedition's navigator, Sebastian Delcano, to bring the ships back to Spain. Only one of the ships, captained by Delcano himself, succeeded in crossing the Indian Ocean, rounding Africa, and arriving safely home in Spain. Out of the 270 men who had set sail from Seville in 1519, only twenty now returned two years later. But their achievement was tremendous. They were the first to sail around, or *circumnavigate*, the world. Magellan's expedition had proved beyond all doubt that the world was round.

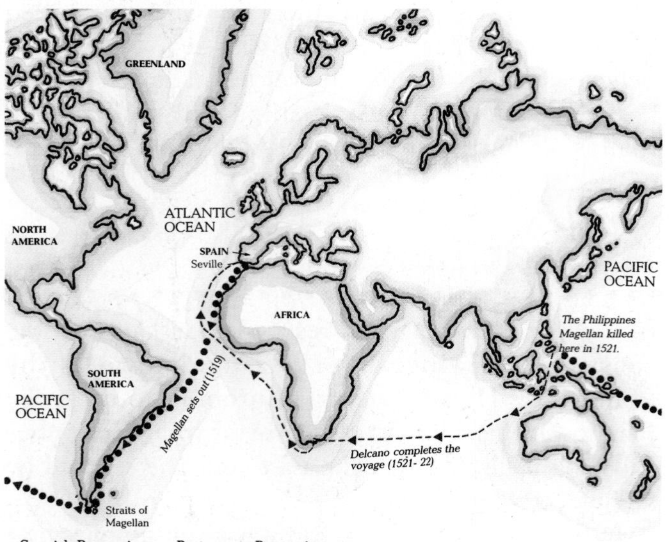

The Voyage of Magellan, 1519–22, the first expedition to sail around the world.

Chapter 26: Review

- In 1519 Ferdinand Magellan, a Portuguese explorer in the service of Spain, set out with five ships and 270 men. His destination was the spice islands off Asia and his route was to go around the coast of South America.

- Magellan's expedition ran into terrible storms as it made its way round the tip of South America, an area which became known as the Straits of Magellan. They then entered a peaceful sea which they called the Pacific.

- By the time Magellan's expedition had landed on the islands off Asia (the Philippines), many of his men had died of starvation and diseases such as scurvy.

- Magellan himself was killed on the islands while helping a local chief in a tribal war. He had been the first European to cross the Pacific Ocean and had shown that the East could be reached by sailing westwards.

- Sebastian Delcano now took charge of the expedition. With only one ship and twenty men, he returned to Spain on 6 September 1522. Magellan's expedition was the first to sail around, or circumnavigate, the world.

CHAPTER 27 The Conquistadores

Most explorers were attracted by the hope of finding great riches in the new lands. While Columbus had failed to bring back these riches, rumours spread of the vast amounts of gold to be found on the mainland of America.

Some Spanish explorers were determined to find out for themselves. This led to the most brutal expeditions during the whole age of discovery—the conquest and destruction of both the Aztec Empire in Mexico and the Inca Empire in Peru.

The men who led these expeditions were known as the *Conquistadores*—the conquerors.

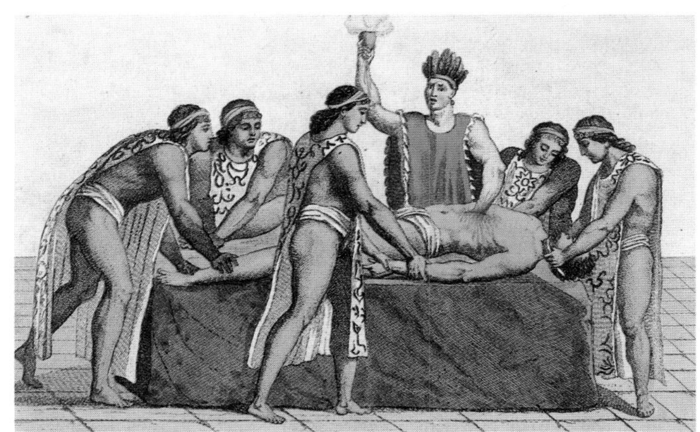

An Aztec priest offering a human sacrifice to his gods. Describe the scene shown here.

Cortés and the Aztecs

Hernán Cortés (1485–1547).

In 1519, a Spanish explorer named Hernán Cortés (1485–1547) left Cuba with a band of followers. They planned to sail to the coast of Mexico. Once ashore, Cortés burned the boats so that there could be no turning back. He then led his little army inland. It consisted of 400 men, fifteen horses and ten cannon. Cortés intended to conquer the rich kingdom of the Aztecs.

The Aztecs were a warlike native Indian people who lived in Mexico. They had not invented the wheel or discovered how to use animals for carrying goods. Aztec priests offered human sacrifices to their gods. Cortés now received help from other tribes which had been conquered by the Aztecs and forced to hand over thousands of their young people for sacrifices to the Aztec gods. Cortés was told that the Aztecs believed that one of their gods would soon return to earth. Cortés decided to pretend that he was this Aztec god.

When Montezuma, the Aztec emperor, heard of the arrival of these white strangers, he firmly believed that they had come down from heaven. He therefore welcomed Cortés and his army when they appeared outside his capital city of Tenochtitlan in November 1519. The Spanish visitors found a splendid, well-organised city built in the middle of a lake and containing nearly a quarter of a million people.

The Aztec welcome was short lived. Many of Cortés's followers stole gold and silver and took over palaces for themselves. The Aztecs rebelled when they

The Aztec emperor, Montezuma, being carried in procession by his people.

The first meeting between Montezuma and Cortés at Tenochtitlan.

Spaniards attacking Aztecs.

saw what was happening. They killed their own king, Montezuma, as well as half of Cortés's army.

Cortés himself escaped, but returned two years later, in 1521, with a much larger force. For eighty days they laid siege to Tenochtitlan. Cortés eventually captured the city and destroyed it, killing tens of thousands of

The conquest of Mexico and Peru by Spanish conquistadores.

Aztecs. In one short battle, Cortés had conquered the Aztec Empire and destroyed its ancient civilisation. He decided to build a new city on the ruins of Tenochtitlan which became known as Mexico City. This city became the capital of the Spanish Empire in America. By 1525, all of Mexico had been conquered by the king of Spain.

The example of Cortés and his followers was later followed by other Spaniards in the Inca kingdom of Peru.

Test your knowledge

1 Why did Cortés and his followers sail from Cuba to Mexico in 1519?

2 What trick did Cortés hope to play on the Aztecs?

3 Name the emperor of the Aztecs.

4 Why did the Aztecs rebel and kill their leader?

5 Name the city which the Spaniards built on the ruins of Tenochtitlan.

6 Why do you think Cortés and his followers were called conquistadores?

Pizarro conquers the Incas

Following the lead of Cortés, another Spanish conquistador, Francisco Pizarro (1470–1541) set out to conquer the Inca kingdom of Peru in South America. The Incas were a much more advanced people than the Aztecs. They were great engineers and builders and produced beautiful works of art in gold and silver. Their emperor was called the Inca, a god-king believed to be descended from the sun.

Francisco Pizarro (1470–1541).

In January 1531, Franciso Pizarro set out from Panama for Peru. He was sixty-one years of age and was about to embark on an adventure which was to make him famous. His aim was to conquer the Incas, a people who lived high up in the Andes Mountains in Peru. He set sail with one ship, 180 men and thirty-seven horses.

The ruins of the Inca empire high up in the Andes Mountains in Peru.

By April 1531, Pizarro and his followers had made contact with the Incas. Curious about these Spaniards, the Inca leader, Atahualpa, agreed to meet Pizarro. Atahualpa lived near the city of Cajamarca and had an army of about 30,000 men.

Pizarro's men capturing the Inca leader, Atahualpa.

Pizarro entered the large square in the centre of Cajamarca and positioned his artillery around it. After a day's waiting, Atahualpa eventually arrived, carried on a litter and escorted by over 3,000 Incas. Pizarro sent a priest to meet the Inca leader and to show him the Bible. When Atahualpa flung the Bible to the ground, Pizarro and his followers immediately attacked the Incas. Atahualpa himself was captured and the astonished Incas fled in terror.

The final conquest

Pizarro held Atahualpa as a hostage. However, the Inca leader hoped to persuade the Spaniards to release him by promising to fill the room where he was imprisoned with gold. Pizarro had no intention of releasing his prisoner and had him strangled to death on 29 August 1533.

With their leader dead, the Inca armies retreated. Pizarro made his way to the royal city of Cuzco which he captured without difficulty. Within a short time, Pizarro and his conquistadores had conquered the Inca civilisation of Peru. So plentiful was the silver in the area that Spanish conquerors were able to make horseshoes from it. In 1540, rich silver mines were discovered in Potosi.

The Incas were skilled craftsmen, as we can see from these wooden cups.

Pizarro himself had become so powerful that he made many enemies among the Spaniards in Peru. On 26 June 1541, a group of his enemies attacked the palace of Lima, and killed Pizarro. It is said that as he died, he drew a cross with his own blood on the ground, kissed it, and cried 'Jesus' as he fell.

Test your knowledge

1 Who were the Incas?
2 Who set out to conquer them in 1531?
3 Name the Inca leader.
4 Why do you think Pizarro killed the Inca leader?
5 Can you say from your reading what kind of man Pizarro was?
6 What do you think were Pizarro's main motives in conquering the Incas?
7 What characteristics did Pizarro and Cortés have in common?

Chapter 27: Review

- Rumours of great riches to be found on the mainland of America encouraged Spanish explorers to find out for themselves. As a result Spanish conquistadores (conquerors) destroyed ancient civilisations like those of the Aztecs in Mexico and Incas in Peru.

- In 1519, a Spanish explorer named Hernán Cortés sailed with over four hundred followers from Cuba and landed in Mexico. The aim was to conquer the Aztec kingdom.

- The Aztecs were a warlike people ruled by their emperor, Montezuma, from his capital at Tenochtitlan. They had conquered neighbouring tribes from which they took thousands of prisoners for human sacrifices to the Aztec gods.

- Montezuma believed that Cortés and his followers were from heaven so he allowed them to enter Tenochtitlan. However, the Spaniards robbed and plundered the city and the Aztecs rose up, killing Montezuma and half of Cortés' army. Cortés himself escaped.

- In 1521, Cortés returned with a larger army and captured Tenochtitlan after a massive slaughter of Aztecs. They destroyed the city and built a new Spanish city named Mexico City on the site. By 1525, the Spaniards had conquered all of Mexico.

- In 1531, another Spanish conquistador, Francisco Pizarro, set out with a small band of followers to conquer the Inca kingdom of Peru.

- The Incas were much more advanced than the Aztecs. They were great engineers and builders and designed beautiful works of art in gold and silver. Their emperor, the Inca, was a god-king believed to be descended from the sun.

- In 1533 Pizarro and his men captured the Inca capital of Cuzco. The Inca emperor, Atahualpa, promised to fill a room with gold as a ransom. However, he was strangled by the Spaniards and his empire was soon destroyed.

- Pizarro became so powerful that he made many enemies among the Spaniards in Peru. In 1541, he was killed in the city of Lima by a group of his enemies.

A Changing World

In this section we have read about the great voyages of exploration and discovery and about the adventurous men who made them possible. These discoveries helped change the world in which we live. In this chapter, we will take a look at the important changes which resulted from the Age of Exploration and Discovery.

Great empires

From his residence at the Escorial Palace in Madrid, the king of Spain ruled over his vast empire overseas.

We have already seen that Spain and Portugal were the two leading countries in the Age of Exploration. Both countries were to gain enormous wealth and power as a result of their discoveries. They conquered many lands and built up powerful empires.

Because both Portugal and Spain were in the race for the same lands, rivalry between them was inevitable. In 1494, both countries signed the *Treaty of Tordesillas* which divided the unknown world between them. Portugal was to gain all new lands to the east and Spain all new lands to the west of a line running through Brazil. The treaty, however, did not prevent rivalry between the two countries. Each continued to send explorers and to grab rich lands before other explorers could arrive.

Take a close look at the map and study the extent of the Spanish and Portuguese empires. Portugal had lands in Africa and Asia, while the Spaniards conquered the people of Central America and Peru.

In the sixteenth and seventeenth centuries, Spain was one of the most powerful countries in the world. The Spanish Empire in America was ruled from Spain by the *Council of the Indies*. The council was responsible for all Church and government appointments in the new empire. Two representatives of the king of Spain, or *viceroys*, lived in America. One was in charge of New Spain (Mexico) and lived in Mexico City. The other ruled over New Castile (Peru) from Lima.

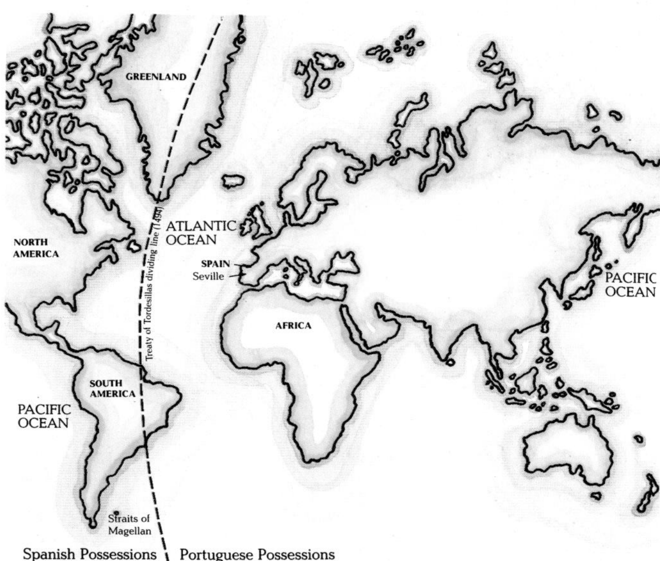

Spanish and Portuguese possessions according to the Treaty of Tordesillas.

Trading goods

There was a great increase in trade between Europe and the new overseas empires. Goods such as tobacco, pineapples, tea, coffee, sugar and chocolates were brought to Europe for the first time. Sheep and horses were introduced to America by the Spanish.

With this great increase in trade to the New World, the Atlantic ports of Europe grew at the expense of the Mediterranean ones. Ports such as Rotterdam and Antwerp prospered, while ports like Venice and Genoa suffered a decline.

Test your knowledge

1 What was the Treaty of Tordesillas?
2 What overseas lands were conquered by the Portuguese?
3 What lands were part of the Spanish Empire?
4 How was the Spanish Empire in America ruled?
5 Name some goods brought to Europe from the New World.
6 Why do you think the Atlantic ports of Europe prospered?

The high price of discovery

The native people of the so-called New World had a terrible price to pay after they were discovered by the Europeans. Disease and slavery were the twin evils which followed quickly in the wake of the invasion by European explorers.

Indians being treated with great cruelty by their Spanish masters.

Two killer diseases carried by the Spanish to the New World were smallpox and typhoid. Smallpox, in particular, devastated the population of Mexico which fell from 11 million to just over 2 million between the years 1519 and 1597.

We have already seen how the natives of the conquered lands suffered greatly at the hands of their European masters. In the last chapter, we read how groups of Spanish explorers—the conquistadores—destroyed the Aztec and Inca civilisations of Central and South America. Traffic in slaves soon grew into a huge business. Most of these slaves were black Africans who were shipped to the American mainland or the Caribbean Islands. In the sixteenth century, over 16,000 slaves a year were transported from West Africa to Spanish and Portuguese America. By the year 1800, about 11 million slaves had been transported from their homes and sold in markets in Europe and the New World.

Slaves were bought and sold in slave markets such as this one in Brazil, South America.

A shrinking world

One of the most important results of the Age of Exploration and Discovery was that knowledge of the world increased greatly. The vast continents of the Americas had been discovered. New trade routes to Asia had been found.

Explorers had proved beyond all doubt that the world was round. A far more accurate map of the world could be drawn in 1550 than was possible in 1450.

The explorers of the fifteenth and sixteenth centuries had therefore led the way in increasing our knowledge of the world about us. Exploration and discovery did not, however, stop there. Others were soon to follow the lead of Columbus and Magellan and venture into unknown parts of the world. By about the middle of the twentieth century, people had discovered and mapped every corner of the planet.

Exploration did not halt at our own frontiers, however. In 1957, the Russians launched the first satellite into space. Four years later, a Russian astronaut named Yuri Gagarin became the first man in space. In 1969, the American astronaut Neil Armstrong became the first man to walk on the moon. The quest for new worlds, which began over 500 years ago, has continued to the present day, as people accept the challenge of entering into the unknown and seeking new frontiers.

Test your knowledge

1 What diseases were brought by the Spanish to the New World?

2 Who became slaves and where were they brought?
3 How did the Age of Exploration and Discovery increase human knowledge of the world?
4 In what way has the quest for new worlds continued up to the present day?

Principal geographical discoveries and conquests

Henry the Navigator
about 1425
Set up a school of navigation.
Sent voyages of exploration along the west coast of Africa.

Bartholomew Diaz
1487
First to reach the southern tip of Africa (Cape of Good Hope).

Christopher Columbus
1492
First to sail westward in search of a new sea route to Asia.
Landed in the West Indies and discovered a new continent—America.

Vasco da Gama
1497–98
Rounded the Cape of Good Hope and reached Calicut in India.

Ferdinand Magellan
1519–22
His expedition was the first to circumnavigate the world.

Hernán Cortés
1521
Conquered the Aztec Empire of Mexico.

Francisco Pizarro
1533
Conquered the Inca Empire of Peru.

Chapter 28: Review

- Rivalry developed between Spain and Portugal over colonies in the New World. In 1494, both countries signed the Treaty of Tordesillas to settle these disputes. Portugal was given all the new lands to the east and Spain the lands to the west of an imaginary line running through Brazil.

- The king of Spain ruled his American empire through his Council of the Indies which made all important appointments in the Church and governments throughout the empire.

- The king of Spain also had two representatives in America known as viceroys. One lived in Mexico City and ruled New Spain (Mexico). The other governed New Castile (Peru) from Lima.

- A huge trade developed between Europe and the New World. Goods such as tobacco, pineapples, tea, coffee and sugar were exported from the New World to Europe, while the Spaniards introduced animals such as sheep and horses to America.

- The native people of America paid a high price for their discovery by Europeans. They suffered terribly as a result of slavery and the diseases introduced by Europeans.

- When the supply of native Indian slaves dried up, they were replaced by millions of black Africans which the Spaniards brought to the New World.

- The Age of Exploration and Discovery, which began 500 years ago, has continued to the present day. In our own century, explorers have discovered new worlds beyond the earth itself.

Reformation and Counter-Reformation

29 The Need for Change

30 Martin Luther and the Reformation

31 John Calvin and the Reformation in Switzerland

32 The Counter-Reformation

The Need for Change

Today, all Christians do not share the same religion. In Ireland, as in many other countries, Christians can be either Catholics or Protestants. Have your ever wondered how these divisions came about?

Before 1500, all the Christian people of Europe belonged to the Catholic Church under the leadership of the pope in Rome. Between 1500 and 1550, however, deep divisions took place in the Christian religion. In some countries, most people remained in the Catholic Church. In other lands such as Germany and England, people rejected the authority of the pope and turned to different religions.

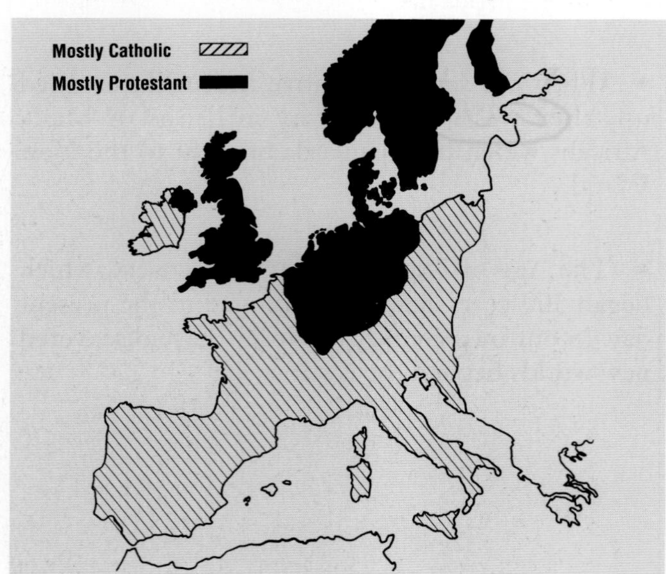

Catholic and Protestant areas in Europe today.

In this section of the book we will see how these changes came about. These changes of religious belief became known as the *Reformation* because they began as attempts to *reform* or improve the Catholic Church. To understand why such reforms began in the first place, we must examine the condition of the Christian Church in Europe around 1500.

A rich and powerful Church

It is clear from this picture of the beautiful Sistine Chapel in Rome that the pope and cardinals were surrounded by great wealth and luxury.

In 1500, the Catholic Church in every country in Europe was rich and powerful. Bishops lived in palaces and owned large amounts of land. Very often, they took part in governments and stayed away from their dioceses to live at the king's court.

Each town and city had several churches run either by ordinary parish priests or by religious orders such as the Franciscans or

This manuscript illustration shows the rich surrounds of a monastery around 1500.

Dominicans. Rich merchants in the towns usually gave large donations of money to their local churches.

In most areas, the priest had a good deal of power over the lives of the local people. There were also courts run by the Church to punish people who were leading bad lives.

Monasteries were another sign of the wealth and power of the Church. There were many of these in every country run by orders such as the Benedictines and Cistercians. Some monasteries owned vast amounts of land. However, they also provided many services which most governments provide today, such as looking after the poor and the sick.

Although much good work was carried out by priests, monks and nuns, there were many abuses in the Christian Church in Europe around 1500.

Abuses in the Church

All too often, Church rulers from the pope down gave most of their attention to worldly matters such as wars and politics. Because they were involved with these problems, they neglected their religious duties. While popes, bishops and abbots were leading lives of luxury, many priests were poor and ignorant men. At this time, some priests could barely read and write.

As you can see from the chart, four abuses in particular were widespread in the Catholic Church by 1500.

Although these abuses existed in every country, nowhere were they worse than in the city of Rome. At this time the Renaissance was taking place in Italy. The popes of the time gave most of their attention to matters like politics, warfare and art.

Abuses

Pluralism
Holding more than one Church position at the same time.

Nepotism
Appointing one's own relations as cardinals or bishops, whether they were suitable or not.

Simony
Buying or selling important Church positions.

Absenteeism
A priest or bishop living away from his own parish or diocese.

One of the most scandalous of all popes was Rodrigo Borgia, who became Pope Alexander VI (1492–1503). He was widely believed to have bribed the cardinals who elected him—the abuse of *simony*. He was also guilty of *nepotism*, since he gave important Church positions to his own children. Another pope, Julius II (1503–13), spent much of his time organising war against his enemies in Italy. By 1500, a complete reform was needed in the Catholic Church, from the pope down to ordinary priests working in the countryside.

It was only a matter of time before somebody led a movement to bring about this reform. As it happened, the issue which triggered off the Reformation was another area where abuses had crept in—the question of *indulgences*.

Test your knowledge

1 Name the two main groups into which Christians in Europe are now divided.
2 Did these divisions exist before 1500? Explain your answer.
3 What type of lives did bishops lead around this time?
4 State two services provided by the monasteries.
5 Explain the following abuses: (a) nepotism; (b) simony; (c) pluralism; (d) absenteeism.
6 Name one pope around this time who led an unchristian life.

The sale of indulgences

According to the teaching of the Catholic Church, an indulgence is a cancelling or a shortening of the time a soul must spent in Purgatory after death. People gaining an indulgence could apply it to themselves or to their dead relations who might already be in Purgatory. Indulgences could be gained by praying, by going to Mass or by giving money to the Church or to charity. Those too poor to give money could gain indulgences simply by praying.

However, preachers travelled around Europe collecting money for indulgences, giving people the impression that only money was required to get a soul into heaven. Many people, however, found these activities scandalous. The following mocking verse dates from the time:

Selling indulgences. Describe what you see in this picture.

'When the coin in the coffer sings
Then the soul to heaven springs.'

In 1517, priests were travelling throughout Europe to preach a special indulgence. They were sent by Pope Leo X (1513–21) to collect money for the rebuilding of St Peter's Basilica in Rome.

When a Dominican friar came to preach the indulgence in Germany, another monk made a public protest. The monk's name was Martin Luther. With his action, the Reformation had begun.

Chapter 29: Review

- Today, all Christians do not share the same religion. In Ireland as in many other countries, they are divided into Catholics and Protestants.
- Before 1500, all the people of Europe belonged to the one Christian Church under the leadership of the pope in Rome.
- Between 1500 and 1550, changes of religious belief came about in many countries in Europe. This time of change became known as the Reformation because it began with attempts to reform or improve the Catholic Church.
- In 1500, the Catholic Church in every country in Europe was rich and powerful. Bishops lived in palaces and often owned vast areas of land.
- Rich merchants usually gave large donations of money to their local churches. In most areas, the priest had a great influence over the lives of the local people.
- Monasteries were another sign of wealth and power in the Church. Some of them owned vast amounts of land. However, they provided food and shelter for the poor and the sick.
- Around 1500, there were serious abuses in the Catholic Church such as nepotism, simony, pluralism and absenteeism.
- Some of the popes around this time gave a very bad example. Alexander VI (1492–1503) lived an immoral life and Julius II (1503–13) was more interested in politics and war than in reforming the Church.
- The practice of selling indulgences was widespread in the Catholic Church around 1500. It led to abuses such as the belief that money alone could bring about the release of a soul from Purgatory.
- In 1517, priests were travelling throughout Europe to preach a special indulgence granted by Pope Leo X (1513–21) who was trying to raise money for the rebuilding of St Peter's Basilica in Rome. A German monk named Martin Luther made a public protest against this, thus beginning the Reformation.

CHAPTER 30

Martin Luther and the Reformation

A dramatic protest

In October 1517, a Dominican friar named John Tetzel came to preach the pope's special indulgence near the town of Wittenberg in Germany. An account dating from the time describes Tetzel's arrival:

'All the priests and monks, the town council, schoolmasters, scholars, men and women and children went out to meet him with banners, songs and processions. Then all the bells were rung. He was conducted into church, a red cross was placed in the midst of the church and the pope's banner was displayed. In short, God himself would not have been welcomed with more honour.'

Martin Luther, a priest and professor at the University of Wittenberg, was very angry when he heard of Tetzel's arrival in the area. On 31 October 1517, he nailed a proclamation called the *Ninety-Five Theses* to the door of the University Church at Wittenberg. In these theses or lists of arguments, Luther condemned indulgences and other abuses in the Church. He asked why the pope did not rebuild St Peter's using his own great wealth. Printed copies of the *Ninety-Five Theses* soon spread throughout Germany. Luther became a hero with many German people who also resented paying taxes to the pope. This was also the time of the Renaissance when many people were questioning old beliefs.

Luther making his dramatic protest on 31 October 1517. At that time, when someone wanted to make a challenge or have a debate, he often pinned a notice like this one on the door of the local church.

Let us now take a closer look at the man who made that dramatic protest in October 1517 and who was soon to start a huge movement of reform in the Catholic Church.

The story of Martin Luther (1483–1546)

Martin Luther (1483–1546).

Martin Luther was born in the German state of Saxony in 1483. His father was a fairly well-off copper miner and a member of the local town council. Young Martin's home life was very strict and from an early age he believed in an angry God who was always eager to punish sinners.

According to his father's wishes, Luther went to university at Erfurt to study law. On 2 July 1505, while returning to the university from a visit home, he was caught out in a terrible thunderstorm. Luther took this as a sign from God and cried out, 'Saint Anne, help me, and I will become a monk.' To his father's great disappointment, Martin Luther entered a strict branch of the Augustinian Order and was ordained a priest in 1507.

Becoming a monk did not bring Luther peace of mind, however. He was convinced that he was a terrible sinner and that he would probably go to hell. In 1510 he visited Rome and was shocked by the bad lives of many churchmen there. Over the next few years, he gradually began to develop the idea that people were totally evil and could do nothing to save their own souls. In Luther's view, only God's grace could save a person's soul. The Catholic Church had always taught that people could save their souls by a mixture of God's grace and their own good works. Luther's idea was known as *Justification by Faith Alone*—only by faith in God could a person be saved, or 'justified'. Suddenly, in October 1517, Luther got an unexpected chance to spread his ideas far and wide by posting up his *Ninety-Five Theses*.

Test your knowledge

1 Name the Dominican friar who preached the pope's special indulgences in Germany.
2 How was he welcomed by the local people?
3 What was the reaction of Martin Luther to his arrival?
4 What dramatic event took place on 31 October 1517 at Wittenberg?
5 When and where was Luther born?
6 Why did he decide to become a monk?
7 Explain Luther's belief in 'Justification by Faith Alone'.

The pope condemns Luther

This famous picture of Pope Leo X was painted by the Italian artist, Raphael. Leo, a son of Lorenzo de Medici of Florence, had been made a cardinal at the age of ten.

When the news of Luther's attack on indulgences first reached Rome, Pope Leo X dismissed it as a small quarrel. He became worried, however, when Luther's ideas began to spread.

Luther soon rejected the pope as head of the Church. He said that Christians should read their Bibles and make up their own minds about what was right instead of obeying popes, bishops and priests.

In June 1520, Pope Leo X issued a papal letter, or *bull*, called *Exsurge Domine* (Arise, O Lord). In this he gave Luther sixty days to *recant* (take back) his teachings. If Luther failed to do this, he would be *excommunicated* (put out of the Church).

Luther and his followers burning the pope's letter and some Catholic books.

On 10 December 1520, Luther publicly burned the pope's letter, together with a number a Catholic books.

The Diet of Worms (1521)

Emperor Charles V clashes with Luther

At the time of Luther's protest, Germany was divided into more than 300 small states, each with its own ruler or prince. Over all of these rulers was Charles V, the Holy Roman Emperor. Although the emperor was the head of all Germany, he had very little power over the princes.

This picture of the Emperor Charles V was painted by the Italian artist, Titian. Charles ruled over a huge empire which included Spain, the Netherlands and Germany.

In April 1521, the parliament of the Empire, known as the *Diet*, met in the town of Worms to consider Luther's ideas. Some of the princes supported Luther because he would be useful to them in their struggle against the Catholic emperor.

On 18 April, Luther himself was called to appear before the Diet. He stated that he would not change his beliefs unless he was proved wrong by the Bible. When he left, there was considerable excitement in the Diet.

On the following day, the Emperor Charles V spoke out against Luther. He said that he would not allow a mere monk, relying on his own judgement, to rebel against the faith held by Christians for over a thousand years. As a result, Luther was condemned by the Diet and declared an outlaw and a *heretic* in the *Edict of Worms* (April 1521).

Luther strongly defends his beliefs in the presence of Emperor Charles V at the Diet of Worms.

Not all of the princes agreed with the attack on Luther, however. The prince in Luther's own area, Frederick of Saxony, now came to his rescue. In the safety of Frederick's castle in Wartburg, Luther worked for nearly a year, translating the New Testament into German and writing pamphlets explaining his religious beliefs. The spread of Luther's ideas was made easier because of the newly invented printing press.

The moveable-type printing press, invented by Gutenberg around 1450, greatly assisted the spread of Luther's ideas.

Test your knowledge

1. How did Pope Leo X react when he first heard of Luther's criticisms?
2. Explain Luther's attitude to the Bible.
3. What was contained in the papal bull, Exsurge Domine (1520)?
4. What was Luther's response to it?
5. Explain what happened at the Diet of Worms.
6. What prince now protected Luther?

Luther's beliefs

Between 1520 and Luther's death in 1546, his religion spread rapidly. It became known as Lutheranism and eventually became the main religion of northern Germany, Norway, Denmark and Sweden. In 1530, the *Confession of Augsburg* was published. This was a statement of the doctrine and customs of the Lutheran Church. Take a look at the chart showing these beliefs and the ways in which they differed from Catholic teachings.

Luther's beliefs	Catholic beliefs
Justification by faith alone Only faith in God would decide who would be saved.	Good works as well as faith were needed to save a person's soul.
The Bible The Bible is the only source of truth and authority for all Christians.	People should not take their own meaning from the Bible. It should be explained to them by the pope and their bishops.
Communion service Luther replaced the Latin Mass with a Communion Service in the German language.	**The Mass** The Mass is truly a re-enactment of the sacrifice of Christ on the Cross and must be said in Latin.
Consubstantiation Both the body and blood of Christ and the bread and wine are present at Communion.	**Transubstantiation** At Communion, the bread and wine are completely changed to the body and blood of Christ.
Two sacraments Baptism and the Eucharist.	**Seven sacraments** Baptism, Penance (Confession), the Eucharist, Confirmation, Marriage, Holy Orders, Extreme Unction (Last Rites).
The priesthood of all believers Priests should not be a special group. People could read the Bible for themselves, so they were as good as priests.	**A separate priesthood** A priest is a special person who is ordained in the sacrament of Holy Orders. Only priests can offer the sacrifice of the Mass and forgive sins in Confession.
A married clergy Luther himself married a former nun, Catherine von Bora, in 1525.	**Priests cannot marry**

Test your knowledge

1 What was Luther's attitude to the Mass?
2 Explain the 'Priesthood of All Believers'.
3 How many sacraments did Luther believe in? Name them.
4 Explain the meaning of Consubstantiation.
5 Whom did Luther marry in 1525?
6 What was the *Confession of Augsburg* (1530)?

Religious war in Germany

While many German princes supported Luther, many others remained Catholics. There now followed almost thirty years of war between the Catholic and Lutheran princes.

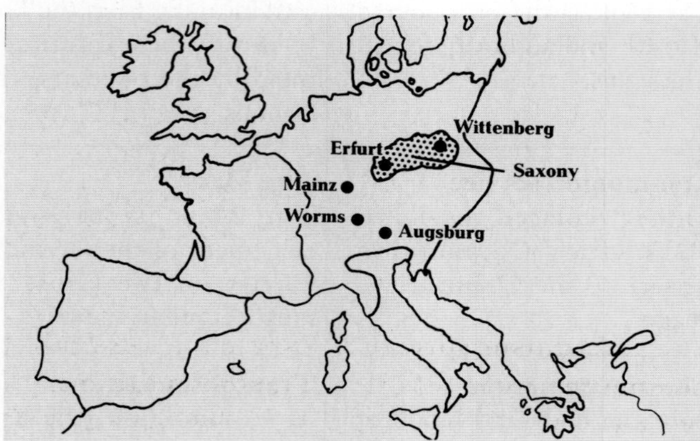

Germany at the time of Martin Luther.

In 1555, after years of fighting, both sides finally reached an agreement. Under the *Peace of Augsburg*, they agreed that each prince should decide the religion of the people. The Peace of Augsburg brought religious peace to Germany after the troubles of the previous thirty years. It was not a lasting peace, however, as religious war broke out again during the next century.

The spread of Luther's ideas

By the time Luther died in 1546, his Lutheran Church was well established. He had protested against the Catholic Church and introduced lasting reforms in doctrines and customs. People who shared Luther's beliefs became known as Protestants. The religious revolution which Luther had started became known as the Reformation.

The Reformation did not end with Luther, however. Other reformers were to bring about even more far-reaching changes than the German monk had ever dreamed of. The main centre of such reform was the small, mountainous country of Switzerland.

Martin Luther

- Born in Germany in 1483.
- Ordained an Augustinian priest in 1507.
- Luther was worried about his own salvation. He came to believe that only faith in God could save a person's soul—Justification by Faith Alone.
- On 31 October 1517, Luther posted his *Ninety-Five Theses* on the door of the University church at Wittenberg. In it, he condemned the sale of indulgences and other abuses within the Catholic Church.
- Luther was excommunicated when he refused to change his beliefs. The emperor later declared him an outlaw, forcing Luther to flee for his life.
- Luther believed that all Christian authority was found in the Bible. He stated that there were only two sacraments and that priests should be free to marry.
- Luther replaced the Latin Mass with a Communion Service in German. He believed that ordinary people were as good as priests—the Priesthood of All Believers.
- By the time Luther died in 1546, his Protestant ideas had spread far and wide. The religious revolution which he had started became known as the Reformation.

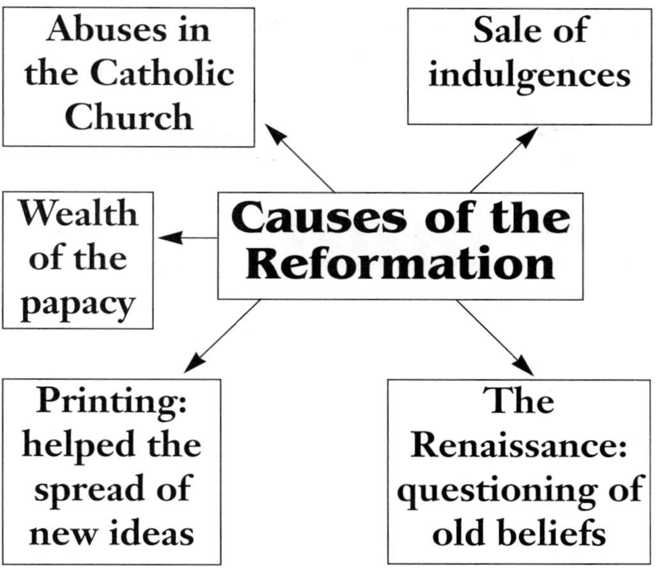

Chapter 30: Review

• Martin Luther was born in the German state of Saxony in 1483. At his father's wish, he studied law but later decided to become a monk. He was ordained a priest in 1507.

• Luther was worried about people's sinfulness. He believed that people were totally evil and could do nothing to save their own souls. They could be saved by God's grace alone. This belief was known as 'Justification by Faith Alone'.

• In 31 October 1517, Luther nailed his *Ninety-Five Theses* to a church door in Wittenberg in protest against the pope's indulgence for those giving money for the rebuilding of St Peter's Basilica. This indulgence was being preached by a Dominican friar called John Tetzel.

• By the end of 1517, Luther had become a hero to many German people who objected to paying taxes to the pope in Rome.

• Luther attacked the power of the pope and said that the Bible should be the only authority for Christians. In 1520, Pope Leo X excommunicated Luther from the Catholic Church.

• At the Diet of Worms (1521) Emperor Charles V clashed with Luther over the new religious teachings. Luther refused to change his views unless he was proved wrong by the Bible. Under the Edict of Worms he was declared an outlaw. However, he was protected by his own prince, Frederick of Saxony.

• After 1521, Luther gave up all ideas of reforming the Catholic Church and started a new religion—Lutheranism. Its main teachings were: Justification by Faith Alone; the Bible as the only authority for Christians; Communion Service instead of the Mass; and two sacraments instead of seven.

• Luther's belief concerning the presence of Christ at Holy Communion is known as Consubstantiation. This meant the presence of both the body and blood and the bread and wine at Holy Communion.

• Lutheranism spread quickly and eventually became the main religion of northern Germany, Norway, Denmark and Sweden. *The Confession of Augsburg* (1530) contained a statement of the main Lutheran beliefs.

• Religious war broke out in Germany between the Catholic and Protestant princes. It lasted for thirty years and only came to an end with the Peace of Augsburg (1555). Under this agreement, the prince in each state was allowed to decide the religion of his people.

John Calvin and the Reformation in Switzerland

John Calvin (1509–64)

John Calvin was born in Noyon in northern France in 1509. He studied theology for a while in Paris, but later became a law student at his father's request. In 1533, Calvin left the Catholic Church to follow Luther's teachings.

John Calvin (1509–64).

It was dangerous to be a Lutheran in France at the time. King Francis I (1515–47) believed that Lutheranism would divide the French people and lead to a civil war. In October 1534, French Lutherans put up posters of a Protestant sermon around the king's castle at Amboise. King Francis I was enraged by this incident. As a result, French Lutherans were severely persecuted.

Fearing for his life, Calvin fled to Switzerland around the end of 1534. He settled in the city of Basle and for the next three years he worked on his great masterpiece, *The Institutes of the Christian Religion*. It was written in Latin and later translated into French and contained all of Calvin's main religious teachings.

Calvinism or Presbyterianism

Calvin's religion was known as *Calvinism* or *Presbyterianism*, from the Greek word *presbyter*, meaning priest. Presbyters, or ministers, were the highest officers in Calvin's Church, as there were no bishops and no pope. Look at the chart to see Calvin's main beliefs.

Calvin's Beliefs

1 Predestination
God has chosen those who are to be saved and those who are to be damned before they are born.

2 The Bible
The Bible is the only authority for Christians to follow.

3 No bishops—only ministers
Calvin's Church contained ministers who were elected by the people to preach the Bible.

4 Christ is not present at Communion
Calvin believed that the bread and wine remained bread and wine at Communion.

5 The power of the Church
Luther had stated that the princes should be the heads of the Protestant Church in their own states. Calvin believed, however, that governments should obey the leaders of the Church.

Test your knowledge

1 Where and when was John Calvin born?
2 Why was it dangerous to be a Protestant in France in 1534?
3 What famous book did Calvin write while he was living in Basle?
4 Why is Calvinism also known as Presbyterianism?
5 Explain the meaning of predestination.
6 Would you agree that Calvinism was a strict religion? Give reasons for your answer.

Geneva—'The City of God'

From 1541 until his death in 1564, Calvin ruled over the Swiss city of Geneva. Here he had an opportunity to put his ideas into practice. He organised his Church along strict lines. There were no bishops and the main officers were preachers, deacons, teachers and elders. The ruling Presbytery was made up of six preachers and twelve elders. The elders were laymen. Calvin gave laymen a lot of power in his Church, including the power of electing their own ministers.

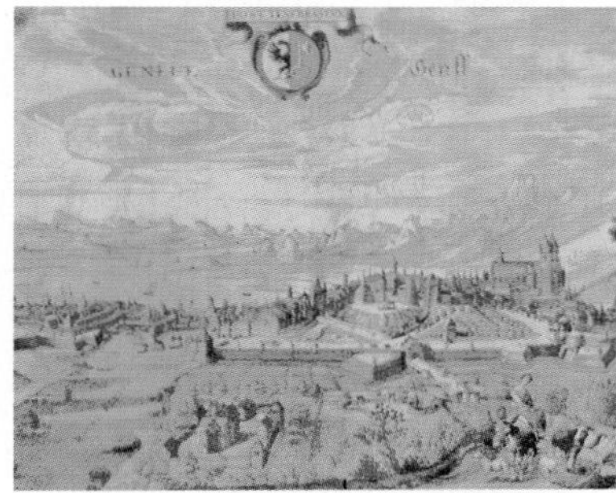

The city of Geneva around the time of Calvin.

The churches of Calvin were very plain and bare compared to Catholic churches.

The Presbytery of Geneva enforced very strict rules. Dancing, gambling, plays and other entertainments were forbidden. Calvin regarded such things as the works of the devil. Church buildings were very bare and simple. There were no crucifixes, statues, altars or stained-glass windows. The main feature in each church was a pulpit. Calvinist preachers wore simple robes and either read from the Bible or preached the word of God. One of the worst punishments in Geneva was excommunication from the Church. An excommunicated person was carefully avoided by others and could no longer earn a living. The death penalty was also used for many offences, including heresy. Because of the strictness of Calvin's rule, Geneva became known as the 'City of God'.

Working with evidence

The following were some of the laws in force in Geneva in Calvin's time.

- The taking of God's name in vain in an oath is to be prevented. Anyone doing this should be told by those hearing it to kneel down and kiss the ground. Those who refuse to do so should be put in prison for twenty-four hours on bread and water.
- The celebration of Christ's birth should be deferred to the Sabbath day following 25 December. There should be no other feast days except one in seven, which we call the Lord's Day.
- Those who have been on pilgrimage, who have observed Catholic feasts or fasts or who have attended Mass should be handed over to the Council of Geneva for punishment.
- Taverns must be closed during church services. Those found drunk shall be fined for a first offence and imprisoned for later offences.
- No one shall play games for gold or silver or stakes of any kind. The punishment for this will be a fine and confiscation of the winnings.

1 What was the punishment in Geneva for taking God's name in an oath?
2 Why do you think Calvin abolished the celebration of Christmas on weekdays?
3 What Catholic religious practices were outlawed in Geneva?
4 What rules were there against the abuse of alcoholic drink?
5 What was the punishment for gambling and betting?

Despite its drawbacks, Calvin's Geneva had a very good record in the area of education. Many schools were set up and in 1559 the Academy of Geneva was established. At first this was a training college for Calvinist ministers. Later it grew into the University of Geneva. Protestants came to Geneva from all over Europe to study at the academy and so observe Calvin's religion for themselves.

The spread of Calvinism

John Knox (1505–72) who brought Calvinism to Scotland.

Calvin's religion spread far beyond Geneva. A reformer named John Knox brought this religion to Scotland. Presbyterianism soon became the main religion of Scotland. From there it spread to Ulster when Scottish settlers arrived after 1600.

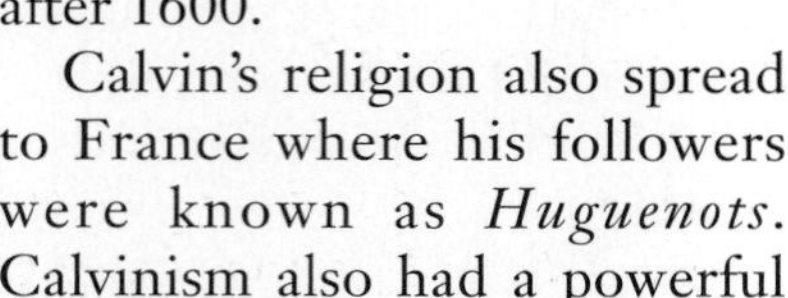

Calvin's religion also spread to France where his followers were known as *Huguenots*. Calvinism also had a powerful influence in the Netherlands. In England, Calvin's followers were known as *Puritans*. Some of these Puritans emigrated to the New World, bringing Calvinism with them.

John Calvin

- John Calvin was born in France in 1509. In 1533, he became a follower of Luther and his teachings.
- In 1534, Calvin fled from France to Switzerland to escape persecution. He remained in Switzerland for the rest of his life.
- Calvin's main religious views were set out in a book called *The Institutes of the Christian Religion.*
- Predestination was one of Calvin's main beliefs. This meant that God had chosen who was to be saved and who was to be damned even before they were born.
- Calvin's Church did not have a pope or bishops. Instead, ministers known as presbyters preached the Bible to the people.
- The headquarters of Calvin's Church was in Geneva, which became known as the 'City of God'. There were very strict rules of conduct in the city, where severe punishments were suffered by those who broke the rules.
- By the time of Calvin's death in Geneva in 1564, his religious ideas had spread to other European countries, including France and Scotland.

Test your knowledge

1 Name the main officials in Calvin's Church.

2 List some activities which were forbidden in Geneva.

3 Describe the inside of a Calvinist church.

4 How was education looked on in Calvin's Geneva?

5 Why was Geneva called the 'City of God'?

6 Who brought the ideas of Calvinism to Scotland?

Chapter 31: Review

- John Calvin was born at Noyon in northern France in 1509. After studying theology, he changed to law at his father's request.
- In 1533, Calvin left the Catholic Church. A year later he fled from France to the town of Basle in Switzerland to escape persecution.
- While in Basle, Calvin wrote the famous book which contained his religious teachings, *The Institutes of the Christian Religion*.
- Calvin's religion was known as Calvinism or Presbyterianism. Its main teachings were: predestination; the Bible as the only authority in religious matters; no bishops, only ministers; a Communion Service instead of the Mass; and a very strict moral code.
- From 1541 until his death in 1564, Calvin ruled over the Swiss city of Geneva. Here he established very strict rules for the people and also set up a good system of education. Calvin's Geneva became known as the 'City of God'.
- A follower of Calvin called John Knox brought Presbyterianism to Scotland. It later spread to the North of Ireland from Scotland.
- Calvin's beliefs also spread to France where his followers were known as Huguenots. In England and America, Calvin's followers were called Puritans.

CHAPTER 32 The Counter-Reformation

We learned in Chapter 29 that abuses within the Catholic Church were among the main causes of the Reformation. We also saw how some reformers like Luther and Calvin left the Catholic Church to form Protestant Churches of their own.

Others, however, believed that the Catholic Church could be improved from within. This reform movement inside the Catholic Church was known as the *Catholic Reformation* or the *Counter-Reformation*. It began with the election of Pope Paul III in 1534.

Paul III (1534–49)

The first counter-reformation pope

Pope Paul III (1534–49).

With the election of Paul III in 1534, a man interested in serious reform was at last the head of the Catholic Church. He appointed a commission of cardinals to prepare a report on abuses. Pope Paul III also set up the *Council of Trent* in 1545 to bring about reform in the Catholic Church.

Cardinal Carafa, who later became Paul IV (1555–59), encouraged Pope Paul to set up the *Roman Inquisition*, a special court to stamp out Protestantism. In 1540, Paul III also gave his approval to the most powerful religious order of the Counter-reformation—the *Jesuits*, founded by St Ignatius Loyola.

St Ignatius Loyola (1491–1556).

The story of Ignatius Loyola (1491–1556)

Ignatius Loyola, a nobleman and soldier, was born in northern Spain in 1491. While fighting against the French at Pamplona in 1521, he was badly wounded. This is his own description of what happened.

Working with evidence

'I was in a fortress besieged by the French. All my companions wanted to surrender if their lives would be spared. They knew that defence was impossible but they took heart when they saw that I was prepared to fight. In the attack a cannon ball struck one of my legs and shattered it completely. Immediately the others surrendered to the French.

After lying twelve days in Pamplona, I was carried on a litter to my father's castle where I became very ill. The leg would not heal. The French surgeons must have set it wrongly. Doctors were called in and began again to butcher my leg. My condition worsened. Doctors said that if I did not improve by midnight I would die. But it pleased Our Lord that, the next day being St Peter's Day, at midnight I began to feel much better, and within a few days I was out of danger.'

1 Why did the companions of Ignatius wish to surrender to the French?
2 What happened to Ignatius during the attack?
3 How do we know from this account that Ignatius' father was a rich man?
4 How did Ignatius explain his eventual cure?

The experience described by Ignatius changed his whole life. While recovering from his injuries, he read a book on the life of Christ and made up his mind to become a priest.

After returning from a pilgrimage to the Holy Land, Ignatius studied at universities in Spain and France. He was a student at the University of Paris at the same time as the Protestant reformer, John Calvin.

While in Paris, Ignatius Loyola gathered six companions around him. On the Feast of the Assumption of Our Lady, 15 August 1534, they took vows of poverty and chastity in a little chapel on the hill of Montmartre. One of Ignatius' companions was a young nobleman, Francis Xavier, who was to become one of the greatest missionaries of all time.

The founding of the Jesuits

In 1540, Pope Paul III approved the rules which Ignatius Loyola had drawn up for his new order, the *Society of Jesus* or the *Jesuits*. Ignatius also wrote a famous book, *The Spiritual Exercises*, to guide the Jesuits in their search to live holy lives.

The Jesuit order spread quickly throughout the Church. It was modelled on an army. The head was called the General, and all Jesuits were taught to obey orders without question. Because of its strict discipline and its loyalty to the pope, the new order was well suited to lead the struggle against Protestantism and to bring the Catholic faith to non-Christian lands. The Jesuits were vital to the success of the Counter-Reformation in certain countries. They succeeded in restoring the Catholic religion in Poland, southern Germany and parts of the Holy Roman Empire (Austria and Czechoslovakia).

Pope Paul III presenting Ignatius Loyola with a papal bull approving the foundation of the Jesuit Order.

Missionaries and teachers

As well as struggling against Protestantism in Europe, the Jesuits sent missionaries to Asia, Africa and America. The most famous Jesuit missionary was St Francis Xavier (1506–52) who reached Japan and brought the Catholic faith to India and the Far East.

The Jesuits were also great teachers. Through education, they believed they could gain influence over rich and powerful Catholics. The Jesuit system of education was very advanced for the time, and they set up schools and colleges all over Europe, including the famous Gregorian University in Rome.

Jesuit churches

The Church of Gesu. This baroque-style building was the main Jesuit church in Rome.

The Jesuits also built many churches. They were completely different from Protestant churches. In contrast to the bare appearance of Protestant churches, the Jesuits began a new style of church architecture called *baroque*. This was a highly decorative form of building which made great use of colour. Jesuit churches were full of paintings and statues of Christ, Our Lady and the saints. Many of them were modelled on the main Jesuit church in Rome, the *Gesu*.

The decorated interior of the Jesuit church at Antwerp.

Test your knowledge

1 Who was the first Counter-Reformation pope? When was he elected?
2 What made Ignatius Loyola change the direction of his life in 1521?
3 Name the order of priests founded by Ignatius Loyola and approved by Pope Paul III in 1540.
4 What famous book was written by St Ignatius?
5 Why were the Jesuits so well suited to lead a campaign against Protestantism?
6 Describe the baroque style of church architecture.
7 What Jesuit became a famous missionary?

The Council of Trent (1545–63)

Soon after the Jesuit order was founded, a council met to plan reform in the Catholic Church. This council, which was so long overdue, met in the little town of Trent in northern Italy.

The Council of Trent had two main aims: to define the teachings of the Catholic Church and to correct its abuses. Some members of the council wished to have discussions with Protestants. Protestants were actually invited to attend, but few of them turned up.

The Council of Trent in session.

The decisions of the Council of Trent

The Council of Trent met on and off for nearly twenty years and finally concluded its work in 1563. Look at the chart to see its main decisions.

While the decisions of the Council of Trent did nothing to break down the barriers between Protestants and Catholics, they at least made the beliefs of the Catholic Church clear to everyone. Also, most of the abuses which had caused the Protestant Reformation now came to an end

Giovanni da Palestrina (1525–94), an Italian musician, was the greatest composer of Church music during the Counter-Reformation. In 1571, he became director of the pope's own choir. The Council of Trent approved of Palestrina's work and he was recognised as the greatest composer of religious music in the Catholic Church.

The decisions of the Council of Trent

Discipline

1 Bishops must live in their own dioceses.
2 Simony and nepotism are strictly forbidden.
3 Seminaries are to be set up in each diocese to educate priests.
4 An index of forbidden books is to be drawn up. No Catholic can read books on this list without permission.

Doctrine

1 Both faith and good works are needed to save a person's soul.
2 Both the Bible and the traditions of the Church must be followed.
3 There are seven sacraments.
4 The Mass is a true sacrifice.
5 Christ is truly present at Holy Communion (transubstantiation).
6 The pope and his bishops are appointed by Christ to rule the Church.
7 Praying to Our Lady and the saints is good and worthwhile.
8 Purgatory exists and Masses and prayers for the dead should be said.

Test your knowledge

1 Name the pope who called the Council of Trent together.

2 What were the two main aims of the Council?

3 What did the Council of Trent decide about the following: (a) the Mass and the Blessed Eucharist; (b) faith and good works; (c) the number of sacraments; (d) prayer to Our Lady and the saints?

4 Name two ways to which the Council of Trent helped to reform abuses in the Catholic Church.

The Court of the Inquisition

The Counter-Reformation brought about a renewal of Catholic doctrine and discipline in the Church. At the same time, however, Catholics went on the attack against the spread of Protestantism.

The most powerful weapon in the fight against Protestantism was the *Court of the Inquisition*. This was a Church court which tried those accused of *heresy* (beliefs against the Catholic religion). People accused of heresy were not allowed to see the witnesses who spoke against them. They could, however, send in a list of their own enemies. If anyone on that list was a witness, his evidence would count for nothing.

Sometimes torture was used to force confessions from people. If they refused to change their beliefs, they were handed over to the government to be burned alive at the stake. If heretics agreed to change their beliefs at the last minute, they were strangled before the fire was lit! For less serious offences, heretics might be made to wear a special yellow garment called a 'San Benito'. They could also serve a term in prison or be punished with a public flogging.

The Inquisition had existed in some European countries during the Middle Ages. It was revived in Rome in 1542 by Pope Paul III. This Roman Inquisition stamped out any Protestantism that existed in Italy. It was also responsible for the condemnation of the brilliant scientist, Galileo.

The Spanish Inquisition

The most frightening Inquisition of all existed in Spain. The Spanish Inquisition had been set up in 1478 by Ferdinand and Isabella as a weapon against Jews and Muslims. It was powerful both in Spain and in the Spanish Empire in America. Those sentenced to death by the Spanish Inquisition were burned during a public ceremony known as *auto da fé* (act of faith). The Inquisition was one of the main reasons why Protestant ideas failed to gain support in any parts of Spain.

Throngs of people gather to see heretics condemned by the Inquisition at an auto da fé at Madrid in Spain.

Reform within the Catholic Church

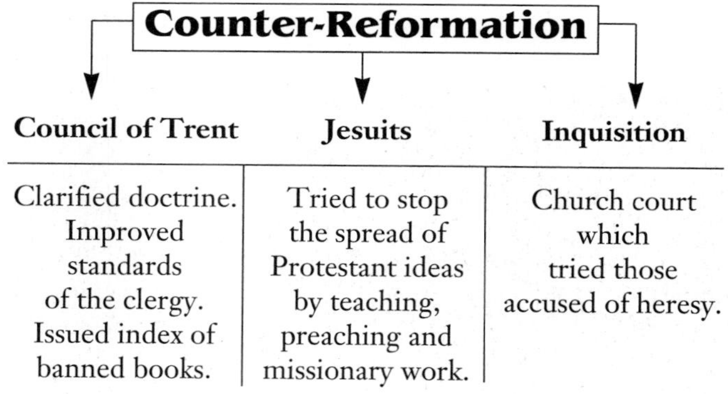

A divided world

In spite of these successes, the Counter-Reformation did not bring about a reconciliation between

Protestants and the Catholic Church. Each side remained bitterly opposed to the other.

One of the worst consequences of the Reformation and Counter-Reformation was the outbreak of religious wars between Catholics and Protestants in Europe. There were religious wars in France between 1560 and 1590 and in the Netherlands around the same time. In Germany, the Thirty-Years War (1618–48) between Catholic and Protestant states brought about widespread loss of life and massive destruction. The Treaty of Westphalia (1648) at the end of this war finally meant the division of Europe into Catholic, Lutheran and Calvinist states.

Although religious bitterness has declined especially since 1900, the effects of the changes which occurred in Reformation times are still present, with Christians in Europe divided into Catholics and Protestants.

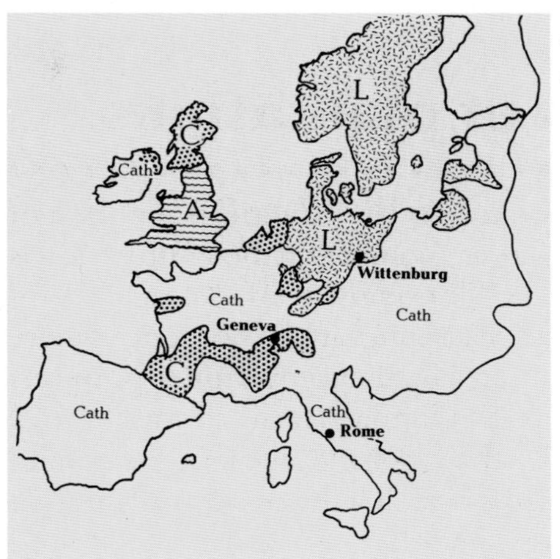

A divided Europe after 1648.

Key:
L = Lutheran
C = Calvinist
A = Anglican
Cath = Catholic

Test your knowledge

1 Name the main offence tried by the Court of the Inquisition.

2 What type of punishment did the Inquisition hand out for lesser offences?

3 For what was the death penalty used?

4 Who set up the Roman Inquisition in 1542?

5 Name the king and queen who established the Spanish Inquisition in 1478.

6 What was an auto da fé?

Chapter 32: Review

• Although reformers like Luther and Calvin left the Catholic Church partly because of the abuses within it, many Catholics believed that the Church could be reformed from within.

• The movement towards reform within the Catholic Church was known as the Catholic Reformation or Counter-Reformation. It began in earnest after the election of Pope Paul III in 1534.

• Paul III (1534–49) was the first pope of the Counter-Reformation. He appointed a commission of cardinals to enquire into abuses in the Church, approved the foundation of the Society of Jesus (1540) and called together the Council of Trent (1545).

• St Ignatius Loyola (1491–1556) founded the Society of Jesus (Jesuits), an order of priests specially trained for missionary work in foreign lands and for the struggle against Protestantism. The order was modelled on an army with a general at the head. Absolute obedience was expected from ordinary members.

• The Society of Jesus expanded rapidly and became a vital part of the Counter-Reformation. Jesuits founded important schools and colleges, converted parts of central Europe back from Protestantism and sent missionaries to distant lands, including the famous St Francis Xavier (1506–52).

• The Council of Trent (1545–63) stressed traditional Catholic beliefs and practices such as salvation by faith and good works, the Mass as a sacrifice, the Real Presence of Christ in the Eucharist, seven sacraments, Purgatory, and the need for prayers to Our Lady and the saints. The council also made disciplinary decisions, such as a ban on simony and nepotism, and an order regarding the establishment of seminaries and an index of forbidden books.

• The Inquisition was the most powerful weapon used by the Catholic Church to stamp out Protestantism.

• The Counter-Reformation, however, did not bring Catholics and Protestants closer together. Although it clearly defined the teachings of the Catholic Church, it also widened the gap between Protestants and Catholics.

Plantation in Ireland

CHAPTER 33 The First Plantations in Ireland

We have already learned that great changes were taking place in Europe around the year 1500. Explorers like Columbus and Magellan were discovering exciting new lands. The Reformation had brought about changes in the religious beliefs of ordinary people throughout Europe.

Ireland shared in many of the changes taking place in the rest of Europe. Both the Reformation and Counter-Reformation influenced the lives of most Irish people in the sixteenth century. At the same time, another type of change was taking place. The English government was attempting to extend control over the whole country of Ireland.

Henry VIII (1509–47) tried to introduce the Reformation into Ireland and to extend English control over the country.

One of the main ways in which the English rulers tried to achieve this aim was to drive the Irish landowners off their land and to replace them with English and Scottish settlers.

This new plan of introducing English and Scottish settlers to take over the land captured from the Irish became known as *plantation*. For the following hundred years, plantations were to play a very important part in the way English governments ruled Ireland.

The idea of plantations

English rulers looked to the American empires of Spain and Portugal as models for their future plans to rule Ireland. Thousands of Spanish and Portuguese settlers had emigrated to America where they were given estates by their governments. In this way, they helped to maintain Spanish and Portuguese rule in these distant lands. From around 1540 onwards, some rich and powerful men in England believed that their governments should carry out plantations in Ireland. As the Irish could not be trusted to support the king of England at all times, they believed that new English settlers loyal to the king should brought over to Ireland. These would then be *planted* or settled on lands captured by the English.

The first plantation took place in Laois and Offaly under the Catholic Queen Mary Tudor in 1556.

Queen Mary Tudor of England and her husband King Philip II of Spain.

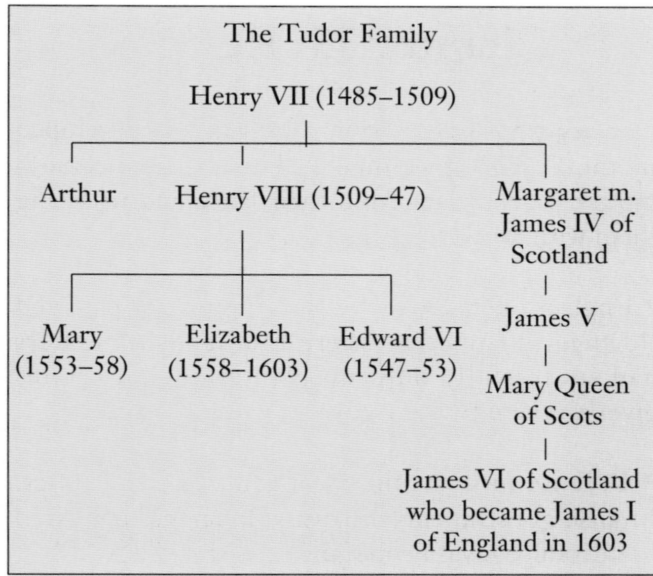

Test your knowledge

1. What was a plantation?
2. How did the empires of Spain and Portugal provide English rulers with models?
3. Why were the Irish not trusted by English rulers?
4. Under which ruler did the first plantation take place in Ireland?

The plantation of Laois and Offaly

Below we can see a picture of the busy town of Portlaoise today. In the year 1556, it became the centre of the first plantation in Ireland.

The modern town of Portlaoise.

In the lands of Laois and Offaly, the Gaelic clans—the O'Mores and the O'Connors—had continued to carry out raids at every opportunity. Several English armies were sent to defeat them. However, the Gaelic clans escaped by retreating into the safety of the surrounding woods and bogs.

When Mary Tudor became ruler of England in 1553, her government decided to capture the lands of the O'Mores and the O'Connors and to give them to English settlers.

Irish clans such as the O'Mores and the O'Connors carried out frequent raids on the Pale.

The scheme of plantation

- Two-thirds of the land was taken from the native Irish and was to be 'planted' by English settlers. The remaining third—the worst land bordering the River Shannon—was set aside for the banished Irish, provided they remained loyal to the queen.

- The English settlers had to build stone houses and keep armed followers in case of attack by the Gaelic clans.

- Settlers were forbidden to mix in any way with the native Irish. They were not to marry into Irish families, to rent land to them, or to hire them as servants.

- The land taken over or confiscated by the English was *shired*, or divided up into counties. Laois became Queen's County, named after Queen Mary. Offaly was renamed King's County, after Mary's husband, King Philip II of Spain.

- Each county had its own main town where the sheriff lived and where the courts were located. Maryborough (present-day Portlaoise) became the principal town in Queen's County. Philipstown (present-day Daingean) was the main town in King's County.

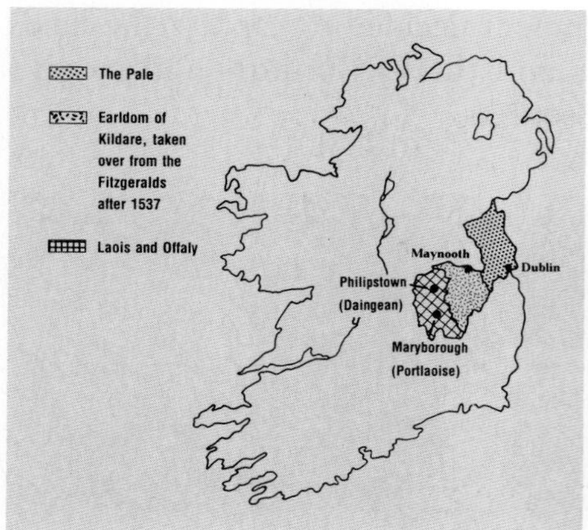

By the use of plantation, the Tudors had further extended English rule in Ireland.

The first plantation—success or failure?

From the beginning, the plantation of Laois and Offaly met with many difficulties. There were not enough English settlers to make the plantation a success. The O'Mores and the O'Connors were not easily defeated. They constantly attacked the new rulers who lived in fear of raids by the Gaelic clans.

However, future English rulers learned a lot from the first plantation and more successful plantations were later carried out in other parts of the country. The new approach, begun by Queen Mary, came to play a very important part in extending English rule throughout Ireland over the following hundred years.

Test your knowledge

1 What new policy was introduced by Queen Mary?
2 What Gaelic chieftains ruled over the lands of Laois and Offaly? In what way did they cause trouble for the English government?
3 How much of the land was given to new settlers?
4 What steps were taken to ensure that the settlers did not mix with the native Irish?
5 Name the two new counties into which the land was divided.
6 How did the towns of Maryborough and Philipstown get their names?
7 Give two reasons why the plantation of Laois and Offaly was not a success.

Chapter 33: Review

• A new approach to ruling Ireland was developed by the English government. This involved removing the Gaelic clans from their lands and replacing them with loyal English settlers.

• English rulers looked to the empires of Spain and Portugal in America where thousands of settlers had successfully built up plantations on estates given to them by their governments.

• Because most of the Irish remained Catholics, English governments distrusted them and preferred to introduce loyal Protestant English settlers.

• The first plantation in Ireland took place at Laois and Offaly during the reign of Queen Mary Tudor (1553–58).

• It was carried out on lands confiscated from the Gaelic clans, the O'Mores and the O'Connors, who had constantly attacked the Pale.

• Two-thirds of the land was set aside for English settlers. The remaining one-third, the worst land bordering the River Shannon, was given to the native Irish.

• English settlers had to build stone houses and keep armed followers for protection. They were forbidden to mix in any way with the native Irish.

• The lands were divided into two counties. Laois became Queen's County after Queen Mary, and Offaly was known as King's County in honour of her husband, Philip of Spain.

• Both counties had a main town: Maryborough (Portlaoise) in Laois and Philipstown (Daingean) in Offaly. Both of these towns contained forts and courthouses.

• The plantation of Laois and Offaly was not a success. There were not enough English settlers and the O'Mores and the O'Connors constantly attacked the plantation.

The Plantation of Munster

Elizabeth I (1558–1603)

On the death of Mary Tudor in 1558, her Protestant half-sister, Elizabeth, became queen of England. She, too, believed that plantations were a good way of extending English rule in Ireland.

The principal plantation in Ireland in Queen Elizabeth's time took place in Munster. The English government was able to carry out this plantation in the 1580s as a result of victory in war. To understand how the land became available, we must take a look at the rebellion which broke out in Munster in 1579.

Rebellion in Munster

The Earl of Desmond was a member of the Fitzgerald family. He was one of the most powerful men in Munster during Elizabeth I's reign. He owned vast areas of land stretching from Dingle in the west to Waterford in the east. Queen Elizabeth disliked the earl and the rest of the Fitzgerald family because they were Catholics.

When the Fitzgeralds rebelled against the queen, English forces marched through most of Munster, plundering and laying waste the territory of the Earl of Desmond and other rebels.

The destruction of Munster

The poet, Edmund Spenser, was in Ireland at the time of the rebellion in Munster. He has given us the following description of these events.

Edmund Spenser (1552–99).

Working with evidence

'Notwithstanding that Munster was a most rich and plentiful country, full of corn and cattle, before one year and a half, the people were brought to such wretchedness, as that any stoney heart would have regretted.

Out of every corner of the woods and glens they came creeping forth upon their hands, for their legs could not bear them. They looked like anatomies of death, they spoke like ghosts crying out of their graves. They did eat of the dead bodies, the very carcasses they took out of their graves.

If they found a plot of watercresses or shamrocks, there they flocked as to a feast for the time ... In a short space there were none almost left, and the most populous and beautiful country was suddenly made void of man and beast.'

1 According to Spenser, what was the condition of Munster before the rebellion?
2 Describe the way the starving people moved.
3 How does Spenser describe their appearance?
4 Give two examples of behaviour which show the extreme hunger of the people.
5 Do you think that Spenser had sympathy for the people of Munster? Explain your answer.

Sir Walter Raleigh (1552–1618) enjoying his first smoke. He was one of the first people to bring tobacco from America to Europe. In the plantation of Munster, Raleigh was given vast estates near Youghal in Co. Cork.

With the complete defeat of the Desmond Rebellion, the vast territories of the earl and his followers were taken over by Queen Elizabeth and preparations were made to plant them with loyal English settlers.

The plantation of Munster

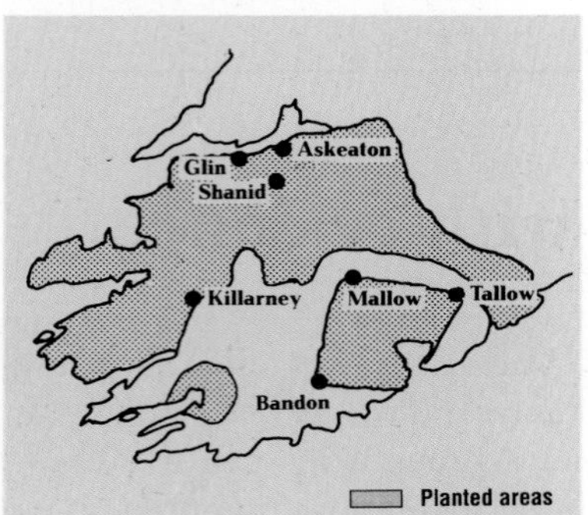

The rebellion in Munster gave the land-hungry English adventurers the opportunity they had been waiting for. The province lay burnt and devastated. Disease and famine were widespread, killing many who escaped death in the wars.

The English government now drew up new maps of the area in preparation for a plantation. Over half a million acres of land were taken from the Earl of Desmond alone. This was scattered throughout Cork, Kerry, Limerick and Waterford.

In 1586, Queen Elizabeth and her advisers approved a plan worked out for the plantation of Munster. The following rules are from the 'Scheme of Plantation' accepted by the queen on 21 June 1586.

Working with evidence

- Her Majesty doth assent that all lands which came into her hands in the Province of Munster shall be divided into estates of 12,000, 8,000, 6,000 and 4,000 acres.
- None shall undertake for himself a greater portion than 12,000 acres.
- None of the English people to be there planted shall make over an estate to the 'mere' Irish.
- No 'mere' Irish shall be permitted in any family there.
- For the next seven years, they shall be defended by garrisons at the queen's charge.

1 What was the largest type of estate under the Munster plantation?
2 Why do you think planters were not allowed to gain estates larger than this?
3 Were the planters allowed to grant land to the 'mere' Irish? Why do you think this was?
4 Why do you think marriage with 'mere' Irish was forbidden to the planters?
5 What protection did the queen offer the settlers in the early years of the plantation?

Although an upper limit of 12,000 acres was set on the size of estates under the Munster plantation, Sir Walter Raleigh, a favourite of Queen Elizabeth, received an estate of 42,000 acres near Youghal, Co. Cork.

These estates were to be rented out to English settlers known as undertakers. They got this name because they undertook or agreed to bring over English customs and the Protestant religion and, above all, to remain loyal to the queen. Many of the undertakers were the younger sons of lords from the western parts of England.

The undertakers were also expected to introduce English methods of farming to Munster and to avoid taking on the native Irish as tenants. The English government hoped that Munster would be loyal to the queen and safe from the threat of Spanish invasion in the future.

How the plantation worked

The plantation of Munster did not work out as well as the English government had hoped. Much of the land had been so badly damaged during the wars that it was difficult to farm it. There was also the constant danger of attack from the Irish who had been driven off their land. As a result, many planters returned to England in disappointment and only about 3,000 English settlers decided to remain. Because so few remained, they had to employ native Irish servants and labourers and to rent out land to them. This made the plantation insecure and likely to suffer from attack in the event of a future rebellion.

Despite these setbacks, those who chose to

remain enjoyed some prosperity for a while. They rebuilt ruined castles and houses, introduced new farming methods and became rich by exporting timber. By 1597, land which had fetched sixpence an acre ten years before was now being let at five times that amount.

The planters also built up plantation towns such as Bandon, Killarney and Tallow. These became centres for trade and the administration of law in the local area. By 1600, however, the new plantation was almost in ruin.

Test your knowledge

1 Describe the condition of Munster after the Desmond Rebellion.
2 How much land belonging to the Earl of Desmond was to be planted with new English settlers?
3 How was the land divided?
4 Who were the undertakers?
5 Write down two reasons why the plantation of Munster did not work out as well as expected.
6 Why were many native Irish servants and labourers employed by the settlers?
7 Name three plantation towns.

The plantation under attack

In their eagerness to build houses and develop their farms, the planters had neglected to provide enough soldiers to defend the plantation. In 1598, when Hugh O'Neill sent an army to Munster under Owney O'More, many of the native Irish and Old English joined in to attack the planters. Those who could not escape to England fled to walled towns such as Youghal, Cork or Limerick where they prepared to set sail for England. Those who failed to escape were killed and their castles and crops were burned.

The English government was to learn some valuable lessons from the plantation in Munster. The next major plantation took place in Ulster during the reign of Elizabeth's successor, James I (1603–25). We will see in the next chapter that much greater care was taken to ensure that the new plantation would be a success.

A planter family flee in terror from attack by the Gaelic Irish.

Chapter 34: Review

• Elizabeth I became queen of England in 1558. She believed that plantations were a good way of extending English rule in Ireland.

• In 1579, the Desmonds in Munster rose in rebellion against Queen Elizabeth. After their defeat, vast lands were confiscated by the English government and made available for plantation by English settlers.

• The plantation of Munster began in 1586 when all the confiscated lands were divided into large estates to be rented to English planters.

• The planters were forbidden to rent their estates to the native Irish or to marry among them.

• Sir Walter Raleigh, a favourite of Queen Elizabeth, was given a vast estate near Youghal in Co. Cork.

• The plantation faced a number of difficulties: the settlers were constantly attacked; many native Irish tenants and servants were employed; and the estates were too large.

• However, the planters introduced new farming methods to Munster as well as building castles and setting up new towns.

• The settlers neglected to defend themselves properly and the plantation was destroyed by the native Irish during a rebellion in 1598. After the defeat of the Irish at the Battle of Kinsale in 1601, the plantation of Munster was restored.

The Plantation of Ulster

The Gaelic chieftains of Ulster

Up to 1600, most of Ulster was still outside the control of the English government. In this part of Ireland the ancient Gaelic way of life still remained largely undisturbed. There were few towns and farming was carried out in the Gaelic manner. Catholic priests enjoyed the protection of the local chieftains.

All of this changed, however, after the Ulster plantation which began in 1609. With the arrival of the settlers from Scotland and England, Ulster would change from being the most Gaelic part of the country to become a stronghold of English customs and the Protestant religion. In order to understand how these huge changes came about, we must first discover how the land in most of Ulster was taken over by the English government.

The Nine Years War

Between 1594 and 1603, the leading Ulster Gaelic chieftains, Hugh O'Neill and Hugh O'Donnell, led a rebellion against the government of Queen Elizabeth. Although the fighting began in Ulster, it later spread throughout the country.

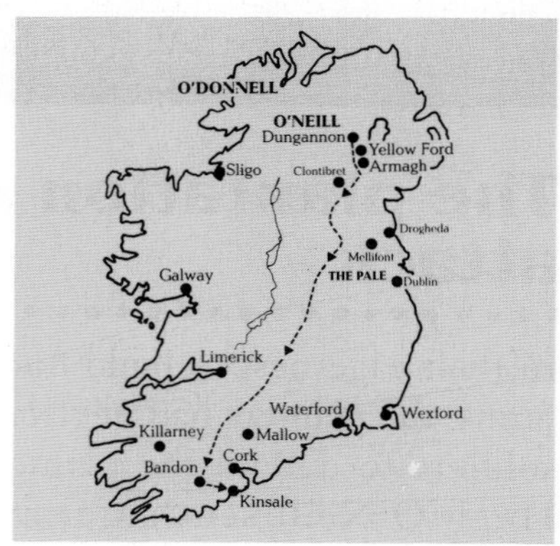

Ireland during the Nine Years War, showing O'Neill's march to Kinsale.

In 1598, O'Neill and his allies gained a huge victory over the English forces at the Battle of the Yellow Ford on the Ulster Blackwater. As we have seen in the last chapter, the rebellion spread to Munster and many English settlers were killed or forced to flee to the walled towns.

The Gaelic chieftains claimed that they were fighting to save the Catholic religion in Ireland. They therefore appealed to the Catholic king of Spain, an enemy of Queen Elizabeth, to send troops to Ireland. When the Spanish troops arrived, they landed at Kinsale in Co. Cork. In the Battle of Kinsale, fought on Christmas Eve in 1601, the English under Lord Mountjoy defeated a combined force of Irish and Spanish troops. This defeat proved decisive for the Gaelic chieftains and their people.

Hugh O'Neill surrendering to Mountjoy at Mellifont in 1603.

The English were determined to destroy the power of the Ulster chieftains. Under the Treaty of Mellifont, signed in March 1603, Hugh O'Neill promised to give up Gaelic customs, to live according to English law, and to allow English officials as sheriffs into his territory.

Some of the English officials were very annoyed that O'Neill and the other Ulster chieftains had been allowed to keep their lands. They had hoped that the government would take over these territories and divide them among English settlers, including themselves.

The new Lord Deputy, Sir Arthur Chichester, travelled around Ulster enforcing English laws and customs. By 1607, O'Neill and the other Gaelic chieftains could no longer put up with the restrictions on their power. They decided to leave Ireland forever.

Test your knowledge

1 Name the two most powerful Gaelic clans in Ulster.
2 Give two examples which prove that before 1600 most of Ulster was outside the control of the English government.
3 Who won the Battle of the Yellow Ford in 1598?
4 Why did O'Neill appeal to the king of Spain for help against Elizabeth I?
5 Name the English commander at the Battle of Kinsale.
6 Explain the outcome of the Battle of Kinsale.
7 What was the Treaty of Mellifont?
8 What did Sir Arthur Chichester do in Ulster after 1603?

The Flight of the Earls

In September 1607, Hugh O'Neill, Earl of Tyrone and Rory O'Donnell, Earl of Tyrconnell, set sail from Lough Swilly for the continent of Europe. They were accompanied by around a hundred followers from the leading Gaelic families in Ulster. O'Neill had been called to London, and knowing that he risked possible execution, he and his followers decided on sudden flight from Ireland. This event has become known as the Flight of the Earls. The Irish people in Ulster were now leaderless and the province was completely in the control of the English government.

The Flight of the Earls.

O'Neill and the other chieftains failed to get the king of Spain and the pope to intervene in Ireland once again. By the time of his death in Rome in 1616, the once-powerful Hugh O'Neill was worn out by blindness, disease and disappointment. Back in Ireland, Sir Arthur Chichester and other English officials were delighted when the Flight of the Earls took place. Now at last they could take control of vast parts of Ulster and hand over land to English and Scottish settlers who would practise the Protestant religion and remain loyal to the king.

The plantation of Ulster

King James I (1603–25) became king of England on the death of Elizabeth I in 1603. Under his rule, the Ulster Plantation took place.

After the Flight of the Earls, six of the nine counties of Ulster were taken over directly by King James I. These counties—Donegal, Derry, Fermanagh, Tyrone, Armagh and Cavan—were to be part of a vast plantation by English and Scottish settlers. Three Ulster counties were not included in this plantation: Monaghan, Antrim and Down.

Co. Monaghan had been taken over by Elizabeth I in 1591 and handed back to its former rulers, the MacMahons and MacKennas, provided that they remained loyal to England. Counties Antrim and Down had already been settled by colonists from Scotland.

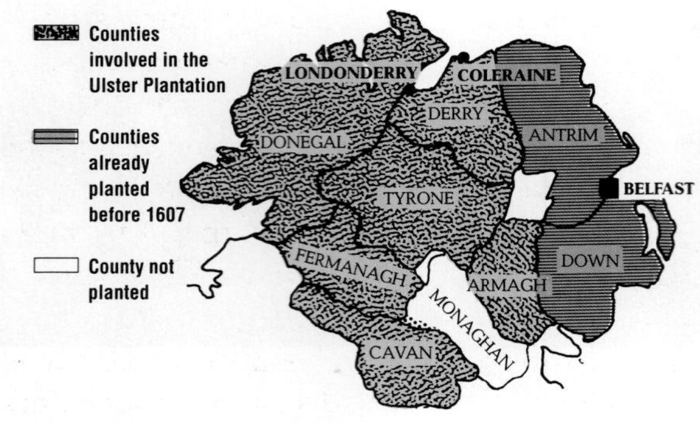

The Plantation of Ulster.

In 1608, Sir Cahir O'Doherty, a Gaelic chieftain in Inishowen, Co. Donegal, rebelled. After his defeat and execution, his lands were added to the plantation area.

Preparations are made

In 1609, English officials and soldiers travelled throughout the six counties which were to be planted. They made a detailed examination of the area and drew up maps. The maps only contained two colours. Land belonging to the Protestant Church of Ireland could not be taken over, so it was shaded in, in one colour. All other land was declared to belong to the king and was given another colour.

When the study of Ulster was completed, nearly 4 million acres were ready for plantation. King James himself was interested in plantations, especially the English one in the American colony of Virginia. He therefore gave his full approval to the new Ulster plantation which he hoped would place loyal Protestants in control of the area.

Test your knowledge

1 What counties in Ulster were taken over by James I after the Flight of the Earls?
2 What did James I plan to do with these counties?
3 What three counties were not to be included in the plantation of Ulster? Why?
4 How much land was to be included in the plantation?

The rules of the plantation

James I and his advisers were determined to avoid the mistakes made during the earlier plantations in Laois-Offaly under Queen Mary and in Munster under Queen Elizabeth I. In both of these earlier plantations, the new English planters had brought few farmers and workers over with them. Instead, they let out farms to Irish tenants and employed Irish workers. The Ulster plantation was to be different: planters were ordered to bring over English and Scottish tenants and craftsmen to build up the new plantation.

Under the plantation rules there were three types of planter: undertakers, servitors and Irish landowners.

Undertakers

These were English or Scottish gentlemen who were to receive estates of 2,000, 1,500 acres or 1,000 acres to rent of £5.33 per 1,000 acres. The rent was low because of the expenses they ran up in bringing Scottish and English tenants to Ulster. They were not allowed to rent land to Irish tenants.

Servitors

These were men who had served the king either as soldiers or as officials. They usually got estates of 1,000 acres at a rent of £8. They were allowed to take Irish tenants.

Irish Landowners

A small part of land was given to Irish gentlemen who were loyal to the king. These people were removed from their old homes, however, and placed near English servitors, who were to watch over them. Irish landowners were allowed to take Irish tenants and had to pay a rent of £10.66 for 1,000 acres.

The undertakers and servitors were expected to build a defensive enclosure, or *bawn*, to defend their settlements from attack by the Irish whose lands they had taken over. Planters with 1,500 acres had to build a stone house inside the bawn. Those with 2,000 acres had to build a castle. In case of attack, the planter and his family, his tenants and their animals could shelter inside the bawn.

A well defended castle of an Ulster planter, surrounded by a bawn.

The Ulster plantation was started in 1609. It developed steadily and by 1618 there were about 40,000 English and Scottish settlers in Ulster. However, the plantation did not work out quite as well as the English government had hoped.

Test your knowledge

1 In what ways was the Ulster plantation going to be different from earlier plantations in Laois-Offaly and Munster?

2 Name the three types of planter to be given land.

3 Who were: (a) the undertakers; (b) the servitors?

4 How were the settlers to defend themselves against attack?

5 When did the Ulster plantation begin? How many settlers had arrived by 1618?

The plantation in action

From the start, the government could not persuade enough undertakers to go to Ulster. As a result, James I forced London trade guilds to take part. These were rich groups of businessmen such as goldsmiths or cloth merchants. They were given Co. Derry at the same rent as the undertakers. These businessmen formed the Irish Society and let out the land to tenants. They built two towns, Coleraine and Derry, which was later renamed Londonderry.

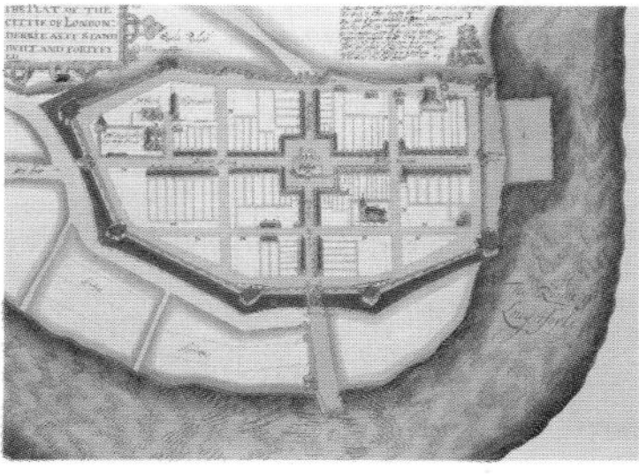

Plan of the plantation town of Londonderry.

The government had another problem to face as well as the shortage of undertakers. Existing undertakers were breaking the rules by renting land to Irish tenants and employing Irish workers. Irish tenants were willing to pay higher rents than English or Scottish farmers. Irish workers were needed to build up the colony as there was a shortage of workers. Despite repeated warnings from the government, undertakers continued to take on Irish tenants and workers.

Conditions were harsh and dangerous for the new settlers. The Irish who had lost their lands often attacked the settlers and drove away their cattle.

Travel was especially dangerous for the planters as they were liable to attack, robbery and even death when passing through wild parts of the countryside.

Most settlers lived in isolated little villages centred on the house of the planter with its protective bawn. A few workers, a teacher and a clergyman with his small church usually completed the settlement. Some of the settlers brought a new style of living to Ulster—the life of the town.

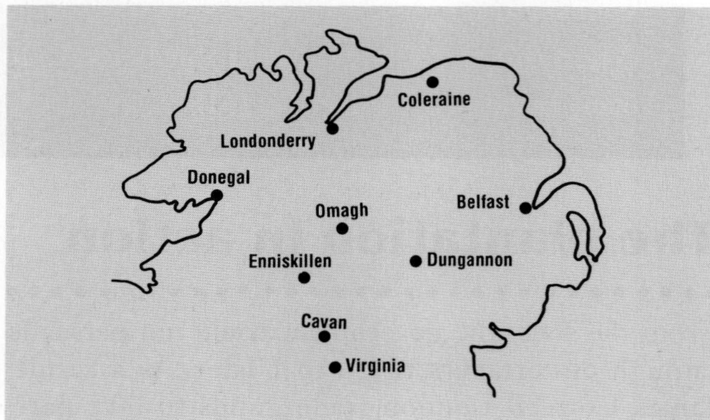

The principal plantation towns in Ulster.

Test your knowledge

1 What were the London trade guilds? What part did they play in the plantation of Ulster?

2 Why did the undertaker rent land to Irish tenants and employ Irish workers?

3 Why were conditions dangerous for the new settlers?

4 Where did most of the settlers live?

The plantation towns

Before the defeat of the Gaelic chieftains and the plantation of Ulster, towns were practically unknown in the province. Only Carrickfergus and Newry existed as towns in 1600. While Gaelic chieftains did not build towns, the English believed that towns were centres of order and civilisation. New towns were part of the plan drawn up for the plantation of Ulster.

The plan of the plantation towns was very simple. There was a square or diamond-shaped market–place in the centre where important buildings such as the church and townhall were situated. Four streets led away from the market–place at right angles. As a means of defence, towns were usually surrounded by high walls or earthen banks. The new towns soon became important, as local markets, fairs and court cases were held there. The sites for the towns were carefully chosen and some of them developed into important centres of population such as Belfast, Enniskillen and Omagh.

The new Ulster towns were usually given a charter by the king which allowed them to be ruled by a council or corporation. These corporations usually contained twelve members known as *burgesses*. Burgesses had to be members of the Protestant Church of Ireland. Each year they elected one of their members to be head of the town. This man was known as the *provost* or the *sovereign*. If a burgess died, the others could elect someone to take his place. Another important privilege held by burgesses was the right to elect members of parliament to represent the town.

Test your knowledge

1 What two towns existed in Ulster before the plantation?

2 Describe the new plantation towns.

3 Name three towns set up as a result of the Ulster plantation.

4 Who were the burgesses?

The results of the Ulster plantation

The Ulster plantation was the first English plantation in Ireland which was largely successful. Although many Irish people remained as tenants in the planted areas, most of the best land in the area was now in the hands of English and Scottish planters. These succeeded in introducing the English language and English customs into Ulster. The Scottish settlers especially brought in a new way of life, completely dependent on hard work, and a determination to get on in life.

The most lasting result of the Ulster plantation concerned religion. The Protestant settlers soon came to outnumber the Catholic Irish in Ulster. Most English settlers belonged to the Church of Ireland which was ruled by King James. The Scottish settlers, however, were mainly Presbyterians or followers of John Calvin. This stern religion was responsible for their hardworking lives. It was also the cause of their bitter hatred of the Catholic religion. From the time of the plantation onwards, Ulster has been divided with the Catholic Irish on the one side and the Protestant descendants of the plantation settlers on the other.

The plantation of Ulster

Flight of the Earls 1607
↓
Plantation of Ulster 1609
↓
Land given to Undertakers, Servitors, Irish Landlords
↓
New Plantation towns— Belfast, Enniskillen, Omagh
↓
Ulster plantation was largely successful

Test your knowledge

1 Was the Ulster plantation a success? Explain why.
2 What customs did the settlers bring to Ulster?
3 What religious beliefs were held by the new Scottish settlers?
4 What religious divisions were created in Ulster as a result of the plantation?

Chapter 35: Review

• In Ulster up to 1600 the Gaelic chieftains controlled most of the land. The ancient Gaelic way of life continued, and there were few towns.

• Between 1594 and 1603, the leading Ulster Gaelic chieftains, Hugh O'Neill and Hugh O'Donnell, led a rebellion against Queen Elizabeth known as the Nine Years War.

• Despite earlier Gaelic victories such as the Battle of the Yellow Ford (1598), the Irish were eventually defeated at the decisive Battle of Kinsale (1601).

• Under the Treaty of Mellifont (1603), Hugh O'Neill promised to give up Gaelic customs, to live according to English law and to allow English officials into his territory.

• In 1607, the Gaelic chieftains of Ulster left Ireland forever. This event became known as the Flight of the Earls and it prepared the way for the plantation of Ulster.

• Six of the nine counties of Ulster were taken over by the English government and a detailed survey took place in preparation for a plantation by English and Scottish settlers.

• Three types of planters arrived in Ulster—undertakers (English or Scottish gentlemen receiving estates of 2,000, 1,500 or 1,000 acres); servitors (men who had served the king as soldiers or officials); and Irish landowners who were loyal to the king.

• By 1618 there were about 40,000 English and Scottish settlers in Ulster. However, not enough undertakers arrived. In addition, land was rented out to Irish tenants, and Irish labourers were employed. The settlers were also constantly attacked by those Gaelic Irish who had lost their land.

• Many new plantation towns were set up. These included Belfast, Enniskillen, and Omagh. Each town usually had a market square in the centre. It had its own charter and was ruled by a council or corporation.

• Overall, the Ulster plantation was a success. English and Scottish customs were introduced into the area and the best land was in the hands of the settlers. As a result of the plantation, Ulster was to have deep religious divisions between Protestants and Catholics.

CHAPTER 36 The Cromwellian Plantation

A land of war and rebellion

For thirty years after the Ulster plantation, there were peaceful conditions both in Ulster and throughout Ireland. All the time, however, the Gaelic Irish in Ulster were waiting for a suitable opportunity to rise in rebellion and drive the Scottish and English settlers from the lands which were once theirs. In October 1641, rebellion broke out in Ulster. Over 10,000 settlers were killed by the Irish rebels and many more fled to the walled towns for safety.

Exaggerated stories soon spread regarding the massacre. Some writers claimed that 300,000 Protestants had been killed, about thirty times the true figure. Protestants in England were outraged at these events and waited for an opportunity to send an army against the Ulster rebels.

For the next eight years, however, England was the scene of a fiercely fought civil war between King Charles I (1625–49) and the extreme Protestants or Puritans led by Oliver Cromwell. The fighting also spread to Ireland where armies supporting both sides fought each other. After the execution of King Charles I in 1649, the new ruler of England, Oliver Cromwell, was free to go to Ireland to gain control of the country and to seek revenge for the massacre of Protestants in 1641.

It was under Cromwell's rule that the last major plantation in Ireland took place. In order to see how that plantation came about, we must first look at the actions of Oliver Cromwell on his arrival in Ireland.

Oliver Cromwell, the Lord Protector of England, landed at Ringsend near Dublin in August 1649 with an army of 12,000 experienced soldiers.

A Protestant artist's view of the sufferings of fellow Protestants in Ulster during the rebellion of 1641.

Test your knowledge

1 What ambition had the Gaelic Irish in Ulster after the plantation had taken place?

2 When did a rebellion break out in Ulster?

3 Describe the fate of the settlers.

4 What was the reaction of English Protestants to the events in Ulster in 1641?

5 Name the English king who was executed in 1649.

6 Who became the new ruler of England?

Cromwell arrives in Ireland

On 13 August 1649, Oliver Cromwell and his army of 12,000 experienced soldiers landed at Ringsend near Dublin. He did not remain in Dublin, but set out with his army for Drogheda. This important town blocked the way to Ulster.

Cromwell's capture of Drogheda and the massacre which followed blackened his name in Ireland forever. Read the following account of Cromwell's capture of Drogheda. It was written by an English army officer.

Cromwell attacking the town of Drogheda.

Working with evidence

'After landing at Ringsend, Cromwell marched into Dublin and gathered his army together at Oxmantown Green, just north of the Liffey. He then marched to Drogheda in order to capture it for the English Commonwealth.

As soon as Cromwell came before the walls of Drogheda, he sent his trumpet player to sound an alarm and call on those inside to surrender up the town. But they answered no, that until they lost their lives they would not hand over the king's soldiers to such a notorious enemy of His Majesty.

After this Cromwell ordered his troops to bombard the walls of the town with cannon fire. After a few days they made a breach in the wall at the south side of the town. Twice Cromwell's men tried to enter through this breach but were beaten back with great loss. At a third attempt, Cromwell himself led them and they succeeded in entering this time but had to fight hard in the streets.

Once the Irish were defeated they were all cut down and killed and no mercy was shown to man, woman or child for twenty-four hours. Not a dozen people escaped out of Drogheda, townspeople or soldiers.

After he captured Drogheda, Cromwell marched south to capture the rest of the country.'

1 What did Cromwell do after landing at Ringsend?
2 Describe Cromwell's actions on reaching the walls of Drogheda.
3 Why did the defenders of Drogheda refuse to surrender?
4 How did Cromwell's army eventually capture the town?
5 Describe the massacre which followed.
6 What did Cromwell and his army do after capturing Drogheda?

Cromwell captures the rest of Ireland

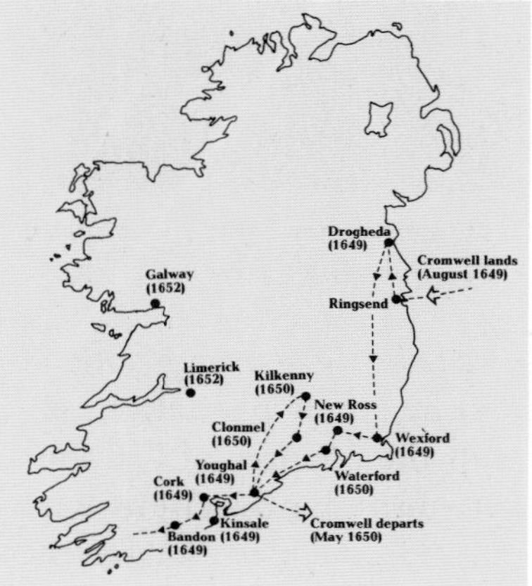

Cromwell's campaign in Ireland.

When news reached other towns of Cromwell's actions in Drogheda, their people surrendered to avoid massacre. Take a close look at the map to see how the rest of Ireland was brought under Cromwell's control.

With Ireland conquered, it now remained for Cromwell and the English parliament to decide what to do with the country.

The Cromwellian plantation

By 1652, Ireland was a country worn out by ten years of warfare. Famine and plague were widespread. Wolves roamed the countryside and even came into the neighbourhood of the towns in search of food.

Because so many men had died in war, and with many Irish soldiers going overseas, large numbers of women and children were unprovided for. The English government had these rounded up and sold as slaves to work in the sugar plantations in the West Indies.

Some Catholic priests were also transported to the West Indies. Anyone who handed over a priest to the authorities was paid a reward of £5. Cromwell and the government hoped that the Catholic religion would die out in Ireland from lack of priests. However, many priests remained in Ireland where they disguised themselves as lay people. They said Mass in the houses of rich Catholics or in desolate places hidden away in the countryside.

Catholics prayed in the open air when they were not allowed the freedom to practise their religion during Cromwell's rule.

Cromwell's principal method of gaining control in Ireland, however, was to be a new plantation. He believed in clearing most of the country of Catholic landowners and of Protestant landowners who remained loyal to the king. He decided to give the land to Englishmen who supported the parliament and to soldiers who had fought for him in the civil war. Cromwell also needed the land to pay the adventurers who had given money to the English parliament in exchange for promises of land in Ireland.

Before a new plantation could take place, however, the land had first to be surveyed and mapped.

Sir William Petty and the Down Survey

In 1653, mapmakers accompanied by soldiers travelled throughout the country, questioning local people, measuring the land and drawing maps. Progress was very slow, however, and those expecting grants of land in the plantation began to complain.

In 1654, Sir William Petty, a thirty-one-year-old army doctor, offered to complete the survey within thirteen months at a lower cost. His offer was accepted by the government and the result was the *Down Survey*, so named simply because the results were written down! Petty's surveyors were guarded by armed soldiers to protect them from the *tories*, or Irish outlaws. Despite all obstacles, the Down Survey was completed on time and Petty was richly rewarded for his work. As well as his fee of over £18,000, he also gained a vast estate near Kenmare in Co. Kerry.

The Down Survey maps were the most accurate to be produced in Ireland until that time. They were the best maps available until Ordnance Survey maps appeared in the 1840s.

Now that the country was surveyed and mapped, Cromwell's government was ready to go ahead with the plantation.

Test your knowledge

1 Why were large numbers of women and children left unprovided for in Ireland by 1652?

2 How did the government deal with these people?

3 What reward was paid to those who handed over the Catholic priests to the authorities?

4 Did Cromwell's government succeed in getting rid of all Catholic priests from Ireland?

5 What landowners did Cromwell wish to clear from their lands?

6 Why did he need land in Ireland?

7 Who was Sir William Petty? With what is his name associated?

8 Why was the Down Survey given its name?

9 Who were the tories in the 1650s?

'To Hell or to Connaught'

Most of Munster, Leinster and Connaught were taken over by Cromwell's government because the landowners in these provinces had fought against the English parliament. Under the *Act of Settlement*

(1652) leaders of the rebellion were to lose all their lands along with their lives. Those who could not prove that they had been loyal to the parliament were to lose part of their lands. They were also to be transplanted to Connaught where they could exchange their old estates for poorer new lands.

All transplanted landowners were ordered to be west of the river Shannon by May 1654. This gave rise to the saying 'To Hell or to Connaught'. They were to be kept in Connaught behind the barrier of the Shannon. There was to be a mile-wide stretch along the Shannon and the west coast reserved for soldiers. This was designed as a means of providing security against the Irish landowners.

Only the landowners were ordered to Connaught. Ordinary farmers and labourers remained behind to work for their new English landlords.

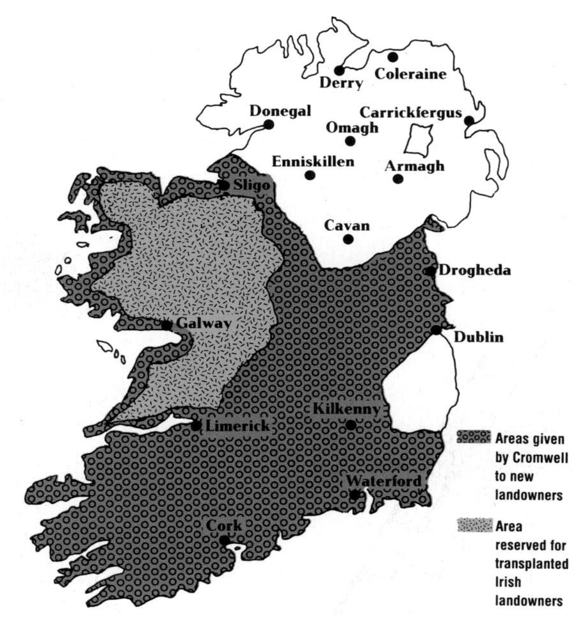

The Cromwellian Plantation of Ireland.

The results of the Cromwellian plantation

The Cromwellian plantation did not work out as well as Cromwell and the English government had hoped:

- Many English adventurers never came to live on their estates but sold them to rich landlords.
- Many soldier-settlers married Catholic women and their children were brought up as Catholics.
- Tories and other Irish outlaws frequently attacked the new planters.

Despite these setbacks, the Cromwellian plantation had important long-term effects on land ownership:

- Before 1641, Catholic landowners owned large parts of Munster, Connaught and Leinster. After the plantation, Catholics were confined to the poorer land west of the Shannon.
- Many of the new landowners and their descendants were *absentees*. They lived in England where they spent the rent collected from their Irish estates.
- All land and property in the towns was taken from Catholics and transferred to Protestants. Catholics lost all positions on town councils. This situation was to last for nearly 200 years.

Although not the largest of the plantations, the Cromwellian plantation had the greatest long-term effect on land ownership. As a result of the changes which it brought about, Ireland became a land deeply divided between Protestant landlords and Catholic tenants for the next two centuries.

Test your knowledge

1 Explain the Act of Settlement (1652).
2 What is meant by the saying 'To Hell or to Connaught'?
3 List two threats to the success of the plantation.
4 What effect had the plantation on Catholic landowners?
5 What is meant by absentees?
6 Explain how Cromwell's government changed the conditions of Catholics in towns.

The Protestant landowners

We have seen in the last few chapters how the land of Ireland changed hands as a result of a number of plantations. Because of the plantations the amount of land owned by Catholics was greatly reduced. Whereas ninety per cent of the land was owned by Catholics in 1600, a hundred years later only fifteen per cent of the land remained in Catholic hands.

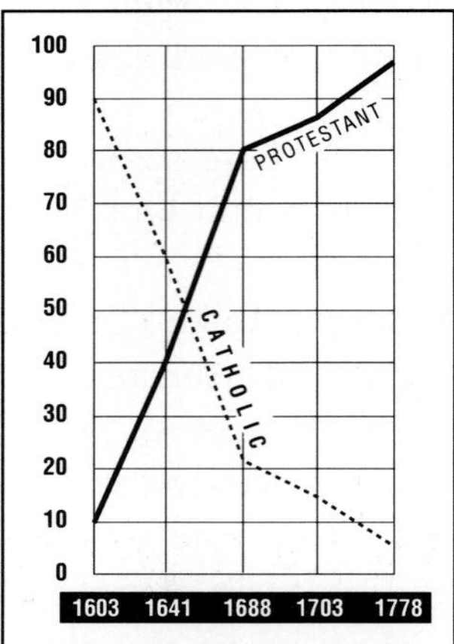

The transfer of land ownership between 1603 and 1778.

As a result of this change in land ownership, a small number of rich Protestant landlords ruled in Ireland. This group became known as the *Protestant Ascendancy*. Because they feared the Catholic masses, they believed in keeping as much land as possible in Protestant hands.

The Protestant landlords rented out the land to Irish tenants. The ordinary people believed that they were tenants on land which had been owned by their ancestors. They never lost hope of recovering these lands whether by violent or peaceful means.

Although the control of land by English landlords often led to violent action on the part of tenants, it would be largely by peaceful means that the plantation settlements were eventually overturned from 1880 onwards and the native Irish became owners of the land once more.

Chapter 36: Review

- For thirty years after the Ulster plantation, there were peaceful conditions throughout Ireland. In 1641, however, a rebellion broke out in Ulster and throughout Ireland.

- Because many Protestant settlers were massacred in Ulster during the Rebellion of 1641, English Protestant leaders planned to gain revenge. Their opportunity arrived when the new ruler of England, Oliver Cromwell, arrived in Ireland with a large army in 1649.

- After his arrival in Dublin, Cromwell marched to the town of Drogheda where he carried out a massacre of the townspeople.

- Frightened by the news from Drogheda, people in the rest of Ireland soon surrendered to Cromwell's armies.

- By 1652, Ireland was a country worn out by ten years of warfare and on the brink of starvation. Cromwell now tried to wipe out the Catholic religion in Ireland by executing or transporting many Catholic priests.

- Plantation was the main method used by Cromwell to control Ireland. He decided to give Irish lands to Englishmen who supported the parliament and to soldiers who had fought for him in the civil war.

- In 1654, Sir William Petty surveyed and mapped the area to be 'planted'. His work was called the Down Survey. His maps were the most accurate yet produced in Ireland.

- Most of Munster, Leinster and Connaught were to be taken over by Cromwell's government for the plantation. All those evicted from their land were ordered to be west of the Shannon by May 1654.

- The Cromwellian plantation did not work out as well as expected. Many English adventurers never came to live on their estates; many soldier-settlers married Catholic women. At the same time, however, the plantation brought about major changes in land ownership.

- Because of the various plantations the amount of Irish land owned by Catholics fell from ninety per cent in 1600 to fifteen per cent by 1700.

- The native Irish never gave up hope of recovering their lost lands. From 1880 onwards, they were to become owners of the land once again.

Political Revolutions

CHAPTER 37

A New Nation is Born

A powerful land

Each year on 4 July, Americans everywhere celebrate Independence Day. On that day, in the year 1776, a small group of men signed a document called the *Declaration of Independence*. This claimed that the United States of America wished to break away from the rule of the king of England.

John F. Kennedy, President of the United States of America 1961–63.

An American postcard celebrating Independence Day.

This event was one of the most important happenings in history. Today, the United States is the richest and most powerful country in the world. Irish emigrants played a very important part in building up this powerful nation. Many presidents of the US were descendants of Irish emigrants, including John F. Kennedy who was assassinated in 1963.

Today, American ideas have a great influence on how we live our lives. Many films and television programmes come from America. Here in Ireland, there are factories and restaurants which have been set up by American business people.

In the next three chapters we will travel back in time and trace the beginnings of this rich and powerful country.

British colonies in North America

We have already seen that Spain and Portugal set up vast empires in Mexico and South America in the sixteenth century. As you can see from the map on page 167, the area at present covering the United States and Canada was developed by British and French explorers and settlers.

A North American Indian chief. The native Indians greatly resented the arrival of settlers from Europe who took over their lands by force.

French settlers took over parts of Canada after a Frenchman named Jacques Cartier discovered the St Lawrence River and founded Montreal in 1535. They also travelled down the Mississippi River and founded the province of Louisiana and the town of New Orleans.

However, the eastern coast of the present-day United States was mostly colonised by English settlers. Indeed, the northern part of this territory became known as New England.

The first English colony was set up by Sir Walter Raleigh. He called the area Virginia in honour of Queen Elizabeth I, the 'Virgin Queen'. The early colonists had to endure dreadful suffering. One of them, George Percy, has left the following account of their troubles.

Working with evidence

'Our men were destroyed with cruel diseases, such as swelling and burning fevers, and by wars. And some departed suddenly but for the most part they died by mere famine. Our food was but a small can of barley sod in water to five men a day, our drink, cold water taken out of the river, which was at flood very salty, at low tide of slime and filth. Thus we lived for the space of five months in this miserable distress, our men night and day groaning in every corner of the fort most pitiful to hear.'

1 List the main causes of death among the soldiers.
2 Describe the food eaten by the men.
3 How was the drinking water contaminated in different ways?
4 For how long did these conditions last?

In search of freedom

Although many English settlers came to North America in search of greater wealth, others came to escape from the persecution in England which they suffered because of their religious beliefs. In the 1630s an English Catholic nobleman, Lord Baltimore, set up a colony north of Virginia called Maryland as a refuge for Catholics fleeing from persecution in England.

Catholics were not the only group to flee from religious persecution in England. Presbyterians or Puritans were also persecuted. These were very strict Protestants, and in 1620 a group of them set sail from Plymouth in southern England for the coast of North America. Known as the *Pilgrim Fathers*, they hoped to reach Virginia in their ship, the *Mayflower*.

The Mayflower, *which carried the Pilgrim Fathers from England to the New World.*

The ship was blown off course, however, and on 15 December 1620, the Pilgrim Fathers landed at Cape Cod, Massachusetts, a few hundred kilometres to the north of Virginia. Although half of the group of around a hundred died in that terrible first winter, the Puritan colony survived and later prospered when more settlers arrived from England. In time the Massachusetts settlers founded other colonies in New England such as Connecticut, Rhode Island and New Hampshire.

Settlers on their way to a prayer service in November 1621 to give thanks for their first successful harvest. Each November, Americans still celebrate this historic event on Thanksgiving Day.

In 1664, British forces captured the settlement of New Amsterdam from the Dutch and renamed it New York. Further south, a Quaker leader named William Penn set

William Penn, who set up the colony of Pennsylvania, reaching an agreement with the native Indians.

up the colony of Pennsylvania as a refuge for persecuted Quakers. To the south of Virginia lay the colonies of North Carolina, South Carolina and Georgia which were lands of huge plantations worked by black slaves.

An American buying slaves in Africa. These people were then shipped to America to work on southern plantations.

Life in the colonies

By 1750 around 2 million people lived in the British colonies in North America. Life was much more comfortable for many colonists than it was for most people in Europe. The largest city in the colonies, Philadelphia, impressed an English naval officer who visited it in 1756.

'The nobleness of the town surprised me more than the fertile appearance of the country. I had no idea of finding a place in America consisting of near 2,000 houses, elegantly built of brick, raised on an eminence with streets paved and spacious, furnished with commodious quays and warehouses employing some hundreds of vessels in its foreign trade and fisheries—but such is this city that very few in England can rival it in its show.'

The Americans were very proud of the growing wealth of the colonies and of their whole way of life. Because of the threat from native Indians and from French settlers on the borders of the colonies, most men were trained in the use of guns. They were therefore well prepared when a war eventually broke out between the forces of Great Britain and the American colonists in 1775.

The British colonies in North America around 1750.

Test your knowledge

1 What area of America was colonised by French settlers?
2 Where was the first English colony in America and who set it up?
3 What difficulties did the early settlers experience?
4 Who were the Pilgrim Fathers?
5 Use the map to name the English colonies in America.
6 Is the naval officer's account of Philadelphia a primary or secondary source?
7 What can we learn about Philadelphia from this source?
8 Why were most men in the colonies trained in the use of guns?

King George III and the American colonies

The struggle for independence from England carried out by the American colonists took place during the reign of King George III who became king of England at the age of twenty in 1760. He was a very stubborn man and was determined that his American subjects should obey all the wishes of the British parliament.

King George III (1760–1820).

In particular, the king and his government ministers believed that the Americans should pay more taxes to cover the cost of sending British soldiers, ships and sailors to protect them. The British parliament in London passed the *Stamp Act* in 1765 to raise more tax in America. This tax placed stamp duties on official documents such as wills and liquor licences as well as on public documents such as newspapers and pamphlets.

The Americans were outraged when news of this reached them from England. Because they did not elect Members of Parliament to the British House of Commons in England, the colonists believed that this parliament had no right to tax them. This belief was known as '*No taxation without representation*' and it was one of the main causes of the American War of Independence.

Because of violent opposition in America, the British parliament repealed, or cancelled, the Stamp Act and replaced it with the *Townshend Acts* which placed large customs duties on glass, paints, lead, paper and tea. The American colonists were in an angry mood and felt that they had been tricked by the British government.

Although people living throughout the colonies were against the new taxes, the strongest opposition was to be found in the town of Boston, the capital of Massachusetts.

A British tax collector being chased out of town by an angry mob in Boston.

Test your knowledge

1 Who was king of England when the colonists began their struggle for independence?
2 Why did the king believe that the Americans should pay more taxes?
3 What was the Stamp Act?
4 How did the colonists react to this?
5 What was meant by 'No taxation without representation'?
6 Why do you think the American colonists felt that they had been tricked by the British government?

Chapter 37: Review

- Each year on 4 July, Americans celebrate Independence Day. This commemorates the Declaration of Independence from Great Britain which was signed on 4 July 1776.

- The Spanish and Portuguese had empires in Central and South America. Farther north, the area at present covering the United States and Canada was developed by British and French colonists.

- The first English colony was set up in Virginia by Sir Walter Raleigh during the reign of Queen Elizabeth I.

- Although many English settlers came to North America to make their fortunes, some came to avoid religious persecution at home. These included Catholics who settled in Maryland, Quakers who came to Pennsylvania and the Puritan Pilgrim Fathers who set up colonies in New England.

- Around 1750, about 2 million people lived in the British colonies in North America. Despite threats from French settlers and Indians, many colonists were prosperous. The largest city, Philadelphia, was rich and spacious.

- During the early years of the reign of King George III (1760–1820), the British government imposed higher taxes on the American colonists to help pay the cost of defending them from attack.

- The Stamp Act (1765) passed by the British parliament in London placed stamp duties or taxes on official documents and newspapers in America.

- Many Americans opposed the Stamp Act because they did not elect MPs to the parliament in London. Their slogan was 'No taxation without representation'.

Americans look for Freedom

Boston town

Ships at anchor in the busy port of Boston.

Boston in Massachusetts was a busy port and many people living there earned their money from foreign trade. When extra numbers of British troops were sent to the town, there were frequent street fights involving soldiers and local gangs. In March 1770, a serious incident known as the *Boston Massacre* took place. After a group of soldiers had been mocked by a local mob they opened fire, killing five and wounding seven.

This famous picture of the 'Boston Massacre' was printed by an anti-British American called Paul Revere. In what way do you think that this may be a biased view?

Immediately anti-British Americans published exaggerated accounts of the massacre in newspapers and pamphlets throughout the colonies. They hoped to turn more and more people against British rule in North America.

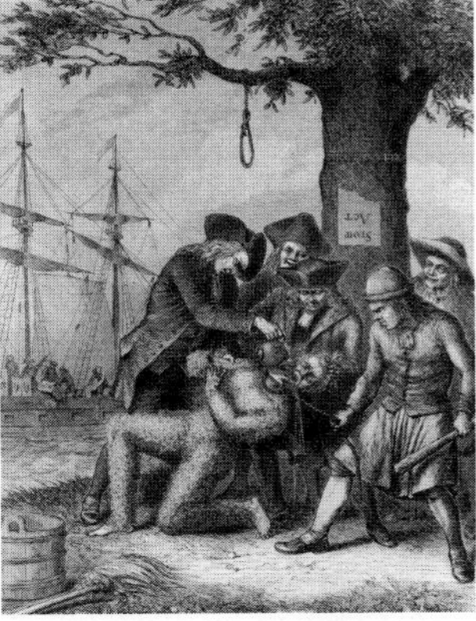

An unfortunate collector of the tea tax is tarred and feathered and forced to drink smuggled tea by some angry citizens of Boston.

Before news of the massacre reached London, the British parliament had already removed the duties on all goods entering North America except for those on tea. These were kept to show that the government in London believed it had the right to tax the American colonists.

The Boston Tea Party (1773)

The Americans refused to pay the tea duty. For the next few years, New England traders smuggled large amounts of tea into the country.

The Boston Tea Party.

In November 1773, English ships carrying tea landed in Boston harbour. Groups of local people asked the owners of the ships to return to London with the tea. When the British governor and the customs officers refused to allow this, the local people held a secret meeting. They decided to go on board the ships and dump the tea into Boston harbour.

A newspaper of the time, the *Massachusetts Gazette*, gives us this account of the exciting events which followed.

Working with evidence

'Just before the end of the meeting a number of brave men, dressed in the Indian manner, approached the door of the Assembly and gave a war whoop which was answered by some in the galleries ... The "Indians" as they were then called made their way to the wharf where the ships lay that had the tea on board. They were followed by hundreds of people who wished to see what would happen. The "Indians" immediately went on board Captain Hall's ship, where they hoisted out chests of tea, moved them up on deck, broke them and emptied the tea overboard. Having cleared this ship they proceeded to Captain Bruce's and then to Captain Coffin's ship ... In the space of three hours they broke up 342 chests which was the whole number in these vessels, and discharged their content into the dock. When the tide rose it floated the broken chests and the surface of the water was filled with the tea.'

1 Why were those who took part in these events known as 'Indians'?
2 What did the 'Indians' do when they went on board Captain Hall's ship?
3 How long did it take them to empty the vessels of all the tea?
4 Do you think this newspaper account is in any way biased? Explain your answer.

Boston is punished

In response to the *Boston Tea Party*, Britain decided to make an example of the town as a warning to the rest of the American colonists. The port of Boston was closed to all trade until the people paid compensation for the tea which had been destroyed. The local assembly elected by the people was closed down and the colony was placed under the rule of the British army. General Gage was sent from England with three regiments of soldiers to see that these orders were carried out.

Many Americans, however, were determined to resist and it was only a matter of time before open warfare broke out between the colonists and the British soldiers.

The first shots are fired

The first shots of the American War of Independence were fired in a small village called Lexington, about thirty kilometres north of Boston.

The Battle of Lexington.

General Gage had received information that rebel supplies of arms and gunpowder were hidden in the town of Concord, north-west of Boston. Under the cover of darkness on the night of 18–19 April 1775, British troops were rowed across Boston harbour. Reaching the northern bank they planned to march to Concord by the shortest route.

Unknown to them, the American rebels knew of all their movements. The most famous American spy was Paul Revere. He crossed the bay before the British and galloped ahead of them, warning the rebels of their arrival. When the British troops arrived at the village of Lexington on their way to Concord, shots were exchanged between them and a group of American colonists who had occupied the village green.

The ride of Paul Revere.

American colonists on the march.

When the troops reached Concord, further fighting took place, with the British troops being forced to retreat to the town of Boston. On that first day of fighting, seventy-three British soldiers and forty-nine American rebels were killed. The Americans now surrounded the town of Boston and laid siege to the British forces inside.

Throughout North America, many people watched the events in Boston with interest. Already, people in other colonies were preparing to join with the rebels of Boston. Their aim was to win freedom from Britain.

Test your knowledge

1 What was the Boston Massacre?
2 Why did the British parliament put a tax on tea?
3 What happened at the 'Boston Tea Party'?
4 How did Britain punish Boston for this incident?
5 Where were the first shots of the American War of Independence fired?
6 Who was Paul Revere?

The Continental Congresses

In September 1774, a group of men from the different British colonies had met in Philadelphia. This meeting was called the *First Continental Congress*. The members of the congress declared their support for the people of Boston and agreed to boycott trade with Britain until their problems were solved. After a six-week session, the First Continental Congress broke up and the members returned to their own colonies to lead the movement for independence.

In May 1775 a *Second Continental Congress* met in Philadelphia. At this stage, most Americans were still loyal to King George III and were very slow to break all connections with Britain.

Thomas Paine, the Englishman who called for the independence of the American colonies from Great Britain in his famous pamphlet, Common Sense.

At the time, however, books and pamphlets were appearing urging Americans to abandon all links with Britain. The most famous of these pamphlets was called *Common Sense* and was written by an Englishman named Thomas Paine.

The Declaration of Independence

On 7 June 1776, a member from Virginia spoke the following words at the Second Continental Congress:

'These United Colonies are, and of right ought to be, free and independent states. They are absolved from all allegiance to the British Crown, and all political connection between them and the state of Great Britain is and ought to be totally dissolved.'

For the following month, the Continental Congress debated whether or not to declare independence from Great Britain. A committee was appointed to draw up a document which outlined their ideas. The task of writing it was given to Thomas Jefferson, a landowner and a lawyer from Virginia. On 4 July 1776, the Continental Congress finally approved the *Declaration of Independence*. It began by stating the reasons why Americans should break away from the rule of Great Britain.

The Declaration of Independence then went on to state one of the most basic beliefs of the American colonists, that governments were there to protect people's rights and that their power came from the people.

Thomas Jefferson (1743–1826) wrote the American Declaration of Independence. Later, he became the third president of the United States.

Because the government of King George III had interfered with their rights, the Americans believed that they had a duty to rebel against it.

The signing of the American Declaration of Independence at Philadelphia on 4 July 1776.

The Declaration then contained a long list of injuries which King George III was accused of inflicting on American colonists. At the end of this he was condemned:

'A Prince, whose character is thus marked by every act which may define a tyrant, is unfit to be ruler of a Free People.'

With the Declaration of Independence, the struggle for American freedom had only begun. To secure that freedom, the colonists would have to defeat the armies of one of the most powerful countries in the world. To lead their forces in that uneven contest the Continental Congress had already, in June 1775, chosen their commander-in-chief. His name was George Washington.

Test your knowledge

1 What was decided at the First Continental Congress?

2 When did the Second Continental Congress meet and what action was taken by it?

3 Who was Thomas Paine?

4 Who drew up the American Declaration of Independence?

5 What, according to the Declaration of Independence, was one of the most basic beliefs of the American colonists?

6 Why do you think the colonists thought that George III was 'unfit to be ruler of a Free People'?

Chapter 38: Review

- Opposition to the British government was strongest in the town of Boston, the capital of Massachusetts. In March 1770, an incident known as 'the Boston Massacre' took place when British soldiers opened fire on a local mob, killing five and wounding seven.

- Before news of the massacre reached London, the British government had already removed all the new taxes on goods entering North America, except for the duties on tea.

- In November 1773, the 'Boston Tea Party' took place. This incident involved local people who dressed as Indians and dumped tea chests from British ships into the harbour as a protest against the hated tea duty.

- In response to the Boston Tea Party, the British government closed the port of Boston and shut down the local assembly elected by the people. It then sent an army under General Gage to the colony to carry out these orders.

- The opening shots of the American War of Independence were fired in Lexington and Concord, in April 1775. As a result of these battles, the British troops were forced to take refuge inside the town of Boston.

- The people of Boston were not alone in their struggle against Great Britain. A Continental Congress consisting of members from most of the thirteen colonies met at Philadelphia to agree on a common plan of action.

- On 4 July 1776, the Continental Congress at Philadelphia passed the Declaration of Independence. This document had been drafted by Thomas Jefferson and it declared the right of the people of the United States to break free from Great Britain.

- With the Declaration of Independence, the struggle for American freedom had only begun. To secure that freedom, the Americans would have to fight a war against Britain. To lead their troops in that war, they chose George Washington as commander-in-chief.

CHAPTER 39 The Story of George Washington

Early days

George Washington, the man chosen by the Continental Congress to command its army, was born in Virginia on 22 February 1732. His father was a landowner who died when George was only eleven years of age.

George Washington (1732–1799).

The young Washington was fortunate, however, as he was then brought up by his step-brother, Lawrence, who treated him very well. After Lawrence's death in 1752, George inherited the family estate in Virginia, known as Mount Vernon, on the banks of the Potomac River. The estate at Mount Vernon consisted of over 8,000 acres and by 1760 nearly fifty black slaves worked there. By the time he was sixteen, George Washington had received some training as a surveyor and had taken part in a number of mapping expedi-

Black slaves working on a plantation similar to George Washington's estate at Mount Vernon.

tions in the wild, unexplored lands in the west. However, Washington now gave up this occupation and managed his lands at Mount Vernon. He became very interested in farm improvements and would have been happy to remain all his life at this occupation.

Washington loved the life of the countryside. Much of his free time was spent riding, fox-hunting and dancing. He also enjoyed playing billiards and cards and running his own horses in races.

The making of a soldier

Like many other wealthy American colonists, Washington was expected to play a part in defending and ruling his local colony, Virginia. Between 1752 and 1758 he served as an army officer in the British forces which protected the colony from French and Indian attacks.

In 1753, George Washington showed great courage and determination when he was ordered to deliver a message to the French commander telling him to withdraw his troops from the Ohio region. Washington travelled over 800 kilometres by boat, foot and horse to deliver the message. He again showed bravery in 1755 during the war against the French. At this time, he was so ill that he rode on a pillow instead of a saddle.

Washington left the army in 1758. He almost immediately married a wealthy widow named Martha Dandridge who already had two children. He now settled down once again to the life at Mount Vernon as a landowner and tobacco planter.

It was not long, however, before George Washington was once again in the public eye. On resigning from the army he was elected to the local assembly which helped the British governor to run Virginia. By the time that assembly was disbanded in 1769 for opposing the stamp duty and other British laws, Washington was already one of Virginia's strongest critics of the British government's rule in America.

Commander-in-chief

Because of his outspoken views, George Washington was chosen as one of the seven Virginian delegates to the First Continental Congress which met at Philadelphia in September 1774. In the following March he was elected to the Second Continental Congress.

One of the most important tasks facing this congress was the appointment of a commander-in-chief of all the colonial troops. On 15 June 1775, George Washington was chosen for this vital post. In his speech to the Continental Congress accepting the position, Washington spoke in the modest fashion that was typical of him:

'Though I am truly sensible of the high honour done me in this appointment, yet I feel great distress that my abilities and experience as a soldier may not be equal to the extensive and important trust. However, as the Congress desires, I will enter upon the great duty and use every power I have in their service, and for the support of the glorious cause.'

Test your knowledge

1 Where was George Washington born?
2 What occupation did he have in the early years of his life?
3 What job did he carry out as an army officer?
4 Why did Washington become a strong critic of Britain?
5 What appointment was he given on 15 June 1775?
6 Read the extract from his speech accepting the position of commander-in-chief. What insight does this give us into Washington's character?
7 To what 'glorious cause' was Washington referring?

The struggle between the British and the Americans

British 'redcoats' fighting against American rebels at the Battle of Bunker Hill.

Four days after Washington's appointment as commander-in-chief, a fiercely contested battle took place at Bunker Hill near Boston. British forces attacked American rebels who had occupied the high ground to the north of the city. The Americans were driven from the hill, but the British suffered huge losses in the battle.

When George Washington arrived near Boston, his aim was to force the British to leave the city. In early March 1776, his army began to bombard Boston with cannon fire. As a result, the commander of the British forces there, General Howe, decided to evacuate the city by sea on 17 March. An anti-British citizen of Boston recorded the event as follows in his diary.

'This morning the British army in Boston, under General Howe, consisting of upwards of 7,000 men, after suffering a shameful blockade for many months past, disgracefully quitted all their strongholds in Boston and Charlestown, fled before the army of the United Colonies, and took refuge on board their ships ... and with such silence and precaution did they embark, that a great part of the inhabitants did not know it until after they were gone.'

With the British driven from Boston, Washington and his army turned their attention to New York which was in American hands. However, after much fighting, the British succeeded in capturing this very important city in September 1776. Washington had no choice but to withdraw his troops inland and build up his armies during the winter of 1776.

George Washington leading his troops across an icy river during terrible winter conditions in 1777.

The year 1777 was to prove a bleak period for the American side in the War of Independence. Large British armies were advancing on American strongholds and on 26 September, the capital city itself, Philadelphia, was captured by British forces under the command of Lord Cornwallis.

The winter at Valley Forge

As Philadelphia was under British control, George Washington and his troops had to spend the following winter at a wild spot called Valley Forge about thirty kilometres to the north-east of the city. Here during the freezing winter months, the soldiers endured terrible hardships. George Washington won their undying admiration by remaining at camp and sharing their suffering.

Miserable conditions in the camp at Valley Forge.

Soldiers who were present at Valley Forge have left some vivid accounts of their suffering. Here is what one of Washington's men wrote about their experiences.

Working with evidence

'On 19 December, the army reached the wooded wilderness, certainly one of the poorest districts of Pennsylvania, the soil thin, uncultivated and almost uninhabited, without forage and without provisions. Here we go into winter quarters ... to enable the army to recruit, to re-equip and to prepare for the opening of the coming campaign, while protecting the country against enemy attacks.'

Late February 1778

'The situation of the camp is such that in all human probability the army must soon dissolve. Many of the troops have no food and their pay is several days overdue. The horses are dying for want of forage ... Our desertions are astonishingly great: the love of freedom which was once alive in those men is overcome by hunger.'

1. How does the writer describe Valley Forge?
2. According to the extract, why did the army set up winter quarters there?
3. What were conditions like for the men by February 1778?
4. How do we know that many men had lost their desire to fight on?

As many as 2,500 men may have died during the six months which the army spent at Valley Forge. However, after this terrible period for the American forces, a source of new hope

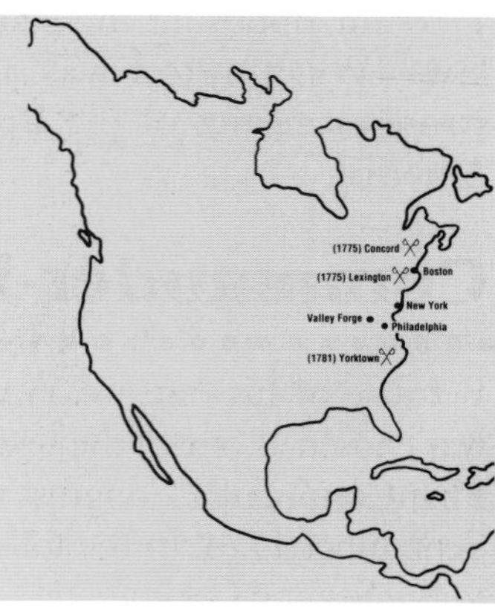

Places and battle sites of the American War of Independence.

appeared in February 1778 when the most powerful country on the continent of Europe—France—joined them in the war against Great Britain. The French saw this as a chance to gain revenge for their defeat by the British in the Seven Years War (1756–63).

The war spreads

A sea battle involving British and American ships during the War of Independence.

The entry of France into the war was to prove decisive in bringing about a British defeat. Before its arrival, the powerful British navy controlled the seas around America. Although the small American navy attacked British ships, it inflicted very little damage on the British navy and its supply vessels.

The statue of Commander John Barry in Wexford. John Barry, who was born in Co. Wexford in 1745, later emigrated to America. When the War of Independence broke out, he joined the US navy and carried out a series of daring raids against British ships. He was later chosen to command the USS United States, *the first purpose-built warship of the American navy. After his death in 1803, he became known as 'The Father of the American Navy'.*

With France now taking part in the war, British ships were no longer safe in the Atlantic Ocean. Also, fewer soldiers could be spared for the war in North America—they were needed to defend Great Britain itself and its other colonies from French attack. The situation further worsened for Great Britain when Spain and the Netherlands entered the war on the American side.

George Washington commanding his troops during the siege of Yorktown.

The victory at Yorktown

The British commander Lord Cornwallis surrenders to George Washington at Yorktown on 19 October 1781.

The decisive battle of the war took place at Yorktown, Virginia, in October 1781. Here George Washington's forces, supported by French troops, trapped a large British army under Lord Cornwallis. As French ships prevented the arrival of the British reinforcements, Cornwallis was forced to surrender to George Washington on 19 October.

As a result of this massive defeat, the British government began peace talks with the French and Americans in Paris.

The Treaty of Versailles

The leading American representative at the peace talks was the famous writer and inventor, Benjamin Franklin, who was American ambassador in Paris. The talks ended in November 1782 and the Treaty of Versailles came into force in September 1783. It was called this because it was signed in the palace of

Benjamin Franklin (1706–90) is regarded as one of the leading 'Founding Fathers' of American independence. He was a printer and publisher by profession and founded the first public library in America. He was also a famous scientific inventor who thrilled audiences with exciting new experiments. He predicted the outbreak of war between Britain and the American colonists and advised his fellow countrymen to unite: 'We must all hang together or assuredly we will all hang separately.' During the War of Independence, Benjamin Franklin was sent as ambassador to America's ally, France. He represented the United States at the successful peace talks which resulted in the Treaty of Versailles.

the king of France at Versailles outside Paris.

In this treaty, Great Britain agreed to recognise the independence of the thirteen North American colonies. The aims outlined in the American Declaration of Independence seven years earlier had now been achieved.

The assistance of the French forces had been important, but the American victory was mainly due to the efforts of the Americans themselves under the powerful leadership of their commander-in-chief, George Washington.

Test your knowledge

1 What happened at Bunker Hill?
2 Read about the British evacuation of Boston. How can we tell that the writer was anti-British?
3 Describe the conditions endured by the soldiers at Valley Forge.
4 What new hope appeared for the colonists in February 1778?
5 What was the decisive battle of the War of Independence?
6 Who was the leading American representative at the peace talks in Paris?
7 What was agreed in the Treaty of Versailles?

The United States of America

Once independence had been achieved, the thirteen states began to plan a new system of government which would allow them not only to keep a lot of power in each state, but also to unite to defend themselves from attack. By 1788, they had agreed on a *constitution*, or basic written law, for the new nation known as the United States of America.

This constitution set up a *federal system* of government. Each state kept its own government and courts for most matters. However, for issues like defence, foreign affairs, currency and the post office, they agreed to elect a single united government with a *president* in charge. He would rule the country and carry on relations with foreign governments.

The law-making body or *Congress* was independent of the president and contained two assemblies—the *Senate* and the *House of Representatives*. The third great independent arm of the government was the court system.

Freedom of speech and a fair system of justice were guaranteed under the American constitution. This was different from most European countries at the time, where people could be thrown in jail for speaking against their rulers. Whereas Europe was ruled by kings, American citizens could elect their own president who stayed in power for a period of four years.

The American system of government

- **Executive**

  PRESIDENT
  (elected by the people for a four-year term)
  Governs the country

- **Legislature**

  CONGRESS: THE SENATE AND THE HOUSE OF REPRESENTATIVES
  (elected by the people)
  Passes laws

- **Judiciary**

  JUDGES
  Tries court cases
  Decides whether laws passed by Congress agree with the Constitution

Capitol Hill in Washington where the Congress of the United States of America meets.

The White House, home of the President of the United States.

The first president

Children with the American flag admiring their first president, George Washington. The thirteen stripes represent the original colonies which won their independence from Britain. There is one star for each state in the United States of America.

George Washington was elected as the first president of the United States in 1789. He was elected for a second four-year term in 1793, and when this was over he retired to his estate at Mount Vernon. At his death on 14 December 1799, Washington was mourned not only in the United States but throughout the world as one of the great generals and leaders of all time.

The influence of the American Revolution

The ideas of democracy and free speech present during the American Revolution soon spread to other countries. In England some people hoped that they could force the government to allow greater freedom in the country.

In Ireland, both Protestants and Catholics hoped to use the ideas coming from America to reduce the power of the British government there. Some people even hoped to follow the example of the Americans and remove the British from Ireland completely.

However, the country which was first to be influenced by the American Revolution was France. As we have already seen, France helped the Americans to win the War of Independence. The king of France was to pay a high price for that victory. The huge cost of running the war almost brought the country to bankruptcy and American ideas like freedom of speech and democracy soon spread throughout France.

In the next chapter, we shall see how these developments paved the way for the outbreak of revolution in France in 1789.

Test your knowledge

1. What do you understand by a federal system of government?
2. In what way was the government of the United States different from the governments of European countries at that time?
3. Who became the first president of the United States?
4. What ideas of the American Revolution soon spread to other countries?
5. Why was the king of France to pay a high price for American victory in the War of Independence?
6. In what ways was Ireland influenced by the ideas of the American Revolution?
7. What country was the first to experience the effects of the American Revolution?

The life of George Washington

- Born in Virginia in 1732. In his early life, he was a surveyor and an army officer on the Western Frontier.
- After his marriage in 1758, he settled down to live as a plantation owner at Mount Vernon in Virginia where he took part in local politics.
- Washington was a delegate from Virginia at the First Continental Congress. He was appointed commander-in-chief of the American troops in June 1775.
- Washington's troops forced the British out of Boston, but they could not prevent the British form capturing New York.
- The year 1777 was a bleak one for Washington's army. They had to spend a bitter winter at Valley Forge after the British captured Philadelphia.

- In 1778, when France, Spain and the Netherlands entered the war on the American side, the situation improved for Washington.
- The decisive battle of the American War of Independence took place at Yorktown, Virginia, in October 1781 when George Washington's army defeated the British under Lord Cornwallis.
- Between 1789 and 1797, Washington served as the first president of the United States. After retiring to Mount Vernon, he died in December 1799.

Chapter 39: Review

- George Washington was born in Virginia in 1732. His father, a landowner, died when the young Washington was only eleven years old. He was brought up by his step-brother, Lawrence, at the family estate in Mount Vernon.
- Washington trained as a surveyor and took part in a number of mapping expeditions in the wild lands in the west.
- On inheriting the Mount Vernon estate in 1752, Washington spent much of his time managing his lands and improving farming methods.
- Like many wealthy Americans, Washington played his part in defending the colony from French or Indian attack. As an army officer between 1752 and 1758, he took a leading part in many dangerous expeditions.
- Because of his outspoken views, George Washington was chosen as one of the members from Virginia at the Continental Congress in 1774.
- On 15 June 1775, the Continental Congress chose George Washington for the all-important post as commander-in-chief of the American armies in the war against the British.
- In March 1776, an army under Washington's command forced the British to retreat from Boston. However, he was defeated at New York and had to withdraw, leaving the city in British control.
- The year 1777 was a bleak time for the Americans. Large British armies were advancing on their strongholds and on 26 September the capital city itself, Philadelphia, was captured.
- Washington and his troops spent the bitter winter of 1777–78 at a bleak spot called Valley Forge, north-east of Philadelphia. Here the soldiers endured terrible hardships such as cold, hunger and disease.
- In February 1778, the Americans were joined by France in the war against Britain. Later on, the Netherlands and Spain also entered the war on the American side.
- The entry of France into the war was decisive in bringing about a British defeat because it reduced the stranglehold which the British navy had held on North America.
- In October 1781, the Americans under Washington defeated a British army under Lord Cornwallis at Yorktown in Virginia. This was the decisive battle of the war. The British government opened up peace talks with the French and Americans at Paris.
- Under the Treaty of Versailles, which came into operation in September 1783, Great Britain agreed to recognise the independence of the North American colonies.
- Once independence had been achieved, the Americans set up a federal system of government. Each state had its own government for most matters, except for nationally important issues like defence and foreign affairs. These were handled by the president and congress of the United States.
- George Washington was elected as the first president of the United States in 1789. On his retirement in 1797, he returned to Mount Vernon where he died in 1799.
- The ideas of democracy and free speech which sparked the American Revolution soon spread to the countries of Europe, including Ireland.

CHAPTER 40

Revolution in France

Six years after the Americans finally gained their independence from Great Britain, far-reaching and exciting changes began to take place in France. Ever since then, the year 1789 has been remembered as the time when the French people rose up in revolt against their government. Because of this revolt and the huge changes which resulted from it, these events have been called the *French Revolution.*

In order to understand why revolution broke out in France, we must see for ourselves what life was like there at the time. Let us begin with the king and queen of France who lived in a splendid palace at the town of Versailles, outside the city of Paris.

The palace of Versailles

The palace and gardens of the kings of France at Versailles.

Look carefully at the pictures of the palace of Versailles. Today this beautiful palace is a museum. Can you see why thousands of tourists still come every year to view this magnificent building and its surrounding gardens?

Guests are entertained in the magnificent Hall of Mirrors at Versailles.

In 1789, these beautifully decorated rooms were the living and working quarters of the king of France and his court. The royal apartments included bedrooms, dining rooms and throne rooms for the king and queen. There was also a private chapel and a theatre where special performances of plays and operas were put on for the royal family.

As well as being the home of the royal family, the palace contained government offices. It was from here that the king and his ministers ruled the country. Also at Versailles there lived many nobles or lords who formed the king's court. They spent much of their time enjoying themselves either at outdoor sports such as hunting or at gambling, especially card playing.

Louis XVI and Marie Antoinette

King Louis XVI of France (1774–93).

At this time, the king of France was Louis XVI who had ruled since 1774 when he was twenty years of age. He was a shy, religious and well-meaning man, but as a ruler he was often weak and indecisive. Louis' favourite pastime was hunting. He and his nobles often hunted in the countryside around Versailles several days a week.

Queen Marie Antoinette.

The wife of Louis XVI was an Austrian princess named Marie Antoinette. Just a year younger than Louis, she had a much stronger personality and tried to dominate her husband. The queen was very extravagant and spent huge sums of money on clothes, jewellery and entertainment. She had a special farm laid out in the grounds of

Versailles. Here Marie Antoinette and the ladies of the court would dress up as milkmaids and shepherdesses, pretending that they were ordinary people.

Although Louis was liked by most French people, Marie Antoinette was hated because of her extravagance and because she came from Austria, a country which had been an old enemy of France.

Test your knowledge

1 Explain why the events which began in France in 1789 have been called the French Revolution.
2 What is to be found at Versailles today?
3 List three types of room included in the royal apartments.
4 Who were the nobles?
5 Who became king of France in 1774?
6 Name the queen of France at this time.
7 What faults did she have?
8 What was the attitude of most French people to: (a) the king; (b) the queen?

A divided country

France before the revolution was a deeply divided country. At the top there was the king, then the lords or nobles. The king had *absolute power.* It was he, and not the parliament, who made the laws. He could also send people to prison without any trial.

A French noble hunting a stag in the grounds of his magnificent chateau.

The nobles lived either at Versailles or on their huge estates in the countryside. A noble's country mansion was known as a *chateau*. A local noble was a very powerful man. He was a judge in the law courts and had great power over the tenants on his estate.

Most bishops at this time were powerful and wealthy and came from noble families.

Next to the nobles were the middle classes, people like merchants, lawyers, doctors and teachers. The middle classes were also known by the French word *bourgeoisie.* The nobles looked down on the middle classes because they had to earn their living through trade or in some career or profession. By the 1780s, however, many middle-class people were objecting to the power and privileges of the nobles.

At the lower end of society were the peasants and workers. In both the towns and in the countryside these workers formed the vast majority of the French population. They had to pay high rents and taxes to keep the king and nobles in luxury. Hard work and hunger were the usual experiences of most people.

Because these conditions existed in France for hundreds of years, the government before the revolution was known as the *ancien régime*, or the ancient government.

France in crisis

By 1788, Louis XVI and his government faced serious difficulties. The country was nearly bankrupt. The cost of fighting in the American War of Independence had been paid for by borrowing. More money could only be obtained by increasing taxes.

As it was, the system of taxation was grossly unfair. A person's tax depended on his position in society. The bishops and priests, known as the *First Estate*, could meet and decide what taxes to vote for the king. The nobles or *Second Estate* were excused from paying many of the existing taxes. This left a huge burden on the rest of the population, or the *Third Estate*, which consisted of merchants, lawyers and shopkeepers in the towns, and the peasants throughout the countryside.

King Louis tried to get the nobles to pay more taxes but they refused. To solve the crisis, the king called together a meeting of the Estates General for May 1789. This was a collection of representatives of

The inside of a French peasant's cottage in the eighteenth century. What does this scene tell you about the living conditions of the poor at the time?

the three estates which came together to advise the king. The last time the Estates General had met was in 1614.

The Third Estate was determined to get its fair share of power and to make the nobles and bishops give up many of their privileges.

The Estates General meeting at Versailles. Can you point out: (a) the clergy; (b) the nobles; (c) the Third Estate (dressed in black)?

The Estates General was opened by King Louis with splendid ceremony at Versailles on 5 May 1789. For the next six weeks, there was a long argument about voting. If you look at the chart you will understand why.

First Estate (Clergy): *308 deputies*
Second Estate (Nobles): *285 deputies*
Third Estate (Commons): *621 deputies*

Cartoons like this from the time of the French Revolution can tell us a great deal about the lives of the people. Point out the people representing each estate. What do we learn about the treatment of the Third Estate?

The nobles and bishops wanted each estate to have one vote. In that way, the First and Second Estates could always outvote the deputies from the Third Estate. However, the members of the Third Estate wanted each deputy to have a vote. In this way, the Third Estate could outvote the other two.

When Louis supported the nobles and ordered the Third Estate to leave their meeting place, its members gathered on the tennis court at Versailles on 20 June. There they swore the famous *Tennis Court Oath*, when they promised to continue to meet until their grievances were solved.

Taking the Tennis Court Oath.

This action forced the king to order members of the other two estates to join with the Third Estate and form the National Assembly. This assembly began the task of drawing up new laws for France.

King Louis, however, soon had other ideas. He tried to bring in troops to close the National Assembly because he feared that it might try to reduce his own power. At this stage, the ordinary people of France entered the revolution for the first time.

Test your knowledge

1 What problems did Louis and his government face in 1788?
2 In what way was the system of taxation in France unfair?
3 Who made up the First and Second Estates?
4 What people were in the Third Estate?
5 What disagreements took place over voting in the Estates General?
6 What was the 'Tennis Court Oath' ?
7 What was the task of the National Assembly?
8 Why do you think the king brought in troops to close the assembly?

The storming of the Bastille

Fearing that the king was about to bring in troops to crush the revolution, mobs roamed through Paris on 12–13 July, searching for weapons in gunsmiths' shops and in military barracks. Some soldiers left their posts to join with the people.

On the 14 July 1789, after an unsuccessful raid for arms on the *Hôtel des Invalides*—the famous

The storming of the Bastille on 14 July 1789.

home for retired soldiers—the crowd marched to the *Bastille*. This huge, fearsome-looking prison had a terrible reputation. Most of the prisoners there had been locked up without trial. The Bastille was, therefore, the symbol of absolute power and unjust rule to the crowd who attacked it in search of weapons.

Nearly a hundred people were killed during the storming of the Bastille. When the mob finally entered the prison, they found only six prisoners, two of whom were insane.

However, the events of 14 July 1789 in Paris saved the National Assembly from being broken up. The citizens of Paris also set an example for the revolution which soon followed throughout the rest of the country.

Test your knowledge

1 Why did the mobs roam through Paris on 12 and 13 July searching for arms?

2 When was the Bastille stormed and why?

3 Why was the Bastille so hated by the people of Paris?

4 Why did the peasants revolt throughout France?

The Rights of Man

On 26 August 1789, the National Assembly passed a law called the *Declaration of the Rights of Man*. Like the American Declaration of Independence, it contained the belief that governments were there to serve the people and to protect their rights.

The National Assembly abolishing the feudal system in France on 4 August 1789.

In the *Declaration of the Rights of Man*, the three great aims of the French Revolution are clearly seen—*liberty, equality and fraternity*. Liberty meant personal freedom under the law. Equality meant that all citizens should be treated in the same manner by the government or the courts. And fraternity was the belief that all people are like brothers.

The events of July and August 1789 were stunning and remarkable. Some people, including the British ambassador in Paris, Lord Dorset, thought that the revolution was over. He wrote to London at the time:

'Thus, the greatest revolution that we know anything of has been effected with the loss of very few lives. From this moment we may consider France as a free country; the king a very limited monarch, and his nobility reduced to a level with the rest of the nation.'

However, despite such hopes for the future, the French Revolution had only begun. Some serious problems were to arise for Louis XVI and for the revolutionaries themselves.

Chapter 40: Review

- Around 1780, France was a deeply divided society. The king and nobles lived lives of ease and luxury. At the same time, millions of peasants experienced poverty and hard work while paying high taxes to maintain the lifestyle of the rich.

- From his palace at Versailles outside Paris, King Louis XVI had absolute power. He could make laws himself and imprison without trial anyone who criticised the government.

- Next to the king, in terms of power and wealth, came the lords or noblemen. They divided their time between Paris or Versailles and their country estates where they lived in huge mansions or chateaux.

- The growing numbers of middle-class people such as doctors, lawyers and merchants resented the power and snobbery of the nobles in France.

- Most of the French population was made up of peasants who worked hard on the land and had to pay high rents and taxes to the nobles and the king.

• Because these conditions had existed for hundreds of years, the government of France before the revolution was known as the *ancien régime*, or the ancient government.

• By 1788, the government of King Louis XVI of France was nearly bankrupt because of the huge cost of fighting in the American War of Independence. Because the tax system was unfair, huge changes would be needed to improve it.

• In May 1789, the king called the Estates General together at Versailles. This form of parliament had last met as far back as 1614. The First Estate represented the clergy, the Second Estate, the nobles and the Third Estate, the common people.

• On 20 June 1789, the members of the Third Estate swore the Tennis Court Oath, refusing to break up until France got a new type of government. As a result, the king forced the other two estates to join them to form the National Assembly.

• Urged on by his wife, Queen Marie Antoinette, King Louis tried to bring in troops to crush the assembly. This led mobs in Paris to storm the Bastille prison on 14 July 1789. As a result the revolution continued.

• In August 1789, the National Assembly passed the Declaration of the Rights of Man guaranteeing equal rights to all French citizens.

• The great slogan of the revolution was 'Liberty, Equality and Fraternity'. Liberty meant freedom under the law. Equality meant that all citizens should be treated in the same way by the government. Fraternity was the belief that all people are like brothers.

CHAPTER 41 France becomes a Republic

In the summer of 1789, while changes were taking place in the government of France, great problems remained for the ordinary people of Paris. Many of the poor were almost starving because of food shortages.

On 5 October, a huge crowd of women from Paris marched to Versailles to see the king and National Assembly. As well as being angry over shortages of bread, they were also enraged at stories that the king's soldiers had insulted the flag of the French Revolution.

The women of Paris march on Versailles.

On 6 October Louis XVI, Marie Antoinette and the royal family were forced to leave Versailles forever and to come to Paris where they lived in the Tuileries Palace. At the same time, the National Assembly voted to transfer to Paris as well.

Around this time, revolutionaries in France began to use this tricolour of red, white and blue. Red and blue were the colours of the city of Paris. White was the king's colour. By placing the white band in the centre, the revolutionaries showed that the king was under the control of the people of Paris. For many years afterwards, this flag was a symbol of revolution. It was flown in many different countries when a rebellion against the government broke out.

The flight to Varennes

The royal carriage is halted by soldiers at Varennes.

Fearing for his life, Louis XVI decided to flee from Paris with his wife and family. At midnight on 20 June 1791, Louis XVI, Marie Antoinette and their family slipped out of the Tuileries Palace into a carriage which awaited them. Their aim was to reach the Austrian Netherlands, a territory ruled by the queen's brother, Emperor Leopold II of Austria. After travelling all day, however, the royal group was recognised and stopped at Varennes, not far from the border. They were forced to return to Paris under armed guard.

The royal family being brought back to Paris by a heavily-armed guard.

The flight to Varennes caused a terrible shock in Paris. Louis was suspected of being in league with foreign enemies of France and all his remaining powers were removed. This gave the assembly a chance to prove that it could rule without the king. It also strengthened the republicans—those people who believed that France would be better off as a republic without any king in charge.

The constitution of 1791

In September 1791, the National Assembly at last completed its main task—the drawing up of a written constitution for France. This set out how the country was to be ruled. It allowed Louis XVI to continue as king, not as an absolute monarch but as a ruler who was bound to obey the laws. Power would be held by the assembly which was to be elected by the people: the king could only delay laws which he did not like for two years.

At this time, small political clubs in Paris and in other cities played a very important role. These clubs were places where people could meet, discuss politics and make plans for the running of the country. The two most famous were the *Girondin* and *Jacobin* clubs. The Girondin Club got its name from the area near Bordeaux in western France called the Gironde. The Jacobins got their name from their main meeting place in Paris, a former Jacobin monastery. Both the Girondin and Jacobin clubs had members in the assembly.

The former Jacobin monastery in Paris which became the headquarters of the revolutionary Jacobin club.

In the spring of 1792, the Girondins and Jacobins in the National Assembly were deeply divided on whether France should go to war against Austria or not. While the Jacobins believed that France was not yet ready for war, the Girondins argued strongly in favour of it. On 20 April 1792, the Girondins got their way when France declared war on Austria. The war which began then was to last on and off for twenty years.

Test your knowledge

1. Why did King Louis decide to flee from Paris?
2. Why do you think the flight to Varennes shocked the people of Paris?
3. How did the constitution of 1791 reduce the power of the king?
4. Name two famous political clubs in France at this time.
5. What country did France go to war against in April 1792?

Revolutionary France goes to war

After all the trouble and upheaval of the previous three years, the French army and navy were in no fit condition to go to war. However, there was a very strong spirit of excitement and pride among the people. They believed that the revolutionary French soldiers would win splendid victories and that they would bring freedom to the rest of Europe.

Despite the bravery and determination of the French soldiers their armies were beaten back by the Austrians. By the summer of 1792, Paris itself was in danger of capture.

France becomes a republic

Many people suspected that Louis XVI and Marie Antoinette hoped for a French defeat in the war so that the Austrian emperor would put an end to the revolution.

During July 1792, there were a number of demonstrations against the king in Paris. Then on 10 August, when bad news reached the city from the battle front, revolutionary soldiers and Paris mobs attacked the Tuileries Palace.

The Paris mob attacking the Tuileries palace on 10 August 1792.

A bloody battle took place resulting in the death of around 800 of the king's troops and 400 of the attackers. The king took refuge in the assembly, but the attackers entered it and forced the deputies to remove Louis XVI from power. This was another turning point in the revolution.

On 21 September 1792, the rule of kings in France which had lasted for over a thousand years came to an end. France was now a republic. A new era had begun. The revolutionaries even drew up a new calendar with 21 September 1792 as the first New Year's Day! At the same time, a new assembly known as the *Convention* was elected.

Massacre in Paris

Between 2 and 6 September 1792, a series of horrific massacres had taken place at prisons in Paris. People suspected of being enemies of the revolution were put to death, including many priests who had refused to take the revolutionary oath. In all, over a thousand people were massacred in this way.

When news of the massacres reached other countries, it turned more and more people against the French Revolution. Foreign governments and peoples were also carefully watching the fate of Louis XVI and the royal family.

Massacres at a Paris prison in September 1792.

Clearly the new French republic needed a strong person to guide it through the early years of foreign wars and internal division. Such a man soon arrived on the scene—he was a Jacobin lawyer named Maximilien Robespierre.

Test your knowledge

1 How did the French armies fare against the Austrians?

2 Why do you think mobs attacked the Tuileries Palace?

3 France became a republic on 21 September 1792. What did this mean?

4 What happened to people suspected of being enemies of the revolution?

Chapter 41: Review

- Food shortages continued in Paris into the autumn of 1789, and on 5 October a huge crowd of women marched on Versailles to confront the king and to demand bread. As a result, the king and his family were forced to leave Versailles and to live in Paris.

- In June 1791, Louis XVI, Marie Antoinette and their family tried to escape from France. They had reached the town of Varennes in the east when they were forced to return to Paris under a heavy guard.

- In September 1791, the National Assembly finished drawing up a constitution for France. It allowed Louis XVI to continue as a ruler with limited powers.

• The new assembly elected in 1791 had a powerful republican minority. It was divided into two main groups, the Girondins and the more extreme Jacobins.

• On 20 April 1792, France declared war on Austria, beginning a period of war in Europe which was to last on and off for over twenty years.

• In August 1792, when bad news reached Paris from the battle front, a mob invaded the Tuileries Palace. They tried to capture the king, and forced the Assembly to remove him from power.

• In September 1792, France was declared a republic. The rule of kings which had lasted for over a thousand years was now at an end. The 21 September 1792 became New Year's Day in the revolutionary calendar. At the same time, a new assembly called the Convention was elected.

• Also in September 1792 a dreadful series of massacres took place in prisons around Paris. Mobs killed prisoners because they suspected them of supporting France's enemies.

• The new French republic clearly needed a strong person to guide it through internal divisions and foreign invasions. Maximilien Robespierre was to be this man.

CHAPTER 42 Robespierre and the Reign of Terror

The story of Maximilien Robespierre–Early days

Maximilien Robespierre was born at Arras in northern France in 1758. His mother died in childbirth and when Maximilien was only eight years of age, his father deserted the family, leaving him, his brother and sisters to be cared for by their grandparents.

Maximilien Robespierre (1758–94).

At the age of eleven, the young Robespierre won a scholarship to a college in Paris where he studied law. In 1781 at the age of twenty-three, he returned to Arras to practise as a lawyer.

Robespierre–the politician

By the time the French Revolution broke out in 1789, Robespierre was already well known to the people of Arras for his outspoken views. The rich were outraged by his attacks on the power of the king. He was elected to the Third Estate by the local people.

Robespierre often contributed to debates in the National Assembly. He was a founder-member of the Paris Jacobin Club and became its president in April 1790. He attacked the calls of the Girondins for war in the winter of 1791–92, believing that France was not yet strong enough. After the king's fall from power and the setting up of a republic, Robespierre's influence increased greatly.

Although he had no sense of humour, Robespierre was highly respected by many people. He had a reputation for being 'incorruptible'—no amount fo money or pressure could force him to change his views. He was to have great power in France from September 1792 onwards, beginning with moves to bring about the trial and execution of King Louis XVI.

The trial and execution of Louis XVI

The main challenge facing the Convention during the autumn of 1792 was how to deal with Louis XVI, who was widely suspected of plotting against the revolution. Although Robespierre believed that the king should be executed without any trial, the members of the Convention decided that they would act as a court to try him.

The trial of the king began on 21 December 1792. The King claimed that the Convention had no right to try him and that, in any case, he was innocent of plotting against the revolution. Eventually, the 693 deputies present found the king guilty and in the middle of January 1793 they voted on his punishment.

Working with evidence

VOTING IN THE CONVENTION ON THE KING'S SENTENCE

16–17 JANUARY

What penalty should be suffered by Louis, former King of the French?

361: death
26: death but with consideration for a reprieve
288: imprisonment, detention, banishment
28: absent

19 JANUARY

Should there be a reprieve in carrying out the sentence on Louis Capet?

310: yes
380: no

20 JANUARY

The National Convention declares Louis Capet, last king of the French, guilty of conspiracy against the national liberty and of assault against national security.
The National Convention decrees that Louis Capet must suffer the death penalty.

1 How many deputies voted for the death sentence for Louis XVI on 16–17 January?
2 What decision was taken by the Convention on 19 January?
3 List the crimes which Convention members found the king guilty of on 20 January.

The execution of King Louis XVI on 21 January 1793.

On 21 January 1793, Louis XVI was brought in a carriage from the Temple prison and publicly executed at the guillotine. An Irish priest, the Abbé Edgeworth, accompanied the king on his last journey. A supporter of the king, M. Bernard, has left the following account of King Louis XVI's execution.

Working with evidence

Paris 23 January 1793.
Wednesday morning.

'My dearest mother,

I commend to you the spirit of the lamented Louis XVI. He lost his life on Monday at half-past ten in the morning, and to the very last he maintained the greatest possible courage.

He wished to speak to the people from the scaffold but was interrupted by a drum-roll and was seized by the executioners who were following their orders and who pushed him straight under the fatal blade. He was only able to speak these words in a very strong voice. "I forgive my enemies. I trust that my death will be for the happiness of my people, but I grieve for France, and I fear that she may suffer the anger of the Lord ..."'

1 How do we know that the writer had great respect for Louis XVI?
2 Did the king meet his death bravely?
3 Was Louis allowed to speak to the people from the scaffold?
4 What were the king's last words concerning his enemies?
5 What fear did he have concerning the future of France?

The execution of Louis XVI caused great shock throughout Europe. Other countries became hostile to France and in February, England and the Netherlands joined in the war against her.

Now that France was at war against the most powerful countries in Europe, its revolutionary leaders looked more and more to Robespierre to guide them through their difficulties.

Test your knowledge

1 Where and when was Robespierre born?

2 What career did he choose?

3 What political club did he help to found in Paris?

4 Why did Robespierre believe that France should not go to war in the winter of 1791–92?

5 Why was Robespierre known as the 'Incorruptible'?

6 Give two reasons why Louis XVI was condemned to death.

The Reign of Terror

The Committee of Public Safety in session.

Because of the difficulties of fighting a war against several enemies, the Convention decided in April 1793 that a small group of its members should run the affairs of the country. This new group was known as the *Committee of Public Safety*. Working side by side with the committee was the *Revolutionary Tribunal* which tried people suspected of being against the revolution. It was to send nearly 3,000 victims to the guillotine, including Queen Marie Antoinette who was executed in October 1793.

The execution of Marie Antoinette on 16 October 1793.

Robespierre and his followers firmly believed that if the revolution in France was to be saved, a *Reign of Terror* was necessary against all its enemies. For a year, Robespierre and his followers were to rule France by means of widespread terror.

In September 1793, a savage *Law of Suspects* was introduced. It stated that anybody denounced to the authorities by a loyal citizen could be condemned as a traitor and sent to the guillotine. Not only in Paris, but throughout all of France, thousands suffered in this way. It is believed that over 40,000 people were killed during the Reign of Terror.

One may wonder how Robespierre managed to stay in power for even as long as a year. He especially enjoyed the support of the tradesmen and shopkeepers of Paris. These people were known as the *Sans-Culottes.*

The Sans-Culottes

As the name suggests, these tradesmen and shopkeepers did not wear the *culottes* or knee breeches of the upper classes. Instead they wore long, straight trousers.

The Sans-Culottes met in groups and expected deputies in the Convention to carry out their wishes. They wanted the price of food kept low, and Robespierre pleased them at first by doing this. The Sans-Culottes were essential to the success of the revolution because of their fierce determination to fight against foreign enemies, as well as against French opponents of the revolution.

Sans-Culottes women were just as courageous as their menfolk. At the height of France's danger from enemy attack, they pawned their wedding rings to raise money for the army and gave away their sheets and clothes for use as bandages.

A Sans-Culottes man and woman.

Test your knowledge

1 What important decision did the Convention reach in April 1793?
2 Explain the role of: (a) the Committee of Public Safety; (b) the Revolutionary Tribunal.
3 Why did Robespierre and his followers start the Reign of Terror?
4 Who were the Sans-Culottes?
5 Why were the Sans-Culottes important in the revolution?

The war in the west

A revolutionary army on the march in the Vendée.

Armies made up of Sans-Culottes troops were used during the Reign of Terror to fight a savage and bloody war in an area in the west of France known as the *Vendée*. Here masses of peasants rebelled against the revolutionary government partly because of its attacks on the Catholic religion. They also rebelled because the government attempted to introduced *conscription*—forcing all men of a certain age to join the army. By the end of 1793, the Vendée royalist rebels had been defeated and the revolutionary armies unleashed a reign of terror in the area. Many people were shot while others were drowned in the River Loire.

Robespierre's hatred of the Catholic peasants in the Vendée was supported by many revolutionaries. By the summer of 1794, however, he had made so many enemies for himself that his own life was in danger.

The death of Robespierre and the end of the Terror

On 10 June 1794, Robespierre had a law passed by the Convention extending the terror and allowing the arrest of members of the Convention themselves. Two weeks later, a French army gained a huge victory over the Austrians. This lessened the need for harsh measures at home.

Instead of relaxing the terror, however, Robespierre made it worse. Between 10 June and 17 July 1794, nearly 1,400 people were executed, an average of 200 a week. Over the previous year the average had been around twenty a week.

On 26 July, Robespierre made a wild speech calling for many more arrests. His enemies now decided to act in case they were next on the list for the guillotine.

During the night of 27–28 July, Robespierre and his friends tried to protect themselves from attack. They failed and awaited arrest within the *Hôtel de Ville* (city hall). Robespierre had apparently tried to commit suicide. A contemporary pamphlet contained this account of his arrest.

The arrest of Robespierre and his followers.

Working with evidence

The arrest of Robespierre

'They went into the Hôtel de Ville and found Robespierre in a room. He was lying on the ground, a pistol shot through his jaw. They picked him up and some of the Sans-Culottes carried him by his feet and his head; there were at least a dozen round him. They tore off his right sleeve, and the back of his blue coat ...

Robespierre was taken to the Committee of Public Safety. The procession paused briefly at the foot of the main stairs: inquisitive people joined the crowd. Some lifted his arm to look at his face. One said, "He isn't dead, he's still warm." Another said, "Isn't that a fine king?" Another: "And suppose it was Caesar's body! Why hasn't it been thrown on the rubbish dump?"

Another citizen said, "I only know of one man who understood the art of tyranny, and that is Robespierre ..."

When his wound was dressed they laid him down again, taking care to put a box under his head as a pillow, they said, "until it was time for him to put his head through the little window" [the guillotine].'

1 When the writer of this account entered the Hôtel de Ville, in what condition did he find Robespierre?
2 How did the Sans-Culottes treat Robespierre?
3 What way did inquisitive onlookers show an interest in him?
4 Why do you think some of them wanted his body thrown on a rubbish dump?
5 Explain the joke at the end of the extract.

The execution of Robespierre on 28 July 1794 brought the Reign of Terror in France to an end.

On the following day, 28 July 1794, Robespierre and his followers were sent to the guillotine where so many of their victims had suffered.

With the death of Robespierre the Terror came to an end. Many consider Robespierre's execution to be the last important event in the French Revolution itself.

After the Revolution

Over the next few years, the people of France attempted to recover from the terror. The pace of change slowed down, and although France remained at war with other countries, rich men at home took charge of the government.

The Convention remained until October 1795 but it was no longer run by extreme Jacobins. It was followed by a government known as the Directory which remained in power until November 1799.

Test your knowledge

1 Why did the peasants in the Vendée region rebel against the revolutionary government?
2 How did the revolutionary soldiers treat the people of the Vendée?
3 Why was Robespierre ousted from power in July 1794?
4 Name the government in power in France between 1795 and 1799.

Robespierre

- Robespierre was born in Arras in 1758. He went to Paris to study, returning home to practise law in 1781.
- Elected as a member of the Third Estate in 1789, he became a founder-member of the Paris Jacobin Club. From 1792 onwards, he held great power in France.
- Robespierre strongly supported the execution of Louis XVI. After more countries joined the war against France in 1793, people looked to Robespierre as a strong leader.
- From April 1793, Robespierre dominated the Committee of Public Safety and the Revolutionary Tribunal—the main groups conducting the Reign of Terror.
- Robespierre was supported by the tradespeople and shopkeepers of Paris, the Sans-Culottes, who fought the enemies of France abroad and the enemies of the revolution at home.
- Robespierre waged a fierce war against Catholic peasants in the Vendée region of western France.
- In June and July 1794, Robespierre worsened the Terror and made many more enemies for himself.
- On 27 July 1794, Robespierre and his followers were arrested. A day later, they were executed at the guillotine.

Chapter 42: Review

• Robespierre was born at Arras in northern France in 1758. He lost his parents at an early age and when he was eleven he won a scholarship to a college in Paris where he studied law.

• By the time he was elected as a member of the Third Estate in the Estates General of 1789, Robespierre was a strong believer in freedom and democracy.

• He was a founder-member of the Paris Jacobin Club and became its president in April 1790. He opposed calls for war in the spring of 1792 because he believed that France was not yet strong enough.

• Robespierre had a reputation for being 'incorruptible'—no amount of money or pressure could force him to change his views.

• After the fall from power of Louis XVI and the declaration of a Republic in September 1792, Robespierre became much more influential. He played a leading role in calling for the king to be punished.

• In December 1792, Louis XVI was put on trial for plotting against the revolution. Although found guilty by a large majority a much smaller majority voted for his execution.

• On the 21 January 1793, the thirty-four-year-old Louis XVI was publicly executed at the guillotine in Paris.

• The execution of the king caused horror throughout Europe. Other countries became more hostile to France and in February 1793, England and the Netherlands joined in the war against her.

• Robespierre and his friends ruled France by means of two powerful groups, the Committee of Public Safety and the Revolutionary Tribunal. Using these they carried out a Reign of Terror against all enemies of the revolution.

• During the Reign of Terror which lasted from September 1793 to July 1794, it is believed that 3,000 people were executed, including Queen Marie Antoinette who was sent to the guillotine in October 1793.

• The Sans-Culottes of Paris were Robespierre's main source of support. These were mostly tradesmen or small shopkeepers. Sans-Culottes women were just as committed to the revolution as their menfolk.

• However, Robespierre was only using the Sans-Culottes for his own purposes and they failed to come to his rescue when his enemies plotted his downfall in July 1794.

• During 1793 and 1794, a savage and bloody war took place in the Vendée region of the west of France between the local people and the revolutionary armies sent to crush their rebellion.

• In June and July 1794, Robespierre stepped up the terror and sent increasing numbers of prisoners to the guillotine. French victory in battle lessened the need for such measures and Robespierre's enemies decided to have him arrested.

• On 28 July 1794, Robespierre and his principal followers perished at the guillotine where so many of their victims had suffered.

CHAPTER 43 Wolfe Tone and the United Irishmen

The Protestant Ascendency

While revolutions were taking place in America and France, Ireland continued under English rule. As you have learned in Chapter 36, from 1700 onwards most of the land in Ireland was owned by Protestant landlords. They also dominated the Irish Parliament in Dublin. Only Protestants could sit in parliament or be members of the government. For this reason the period was called the time of the Protestant Ascendancy or control.

The majority Catholic population had very few rights and suffered from a series of laws against their religion known as the Penal Laws. While most Irish Protestants supported the existing situation some tried to end the Penal Laws and even reduce or remove the power of the British government in Ireland. One such man was Wolfe Tone

Theobald Wolfe Tone (1763–98)

Tone was born in Dublin in June 1763. The son of a Protestant coachmaker, Peter Tone, and his wife, Margaret, he was given a good education and entered Trinity College in 1781. He was very interested in politics and won medals for his speeches in the College Historical Society.

Theobald Wolfe Tone (1763 –98).

In July 1785, Tone ran off with and married a young girl called Matilda Witherington to whom he remained devoted for the rest of his life. Now a married man, he set about choosing a career and decided to become a barrister. After studying law in both Dublin and London, he qualified as a barrister in February 1789.

Throughout this time, Tone kept up his interest in politics. He was delighted when the revolution broke out in France in the summer of 1789. He began to write pamphlets in which he called for greater freedom for the Irish people. As a result, he was closely watched by the British authorities in Dublin Castle, especially when it became clear that he intended to mix with other people who shared his point of view.

The beliefs of Wolfe Tone

Wolfe Tone believed that the Irish parliament was a corrupt assembly of rich Irish Protestants from which Catholics and Presbyterians were excluded. Because the Presbyterians of the north of Ireland had also suffered under the penal laws, Tone hoped that they might join with Catholics to rebel against the British government.

A number of people in Belfast at this time shared Tone's admiration for the French Revolution. They planned a great celebration in July 1791 for the second anniversary of the Fall of the Bastille.

Wolfe Tone wrote a *Journal* which helps us to understand many of his beliefs. This is a very valuable primary source for students studying his life and times.

Tone's three main aims were:

- To achieve complete separation from England for Ireland. Following the example of America and France, he wanted to set up a republic in Ireland.
- To use violence to achieve this.
- To unite Irishmen of all religions—Catholic, Protestant (Church of Ireland) and Dissenter (Presbyterian) in a struggle for Irish freedom.

The founding of the United Irishmen

To achieve these aims, Tone and his followers founded a new society in Belfast on 18 October 1791. They called themselves the *Society of United Irishmen*, as one of their main aims was to unite all Irishmen against England. A Dublin branch of the new society was founded less than a month later on 9 November.

Thomas Russell, one of the earliest associates of Wolfe Tone and a founder of the Society of United Irishmen in Belfast in 1791.

James Napper Tandy, became the first secretary of the Dublin Society of United Irishmen. In later years, he was one of the leading United Irishmen in Dublin.

The leaders of the United Irishmen were mainly professional men—merchants, lawyers, doctors. As in France, it was members of the middle class who mainly became revolutionary leaders. At the outset, most of the United Irishmen were Protestants. However, Catholics soon began to join in large numbers although the Catholic bishops were completely opposed to the movement.

Tailor's Hall, Dublin, where the Dublin Society of United Irishmen met during the 1790s.

Test your knowledge

1. When and where was Wolfe Tone born?
2. How do we know that he was interested in politics while still a student at Trinity College, Dublin?
3. What career did he decide to follow?
4. List Tone's three main political aims.
5. Name the society founded by Tone and his followers at Belfast in October 1791.

The United Irishmen are outlawed

When war broke out between England and France in 1793, all revolutionaries like Tone were suspected of being in league with the French. In order to avoid arrest, Tone left Ireland in 1794 and went to America.

The Society of United Irishmen was now declared illegal. However, they ignored this ban and continued to operate as a secret, oath-bound society. The United Irishmen now waited for the right moment to rise in rebellion against the British government.

Tone only remained in America for a year and a half. In January 1796, he left his wife and family there in the care of friends and sailed for France. In the following month he arrived in Paris. His mission—to convince the French government to send an invasion force to Ireland.

The French connection

As France was at war with Britain, the French government was quite willing to consider an attack through Ireland. During his stay in Paris, Tone often met government ministers. After many delays, the French government agreed to send a fleet with 15,000 soldiers to Ireland. It was to be commanded by the brilliant and experienced young general, Lazare Hoche.

Failure at Bantry Bay

The French landing at Killala Bay, August 1798.

On 15 December 1796 the fleet of forty-three vessels set sail for Ireland. Bad luck dogged the expedition from the outset and when it arrived off Bantry Bay, Co. Cork on 21 December, the weather was appalling. Some of the ships, including Tone's, were to remain off-coast for seventeen days, unable to land.

To the great relief of the British government, the French expedition had to return home. While Tone was to remain in France working hard for the sending of another expedition, the British government in Ireland began to take very severe measures to prevent the outbreak of rebellion.

Test your knowledge

1 Why did Tone have frequent meetings with government ministers in Paris?
2 Name the commander chosen to take charge of a French fleet which was to invade Ireland.
3 When did the fleet set sail from France?
4 What misfortune dogged the French expedition as it arrived off the coast of Ireland in December 1796?
5 What work did Tone continue to do on his return to France?

The road to rebellion: 1796–98

The government in Dublin Castle was well aware of the plans of the United Irishmen. From the start it had paid spies to infiltrate the movement. The most famous of these spies was Leonard McNally, a prominent United Irishman. As a barrister he was later to defend Tone and other leaders at their trials. All the time, however, he had been acting as a secret informer for the British.

With detailed information on the United Irishmen, the government decided to crush the movement before it became too strong. Laws were passed banning the importation of arms into Ireland and giving the authorities wide powers to search houses and to arrest suspects. Swearing a secret oath was made a hanging offence.

Pitch-capping and half-hanging were methods used by the army to stamp out rebellion in Ireland.

As the government believed that the United Irishmen were strongest in Ulster, the campaign of disarming them began there. In the spring of 1797, an army under General Lake unleashed a reign of terror in order to collect weapons. Soldiers were given complete freedom to search houses as they pleased. The homes of suspected United Irishmen were burned to the ground and many people were flogged or shot by the soldiers. As a result over 6,000 weapons were collected within two weeks.

Alarmed at the government success in Ulster, the leaders of the United Irishmen realised that to have any chance of success, a rebellion would have to begin soon—with or without French help.

The government strikes

By early 1798, the government at Dublin Castle heard reports that up to 300,000 men had joined the United Irishmen. Although the numbers might have been greatly exaggerated, and although most of the rebels were only armed with pikes, the government decided to strike first and arrest the principal United Irishmen in Dublin.

On 12 March, several leaders of the movement were arrested in Dublin, including twelve who were taken by surprise during a secret meeting at the house of Oliver Bond, a prominent United Irishman.

Lord Edward Fitzgerald, son of the duke of Leinster, had been placed in charge of plans for the rising. He escaped arrest in March and managed to go into hiding in Dublin. He spent the next two months making secret arrangements for the rising which was eventually planned for 24 May 1798. However, four days earlier, he was betrayed to the authorities and arrested in a house in Thomas Street, Dublin. Wounded during the arrest, he died in prison two weeks later.

Lord Edward Fitzgerald (1763–98).

While the leaders were being rounded up, the government began another drive to disarm ordinary members of the United Irishmen throughout the country. At the end of March, martial law was imposed. This meant that the army had complete power over the people. Soldiers went from place to place, hanging and flogging suspects and burning their houses. Half-hanging and pitch caps of boiling tar were other methods of torture widely used. Pikes were often hidden in the thatch of houses and, whenever these were discovered, the houses were burned to the ground. Blacksmiths were usually the first men in a village to be arrested and tortured to make them reveal the location of pikes. In spite of these conditions and with most of the leaders captured, the long-awaited rising broke out in various parts of the country on 24 May 1798.

Lord Edward Fitzgerald being fatally wounded during his arrest in Thomas Street, Dublin, in May 1798.

Chapter 43: Review

- Theobald Wolfe Tone was born in Dublin in 1763. His father, Peter Tone, was a Protestant coachmaker. In 1781 the young Tone entered Trinity College, Dublin.

- While at Trinity College, Tone became very interested in politics and won medals for his speeches. In July 1785 he ran off with and married a young girl named Matilda Witherington.

- Tone decided to become a barrister and after studying law in both Dublin and London, he qualified in February 1789.

- He was very pleased when revolution broke out in France in 1789 and he began writing pamphlets in which he called for greater freedom for the Irish people.

- In his Journal, Tone set out his main political beliefs. These included complete separation between Ireland and England which was to be achieved by force if necessary. He hoped to unite all Irish people—Catholics, Protestants and Presbyterians—to achieve this.

- To work for these aims, Tone and his followers set up the Society of United Irishmen in Belfast in October 1791. Within a month, a Dublin branch of the new society had been formed.

- At the start, most United Irishmen were Protestants. However, soon Catholics began to join in large numbers, although the Catholic bishops were completely opposed to the movement.

- After war broke out between Great Britain and France in 1793, the Society of United Irishmen was declared illegal. It did not break up, however, but became a secret, oath-bound society.

- In 1794, Tone went to America to avoid arrest but in January 1796 he sailed for France in an effort to persuade the French government to send an invasion force to Ireland.

• After many delays, the French government sent an expedition of 15,000 soldiers to Ireland in December 1796. It was commanded by General Lazare Hoche and Wolfe Tone was on board one of the ships as a French officer.

• The French fleet spent seventeen days off Bantry Bay in Co. Cork, in atrocious weather, in a hopeless attempt to land. Tone had to look on in helplessness. In the end the fleet had to return to France without landing in Ireland.

• The government in Dublin Castle was well aware of the plans of the United Irishmen. It had many spies in the movement including Leonard McNally, one of the leading United Irishmen.

• In 1797, a campaign of disarming the country began. The British soldiers used forms of torture like flogging, pitch-capping and half-hanging to collect weapons and to gather information about the Untied Irishmen.

• In March 1798, the leading United Irishmen in Dublin were arrested. Lord Edward Fitzgerald now took charge until he was arrested and fatally wounded in Dublin in May. By this time, however, the rising was arranged for 24 May 1798.

CHAPTER 44 The 1798 Rising

The mail coach signal—the rebellion begins in Leinster

Before dawn on 24 May 1798, groups of United Irishmen were placed along the roads leading to the country from Dublin. They had orders to stop the mail coaches—this was to be signal to the rebels in the country that the rising had begun.

A mail coach being halted by rebels, May 1798.

Only one coach was stopped successfully—the Belfast mail coach was captured and burned at Santry in north Dublin. The Munster mail coach got almost as far as Naas when it was attacked and its passengers hacked to death by a group of rebels. The rising had begun. Before the year 1798 was over, the rebellion would cost 30,000 lives.

Although the rising had started in north Leinster, it was easily put down by government forces. Within a week, the rebels in Kildare and Carlow had been defeated and roads were re-opened for troops to march from Dublin to the country. By this time, however, the United Irishmen in Ulster had risen in rebellion.

The rising in Ulster

The government had long feared a rising in Ulster. They were particularly alarmed at the united movement involving Presbyterians and Catholics in the north-east. The

Henry Joy McCracken is hanged outside his own house in Lisburn, Co. Antrim.

disarming of Ulster in 1797 did not stop the United Irish leaders from planning a rebellion.

On 7 June, Henry Joy McCracken, a young Presbyterian cotton manufacturer, began a rebellion in Ulster by leading 3,000 rebels in an attack on the town of Antrim. Two days later, the rising spread to Co. Down where the leader was a young Protestant draper from Lisburn called Henry Monroe. After a week of fighting, the rebellion in Ulster was crushed by British troops. Both McCracken and Monroe were captured and hanged.

Fighting in Ulster during the 1798 Rebellion.

Unlike the rising in Ulster, which was short–lived, a rebellion broke out in Wexford which was to prove the most serious threat of all to British rule in Ireland during 1798.

Test your knowledge

1 What was to be the signal for the rising to begin in Leinster?
2 How many people would die in the rebellion before the year 1798 was over?
3 How long did it take the government to suppress the rising in north Leinster?
4 Why did the government particularly fear the rising in Ulster?
5 Name the leader of the rebellion in Antrim.

Rebellion breaks out in Wexford

By May 1798, the county of Wexford was in a very dangerous state. It contained a fairly large Protestant population and there was great tension and bitterness between local Protestants and Catholics.

On 20 May, government soldiers began a campaign of hanging, flogging, and pitch-capping in Wexford. One particular atrocity spread panic among the people. On 27 May, twenty-eight prisoners were massacred by a Protestant mob at a ball-alley in the town of Carnew. When the news reached Father John Murphy of Boolavogue, he agreed to lead the people in a rebellion.

The rebels gained more and more recruits as each day passed. Within a few days, they won their first victory when they defeated a group of soldiers at Oulart Hill. Although most of the rebels were only armed with pikes and scythes, their vast numbers guaranteed some early victories in battle.

When the rebels captured Enniscorthy, the second town in the county, the road lay open to the town of Wexford itself.

Wexford captured

After the capture of Enniscorthy by the rebels, Protestants from there and the surrounding areas crowded into Wexford for protection. As the vast rebel army approached, the garrison defending the town departed, leaving it undefended. Most Protestant men were imprisoned because they were suspected of being loyal to the British government. The moment that rich Protestants had long dreaded had arrived—the French Revolution had spread to Ireland. They now found that their servants, tradesmen, tailors and shopkeepers were in control.

Rebels burning furniture from the Protestant church at Enniscorthy after they had captured the town.

Fears that the rebels lacked discipline were completely justified. In times of threat, they could become a bloodthirsty mob. Two appalling incidents occurred during the rebel occupation of Wexford.

On 5 June, a large group of Protestant prisoners was massacred at a place called Scullabogue in south Wexford. When a group of rebels set fire to a barn, over a hundred men, women and children were burned to death as a result.

A similar incident took place at Wexford Bridge

on 20 June. As government troops were marching on Wexford, Protestant prisoners were taken from the town jail by a mob. In all, ninety-seven people were piked to death on the bridge.

On the 5 June, the day of the Scullabogue massacre, the rebels met with their first major defeat when they failed to capture the important town of New Ross. The government was now able to mount a counter-attack and pour troops into Co. Wexford.

The massacre at Scullabogue.

Test your knowledge

1 Explain the dangerous condition of Co. Wexford in May 1798.
2 What campaign was begun by the authorities on 20 May?
3 Why did Father John Murphy of Boolavogue agree to lead a rebellion?
4 Describe the early victories of the rebel army.
5 Describe the massacre at Scullabogue.
6 What appalling incident took place at the bridge in Wexford town?
7 What happened at New Ross on 5 June 1798?

Vinegar Hill

At the start of the rebellion, Father John Murphy had established a camp on Vinegar Hill near Enniscorthy. As the British forces advanced, the rebels gathered on Vinegar Hill. Here on 21 June, the rebel force of 20,000 men was attacked by an army under General Lake. Pikes and scythes were no match for the artillery of a regular army. General Lake gained a complete victory and forced the rebels from Enniscorthy. Some rebels fled to Wicklow and continued to fight. But the defeat of Vinegar Hill and the capture of Wexford town, which soon followed, marked the end of the rebellion in the south-east.

The rebel camp at Vinegar Hill.

The defeat of the Wexford Rising at Vinegar Hill, 21 June 1798.

The soldiers under Lake's command scoured the country for rebels, hanging many suspects and burning houses as they proceeded. Bagenal Harvey, Father John Murphy and the other leaders were captured, hanged and their heads placed on spikes as a warning.

With the defeat of the Wexford Rising, it appeared the government had succeeded in stamping out the United Irishmen's rebellion. However, there was one more rising still to come in that fateful year of 1798.

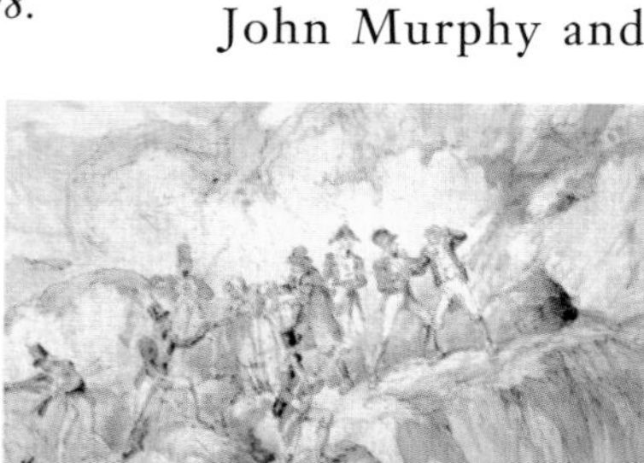
After the Battle of Vinegar Hill, the British forces searched the countryside for rebels on the run. Here they are seen capturing some fugitives, including the leader Bagenal Harvey.

The year of the French

As the rebellion was being crushed in Ireland, Wolfe Tone continued to press the French government to send another expedition to Ireland. In July 1798, the French agreed to send troops the following month, and on 24 August, General Humbert landed at Killala, Co. Mayo, with a thousand soldiers. Although they arrived after the rebellion had been put down in the rest of the country, men from all over Connaught came to join them.

From Killala, General Humbert and his army went on to capture the nearby town of Ballina. He then marched his men over the mountains and launched a surprise attack on the British forces in Castlebar, commanded by General Lake, who had recently arrived from Wexford. Lake and his troops fled on the approach of the French and Irish. In their rush to escape, they left muskets and cannon behind. This victory of Humbert's became popularly known as the *Races of Castlebar*.

Places connected with Wolfe Tone and the Rebellion of 1798.

After this victory, Humbert set up a provisional government of Connaught. John Moore, the younger brother of a Catholic landlord from Mayo, became its president. When reinforcements from France failed to arrive, Humbert decided to leave Connaught and march towards Dublin.

All the time the government was gathering reinforcements. On 6 September, Humbert's small force of around 850 men was defeated at Ballinamuck, Co. Longford by a British army of around 10,000 under the command of Lord Cornwallis and General Lake.

The short-lived expedition of the French had come to a sudden end.

The French under General Humbert surrender at Ballinamuck.

The death of Wolfe Tone

In October 1798, a French expedition of 3,000 men sailed into Lough Swilly in Co. Donegal. Wolfe Tone was on board the flagship, the *Hoche*. After a fierce sea battle, the British fleet was victorious.

Tone was among the French army officers taken prisoner. Recognised at once, he was immediately sent to Dublin to stand trial. Charged with treason, his trial took place on 10 November. He admitted all charges against him and then read a statement explaining his actions. As a last request, Tone asked that he be shot like a soldier.

Lord Cornwallis, the Lord Lieutenant, refused this request and Tone was sentenced to be hanged by the public hangman on 12 November. Early that morning, he cut his throat in prison. He lingered on in great pain for a week and died on the morning of 19 November 1798.

As a revolutionary leader, Wolfe Tone has an important place in Irish history. Because of his belief that the solution to Ireland's problems was an independent republic, he has become known as the *Father of Irish Republicanism*. Many people admired his republican views and his desire to unite Irish people of all religions. Many others, however, criticised Wolfe Tone's belief in the use of violence in order to achieve complete separation from Great Britain.

Why the 1798 Rising failed

The 1798 rebellion of the United Irishmen failed for a number of important reasons. Apart from Wexford, only a small minority of people were prepared to take up arms against the government. The leaders of all religions condemned the United Irishmen and the rising. As well as Protestant and Presbyterian leaders, the Catholic bishops strongly opposed it. So did most Catholic priests. Father John Murphy and the small number of other rebel priests were very much the exception.

From the outset, the British government had a very efficient spy network. It provided information on the United Irishmen from local level right up to the secret meetings of the leaders.

The poorly-armed and ill-disciplined rebel forces were no match for the well-armed regular troops who were commanded by experienced generals. In addition to this, when the regular French troops arrived in August 1798, the rebellion was all but over.

The rising of 1798 had one result which was completely at variance with Wolfe Tone's hopes. Instead of drawing Irish people of different religions closer together, it actually drove them further apart. Protestants and Presbyterians in the north of Ireland were particularly horrified at the massacre of Protestants in Wexford. In the years which followed, most of them began to see the connection with England as being essential to their well-being and prosperity.

Test your knowledge

1 Describe the outcome of the Battle of Vinegar Hill.
2 Name the British commander at the battle.
3 What punishment was meted out to the leaders of the rebellion in Wexford?
4 Where did General Humbert and a thousand troops land in Ireland in August 1798?
5 What were the 'Races of Castlebar'?
6 What happened at the Battle of Ballinamuck?
7 Describe the capture and arrest of Wolfe Tone.
8 Why is Tone known as 'The Father of Irish Republicanism'?

Wolfe Tone

- Wolfe Tone was born in Dublin in 1763. Educated at Trinity College, he later trained as a barrister.
- Tone welcomed the French Revolution. In 1791, he set up the society of United Irishmen in Belfast and Dublin.
- Tone's main political aims were to break the connection between Ireland and England by violent means and to unite Irish people of all religious beliefs in a struggle against England.
- In 1794, Tone went to America to escape arrest. In 1796 he sailed for France where he tried to persuade the revolutionary government to send soldiers to Ireland.
- In December 1796, Tone was part of a French expedition which failed to land at Bantry Bay in Cork because of bad weather.
- Throughout 1797 and most of 1798, Tone remained in France, urging the government to send troops to Ireland. In October 1798, he was arrested by British forces off the coast of Donegal on his arrival as part of another French expedition.
- Tone was brought to Dublin where he was tried, found guilty of treason and sentenced to death by hanging. To avoid this, he cut his own throat and died in prison a week later on 19 November 1798.

Chapter 44: Review

- The signal for the rising to begin throughout the country on 24 May 1798 was the stopping of the mail coaches from Dublin. Before the year 1798 was over, the rebellion which began that day would cost 30,000 lives.
- The rising in north Leinster was easily put down by government troops and soon the roads between Dublin and the country were re-opened.
- On 7 June the rising in Ulster began when Henry Joy McCracken, a Presbyterian cotton manufacturer, led the attack on the town of Antrim. Two days later, a young Protestant draper from Lisburn, Henry Monroe, began a rising in Co. Down.
- After a week of fighting, the rebellion in Ulster was crushed by British troops and both leaders, McCracken and Monroe, were captured and hanged.

• The most serious threat to British rule in Ireland in 1798 began when a rising broke out in Co. Wexford on 27 May. It began at Boolavogue when the local Catholic priest, Father John Murphy, agreed to lead the people in rebellion.

• The Wexford rebels were armed mostly with pikes and scythes. They won their first victory at Oulart Hill. They then captured Enniscorthy and Wexford town itself.

• In Wexford town, local Protestants were kept under guard by the rebels as they were suspected of supporting the British government.

• Two appalling incidents took place during the rebel control of Wexford. At Scullabogue, Protestant men, women and children were burned to death in a barn. At Wexford Bridge, Protestant prisoners were massacred by the rebels.

• Having failed to capture New Ross, the rebels gathered at Vinegar Hill hear Enniscorthy. Here, on 21 June they were defeated by British forces under General Lake. After this victory, the troops scoured the countryside burning houses and hanging many rebel suspects.

• On 24 August 1798, a French expedition of a thousand soldiers, under the command of General Humbert, landed at Killala Bay in Co. Mayo. Although they arrived after the rebellion had been put down in the rest of the country, men from all over Connaught joined them.

• After their victory at Castlebar, Humbert and his French and Irish followers marched towards Dublin. However, they were defeated at Ballinamuck, Co. Longford by a much larger British army.

• In October 1798 Wolfe Tone was captured on board a French warship off the coast of Donegal. He was immediately sent to Dublin to stand trial for treason against the king of England.

• Found guilty at his trial and condemned to hang, Tone requested that he be shot like a soldier. When this was refused, he attempted to commit suicide by cutting his throat. He lingered in great pain for a week and died on 19 November 1798.

• Because of his belief that the solution to Ireland's problems lay in an independent Irish republic, Wolfe Tone became known as the 'The Father of Irish Republicanism'.

• The 1798 rising failed for a number of reasons. Only a small minority of people supported it, and religious leaders condemned it. The British government had an efficient spy system and poorly-armed rebels were no match for well-armed, disciplined regular soldiers.

• Instead of drawing Irish people of different religions closer together, the events of 1798 drove them further apart. After that date, almost all Protestants looked on the connection with England as essential for their safety and well-being.

The Life of the People—Industrial England and Rural Ireland

CHAPTER 45 The Agricultural Revolution

Britain in 1750

Today around 60 million people live in Great Britain. Most of these work in factories or offices and live in towns or cities.

In the year 1750, Britain had a population of 7 million. The vast majority of the people worked long hours on the land where they barely grew enough food for themselves. Unlike today, Britain was then a country of small villages.

The only type of industry to be found in Britain in 1750 was carried out in tiny workshops or in people's homes. All work was done slowly by hand. As a result, the number of goods produced was very small.

A woman spinning wool slowly by hand. This was the kind of industry carried out around 1750.

Unlike today, when people think of travelling great distances, most people in 1750 rarely travelled outside their own villages. Roads were poor and a journey by coach was long, uncomfortable and dangerous.

By 1800, however, great changes were in the air. Children born at that time were to grow up in a world which was to be vastly different from that of their grandparents' generation. In this chapter, we will take a closer look at some of these changes.

A time of change

From around 1750, the population of Britain was beginning to rise rapidly. Study the figures and graph which show this increase. Around this time, people were marrying at a younger age and, as a result of this, more children were born. The *birth rate* (number of children born in a year per 1,000 people in the population) was increasing. People were also living longer because of better food, a more varied diet, and the use of vaccination to overcome some killer diseases. Therefore, the *death rate* (number of people who died per 1,000 of the population) decreased at this time.

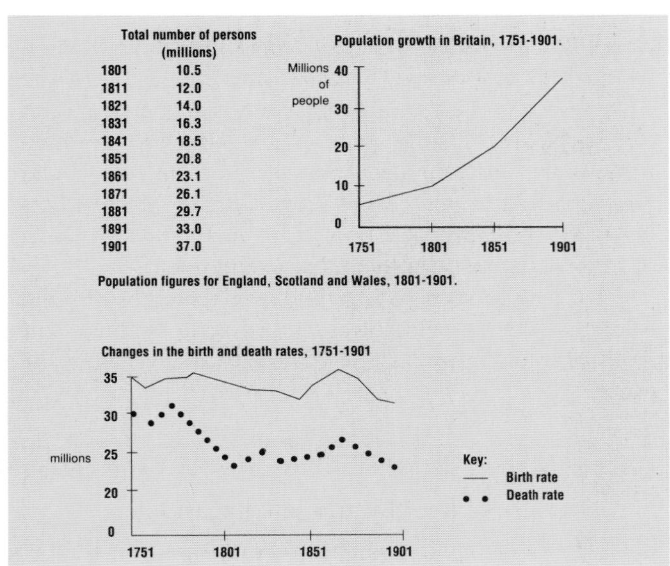

	Total number of persons (millions)
1801	10.5
1811	12.0
1821	14.0
1831	16.3
1841	18.5
1851	20.8
1861	23.1
1871	26.1
1881	29.7
1891	33.0
1901	37.0

Population figures for England, Scotland and Wales, 1801-1901.

It should now be clear that the population of Britain was growing rapidly by the year 1800 because of a rising birth rate and a falling death rate. Many of these extra people no longer lived in the countryside but moved to the new towns which were expanding quickly at this time. Look carefully at the pie charts. They show how the number of people living in the towns has greatly increased from around 1750 onwards.

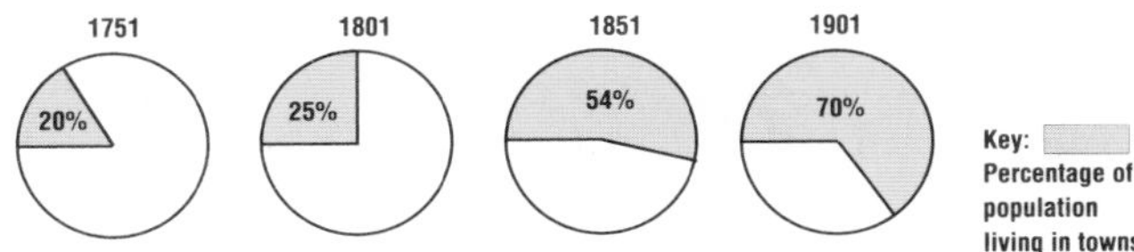

The increase in the population of towns.

The importance of population growth

The growing population of Britain created a number of problems and challenges. In the towns, many people lived in miserable conditions, with overcrowded houses lining dirty streets. They worked in big factories where they sweated long hours for little money.

In the countryside, more food was now needed to feed the rapidly rising population. Old ways of farming which had remained unchanged for hundreds of years were no longer good enough. New and better methods were urgently needed.

The changes taking place at this time in both town and country were so great that the word 'revolution' has been used to describe them. The changes in the countryside have been called the *Agricultural Revolution*. The changes in the towns and factories have been called the *Industrial Revolution*.

We will now look more closely at the first of these revolutions and at the people who helped to bring it about.

Test your knowledge

1 By how much did the population of Britain increase in the years 1750 to 1850?
2 What is meant by birth rate? Why did the birth rate in Britain increase around 1750?
3 What is meant by death rate? Why did the death rate in Britain decrease around 1750?
4 Where were many of the extra people living by the early years of the nineteenth century?
5 In what conditions did many of the people in the towns live?
6 Why was more food needed?
7 What do you understand by the term 'revolution'? Why do you think this term has been used to describe what was happening in Britain around 1800?

Life on the land

In 1750, most of the land of Britain was owned by powerful landlords. Each landlord lived with his family in a huge mansion on his vast estate. Most of these landlords were very well off and some were enormously wealthy. At this time, one of the richest men in Britain was the Duke of Devonshire, with an income of £50,000 a year (an average workingman in 1800 earned less than £50 a year). Look closely at the pictures and see what they tell you about the lifestyle of the landlord and his family.

Landlords made their money by renting lands to farmers who were known as *tenants*. Some tenants rented a lot of land and were able to grow more food than their families needed. They made more money by selling their surpluses to local markets.

The country mansion of a landlord and his family.

Hunting was the favourite pastime of the rich in the countryside.

Harvest time on the land.

Most tenants, however, had very small farms. Many of them could not grow enough food for their families and had to work part-time as labourers for the larger farmers.

Most labourers lived in miserable conditions of poverty. The following description of labourers' cottages was written by a doctor around 1800. It highlights the dreadful conditions in which so many labourers lived.

Working with evidence

'Most of the cottages are of the worst kind: some were mud hovels with cesspools of filth close to the doors. The mud floors of many are much below the level of the road and in wet seasons are little better than so much clay. In many of the cottages I visited, the beds stood on the ground floor, which was damp three parts of the year; scarcely one had a fireplace in the bedroom, and one had a single, small pane of glass stuck in the mud walls as its only window, with a large heap of wet and dirty potatoes in one corner. Persons living in such cottages are generally very poor, very dirty and usually in rags, living almost wholly on bread and potatoes.

I have often seen springs bursting through the mud floors of some of the cottages, and little channels cut from the centre under the doorways to carry off the water.'

1 Make a list which illustrates why the cottages were unhealthy and uncomfortable.
2 What food was eaten by the people living in the cottages?
3 How were they dressed?

Take a look at the chart which tells us more about the miserable conditions of the labourer and his family.

WEEKLY INCOME	
Husband's wages	40 p
Wife's work at harvest time	2.5p
Total	42.5p

The following information was collected by a clergyman in 1787. It dealt with some of the labourers living in his parish. The family in this example consisted of a husband, a wife and five children.

WEEKLY COSTS	
Flour	31p
Bacon	3p
Sugar, tea, butter, lard	5p
Soup	1p
Candles	1.5p
Thread	1.5p
Total	43p

A yearly expenditure of £6 added another 11.5p per week to weekly costs. What problems did this family face in surviving? What would happen if the cost of flour increased?

Yearly costs	
Rent	£2.00
Fuel	50p
Clothing	£3.50
Total	£6.00

Open-field farming

In 1750, a landlord's estate was generally divided into three huge unfenced or 'open' fields. Each field was then divided into one-acre strips of land which were rented out to tenants. In any one year, only two of the three fields were cultivated with crops. The other field was always left *fallow* or uncultivated. This allowed the soil to rest and to restore its goodness. There was also *common land* on the estate where anyone could graze cattle. Those who had no land—the *squatters*—often used this land to graze a single cow. This kind of farming was known as *open-field farming*, a system which had been followed in Britain for many hundreds of years. Look carefully at the diagram and examine more closely how open-field farming worked.

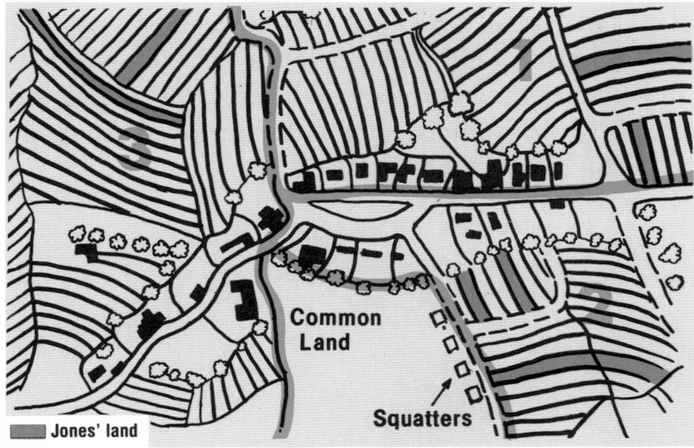

The open-field system of farming. Note the three large fields at 1, 2 and 3. Each contained one-acre strips of land used by different farmers. In the diagrams you will see that farmer Jones has strips of land in each of the three fields.

The case against open-field farming

We have already learned that there was a large increase in Britain's population from around 1750 onwards. This led to a demand for more and more food. The open-field system, however, was not able to meet this demand for increased food production.

For many years, some landlords had wanted to enclose or fence in their land. They had a number of reasons for this. Work on open-field farms was slow and inefficient. Since there were no fences between strips of land, weeds could easily spread. The good work of one farmer could be quickly undone by the carelessness of a neighbour. The farmer lost much valuable time in travelling between his different strips of land, which were usually not side by side but scattered throughout the estate. As animals mixed freely together on the common land, cattle diseases spread rapidly. Furthermore, as one field was always left fallow, the village land was never used to its full potential.

Look at the map of an open-field farm and see how many of these disadvantages you can identify from it.

Enclosing the land

Because of all these drawbacks, there were growing demands—especially by landlords themselves—to put an end to the open-field farms and to fence in, or enclose, all the land.

Like many changes, *land enclosure* was to be welcomed by some and opposed by others. Many labourers feared that the new enclosed farms would require fewer workers and that they would lose their jobs as a result. In addition, many poor people who had no land but had been allowed to graze a cow on the common, could no longer do so.

Landlords who wished to enclose their land had to apply to parliament for permission. As most members of parliament were themselves rich landlords, hundreds of *Acts of Enclosure* were passed. As a result, millions of acres of land were enclosed by 1800 as the old open fields were broken up into individual farms.

Examine the map of the enclosed farm. Compare it with the open-field farm.

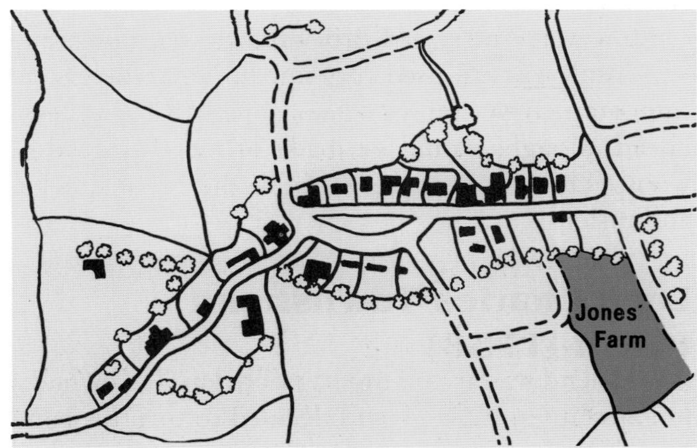

The enclosed farm system. Notice how the same estate has changed as a result of enclosure. It has been fenced off into larger farms. Farmer Jones' land is now all together in one single farm. The common land has also been enclosed as a farm.

Test your knowledge

1 What was open-field farming?
2 State two drawbacks in this method of farming.
3 Why was there a growing demand to put an end to the open-field system?
4 What was meant by land enclosure? Why did some people oppose it?
5 What did a landlord have to do before enclosing his land?

Three men of change

Other changes in farming were taking place at the same time as land enclosure. New machines were making work on the land easier. Both crop-growing and cattle-rearing were greatly improved. Three men played an important part in these changes.

Jethro Tull (1674–1741)

In the open-field farms, seeds had always been planted by hand until a man named Jethro Tull thought of a method of sowing seeds mechanically. In 1701, he invented a *seed drill* which planted seeds in even rows.

A seed drill in action.

However, Tull's seed drill often broke down and as a result was not used very much. Nevertheless, an important first step had been taken. In the years ahead, ploughs would be made of metal instead of wood. This would make work on the farms quicker and easier.

Lord Charles Townshend (1674–1738)

Townshend was at one time a politician. He owned a huge estate in Norfolk and decided to turn his hand to farming his own land.

He developed a famous system of *crop rotation*. The diagram shows how this system worked.

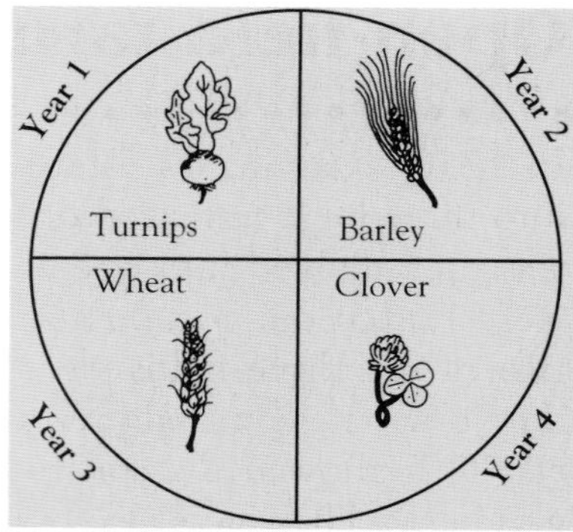

A different crop was grown in the field each year. This gave the land a chance to renew its goodness.

Robert Bakewell (1725–95)

Under the open-field system, cattle mixed freely together and disease spread rapidly among them.

Robert Bakewell wanted to improve the quality of sheep and cows which, at the time, were very thin and unhealthy. He took cattle off the common land and placed them in enclosed fields. By selectively breeding the animals, he greatly improved the quality of the herd.

Robert Bakewell (1725–95) brought about great improvements in the quality of livestock, especially sheep.

The results of change

In this chapter we have seen some of the changes which were happening in Britain around 1800. The Agricultural Revolution was changing the face of the countryside. Open-field farms were replaced by new enclosed farms. Better farming methods were also developed, such as crop rotation and selective animal breeding.

Arthur Young (1741–1820) was the best-known writer on farming matters of his day. He was in no doubt that the changes were all for the better. In 1768, he described what he saw in Norfolk.

'All the country was a wild sheep walk before the spirit of improvement seized the inhabitants, and this great spirit has had amazing effects. Instead of boundless wilds and uncultivated wastes inhabited by scarcely anything but sheep, the country is all cut into enclosures, cultivated in a most efficient manner, well peopled and yielding a hundred times the produce that it did in its former state.'

It is true, as Arthur Young says, that the new farming methods produced far more food. However, his enthusiasm for the changes made him overlook some of the problems caused by these new methods.

Many small farmers and labourers were now no longer able to make a living on the land. Those who wanted to introduce improved farming methods favoured larger farms. This was because large farmers were usually the ones with the money to change to the new methods. In addition, many small farmers could not afford the cost of enclosure and, as a result, left the land. The squatters who had grazed their cattle on the common land were also forced to move on.

Many of those who left the countryside because of the agricultural changes now flocked into the towns in search of work in the new factories. In this way, the changes in the countryside prepared the way for the Industrial Revolution in the towns.

Test your knowledge

1 What did Jethro Tull invent? In what way was this invention an important first step?

2 What new method of farming did Lord Townshend develop on his Norfolk estate?

3 How did Robert Bakewell improve the quality of cattle?

4 Who was Arthur Young? What were his views on the new changes in farming methods?

5 How did the changes in the countryside cause problems for many people?

Chapter 45: Review

• Great changes were taking place in Britain around the year 1800. The population was rapidly increasing. As a result, more food had to be grown and more goods such as cloth had to be produced. The changes in the countryside were known as the Agricultural Revolution, while the changes in the towns were called the Industrial Revolution.

• In 1750, open-field farming was practised throughout Britain. This consisted of three huge, unfenced fields which were divided into one-acre strips and then rented out to tenants.

• The open-field farmers could not produce enough food for the growing population. Weeds spread rapidly and animals could roam freely throughout the estate. There was a great demand to enclose farms.

• Land enclosure was greatly welcomed by the landlords. But some tenants and labourers, afraid that they would have to leave the land, were against it. However, soon millions of acres of land were enclosed, and the open fields were broken up into individual farms.

• Other changes in farming methods were also taking place at this time. Jethro Tull invented a seed drill to sow seeds. Robert Bakewell improved the quality of sheep and cows by a process of selective breeding. Lord Charles Townshend developed a famous system of crop rotation on his Norfolk estate which improved the quality of the soil.

• All these changes in the countryside improved the quality and production of food which was needed to feed the growing numbers in the towns. Also, the small farmers and labourers who were forced off the land now went to new factory towns in search of work.

The Workshop of the World

Today, many people live in cities or towns and work in factories. These factories produce a great variety of goods which are made by machines.

People did not always live and work in this way, however. Around 1750, most work was not carried out in factories but in small workshops which were usually attached to people's homes. Here small quantities of goods–especially clothing– were made slowly by hand.

Because this small-scale industry was based in the home, it was called *domestic industry*.

Domestic industry: women spinning yarn in the home, using simple hand-worked spinning wheels. Spinning involved the making of a long yarn out of raw wool.

The heavier work of weaving was carried out by the men, using a hand loom. Weaving involved the making of the yarn into finished cloth.

We learned in the last chapter that the population of Britain was growing rapidly from around 1750 onwards. This was to result in a much greater demand for goods. Gradually, work done by hand was to be replaced by machines which could produce greater quantities of goods more quickly and cheaply. The small domestic workshops gradually disappeared. From then on, most work was to be carried on in big factories which were located in towns.

This changeover from domestic to factory industry has been called the *Industrial Revolution*. The first Industrial Revolution in the world took place in Britain between the years 1750 and 1850.

Britain: The world's first industrial power

Britain became the first industrial country in the world for the following reasons:

We will now look at the first industry to be affected by these changes: cloth-making.

Test your knowledge

1 What was domestic industry?
2 Why was there a demand for more goods around the year 1800?
3 What was the Industrial Revolution?
4 What country was the first to have an Industrial Revolution?
5 State two causes of the Industrial Revolution.

The cotton factories

If you had lived around 1750, your clothes would have been made from wool. Fifty years later, most of your clothes would have been made from cotton. By 1800, cotton manufacturing had become Britain's greatest industry. Look at the graph and see for yourself how quickly this industry grew.

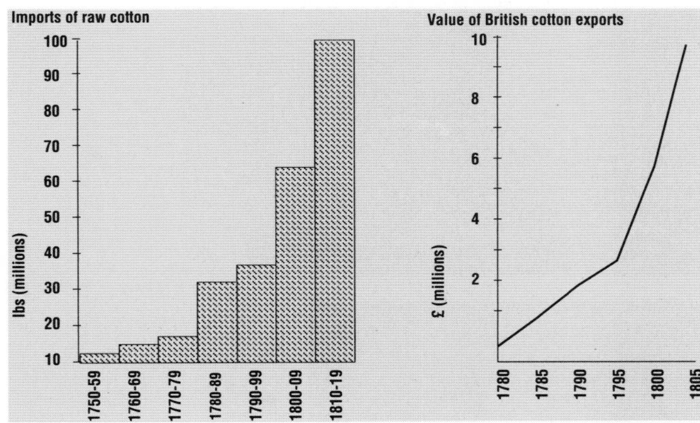

Woollen and cotton clothes were originally made slowly by hand in people's homes. By 1800, new machines had been invented which greatly speeded up the production of cloth and led to the building of large factories.

The earliest factories were located in the countryside near rivers or streams. The machines used in these mills were run by water power.

Here the power of water is being used to operate the machinery in a mill. These early mills were located in the countryside near a river.

Examine the drawings showing some of the machines which greatly changed the cloth-making industry.

SPINNING JENNY
James Hargreaves (1765)

Allowed one spinner to spin eight yarns at a time.

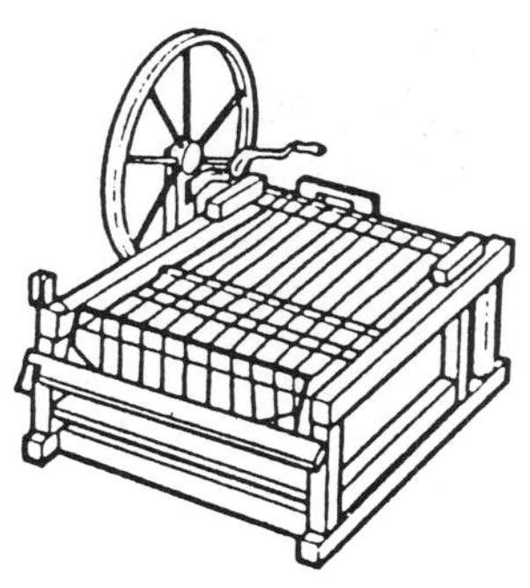

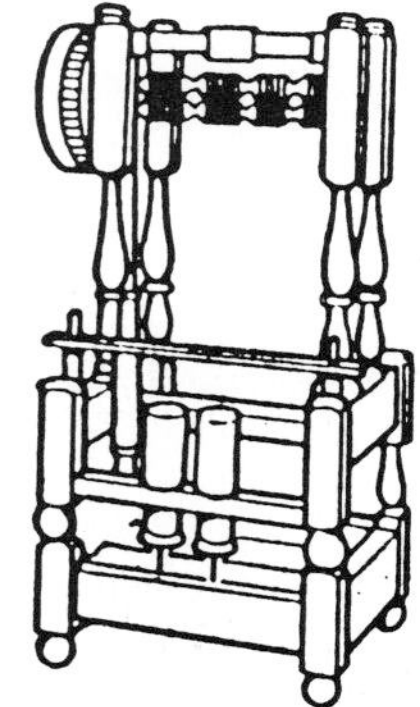

WATER FRAME
Richard Arkwright (1768)

Allowed the spinning of hundreds of yarns at the same time. It was run by water power.

SPINNING MULE
Samuel Crompton (1779)

Better than the water frame and made finer thread. Needed a skilled operator.

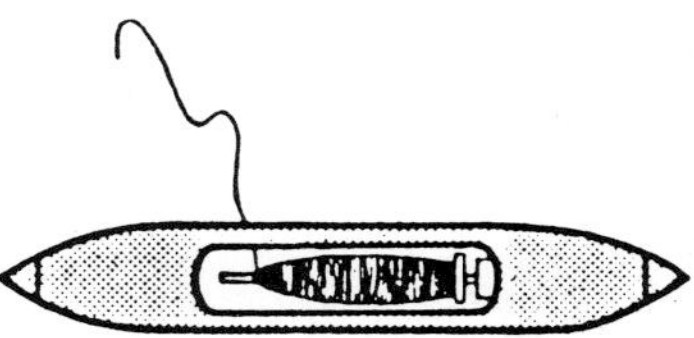

FLYING SHUTTLE
John Kay (1733)

Allowed one weaver to double the work.

POWER LOOM
Edmund Cartwright (1785)

Greatly speeded up the weaving of cloth. It was run by steam power.

Workers operating the new spinning machinery in a factory.

The power of steam

By the early 1800s, many cotton factories were using steam power to run their machines. The use of steam to power machines was the greatest discovery of the Industrial Revolution. Before this, wind, water and the muscles of people and animals were the only ways of producing power.

The first successful steam engine was invented in 1705 by a man named Thomas Newcomen. Newcomen's engine was only used for pumping water out of mines. Although it was unreliable and often broke down, this engine was not improved on for almost sixty years.

James Watt—engineer and inventor—looking at the steam coming from a kettle.

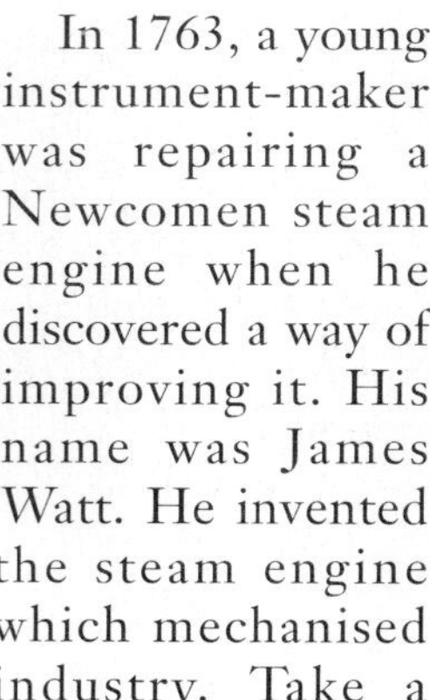

In 1763, a young instrument-maker was repairing a Newcomen steam engine when he discovered a way of improving it. His name was James Watt. He invented the steam engine which mechanised industry. Take a close look at the picture of Watt's engine. Its rotary motion could turn big machines in factories. The steam engine also led to some huge changes in transport.

Watt's pumping engine, on display in the Science Museum in London.

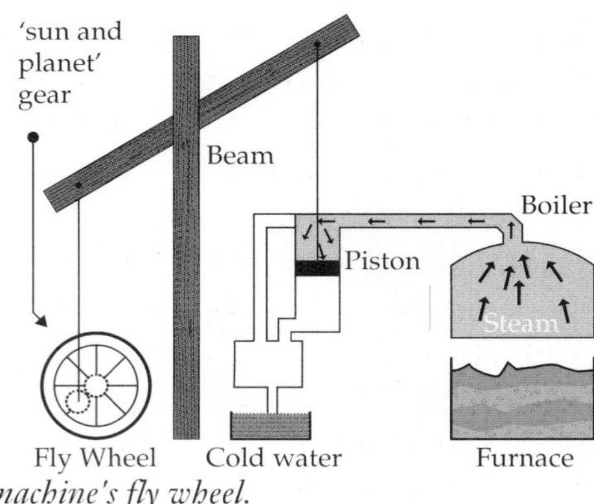

Watt's steam engine. Steam from the boiler forces the piston down and up, causing the beam to move as well. The beam in turn drives the 'sun and planet' gear, which moves the machine's fly wheel.

Let us now take a look at two industries which were greatly changed by the new invention of steam power—coal-mining and iron-making.

Down the mines

Inside a coalmine.

A night-time view of a coal-mining area.

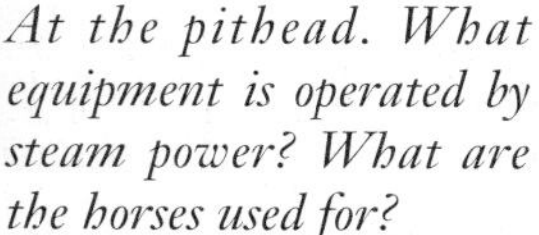

At the pithead. What equipment is operated by steam power? What are the horses used for?

Coal was the most important fuel to be used during the Industrial Revolution. It was needed to power the steam engines, to make iron goods and to run trains. Many of the new factories were built close to the coal mines.

Coal-mining was always a hard and dangerous job. Water usually flooded the shafts when the miners dug below a certain level. At first, this water prevented them from digging to deeper levels where the best coal was to be found. Newcomen's steam engine helped to solve this problem because it could successfully pump water out of the mines.

However, it took much longer to mechanise the other aspects of mining. Horses were used to wind baskets of coal to the top of the shaft. Eventually new mechanised winding equipment was installed at the mines, and the steam engine soon replaced the horses as the main means of transporting coal from the mines to ships on a nearby river.

Despite these advances, work in the mines remained slow, hard, and dangerous. Study the following sources. They tell us about the dangers faced by the miners in their daily work.

Working with evidence

Source A

A newspaper report describing a visit to a mine in 1859.

'You have a candle stuck into a bit of moist clay. With this, your eyes become used to the gloom and you can now explore the mine. You pass the stables, which in a pit have a curious indescribable smell. You see the roof bulging in and bending down the cross timbers that rest on stout upright "trees" for support. A door, kept by a boy who sits all day, pent up in darkness, opens to admit us. We come in sight of boys drawing coals to the wagons. These appear like imps, while men, naked to the waist, toiling in deep twilight and black coal-dust, wielding picks, look like full-grown demons. The "holders" or "hewers" are squatting on their haunches, lying on their sides, stooping and bending double to get out the underclay from beneath the bed of coals.'

Source B

The following is a description of an explosion at Felling Colliery on the Durham coalfield in 1812.

'The deep caverns, where the explosion first vent its fury, confined the eruption too much for its utmost noise to be heard on the surface. But for half a mile around, the trembling vibration of the earth could be heard, and for four or five miles an alarm was created by the slow and hollow rumblings in the air. Immense quantities of coal, pieces of wood, and dust drove high into the atmosphere, and the lacerated remains of several bodies were thrown up the shaft. The roads and paths were covered in all directions with pieces of coal and coal dust. Machinery about the shaft was blown to pieces or set on fire, and the town of Haworth, located near the mine, was covered in darkness.'

Source C

Look at the following figures on deaths in the mines of Britain in 1838.

	Age		
Cause of death	*under13*	*13–18*	*over 18*
Fell down shaft	14	16	36
Drawn over pulley	3	–	3
Fall of stone down shaft	1	–	3
Drowned	3	4	15
Fall of stone or coal	14	14	69
Crushed	–	1	1
Explosion of gas	13	18	49
Suffocated	–	2	6
Explosion of gunpowder	–	1	3
By tram wagons	4	5	12

1 What did the writer in Source A use to find his way in the mines?
2 Who opened the door for him?
3 What work was carried out by the boys in the mines?
4 Why do you think the writer described the men as 'full-grown demons'?
5 Source B describes an explosion at Felling Colliery. How did people in the neighbouring area know what had happened?
6 What was thrown up the shaft?
7 What happened to the machinery near the shaft?

8 Source C shows us that an explosion like that at Felling was only one danger facing miners during the Industrial Revolution. Add up the numbers of people killed for each cause and write down the totals in numerical order of importance.

9 What was the total number who died in the mines in 1838?

Iron and steel

The manufacture of iron. What processes in the making of iron can you identify in this picture?

From around 1780 onwards, iron began to replace wood as the main building material. It was used in the construction of bridges, factories, ships and trains. Huge ironworks were built around the country, close to the deposits of coal and iron ore. Look carefully at the chart and see how quickly the iron industry grew from around 1800 onwards.

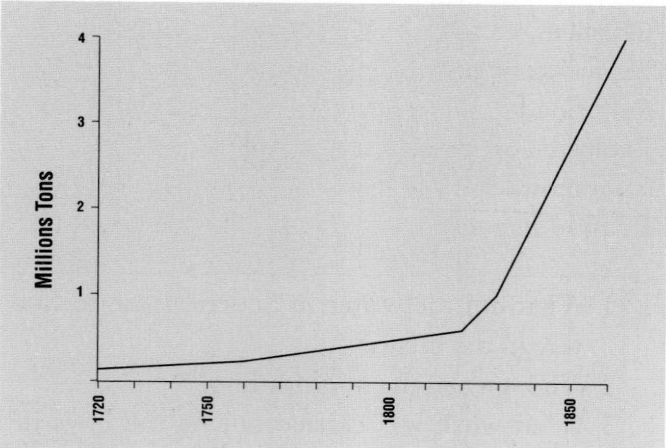

Pig iron output 1720–1860.

You have already seen the important part played by new inventions in the expansion of the cotton industry. The production of cheaper and better-quality iron was also made possible by new inventions. Three men helped bring about important changes in iron production.

Abraham Darby

When iron ore is taken from the ground, it first has to be heated or smelted in blast furnaces. All the impurities are then removed and the remaining iron is cooled to form pig iron.

At first, charcoal was used to run the blast furnaces. In 1709, Abraham Darby discovered that coke could be used instead of charcoal. As coke was far cheaper and in greater supply, pig iron could be made more cheaply than ever before. By 1850, Britain was producing half the pig iron of the world.

Henry Cort

Sometimes the pig iron was reheated and hammered into bars of wrought iron. This wrought iron was a tough metal and used for making horseshoes, nails, picks and spades. In 1794, Henry Cort thought of a way of making cheaper wrought iron.

He called his method 'puddling and rolling'. Puddling involved reheating the pig iron with coke and stirring it with iron rods to remove all the impurities. Rolling involves passing the pig iron between iron rollers which made it into slabs of wrought iron.

Henry Bessemer

The Bessemer process of steel making.

Henry Bessemer invented a converter which processed pig iron into steel by blowing air through the melted iron in a furnace. The pictures show how this worked. The Bessemer Process resulted in the production of better and cheaper steel.

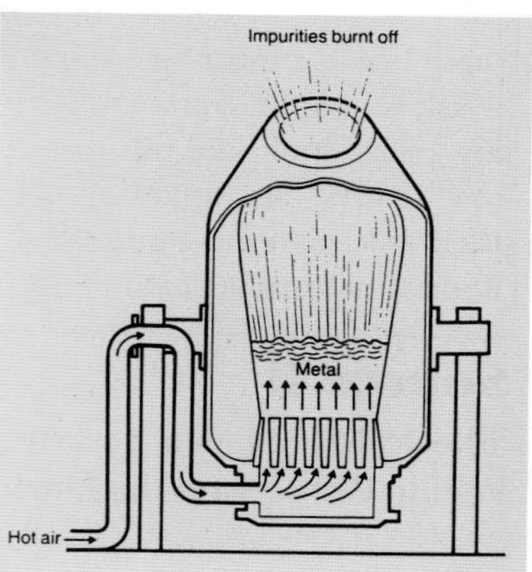

The Bessemer converter for processing pig iron into steel.

Test your knowledge

1 Name two inventions which helped change the clothing industry.
2 How was coal used during the Industrial Revolution?
3 For what purpose was the steam engine first used in coal mines?
4 In what ways was work in the mines slow, hard and dangerous?
5 Why was there a great demand for iron during the Industrial Revolution?
6 What improvements did Abraham Darby bring about in iron-making?
7 What was 'puddling and rolling'? Who invented this process?
8 Who developed a new way of processing steel?

The Great Exhibition of 1851

In this chapter, we have seen that Britain had made great advances in industry from around 1750. The country had certainly earned the title 'Workshop of the World'.

Everyone could see and admire the results of British industry during the Great Exhibition which was held in London in 1851. A special glass building, known as the Crystal Palace, was built to house this huge display which exhibited machines and products from many countries.

Over 20,000 people crowded into the Crystal Palace to see Queen Victoria open the Great Exhibition on 1 May 1851. During its 140 days, there were over 6 million visitors. Many came on special excursions from all parts of the country. The crowds marvelled at the latest developments in steam engines, pottery and furniture.

However, the Industrial Revolution also had its darker side. For many people, living and working conditions remained appalling. In the next chapter, we will examine this darker side of life in the new factory towns.

Crowds gather to see the wonders of industry inside the Crystal Palace during the Great Exhibition of 1851.

Chapter 46: Review

• Before the coming of factories and machines, industry took place in small workshops which were usually attached to people's homes. This system was known as domestic industry.

• By 1800, great changes were taking place in Britain. New machines were being invented and industry now moved to factories which were located in new towns. This changeover from domestic to factory industry became known as the Industrial Revolution.

• Britain was the first country in the world to experience an Industrial Revolution. This was because its increase in population resulted in a demand for more goods. Britain had large supplies of coal and iron which were needed to work the new machines. It had many rich businessmen who were willing to invest money in new industries.

• Steam power was the greatest invention during the Industrial Revolution. While Thomas Newcomen invented the first successful steam engine, James Watt was the man who perfected it.

• Textiles or cloth-making had, for a long time, been one of Britain's greatest industries. Under the domestic system, the two processes of spinning and weaving had been carried out slowly by hand in small workshops.

• With a growing population, there was a great demand for more cloth. New ways were found of speeding up production. The more important inventions were the spinning jenny (1765, James Hargreaves), the water frame (1768, Richard Arkwright), and the power loom (1785, Edmund Cartwright).

• Coal was needed to work the new machines. In the early days, coal-mining was all done by hand and there were great dangers involved in it. Steam power increased the demand for coal and also helped to mechanise the industry. New winding equipment was installed and steam engines were used to take the coal from the mines to a nearby canal or river.

• Iron was also in great demand at this time, and new ways of processing it were developed. Abraham Darby discovered that coke could be used instead of charcoal to make pig iron. Henry Cort developed a new way of making cheaper wrought iron called 'puddling and rolling'.

• The great industrial developments of this time, in both Britain and Europe, were shown to the world in a Great Exhibition which took place in London's Crystal Palace in 1851.

CHAPTER 47 Life in the Factory Towns

In the last chapter, we studied some of the vast changes which came about in Britain as a result of the Industrial Revolution. Thousands of people crowded into the towns in search of work in the new steam-powered factories.

Workers relaxing at dinner hour outside the factory.

The Industrial Revolution was to make some people very rich. Factory owners and businessmen reaped handsome profits from their investments. However, in the early days especially, the factory workers and their families lived and worked in conditions of terrible misery and poverty.

In this chapter we will examine for ourselves the life and times of these factory workers.

The working day

Before the new steam-powered machines were invented, processes such as spinning and weaving were carried out by skilled men and women. The new machines, however, could be easily operated by people who had no special skills. Because of this, those who worked in the new factories were mostly unskilled. With such a great supply of unskilled men and women, factory owners could make their employees work long hours for very low wages.

Take a look at the chart. It shows the typical day of a person working in a cotton mill in the early nineteenth century. As you can see, the working day in such a factory was long and disciplined.

Working with evidence

The following account describes the appalling working conditions in the cotton industry early in the nineteenth century.

> 'Some of these lords of the loom have, in their employ, thousands of miserable creatures. In the cotton-spinning work these creatures are kept fourteen hours in each day, locked up, summer and winter, in heat of 80 to 84 degrees. The rules which they are subjected to are such as no negro slaves were ever subjected to.
>
> Observe too that these creatures have no cool room to retreat to, not a moment to wipe off the sweat, and not a breath of air to come between them and infection. The door of the place where they work is locked, except half an hour at tea time. The workers are not allowed to send for water to drink. If any spinner is found with his window open, he is to pay a fine of one shilling.
>
> Not only is there not a breath of sweet air, but, for most of the time, there is the terrible stink of the gas, mixed with the steam. There is dust and what is called cotton flyings, which the unfortunate creatures have to inhale. And the fact is that all men are rendered old and past labour at forty years of age, and that children are rendered decrepit and deformed, and thousands of them are slaughtered by consumption before they arrive at the age of sixteen.'

1. What do you think the writer means by the 'lords of the loom'?
2. How many people does one of these employ?
3. Make a list of the ways in which the writer feels that factories are unpleasant.
4. What happens to workers who break the rules of the factory?
5. What happens to many people as a result of working in the factories?
6. What do you think is the writer's opinion of the factory owners?
7. Name the terrible disease that killed many child workers before they were sixteen years of age.

Children at work

Because wages were so low, children were sent to work so that families could survive. Children as young as six or seven years of age often worked twelve to fourteen hours a day. In cotton mills, their small hands were used for tying thread together. In coal mines, they worked in dark damp, underground passages where the younger ones opened and shut trap doors.

Children at work in a cotton mill. What does this tell us about the dangers they faced?

The older children worked in the mines as 'hurriers'. Their job was to drag wagons full of coal, called *corves*, from the pit to the bottom of the shaft where they were then wound to the surface. These hurriers were usually the children of the 'hewers', the men who dug the coal and loaded it into the trucks.

The life expectancy of these children was very low. Their backs were deformed from crouching and bending. Their eyesight was poor because of the dark, dreary atmosphere in which they worked. Their lungs and breathing were very badly damaged by the smoke and other gases which they constantly inhaled.

Housing conditions

At first factory owners built good houses for their workers. Those who worked in the first mills, which were often built beside streams in the countryside, lived in solid redbrick houses nearby.

All of this changed when industry moved to the towns and cities. With thousands of people looking for work, housing was in very short supply and overcrowding became a great problem. As towns became industrialised, many people moved away from the centres. Their houses, fallen into terrible decay, became the new homes of the factory workers.

The poor lived in terrible slums, like these in London.

Several families lived in each house, with one or perhaps two families to each room. The conditions of poverty in which these families lived were appalling. The floors of the houses were bare, and the walls and ceilings were damp. There was very little furniture and the beds consisted of old straw or hair mattresses stretched on the floor.

Inside a Manchester slum around 1850. What can you learn from this about the housing conditions of the poor?

The cheapest and most common type of accommodation for factory workers and their families was a cellar. These cellars were dark, damp and dirty. The population of the city of Manchester at the time was 80,000. About 15,000 of them lived in cellars. The following evidence will give a clearer picture of the terrible conditions in which these people lived.

Working with evidence

Source A

This is the report of a doctor describing conditions in a cellar in 1842.

> 'I have been in one of these damp cellars, without the slightest drainage, every drop of wet and every piece of dirt and filth having to be carried up into the streets. Beds are overlaid with sacks for five persons. There was scarcely anything in the room to sit on, but a stool or a few bricks. The floor, in many places, is absolutely wet, and there is also a pig in the corner.'

Source B

These are the results of a survey carried out by Dr James Kay on housing conditions in Manchester in 1832.

District	No. of houses inspected	No. of houses reported as requiring whitewashing	No. of houses reported as requiring repair
1	850	399	128
2	2489	898	282
3	213	145	104
4	650	279	106
5	413	176	82
6	12	3	5
7	343	76	59
8	132	35	30
9	128	34	32
10	370	195	53
11	113	33	23
12	757	218	44
13	481	74	13
TOTAL	6951	2565	960

District	No. of houses reported as damp	No. of houses reported as ill-ventilated	No. of houses reported as wanting lavatories	No. of streets containing human and other refuse
1	177	70	326	64
2	497	109	755	92
3	61	52	96	28
4	134	69	250	52
5	101	11	66	12
6	–	–	5	2
7	86	21	79	17
8	48	22	20	7
9	39	19	25	20
10	54	2	232	23
11	24	16	52	4
12	146	54	177	23
13	68	7	138	8
TOTAL	1435	452	2221	352

1 Describe the conditions seen by the doctor on his visit to the cellar.
2 What furniture was in the room?
3 Look at the Housing Survey carried out by James Kay. List the faults noted by him.
4 What seems to be the worst problem detected by Kay?
5 What overall impression do you get of housing in Manchester from Kay's survey?

Disease

Because of the filthy conditions in which many people lived, disease was a constant danger during the Industrial Revolution. The dreaded diseases of the time were typhus, typhoid, and cholera. Cholera was the most feared disease of all. Over half of those who got it died, and death was usually sudden and painful. At the time, people did not understand what caused cholera. They believed that it was caught from poisons floating in the air. It was much later before people understood that cholera was caused by a germ present in dirty drinking water or impure food.

Poor people, weakened by disease, wait for help outside a hospital ward.

In 1842, a man named Edwin Chadwick wrote a report called *The Sanitary Condition of the Labouring Population of Great Britain*.

This is how he describes the conditions of some victims of disease.

'In the year 1836–37, I attended a family of thirteen, twelve of whom had typhus fever, without a bed in the cellar, without straw or timber shavings. They lay on the floor and so crowded was it that I could scarcely pass between them.

In another house, I attended fourteen patients. There were only two beds in the house. All the patients, as lodgers, lay on boards and, during their illness, never had their clothes off.

It will be seen that, in the township of Manchester, a population of nearly 80,000, one twenty-eighth are swept away annually, whilst in a favoured suburban district, no more than one sixty-third die.'

Entertainments

In this chapter, we have painted a very bleak picture of life and work in the early nineteenth-century towns. Although working hours were very long, workers did enjoy some leisure activities which helped them to escape from their misery, at least for a short while.

A London public house or "gin shop" around 1820.

Drinking was a very popular pastime in those days. Public houses usually opened before six in the morning and did not close until after midnight. There was no age limit for drinking.

Bull-baiting had been a very popular 'sport' at one time. In this 'sport', a dog had to try and seize a bull's nose ring and hold on to it. If the bull was too quick for the dog, it was tossed into the air. Bets were laid as to which dog would succeed.

While attempts were made to stop bull-baiting around 1800, cock-fighting remained a very popular pastime in the early years of the nineteenth century. This took place in any open space or in a specially built cock-pit where the excited crowds would place bets.

Crowds watch dog-fighting and cock-fighting.

Crowds gather to watch a prize fight.

Boxing with bare fists was also very common. It was known as prize fighting. Huge crowds placed bets on fights, which often took place in the open air and lasted for hours.

Some workers, however, spent their leisure time trying to improve their working conditions and to advance the education of workers.

Chapter 47: Review

• For the factory workers and their families, life in the new factory towns was often terrible. Most of the workers were unskilled. The working day was very long; wages were very low; accidents were frequent and fines were imposed for breaking factory rules.

• Children did a variety of work. Some worked in terrible conditions in the coal mines and textile factories. Others worked as chimney sweeps. The life expectancy of these children was very low.

• Housing and living conditions were also very bad. While the early factory workers lived in solid houses, housing in the new industrial towns was in very short supply. Houses consisted of tenement-style buildings which were divided into a number of rooms, with one or more families to a room.

• Disease was a terrible problem in the industrial towns. Killer diseases such as cholera, typhus and typhoid spread rapidly in the filthy conditions.

• Drunkenness and crime were two growing problems in industrial towns throughout Europe in the nineteenth century.

• The pastimes of the workers included bull-baiting, cock-fighting and bare-fisted boxing. Huge crowds attended these events and there was a lot of betting on the results.

CHAPTER 48

The Transport Revolution

While all the important changes were taking place in mines and factories during the Industrial Revolution, vast improvements also came about in travel and transport. At this time, roads were greatly improved and canals were built throughout the countryside. By far the greatest development in transport was the invention of the railway. These changes were so great that the words *Transport Revolution* have been used to describe them.

On the road

Travel by coach

By 1750, travellers by road faced problems unknown to the modern traveller. The passengers on board a horse-drawn coach were jolted from side to side as they travelled over rough, pot-holed roads which became like muddy swamps during the winter months. People often arrived at their destination dirty and exhausted, but lucky if they had escaped the attention of the highwayman.

A coach about to leave London.

One traveller has given us the following description of his journey on the outside of a coach in 1782.

> 'The getting up was the risk of one's life; and when I was up I was obliged to sit just at the corner of the coach, with nothing to hold by, but a sort of little handle fastened on the side. I sat nearest to the wheel; and the moment that we set off, I fancied that I saw a certain death awaiting me. All I could do was to take still faster hold of the handle and to be more and more careful and keep my balance.
>
> The coach now rolled along with speed, over the stones through the town, and every moment we seemed to fly into the air: so that it was almost a miracle that we stuck to the coach and did not fall. We seemed to be thus on the wing, and to fly, as often as we passed through a village, or went down a hill.'

From this account, it is clear why people living at that time did not travel by coach for pleasure. They only set out on such a hazardous and uncomfortable journey when they had to.

A coach proceeding slowly on its way.

Turnpike Trusts

From around 1750 onwards, attempts were made to improve the state of the roads. Companies known as *Turnpike Trusts* were given charge of a stretch of road. They then levied a payment or toll on the travellers using it. The tolls collected were used to maintain the road and keep it in good condition.

Passing through the toll gate.

Toll houses were built on the busy roads. These were six-sided in shape and had umbrella-type roofs. The toll-keeper had six points from which to see the approaching traffic.

The writer, Daniel Defoe (the author of *Robinson Crusoe*), has described the great improvements which the Turnpike Trusts brought about in one of the roads on which he travelled.

> 'These roads were once deep, in times of floods dangerous and at other times, in winter, scarce passable. They are now so firm, so safe, so easy to travellers and carriages as well as cattle, that no road in England can yet be said to equal them. This was first done by the help of a turnpike.'

The chart shows how the number of Turnpike Trusts grew between 1750 and 1836.

	No. of Turnpike Trusts	*Mileage of Turnpike Roads*
1750	**143**	**3,400**
1770	**500**	**15,000**
1836	**1000**	**22,000**

While the Turnpike Trusts helped to improve the conditions of roads, ways were also found of making better roads. Two men were largely responsible for these developments: Thomas Telford and John MacAdam.

Thomas Telford

The magnificent Menai Suspension Bridge in North Wales designed by Thomas Telford.

Telford was a Scotsman and a great road engineer. He realised that roads needed a firm foundation. The diagram shows how his roads were built.

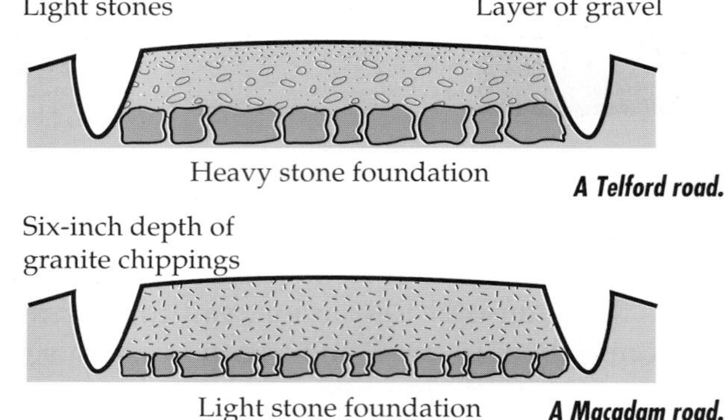

John MacAdam

MacAdam was another outstanding road engineer and Telford's great rival. In the following extract, you can read about his ideas on road-building.

> 'The first operation in making a road should be the reverse of digging a trench. The road should not be sunk below but rather raised above the level of the land beside it, and care should be taken that there be a sufficient fall to take off the water. The roadmaker should next secure the road from rain water by means of a solid road of clean, dry stone or flint, so selected, prepared and laid as to be perfectly impervious to water. This cannot be done unless the greatest care be taken that no earth, clay, chalk or other matter that will hold water be mixed with the broken stone. This must be prepared and laid as to unite by its angles into a firm, compact body.
>
> The thickness of such a road does not matter. Experience has shown that, if water passes through the soil, the road, whatever its thickness, loses its support and goes to pieces.'

Test your knowledge

1 What was the condition of English roads around 1750?

2 According to one traveller, what were the dangers of travelling on the outside of a coach in 1782?

3 What were Turnpike Trusts?

4 According to the writer Daniel Defoe, what improvements did Turnpike Trusts make to roads on which he travelled?

5 How did Thomas Telford go about building his roads?

6 Read MacAdam's views on road-building. What was the first operation in making a road? How was the road to be secured from rain water?

Travelling by canal

Road transport was of little use in carrying heavy loads such as coal over long distances. The solution lay in transport by water. From around 1750, a network of internal waterways known as canals were built throughout the English countryside.

A barge makes its way along a canal.

In 1759, the Duke of Bridgewater hired an engineer named James Brindley to build a canal linking his coal mines with the town of Manchester, a few kilometres away. As a result of this project, coal could be delivered from the duke's mines to Manchester at half the price it had cost to bring it by road. The age of the canals had arrived.

A network of canals and bridges soon criss-crossed England. Heavy goods such as coal, iron, timber and stone could now be easily carried over long distances at low cost.

Work begins on a tunnel along the Bridgewater canal.

Although the canals were used in the beginning mainly for carrying goods, they were later used for carrying passengers as well.

The age of the railway

Canals were only popular for a short time. They were soon to be overtaken by the greatest single development in the Transport Revolution—the invention of the railways.

The first railways consisted of horse-drawn wagons which carried coal over short distances. Wooden tracks were built to help the movement of these wagons.

Steam carriages such as this were first driven on the roads and caused quite a stir among the local passers-by.

James Watt (1736–1819).

The circular track known as 'Catch-me-who-Can' designed by Richard Trevithick in 1808.

The real advance came when the rotary steam engine, invented by James Watt, was used to draw a carriage. The first 'steam carriages' did not run on tracks but on public roads. They must have caused quite a stir among the horse-drawn traffic as they rattled their way noisily through the busy streets.

The steam carriages were soon abandoned and locomotives running on special rails were built. The first locomotive running on its own track was built in 1804 by a man named Richard Trevithick.

Carrying iron ore and about seventy people, Trevithick's engine took four hours and five minutes to travel a distance of fifteen kilometres.

The first railway: From Stockton to Darlington

The opening of the Stockton to Darlington railway on 27 September 1825.

It was September 1825. About 50,000 excited spectators watched the making of history. On that day, the first public railway, linking the towns of Stockton and Darlington, was opened. The following source describes the events of that exciting day.

Working with evidence

'Throughout the whole distance the fields were covered with elegantly dressed ladies, and all kinds of spectators. The bridges were lined with spectators cheering and waving their hats. At Darlington all the people of the town were out to witness the procession.

The procession was not joined by many horses and carriages until it approached within a few miles of Stockton; and here the situation of the railway, which runs parallel and close to the turnpike road, gave them a fine opportunity of viewing the procession. Numerous horses, carriages, carts and other vehicles travelled along with the engine and her huge carriages, and at one time the passengers by the engine had the pleasure of accompanying and cheering their brother passengers by the stagecoach, which passed alongside, and of observing the striking contrast exhibited by the power of the engine and of horses; the engine with her six hundred passengers and load and the coach with four horses, and only sixteen passengers.'

1. Describe the scene throughout the whole distance of the railway.
2. What joined the procession a few miles outside Stockton?
3. What ran parallel to the railway?
4. What striking contrast did the writer notice along the route?

The Rainhill trials

Excitement during the Rainhill Trials.

The first passenger railways to be built connected the towns of Manchester and Liverpool. The owner of this railway decided to hold a competition to find the best locomotive to pull the carriages. This competition was known as the *Rainhill Trials*. Rainhill was the area chosen for the trials because of its flatness.

'On the morning of 6 October 1829, the ground at Rainhill presented a lively appearance, and there was much excitement as if the St Leger were about to be run. Many thousand spectators looked on, amongst whom were some of the first engineers of the day. A stand was provided for the ladies; the "beauty and fashion" of the neighbourhood was present, and the side of the railroad was lined with carriages of all descriptions.'

The winners of the £500 prize were two of the greatest engineers of the time—George and Robert Stephenson. The locomotive designed by them was called the *Rocket*.

Stephenson's Rocket.

On its opening trip along the Manchester-Liverpool line, the Rocket pulled carriages at the rate of sixteen kilometres per hour. Among the excited passengers was the Prime Minister, the Duke of Wellington. This great and exciting event had its tragic side, however. One of the spectators, a Member of Parliament called William Huskisson, was killed by the locomotive.

Railway fever

Accidents like this one were quite common in the early days of the railway. This was one reason why some people were against the building of railways.

Opposition to them was very strong. Landlords and farmers were against railways because they came through their land. Coach owners and canal operators were afraid that the trains would take business away from them:

> 'The people would be smothered in tunnels, and those that escaped suffocation would be burned in the carriages. Eton College opposed it because it would damage the discipline of the school and would be dangerous to the morals of the pupils. A farmer objected because his cows might be killed. A landowner objected because no public benefit would compensate for destroying the beauties of his estate. The water in the Thames would be decreased, and the supply for Windsor Castle would be destroyed.'

An engine passes through a tunnel during the early days of the railway.

An early train leaving the city of London and heading for the open countryside.

A railway cutting being built by workers, known as navvies.

Despite the strong opposition, however, the railway 'mania' had gripped the country. From the 1830s on, many new railway lines were constructed. Each railway company had to get special permission from parliament to build the railway lines. Take a close look at the chart showing the growth of the railways during the nineteenth century.

The building of the railways was a great engineering achievement. Tracks had to be laid, bridges and viaducts built, and tunnels carved out of solid rock. One of the greatest railway builders of the century was a man named Isambard Kingdom Brunel.

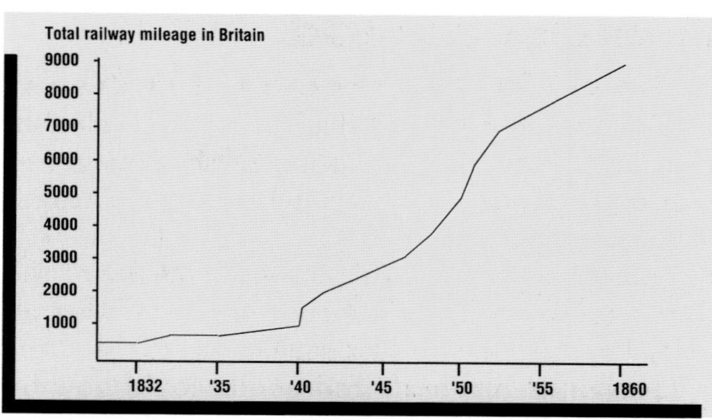

Travel by rail

1ST CLASS

The comfort of passengers on the early trains depended on how much they could afford. Look at these pictures. What do you think they tell us about conditions of travel by rail?

2ND CLASS

3RD CLASS

Test your knowledge

1 What were steam carriages?
2 Who built the first steam locomotive?
3 When was the first public railway opened? What towns did it link?
4 What were the Rainhill Trials? Who won them?
5 Why did some people oppose the development of the railways?
6 Name one of the greatest railway builders of the nineteenth century.
7 In what ways did first-class travel differ from third-class travel?

A smaller world

It should be clear by now that the word 'revolution' provides a suitable description of the changes in transport which came about during the nineteenth century.

Improvements in roads, the rise and fall of the canals and especially the arrival of the railways all helped to make the world a 'smaller place'.

Heavy raw materials and goods could now be transported more quickly and over longer distances than ever before. This greatly helped the Industrial Revolution to take place. The railways in particular led to great growth in the iron and steel industries. Many towns which were located on the railway lines experienced rapid growth.

Thousands of unskilled workers (navvies) were employed in building canals and railways. The tunnels, viaducts and bridges built during the nineteenth century are clear proof of the engineering achievements of the time.

The Great Eastern *steamship was designed by a great engineer named Isambard Kingdom Brunel (1806–59). For many years the* Great Eastern *was the largest ship in the world.*

Perhaps the greatest single outcome of the Transport Revolution was that it made cheap, rapid and comfortable travel available to more and more people. Towards the end of the century, trains provided cheap daily excursions which allowed people to escape for a while from their everyday troubles. Seaside towns prospered greatly as a result. A new age of mass travel was about to begin.

Chapter 48: Review

- Great changes in transport and travel also took place around the year 1800. These changes were so great that the words Transport Revolution have been used to describe them.

- Travel by road greatly improved. Turnpike Trusts improved the condition of the roads, while men like Thomas Telford and John MacAdam greatly improved their quality.

- Canals were built throughout the country to carry heavy goods such as coal. The first canal was built by James Brindley in 1759. It linked the Duke of Bridgewater's coal mines with the town of Manchester.

- The greatest development in transport at this time was the railway. The first steam carriages ran on roads but were not a success. They were soon replaced by locomotives running on special rails.

- The first locomotive was built in 1804 by Richard Trevithick. However, George Stephenson was the greatest engineer in the early days of the railways. He invented a famous locomotive known as the *Rocket*.

- The first railway was opened between Stockton and Darlington on 27 September 1825. It was such a success that in 1829 a railway linking the cities of Manchester and Liverpool was opened.

- Railway companies were set up throughout the country and competition between them was fierce. Soon railways had been built throughout most of Britain.

- The building of railways was carried out by thousands of unskilled labourers known as navvies.

- I. K. Brunel was one of the greatest of all railway engineers. He built railways throughout the country, but he also had a great interest in developing steamships. His two most famous steamships were the *Great Western* and the *Great Eastern*.

- The Transport Revolution, especially the arrival of trains, brought about huge changes. It greatly helped the Industrial Revolution but, above all, it provided rapid, comfortable and cheap travel to more and more people, thus making the world a 'smaller place'.

Life in the Irish Countryside

Living on the land

Unlike Great Britain, most people in Ireland in 1850 lived in the countryside. In contrast to the huge cities of Manchester, Birmingham and London, there were very few large towns in Ireland. As you can see from the map, only Dublin, Belfast and Cork had populations over 50,000 in the year 1851.

The only part of Ireland to experience the Industrial Revolution at this time was the area around Belfast in the north-east. In the rest of the country, like the people of England before 1750, the vast majority of the Irish population earned their living on the land.

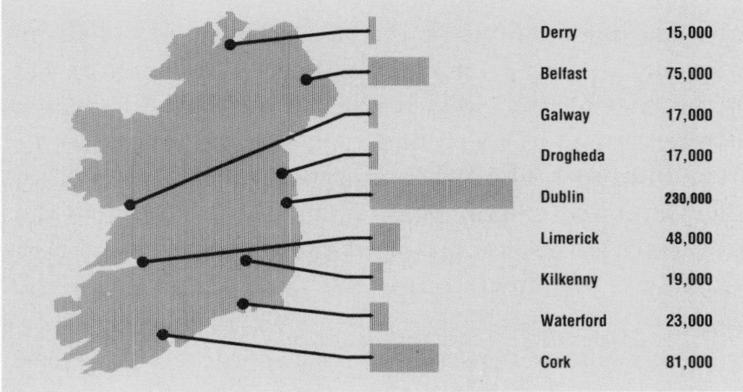

The landlord and his mansion

Around 1850, all the land of Ireland was owned by just a few thousand landlords. Most landlords were Protestants and were descended from English settlers who had come to Ireland during the plantations.

The country mansion of a landlord and his family in Ireland.

A landlord and his family pose for the artist in the beautiful reception room of their house.

A landlord and his family lived on a huge estate in a large country mansion which the local people called the 'big house'. You can see from the pictures what life was like in the 'big house'.

The landlord and his family were waited upon by a host of servants. Indoor servants included butlers, cooks, footmen and maids, while outdoor servants consisted of gardeners, groundsmen and the grooms who tended the horses.

Hunting was a very popular pastime enjoyed by the rich in the countryside.

Dinner in such a household was very formal. The meal was announced by the butler at 8 pm and usually began with soup or fish. The main course had a choice of two meats, followed by cheese, dessert and a glass of port. The ladies would then withdraw while the men would smoke cigars, sip brandies and talk of hunting or perhaps politics.

Some landlords were very interested in their estates. However, many others remained absent from their lands for long periods.

A landlord and his wife enjoying a drive in the countryside.

These men, known as *absentee landlords*, left their lands in the charge of agents or middlemen who rented it to tenant farmers.

Farmers and labourers

The tenant farmer either rented his land from the landlord or from his agent or middleman. However, there were great differences of wealth among tenant farmers themselves. They can be divided into three main groups.

Large tenant farmers

These were well-to-do farmers who rented land over thirty acres. They enjoyed a good standard of living and had great security on the land as most of them were *leaseholders*. This meant that they signed a lease or contract with the landowners allowing them to use the land for a set period of time, usually thirty-three or ninety-nine years. As long as a leaseholder paid his rent, he could not be evicted or removed from his farm.

Large tenant farmers lived in well-furnished, two-storeyed stone houses. These families were well fed and ate meat regularly.

Small tenant farmers

Most tenant farmers were not as well off as this. Smaller farmers rented between five and thirty acres. They were most plentiful in the West of Ireland.

Small farmers and their families lived in one-storeyed houses with little furniture. Their diet included potatoes, oatmeal and milk. They only had meat on special occasions, such as Christmas.

Labourers

Even worse off than the small farmers were the landless labourers. Having no farms of their own, they usually rented a small piece of land to grow potatoes. They also had to work for larger farms to earn enough money to survive. The average daily wage of a labourer at this time was around five pence.

Before the Famine many poor people lived in mud cabins such as these.

Housing conditions in the countryside

We can learn a great deal about the housing conditions of most people in the Irish countryside around 1850 from drawings in newspapers and from written accounts by the people at the time. The following descriptions were given by Mr and Mrs S. C. Hall who travelled around the country examining the lifestyle of the people.

Working with evidence

Source A: The cabins of the poor

'Cabins are often whitewashed now—a practice which was introduced during the terrible visitations of cholera. Very often there is not only no window, but no chimney, with chinks in the door alone providing light. The thatched roof is rarely kept in repair and the rain drips through.

Many of them—indeed most of them—consist of but one apartment, in which the whole family of grown-up men and women eat and sleep. There is generally a bed in a corner for the father or the "old people", for a cabin is rarely found in which there is neither a grandfather or grandmother. The other members of the household commonly rest upon straw or heather. The pig—the never-absent guest—a cow, if there is one, and, occasionally, a few fowl occupy the same chamber for the night.

The furniture consists of an iron pot to boil potatoes; a rude dresser sometimes, a couple of three-legged stools, a couple of stone seats on either side of the turf fire, a table (not always) and a kish, or wickerwork basket, into which the potatoes are thrown when cooked.'

Source B: The house of a larger farmer

'There was no upper storey, but there was a room branching off to the right and another to the left of the "kitchen, parlour and hall"—the sleeping rooms of the family and decently furnished.

The first object that attracted our attention was a chair made of elm with the pieces nailed together. We next observed a quern or hand mill. In appearance it took the form of two rounded stones.

The corn was generally dried out in an iron pot over a slow fire and constantly stirred to prevent it from burning. When it arrived at a certain degree of crispness, it was taken out to be ground. Two women generally worked the quern.

The next object that attracted our notice was a wooden drinking cup. It was a simple rounded cup with a single handle—and such indeed are common in this country.

There was also a primitive gridiron to "broil the red herrings". It was made from a piece of twisted metal and a candlestick.

The dresser we saw was well garnished with plates. There were three or four three-legged stools and at either side of the chimney was a stone seat. A saddle hung upon a peg and a smoke-dried shelf above the chimney was also garnished with plates.

There was a pair of oddly-shaped tongs to place the turf on the fire, a churn, a rafter to hang the clothes upon, a salt-box, a trough for the pig (who, although living in his own house, was an occasional visitor). There was also an iron pot, of course, and a crook fastened up the chimney to hang the pot upon. There were two wheels in the kitchen, the wheel for the wool and the wheel for the flax.

The roof of the cottage was sound. The windows were whole, and opened and shut. The pig had his separate apartment and there was a stable for the cow and the horse.'

1 Why were the cabins whitewashed?
2 Explain why the cabins of the poor were often dark and damp.
3 Did the poor respect older members of the family? How do we know this?
4 What 'guests' join the poor families indoors at night?
5 Describe the furniture in these poor cabins.
6 How did the sleeping arrangements of the families of larger farmers differ from those of the poor?
7 What is a quern? Describe its appearance.
8 List two cooking utensils found in the home of the large farmer.
9 What evidence is there inside the house which suggests that the family owned a horse?
10 Explain the function of the two wheels in the kitchen.
11 Do you think that the account written by Mr and Mrs Hall is a good primary source? Give reasons for your answer.

Customs, traditions and pastimes

Poor country children making their own entertainment in the form of music and dance.

Life was not a continual misery for those living in the Irish countryside. There were many occasions for fun and entertainment at that time.

Wren boys in Co. Kerry.

• *Fairs and markets* were places of great activity and excitement where the people could forget their troubles for the moment. At fairs there was a great haggling over prices and people travelled from far and wide to do business, at the same time enjoying a day out. Dancing and music were part and parcel of the fair day. Heavy drinking, especially of poteen, often led to disorder and fighting in the streets. Two of the most famous fairs took place at Ballycastle, Co. Antrim and Donnybrook in Dublin.

A faction fight.

• *Weddings and wakes* were also occasions for entertainment. Early marriages were very common and were frequently arranged by the local matchmaker. The marriage prospects of the girl depended on the size of the dowry, or payment, that her father could afford to make to her future husband.

A wake was usually held when a person died. Relations, friends and neighbours used to gather in the house of the dead person where there would be singing, dancing, eating, snuff-taking and card playing. Often 'keeners' would attend wakes and funerals. These were women who wailed and lamented over the body of the dead person.

• *Sports and games* were also greatly enjoyed by country people. Horseracing was very popular and regattas, involving currachs, were organised along the west coast. Hurling, of course, was a very popular sport but in the absence of any rules it was often extremely tough and might even lead to multiple injuries.

We have many accounts of 'entertainments' in nineteenth-century Ireland. The following is a description of a wake which took place at Tallaght in Co. Dublin. Tallaght was then in the middle of the countryside. This account was given by a local farmer named Malachi Horan.

Working with evidence

'I know the clergy are against wakes. At least they are against the bad conduct that went on at some of them. And rightly so. But there is sense in wakes too. Sure, what man at all would be sorry for a friend to go to heaven? A prayer for him that's gone and a song for him that's left—that's a wake for you.

The coffin is put in the best room—and no harm either. It rests on a coffin bearer. This is made of two eight-foot poles with three slats joining them. The ends of the middle slat come out beyond the poles so, with the four pole-ends and the middle slat, you would have six handles for the bearers.

There would be five or seven candles and them put standing around the coffin. When all the people came together, they would say the rosary. They would be saying it three times before the night was over. Tea was most generally drunk twice. This they would take sitting by the turf fire.

Pipes and pigtail tobacco were given to every man. The young blackguards who had not manhood to smoke used to take the pipes and with them crack the next man's clay pipe. Then, maybe, they would fall to pelting each other with the broken pieces. That's the way rows would start.

We played many a game at the wakes. We had to. It was a mortal hard thing for a man to keep awake all night, and it, maybe, on the head of a heavy day's work.'

1 Why were the clergy against wakes?
2 Complete Malachi Horan's definition of a wake: 'A prayer for him that's gone ...'
3 Explain how the coffin bearer was made. You may draw a sketch if you wish.
4 How many candles were usually placed around the coffin?
5 What prayer was said three times during the night at the wake?
6 Describe the rowdy conduct of the 'young blackguards' during the wake.
7 Why were many games played during the wake?

Chapter 49: Review

• Unlike Great Britain, most people in Ireland around 1850 earned their living by working on the land.

• The land of Ireland was owned by just a few thousand landlords who were mostly Protestant. Some, known as 'absentee landlords', never visited their estates but employed agents to collect their rents and run their affairs.

• Landlords and their families led lives of ease and luxury in their mansions on country estates. They enjoyed entertainments such as hunts and banquets.

• Tenant farmers in Ireland could be divided into large farmers, who usually held their land on a lease, and small farmers, who had little security.

• The poorest section of the Irish countryside were those labourers who had no farms of their own. They grew potatoes on a small patch of land and worked for larger farmers.

• There were huge differences between the one-room cabins of the poor and the better living conditions of the larger farmers.

• Fairs, markets, weddings and wakes provided occasions for enjoyment among the ordinary people.

The Great Famine

Problems on the land

People living in the Irish countryside faced many difficulties in the first half of the nineteenth century. Landlords often charged very high rents known as *rackrents*. Tenants who were unable to pay were evicted. A force of police and soldiers would arrive with a crowbar to knock down the tenant's cabin. This group became known as the 'crowbar brigade'. Men women and children, together with all their belongings, were then placed on the side of the road. They looked on helplessly while their cabin was knocked down.

Describe what you see in this eviction scene.

Although there was often hardship in the countryside in the nineteenth century, one terrible disaster stands out above all others—the *Great Famine* of 1845–50. The Famine resulted in important and far-reaching changes in life in Ireland for many years afterwards. To understand why this disaster happened, we must first take a look at the huge rise in population in the country during the first half fo the nineteenth century.

The population of Ireland

We have already seen how the number of people living in Britain increased greatly around 1750 onwards. Can you remember the causes of this increase?

Take a close look at the chart and see how the population of Ireland also expanded at this time.

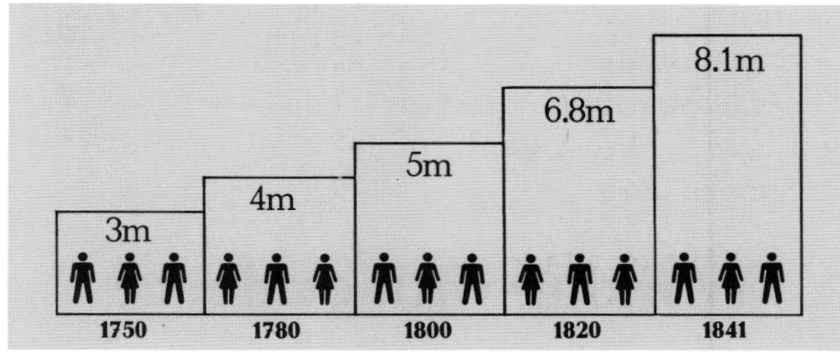

The population of Ireland, 1750–1841.

In the early years of the nineteenth century, the birth rate in Ireland increased. This was because many people married at a very early age and had large families. These early marriages took place because a farmer divided his land among his children when they married. Large families could then be raised on a small patch of land which was used to grow potatoes.

In Britain, industry provided jobs for the expanding population. In Ireland, however, the land remained the only major source of employment. It was only through working on the land that most people earned enough money to feed themselves, as well as providing food for a growing population.

The over-dependence of millions of people on the potato could lead to disaster if this crop failed. This is exactly what happened in Ireland during the years of the Great Famine.

Famine strikes

The disease of blight which attacked the potato crop in the autumn of 1845 marked the beginning of the Great Famine in Ireland. Hunger and famine, common in Third World countries today, were by no means unusual in the Ireland of that time. However, successive crop failures made the Great Famine of 1845–50 worse than any previous one in Ireland. It had a terrible impact on the country for generations.

Terrible scenes at Skibbereen, Co. Cork during the Famine.

The spread of famine throughout the country led to hunger and starvation on a vast scale. However, most deaths resulted not directly from starvation but from diseases such as typhus, dropsy and other fevers.

A puzzled farmer discovering rotten potatoes in the ground.

The following horrific account was written by a Cork magistrate. It describes scenes he saw in the town of Skibbereen, West Cork, in December 1846.

Working with evidence

'Being aware that I should have to witness scenes of frightful hunger, I provided myself with as much bread as five men could carry and, on reaching the spot I was surprised to find the wretched hamlet deserted. I entered some of the hovels to find out the cause, and the scenes that I witnessed were such that no tongue or pen can convey the slightest idea of. In the first, six famished families and ghastly skeletons, to all appearances were dead, were huddled in a corner on some filthy straw, their only covering what seemed ragged horse-cloth and their wretched legs hanging about, naked above the knees. I approached in horror, and found by a low moaning they were alive, they were in fever—four children, a woman and what had once been a man. In a few minutes I was surrounded by at least 200 such phantoms. By far the greater number were raving either from starvation or from fever. Their awful yells are still ringing in my ears, and their horrible appearances are fixed upon my brain.

The same morning the police opened a house on the adjoining lands, which was observed shut for many days, and two frozen corpses were found lying upon the mud floor, half devoured by rats. A mother, herself in a fever, was seen the same day to drag out the corpse of her child, a girl of twelve, perfectly naked, and leave it half covered with stones. In another house the doctor found seven wretches lying, unable to move, under the same cloak—one had been dead for many hours, but the others were unable to move either themselves or the corpse.'

1. Why did the magistrate bring bread with him to visit the hamlet?
2. What did he find when he first arrived?
3. What did he see in one of the hovels?
4. How does he describe the people who surrounded him?
5. What was discovered by the police?
6. Do you think that this account conveys the horror of the Famine? Why?

Helping the famine victims

Look carefully at the following pictures and see what they can tell us about the help given to people during the years of Ireland's Great Famine.

People come to buy 'Indian Meal' on sale during the Famine. This was American maize sold to the poor at low cost in special food depots.

A soup kitchen during the Famine. Soup kitchens were set up in 1847 and provided free soup for starving Famine victims. Charitable organisations such as the Quakers opened their own soup kitchens.

Crowds seeking assistance outside a workhouse during the Famine. Workhouses had first been set up in Ireland in 1838 to help those who could not support themselves. During the Famine starving masses of people flocked to the workhouses. As a result they became totally overcrowded. Because of this, the government decided to give outdoor relief to those who were not resident in them. In 1849 alone almost a million people were given assistance in the workhouses while almost the same number received outside relief.

Chapter 50: Review

- There were many difficulties facing people in the Irish countryside. Landlords often charged high rents known as rackrents.

- Tenants were often evicted from their land for not paying their rent or because the landlord wanted the land for someone else. The group of policemen and soldiers present at evictions became known as 'the crowbar brigade'.

- By 1845, the population of Ireland was over 8 million. In the absence of large-scale industrialisation, most people depended on agriculture for a living.

- On the eve of the Famine, one Irish family in three lived in one-roomed mud cabins. They had barely enough food to eat and were heavily dependent on one crop—the potato.

- The failure of the potato crop in the autumn of 1845 marked the beginning of the Great Famine in Ireland. This was caused by a potato blight which had spread from North America and England.

- After the blight of 1845, it was hoped that the next year's crop would be saved. However, the potato crop of 1846 was a total failure and the starvation and death which followed led to 1847 becoming known as 'Black 47'. Famine conditions lasted until 1848, although conditions improved slowly after that.

- The spread of the Great Famine throughout the country led to starvation on a massive scale. In addition, many deaths were caused by the spread of diseases such as typhus.

- The workhouses became totally overcrowded during the Famine. As a result, they were breeding grounds for deadly diseases.

- Private charities played an important part in relieving distress during the Famine years. The Quakers, in particular, set up soup kitchens throughout the country before the government finally decided to open some of its own.

A Changing Countryside

Population

By 1850, the worst of the Great Famine had passed. However, the country did not recover from the effects of this terrible catastrophe for many decades. Almost a million died from starvation and disease, while another million left the country in desperation.

Labourers and small farmers were the hardest hit. Many of them were evicted from their land because they were unable to pay their rents. Their numbers fell drastically as a result of death and emigration.

The farms left behind by these groups were now joined together to form larger holdings. Take a close look at the chart and see how farm sizes increased between 1841 and 1851.

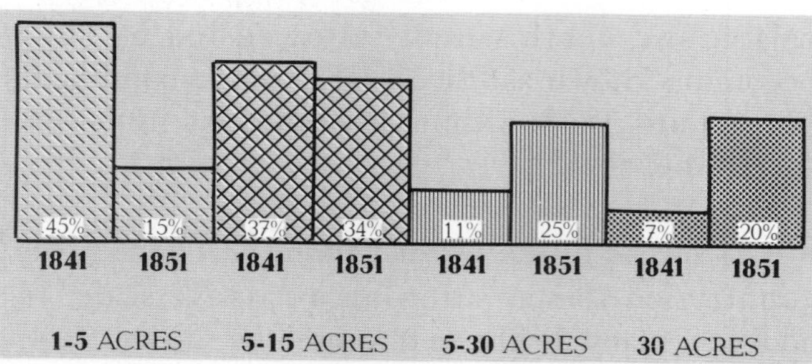

Changes in farm sizes in Ireland, 1841–51. After the Famine, the size of the average Irish farm was larger. This was the result of an end to subdivision and a change from tillage to pasture, which required larger farms.

The Famine ended around 1850, but the population of Ireland continued to fall for over a hundred years. From 1850 on, Irish farmers no longer subdivided their land. Instead, they passed the farm on to the eldest son. He could not marry until he took over the family farm, usually after the death of one or both parents. Because of the fall in the marriage rate, there was also a fall in the birth rate. This contributed to the steady drop in population experienced in Ireland until the 1960s.

For the other children on the farm, there was often only one option—emigration. Emigration has remained part of Irish life right to the present day.

Examine the chart carefully and see how the Irish population, unlike that of Britain, continued to drop after the Great Famine.

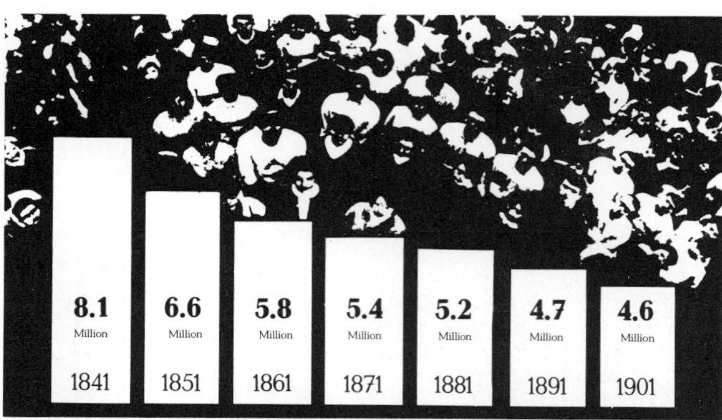

Irish population decline, 1841–1901.

Test your knowledge

1. By how much did the Irish population drop during the Famine?
2. What groups were the hardest hit by the famine?
3. Look at the chart showing farm size. Can you explain why this increased as a result of the Famine?
4. How did the ending of subdivision affect marriage rates in Ireland after the Famine?
5. What effects had dropping marriage rates on the Irish population?
6. What was often the only option open to the younger children on the farm?
7. Look at the chart showing Irish population figures since the Famine. What was the overall trend? How does it differ from: (a) what had happened in the years before the Famine; and (b) what was happening in Britain during the same period?

Emigration

Passengers on board an emigrant ship.

For many people during the Famine, there was a stark choice between death and emigration. As a result, hundreds of thousands of people fled from the country in order to survive. Masses of people flocked into British ports such as Liverpool. Many arrived in a terrible condition, carrying diseases and needing immediate attention.

Overcrowding below decks.

From Britain many emigrants set sail for Canada and the United States. The traffic in people became so great that direct sailings began from Ireland to North America.

Conditions on many of the emigrant ships were atrocious. Vast numbers of people were huddled together on old, overcrowded and unsafe vessels. Food and sanitation were appalling and disease, drunkenness and death were rampant. Some of the ships sank on the way. Because of this, these craft came to be called 'coffin ships'.

When the emigrants arrived in Canada, they had to go into quarantine on Grosse Island, on the St Lawrence River near Quebec. Read the following account written by a doctor describing the condition of some of these emigrants.

Working with evidence

'On boarding the boat I found the passengers in a most wretched state of filth and disease. No order or rules had been kept, or any attempt at enforcing cleanliness. Their excrement and filth had been thrown into the ballast, producing a stench which made it very difficult to remain any length of time below. I found twenty-six cases of fever, and received the names of twenty others, including the captain, who had died on the passage. The voyage had extended to the unusual length of seventy-two days. On landing the passengers at the sheds, I had to send fifty more to hospital and six have died since landing. The remainder, though weak, are healthy at present, and have been made to clean themselves, their clothing and bedding, those of them that had any, but most of them are without a second change of clothes.

The causes which have produced disease and death among these passengers are those so often stated by me in my annual reports:

1 Want of cleanliness and want of ventilation.
2 Lack of food and water, and that of an unwholesome quality.
3 Overcrowding.

These causes produce fever, and once disease sets in, the stench from the bodies of the sick, dying and dead confined in the hold (the captain was kept two or three weeks on board after death), soon made the whole atmosphere unfit to breathe. The captain, from all accounts, was a man unfit to take charge of a passenger vessel. He was in ill health and a drunkard.

The passengers were not provided by the vessel with any food: their own stock was soon eaten. The bunks were badly put up, and came down on the starboard side two or three days after leaving. The vessel itself is the oldest in North England, being 83 years old.

The numbers of passengers put on board exceeded by sixty or seventy the number allowed to the tonnage of the vessel.'

1 What conditions were found by the doctor on board the ship?
2 How long had the journey taken?
3 How many passengers had died during the voyage?
4 According to the doctor, what causes disease and death among the passengers?
5 What is his opinion of the captain?
6 The doctor is very critical of the ship. State three examples which show that the passengers were badly looked after.

The horrific scenes which you have just read about took place during the Famine years. However, we have already seen that emigration continued from Ireland for many decades after this. Look carefully at the chart which shows Irish emigration figures during the nineteenth century.

Emigration from Ireland, 1841–1900.

The Irish language

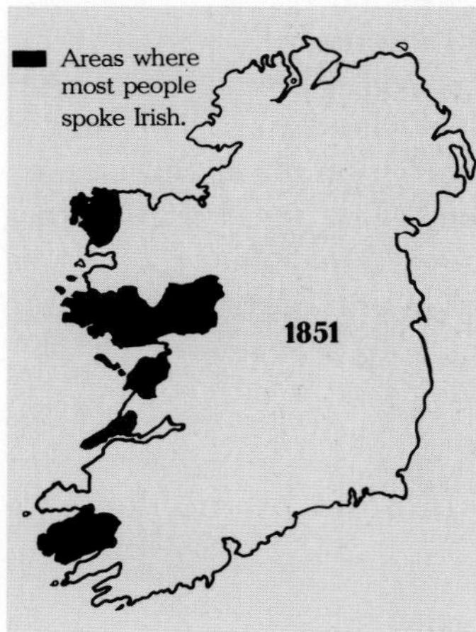

The Irish-speaking areas of the south and west suffered most from death and emigration, both during and after the Famine. The numbers of Irish speakers fell drastically as a result. These areas continued to experience high levels of emigration in the following decades.

Between 1851 and 1891, the areas where nearly everyone spoke Irish had been much reduced in size.

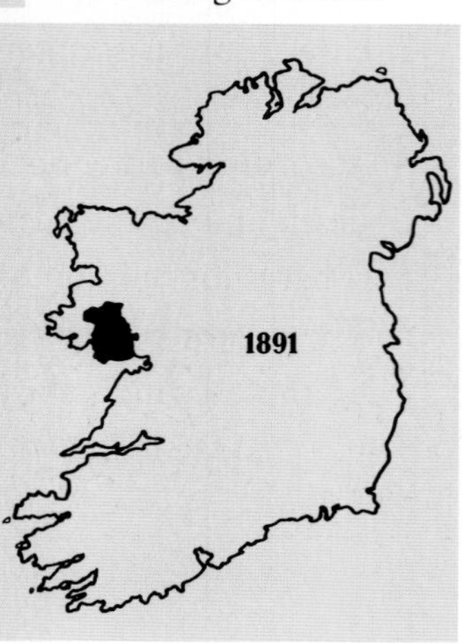

Study the maps showing the decline in the numbers of Irish speakers in the years after the Famine.

Test your knowledge

1 How many people emigrated during the Famine years?
2 What were coffin ships?
3 Describe conditions on board these ships.
4 How did the Famine affect the Irish-speaking areas of Ireland?

Different worlds

By now you should clearly understand the difference between rural Ireland and industrial Britain around 1850. While more and more people in Great Britain crowded into the factory towns, most Irish people continued to live in the countryside.

The rapid growth of the British population was in marked contrast to the fall of the Irish population. In Britain, people migrated from country to town, while in Ireland, people leaving the land emigrated from the country.

For the vast majority of people, whether they lived in rural Ireland or industrial England, life around 1850 was a daily struggle. However, as the nineteenth century advanced, living and working conditions improved.

Chapter 51: Review

• The population of Ireland fell by about 2 million during the Great Famine. Almost a million died from starvation and disease while another million emigrated.

• The Famine had clearly shown the dangers of subdividing land. From then on, it became the practice for the eldest son to inherit the whole farm.

• After the Famine, marriages in Ireland were fewer and people tended to marry at a later age. This led to a fall in the birth rate which, along with emigration, accounted for the fall in the Irish population over the following decades.

- Conditions aboard emigrant ships were often appalling. As a result these became known as 'coffin ships'.

- The Famine had a huge impact on the decline of the Irish language. The areas which suffered most in terms of death and emigration were those in which the language had once been strongest.

- From 1850 onwards, the rapid growth of the British population was in marked contrast to the fall in the population of Ireland.

- While Great Britain became more and more industrialised, Ireland remained largely dependent on agriculture.

- Life for most people in industrial England and rural Ireland around 1850 was a daily struggle. However, as the nineteenth century advanced, both living and working conditions improved.

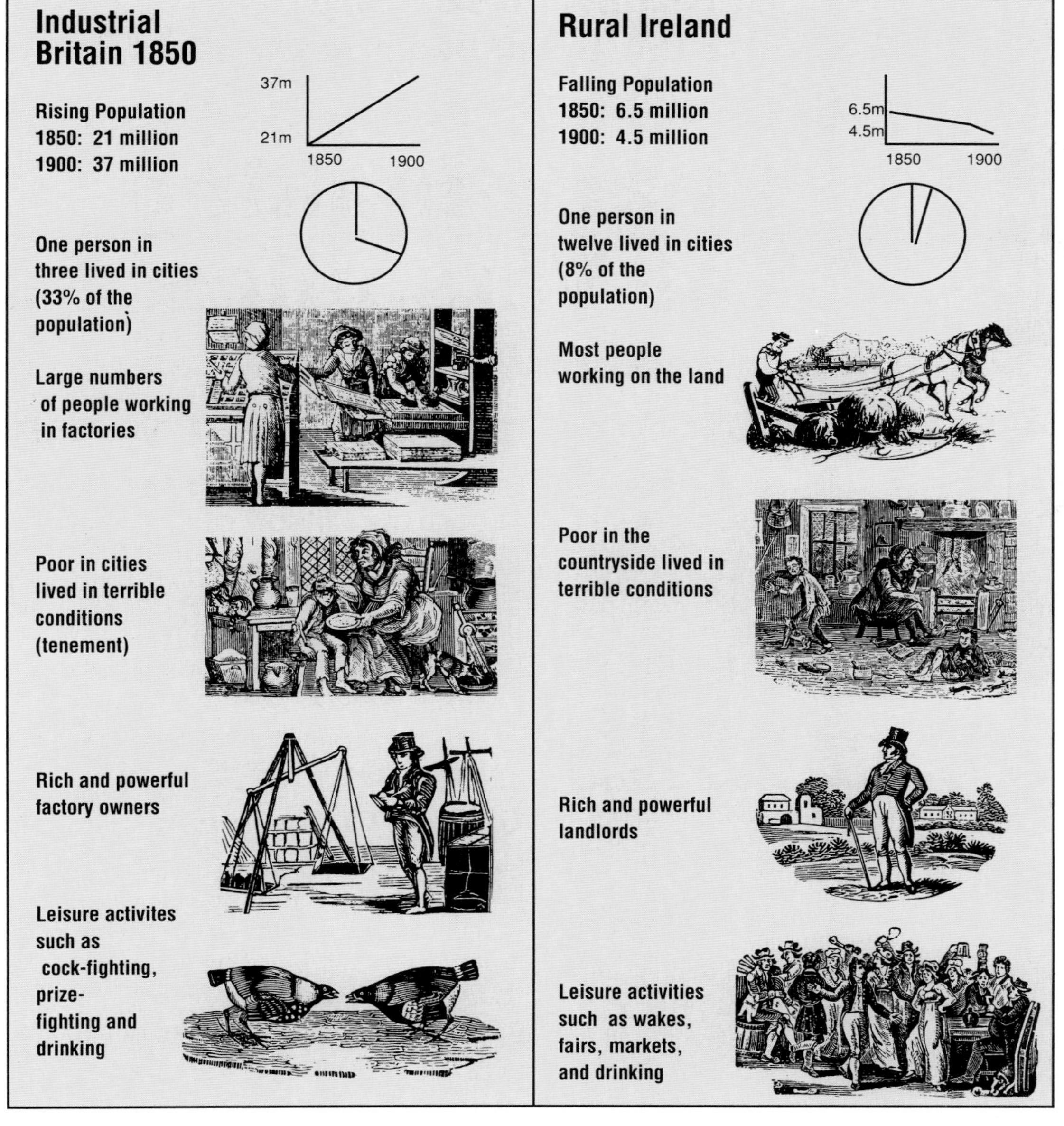

International Relations in the Twentieth Century

CHAPTER 52 Peace-making at Versailles

In November 1918, the First World War (1914–18) came to an end. Millions had fought in the war, believing it to be 'the war to end all wars'. For the first time in history war had influenced the everyday lives of whole populations. At its conclusion millions of men lay buried in the battlefields of Europe and many more returned home wounded.

Soldiers cutting through the barbed wire defences of enemy trenches.

Therefore, when the statesmen of the victorious Allied countries met they had a mission to draw up a peace settlement that would prevent war in the future. This important peace conference opened in Versailles near Paris in January 1919.

The leaders of Versailles

Woodrow Wilson of the United States

President Wilson came to the peace conference with his own *Fourteen-Point Plan*. This plan declared that the people of each nation should have the right to choose their own government — *self-determination*; Germany should be treated fairly; the arms race should be ended; and a *League of Nations* should be set up to preserve peace in the world.

George Clemenceau of France

Clemenceau was known as 'The Tiger'. He had been prime minister of France during the last years of the war. His main interest was that France should never again be invaded by Germany. He proposed that Germany pay a huge sum as compensation for the damage done to French territory and that steps be taken to make the border between France and Germany secure. He was determined to deal harshly with Germany.

David Lloyd George of Great Britain

Lloyd George had fought and won an election in December 1918 on the promise to make Germany pay. Like Clemenceau, he was determined to make the Germans compensate the Allies for the destruction caused by the war. Britain had gone heavily into debt in order to finance her war effort. As a result, anti-German feelings ran very high in the country.

Vittorio Orlando of Italy

Orlando, the Italian prime minister, represented his country at Versailles. Italy entered the war on the Allied side in 1915, although it had earlier been part of the Triple Alliance with Germany and Austria-Hungary. Italy now hoped to gain some Austrian territory at the peace conference.

Test your knowledge

1 Name the four main leaders at the Versailles Peace Conference.
2 Which two shared common views on the treatment of Germany?
3 What plan did President Wilson bring to the conference? Outline some of its provisions.

The Treaty of Versailles

The signing of the Versailles Peace Treaty on 28 June 1919.

Discussions continued among the Allied leaders at Versailles between January and June 1919. *The Treaty of Versailles* between the Allied powers and Germany was finally signed on 28 June 1919, exactly five years after the first shot of the war had been fired at Sarajevo.

Read the following extracts from the Treaty of Versailles.

Working with evidence

Article 231
The Allied governments affirm, and Germany accepts, the responsibility of Germany and her allies for causing all the loss and damage to which the Allied governments and their peoples have been subjected as a result of the war.

Article 232
The Allied governments require, and Germany undertakes, that she will make compensation for all the damage done to the civilian population of the Allied powers and to their property during the war.

Article 428
As a guarantee that the treaty shall be carried out, the German territory to the west of the Rhine will be occupied by Allied troops for fifteen years.

Article 160
The German army must not comprise more than seven divisions of infantry and three divisions of cavalry. The total number in the army must not exceed 100,000 men. The army shall be devoted exclusively to the maintenance of order within the territory and the control of frontiers.

1 Article 231 was known as the 'War Guilt' Clause. Explain why.
2 Would you consider that this clause was fair to Germany?
3 What did Germany undertake to do under Article 232?
4 What limit was set on the size of the German army?
5 Explain the precautions take by the Allies to make sure that the Germans would carry out the terms of the treaty.

As well as having its army reduced, Germany's navy was to be reduced to six small battleships. The German air force was abolished.

However, all of these conditions were over-

As the delegates left Versailles for home, many of them failed to grasp that decisions taken at the Conference would lead to serious problems in the future.

What view of the Versailles Treaty is shown in this German cartoon?

shadowed by the main results of the Treaty of Versailles — huge losses of territory by Germany. As well as losing all their overseas colonies, the Germans lost about one-eighth of their land and population in Europe.

Germany lost Alsace-Lorraine to France, and land to Poland in the east, to Denmark in the north and to the new state of Czechoslovakia in the south.

Changes in central and eastern Europe

Territorial changes in Europe after the Versailles Conference, 1919.

As a result of the Versailles Conference, there were vast changes in central and eastern Europe. As you can see from the map, the old empire of Austria-Hungary, defeated in the war, was completely broken up. Austria and Hungary became two small independent states, while two completely new states ruled by Slav peoples were established. These were Czechoslovakia, with its capital at Prague, and Yugoslavia, with Belgrade as its capital city. As part of the Versailles settlement, any future union of Germany and Austria was strictly forbidden.

Poland, which had ceased to be a separate state around 1800, now recovered its independence from Austria, Germany and Russia.

Despite President Wilson's ideas on national self-determination, there were many national minorities in the new states set up at Versailles. Since many different races had settled in central and eastern Europe, this could not be avoided. It was to be a source of tension and conflict in the years ahead.

The League of Nations

A meeting of the League of Nations at Geneva.

What weakness of the League of Nations is highlighted in this contemporary cartoon?

The statesmen at Versailles accepted President Wilson's idea for an international peace-making organisation and in 1920, the League of Nations was founded. Its headquarters was at Geneva in Switzerland. The League was organised as follows:

The Assembly — It met once a year. Each member country had one vote and it looked after the League's main business.

The Council — A smaller body than the Assembly, it had some permanent members such as Britain and France and some who were elected every year. It met several times a year to deal with business when the Assembly was not meeting.

The Secretariat — A permanent body of officials, it was the League's 'Civil Service'.

Council	Assembly	Secretariat
4 large powers (Britain, France, Italy and Japan) + representatives from 9 other countries.	(Representative of all member states) USA never joined. Germany was allowed to enter in 1926 but left in 1933. Russia did not join until 1934.	(Civil Service of League.)

The organisation of the League of Nations.

Although the League carried out important work in areas such as health and justice, it was to fail in its main aim of preventing future war. It was weakened from the outset when the most powerful nation in the world, the United States of America, failed to join. President Wilson toured America trying to persuade his fellow countrymen and women that the US should join the League. He prophesied what would happen if they did not join:

> 'I can predict with absolute certainty that within another generation there will be another world war.'

However, the American Senate voted to stay out of the League of Nations, a policy known as *Isolationism* (that is, Americans wished to remain 'isolated' or apart from European disputes).

As well as lacking American participation, the League of Nations had no armed force to put its decisions into operation. With the US refusing to take part, Great Britain began to spend less money on defence and to keep out of continental European affairs. This left France to face a bitter and resentful Germany without much international support.

The future of peace in Europe was not based on any secure foundations, despite all the promises that World War I would be 'the war to end all wars'.

Test your knowledge

1 What did the Treaty of Versailles contain regarding:
   (a) The German navy?
   (b) The German air force?
2 Name two countries which gained former German territory in 1919.
3 List three new states on the map of Europe in 1919.
4 Did the Versailles settlement introduce complete national self-determination? Explain your answer.
5 List the three main parts of the League of Nations.
6 Give two reasons why it failed to prevent war in the future.

Chapter 52: Review

- In January 1919, the victorious Allied leaders met at Versailles outside Paris to draw up peace treaties with Germany and the other defeated countries and to plan the shape of the post-war world.

- President Woodrow Wilson represented the United States of America. He came with a Fourteen-Point Plan which included the right of each people to choose their own government and a proposal for a League of Nations.

- France was represented by her prime minister, Georges Clemenceau, who wanted to impose harsh conditions on Germany to make sure that she was never in a position to invade France again.

- David Lloyd George, the prime minister, represented Great Britain. Like Clemenceau, he was determined to make Germany pay for the destruction caused by the war.

- In the Treaty of Versailles, Germany was made to accept responsibility for the war — the 'War Guilt' Clause; had to pay huge sums of money to the winning countries — Reparations; and lost a lot of territory including Alsace-Lorraine.

- Germany also lost its air force and most of its

army, and the navy was to be strictly limited in size. German troops were not to be allowed in the Rhineland and all German overseas colonies were lost to the Allies.

• The Austrian Empire was broken up into a number of small countries including Austria, Hungary, Czechoslovakia and Yugoslavia.

• Poland, which had been divided between Austria, Germany and Russia, became an independent country.

• The League of Nations was set up as an international organisation with its headquarters at Geneva. It did not succeed in its main aim of preventing future war.

CHAPTER 53

Russia under Stalin

The Russian Revolution

In 1917, as a result of a revolution Russia became the first country in the world to be ruled by a Communist government. Before this the ruler of Russia had been the Tsar, an all-powerful leader who had governed without a parliament.

Revolutionaries attacking an office in St Petersburg in October 1917.

The leader of the Russian Revolution was Lenin. By the time of his death in 1924, despite famine and civil war, Communism was firmly established in Russia. Lenin's successor as leader of Russia was to be Joseph Stalin.

Joseph Stalin

In 1879, Joseph Stalin was born into a peasant family in the southern Russian region of Georgia. At an early age he became interested in revolutionary ideas and joined Lenin's Bolshevik Party. Stalin spent most of the period between 1907 and 1917 in prison for his political activities. He played a small part in the October Revolution of 1917, but was unknown at the time.

In 1922, Stalin was appointed General Secretary of the Russian Communist Party. This was to mark the beginning of his extraordinary rise to power. Through this position he became familiar with the workings of the party and was able to build up vital contacts within it.

Joseph Stalin (1879-1953).

Lenin was deeply suspicious of Stalin's ambition. In his final testament, or will, written shortly before his death, Lenin tried to warn the party against choosing Stalin as leader:

> 'Comrade Stalin, having become General Secretary, has concentrated an enormous power in his hands; and I am not sure that he always knows how to use that power with sufficient caution...Stalin is too coarse, and this fault is insupportable in the office of General

> Secretary. Therefore I propose to the comrades to find a way to remove Stalin from that position and to appoint to it another man who in all respects differs from Stalin — more patient, more loyal, more polite, more attentive to comrades.'

This document was suppressed by Stalin and it did not become publicly known until many years later. After Lenin's death in 1924, Stalin engaged in a power struggle to succeed Lenin as leader.

Stalin's main rival and the person most favoured by Lenin was Leon Trotsky. By 1926, Stalin had outwitted his rival and in that year he had Trotsky and his wife expelled from Russia. By 1928, Stalin had become dictator of the Soviet Union.

During the following years, Stalin set about crushing all opposition to his rule. He believed in a policy called *Socialism in One Country*. All efforts should be made to make the USSR fully socialist before attempting to spread revolution throughout the world. Making the USSR fully socialist would involve drastic changes in Soviet agriculture and industry.

The collectivisation of agriculture

At the time of Lenin's death, Russian agricultural methods were primitive and levels of production

Threshing rye on a collective farm.

were low. Stalin saw that better farming methods and higher levels of production would provide more capital which could then be channelled into industrial development. Workers could also be transferred from the land to the cities where they would be employed in industry.

Stalin set about modernising Russian agriculture through a policy known as *collectivisation*: the peasants were required to join their farms together and work the land collectively as state employees. The wealthy peasants known as Kulaks fiercely resisted collectivisation. Some destroyed their property and livestock rather than surrender their possessions to the state. Stalin, however, ruthlessly enforced his policy of collectivisation and put down all resistance. While some 25 million one-family farms were now replaced by 300,000 collective farms, the cost in human terms was huge. It is estimated that around 5 million families disappeared during the years of collectivisation.

Test your knowledge

1 What was collectivisation?

2 Why did Stalin adopt this policy?

3 Who were the Kulaks? How did they react to Stalin's policy of collectivisation?

The industrialisation of Russia: Five-Year Plans

The industrialisation of Russia was Stalin's greatest achievement. He transformed a backward agricultural land into a modern industrialised country by means of three *Five-Year Plans*. They were designed to increase industrial production, especially in iron and steel, and they resulted in great achievements:

- New industries were set up.
- Many workers were transferred from the land to the factory.
- New power stations were constructed.
- Transport was vastly improved, with the Moscow Underground Railway being one of the greatest achievements.
- Education, especially literacy levels, was greatly improved.

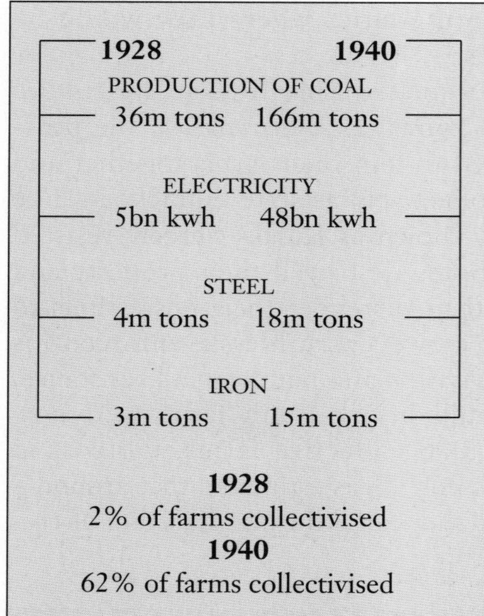

	1928	1940
PRODUCTION OF COAL	36m tons	166m tons
ELECTRICITY	5bn kwh	48bn kwh
STEEL	4m tons	18m tons
IRON	3m tons	15m tons

1928
2% of farms collectivised
1940
62% of farms collectivised

Results of Stalin's Five-Year Plans in Russia.

Hard work was encouraged and rewarded while lack of effort was dealt with severely. Propaganda was constantly used to encourage higher levels of production. One young miner named Alexei Stakhanov was set up as a model for other Soviet workers to imitate.

> 'In August 1935, a miner, Alexei Stakhanov, pondered over his highly skilled task of operating a pneumatic drill or coalcutting machine. He had the idea that he could cut more coal if he could concentrate all his effort and attention on cutting, while the operation of removing the coal was performed by other members of the team, who were also concentrating on their own particular processes.
> The result was immediately amazing. Instead of the usual six or seven tons per shift, Stakhanov began to cut 102 tons in one shift. The idea spread to other industries.'

Within a short period of ten years, Russia had experienced dramatic industrial growth. By 1930 she was ranked among the great industrial powers of the world. Russia's industrial revolution had been achieved at tremendous cost, however. Forced labour had been widely used, overall living standards remained very low, and consumer goods were in very short supply.

Massive hydroelectric power stations like this were built in Russia during the Five-Year Plans.

Building a canal in the 1930s.

Test your knowledge

1 How did Stalin set about industrialising Russia?
2 State four steps introduced under the Five-Year Plans.
3 'Russia's industrial revolution had been achieved at tremendous cost.' Do you agree with this statement? Explain your answer.
4 Give an example of how propaganda was used to encourage high levels of production among workers.

The purges and show trials of the 1930s

Stalin had shown his terrible ruthlessness in dealing with those who in any way resisted his policies of collectivisation and industrialisation. By the 1930s, he had become deeply suspicious of those around him and was determined to exterminate all possible enemies, especially anyone who had association with Trotsky. In 1933, therefore, he began a great purge of all his enemies.

Stalin used his secret police, the *Cheka* (NKVD), to carry out this policy of extermination. During the 1930s, countless numbers of people were visited by the NKVD in the middle of the night. They were taken away and never seen again. Others were arrested and made to face 'show' trials where they were forced to confess to crimes which they had never committed. Leading Russian politicians, beaten up and threatened beforehand, confessed to plotting the overthrow of Stalin. They were then found guilty on the basis of their own confessions and executed.

This is one victim's account of the interrogation methods used by the secret police.

> 'The torture began...The five men beat viciously. They beat with fists, feet, birch rods, tightly braided towels; they beat with anything anywhere...The more they beat the more brutal they became...How long they beat me I don't know...
>
> My shirt had turned to bloody shreds. I lay on the floor in a pool of blood. My eyes were swollen. With difficulty I raised my eyelids and as if in a fog saw my torturers. They were smoking, taking a rest. Someone came up to me and just then something very painful burned my body. I was convulsed with pain. And they laughed. Then it burned again, again, again...I understood. They were putting out their cigarettes on my body.'

Millions of people died in the great purges while countless others were sent to forced labour camps in Siberia. Read the following description of life in such a camp.

> 'It took twenty to thirty days to turn a healthy man into a wreck. Working in the camp mine sixteen hours a day, without any days off, with systematic starvation, ragged clothes, sleeping in a torn tent at sixty below zero, did the job. Beatings by the foremen, by the ringleaders of the thieves, by the guards, speeded up the process.
>
> Prisoners were taken out to work during the worst frosts. The barracks were not given enough heat, clothing would not dry out. Prisoners were given third-hand clothing, mere rags, and often had only cloth wrapping on their feet. Their torn jackets did not protect them from the bitter frost, and people froze in droves.'

By the time the purges eased in 1938, nearly half the officers in the Red Army had been killed on the orders of Stalin.

Chapter 53: Review

- After Lenin died in Russia in 1924, a leadership struggle took place between Leon Trotsky and Joseph Stalin. Stalin won this struggle and by 1928 he was the undisputed ruler of the Soviet Union.

- Stalin believed that all efforts should be made to make Russia fully Communist before attempting to spread revolution throughout the world. This policy was known as *Socialism in One Country*.

- Stalin set about bringing all farms under state control. This was known as collectivisation and led to fierce resistance from the wealthier Russian peasants known as Kulaks.

- In a series of Five-Year Plans, Stalin set about changing the Soviet Union from a backward agricultural country into a modern industrial one.

- Although by 1939 the Soviet Union ranked among the great industrial powers of the world, this was achieved at great human cost — forced labour had been widely used.

- During the 1930s, Stalin eliminated all opposition in the great purges and show trials which resulted in the death or imprisonment of millions of people.

CHAPTER 54 Benito Mussolini and the Rise of Fascism

The fascist dictators

In the 1920s and 1930s, a new form of government emerged in some important European countries. Existing democratic governments were replaced by dictatorships. In a democracy, a government is elected by the people, controlled by a parliament and can be replaced in a general election. In a dictatorship, however, one man rules without the control of parliament and cannot easily be removed from power.

The three principal dictators in Western Europe between the two World Wars were Mussolini in Italy, Hitler in Germany and Franco in Spain. These dictatorships had a number of characteristics in common:

- The dictators outlawed all opposition to their rule, exercising complete control over the lives of the people. This system was known as *totalitarianism*.
- Everything centred on the personality of the dictator himself who demanded the full loyalty and obedience of every citizen. The army and the police were used to enforce this loyalty.
- The dictators were extremely nationalistic: they encouraged all citizens to love their country without question.
- The dictators were strongly anti-Communist and were determined to rid their countries of any Communist influences.

There were a number of reasons why dictators came to power in Europe in these years:

- In a time of economic depression with high unemployment, people lost faith in their existing democratic governments and turned to the dictators in despair.
- Many people feared the spread of Communism and looked to the dictators to prevent this from happening.
- After World War I, many countries, especially Italy and Germany, felt that they had been wronged by the Versailles settlement. The dictators exploited this resentment and promised a return to national greatness.

Test your knowledge

1 What new form of government emerged in some European countries between the two World Wars?
2 What do you understand by the terms: (a) democracy, (b) dictatorship and (c) totalitarianism?
3 Name the three most important dictators in Western Europe and the countries they ruled.
4 State any three features which the dictators had in common.
5 Why did so many people support dictators between the wars?

The life and times of Mussolini

The early years

Benito Mussolini was born in northern Italy in 1883, the son of a blacksmith and a schoolmistress. He started his career as a teacher but soon turned to journalism. He showed an early interest in politics and became a socialist. Mussolini later turned away from Socialism and in 1915 he joined the Italian army to fight in World War I. He was wounded in 1917 and returned to his work as a journalist.

Along with most Italians, Mussolini believed that Italy had been badly treated at the Versailles Peace Conference. Italy had hoped to gain more territory at Austria's expense, but was bitterly disappointed.

In addition, Italy suffered a severe economic depression after the war. Prices soared, unemployment increased, and strikes and street disturbances were widespread. Weak Italian governments were unable to cope with this crisis. Mussolini saw the need for a new political movement to deal with this situation.

Mussolini addressing a meeting of his followers.

On 23 March 1919 he founded the Fascist Party — *Fascio di Combattimento* — in Milan. This party stood for the following:

- Strong, decisive leadership under the party leader.
- Law and order — the movement got its name from *fasces*, a bundle of rods carried before a governor in ancient Rome as a symbol of authority.
- A belief in Italy's greatness and the need to build up her armed strength.
- Mussolini's party was deeply anti-Communist and brought itself into the public view by clashing with Communist strikers.

Mussolini's path to power

Between 1919 and 1922, Mussolini and the Fascists went from strength to strength. Mussolini organised a series of meetings and demonstrations throughout Italy. At these he was surrounded by his armed followers who were known as *Blackshirts* due to the colour of their uniform. These Blackshirts fought in the streets with the Communists and other opponents. Mussolini claimed that Communists were not loyal Italians but followers of Russian Communist rulers. Industrialists and businessmen supported Mussolini's party because they came to see it as the only means of preventing a Communist takeover.

In October 1922, the Fascists took part in the famous *March on Rome* in an effort to seize power. Their plans succeeded when King Victor Emmanuel invited Mussolini to form a government. Mussolini organised a huge victory celebration in Rome on 31 October 1922 in which some 25,000 Blackshirts marched.

Mussolini leading the Fascist March on Rome in October 1922.

Test your knowledge

1 Where and when was Mussolini born?

2 Give two reasons why Mussolini saw the need for a new political party in Italy in the years after World War I.

3 What new party did Mussolini found? State two beliefs which it had.

4 Who were the Blackshirts? Why were they so named?

5 Why did many industrialists and businessmen come to support Mussolini's party?

6 What was the 'March on Rome' and what was its result?

Mussolini: The years of power

Once Mussolini was safely in power, he set about creating a Fascist dictatorship in Italy. He gradually eliminated all opposition to his rule. The Socialist leader, Matteotti, was murdered by Fascist Blackshirts in 1924. In the following year, all political parties, except the Fascist Party, were banned.

By then Italy had become a *police state* — Mussolini's police and Fascist followers dealt violently with any opponents of the government. The

Italian parliament no longer had any power in running the country. Free trade unions were abolished and strikes outlawed. Italy had become a one-party state ruled by a dictator.

In the early years of his rule, Mussolini had the support of most Italians. Propaganda played a large part in his popularity. He became known as *Il Duce*, the leader who could do no wrong. His portrait was displayed in all public places. Fascist slogans were seen everywhere and schoolchildren were instructed to admire and be loyal to Il Duce.

While Mussolini had set up a totalitarian state in which the government had full control, he had a number of important achievements to his credit:

Activity

Identify examples of Fascist propaganda in the following pictures.

Fascist women march past Mussolini.

A Fascist demonstration in Milan.

Mussolini dressed as a peasant.

The triumphant arrival of Mussolini in Turin.

Achievements of Mussolini

- Unemployment was greatly reduced.
- A huge programme of public works was implemented by the government: new motorways were built; railways were electrified and wasteland reclaimed (the most famous project was the draining of the Pontine Marshes near Rome).
- Food production, especially wheat, was greatly increased.
- In 1929, an agreement, or *concordat*, called the *Lateran Pact* was signed between Mussolini and the pope. The independent Vatican City State was set up in Rome with the pope as its ruler. This finally brought an end to many years of disagreement between the pope and the Italian government.

A meeting between Pope Pius XI and Mussolini.

The building of an empire

Building up an overseas empire for Italy was one of Mussolini's deepest ambitions. He was determined to expand and equip the Italian armed forces so that they could rival the best in the world. One of his first priorities was to gain revenge for the defeat of an Italian army by Abyssinia (Ethiopia) back in 1896. As leader of Italy, he still had vivid memories of that defeat:

> 'That day I was ill. At about ten o'clock one of my school friends ran into the dormitory with

an open newspaper shouting "Read! Read!". I grabbed the newspaper. From the first page to the last it talked of nothing but the disastrous battle — 10,000 dead and seventy-two cannons lost. Those figures are still hammering in my skull.'

In October 1935, Mussolini realised his life's ambition when Italian forces invaded Abyssinia. Although that country's ruler, Emperor Haile Selassie, appealed to the League of Nations for help, no decisive action was taken against Italy.

The Abyssinians resisted the Italian invasion, but they were no match for Mussolini's forces who used modern methods of warfare, including bombing and poison gas.

By this time, a new Fascist dictator had emerged in Germany — Adolf Hitler. Over the next few years, Mussolini and Hitler were to become close allies.

Test your knowledge

1 Outline three steps taken by Mussolini to make Italy a dictatorship.
2 How did Mussolini use propaganda to increase his popularity?
3 By what name did Mussolini become known?
4 What forms of public work did Mussolini implement?
5 What was the Lateran Pact?
6 State one of Mussolini's deepest ambitions.
7 Why did Italian forces invade Abyssinia in 1935?

Chapter 54: Review

• In Western Europe during the 1920s and 1930s, democracy was replaced by dictatorships in a number of countries. Under a dictatorship, all opposition was outlawed and the state exercised complete control over people's lives.

• The three main dictators in Western Europe in these years were Adolf Hitler, Germany; Benito Mussolini, Italy; and Francisco Franco, Spain.

• These dictators were all strongly anti-Communist. They were also extremely nationalist — that is, they encouraged their citizens to live and die for their country without question. They were also Fascist — a word which originated in Italy and came to mean a government which allowed no opposition to its rule.

• Bad economic conditions and the threat of Communism were used by the dictators as a means of gaining power.

• In 1919, Mussolini founded the Fascist Party in Milan. This stood for strong, decisive government and Italy's return to greatness. Mussolini was surrounded by a group of armed followers known as Blackshirts.

• Following a threat of a march on Rome, Mussolini came to power in 1922. He quickly set about creating a Fascist dictatorship in Italy. Before long, Italy had become a one-party police state ruled by a dictator. Propaganda played a large part in accounting for Mussolini's early popularity.

• One of Mussolini's deepest ambitions was to build up an overseas empire for Italy. In 1935, Italian forces invaded Abyssinia in revenge for Italy's defeat by that country in 1896.

Germany under Hitler

The Weimar Republic: 1919–33

In 1919, Germany's leading politicians met in the town of Weimar to decide how their country should be governed. They drew up a new constitution which provided for the establishment of a democratic republic. This form of government, known as the *Weimar Republic*, was to rule Germany until 1933. Its *Reichstag* or parliament was elected by the people. The head of the government was known as the *chancellor*. There was also a head of state elected by the people and known as the *president*.

The new government faced a number of serious problems in the years ahead:

- Some Germans blamed the politicians of the Weimar Republic for accepting the humiliating Treaty of Versailles.
- The German economy was in a state of depression after the war. Unemployment was very high, prices continued to rise and vast reparation payments crippled the economy. The worst year was 1923, when inflation reached huge levels and money became almost worthless.

For the most part, Weimar politicians were weak and indecisive and failed to face the country's problems. However, one politician, Gustave Stresemann, emerged above the others. Under his direction, the German economy began to recover with the aid of American loans.

Stresemann died in 1929 at a time when his country needed him most. The coming of the Great Depression in 1929 threw the German economy into another decline. American loans were withdrawn and the German people once again faced soaring inflation and unemployment. They now lost all faith in the Weimar Republic and turned increasingly towards more extreme groups which were offering them a way out of the Depression.

One such group was the Nazi Party. Its leader was Adolf Hitler.

Test your knowledge

1 What type of government was set up in Germany in 1919?

2 Why was this government known as the Weimar Republic?

3 State two problems facing German politicians in the 1920s.

4 Who was the most able politician in Weimar Germany? What contribution did he make to his country?

5 Why did the fortunes of the German economy experience a new drop in 1929?

Adolf Hitler: The early years

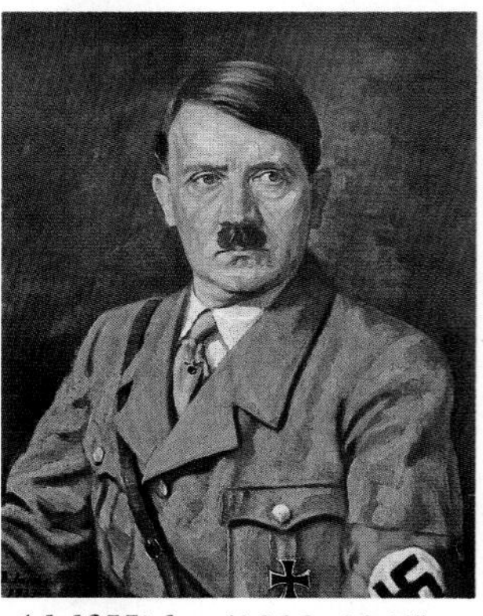

Adolf Hitler (1889-1945).

Adolf Hitler was born in Austria on 20 April 1889, the son of a customs officer. Both his parents died while he was still at school. After leaving school Hitler applied for a place in the academy of art in Vienna. Although he was not accepted in the art school, he still went to live in Vienna. While there, Hitler became interested in politics and for many years lived the life of a 'down-and-out' in Vienna. It was here that he developed much of his hatred of the Jews, whose wealth he resented.

When World War I broke out, Hitler joined the German army and fought for four years on the Western Front where he was decorated three times for bravery. After the war, he was employed as a government spy in Munich with the task of keeping an eye on revolutionary groups. It was here that he came in contact with a small group known as the *National Socialist German Workers Party* (*Nazi Party*). Hitler joined this group and quickly became its leader. In 1923 he organised a rebellion against the government in Munich. This failed and he was imprisoned for over a year as a result.

Hitler's political ideas

While in prison, in 1924, Hitler wrote his famous book called *Mein Kampf* (*My Struggle*). In his book he set out his main ideas for the future of Germany:

- Hatred of the Jews — Hitler blamed the Jews for all of Germany's problems, especially its defeat in World War I.
- Hatred of Communism — He was determined to rid Germany and the world of Communism which he saw as a great threat.
- The Master Race — Hitler believed that the Germans were the Master Race, or Aryans, who were destined to rule the world. He wanted Germany to expand eastwards and use the local people as slaves.
- A belief in Germany's greatness — Hitler was determined that Germany should become a great power again and that the Versailles Treaty should be wrecked.
- All Germans should be reunited under one single leader.

Test your knowledge

1 When and where was Hitler born?
2 What ideas did Hitler develop while in Vienna?
3 How did Hitler come to join the Nazi Party? What was the full name of that party?
4 Why was Hitler imprisoned in 1923?
5 What famous book did Hitler write in 1924?
6 Write down three ideas outlined by him in that book.

Hitler's path to power

Hitler salutes supporters from a car.

Between 1924 and 1929, Hitler and the Nazi Party were almost unknown in Germany. Owing to economic improvements at home, these were good years for most Germans. Hitler's great opportunity came, however, when severe economic depression hit Germany after the Wall Street Crash in America in 1929. Massive unemployment and soaring prices led to a crisis in Germany. The existing democratic government was unable to deal with these serious problems. More and more, Germans turned in desperation to the Communists or the Nazis to find an answer to their problems.

Hitler played especially on people's fears and promised a way out of the crisis. He was a powerful public speaker who was able to stir the emotions of an audience. This is one Nazi's recollection of the power of Hitler's oratory:

> 'I don't know how to describe the emotions that swept over me as I heard Adolf Hitler. His words were like a scourge. When he spoke of the disgrace of Germany, I felt ready to spring on any enemy. His appeal to German manhood was like a call to arms; the gospel he preached, a sacred truth. I forgot everything but the man. Then, glancing around, I saw that his magnetism was holding these thousands as one. The intense will of the man, the passion of his sincerity, seemed to flow from him into me. I experienced an exultation that could be likened only to religious conversion.'

Hitler addressing a Nazi rally.

Like Mussolini, Hitler used propaganda in the form of massive rallies and cinema newsreels to gain more support. He was surrounded by groups of armed followers or storm troopers known as the SA and the SS. These groups terrorised all opposition, especially Communists and Jews.

Many industrialists and businessmen supported Hitler because of his opposition to Communism. In total despair, many Germans now came to see Hitler as their only hope. In the election of July 1932, the Nazi Party won more seats than any other party. Six months later, Hitler was invited by President Hindenburg to form a government. The 'down-and-out' of Vienna had now become the Chancellor of Germany.

German Elections 1928–32

1928 Nazis win 12 seats	**1932 (July)** Nazis win 230 seats
1930 Nazis win 107 seats	**1932 (November)** Nazis win 196 seats

Test your knowledge

1 Why were the Nazis almost unknown in Germany between 1924 and 1929?
2 Why did Hitler's fortunes begin to turn after 1929?
3 What methods did Hitler use to increase his support?
4 Why did many industrialists and businessmen come to support Hitler?
5 Why was the election in July 1932 so important for Hitler?

Hitler in power

Once in power, Hitler was determined to set up a dictatorship in Germany. His first opportunity came when the Reichstag building was burned to the ground on 27 February 1933. Hitler blamed the Communist Party for this act and accused them of plotting against the state. As a result, some 4,000 Communist Party officials were arrested.

In March 1933, Hitler forced parliament to pass the *Enabling Act*. This allowed him to rule without the aid of parliament for a period of four years. He was now firmly on the road towards becoming a dictator. All other political parties were soon banned. By the summer of 1933, the Nazi Party was the only legal political organisation in Germany. Newspapers, radio and cinema were strictly censored and forced to present Nazi views.

A victory march of Hitler's brown-shirted supporters after he became chancellor.

Hitler's position was further strengthened when President Hindenburg died on 2 August 1934. Hitler now became both president and chancellor of Germany. From then on, Hitler was known as *Der Führer* (the leader) and his motto became *Ein Reich, Ein Volk, Ein Führer*—One Empire, One People, One Leader. He called his government the *Third Reich*, or the Third Empire, which, he boasted, would last a thousand years.

Members of the Nazi Youth Movement, organised by Hitler throughout Germany.

Young people were instructed to be loyal to the German state and the Führer from an early age. A *Hitler Youth Movement* was organised for this purpose. The following order, which was issued by the Ministry of the Interior, stated the purpose of education in the Third Reich:

> 'The principal task of the school is the education of youth in the service of manhood and the state in the National Socialist spirit. At the beginning of every lesson, the teacher goes to the front of the class, which is standing, and greets it by raising his right arm, with the words "Heil Hitler"; the class returns the salute.'

Hitler set up a police state in Germany with his infamous secret police — *the Gestapo* — dealing ruthlessly with all opposition. During the 1930s, concentration camps were opened to deal with enemies of his rule, especially Communists and Jews. The Jews were to suffer most at the hands of the Nazi state.

The Jews

What does this picture tell you about the treatment of Jews in Nazi Germany?

In November 1935, the *Nuremberg Laws* were passed. These deprived Jews of all citizenship rights, forbade a Jew to marry a German, and forced all Jews to wear a special badge (the Star of David) to identify themselves. As a result of these laws, many Jews such as the famous scientist, Albert Einstein, fled from Germany.

Jews, fleeing from Germany on board a train, are caught trying to take their valuables with them.

Worse, however, was yet to come. In Berlin on 9-10 November 1938, Jewish property was attacked and burned. This incident, which caused the massive destruction of shops and synagogues, became known as 'The Night of the Broken Glass' (*Kristallnacht*).

The following eye-witness account tells about this dreadful night:

> 'Jewish buildings were smashed into and the contents demolished or looted. In one of the Jewish sections, an eighteen-year-old boy was hurled from a third-storey window to land with both legs broken. Jewish shop windows by the hundred were smashed throughout the entire city. Three synagogues were fired by incendiary bombs. Having demolished dwellings and burned most of the moveable effects on the streets, they threw many of the trembling inmates into a small stream, commanding horrified spectators to spit at them, defile them with mud, and jeer at their plight. There is much evidence of physical violence, including several deaths.'

In the years ahead, Hitler was to put his plan for the total elimination of the Jews into operation. It was known as *The Final Solution*.

Test your knowledge

1 What was the Enabling Act?

2 What name did Hitler adopt? What was his motto? What do you understand by this motto?

3 Who were the Gestapo?

4 How did Hitler deal with enemies of his rule?

5 What were the Nuremberg Laws?

Chapter 55: Review

- Between 1919 and 1923, Germany was ruled by the Weimar Republic, a democratic form of government. The greatest statesman of these years was Gustave Stresemann who helped Germany to recover after the defeat of World War I.

- However, the economic depression which hit Germany in 1929 helped Adolf Hitler and the Nazi Party come to power in January 1933.

- Hitler's main beliefs included a commitment to Germany's greatness, a hatred of Jews and Communists, and the idea that the Germans were a Master Race, superior to other peoples.

- Hitler was a powerful speaker who was able to stir the emotions of an audience. Like Mussolini, he used propaganda in the form of massive rallies and cinema newsreels to gain support.

- Once in power, Hitler banned all other political parties as well as trade unions. When President Hindenburg died in August 1934, he took over that office and became known as *Der Führer* (the leader). Under the 1935 Nuremberg Laws, Jews were deprived of their civil rights.

Civil War in Spain

The path to war

Between 1936 and 1939, a fierce civil war took place in Spain. In 1931, the king of Spain had been overthrown and a republic was set up. For the next five years, the Republican government tried to bring in reforms to improve the lot of the poorer people.

- In towns and cities, workers' conditions were improved.
- In the country, attempts were made to divide large estates among the peasants.

Many of those supporting the Spanish Republic were Communists or Socialists who wanted to introduce sweeping changes to Spain. They wished to take land from the rich landowners and place it under the control of the peasants. They wanted workers to control the factories. And above all, they wished to reduce the power and influence of the Catholic Church. These groups joined together to form the *Popular Front* and won an election in February 1936.

The success of this group greatly alarmed the old ruling class made up of rich landowners, businessmen, army officers and Church leaders. These people now looked to the Spanish Fascist Party (*Falange*) for protection. In July 1936, General Francisco Franco, leader of the Fascists, led a revolt in Spanish Morocco against Spain's Republican government. This revolt soon spread to Spain itself — the Spanish Civil War had begun.

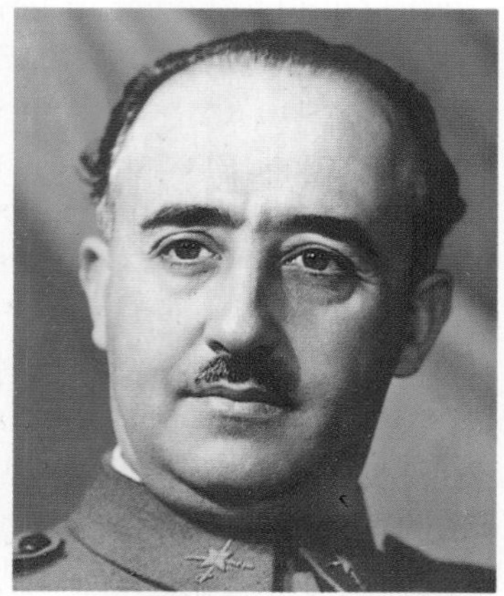

General Francisco Franco.

The war rages

Many army garrisons in Spain supported Franco - his followers became known as the *Nationalists*. Franco's opponents, the *Republicans* — mostly Communists and Socialists — had their strongest support in the province of Catalonia where industrial workers were most numerous.

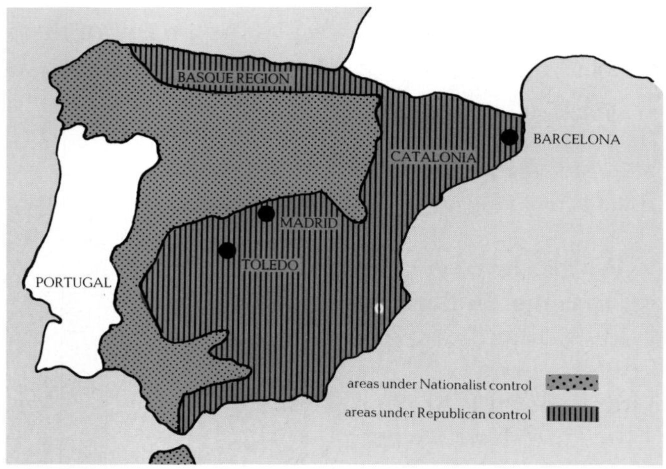

Spain was deeply divided between Nationalist and Republican areas during the Civil War, 1936-39.

Republicans marching in Madrid in July 1936. Notice the women carrying guns.

The war was fought with great cruelty on both sides. The Republican forces were strongly opposed to the Church's influence in Spain. They murdered many priests and nuns and burned churches. The Nationalists conducted ruthless mass killings of their captured opponents.

Republicans kill a Catholic monk in Barcelona.

Hitler and Mussolini sent arms and soldiers to their fellow Fascist, General Franco. From Soviet Russia, Stalin sent aid to the Republicans. An International Brigade was organised in which men from all over the world (including Ireland) went to Spain to fight for the Republicans in an effort to defeat Franco and Fascism. But many others, strongly opposed to Communism, supported Franco. Ireland's Eoin O'Duffy and some of his followers went to Spain to fight for Franco.

The bombing of Guernica

One of the most horrific incidents of the war was the German bombing of the town of Guernica on 26 April 1937. The following account, written by a local priest, gives us a vivid report of that terrible event:

> 'Late in the afternoon of 26 April I was going by car to rescue my mother and my sister. We reached the outskirts of Guernica just before six o'clock. The streets were busy with the traffic of market day. Suddenly we heard the siren and trembled.
>
> Soon, an aeroplane appeared over Guernica, followed by a squadron of seven planes, followed a little later by six more, and this in turn by a squadron of five more. All of them were Junkers [German aircraft]. Meanwhile, Guernica was seized by a terrible panic. For more than an hour these eighteen planes dropped bomb after bomb on Guernica. The sound of the explosions and of the crumbling houses cannot be imagined. Bombs fell by thousands. Later we saw the bomb craters. Some were sixteen metres in diameter and eight metres deep.
>
> The aeroplanes left around seven o'clock and then there came another wave of them, this time flying at immense altitude. They were dropping incendiary (fire) bombs on our martyred city. The new bombardment lasted thirty-five minutes, sufficient to transform the town into an enormous furnace. Even then I realised the terrible purpose of this new act of vandalism. They were dropping incendiary bombs to try to convince the world that the Basques had fired their own city.
>
> When it grew dark, the flames of Guernica were reaching the sky, and the clouds took on the colour of blood, and our faces too shone with the colour of blood.'

What view of Guernica is conveyed in Picasso's famous painting?

The war ends

Franco's troops fighting for control of Madrid at the end of the Civil War.

In the spring of 1939, Franco's Nationalist army was finally victorious. Its soldiers had been better trained and it had received more foreign aid than the Republicans. Furthermore, while the Nationalist side was totally united under Franco, there had been deep divisions in the Spanish Republic between various political parties.

Once in power, Franco set up a Fascist dictatorship, outlawing all political parties except his own. Free trade unions were banned and a strict censorship was imposed on the press and the radio. Under the Republic, regions like the Basque country and Catalonia were given a certain amount of freedom. Franco, however, ruled all of Spain centrally from Madrid.

Test your knowledge

1 Who were the Republicans?
2 What groups of people were against the Republic?
3 By what name was the Spanish Fascist Party known? Who was its leader?
4 Name the two sides in the Spanish Civil War.
5 What part did Mussolini, Hitler and Stalin play in the Spanish Civil War?
6 Why did many people go to Spain to fight for: (a) the Republicans; (b) the Nationalists?
7 Give three reasons why Franco won the Civil War.
8 How did Franco go about setting up a dictatorship in Spain?
9 What do you think Franco's Spain had in common with Mussolini's Italy and Hitler's Germany?

Chapter 56: Review

• In Spain, a fierce civil war took place from 1936 until 1939 between supporters of the Republican government and the Nationalist forces under General Francisco Franco. The Republic was largely supported by Communists and Socialists, while Franco had the backing of rich landowners and the Catholic Church.

• There was much international involvement in the Spanish Civil War. Hitler and Mussolini sent arms and soldiers to help their fellow Fascist, Franco. From Soviet Russia, Stalin sent aid to the Republicans.

• The war ended in the spring of 1939 when Franco's forces were finally victorious. His soldiers had been better trained and the Nationalist side had received more aid than the Republicans.

• Once in power, Franco set up a Fascist dictatorship in Spain, outlawing all political parties except his own.

The Steps towards War

Hitler's foreign policy

Hitler's foreign policy had four main aims:

- To make Germany a great power again.
- To gain revenge for the humiliation of the Versailles settlement.
- To unite all German-speaking peoples under one leader.
- To expand eastwards and enslave the Jews and the Communists.

Hitler dismantles the Treaty of Versailles

In the 1930s, Hitler set about making Germany a strong nation again. He particularly wanted to reverse the humiliating aspects of the Treaty of Versailles. Although the treaty had set strict limits on the size of Germany's army and navy, Hitler ignored it. He introduced *conscription* in 1935 and Germany soon had an army far greater than the 100,000 soldiers permitted under the Treaty of Versailles. Hitler also built up the German navy and the air force (the *Luftwaffe*).

Hermann Goering became head of the German airforce, the Luftwaffe.

Mussolini's visit to Hitler after the formation of the Rome-Berlin Axis.

Celebrations in Tokyo following the alliance between Germany, Italy and Japan.

In 1933, Hitler took Germany out of the League of Nations. When Mussolini invaded Abyssinia, Hitler formed an alliance with him known as the *Rome-Berlin Axis* (1936). Around the same time, Germany also formed an alliance with Japan. Relations between Germany, Italy and Japan were now firmly established in the form of the *Rome-Berlin-Tokyo Axis.*

The Rhineland is reoccupied

Under the Treaty of Versailles, Germany was forbidden to station soldiers in the Rhineland zone. Hitler defied this and sent troops into the zone in March 1936. The French were both angered and frightened by this move. The British, on the other hand, were not prepared to take action because they regarded the Treaty of Versailles as being

German troops entering the Rhineland in March 1936. What is the reaction of the local people?

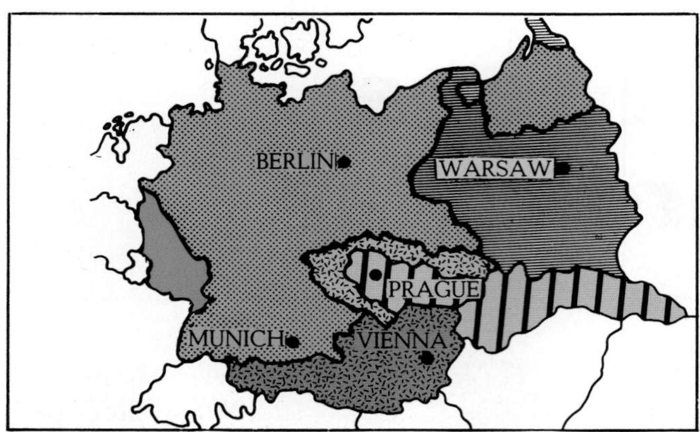

The expansion of Germany under Hitler.

too harsh on Germany. As a result of Hitler's move into the Rhineland, the French built a line of forts along their border with Germany—the *Maginot Line*. The Germans, in turn, built the *Siegfried Line* of defensive forts along their side of the border. Meanwhile, Hitler's successful reoccupation of the Rhineland encouraged him to expand further.

- By 1935 Hitler had increased the size of the German army and had built up the navy and airforce.
- Hitler enters the Rhineland (1936)
- Hitler annexes Austria (The Anschluss) (March 1938)
- Hitler takes over the Sudetenland area of Czechoslovakia (September 1938)
- Hitler takes over all of Czechoslovakia (March 1939)
- Hitler invades Poland (1 September 1939)

Test your knowledge

1 State three steps taken by Hitler to dismantle the Treaty of Versailles.

2 How did the French and British react to Hitler's invasion of the Rhineland?

3 What were: (a) the Maginot Line; (b) the Siegfried Line?

Germany annexes Austria

It was now clear to Hitler that the League of Nations could do nothing to prevent German expansion. The League had already failed to take action when Italy invaded Abyssinia and when Japan invaded part of China. This encouraged Hitler to make his next move: the take-over of Austria, the land of his birth.

Hitler believed that all German-speaking people should be united under one leader. Many Austrians also desired union with Germany. This policy was known as the *Anschluss*. There was a powerful Nazi Party in Austria and Hitler put pressure on the Austrian government to give important positions to members of that party. Finally, in March 1938, Hitler invaded Austria, having first secured Mussolini's agreement.

Nazi troops marching in Vienna after the German annexation of Austria in March 1938.

Britain and France did not interfere, although the Anschluss was forbidden by the Treaty of Versailles. Hitler made a triumphant visit to Austria and announced that the country would become a part of the Third Reich.

The man who had once been a down-and-out artist in Vienna had now returned as the city's victorious ruler.

Test your knowledge

1 What was meant by Anschluss?

2 When did Hitler annex Austria?

3 What was Britain's reaction to this move?

The Munich conference and the German invasion of Czechoslovakia

In the autumn of 1938, Hitler made his next move. He turned his attention to the German-speaking section of Czechoslovakia, the Sudetenland, where over 3 million Germans lived. The leader of Czechoslovakia, Eduard Benes, appealed to the other European powers for help and in September 1938 a conference was held at Munich to discuss the issues involved. Hitler, Mussolini, Deladier, the French leader, and Chamberlain, the British prime minister, were the main participants.

At this conference, Chamberlain continued Britain's policy of *appeasement*—he believed that by agreeing to German demands, Hitler would be satisfied and war in Europe would be prevented.

Neville Chamberlain showing his written agreement with Hitler on his return home from the Munich Conference.

German troops welcomed into the Sudetenland.

Appeasement was popular in Britain because many people felt that the Treaty of Versailles had been too harsh on Germany. Many people in Britain also dreaded a return to the trench warfare experienced in World War I, with its huge cost in numbers of dead and wounded. Britain and France therefore agreed at Munich that Hitler should take over the Sudetenland in return for a promise that he would make no further demands.

1 How did Churchill and Chamberlain differ over Munich?
2 Suggest reasons for their differences.
3 Why do you think Chamberlain's views were more popular in Britain at the time?
4 How do you think Czechoslovakia reacted to the Munich Agreement?

Following Hitler's invasion of Czechoslovakia, Britain prepares for war by building trenches in the middle of London as a protection against air raids.

Hitler soon showed his disregard for the agreement reached at Munich. In March 1939, Germany took over the rest of Czechoslovakia. For the first time, Hitler had taken control of a non-German-speaking people. It was only now that Britain fully realised the German threat. Chamberlain introduced conscription in Britain and promised to go to war if Germany invaded Poland.

Working with evidence

Two Views of Munich

(*a*) Neville Chamberlain said on his return from Munich:

> 'My good friends, for the second time in our history, a British Prime Minister has returned bringing peace with honour...I believe it is peace for our time.'

(*b*) Winston Churchill commented on the Munich Agreement:

> 'We have suffered a total and unmitigated defeat. All is over...I think you will find that in a period of time Czechoslovakia will be engulfed in the Nazi regime. We have passed an awful milestone in our history, when the whole equilibrium of Europe has been deranged...And do not suppose that this is the end. This is only the beginning of the reckoning.'

Test your knowledge

1 Why did Hitler want to take over the Sudetenland?
2 Who was the prime minister of Britain in 1938?
3 What was meant by appeasement? With which country is this policy most associated?
4 What was decided at Munich in 1938?
5 How did Hitler show his disregard for the Munich Agreement?
6 How did Hitler's invasion of Czechoslovakia in March 1939 differ from his earlier moves?
7 How did Chamberlain respond to the German take-over of Czechoslovakia?

The invasion of Poland

Poland was the next country in Hitler's plans for German expansion eastwards, a policy known as *Lebensraum* (living space). Realising this, Britain and France now tried to form an alliance with the Soviet Union in the face of the Nazi threat.

Stalin, concerned only for the security of the Soviet Union, did not trust them. In a desperate effort to keep Russia out of another war, Stalin came to an agreement with Hitler in August 1939 known as the *Nazi-Soviet Non-Aggression Pact*. Stalin agreed to stand aside while Germany invaded Poland, and both he and Hitler secretly agreed to divide Poland between them. On 1 September 1939, Germany invaded Poland. Two days later, Britain and France declared war on Germany. World War II had begun.

Molotov and Ribbentrop, the Soviet and German foreign ministers, signing the Nazi-Soviet Non-Aggression Pact in August 1939. This pact ensured that, in the event of war, Hitler could concentrate on defeating Britain and France and avoid fighting on two fronts. Stalin desperately wanted to avoid Russian involvement in war. Having failed previously to persuade Britain and France to form an alliance with him against Hitler, he came to an agreement with the Nazi dictator in order to keep war from the USSR as long as possible.

Contemporary cartoon showing Hitler and Stalin at the time of the Nazi-Soviet Pact. What is the main message being conveyed?

Chapter 57: Review

- During the 1930s, Hitler built up Germany's armed forces and took the country out of the League of Nations. In 1936 he formed an alliance with Mussolini — the Rome-Berlin Axis — and later extended this to include Japan.

- In March 1936, Hitler's troops reoccupied the Rhineland. This was forbidden under the Treaty of Versailles but Great Britain and France took no action to stop it.

- In March 1938, Hitler again broke the Versailles settlement when he marched into Austria and joined it to Germany — a policy known as the Anschluss.

- At the Munich Conference in September 1938, Britain and France agreed to allow Hitler to take over the Sudetenland area of Czechoslovakia. The British prime minister, Chamberlain, returned from the conference claiming that he had secured 'peace for our time'.

- In March 1939, Hitler took control of a non-German people for the first time when he conquered the rest of Czechoslovakia. Britain now promised support to Poland if Hitler attacked that country.

- In August 1939, Hitler signed an agreement with the Russian Communist leader, Stalin, known as The Nazi-Soviet Non-Aggression Pact. In a secret clause they agreed to divide Poland between them.

- On 1 September 1939, Hitler invaded Poland. Great Britain and France then declared war on Germany. World War II had begun.

The World at War

Blitzkrieg: Poland is overrun

On 1 September 1939, Germany invaded Poland. Hitler launched a new type of warfare — *blitzkrieg* or lightning war. This was a combination of rapid tank movements on the ground and heavy bombing from the air. Soon Poland was completely overrun by the might of the German war machine.

German planes get ready to launch a blitzkrieg *or 'lightning war'.*

After Germany's conquest of Poland, there was a lull in fighting lasting for nearly six months during the winter of 1939–40. This was known as 'the Phoney War'. It was not until the spring of 1940 that war in Europe got fully under way.

Newspaper headlines in London announcing the outbreak of World War II.

1940: German attacks on the West

In April 1940, Hitler conquered Norway and Denmark. On 10 May, he launched a successful attack on Belgium and Holland. Hitler's armies then overran France in a matter of weeks, to the surprise of many people, and the French government surrendered on 24 June. Britain now stood alone to face the German attack.

German troops occupy Paris, May 1940.

A British Expeditionary Force (BEF) had arrived in France to assist the French in their fight against Hitler. With the rapid defeat of France, this force was trapped at the port of Dunkirk in northern France. A spectacular rescue attempt followed. Over a period of six days, a huge assortment of ships, including warships and pleasure boats, arrived from England and braved the German bombs to rescue over 300,000 soldiers.

Fighting in Dunkirk in May 1940.

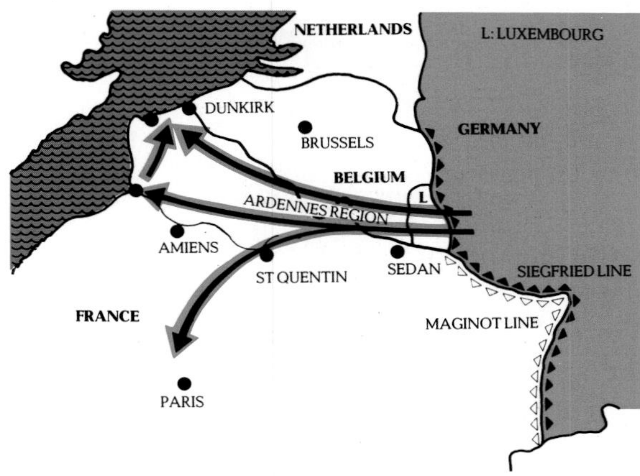

Hitler launched a lightning attack on the West in the Spring of 1940.

Read the British and German accounts of these events. What differences do you notice?

Source A (BBC news bulletin, 31 May 1940)

'All night and all day, men of the undefeated British army have been coming home. From the many reports of their arrival and of interviews with the men, it is clear that if they have not come back in triumph, they have come back in glory; that their spirits are as high as ever; that they know that they did not meet their masters; and that they are anxious only to be back again soon — as they put it — "to have a real crack at Jerry".'

Source B (Official German bulletin, 4 June 1940)

'The full extent of our victory in Holland, in Belgium and in the north of France can be measured by enemy losses in men and material. The English, French, Dutch and Belgians have lost 1,200,000 as prisoners, plus dead and wounded. The arms and equipment of the whole Allied army, including tanks and vehicles of every type, have also been destroyed or captured.'

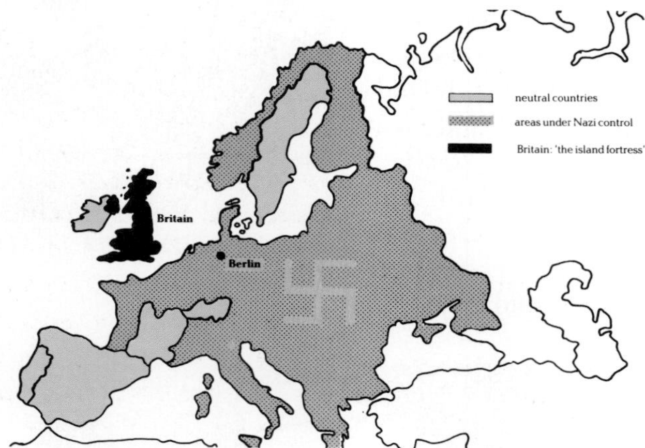

After the fall of France in June 1940, Britain stood alone against the power of Nazi Germany.

In the meantime, the British prime minister, Neville Chamberlain, had resigned and was replaced by Winston Churchill. Churchill was determined to lift the spirits of the British people and resist the German attack to the end. Here is what he told the House of Commons on 4 June 1940.

'...we shall defend our island whatever the cost may be, we shall fight on the beaches, we shall fight on the landing grounds, we shall fight in the fields and in the streets, we shall fight in the hills; we shall never surrender.'

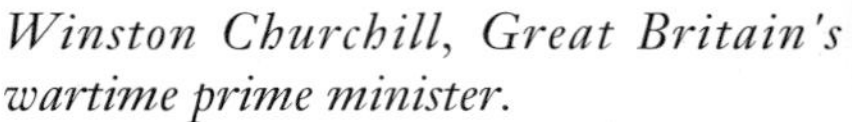

Winston Churchill, Great Britain's wartime prime minister.

Test your knowledge

1 What new method of warfare did Hitler use in his attack on Poland in September 1939?

2 What was the 'Phoney War'? Why was it so named?

3 What new offensive did Hitler launch in the spring of 1940?

4 What happened at Dunkirk?

5 Who replaced Chamberlain as prime minister of Britain in 1940?

The Battle of Britain

After the defeat of France in June 1940, Hitler planned an invasion of Britain (*Operation Sealion*). Before he could attempt this, however, he first needed to control the air space. A huge battle took place in September 1940 between the German airforce, the *Luftwaffe*, and the British Royal Air Force (RAF). This air battle was known as the *Battle of Britain*. With the aid of radar, the RAF successfully repelled the German attack. Around a thousand British pilots of Fighter Command bore the brunt of the fighting and about 400 of these were killed in action. Churchill later paid tribute to the RAF when he commented:

'Never in the field of human conflict was so much owed by so many to so few.'

War in the air during the Battle of Britain.

Bomb damage in London during the Blitz.

Sheffield under attack during the Blitz.

Londoners emerging from an underground shelter after a bombing raid.

While Hitler postponed his plans to invade Britain, he continued to bomb London and extended the bombing campaign to other British cities. This marked the beginning of the 'Night Blitz'. Between 7 September and 13 November 1940, there was only one night when London escaped bombing, with an average of 163 German bombers flying over the city each night. The bombing of British cities, including London, Coventry, Southampton and Belfast, resulted in the deaths of 40,000 civilians and the injury of 46,000 others.

June 1941: Germany attacks Russia

German tanks invading Russia in June 1941.

On 22 June 1941, Hitler broke the Nazi-Soviet Pact of 1939 by invading Russia. This was known as *Operation Barbarossa*. The Soviet Red Army was not prepared for this attack. It was poorly equipped and much of its aircraft and weaponry was outdated. Within a very short time the German army had made rapid advances towards Leningrad and Moscow. By October, Moscow was almost a deserted city — only Stalin and his advisers remained on in the Kremlin, the Russian seat of government.

The German invasion of Russia (Operation Barbarossa), 1941. By December 1941 German troops had captured vast stretches of Russian territory, almost reaching Moscow, the capital city.

When the Russian winter set in, the German advance froze to a halt. This gave Stalin the breathing space he needed. The huge Russian army, under the command of Marshal Zhukov, was rebuilt and moved into action. The German advance was halted outside Moscow, but the great turning point came in the winter of 1942–43 at Stalingrad.

The German Sixth Army under General von Paulus began its attack on Stalingrad in September 1942. By the middle of November, most of the city had fallen to the Germans in street-by-street fighting. However, Marshal Zhukov now came to the aid of the city with an army of a million men which completely surrounded the Germans. Von Paulus asked Hitler for permission to surrender but this was refused.

'Surrender is forbidden. The army will hold their positions to the last man and the last round of ammunition.'

Street-by-street fighting between Germans and Russians in Stalingrad.

For over two months, the Russians attacked the starving, frozen Germans. When von Paulus finally surrendered at the end of January 1943, out of a Germany army of 300,000 only 97,000 survived.

The German advance in Russia is blocked by the extreme cold.

Hitler's invasion of Russia had been a serious error, resulting in massive casualties on both sides. The war in Russia had been fought with terrible savagery and brutality. Millions of Russians perished in the course of the campaign.

Test your knowledge

1 What was Operation Barbarossa?

2 Why do you think the Germans advanced rapidly through Russia?

3 What happened at Stalingrad? What was its outcome?

4 Do you think the Russian campaign was a serious error on Hitler's part? Give reasons for your answer.

Pearl Harbor (December 1941)

America enters the war

Throughout the 1930s, the heavily populated Japanese Empire had looked greedily on American, British and French possessions in the Pacific. In 1936, the Japanese made an alliance with Hitler and Mussolini with a view to future expansion.

American ships burning after the Japanese attack on Pearl Harbor.

On the morning of Sunday, 7 December 1941, the Japanese air force launched a surprise attack on the US naval base at Pearl Harbor in Hawaii. When the Japanese finally departed, eight battleships were badly damaged, many aircraft were destroyed on the ground and 2,403 Americans were dead. This attack brought the United States immediately into the war on the side of Great Britain and the USSR. Ever since the beginning, America had been sympathetic to the Allied side and had given equipment to Britain and France in a scheme known as 'Lend-Lease'.

American propaganda poster following the attack on Pearl Harbor.

America's entry was a vital turning point in the war. From then on the American president, Franklin D. Roosevelt, co-operated closely with Churchill in planning the Allied military campaigns. The might of American manufacturing industry and finance was to play a key role in the eventual Allied victory.

Test your knowledge

1 What event brought America into the war?
2 Who was the president of America during World War II?
3 Why was America's entry into the war of such importance?

1942–43: The tide turns

In North Africa, the presence of the Afrika Corps of the German army under General Rommel was a serious threat to British interests in Egypt, especially the Suez Canal. The British Eighth Army, under General Montgomery, was strengthened by American aid and defeated Rommel's forces at the Battle of El Alamein in October 1942. In the following month, the American General Eisenhower led an army into Algeria and Morocco in North Africa (*Operation Torch*) and forced the remains of Rommel's Afrika Corps to surrender.

British forces in action during the Battle of El Alamein.

In July 1943, Eisenhower's forces combined with Montgomery's Eighth Army to invade Sicily. They proceeded from there to mainland Italy. Due to difficult countryside and fierce German resistance, their progress was slow — Rome did not fall to the Allies until June 1944. With the arrival of the Allies, some Italians rose against Mussolini and imprisoned him. However, he was rescued in a German parachute raid and brought north. In the meantime, a new pro-Allied government took over in Italy. Mussolini once again fell into the hands of his enemies. This time he was put to death and his body hanged in public. The Allied victories during 1942 and 1943 — in North Africa, Stalingrad and Italy — marked the beginning of the end of Nazi domination.

General Rommel, German Commander in North Africa.

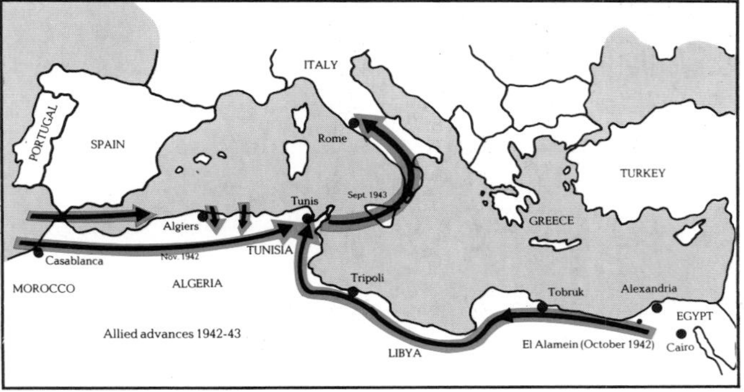

The tide turned for the Allies in 1942–43 as they conquered North Africa and advanced from there into Sicily and Italy.

Test your knowledge

1 Name the commanders of the British and German forces in the Battle of El Alamein.
2 Who led the Allied forces in the invasion of North Africa?
3 What happened to Mussolini when the Allies entered Italy?
4 Name three Allied victories which showed that the tide was turning against Hitler.

Chapter 58: Review

• Hitler's new tactic, which he used against Poland, was known as *blitzkrieg* or lightning war. German troops soon conquered the country and after that there was a lull in the fighting until the following spring ('the Phoney War').

• In April and May 1940, Hitler attacked and conquered Norway, Denmark, Belgium and Holland. He also attacked France which, to the great surprise of many, surrendered to Germany on 24 June. Britain now stood alone against Hitler.

• In a dramatic rescue attempt, over 300,000 British soldiers were brought from Dunkirk to England in June 1940. The new British prime minister, Winston Churchill, was determined to resist the German attack to the bitter end.

• In a huge air battle in September 1940 between the British Royal Air Force and the German *Luftwaffe* (The Battle of Britain), the British successfully beat off the German attack.

• Following his failure to invade Britain, Hitler launched a blitz of night bombings on British cities throughout the following autumn and winter.

• On 22 June 1941, Hitler attacked Soviet Russia in an invasion known as Operation Barbarossa. The Germans made huge advances at first but were halted before reaching the three main cities of Moscow, Leningrad and Stalingrad.

• In the winter of 1942–43, World War II reached a major turning point when the German army surrendered to the Russians at Stalingrad. After that the Russians began to push the Germans back on the Eastern Front.

• The United States of America had entered the war in December 1941 when Germany's ally, Japan, attacked a naval base at Pearl Harbor. American entry was to eventually turn the tide in favour of the Allies.

• At the Battle of El Alamein in North Africa in October 1942, the British Eighth Army under General Montgomery defeated the German Afrika Corps of General Rommel. In the following month, the American General Eisenhower led an American army into Algeria and Morocco (Operation Torch).

• In July 1943, a combined force of British and American soldiers invaded Sicily and went on from there to Italy where they met with fierce German resistance — the city of Rome only fell to the Allies in June 1944.

Towards Allied Victory

D-Day: Allied landings in France

For a long time, Stalin had been demanding that Britain and America open a second front in the west to relieve pressure on Russia. On 6 June 1944, the long-awaited D-Day (D for deliverance) occurred. A huge Allied force, under the command of General Eisenhower, crossed the English Channel and landed in Normandy in northern France. This invasion was known as *Operation Overlord*. A bridgehead some 80 kilometres wide was specially built for the invasion. Despite fierce German resistance and heavy casualties, nearly a million Allied soldiers had landed in France by the end of June.

General Dwight D. Eisenhower, the American general who was in command of Operation Overlord.

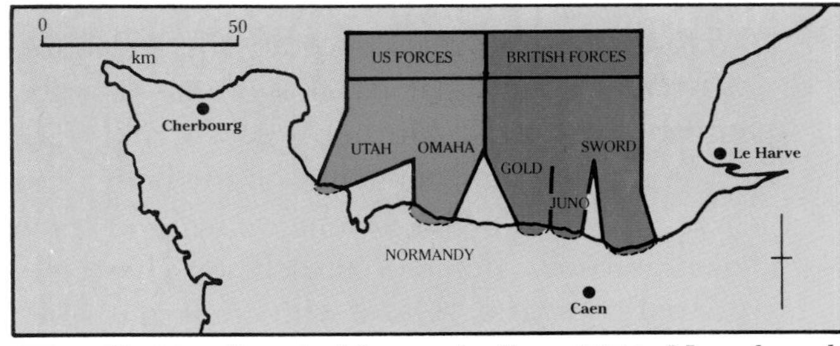

The Allied landings in Normandy, June 1944. Note the code names for the beaches (e.g. Utah).

Allied soldiers were also parachuted into France where they linked up with local Resistance groups. These sabotaged transport and communications networks in an effort to disrupt the German forces. On 18 August, Paris was liberated from German control. The Allies now moved on towards Belgium.

The war in Europe ends

General Charles de Gaulle marching through Paris in triumph in August 1944 following the Allied liberation of the city from German control. De Gaulle had fled to London after the fall of France in June 1940. From there he played a key part in directing the French Resistance Movement.

Members of the French Underground or Resistance Movement planning an attack on German defences during the Allied invasion of France.

By the end of 1944, both France and Belgium were freed from German control. The Allies now advanced towards Germany on two fronts. They continued to bomb German cities, which led to huge civilian casualties. One of these attacks was the bombing of Dresden in February 1945, which resulted in the loss of some 135,000 lives. From the east, the Red Army was making rapid progress, while British and American troops were closing in from the west. The Germans had not lost all hope, however. In December 1944, they tried to drive the Allies back into the

Allied bombing of a German city.

Ardennes region of France and Belgium in a battle known as the Battle of the Bulge.

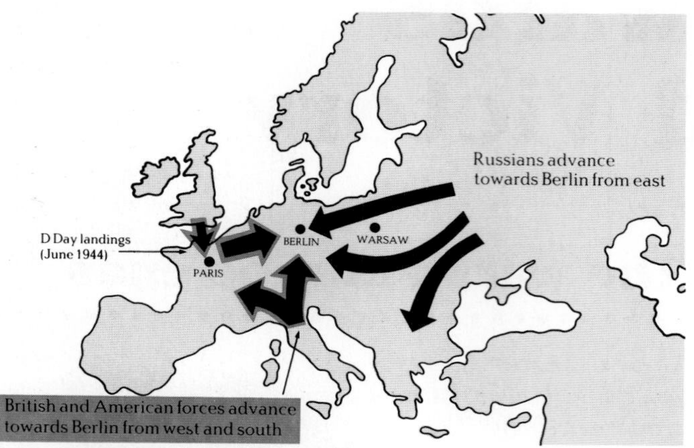

Allied forces advancing towards Berlin.

By 1945, Hitler's position was becoming desperate. His last hope rested in his newly developed V1 and V2 rockets, but these failed to break the Allied advance. On 30 April 1945, with the Russian army entering Berlin, Hitler and his wife, Eva Braun, committed suicide in their underground bunker. On 7 May 1945 the Germans surrendered unconditionally. The war in Europe was over.

Life in Nazi-occupied Europe

Members of the International Red Cross Movement clearing out concentration camps.

The war in Europe left a heavy toll of death and destruction in its wake. The full extent of the horrors of Nazi rule became clear as the Allies liberated German-occupied territory. In a plan known as 'The Final Solution' Hitler had exterminated some 6 million Jews in concentration camps throughout Europe such as Auschwitz, Dachau and Treblinka.

The following is one survivor's account of life in Auschwitz.

'Total obedience, total humiliation. It was no use trying to predict logically what they would do. Yet at the same time you had to be somehow a step ahead. You had to develop special antennae...Above all keep away from those who said it wasn't worth trying to go on. Despair was contagious. There was one period when illness had almost the same awful effect on me. It started with a night when I couldn't sleep, tired as I was. I tossed and turned, hot and shivery, icy cold and bathed in sweat. Was it typhus? Nearly everyone caught it sooner or later. It was as common a killer as the SS.

[Kitty Hart was then taken to the hospital block where her mother was working.] The block was full. I was put on to a single bunk which already had three occupants. One patient had diphtheria, another malaria and third had typhus...I heard myself crying for water. Then I must have been unconscious for a long time. Then awake, or half awake, I thought I could see oranges, grapes and cool drinks at the foot of my bunk and screamed for them. Mother was there and I cursed her for being so cruel...

One day as I lay unconscious there was a selection. All those unable to get up were taken to be gassed. Mother saw what would surely happen to me. She pushed me inside a straw mattress and laid a corpse on top of me, praying I would keep still and not start raving and singing, as I had been doing some hours earlier. The SS doctor passed the bunk. The corpse was taken away. The incurably sick were taken also. I was still alive...

During my convalescence another selection was carried out. That day I was able to walk, but not very well. Mother was worried, too, about the sores and scratches on my body. And I was far too thin. One by one we had to parade naked outside. Mengele himself was there. He ordered us to run. Those who could not summon up the energy to run were sent to the left, the others to the right. I gathered all my strength, began to run and somehow made it. But Mengele was staring hard at my pimply body. He made me turn round, then round again, while he hesitated...and at last he pointed to the right.'

Kitty Hart, *Return to Auschwitz*, 1981.

Joy on the faces of Jewish children as they are released from Dachau concentration camp on 12 May 1945.

Millions of people in the occupied countries were sent to work as forced labour in Germany. Not everyone submitted peacefully to German domination. Resistance groups sprang up throughout Europe, most notably the *French Resistance* and Marshal Tito's *Partisans* in Yugoslavia.

Leading Nazis on trial at Nuremberg in 1946.

The Allies were determined to bring the leading Nazi war criminals to justice. In a series of trials held in Nuremberg between November 1945 and September 1946, twelve leading Nazis were sentenced to death for crimes against humanity. Of these Goering, the leader of the Luftwaffe, committed suicide and the eleven others were hanged.

Test your knowledge

1 What happened on 6 June 1944?

2 Who was the commander of the D-Day landings?

3 Why was the German position in Europe becoming desperate by 1945?

4 What was the Final Solution?

5 What happened at Nuremberg between November 1945 and September 1946?

The war in the Pacific

While the war in Europe had ended, the struggle in the Pacific between the Japanese and the Americans still raged. Soon after Pearl Harbour, the Japanese proceeded to attack the British and French empires in the Pacific. In June 1942, the Japanese and the American fleets confronted one another off the island of Midway. In the Battle of Midway, the Americans sank four Japanese carriers. The Japanese never really recovered from their defeat in this battle, which was a turning point in the war in the Pacific.

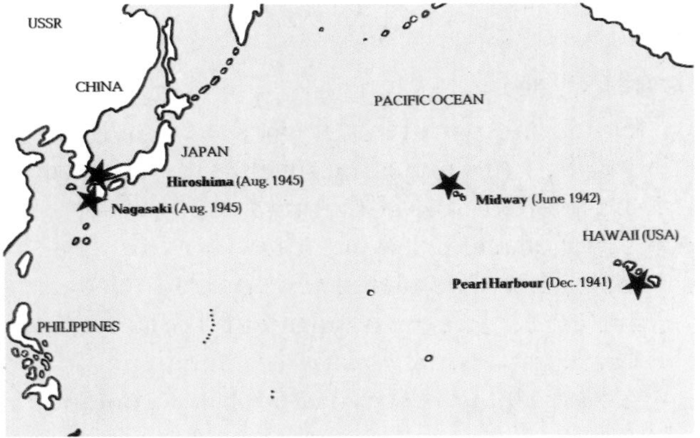

Warfare in the Pacific, 1941–45.

After this victory, the Americans began to retake the Pacific islands. By 1944, although the Japanese were effectively beaten, they refused to surrender. At this stage of the war, the casualties were huge as most Japanese soldiers chose to die rather than surrender.

The atomic bomb is dropped: World War II ends

Throughout the war, American and British scientists had been developing the atomic bomb. Harry S. Truman, who succeeded Roosevelt as president of the US in April 1945, decided to drop the atomic bomb on Japan.

On 6 August 1945 a single American plane, the *Enola Gay*, flew over the city of Hiroshima in southern Japan. It was carrying the most destructive bomb the world had ever seen. After the bomb was dropped, the city of Hiroshima was reduced to rubble.

Some 80,000 people were burned to death on the first day and thousands died in agony in the weeks and months ahead. A second atomic bomb was dropped on the Japanese city of Nagasaki, killing a further 60,000 people.

The destruction of Hiroshima.

The after-effects of both bombs were horrific, with thousands suffering and dying from radiation in the years ahead. Read the following accounts, written by victims of the atomic bombs.

Source A

'Someone shouted "A parachute is coming down". I responded by turning in the direction she pointed. Just at that moment, the sky I was facing flashed. I don't know how to describe that light. I wondered if a fire had been set in my eyes. The next moment I was knocked down flat on the ground. Immediately things started falling down around me. I couldn't see anything. Soon I noticed that the air smelled terrible. Then I was shocked by the feeling that the skin on my face had come off. Then the hands and arms from the elbows to the fingernails, all the skin of my right hand had come off and hung grotesquely.'

Source B

'I ran to the railway bridge. On the far side, crowds of maddened people were running like lemmings, trying to get across the river. In the middle of the bridge lay four or five bodies, unrecognisable as human beings, but still moving. Their skin hung from them like strands of seaweed! Instead of noses, holes. Their eyes and hands were so swollen as to be shapeless. There were still fifty or sixty clinging to red-hot rails. In their terror of dying, they clawed their way over one another, their eyes hanging from their sockets, pushing one another into the river and screaming all the time.'

The Japanese, stunned by these events, surrendered on 10 August 1945, bringing World War II to an end.

The Japanese surrender to the American General MacArthur on board the USS Missouri *in Tokyo Bay on 1 September 1945.*

American troops arriving in Tokyo in 1945.

Test your knowledge

1 In what sense was the Battle of Midway a turning point in the war in the Pacific?

2 Who made the decision to drop the atomic bomb on Japan?

3 Describe the effects of the atomic explosions in Hiroshima and Nagasaki.

4 When did the war in the Pacific end?

The legacy of World War II

World War II had been the most destructive war in history. At its end, around 40 million people lay dead. Millions of others were wounded or homeless, and cities and towns throughout Europe were almost totally destroyed. Unlike World War I, civilian populations had been direct targets.

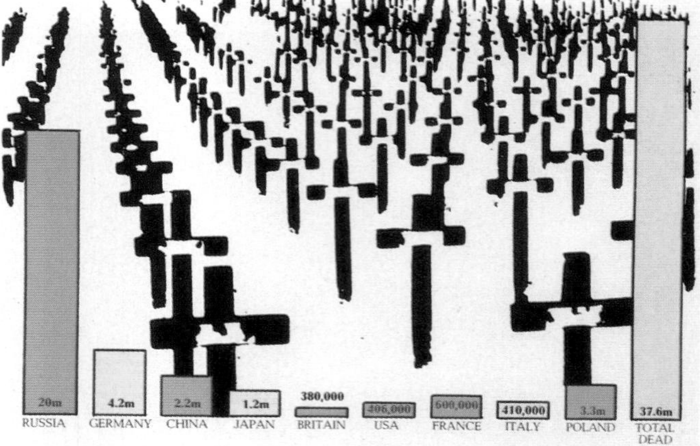

Even before the end of the war, Allied leaders were drawing up plans for rebuilding Europe. Stalin,

Churchill, Roosevelt and Stalin, the three wartime Allied leaders, at the Yalta Conference, February 1945.

Roosevelt and Churchill had met at Tehran (October 1943) and at Yalta (February 1945) to plan a future shape of Europe after its liberation from Nazi occupation. The Allies met again at Potsdam in July 1945 to decide on the joint rule of Germany. However, while the Allies had won the war, they were to find it much harder to agree on the type of Europe they now wanted.

Important dates and events of World War II

1 September
1939
Germany invades Poland

3 September
1939
Britain and France declare war on Germany

April-May
1940
Germany overruns Norway, Denmark and the Low Countries

June
1940
The Fall of France

September
1940
The Battle of Britain

June
1941
The German invasion of Russia

December
1941
Pearl Harbour — America enters the war

June
1942
Japanese defeat at the Battle of Midway

October
1942
The Battle of El Alamein — German defeat in North Africa

January
1943
Russian victory at the Battle of Stalingrad

July
1943
Allied invasion of Italy

June
1944
D-Day: Allied landings in France

May
1945
The war ends in Europe

August
1945
Atomic bombs dropped on Japan. End of World War II

Chapter 59: Review

• On 6 June 1944 (D-Day) the Allies (Britain and America) launched an attack on the coast of Normandy in France (Operation Overlord). On 18 August, Paris was liberated from German control and the French leader, General de Gaulle, set up his headquarters there.

• By the end of 1944, both France and Belgium were cleared of German troops. However, in December Hitler launched a last unsuccessful attack in the Ardennes region of France and Belgium (The Battle of the Bulge).

• On 30 April 1945, with Russian soldiers closing in on Berlin, Hitler committed suicide in an underground bunker in the centre of the city. A week later, Germany surrendered unconditionally to the Allies, bringing the war in Europe to an end.

• The war in the Pacific continued, however, and only ended when the Americans dropped atomic bombs on the Japanese cities of Hiroshima and Nagasaki in August 1945. As a result, the Japanese surrendered unconditionally and World War II finally came to an end.

• When the Allies liberated Europe, they discovered the full horrors of the Nazi concentration camps. As part of Hitler's Final Solution some 6 million Jews had been killed, along with other enemies of the Nazi regime.

• In the countries occupied by Germany during the war, resistance movements of local people had grown up. Two of the most famous were the French Resistance and the Partisans of Marshal Tito in Yugoslavia.

The Cold War: 1945–53

The age of the Superpowers

At the end of World War II, much of Europe lay in ruins, with millions dead, cities destroyed and economies shattered. Only the United States of America and the USSR emerged as great powers after 1945.

The devastated condition of the German city of Berlin in 1945. Conditions such as this were to be found throughout Europe as a result of bomb damage during World War II.

Of all the countries involved in World War II, the United States had suffered least. The American mainland had never been invaded or bombed. At the same time, American agriculture and industry enjoyed a boom period while providing food and equipment for the war effort. In 1945, the American economy was by far the strongest in the world.

The USSR, or Soviet Union, on the other hand, had suffered huge casualties and massive destruction during the war. In 1945, however, the Soviet Union emerged with the largest army in the world which, in a short time, would control most of Eastern Europe.

With Europe weakened by the ravages of war, the United States and the Soviet Union dominated world affairs from 1945 onwards. Because of their size, power and influence, these two countries became known as the *Superpowers*. After the final defeat of Hitler's Germany, their friendship soon turned into bitter mistrust and rivalry. Before this happened, however, they worked together to set up a new world peace-keeping organisation - the *United Nations*.

The United Nations

The UN Security Council in session in New York.

Many lessons were to be learned from World War II. The Allied leaders realised that co-operation between the nations of the world was essential to ensure peace in the future. As the League of Nations had failed to prevent the outbreak of war, Roosevelt, Stalin and Churchill set about planning a new and stronger organisation which became known as the United Nations.

In April 1945, fifty countries signed the United Nations Charter in San Francisco. This international organisation aimed to preserve world peace through co-operation and joint action. New York was to be the headquarters of the United Nations. The organisation had three main parts:

The General Assembly: Each member country has a representative in this group which discusses world problems and the business of the UN.
The Security Council: This group is always in session to deal with any world crisis. It has eleven members, five of which are permanent (US, USSR, Britain, France and China).
The Secretariat: This is the civil service of the UN which is responsible for the day-to-day running of the organisation.

The most powerful figure in the UN is the Secretary General who is elected by the General Assembly. Since its foundation there have been six Secretaries—General Trygve Lie (Norway); Dag Hammarskjold (Sweden); U Thant (Burma); Kurt

Waldheim (Austria); Javier Perez de Cuellar (Peru) and Boutros Boutros Ghali (Egypt).

Irish soldiers on United Nations peacekeeping duties in Lebanon.

Unlike the League of Nations, the UN has its own peacekeeping force drawn from the armies of member nations. This force has served in various trouble spots around the world, including Cyprus, the Congo and Lebanon. The Irish army has played an important part in these peacekeeping operations.

In addition to preserving the peace, the UN has become actively involved in attempts to improve social and economic conditions throughout the world. For this purpose it set up the following bodies:

The World Health Organisation (WHO): This organisation concerns itself with fighting disease and improving standards of health throughout the world.

United Nations International Children's Emergency Fund (UNICEF): It cares for children in the underdeveloped countries and assists children who are victims of war or natural disasters.

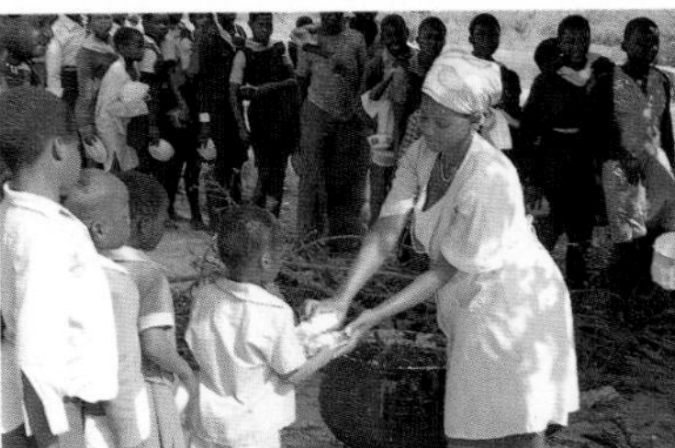

The work of FAO and UNICEF: (top) Nigerian farmers receiving tools. (bottom) South African children queue for food.

United Nations Educational, Scientific and Cultural Organisation (UNESCO): It aims to spread knowledge and understanding among people of different races, religions and cultures.

Food and Agriculture Organisation (FAO): This organisation attempts to improve would agriculture and food supplies.

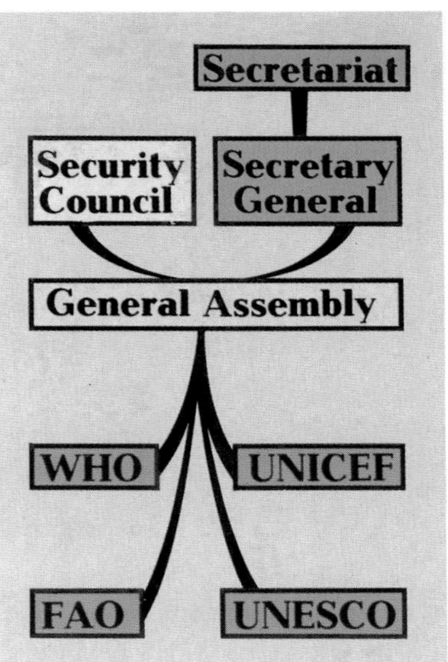

The organisation of the United Nations.

Despite the good work carried out by the United Nations since 1945, it was weakened from the start by the disagreements between the two Superpowers. These disagreements, which never led to an actual outbreak of fighting, became known as the *Cold War*.

Test your knowledge

1 Describe the condition of European countries at the end of World War II.

2 Why did the United States emerge in a strong position after 1945?

3 How was the Soviet Union affected by World War II?

4 When was the United Nations organisation set up? What was its main aim?

5 Explain the role of the Security Council in the United Nations.

6 Who is the most important person in the UN?

7 Name two countries in which UN peacekeeping forces have served.

The Cold War begins

It was not surprising that the United States and the Soviet Union should quarrel once their common enemy had been defeated in 1945. As you can see from the chart, they had very different beliefs concerning how countries should be run.

USA	USSR
• A private enterprise Capitalist economy • Freedom of speech • Free multi-party elections • Free trade and Capitalism should spread throughout the world	• A state-controlled Communist economy • Strict government control over books, newspapers, radio • Only one party, the Communist Party, allowed to stand for election • Worldwide spread of Communism

Because the Cold War was a disagreement over basic beliefs or ideologies, it was known as an *ideological conflict*. This ideological conflict between the Capitalist USA and the Communist USSR added a strong extra element of bitterness to the ordinary rivalry which already existed between the great powers. It also helps to explain the bitter propaganda war carried out by both sides during the Cold War.

Eastern Europe during the Cold War.

Stalin was determined to establish Russian control in the countries of Eastern Europe which the Red Army had liberated from Nazi control. Twice in the twentieth century, Russia had been invaded. As a result, Stalin declared that friendly governments in Eastern Europe were vital for Russian security. By 'friendly', the Russian leader meant Communist governments under his control.

American and British leaders saw matters differently. They believed that there should have been free elections in Eastern Europe to let the people decide on their own form of government. After all, the British claimed, had they not gone to war in 1939 to support Poland, one of the countries now under Russian control?

Truman: a new president

Atlee, the new British Prime Minister, Truman and Stalin at the Potsdam Conference in July 1945.

President Franklin D. Roosevelt of the USA died suddenly in April 1945. He was succeeded by his vice-president, the strongly anti-Communist Harry S. Truman. At the Potsdam Conference in Germany in July 1945, Truman was determined not to make any concessions to the Soviet Union. Many people believed that his decision to drop the atomic bomb on two Japanese cities in August 1945 had another motive besides saving the lives of American soldiers who would have had to invade Japan. Truman's 'hidden motive' may have been that American possession of the atomic bomb would act as a warning to the Russians and remind them of how powerful the US was.

From then on, relations between the Superpowers went from bad to worse. By the start of 1946, the Cold War had well and truly begun.

Working with Evidence

Read the following extracts and answer the questions which follow.

(a) Winston Churchill's 'Iron Curtain' Speech
In March 1946, Churchill spoke of the growing divisions in Europe in a speech at Fulton, Missouri in the USA. In it he coined the famous phrase 'the Iron Curtain'.

> 'From Stettin in the Baltic to Trieste in the Adriatic, an Iron Curtain has descended across the Continent. Behind that line lie all the capitals of the ancient states of central and eastern Europe. Warsaw, Berlin, Prague, Vienna, Budapest, Belgrade, Bucharest and Sofia, all these cities and the populations around them lie in the Soviet sphere, and are all subject, in one form or another, to a very high and increasing measure of control from Moscow. In other countries Communist parties or fifth columns constitute a growing challenge and peril to Christian civilisation.'

(b) Stalin's reply to Churchill

> 'Mr Churchill now takes the stand of the war-mongers, and he is not alone. He has friends not only in Britain, but in the US as well.
> The following circumstances should not be forgotten. The Germans made their invasion of the USSR through Finland, Poland, Rumania, Bulgaria and Hungary. Governments hostile to the Soviet Union existed in those countries. As a result of the German invasion, the Soviet Union's loss of life has been several times greater than that of Britain and the United States put together. How can anyone who has not taken leave of his senses, describe the peaceful aspirations of the Soviet Union in Eastern Europe as expansionist tendencies on the part of our State?'

1 What do you think Churchill had in mind when he used the expression 'Iron Curtain'?
2 Would you agree that he was in favour of the unity of European peoples? Prove your answer.
3 What form of control, according to Churchill, was 'high' and 'increasing' in Eastern Europe?
4 Show how Churchill sums up the ideological conflict taking place in the world in the final sentence.
5 What serious accusation did Stalin make against Churchill in his reply?
6 Like Churchill, Stalin too lists various areas in Eastern Europe. However, the Soviet leader did it for a different reason. What was his reason?
7 What contrast did Stalin make between the suffering of Russians and their Western Allies during World War II?
8 Can you explain how Stalin saw his conduct in Eastern Europe as 'peaceful', while Western leaders regarded it as 'expansionist'?

The Truman Doctrine and the Marshall Plan

In 1947, President Truman of the US took two important steps which made it clear that he was determined to prevent the further spread of Communism in the world. In March, he proclaimed the *Truman Doctrine*. In June, his Secretary of State, George Marshall, announced the *Marshall Plan*.

General George Marshall, the US Secretary of State, who announced the Marshall Plan.

The Truman Doctrine involved a foreign policy known as *containment*. By this, Truman meant that he would give help to any country trying to stop or 'contain' the spread of Communism, either in the form of attack from outside or revolution within. Truman said:

> 'I believe that it must be the policy of the US to support free peoples who are resisting attempted subjugation by armed minorities or by outside pressures.'

At the time, the US was sending support to the governments of Greece and Turkey which were fighting against Communist rebels. However, Truman did not believe that military help was enough. He realised that people often supported Communists because they promised relief from poverty and hardship. On this subject, Truman commented:

> 'I believe that our help should be primarily through economic and financial aid which is essential to economic stability and orderly political processes. The seeds of totalitarian regimes are nurtured by misery and want. They spread and grow in the evil soil of poverty and

strife. They reach their full growth when the hope of a people for a better life has died. We must keep that hope alive.'

As Truman had hinted in his speech, the US government was planning to give economic aid to other countries. Europe in particular was singled out for assistance. If the countries of Western Europe could rebuild their shattered economies, they would not only be in a stronger position to resist Russian expansion; they would also provide markets for American exports. The American offer of economic aid was contained in the Marshall Plan of June 1947. European countries, including those behind 'the Iron Curtain', were offered *Marshall Aid*. After Stalin had forced the governments in Eastern Europe to reject the offer, only those in the West benefited from it.

Within a year of the announcement of the Marshall Plan, one of the most serious crises of the Cold War developed in the very nerve-centre of East-West tension, the city of Berlin.

Test your knowledge

1 Explain what is meant by an 'ideological conflict'?
2 Who became president of the USA in 1945?
3 What is meant by 'containment'?
4 State one weakness in the Truman Doctrine.
5 What was the Marshall Plan?
6 How did Stalin react to it?

The Berlin Blockade and Airlift

At the Yalta Conference in 1945, the Allied powers had decided to divide Germany into four occupation zones after the war. The USA, Britain and France were to occupy zones in the west while the Russians would control the eastern part of Germany. This division was supposed to be a temporary measure, leading eventually to the reunification of Germany. Stalin, however, had other plans. He wanted Germany to remain permanently weak and divided.

In June 1948, a serious crisis developed between the Superpowers over the city of Berlin. Although inside the Russian zone, Berlin itself was divided into four zones, including an eastern section under Russian Communist rule and three western zones under the USA, Britain and France. When the Western powers introduced currency reforms into West Berlin, Stalin tried to force them out of the city. On 23 June 1948, he cut off all road and rail links between West Berlin and the western zones of Germany. Electricity which came from the Russian sector of Berlin was also cut off.

Children from West Berlin look on as an American airplane arrives with essential supplies during the blockade.

The American, British and French governments responded by deciding to supply West Berlin with food, fuel and other essentials from the air. The *Berlin Airlift* was a huge achievement in terms of organisation. Over 2 million people were kept alive in West Berlin until the Russians admitted defeat and re-opened the transport routes in May 1949.

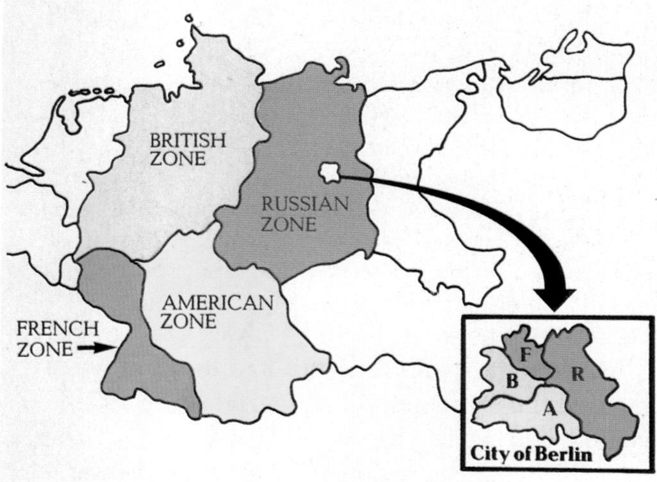

The Allied division of Germany and of the city of Berlin into four occupation zones after World War II.

Although the Superpowers had avoided the outbreak of a third world war over Berlin, the incident led to increased tension between East and West. It also deepened the division of Germany into a Capitalist West and a Communist East. The Berlin Crisis had also shown the Western countries that Russian expansion was a constant threat.

The North Atlantic Treaty Organisation (NATO)

In April 1949, the USA, Canada, and ten Western European countries signed a defence pact known as the *North Atlantic Treaty Organisation* (NATO). An attack on any member of the alliance would be regarded as an attack upon them all. The USA and Britain had nuclear weapons. In the year that NATO was established, the Soviet Union also produced its own atom bomb. As a result, tension between East and West reached an even higher level. The Cold War was now at its height. Each side confronted the other with the threat of nuclear weapons and a constant barrage of propaganda. Huge stockpiles of weapons were built up and large numbers of spies were active on both sides of the Iron Curtain.

Test your knowledge

1. What decision concerning the future of Germany was taken at the Yalta Conference in 1945?
2. What plans had Stalin for Germany?
3. Why did the Russians blockade West Berlin in June 1948?
4. Describe the response of the Western powers.
5. When was NATO founded? Which non-European powers were members?
6. Would you agree that the Cold War was at its height in 1949? Explain your answer.

The Korean War

In June 1950, war broke out in the Far Eastern country of Korea when the Communist North attacked its non-Communist neighbour to the South. This was a further incident in the Cold War because the Soviet Union supported and armed the North Koreans while the Americans assisted South Korea.

UN forces at the front line during the Korean War, in February 1951.

After the entire country had been freed from Japanese control at the end of World War II, the Russians had occupied the North, where they set up a Communist government under Kim Il Sung. In the South, the Americans allowed free elections which resulted in a non-Communist government led by Syngman Rhee. As in Germany, it was originally hoped to unite both zones, but the Cold War divisions between the USA and the Soviet Union prevented this.

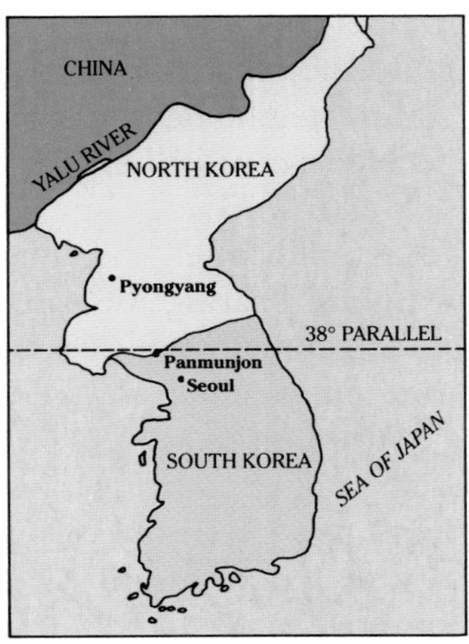

The Korean War, 1950–53.

It is unclear whether the Russians forced the North Koreans to attack the South in June 1950. It could well have been an effort by Stalin to compensate for his failure with the Berlin Blockade. However, it may have been the new Communist Chinese government of Mao Tse Tung, in power since 1949, which encouraged the North Koreans to start the war.

Mao-Tse-Tung, Communist leader of China for over twenty-five years.

President Truman immediately went to the United Nations to get support for South Korea. As the Russians were boycotting the UN, they were not present to veto action against North Korea. It was decided to send United Nations forces to defend South Korea, although in practice most of the troops who went to Korea were Americans in UN uniforms. The American general, Douglas MacArthur, was placed in command.

Having expelled the North Koreans from the South, MacArthur's forces invaded North Korea. At this stage, the Chinese leader, Mao Tse Tung, ordered 300,000 soldiers to cross the Yalu River and go to the assistance of the North Koreans. The war which began between the two Koreas had now become a conflict between the USA and China.

General MacArthur wished to attack bases in China and urged President Truman to use atomic weapons. Fearing Russian involvement and the possible outbreak of nuclear war, Truman sought to end the conflict and dismissed MacArthur in April 1951.

Although peace talks began in July 1951, they were to drag on for two years. Eventually, on 27 July 1953, peace terms were signed at the North Korean city of Panmunjom. As a result, the two Koreas returned to the pre-1950 position after a war which had cost many lives.

For the USA, the settlement was a satisfactory solution to the Korean War. Containment as outlined in the Truman Doctrine had been put into action. Although relations with China were now at a low ebb, American relations with the USSR were about to improve slightly as two new leaders came to power in both Washington and Moscow.

Test your knowledge

1 Explain how war broke out in Korea in June 1950.
2 Why was this an incident in the Cold War?
3 How did the situation in Korea resemble what had happened in Germany?
4 Name the Communist leader of China.
5 Explain the role of the United Nations in the Korean War.
6 Why did the Chinese become involved in the war?
7 Explain the outcome of the Korean War.

Chapter 60: Review

• At the end of World War II, much of Europe lay in ruins, and the USA and the USSR emerged as the two Superpowers.

• In April 1945, the United Nations was set up in order to preserve world peace through international co-operation. The three main parts of the UN are the General Assembly, the Security Council and the Secretariat.

• The most powerful figure in the UN is the Secretary General. The UN has set up agencies such as UNICEF to improve social and economic conditions around the world.

• While the two Superpowers had been allies in the war against Hitler, there were fundamental differences between them. The USA was Capitalist with a two-party democratic system of government, while the USSR was a one-party Communist state.

• By 1946, deep divisions had emerged between the USSR under Stalin and the USA under Truman. While there was great rivalry between them it stopped short of open warfare. This state of affairs was known as the Cold War.

• In 1947, President Truman announced the Truman Doctrine. This involved a foreign policy known as containment. By this Truman meant that he would give help to any country trying to stop or 'contain' the spread of Communism.

• In June 1948, a crisis occurred over the city of Berlin which, along with Germany, had been divided into four occupation zones at the end of the war. The Russians tried to force the Western Allies out of the city by means of a blockade. This plan failed, however, when the Americans organised the Berlin Airlift to supply essential goods to West Berlin.

• In 1949, Western European countries joined the USA and Canada to form a military alliance known as NATO.

• The Korean War started in June 1950, between Communist North Korea and pro-American South Korea. Involving both the USA and China, it ended with a truce in July 1953.

Peaceful Co-existence

From Stalin to Khrushchev

During 1953, both Superpowers experienced changes of leadership. In January, Dwight D. Eisenhower, the former general who had led the Allied forces in World War II, succeeded Harry Truman as president of the United States. One of his main objectives was to bring about a quick end to the Korean War.

Nikita Khrushchev, who had emerged as leader of the Soviet Union by 1956.

On 5 March, Joseph Stalin died in Moscow. For twenty-five years he had ruled the Soviet Union with his iron will. Since 1945 he had controlled all of Eastern Europe as well. It remained to be seen if his successors could maintain the same level of control.

For a few years there was a collective government in Moscow as a number of influential Communist party leaders shared power. By 1955, Nikita Khrushchev had emerged as the clear leader. Under his leadership, the first thaw in the Cold War began to take place.

A thaw in the Cold War

The first signs of the Russian desire to improve relations with the West were seen at the Korean Peace Settlement of July 1953 when the Soviet leaders encouraged the Chinese to agree to a settlement.

In 1955, the USSR and the Western powers, the USA, Great Britain and France, agreed to end the occupation of Austria and to establish the country as an independent, neutral state.

Events at the United Nations in 1955 also showed a thaw in the Cold War. In that year, both Superpowers lifted their objections to a number of other countries joining the UN. Up to then, the US had prevented friends of the Soviet Union from joining, while the Russians had prevented the membership of pro-American countries. The Republic of Ireland, seen by the Russians as friendly to the USA, was allowed to join the United Nations under this new arrangement.

The Warsaw Pact (1955)

Despite this slight thaw in the Cold War, the Soviet leaders did not neglect the primary aim of Russian security. As a response to NATO, they set up a Communist defence pact in Eastern Europe in 1955. Because the agreement was signed at Warsaw, the Polish capital, it was known as the *Warsaw Pact*. Its members agreed to place their armed forces under the command of a Russian general.

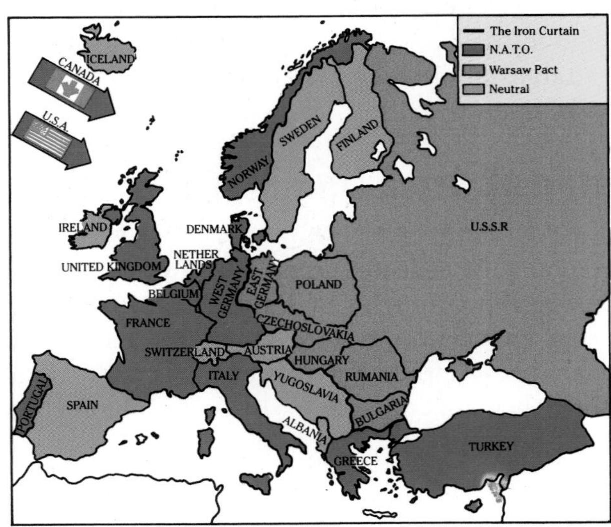

Europe in 1955, divided between NATO and Warsaw Pact countries.

From then on, two rival alliances, NATO and the Warsaw Pact, faced each other across the 'Iron Curtain' which ran down the middle of Europe.

Test your knowledge

1 Who became president of the USA in 1953?
2 When did the Soviet leader, Joseph Stalin, die?
3 How was the Soviet Union ruled after Stalin's death?
4 Explain the Austrian settlement of 1955.
5 How did the thaw in the Cold War influence affairs at the United Nations?
6 What was the Warsaw Pact? When was it founded?

Peaceful co-existence

Nikita Khrushchev and the other Soviet leaders who succeeded Stalin relaxed the control of the secret police in the Soviet Union. In a surprising speech to the Congress of the Communist Party in February 1956, Khrushchev condemned Stalin as a tyrant and a dictator.

Khrushchev also began to change the way Soviet leaders spoke about the outside world. Lenin and Stalin had declared that Communism would eventually overthrow Capitalism throughout the world. While Khrushchev also believed this, he saw it as something which would happen in the distant future. In the meantime, the Soviet Union and her Communist allies should have friendly relations with Capitalist countries. This policy was known as *peaceful co-existence*.

Unrest in Eastern Europe

The policy of peaceful co-existence was put under strain in the countries of Eastern Europe. These Warsaw Pact countries were often known as Russian *satellites* because they were under the overall control of the Soviet government in Moscow. Only the presence of the Red Army kept the unpopular Communist governments in power in these countries. If their peoples had been allowed to hold free elections, they would have turned the Communists out of government.

Harsh economic policies made many of these governments unpopular. Another cause of complaint was the persecution of people because of their religious beliefs. Practising Christians found it hard to get jobs. Even in largely Catholic countries like Poland and Hungary, bishops and priests were imprisoned, churches were closed and religious education was banned in the schools.

A few months after Stalin's death, people in East Germany rebelled against the Communist government in June 1953. The rising was crushed by the Red Army. Over 400 people died when unarmed workers found themselves helpless against tanks and machine guns.

In 1956, a rising also took place in Poland. As a result the government allowed greater freedom. However, the country still remained under a Communist government and continued to be part of the Warsaw Pact.

The most serious of all the anti-Soviet rebellions in Eastern Europe, however, took place in Hungary in 1956.

Test your knowledge

1 What was surprising about Khrushchev's speech to the Communist Party Congress in 1956?
2 Explain the meaning of 'peaceful co-existence'.
3 Give one reason why this policy was followed.
4 What were the 'Russian satellite countries'?
5 State two reasons why Communist governments in Eastern Europe were unpopular.
6 What occurred in East Germany in June 1953?
7 What was the result of the rising in Poland in 1956?

A Rising in Hungary (1956)

Events in Poland influenced people in Hungary who longed to achieve complete freedom from the Soviet Union. In October 1956, a huge uprising against the Russians took place in the Hungarian capital, Budapest.

By the time the Hungarian Rising had been crushed on 7 November, 25,000 Hungarians and

3,500 Russians lay dead in Budapest. The Hungarian leader, Imre Nagy, who wished to break away from Russian control, was executed and replaced by a pro-Russian Communist.

Although the Hungarians had appealed to the United States and other Western countries for help during the rising, they only received words of support. Any action by the West in their favour could have led to nuclear war.

Hungarians celebrate the capture of a Soviet tank during the uprising of 1956.

Soviet tanks on the streets of Budapest in 1956.

Despite the improvements in relations between the Superpowers after Stalin's death, events in Hungary in 1956 proved that a vast gulf still existed between Communist-controlled states on the one hand and those in favour of free speech and free elections on the other.

The Berlin Wall

President John F. Kennedy meeting Khrushchev in Vienna in June 1961.

In January 1961, John F. Kennedy replaced Eisenhower as president of the USA. When he and Khrushchev met for the first time in Vienna the following June, the sixty-seven-year-old Soviet leader was not impressed by the younger American president. Kennedy was forty-four at the time. Khrushchev mistakenly thought that Kennedy would turn out to be weak. Khrushchev was in difficulty at home because of the poor performance of the Russian economy. So he decided to attempt an aggressive policy towards the West. The first example of this was seen in Berlin.

The divided city had been free of major incidents since the East German uprising of 1953. In 1958, Khrushchev had tried and failed to get the Western powers to leave West Berlin. By 1961, vast numbers of East German citizens were moving to the more prosperous West Germany by travelling first to West Berlin. Indeed since 1945, the German Democratic Republic (East Germany) had lost over 3½ million citizens who had fled to the West.

The visit of President Kennedy of the USA to West Berlin and the Berlin Wall in June 1963.

On the morning of 13 August 1961, Berliners awoke to find a wall of barbed wire dividing Communist East Berlin from the rest of the city. Families were divided, homes bricked up, watch towers were built and border guards were told to shoot to kill.

The East German leader, Walter Ulbricht, declared that he was protecting his country from economic ruin by the Capitalist West. In non-Communist countries, however, people were horrified at the construction of the *Berlin Wall.* For them, it was a proof that Communism had failed if Communist governments had to imprison their peoples in this manner.

People made heroic attempts to escape across the Berlin Wall and many died in the attempt. In June 1963, President Kennedy visited West Berlin to express his solidarity with the people there.

As with the Berlin Blockade before it, the Berlin Wall added to the tension between the Superpowers and prolonged the bitterness of the Cold War.

The Cuban Missile Crisis (1962)

Despite Khruschev's belief in peaceful co-existence, both Superpowers continued to build up their supplies of weapons, especially nuclear missiles. Still believing that he could gain an advantage over President Kennedy, the Soviet leader decided to intervene in the island of Cuba in the Caribbean.

Fidel Castro, the Communist leader of Cuba.

In 1959, a successful Communist revolution had taken place in Cuba under the leadership of Fidel Castro. As Cuba is only about 150 kilometres from the coast of Florida in the USA, American leaders were greatly concerned. The USA immediately banned all trade with Cuba. At the same time, the USSR came to the assistance of Castro. The Russians agreed to buy Cuba's entire sugar crop and to send economic aid to the island.

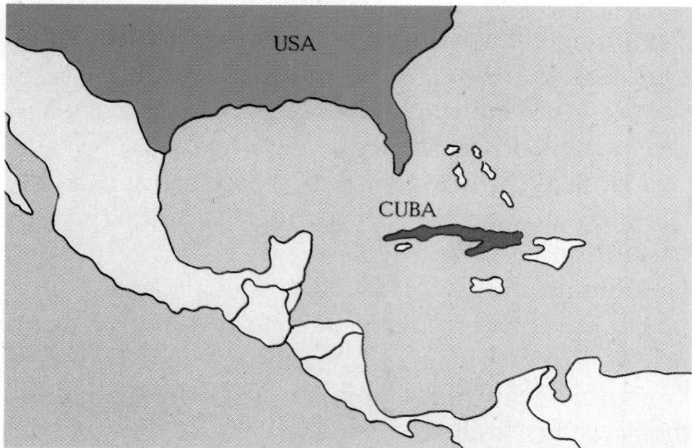

Communist Cuba under Fidel Castro had close relations with the USSR.

Khrushchev went a step further, however. In 1962, he began to place secret missile sites in Cuba. When Kennedy demanded their removal, the crisis which followed became known as the *Cuban Missile Crisis*. It was one of the most serious developments of the Cold War and brought the world to the brink of a disastrous nuclear conflict between the Superpowers.

An American photograph of a Soviet missile base on the island of Cuba.

From aerial photographs, the Americans were able to observe the construction of the missile sites in Cuba. On 13 September 1962, Kennedy issued a strong warning:

> 'If at any time the Communist build-up in Cuba were to endanger or interfere with our military security in any way, or if Cuba should ever become an offensive military base for the Soviet Union, then this country will do whatever must be done to protect its own security and that of its allies.'

However, when Kennedy spoke to the Soviet foreign minister, Andrei Gromyko, he was assured that Khrushchev had no intention of sending nuclear missiles to Cuba. Kennedy now had three choices: give in to the Soviet Union; attack the missile sites in Cuba; or blockade the island and prevent Soviet ships from arriving there with weapons. He decided on a blockade, as an attack could start a nuclear war. Kennedy could not give in because, if the missiles were set up in Cuba, many American cities would be within their range.

When Russian ships were only half an hour's journey from the American fleet near Cuba, they suddenly stopped and turned back. Khrushchev had decided that his gamble could not succeed. To save face, he had promised that he would withdraw the missiles if the USA agreed not to invade Cuba. Kennedy accepted these terms and the world was relieved that nuclear war had been avoided.

The Cuban Missile Crisis was an important turning point in the Cold War. Although the

Superpowers continued to be keen rivals, never again did they come so close to all-out nuclear war. Indeed, a special telephone known as the *Hotline* was established between the US president's headquarters, the White House, and the headquarters of the Soviet leader, the Kremlin in Moscow. This was set up in order to make communication easier during a crisis. The Superpowers also began efforts to reduce the level of armaments in the wake of the Cuban Missile Crisis.

Test your knowledge

1 Who became president of the US in 1961?
2 Why did Khrushchev decide on an aggressive policy against the West?
3 How many citizens fled from the German Democratic Republic (East Germany) between 1945 and 1961?
4 When was the Berlin Wall built and why?
5 Name the Communist leader who came to power in Cuba in 1959.
6 How did the Cuban Missile Crisis start?
7 Why did President Kennedy take action?
8 What did the two leaders agree to do in order to end the crisis?

The Space Race

Yuri Gagarin—the first man in space.

During the 1960s, space exploration was another area in which keen rivalry existed between the Superpowers. Despite the harsh economic conditions which the people were experiencing, the Soviet leaders spent vast amounts of money on their space research programme. In 1957, this led to a sensational breakthrough when a Soviet rocket launched an artificial satellite, the *Sputnik*, into orbit around the earth.

Four years later, the Russians recorded another first in space exploration. In 1961, the Russian cosmonaut, Major Yuri Gagarin, became the first man to go into orbit around the earth.

Edwin ('Buzz') Aldrin walking on the moon in July 1969.

The Americans were shocked by these early Soviet successes in space exploration. Up until then, they had believed that they were the world leaders in this area. The US government now stepped up its programme of space exploration. As rockets could also be used to launch weapons, space exploration became closely linked with the arms race.

Throughout the 1960s, both Russians and Americans conducted a *Space Race* to place the first man on the moon. In 1969, the Americans won the race when Neil Armstrong and Edwin ('Buzz') Aldrin from the spaceship *Apollo 11* became the first men to land on the moon.

From then on, American astronauts and Soviet cosmonauts have carried out longer and longer journeys of space exploration. At the same time, unmanned satellites have been sent vast distances from which they continue to transmit information back to earth.

The space race, which began as a contest between the Superpowers, has greatly increased people's knowledge of the vast universe of which the earth is just a small part.

The Brezhnev era

Although Khrushchev had led the USSR during the great early achievements in space exploration, his popularity as a leader suffered because of troubles in the Russian economy. Although most Russians were proud of their space exploration programme, they wondered why a government which could carry this out could not end food shortages and improve overall living conditions. In October 1964, Khrushchev was removed from the leadership by a majority of his colleagues. Unlike previous situations in the USSR, he was not executed or placed in prison but was allowed to retire quietly.

Khrushchev was replaced as leader by Leonid Brezhnev. Under Brezhnev and his colleagues, Khrushchev's policy of allowing criticism of Stalin was outlawed. Writers and others who criticised the government were placed in prisons or mental hospitals. This, in turn, worsened relations with the US and the rest of the world.

Leonid Brezhnev became leader of the Soviet Union in 1964.

The Brezhnev Doctrine

Alexander Dubcek, the reforming leader of Czechoslovakia.

In 1968, Soviet troops intervened in Czechoslovakia to bring down the government of Alexander Dubcek, a reforming Communist leader. Although there was little bloodshed, unlike Hungary in 1956, the basic situation was the same. The Soviet Union would intervene to preserve hardline Communist regimes in the satellite states of Eastern Europe. Indeed, this claim to the right of intervention became known as the *Brezhnev Doctrine*.

Despite the harshness of the government in the USSR during the Brezhnev period, there was some signs of a desire for peaceful co-operation. These were mainly found in the area of arms reduction which we shall read about in the next chapter.

Soviet tanks rolling into Prague in August 1968.

Test your knowledge

1 What was the *Sputnik*? When was it launched?
2 Name the first Russian cosmonaut in space.
3 Who were the first men to land on the moon?
4 Why was Khrushchev removed from power in 1964?
5 How did Brezhnev's policies differ from Khrushchev's?
6 What took place in Czechoslovakia in 1968?
7 Explain the 'Brezhnev Doctrine'.

Chapter 61: Review

- In the 1950s Eisenhower replaced Truman as American president. Within a few years of Stalin's death in 1953, Nikita Khrushchev emerged as leader in the USSR. Khrushchev believed in a policy known as peaceful co-existence.

- The USSR continued to maintain strict control over Eastern Europe. A rising took place in Hungary in 1956 against Soviet control. However, it was ruthlessly put down by the USSR.

- In January 1961, John F. Kennedy replaced Eisenhower as president of the USA. Khrushchev decide to attempt an aggressive policy towards the West. The first example of this was seen in the erection of the Berlin Wall, cutting off contact between the East and the West.

- The Cuban Missile Crisis in 1962 was probably the most serious episode of the Cold War. A nuclear war was avoided when Kennedy forced Khrushchev into withdrawing Soviet missiles from the island of Cuba.

- During the 1960s, space exploration was another area of keen rivalry between the Superpowers.

- In 1964, Leonid Brezhnev became the new leader of the Soviet Union. Despite the harshness of his government in the USSR, there were some signs of a desire for peaceful co-operation with the West.

The Age of Détente

During the 1960s, the policy of peaceful co-existence between the Superpowers was taken a step further. They began to move towards more friendly relations. This movement was known as *détente*, which means an easing of the strained relations which had existed up to then. The area in which détente was most in evidence was the attempt to limit the spread of nuclear weapons.

Arms limitation

In 1963, the first step was taken along the road to arms reduction between the Superpowers. In October of that year, a *Test Ban Treaty* was signed in Moscow between the USA and the USSR. This outlawed nuclear testing in the air, in space and underwater. Many other countries added their names to the treaty.

One serious problem facing the Superpowers was the possibility that smaller states would develop nuclear weapons. To prevent this they signed a *Non-Proliferation Treaty* in 1968. Under this agreement, existing nuclear powers agreed not to help non-nuclear states to develop nuclear weapons.

In 1972, the *Strategic Arms Limitation Talks* (SALT) began between the Superpowers. The agreement, known as SALT 1, limited the number of nuclear missiles held by the USA and the USSR.

President Richard Nixon of the US and the Soviet leader, Leonid Brezhnev, sign a SALT Agreement in Moscow in 1972.

In 1979, SALT 2 placed further limits on the number of these missiles.

During the 1980s, arms limitation talks between Washington and Moscow proceeded further. However, the Soviet leaders insisted on a halt to an American reseaıch project known as *Star Wars*. Star Wars involved the development of weapons which could shoot down enemy missiles in space. It was a favourite project of Ronald Reagan, president of the United States from 1981 to 1988.

Despite disagreement concerning Star Wars, the Superpowers continued with negotiations on arms reductions. Along with other benefits, it would help their economies if they could spend less on weapons.

Human Rights and the Helsinki Conference (1975)

Throughout the 1970s and 1980s, people in Western Europe and America expressed grave concern over the treatment of people who criticised the governments in Communist countries. These critics were known as *dissidents* because they expressed dissent or disagreement with the policies of their Communist rulers. In the USSR and other Communist countries, they were frequently placed in prisons or mental hospitals. Prominent Russian dissidents included the famous novelist, Alexander Solzhenitsyn, and the brilliant scientist, Andrei Sahkarov. Solzhenitsyn was

Alexander Solzhenitsyn, the Soviet author and dissident. His first great novel, A day in the life of Ivan Denisovich, *exposed the conditions in a Siberian labour camp.*

persecuted because he exposed the conditions in Soviet labour camps and Sahkarov because he criticised the nuclear weapons programme.

Dr Andrei Sakharov, the Soviet scientist and dissident and winner of the Nobel Peace prize.

Many people in the West argued that any future military or economic co-operation with Communist countries should include commitments from them that the human rights of all citizens in these states would be respected. In 1975, a conference took place at Helsinki in Finland in which these human rights issues were discussed. It resulted in the *Helsinki Declaration on Human Rights*, which was signed by all the states which took part. In Europe, every state except Albania signed the agreement.

Despite the Helsinki Agreement, there were repeated cases of the denial of human rights in the Soviet Union and Eastern Europe. Human rights in the USSR and in Eastern Europe, however, improved greatly when a new Soviet leader came to power in 1985. His name was Mikhail Gorbachev.

Test your knowledge

1 Explain what is meant by détente.
2 What was agreed under the Test Ban Treaty (1963)?
3 Why did the Superpowers sign the Non-Proliferation Treaty in 1968?
4 What do the initials SALT stand for?
5 Who were the dissidents?
6 Name two famous Russian dissidents.
7 What was agreed at Helsinki in 1975?

President Gorbachev in power

Glasnost and Perestroika

From the outset, President Gorbachev made it clear that he wanted to introduce reforms in the Soviet Union. In order to improve living conditions at home, he needed the assistance of the US and other Western states. He also genuinely wished to end the Cold War and to improve relations between East and West.

Mikhail Gorbachev.

Gorbachev's two main approaches to reforming the Soviet Union were *glasnost* and *perestroika*. *Glasnost* is a Russian word for 'openness'. Gorbachev believed that criticism of mistakes made by Soviet governments should be allowed. He believed that such openness, or *glasnost*, would lead to reforms and improvements in the Soviet economy and in society generally. As part of his policy of *glasnost*, Gorbachev extended the hand of friendship to many leading dissidents. He allowed freedom of speech in television, radio, books and newspapers. This restoration of human rights to Soviet citizens greatly pleased people in the west and led to improved relations with the Soviet Union.

By *perestroika*, Gorbachev meant a restructuring of the Soviet economy which would reduce the level of state control and allow a certain amount of private enterprise. He did this in order to improve living conditions for the Soviet people.

President Gorbachev with US President Ronald Reagan in New York in 1988. As part of the spirit of glasnost, *visits between American and Soviet leaders became more frequent.*

Gorbachev did not restrict his reforms to the Soviet Union alone. He allowed Russia's 'satellites' in Eastern Europe to press ahead with reforms themselves. In these countries this decision was to have startling results.

The collapse of Communism in Eastern Europe

With the death of Leonid Brezhnev came the end of the Brezhnev Doctrine. Instead, Mikhail Gorbachev decided that the Soviet army would not intervene to keep unpopular Communist regimes in power. As a result, these governments collapsed one after another and were replaced by democratically elected rulers.

A Solidarity march in Poland. The movement's leader, Lech Walesa, was elected President of Poland in 1990.

In Poland, there was a powerful trade union movement. Known as *Solidarity*, it was under the leadership of Lech Walesa. While the Communists held power in Poland, Solidarity members were harassed by the police. However, in 1989, Solidarity provided many of the members of Poland's first democratically elected government in over fifty years.

The fall of Communism in Eastern Europe.

Like Poland, the Communist regimes in Hungary and Czechoslovakia came under pressure from the ordinary people and were replaced by freely elected governments. In Czechoslovakia, the new president, Vaclav Havel, was a playwright and former dissident who had been imprisoned many times for his beliefs by the Communist rulers.

Bulgaria, Yugoslavia and Rumania also witnessed the collapse of Communist regimes. In Rumania, the revolution only came about with a great deal of bloodshed. In December 1989, the Communist dictator Nicolai Ceaucescu, a ruthless tyrant, was overthrown by a popular revolution. As the world looked on, people could see the events unfold on their television screens. Pictures of the fighting were broadcast and the new government even released scenes from the trial and execution of Ceaucescu and his wife.

Rumanian soldiers take to the streets in Bucharest to bring down the government of Nicolai Ceaucescu.

Nicolai Ceaucescu, the Communist dictator of Rumania who was executed in December 1989.

By far the most exciting changes, however, took place in East Germany. Berlin, the scene of many conflicts during the Cold War, was to be at the centre of its last act in the autumn of 1989.

Test your knowledge

1 Did President Gorbachev wish to introduce changes in the Soviet Union? Explain your answer.
2 Explain the meaning of: (a) *glasnost*; (b) *perestroika*.
3 How did the condition of dissidents in the USSR improve under Gorbachev?
4 What was Gorbachev's attitude to the 'satellite' states in Eastern Europe?
5 What is Solidarity? Who was its leader?
6 Who was Vaclav Havel?
7 Name the Rumanian dictator who was overthrown in December 1989.

Germany reunited

In the summer of 1989, the government of Hungary opened up its border with Austria. Thousands of East Germans travelled immediately to Hungary in order to reach West Germany through Austria. For nearly thirty years, the Berlin Wall had closed off the last exit in the Iron Curtain. Now, once again, East Germans availed of any opportunity to flee to the more prosperous Capitalist West Germany.

People from East Berlin receive a great welcome as they cross over to the West.

The East German Communist leader, Erich Honecker, called on the Hungarians to seal their borders, but his request was refused. Throughout the autumn of 1989, people began to protest publicly against the Communist government on the streets of East German towns such as Leipzig, Dresden and East Berlin. On 18 October, Honecker was replaced as leader by a reforming Communist, Egon Krenz. Events were now moving at a fast pace. On 9 November, Krenz's government agreed to open the Berlin Wall.

Jubilant crowds make their way over the Berlin Wall on the night of 9-10 November 1989.

It was now obvious that, given free elections, most East Germans would vote for unity with West Germany. On 18 March 1990, the first free elections since 1933 were held in East Germany. There was a clear majority in favour of unity with the West. On 1 July, the two German economies were united with a single currency in operation. Finally, on 3 October 1990, Germany became a united country once again under the government of the former West German chancellor, Helmut Kohl.

Before German unity could come about, the four former World War II Allied powers—the USA, the USSR, Britain and France—had to agree. Cold War divisions had kept Germany divided. The ending of this division was a sign that the Cold War was coming to an end. President Gorbachev of the USSR even agreed that the united Germany could become a member of NATO. Many people, however, wondered if NATO would last indefinitely if Cold War divisions were ended.

The Superpowers in Agreement

A US paratrooper in the Saudi-Arabian desert during the Gulf War.

By 1990, it was clear that the Superpowers were in agreement on many issues. Nowhere was this more evident than in the United Nations. We have seen already how both the United States and the Soviet Union had often used their power of veto in the UN Security Council during the Cold War. This prevented the United Nations from taking decisive action in various trouble spots throughout the world.

By the late 1980s, however, it became clear that the two Superpowers were willing to co-operate in the United Nations in the cause of world peace. They agreed on united action in areas such as South Africa and the Middle East. When the ruler of Iraq, Saddam Hussein, invaded neighbouring Kuwait in August 1990, the US and USSR agreed at the United Nations to send a peace-keeping force to the area. Such agreement was unthinkable even a few years previously.

With the Cold War drawing to a close, many people hoped that the two Superpowers were entering into a new age of co-operation. It was hoped that reduced spending on armies and weapons would pave the way for a more determined attack on the real enemies of the human race such as ignorance, poverty and starvation in the Third World and elsewhere.

Presidents of the USA and Soviet Leaders after 1945

Presidents of the USA

Harry Truman 1945–53
Dwight Eisenhower 1953–60
John Kennedy 1961–63
Lyndon Johnson 1963–69
Richard Nixon 1969–74
Gerald Ford 1974–77
Jimmy Carter 1977–81
Ronald Reagan 1981–89
George Bush 1989–93

Soviet Leaders

Joseph Stalin 1928–53
Nikita Khrushchev 1953–64
Leonid Brezhnev 1964–82
Yuri Andropov 1982–84
Konstantin Cernenko 1984–85
Mikhail Gorbachev 1985–91

Chapter 62: Review

• During the late 1960s the two Superpowers began to move towards friendly relations. This movement was known as détente. It was most evident in the attempt to limit the spread of nuclear weapons.

• The cause of arms limitation was advanced in the following agreements: Test Ban Treaty; Non-Proliferation Treaty; SALT 1; and SALT 2.

• There was also some advance in the area of human rights. Many people in the West were very concerned over the treatment of those who criticised the governments in Communist countries.

• In 1985, Mikhail Gorbachev became leader of the Soviet Union. He had two new approaches to reforming the Soviet Union: *glasnost* and *perestroika*. By *glasnost*, he meant a new openness. *Perestroika* meant a restructuring of the Soviet economy in order to reduce the amount of state control.

• A new wave of reforms also took place in the countries of Eastern Europe. In countries like Poland, Hungary and Czechoslovakia, Communist regimes came under pressure from the ordinary people and were replaced by freely elected governments.

• The most exciting changes took place in East Germany. On 9 November 1989, the new Eastern German leader, Egon Krenz, agreed to open the Berlin Wall. On 3 October 1990, Germany became a united country once again under the government of the former West German chancellor, Helmut Kohl.

Political Developments in Ireland in the Twentieth Century

A Divided Land

Ireland under the Union

If you were growing up in Ireland over a hundred years ago, you would have seen reminders everywhere of the connection with Great Britain. Each letter box was painted red and decorated with the letters V.R. *(Victoria Regina)*, in honour of Queen Victoria. The British flag, the Union Jack, flew from the top of important buildings and British soldiers in their red uniforms were a regular sight on the streets of towns and cities. In maps on the school-room wall, Ireland was coloured red, along with the rest of the British Empire.

The Houses of Parliament at Westminster in London where Irish lords and MPs attended the British parliament from 1801 onwards.

Queen Victoria on a visit to Dublin in 1900.

At this time, Ireland was part of a United Kingdom which also included England, Scotland and Wales. Since the abolition of the old Irish parliament in 1800, all Irish MPs attended the British parliament at Westminster in London. Ireland was ruled directly by the British government.

The Unionists

Around 1880, about a quarter of the people living in Ireland were quite happy to be ruled by the British government. Because they supported the full union between Great Britain and Ireland, they were known as *Unionists*. Although some better-off Catholics supported the Union, the vast majority of Unionists were Protestants, mainly members of the Church of Ireland or the Presbyterian Church. Most of them lived in Ulster where around a million Protestants, from the poorest workers to rich lords and businessmen, supported the Union. In the rest of Ireland, Unionists were usually landlords or businessmen who formed a small minority of the local population.

Shipyard workers in Belfast around 1900. The majority of people living in Belfast were Protestants and Unionists.

Because of their deep loyalty to the queen of England and the belief that British governments protected them, the Unionists' great fear was that the Catholic majority in Ireland would one day succeed in setting up some form of government which was independent of Great Britain.

Irish Nationalists

While the Unionist minority in Ireland was content with the connection with Great Britain, over three-quarters of the population of Ireland had a different political outlook. The people who formed this majority were known as Irish Nationalists because they believed that the Irish nation should be ruled by the Irish people. While they shared a belief in self-government, Irish Nationalists were deeply divided over the means of achieving their aims. Some groups were in favour of using violence against Britain, but others relied on peaceful methods. Because of this, two main types of Irish Nationalist can be identified.

- *Constitutional Nationalists:* They worked through the British parliament and used arguments and the support of the people to achieve their aims. Realising that British governments would never give Ireland complete independence without war and bloodshed, they agreed to struggle for Irish self-government inside the British Empire. Daniel O'Connell was the leading example followed by Constitutional Nationalists.
- *Physical Force Republicans:* They followed Wolfe Tone's belief in complete separation from Great Britain and hoped to achieve this by an armed uprising. While Constitutional Nationalists often enjoyed widespread public support, physical force movements were usually secret societies supported by small minorities.

After the passing of the Act of Union (1800), Irish Nationalist movements of both types grew from time to time. After the death of Daniel O'Connell (1847) and the Great Famine, Nationalists were weak and divided for a number of years. In 1856, however, a new movement was founded which had a lasting influence on Irish Nationalists in the years ahead. This was the Fenian Movement.

Test your knowledge

1. Explain the term 'Unionist'.
2. To which religious denominations did most Unionists belong?
3. How was the position of Unionists in Ulster different from their position in the rest of Ireland?
4. What was the great fear of Unionists?
5. Who were the Irish Nationalists?
6. List the two main types of Irish Nationalists.

The Fenian Movement

The *Fenian Movement*, or *Irish Republican Brotherhood*, (IRB) was set up with the aim of organising a rebellion against British rule in Ireland. A Fenian rising eventually took place in March 1867.

Although the rebellion of 1867 was a total failure, the IRB did not die, but lived on to plan future attacks against the British government in Ireland. After the execution of a group of Fenians known as the Manchester Martyrs in November 1867, many people in Ireland began to sympathise with them.

Fenian prisoners being brought to jail in Cork.

The Irish in America continued to support the Irish Republican Brotherhood. Even British politicians were influenced by the Fenians; by highlighting Irish problems, they forced leading politicians in London to improve conditions for the Irish people.

After the defeat of the Fenian rebellion, Constitutional Nationalists made another attempt to secure self-government for Ireland. They were to be guided by Isaac Butt, a barrister who had first come to the attention of the public when he defended Fenian prisoners at their trials.

Isaac Butt and the Home Rule Party

In 1870, Isaac Butt, the son of a Church of Ireland clergyman, founded the Home Rule Party. Butt was not satisfied that either of the two main British parties, the Conservatives and the Liberals, gave proper attention to Irish problems.

Isaac Butt, the founder of the Home Rule Party.

Butt not only believed that Irish MPs should form their own party. He also wanted the return of an Irish parliament in Dublin which would have control over Irish affairs. He was willing to allow the British parliament to continue to run matters like foreign affairs, defence, customs, and the post office, with Ireland remaining part of the British Empire under the queen. This belief in limited self-government was known as *Home Rule*. For the next fifty years, this new political party was to enjoy the support of the vast majority of the people of Ireland.

In the general election of 1874, against all odds, Butt's Home Rule Party won fifty-nine seats at Westminster. This success was partly due to the Secret Ballot Act (1872) which finally gave tenants the freedom to vote without interference from their landlords.

By the time of Butt's death in 1879, an up-and-coming young MP for Co. Meath was ready and willing to lead the party. His name was Charles Stewart Parnell.

Test your knowledge

1 What was the main aim of the Fenian Movement?

2 Was the movement limited to Ireland? Explain your answer.

3 Who were the 'Manchester Martyrs'?

4 Why did Isaac Butt found a new political party in 1870?

5 Explain the meaning of 'Home Rule'.

6 How did Butt's party perform in the 1874 general election?

Chapter 63: Review

- In 1800, the old Irish parliament was abolished and Ireland was governed directly by the British government.

- About a quarter of Irish people supported the full union between Britain and Ireland. They were called Unionists and lived mainly in Ulster.

- The majority of Irish people were Nationalists. They believed that the Irish nation should be ruled by Irish people themselves. Constitutional Nationalists aimed for Irish self-government within the British Empire by peaceful means. Physical force Republicans wanted to gain full independence from Britain by means of armed rebellion.

- The Fenian Movement was the nineteenth century's most famous example of physical force Republicanism. Although the Fenian Rebellion of 1867 was a total failure, the IRB did not die out but lived on to plan future attacks against the British government in Ireland.

- Isaac Butt founded the Home Rule Party in 1870. He wanted Ireland to have its own parliament again, while still remaining part of the British Empire. Fifty-nine Home Rule MPs were elected in the general election of 1874.

The Age of Parnell

Charles Stewart Parnell (1846–91)

Charles Stewart Parnell (1846-91).

In 1846, Charles Stewart Parnell was born at Avondale, Co. Wicklow, into a family of Protestant landowners. He was educated in England where he attended Cambridge University. While there he developed a hatred of British rule in Ireland. He may have been influenced by his American mother who held strong anti-British views.

Although distant and shy in company, Parnell was a very ambitious man. Soon after his entry to the British parliament in 1875 as an MP for Co. Meath, he began to make a name for himself when he defended the Fenian Manchester Martyrs.

Parnell being removed from the British House of Commons for disrupting the business of parliament.

When Parnell became leader of the Home Rule Movement in 1880, most Irish people hardly knew what Home Rule meant and had little interest in it. Survival on the land was the main issue affecting their everyday lives. A terrible crisis had hit the Irish countryside around 1878. Before Parnell could even begin to campaign for Home Rule, he first had to tackle the problems facing the people on the land.

The crisis on the land

Most tenant farmers in Ireland were very insecure on the land. They could be evicted from their cottages and farms whenever it suited the landlord. By the 1870s, however, evictions usually took place only when tenants failed to pay their rents. Around 1878, a serious crisis hit the Irish countryside.

- There were a number of bad harvests.
- Prices for Irish farm products fell as cheaper grain was imported from America.
- In British markets, Irish meat could not compete with cheaper imports from Argentina, New Zealand and Australia.

An eviction scene in Ireland.

Eviction and starvation on a scale not experienced since the Great Famine of the 1840s now faced thousands of farmers and their families throughout

Michael Davitt (1846-1906), the founder of the Land League, was evicted with his family from a farm in Mayo when he was only five years of age. After emigrating to England, he lost his right arm in an accident while working in a cotton mill. In 1870, he was jailed for fifteen years for Fenian activities in England. It was on his release in 1877 that he witnessed the horrific conditions of people in the West of Ireland. As a result, he established the Land League to help tenant farmers to work together to seek a reduction in rents and to prevent evictions.

the country, especially in the West of Ireland. At this stage, a remarkable man named Michael Davitt, a former Fenian prisoner on parole from jail in England, set up the *Land League* so that tenants could organise themselves to resist evictions.

Founded by Davitt in Co. Mayo in 1879, the Land League had the following aims:

- To stop evictions and to get reductions in rent for tenants.
- In the longer term, to ensure that tenant farmers replaced landlords as owners of the land.

As Irish landlords had the powerful backing of the British government, Davitt decided to step down as leader and allow Parnell to unite the Home Rule Party and the Land League in the struggle for the rights of tenant farmers.

An attack on unsuspecting landlords during the 'Land War'.

For three years, from 1879 to 1882, a widespread upheaval known as the *Land War* took place throughout Ireland. Although the movement was meant to be a peaceful one, violence often broke out as landlords, their agents, and people taking over the land of evicted tenants were attacked and sometimes murdered.

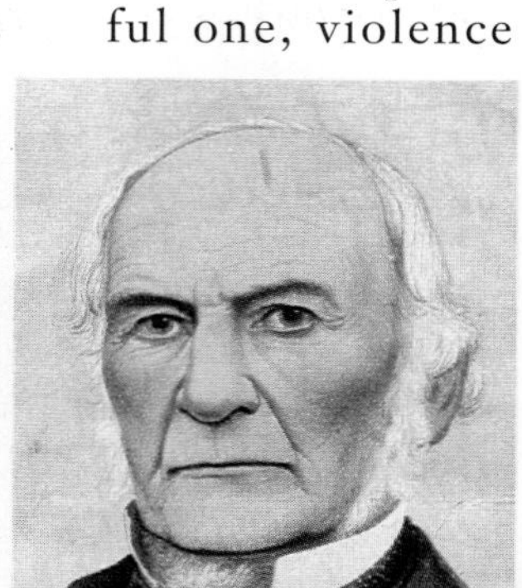

William Gladstone, the British Prime Minister.

In parliament, Parnell led the struggle against the British government which was headed by the prime minister, William Gladstone. In response to the widespread unrest in Ireland, Gladstone decided on two main approaches: harsh laws to impose order, and a Land Act bringing about improvements in the conditions of tenants.

When the Land Act was passed in 1881, Parnell condemned the act because it did not help the tenants as much as he had wished. As a result of his continuing campaign against the British government, Parnell was arrested and spent the winter of 1881–82 in Kilmainham jail, Dublin. He now became an even more popular hero than ever.

While Parnell and other leaders were in prison, they instructed the tenants not to pay any rent. As a result, violence increased on a huge scale throughout the countryside. Gladstone realised that if he reached an understanding with Parnell, the Irish leader would control the more extreme members of the Land League. In April 1882 an agreement was reached known as the *Kilmainham Treaty.* Gladstone released Parnell and his followers and promised to further improve the 1881 Land Act. In return, Parnell agreed to call off the rent strike and to accept Gladstone's Land Act.

Later British governments went further than Gladstone by advancing loans to tenants to help them buy out their farms from the landlords. As a result, from around 1900 onwards, most Irish farmers owned their own farms and there were very few landlords left in the country. The main leaders in the movement which led to this important change were undoubtedly Michael Davitt and Charles Stewart Parnell.

The Kilmainham Treaty of 1882 was a major turning point in Parnell's career. From then on he gave less and less attention to the land problem and concentrated on winning Home Rule for Ireland.

Test your knowledge

1. When and where was Parnell born?
2. How did he come to the attention of the public after entering the British parliament?
3. Who founded the Land League?
4. Explain what is meant by the 'Land War'.
5. What was William Gladstone's response to the Land War?
6. Explain the agreement known as the 'Kilmainham Treaty'.
7. How was this a turning point in Parnell's career?

The Phoenix Park Murders

A week after Parnell's release from Kilmainham jail, a terrible event took place in Dublin which would create difficulties for him in the future. On the evening of 6 May 1882, the new Chief Secretary, Lord Frederick Cavendish, and the Under-Secretary, Thomas R. Burke, were brutally murdered

The Phoenix Park Murders, May 1882.

as they walked in the Phoenix Park. The murder was carried out with surgical knives by a violent secret society known as 'the Invincibles'. Most of those responsible were later tried and hanged for the murders.

People in England and Ireland were horrified by the Phoenix Park murders. They left a terrible impression on Parnell, who wanted to give up politics as a result. Gladstone, equally horrified at the murders, managed to persuade Parnell to remain on as leader of the Home Rule Party. The years ahead were to truly test the ability of the Irish leader.

The organisation of the Home Rule Party

When the Land League was banned by the government in October 1881, Parnell replaced it by a new organisation called the *National League*. He had very strong control over this and he used it in his campaign for Home Rule. The National League:

- Chose Home Rule candidates in general elections.
- Collected money for the party.
- Organised support on a local level throughout the length and breadth of the country.

As well as improving party organisation at home, Parnell also tightened his control over Home Rule MPs at Westminster. All Home Rule candidates agreed that, if elected, they would always vote together as a group at Westminster. This was known as a *party pledge* and any MP breaking it was expected to resign his seat in parliament. This gave Parnell a united party which could exert great influence in Westminster.

A great opportunity arose when a general election was called in November 1885. In this election, eighty-six Home Rule MPs were elected. These MPs found themselves in a powerful position, as neither the Conservatives nor the Liberals had enough seats to form a government on their own.

Parnell first of all decided to support the Conservatives with Lord Salisbury as prime minster. However, despite the new powerful position of the Home Rule Party, both British parties were still against Home Rule. All of this was to change dramatically in the months ahead.

The number of seats held by each party after the 1885 election.

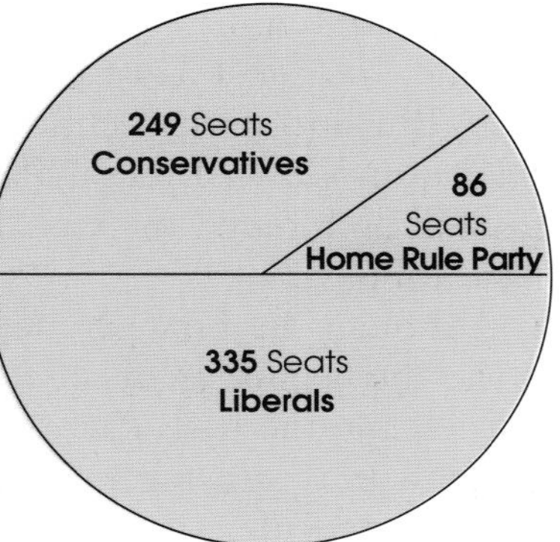

Test your knowledge

1. What were the Phoenix Park Murders?
2. State two ways in which Parnell improved the organisation of the Home Rule Party.
3. In what way did Parnell's party find itself in a powerful position after the 1885 election?
4. Name the leader of the Conservative Party at this time.

Gladstone supports Home Rule

In December 1885, Gladstone, leader of the opposition Liberal Party, made the dramatic announcement of his support for Home Rule. In January 1886, the Conservative government fell from power when the Home Rule Party joined the Liberals to defeat it.

The Liberal Prime Minister, William Gladstone, introducing the first Home Rule Bill in the British House of Commons in 1886.

Gladstone and the Liberal Party, with the help of the Home Rule MPs, formed a government which for the first time ever supported Home Rule for Ireland. In April Gladstone brought the First Home Rule Bill into parliament. However, groups within Gladstone's own Liberal Party refused to support the bill and joined the Conservatives to defeat it in June 1886.

Although the First Home Rule Bill was defeated, it was the beginning of the Liberal Alliance in which Parnell and the Irish Party continued to support the Liberals in return for a promise to continue to support Home Rule.

The Conservatives in power

'Killing Home Rule with Kindness'

After the failure of the First Home Rule Bill, Gladstone's Liberal government fell from power. In the general election which followed, the Conservatives won a huge majority and returned to power with Lord Salisbury as prime minister. They remained in power until 1892.

The Conservatives continued to oppose Home Rule. However, they hoped to lessen support in Ireland for Home Rule by bringing about other improvements in the country. Under the Ashbourne and Balfour Land Acts, the government made loans available to tenant farmers to buy their farms from the landlords. In 1891, a *Congested Districts Board* was set up to help the poorer areas of the West of Ireland by promoting local schemes of road, rail and pier building.

These various improvements were part of a policy known as *Killing Home Rule with Kindness*. However they failed to lessen support for Home Rule in Ireland.

The Pigott Forgeries

In the meantime, the Conservatives and other enemies of Parnell set out to discredit the Irish leader. In the spring of 1886, the powerful London newspaper, *The Times*, published a series of articles known as 'Parnellism and Crime'. *The Times* claimed that Parnell supported the Phoenix Park Murders in 1882! To prove this, the paper printed letters which were supposedly written by Parnell. When these claims were investigated by a special commission set up by parliament, it was discovered that the letters had been forged by a journalist called Richard Pigott who eventually fled to Spain where he committed suicide. Parnell was found to be innocent and his fame increased even more. He was now at the height of his power.

Test your knowledge

1 What important change of policy did Gladstone make towards the end of 1885?
2 What happened to Gladstone's First Home Rule Bill in June 1886?
3 What is meant by 'Killing Home Rule with Kindness'?
4 What were the Pigott Forgeries? How did they affect Parnell's career?

The fall of Parnell

In November 1890, the news of Parnell's involvement in a divorce case in London shocked people throughout Britain and Ireland. Parnell had been having a love affair for many years with a married woman, Katharine O'Shea. When her husband, Captain William O'Shea, sued for divorce, the 'scandal' became public knowledge.

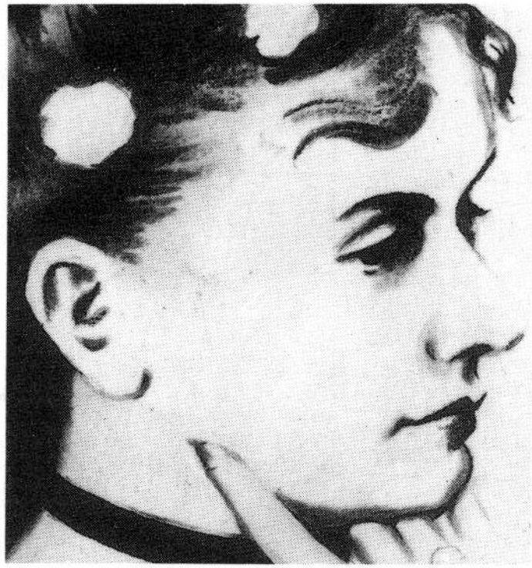

Katharine O'Shea, who married Parnell in 1891 after her marriage to Captain William O'Shea ended in divorce.

There was an immediate outcry in Ireland and Britain. Some people said that Parnell should resign, while others said his private life was his own business. Matters came to a head when Gladstone declared that he could not continue to support Home Rule if Parnell remained as leader of the Irish Parliamentary Party. The Irish Catholic bishops also believed that Parnell should resign.

The Irish Party itself met to consider the whole

Parnell addressing a hostile crowd in Kilkenny during a by-election campaign in 1891.

question in Committee Room 15 of the House of Commons at Westminster in early December 1890. Parnell used his position as chairman to delay the taking of a vote on his leadership. Eventually, a majority of the MPs present left the room and elected Justin McCarthy as their leader. The Irish Party, so noted for its unity during the 1880s, was now bitterly split into two groups—for and against, Parnell. Rejected by a majority of his parliamentary colleagues, Parnell now decided to look for the support of the Irish people.

The death of Parnell

Throughout 1891, Parnell put his own candidates forward in three by-elections in Ireland and suffered three successive defeats. During the campaigns, he had to put up with much personal abuse, including mud-slinging and stone-throwing. He finally married Katharine O'Shea in June 1891.

Although Katharine begged him to retire from public life, Parnell continued with the struggle. Worn out from exhaustion and disappointment, Parnell died at Brighton on 6 October 1891 at the early age of forty-five.

His funeral at Glasnevin cemetery in Dublin was one of the biggest ever seen in the city. The death of the 'Uncrowned King of Ireland' was deeply mourned. Those who lined the streets to see the funeral procession realised that they were witnessing the end of an era in Irish history. Things would never be quite the same again.

The funeral of Parnell passing by the old Irish Parliament buildings at College Green, Dublin.

Test your knowledge

1 Who was Katharine O'Shea?
2 What news broke in November 1890?
3 Describe the public reaction to this news.
4 How did Gladstone react?
5 What happened in Committee Room 15 in December 1890?
6 How did Parnell's fall from power affect the Home Rule party?

Chapter 64: Review

- In 1875, Charles Stewart Parnell was elected Home Rule MP for Meath. However, during the 1870s most Irish people were far more concerned with making a living on the land than with political issues like Home Rule.

- In the late 1870s, a serious crisis hit the Irish countryside. Many families faced hunger and eviction on a scale not witnessed since the Famine.

- In 1879, Michael Davitt set up the Land League with the aim of protecting tenant farmers from eviction. Parnell became leader of the Land League and the Home Rule Party.

- Between 1879 and 1882, the Irish countryside was in a state of crisis. This was known as the Land War. In 1881 William Gladstone, the British prime minster, introduced a Land Act which improved the conditions of Irish tenants.

- When Parnell condemned the Land Act for not helping tenants as much as he wished, he was imprisoned in Kilmainham jail.

- In April 1882, Parnell reached an agreement with Gladstone known as the Kilmainham Treaty. From then on, Parnell gave less attention to the land question and devoted his time to gaining Home Rule for Ireland.

• The Phoenix Park Murders of 6 May 1882 horrified most people in Britain and Ireland. The Chief Secretary and the Under-Secretary were murdered by a group called the Invincibles.

• From 1882, Parnell concentrated on building up a strong Home Rule Party in Westminster. In the general election of 1885, his party won eighty-six seats. He was in a very strong bargaining position as neither of the two British parties could form a government without his help.

• Towards the end of 1885, Gladstone, leader of the Liberal Party, agreed to support the cause of Home Rule. He became prime minister, with Parnell's help, in February 1886. The following April, Gladstone introduced the First Home Rule Bill, but it was defeated in the House of Commons.

• The Conservatives continued to oppose Home Rule. They had a policy called 'Killing Home Rule with Kindness'. This involved bringing in improvements on the land in the hope that the Irish would then forget about Home Rule.

• In November 1890, news broke of Parnell's involvement in a divorce case between Captain William O'Shea and his wife Katharine. Gladstone and the Irish Catholic bishops called for Parnell's resignation. At a meeting of the Irish Home Rule Party, Parnell was deposed as leader.

• Parnell refused to accept this verdict and decided to look for support in Ireland. He lost three by-elections and died on 6 October 1891. His fall from power and death left the Irish Home Rule Party deeply divided into two groups.

The Gaelic Revival

Ireland's identity

By the time of Parnell's death in 1891, small groups of people throughout Ireland were beginning to wonder if Home Rule was the answer to all of the country's problems. More and more Irish people were turning away from their native customs and pastimes in favour of English ones. If this trend continued, it was feared that Ireland would lose its cultural identity and become like an English province. To prevent this from happening a number of important organisations were set up to preserve Ireland's cultural heritage. They were founded by small groups of people but grew and developed into a powerful movement catering for a wide variety of activities including sport, language, literature, drama and politics.

The first such movement to be founded was the *Gaelic Athletic Association* (GAA).

The Gaelic Athletic Association (GAA)

On 1 November 1884, a group of seven men met in Hayes' Hotel, Thurles, Co. Tipperary. They were brought together by a common concern for the future of the traditional Irish games of hurling and football. These traditional pastimes were under increasing threat from the spread of English sports; soccer, for example, had become especially popular after the formation of the Irish Football Association in 1880. From the 1860s, rugby

The Tipperary hurling team which won the first All-Ireland championship in 1887.

football had spread among the upper classes and the Irish Football Union was founded in 1874. Alarmed by these developments, the seven men who met in Thurles in November 1884 founded the Gaelic Athletic Association (GAA).

The aim of the new movement was to promote traditional Gaelic games and, above all, to give them official rules and standards. Up to this time, hurling had no rules, and hurling matches frequently developed into brutal events resulting in numerous injuries.

Michael Cusack, the founder of the Gaelic Athletic Association (GAA).

Michael Cusack (1847–1906), a teacher from Co. Clare, was the leading figure in the new organisation and became its first secretary. A Tipperary athlete named Maurice Davin became the first president of the association. Archbishop Croke of Cashel, Charles Stewart Parnell and Michael Davitt were among the GAA's patrons.

From its foundation, many IRB men were involved in the GAA and used it as a recruiting ground for new members. It was, therefore, strongly anti-British and imposed on its members a 'ban' on the playing or viewing of foreign sports. This 'ban' remained in operation until the 1970s.

Archbishop Thomas Croke of Cashel, one of the first patrons of the GAA, helped to prevent the young organisation from falling under the control of the Fenians. He was a life-long supporter of Gaelic games and other forms of Irish culture.

GAA clubs sprang up throughout the country and had a major impact, especially in rural areas where they provided much-needed leisure activities. Competitions were organised between clubs and Sunday became the traditional day for matches. The first All-Ireland finals were held in 1887.

Test Your Knowledge

1. Why do you think traditional Irish games and pastimes were under threat in the late nineteenth century?
2. Where and when was the GAA founded?
3. What was the aim of the new organisation?
4. Name two of the founders of the GAA. State what position each held within the organisation.
5. Who became the first patrons of the GAA?
6. 'From its foundation, the GAA was very anti-British'. Give two examples to show this.
7. When were the first All-Ireland finals held?

The Gaelic League

By the closing years of the nineteenth century, the Irish language, like Gaelic games, had been under increasing threat from the spread of English influence. While no single cause may be given for this great decline in the use of Irish, the following points taken together help us to explain what happened.

- The Great Famine (1845–49) resulted in death and emigration, especially in the West of Ireland where Irish was mostly spoken.

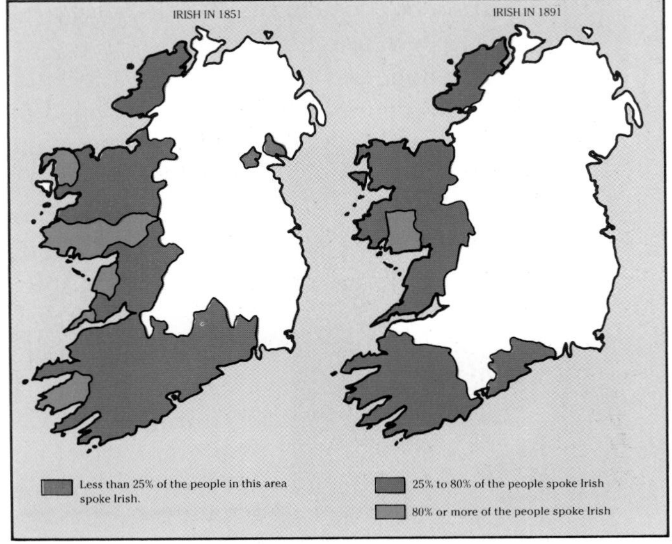

The decline of the Irish language. Between 1851 and 1891 the areas where nearly everyone spoke Irish had become much smaller.

- Children were taught in the national schools through English. Parents co-operated with teachers in discouraging children from talking in Irish.
- English was associated with progress; Irish became identified with poverty and backwardness.
- English was also the language of politics, and all leading Irish politicians, from O'Connell to Parnell, spoke English.

Concerned about the poor state of the Irish language and culture, Douglas Hyde, the son of a Church of Ireland rector from Co. Roscommon, founded the *Gaelic League* in 1893. He had a great love for the Irish language and became the first president of the League. Eoin MacNeill, an Irish scholar from Co. Antrim, became its first secretary. The League had three main aims:

1. to restore Irish as the spoken language of the country;
2. to encourage the writing and publication of Gaelic literature;
3. to remove English cultural influence from Ireland (Hyde called this the 'de-anglicisation of Ireland').

The Gaelic League hoped to achieve these aims by:

- The organisation of Irish classes throughout the country run by travelling teachers known as *timirí* (these travelled around the country using the newly-invented bicycle).
- The publication of its own newspaper, *An Claidheamh Soluis* (Sword of Light).
- The publication of books in the Irish language.
- The holding of *feisenna* and *ceilis*.

The Gaelic League gave its members a greater sense of their Irish identity. Douglas Hyde hoped to keep the movement totally separate from politics, but in this he failed. For many people, such as Patrick Pearse, the Gaelic League formed a stepping stone on the road to open involvement in violent Republican organisations.

Douglas Hyde, the Gaelic scholar and writer who was first president of the Gaelic League.

Eamon de Valera, a member of the Gaelic League, giving an Irish class in 1912.

Test your knowledge

1. Why was there cause for concern about the Irish language in the closing years of the nineteenth century?
2. State three reasons for the decline of the Irish language.
3. Who founded the Gaelic League? What were the aims of this organisation?
4. Who were the *timirí*?
5. What newspaper was founded by the Gaelic League?
6. Why do you think the organisation provided a stepping stone for some towards involvement in violent Republican movements?

The Abbey Theatre

While members of the Gaelic League were trying to promote new stories, plays and poems in the Irish language, there was also a new and exciting movement based on writings about Ireland in the English language. These writings are known as *Anglo-Irish literature*.

William Butler Yeats (1865-1939).

The most brilliant Anglo-Irish writer at this time was a young poet called William Butler Yeats (1865-1939). He believed that Ireland could and should have writers who could be as good as any in the world. Instead of writing in the fashion of Britain, Europe or America, Yeats believed that Irish writers should explore Irish topics in their works. Therefore in 1899, along with Lady Augusta Gregory and Edward Martyn, Yeats founded the *Irish Literary Theatre* with the aim of writing and producing plays on Irish topics. In 1904, the Abbey Theatre in Dublin became the company's new headquarters where all their most famous plays were produced.

Lady Augusta Gregory, one of the founders of the Abbey Theatre.

Many of these plays concerned Irish history or folklore and they encouraged resistance to British rule in Ireland. For the opening of the Abbey Theatre in 1904, Yeats wrote *Cathleen Ni Houlihan* with the beautiful Maud Gonne, whom he greatly admired, in the title role. This play was set in Mayo during the rebellion of 1798 and Cathleen Ni Houlihan was the representation of Ireland as an old woman calling on her sons to fight. At the end of the play, she calls a young man away from his wedding in order to fight and die in the rebellion. The play ends with the lines:

'Did you see an old woman going down the path?'

'I did not; but I saw a young girl, and she had the walk of a queen.'

Those who were at the play said that these lines caused great excitement. After the Easter Rising of 1916, Yeats wondered if he had encouraged people to join in the fighting:

'Did that play of mine send out
Certain men the English shot?'

The Abbey Theatre, which was opened in 1904.

As well as patriotic plays, there were also plays about life in the countryside. One of these, *The Playboy of the Western World* by John Millington Synge, caused riots in the Abbey in 1907 when young Nationalists believed that ordinary Irish country people were being mocked.

By 1910, the Abbey Theatre had gained a reputation as one of the finest in the world. Along with the GAA and the Gaelic League, it emphasised Ireland's special cultural identity which was separate and distinct from Britain's.

Test your knowledge

1 Who founded the Irish Literary Theatre?

2 What is meant by Anglo-Irish Literature?

3 What theatre became the headquarters of the Literary Theatre in 1904?

4 What was the main idea in Yeats's play, *Cathleen Ni Houlihan*?

5 Who was John Millington Synge? What was his most famous work?

6 In what way do you think the Abbey emphasised Ireland's unique cultural identity?

Arthur Griffith and Sinn Féin

Not all the movements founded at this time were concerned with cultural activities. One new organisation emphasised the need for Ireland to industrialise and to become above all self-sufficient in economic terms. This was *Sinn Féin*, founded by Arthur Griffith in 1905.

Arthur Griffith (1871-1922), the founder of Sinn Féin.

Born in Dublin in 1871, Griffith was a printer by trade. After spending some years in South Africa he returned to Ireland in 1898 and founded his own newspaper, the *United Irishman*. Although he favoured Ireland's total separation from Britain, he realised the difficulty of attaining this. He proposed instead for Ireland the Austro-Hungarian system of government known as *dual monarchy*. This would involve a separate parliament in Dublin under the British crown. Griffith said that Irish MPs, when elected, should refuse to take their seats in the Westminster parliament *(abstention)* and should instead set up their own parliament in Ireland.

In economic matters, Sinn Féin called for industrial growth to be achieved by means of tariff protection. It wanted Ireland to become self-sufficient and self-reliant—the words Sinn Féin mean 'we ourselves' or 'ourselves alone'. However, this organisation did not play an important part in Irish affairs until after 1916.

Test your knowledge

1 Who founded Sinn Féin and when?
2 What was meant by dual monarchy?
3 Sinn Féin favoured a policy of parliamentary abstention. What was meant by this?
4 What did Sinn Féin mean by tariff protection?
5 Sinn Féin wanted Ireland to become self-sufficient and self-reliant. Explain these terms.

Chapter 65: Review

• The Gaelic Athletic Association (GAA) was founded at Thurles, Co. Tipperary on 1 November 1884. Its aims were to promote Gaelic games and to give them official rules and standards. Michael Cusack, a Clare man, was its first secretary and Maurice Davin of Tipperary became its first president. Archbishop Croke of Cashel, Charles Stewart Parnell and Michael Davitt were its first patrons.

• The Gaelic League was founded in Dublin in July 1893 with the aim of reviving the Irish language. Douglas Hyde was the league's first president, while Eoin MacNeill was its first secretary. The organisation founded its own newspaper, *An Claidheamh Soluis*, and sent travelling teachers (*timirí*) around the country to run classes in Irish.

• In 1899, the Irish Literary Theatre was founded by W.B. Yeats, Lady Gregory and Edward Martyn with the aim of writing and producing plays on Irish topics. In 1904 the Abbey Theatre in Dublin became its new headquarters and its most famous playwright was John Millington Synge whose *Playboy of the Western World* caused riots in the Abbey in 1907.

• Arthur Griffith founded Sinn Féin in 1905. This organisation wanted Ireland to become self-sufficient, that is, supplying its own people with adequate food and employment. Griffith believed in a dual monarchy for Ireland and Britain, which meant that the king of England would also be king of Ireland, but that Ireland would have its own parliament.

The Home Rule Crisis: 1912–14

Home Rule on the way

After Parnell's death in 1891 and the bitter split in the Home Rule Party, many people lost respect for its members and believed that Home Rule would not be passed for a very long time. In 1893, Gladstone had succeeded in getting his Second Home Rule Bill passed by the House of Commons, but it was decisively rejected by the House of Lords. The opponents of Home Rule, the Conservatives, were then in power continuously from 1895 until 1906.

John Redmond, who became leader of the re-united Irish Parliamentary Party in 1900.

Although the Irish Home Rule Party was reunited in 1900 under the leadership of the Parnell supporter, John Redmond, few people in Ireland believed that Home Rule was on the way. Indeed, many young people preferred to become involved in the GAA, the Gaelic League and other cultural movements, rather than in the Irish Parliamentary Party.

In 1910, however, John Redmond and his party became very influential in London when the Conservatives and Liberals were almost evenly balanced in the British House of Commons. The eighty-two Irish MPs now held the balance of power. Not since Parnell's time in 1885 had the Irish party enjoyed this position.

The Liberal government of H.H. Asquith was dependent on the Irish MPs to stay in power. As a condition of his support, Redmond insisted that a Home Rule Bill be introduced. The hopes of the Irish Nationalists were high. As a result of the Parliament Act (1911), the House of Lords could no longer completely reject a law. They could only delay it for two years. When the Third Home Rule Bill was passed in the House of Commons in 1912, it appeared that nothing could prevent it from becoming law by 1914.

The Liberal Prime Minister, H.H. Asquith, who needed the support of the Irish Parliamentary Party in order to stay in power after 1910.

Although under the bill the powers of an Irish parliament would be quite limited, Redmond and his followers were prepared to accept it as a big improvement on direct rule from London.

However, neither the British Liberal Party nor their Irish supporters fully realised the strength of resistance to Home Rule among Irish Unionists and British Conservatives.

Ulster says 'no' to Home Rule

Ulster Protestants were determined to block the Third Home Rule Bill. They began to organise an anti-Home Rule campaign throughout Ulster. They opposed Home Rule for three main reasons:

- *Religious:* They feared that, in a Home Rule parliament with a Catholic majority, Protestants would be treated unfairly. This belief was summed up in the slogan *Home Rule is Rome Rule*.
- *Political:* They were loyal to the king of England and wished to remain under the direct rule of the British government.
- *Economic:* Ulster had prospered under the Union since 1800. Unionists feared that a Home Rule parliament in Dublin would pass laws which would damage trade and industry in the province.

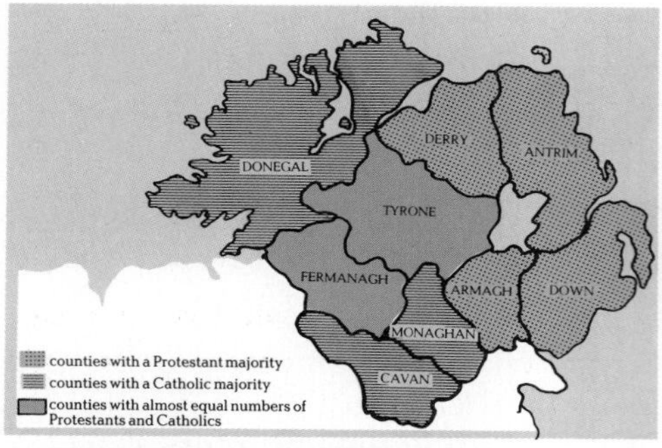

Catholic and Protestant divisions in Ulster about 1910.

Edward Carson signing the Ulster Covenant.

Crowds outside Belfast City Hall cheer the signing of the Solemn League and Covenant in 1912.

Edward Carson, a Unionist MP for Trinity College, and James Craig, an MP for Down since 1906 and a millionaire businessman, were the leaders of the Unionist campaign. In September 1912, they drew up the *Ulster Solemn League and Covenant.* This pledged resistance to Home Rule and was signed by over 250,000 Protestant men throughout Ulster.

The Ulster Volunteers

The Ulster Unionists, supported by the Conservatives under their leader, Andrew Bonar Law, were prepared to resist Home Rule by force if necessary. To this end they set up the *Ulster Volunteers* early in 1913. They were a force of loyal Ulstermen determined to go to any lengths to block Home Rule. The Ulster Volunteers, under the leadership of Carson and Craig, grew steadily in number throughout 1913. They drilled and took part in military manoeuvres and prepared to seize control of the province in the event of Home Rule becoming law.

The Irish Volunteers

Meanwhile, Irish Nationalists paid close attention to events in the North. Eoin MacNeill, a founder member of the Gaelic League, wrote an article called 'The North Began'. In this article, he called for the setting up of a similar volunteer force in the South in order to defend Ireland's right to Home Rule. In response to this article, a meeting of Irish Nationalists took place at the Rotunda in Dublin on 25 November 1913. It was at this meeting that the *Irish Volunteers* were formed. Many members of the Irish Republican Brotherhood (IRB) joined this new force. They hoped to use it when the time was right to stage a rebellion. By the summer of 1914, more than 100,000 men had joined the Irish Volunteers.

A group of Irish Volunteers drilling with hurleys in 1914.

Test your knowledge

1 Who were the Ulster Volunteers? Why were they set up?

2 Who led this group of Ulstermen?

3 Who wrote the article 'The North Began'? What was its immediate outcome?

4 When were the Irish Volunteers set up? What was the purpose of this organisation?

5 Why did many IRB men join this force?

1914: Ireland on the verge of war

In the early months of 1914, many people believed that Ireland was on the brink of civil war. In this year, the Ulster Volunteers and the Irish Volunteers illegally imported arms and ammunition. The stage now seemed set for a war between North and South.

The Larne gun-running

On 24 April 1914, the Ulster Volunteers illegally imported arms from Germany. Most of these arrived

The Larne gun-running.

safely ashore at the Co. Antrim port of Larne. The cargo numbered some 24,000 rifles and 3 million rounds of ammunition.

Although the British government knew what was going on, no effort was made to seize the arms or to arrest those involved. This was an important triumph for the Ulster Volunteers. They could now back up their campaign against Home Rule with force of arms.

The Howth gun-running

The Irish Volunteers smuggled arms into the country at Howth, Co. Dublin, on 26 July 1914. The ship used was Erskine Childers' yacht, the *Asgard.* Hundreds of Volunteers helped to unload the arms and to take them safely away. On their way back to Dublin, the Volunteers were challenged by the army and police but managed to get the weapons away safely. Later that day, when British soldiers were marching along Bachelors Walk, they were jeered by local onlookers. The soldiers opened fire on the crowd, killing three and injuring thirty-eight.

The Howth gun-running.

World War I begins—Home Rule is shelved

The Third Home Rule Bill, passed in 1912, was due to become law in the autumn of 1914. John Redmond and his followers were about to see their hopes come true. These hopes were dashed when World War I broke out in August 1914. The British government now decided to postpone Home Rule until after the war. As soon as the war broke out, the Ulster Volunteers showed their loyalty by joining the British army and marching off to fight for the empire.

The Irish Volunteers split

World War I was not so simple an issue for the Irish Volunteers. In September 1914, in a speech at Woodenbridge, Co. Wicklow, John Redmond strongly urged the Volunteers to fight for Britain in the war. He hoped that, in return, Britain would grant Home Rule at an early date.

An Irish recruiting poster during World War I.

This speech brought about a split in the Irish Volunteers. The vast majority followed Redmond's call and changed their name to the National Volunteers. A minority of 10,000, under the leadership of MacNeill, refused to fight for Britain and retained the name Irish Volunteers.

Test your knowledge

1 What happened at the port of Larne on 24 April 1914?

2 What was the reaction of the British government to this event?

3 What event occurred at Howth on 26 July 1914?

4 What ship was used? Who assisted in unloading its cargo?

5 What happened at Bachelors Walk, Dublin, later the same day?

6 Ireland seemed to be on the brink of civil war in 1914. Explain why.

7 What led to a split among the Irish Volunteers?

Chapter 66: Review

• From 1910 onwards, the British Liberal government under H.H. Asquith needed the support of the Irish Home Rule Party under John Redmond in order to stay in power. In return for this support, Asquith promised to bring in a Home Rule Bill for Ireland at the earliest possible opportunity.

• The Third Home Rule Bill was passed by the British House of Commons in 1912 but was immediately rejected by the House of Lords. However, as the House of Lords could only delay a bill for two years, it was due to become law in 1914.

• Ulster Unionists and British Conservatives were bitterly against Home Rule. Edward Carson and James Craig drew up the Solemn League and Covenant (1912) which was signed by over 250,000 Ulster Protestants opposed to Home Rule. In 1913 they set up the Ulster Volunteers which was a force of loyal Ulstermen determined to block Home Rule at all costs.

• On 25 November 1913, the Irish Volunteers were set up in Dublin under the leadership of Eoin MacNeill. Their aim was to defend Ireland's right to Home Rule. Many IRB men joined the Irish Volunteers and hoped to use them to organise a rebellion against British rule in Ireland.

• On 24 April 1914, the Ulster Volunteers landed arms illegally at Larne, Co. Antrim. On 26 July, the Irish Volunteers landed guns at Howth, Co. Dublin.

• When World War I broke out in August 1914, the British government decided to put off Home Rule until the war was over.

• The Ulster Volunteers immediately responded to the war by joining the British army. However, when John Redmond advised the Irish Volunteers to do the same, a split occurred in the organisation. The majority, known as the National Volunteers, followed Redmond's call, while the minority under Eoin MacNeill refused to fight for Britain and kept the name Irish Volunteers.

Chapter 67 Rebellion in Ireland: 1914–18

A revived IRB

As we have seen, the IRB was a secret illegal organisation waiting for the right opportunity to stage a rebellion against British rule in Ireland. They were also members of the Irish Volunteers and hoped to use that organisation when the time came to stage a rebellion. When the split came in the Volunteers, the IRB members were among those who refused to answer Redmond's call to join the British army.

By this time several young men, including Sean Mac Diarmada and Patrick Pearse, had been recruited into this secret organisation. Both they and older Fenians like Thomas Clarke welcomed Britain's involvement in World War I. They saw this as Ireland's great opportunity to strike another blow for freedom. This view was summed up in the phrase: 'England's difficulty is Ireland's opportunity'.

Patrick Pearse (1879–1916)

Born in Dublin in 1879, Patrick Pearse was the son of an English stone cutter and an Irish mother. He received his early education in the Christian Brothers' school, Westland Row, and later trained as a barrister. From an early age, Patrick showed an interest in the Irish language and became a member of the Gaelic League. In 1903 he became editor of the League's newspaper, *An Claidheamh Soluis*.

Thomas Clarke, the elderly Fenian whose tobacco shop in the centre of Dublin was used by the IRB for secret meetings in the years before 1916.

Pearse spent his summers in a cottage he built at Rosmuc in the Connemara Gaeltacht. He was very interested in education and opened a bilingual school, St Enda's, at Cullenswood House, Ranelagh, in Dublin. In 1910, 'The Hermitage', Rathfarnham, Dublin, became the new home for Pearse's school. Subjects taught included the Irish language, history, legends and nature study. He inspired his students with a love of Ireland.

Patrick Pearse was committed to the cause of Irish freedom and he joined the Irish Volunteers and the IRB. He became convinced that freedom could only be achieved by the spilling of Irish blood. He made this clear in 1915 when he spoke at the graveside of the old Fenian, O'Donovan Rossa. He ended this graveside oration with the words: 'Ireland unfree shall never be at peace'. From then on, Pearse and other IRB leaders plotted an early rebellion.

Patrick H. Pearse (1879-1916).

Test your knowledge

1 Why did many IRB members join the Irish Volunteers?

2 How did the IRB view Britain's involvement in the World War I?

3 How did Patrick Pearse show his interest in the Irish language?

4 What do you think was unusual about Pearse's school at St Enda's?

5 In what way did Pearse believe that Irish freedom could be achieved?

6 What famous speech did he make in 1915?

Preparations for a rising

In January 1916, the Supreme Council of the IRB decided to hold a rising around Easter. Those involved in this decision included Thomas Clarke, Patrick Pearse, Sean Mac Diarmada, Eamonn Ceannt and Joseph Plunkett. Meanwhile, James Connolly and the Irish Citizen Army were planning their own rebellion. When the leaders of the IRB learned of this, they persuaded Connolly to join forces with them.

Members of the Irish Citizen army outside their headquarters at Liberty Hall, Dublin, in 1916. This group had been founded by Connolly in 1913 to protect workers in their clashes with the police during the long strike and lock-out in Dublin in 1913.

Both the Irish Volunteers and the Citizen Army marched through the centre of Dublin on St Patrick's Day 1916, while Eoin MacNeill, the Volunteer leader, looked on. The IRB had chosen Easter Sunday, 23 April 1916 as the date of the rising.

Plans go wrong

A DIARY OF EVENTS, HOLY WEEK 1916

Holy Thursday, 20 April 1916

The IRB had kept their plans for the Easter Rising top secret. It was not until as late as this that Eoin MacNeill, commander of the Volunteers but not himself a member of the IRB, discovered these plans. MacNeill believed that a rising could not succeed because of lack of arms.

As the IRB needed MacNeill's support, they forged a document known as *The Castle Document* which stated that the government was about to suppress the Volunteers and arrest its leaders. The IRB also told MacNeill of the expected arrival of arms from Germany.

Good Friday, 21 April 1916

A German boat, the *Aud*, full of arms and ammunition, arrived off the Kerry coast.

Sir Roger Casement, a former British diplomat who had organised this arms supply, arrived on board a German submarine. He shaved off his beard

Sir Roger Casement, the former British diplomat who travelled to Germany for the IRB to seek German support for a rising against Great Britain.

in an effort to hide his identity and arrived ashore at Banna Strand, Co. Kerry. Despite his precautions, however, he was almost immediately arrested. The *Aud* was also captured.

Holy Saturday, 22 April 1916

The *Aud*, while being escorted into Cork harbour, was scuttled by her crew. MacNeill learned of this and also discovered that the so-called 'Castle Document' had been a forgery. He immediately set about cancelling all Volunteer activities for the following day.

Easter Sunday, 23 April 1916

MacNeill's order forbidding all Volunteer movements for that day was published in the *Sunday Independent*. Because of this, the Rising could not take place on Easter Sunday. However, the IRB leader decided to have a rising on the following day, Easter Monday.

The Rising begins

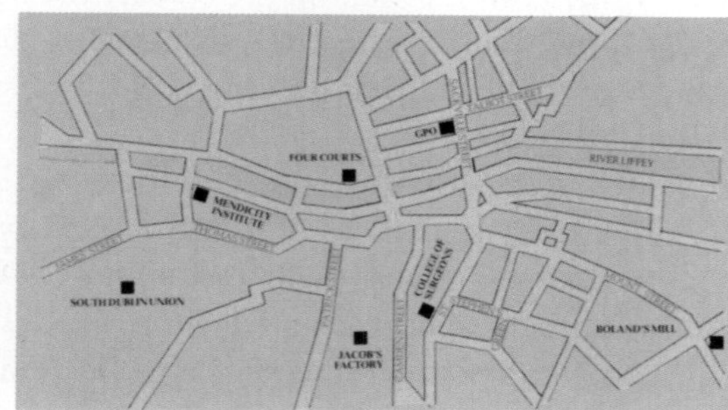

Buildings in Dublin occupied by the rebels during Easter Week, 1916.

The centre of Dublin was deserted and peaceful on this bank holiday Monday. Ordinary Dubliners were completely taken by surprise when they saw groups of armed Volunteers capturing important buildings throughout the city—the Rising had begun.

The rebels chose the General Post Office as their headquarters. From its steps, Patrick Pearse read the *Proclamation of the Irish Republic* to a small and bewildered group of onlookers. The tricolour was raised on the roof of the building. Other centres manned by the rebels included St Stephen's Green, the Four Courts, Boland's Mill, Jacobs, and the South Dublin Union in James's Street. However, they failed to capture Dublin Castle, the headquarters of the British government in Ireland.

Two artists' views of fighting in Dublin during Easter Week 1916. In the first painting, the wounded James Connolly is shown on a stretcher. The second painting is by Thomas Ryan.

The Rising fails

The outbreak of the Rising in Dublin took the British authorities completely by surprise. There were only 2,500 troops based in the city and many of them had gone off to the Fairyhouse Races on that bank holiday Monday. However, by Tuesday, troops and artillery were pouring into Kingstown harbour. Some 12,000 British soldiers had arrived by Thursday.

The only real resistance which the incoming soldiers faced was at Mount Street bridge where a group of about seventeen rebels from Eamon de Valera's garrison at Boland's Mill fired on the soldiers from nearby houses. Many British soldiers were killed before the army eventually stormed the doorways with hand grenades. Another rebel garrison which offered strong resistance was the South Dublin Union in James's Street.

By midweek, however, it was becoming increasingly obvious that the rebels were fighting a losing battle. On Wednesday, a gunboat, the *Helga*, sailed up the Liffey and began to shell Liberty Hall and other buildings. During the next few days, the sounds of gunfire could be heard throughout the city and many buildings, including the GPO, were burning. Looting of shops was widespread as people from nearby tenements took advantage of the confusion. Women could be seen wearing stolen fur coats and wheeling prams which were full of stolen goods.

The centre of Dublin in ruins after the Easter Rising.

The British forces gradually closed in on the rebels, whose situation was hopeless by the end of the week. At 3 pm on Saturday, 29 April, Pearse, shocked by the number of civilian casualties, surrendered unconditionally to General Maxwell, the British commander. The Easter Rising had ended in failure.

In all, owing to confusion before the Rising, only about 2,000 rebels had fought, and there was little activity in the rest of the country. Casualties had been very high—about 450 people were killed and another 2,600 wounded, most of them civilians. The damage to property had also been considerable, amounting to about £2½ million. Therefore, for most Dubliners, the Rising had been a major inconvenience, resulting in a costly loss of life and destruction of their city.

Test your knowledge

1 What did the IRB decide to do in January 1916?
2 Why did MacNeill disapprove when he heard of the IRB plans to hold a rising?
3 What part did Sir Roger Casement play in the events leading up to the 1916 Rising?
4 Why did the IRB change the date of the Rising?
5 What buildings did the rebels occupy?
6 What steps did the British authorities take to deal with the Rising?
7 How had ordinary Dubliners regarded the Rising?

After the Rising

Volunteers surrendering to British forces.

Huge numbers were arrested after the Rising and brought to Richmond Barracks for questioning. As the arrested leaders of the Rising were marching through Dublin, they were jeered and taunted by onlookers. The military was now in charge of the city, the streets were cleared and a curfew was enforced.

Military courts were set up to try the rebels. Fifteen men were shot between 3 and 12 May, including the seven signatories of the Easter Proclamation—Clarke, Pearse, Connolly, Ceannt, Mac Diarmada, Plunkett and MacDonagh. Roger Casement was hanged in August. Some of those sentenced to death, including Eamon de Valera and Countess Markievicz, had their sentences changed to life imprisonment. The vast majority of those who took part in the Rising were sent to internment camps in Britain.

Eamon de Valera under arrest

The following account clearly shows the effect which the harsh treatment of the rebels had on many Irish people:

> 'The executions, which followed the defeat of the Volunteers, horrified the nation...The first open manifestation of the deep public feeling aroused by the executions was at the Month's Mind for the dead leaders. A Month's Mind is the Mass celebrated for the soul of a relative or friend a month after his death. It was the first opportunity that sympathisers of the rebels had to come out in the open. I went with my father to the first of the Month's Minds, which was for the brothers Pearse, at Rathfarnham. We arrived well in time for Mass

but could not get into the church and the forecourt was packed right out to the road. I was surprised to see so many well-dressed and obviously well-to-do people present...I went to other Month's Minds with my father—to Merchant's Quay, John's Lane and other city churches. For us young people these Masses were occasions for quite spontaneous demonstrations, shouting insults at the Dublin Metropolitan Police who were always around but, having learned their lesson during the 1913 strike, were anxious to avoid trouble...'

C.S. Andrews, *Dublin Made Me*

The revival of Sinn Féin

Britain had regarded the 1916 Rising as a Sinn Féin rebellion. Its leader, Arthur Griffith, was placed under arrest. However, Sinn Féin was not directly involved in the Rising but it benefited from being associated with its dead martyrs. Those who sympathised with the Rising came to rally around Sinn Féin, and the party grew steadily.

Republican prisoners, including Countess Markievicz, receiving an enthusiastic welcome home after their release from internment camps in England.

The rebels who arrived home from internment camps in 1916–17 quickly joined the ranks of Sinn Féin and the re-organised Volunteers. In October 1917, Eamon de Valera, the senior survivor of the 1916 Rising, took over the leadership of the new Sinn Féin and the Volunteers.

The increased support for Sinn Féin was clearly seen in a number of by-election victories. Count Plunkett, the father of the executed 1916 leader, won a seat in North Roscommon in February 1917. In July of the same year, de Valera himself won a by-election in East Clare. Neither of them took his seat at Westminster.

An anti-conscription meeting, 1918. Sinn Féin was prominent among the groups which organised opposition to conscription.

World War I ends

While the events recorded in this chapter were taking place in Ireland, around 300,000 Irishmen were fighting for Britain in World War I. Of these men, 50,000 were killed in action. Although all those soldiers had volunteered for service, an attempt was made to bring conscription into Ireland in 1918. Sinn Féin organised an anti-conscription campaign which further increased their popularity. As a result, the government dropped the scheme.

The war finally ended in November 1918. Those returning home found conditions in Ireland totally changed. Back in 1914, most Irish people had supported Home Rule but now, more and more people wanted a separate Irish Republic.

This important change was very clearly shown in the results of the general election of December 1918. Out of 106 seats, Sinn Féin won seventy-three while the Home Rule Party, now under the leadership of John Dillon, won a mere six. The Unionists won twenty-six seats. The newly elected Sinn Féin MPs refused to attend the Westminster parliament.

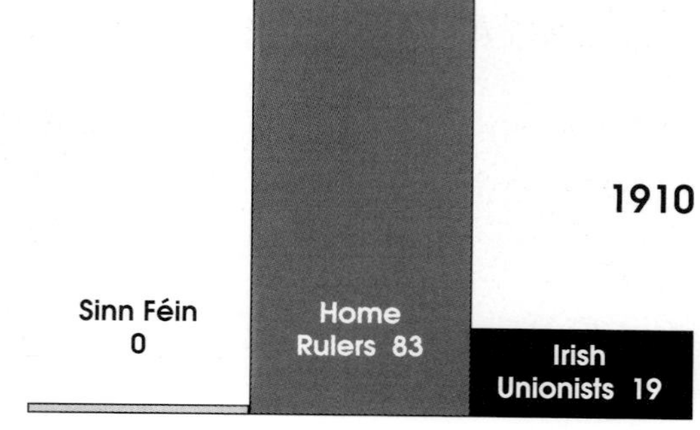

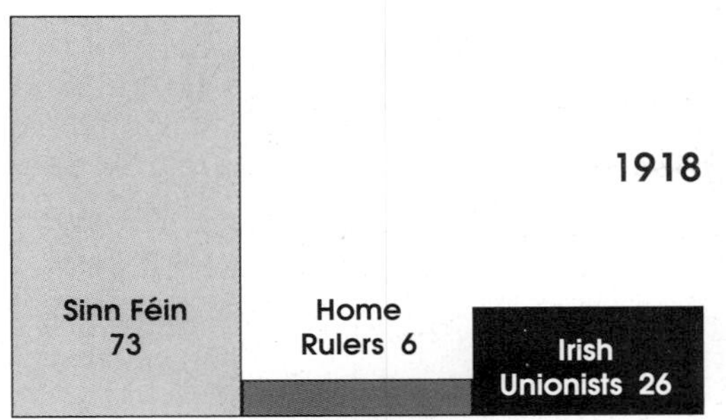

These two bar graphs clearly show the changes in strength of the main Irish political parties between 1910 and the general election of 1918.

The scene was now set for a clash between Sinn Féin and the British government.

Test your knowledge

1 What was the first popular view of the 1916 Rising?
2 How was this view to change in the succeeding months?
3 Why do you think the death sentences imposed on de Valera and Countess Markievicz were changed to life imprisonment?
4 In what way did Sinn Féin benefit from the 1916 Rising?
5 Name two by-election victories secured by Sinn Féin throughout 1917.
6 What role had Irishmen played in World War I?
7 What was the result of the 1918 general election? What do you think was so revolutionary about this result?

Chapter 67: Review

- The IRB welcomed the outbreak of World War I, as they saw it as an opportunity to stage a rebellion against British rule in Ireland—'England's difficulty is Ireland's opportunity'.

- P.H. Pearse (1879–1916) became a leading member of the IRB. He had earlier been editor of the Gaelic League newspaper, *An Claidheamh Soluis.* He was very interested in education and opened his own school, St Enda's.

- The Supreme Council of the IRB settled on Easter Sunday, 1916, as the date of a rising. Connolly and the Citizen Army were persuaded to join forces with the IRB.

- Roger Casement, who had arranged the delivery of arms, was arrested in Co. Kerry. MacNeill now decided to withdraw from the Rising and cancelled all Volunteer activities arranged for Easter Sunday.

- The IRB decided to hold the Rising on the following day, Easter Monday. The rebels took over various building in Dublin including the GPO, the South Dublin Union and Boland's Mills. Patrick Pearse, as Commander-in-Chief, read the Proclamation of the Irish Republic outside the GPO—the rebel headquarters.

- By the end of Easter Week, the rebels were hopelessly outnumbered by British troops. Much of the city centre lay in smoking ruins. On Saturday, 29 April, Pearse surrendered unconditionally to General Maxwell, the British commander.

- In the beginning the people of Dublin were very angry with the rebels. However, this anger soon changed to sympathy after fifteen of the rebel leaders were shot between 3 and 12 May. Most of those who had taken part in the Rising were sent to internment camps in Great Britain.

- When the 1916 rebels were released from imprisonment, they rallied around the Sinn Féin Party and chose Eamon de Valera, the senior surviving officer of the Easter Rising, to be their leader. The re-organised Sinn Féin Party grew quickly and in the 1918 general election, it won seventy-three out of the 106 Irish seats in the British parliament.

Troubled Times in Ireland: 1919–23

The First Dáil

On 21 January 1919, an historic event took place at the Mansion House in Dublin. Sinn Féin MPs, having refused to take their seats in the British parliament, met and set up a parliament of their own. This became known as the *First Dáil*. Many Sinn Féin MPs were either in prison or on the run—therefore only twenty-seven of them were present in the Mansion House on that day. This small group met for two hours and made the following decisions:

- They supported the declaration of an Irish Republic made at Easter 1916.
- They agreed to a democratic programme that promised widespread reforms in the areas of economy, education and poor law.
- Seán T. O'Kelly was elected to head an Irish delegation to the Versailles Peace Conference where they hoped to win support for their views.

Eamon de Valera, the most senior member of Sinn Féin, was in prison when the First Dáil met. In his absence, Cathal Brugha acted as president. However, de Valera escaped from prison the following month and was elected president of the Dáil on 1 April 1919. He appointed a cabinet of ministers to take over the running of the country: Arthur Griffith (Home Affairs), Michael Collins (Finance), Cathal Brugha (Defence), William T. Cosgrave (Local Government), Countess Markievicz (Labour), Eoin MacNeill (Industries), Count Plunkett (Foreign Affairs) and Robert Barton (Agriculture).

A meeting of the First Dáil at the Mansion House, Dublin, in 1919.

The British government soon declared Sinn Féin and the Dáil to be illegal. The stage was set for a war between Britain and Ireland to decide who would govern the country. The War of Independence was about to begin.

Test your knowledge

1. What historic event took place at the Mansion House in Dublin on 21 January 1919?
2. Who formed the first Dáil? What did its members stand for?
3. Why were only twenty-seven MPs present at the first meeting of the Dáil?
4. Who became president of the Dáil in April 1919?

The War of Independence—the fighting begins

On the same day that the First Dáil met in Dublin, the first shooting of the War of Independence took place in Co. Tipperary. A group of Volunteers, in search of arms, attacked a number of policemen of the Royal Irish Constabulary (RIC) near the town of Soloheadbeg in Co. Tipperary. Many of the early attacks were on RIC barracks in search of arms, but later, British soldiers also came under attack.

There followed two and a half years of guerrilla-type warfare between Irish Republicans and the British forces.

Michael Collins (1890–1922)

Michael Collins was the most important Irish military leader during the War of Independence. Born in Co. Cork in 1890, he went to London at the age of fifteen to work in the British Post Office. He soon became a member of the IRB and the Irish Volunteers and returned to Ireland for the 1916 Rising.

Michael Collins (1890-1922).

Collins did not make his mark on events until after his release from prison at the end of 1916. He then set about re-organising the Volunteer movement which now became known as the *Irish Republican Army (IRA).*

During the War of Independence, Collins directed IRA activities. He master-minded his own spy network which successfully countered the British spying system. The British government offered a reward of £10,000 for the capture of Collins. To them he was the most wanted man in Ireland.

Guerrilla warfare in Ireland

The War of Independence consisted of attacks and reprisals on the part of the British forces and the IRA. The IRA used guerrilla warfare against the British forces—that is, small groups carried out surprise attacks and then withdrew quickly. Ordinary people, going about their daily work, were often innocent victims of terror and violence.

The Black and Tans

In the early months of 1920, law and order was breaking down throughout Ireland. To cope with this crisis, the British government in March 1920 sent over a new force which became known as the *Black and Tans*. Many of these had fought in World War I and could not find employment after the war. They were attracted to Ireland by the high wages of ten shillings (50p) a day. Due to a shortage of police uniforms, this force wore a mixture of dark green and khaki which led to their name, the Black and Tans. Used to war and adventure, they let loose a reign of terror in Ireland.

A group of Black and Tans carrying out a raid on Liberty Hall, Dublin.

Police and British soldiers attack a farm used by the IRA.

A smaller force, the Auxiliaries, were sent to Ireland in August 1920. These consisted of ex-army officers who were given great freedom in the methods they used. Like the Black and Tans, they used widespread terror against both the IRA and the civilian population.

The Flying Columns

The IRA was organised in small groups which conducted hit-and-run attacks on the crown forces. Such groups were known as *Flying Columns*. The IRA were not in uniform and were able to escape quickly into the local countryside where they had many supporters among the local people. Famous leaders of Flying Columns included Ernie O'Malley, Liam Lynch, Sean MacEoin and Tom Barry. The Black and Tans and the Auxiliaries found the tactics of the IRA impossible to defeat. As a result they carried out acts of revenge on the local civilian population and on public figures who were known to be sympathetic to the IRA.

An IRA Flying Column during the War of Independence.

1920: A Year of Terror

1920 was the most violent year in the War of Independence.

- In March, Tomás MacCurtain, the Sinn Féin Lord Mayor of Cork, was shot dead in his house by Crown forces.
- On 25 October, Terence MacSwiney, the next Lord Mayor of Cork, died in Brixton prison, London, after a hunger strike lasting seventy-four days.

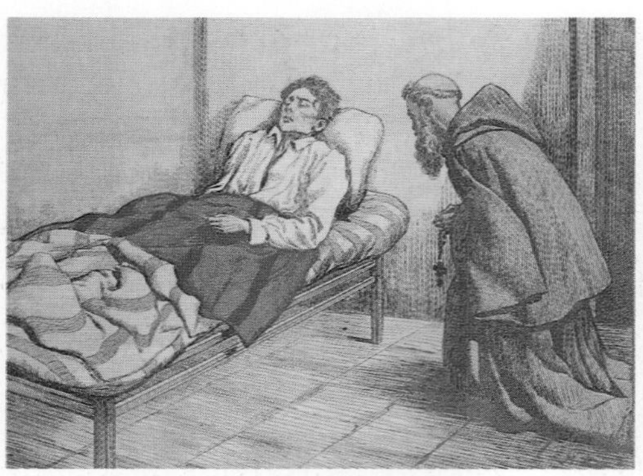

Terence MacSwiney, Lord Mayor of Cork, on hunger strike.

- On 1 November, Kevin Barry, an eighteen-year-old university student, was hanged in Mountjoy Jail, Dublin, for his part in an IRA ambush.
- Sunday, 21 November, was to become known as 'Bloody Sunday'. Collins had discovered the hide-outs of a number of undercover British agents in Dublin. Beginning at 9 am, his hit squad assassinated fourteen of them. On the same afternoon, the Black and Tans, in an act of reprisal, opened fire on a crowd watching a football match between Dublin and Tipperary at Croke Park. Twelve people, including one of the Tipperary players, were killed and another sixty were injured.

Kevin Barry, the eighteen-year-old medical student who was hanged in Mountjoy Jail, Dublin, in November 1920 for his part in an IRA ambush.

IRA prisoners in Mountjoy Jail, Dublin, go on hunger strike.

On the night of 10-11 December, the Black and Tans and the Auxiliaries set fire to a large part of the centre of Cork city. This was a reprisal for the IRA ambush, under the command of Tom Barry, at Kilmichael, Co. Cork, on 28 November.

Test your knowledge

1 What incident marked the beginning of the War of Independence?

2 Who was the most important Irish military leader during the War of Independence?

3 What new name did the Volunteers take?

4 What type of fighting took place during the War of Independence?

5 Who were the Black and Tans? How did they get their name?

6 Who were the Auxiliaries?

7 What were the Flying Columns? Name one of their most famous leaders.

8 What happened in Dublin on 'Bloody Sunday', 21 November 1920?

Deadlock: a truce is declared

By 1921, the War of Independence had almost reached a deadlock. While the British controlled the major towns, the IRA had a firm grip on the countryside.

The Dáil had also set up its own government departments and courts: more and more people were now using these and ignoring the British ones. By the middle of 1921, morale among both the British and IRA had reached a very low point. Ordinary people, both in Britain and Ireland, longed for an end to the violence and the terror. In July 1921, both sides agreed to a truce.

De Valera and Lloyd George, the British prime minister, met in London. While no agreement was reached at this meeting, they did arrange for peace talks to begin in London the following October.

The Irish delegates at the Treaty negotiations in London in the autumn of 1921.

A peace treaty is signed

David Lloyd George, the British Prime Minister who negotiated the Anglo-Irish Treaty.

In October 1921, an Irish delegation went to London to arrange a treaty with the British government. This delegation consisted of Michael Collins, Arthur Griffith, George Gavan Duffy, Eamonn Duggan and Robert Barton. De Valera, the president of the Dáil, did not go. This caused a major surprise at the time. The Irish group had no experience of talks at this level. They faced an experienced British team which included Lloyd George, Winston Churchill and Austen Chamberlain. The Treaty drawn up by the British contained the following points:

- The twenty-six counties of Ireland were to be given 'Dominion Status'. Under this, Ireland would become a member of the British Commonwealth and would be known as the 'Irish Free State'.
- While the Irish Free State would have its own government, parliament and army, members of the parliament would have to take an oath of allegiance to the king of England.
- The British army was to remain in possession of certain Irish ports which were known as the 'Treaty Ports'.
- This treaty only covered the twenty-six counties of Southern Ireland, as the Government of Ireland Act (1920) had set up a separate parliament in Belfast under the British king. However, a boundary commission was to be set up with the task of redrawing the border between North and South.

The Irish delegation, under severe pressure from Lloyd George, signed the Treaty on 6 December 1921. They now had to convince the Irish at home that acceptance of the Treaty was the only way forward.

Test your knowledge

1 Why did both sides want a truce?
2 Name the members of the Irish delegation who went to London to negotiate a treaty in October 1921.
3 State two terms of the Treaty.
4 Why was the Boundary Commission set up?
5 Do you think the Irish delegation performed well? Give reasons for you answer.

Country divided over Treaty

When the Irish group arrived back in Ireland after signing the Treaty, they found a sharply divided country. Most ordinary people were relieved that the war had ended; however, others saw the Treaty as a 'sell-out' to the British.

The debate on the Treaty began in the Dáil on 14 December 1921. De Valera was against the Treaty. He objected to the oath of allegiance and would only accept a full Irish Republic. Those supporting de Valera included Austin Stack, Cathal Brugha and Erskine Childers.

Michael Collins and Arthur Griffith strongly defended the Treaty. They saw it as the best deal there was in the circumstances. The only alternative to acceptance of the Treaty was the renewal of war. They also argued that the Treaty was a good beginning along the road to greater freedom. It would, in Collins' words give Ireland 'the freedom to win freedom'.

The vote on the Treaty was taken in the Dáil on 7 January 1922: sixty-four voted for it and fifty-seven against. De Valera resigned from the presidency of the Dáil and was replaced by Arthur Griffith. The new Free State government now prepared to take over from the British who were leaving the country. The IRA was also bitterly divided over the Treaty. While one faction supported Collins and became absorbed into a new national army, another faction prepared to take up arms against old colleagues who supported the Treaty.

The Civil War begins

In April 1922, the anti-Treaty IRA or *Irregulars*, under the command of Rory O'Connor, occupied the Four Courts in Dublin.

As tensions were mounting in the city and in the country, both sides attempted to avoid a war which would involve the murder of friends and comrades. They agreed to hold an election in June 1922. This election, however, only increased the tension and the bitterness: fifty-eight pro-Treaty TDs were elected while only thirty-five anti-Treaty TDs were returned. Matters came to a head when Sir Henry Wilson, a hardline Unionist and military adviser to the Northern Ireland government, was assassinated in London by two IRA men.

The shelling of the Four Courts, during 1922.

On 28 June, Michael Collins, under pressure from the British government, ordered the Free State army to shell the Four Courts. The Civil War had begun.

Dublin was the first scene of the fighting. The fierce street battles, which took place around O'Connell Street, ended in the total defeat of the anti-Treaty forces, Cathal Brugha being among the casualties.

Irregular soldiers surrendering to Free State forces in Dublin during the Civil War.

After their defeat in Dublin, the Irregulars held out in Munster. By the end of August 1922, after ferocious fighting, all the towns of that province were in Free State hands.

The deaths of two leaders

In the meantime, the Free State government had lost its two leading figures. On 12 August 1922, Arthur Griffith died suddenly of exhaustion at the age of fifty. Ten days later, Michael Collins was shot dead in an ambush in Co. Cork. His death at the age of thirty-two was a tragic loss to the new state.

The funeral of Arthur Griffith passing through Dublin.

Many Republicans are executed

William T. Cosgrave became the new leader of the Free State government. Cosgrave and his leading ministers in the Free State government, Kevin O'Higgins and Richard Mulcahy, were determined to deal severely with the Irregulars. They set up military courts with the death penalty for those found carrying arms. Under these new laws, from December 1922 many Republicans, including Erskine Childers and Rory O'Connor, were executed and some 12,000 other were interned. The Irregulars in turn attacked members of the Dáil and Senate. The Civil War had now entered its bloodiest phase.

The Civil War ends

By the spring of 1923, the Free State government had gained firm control over the country. General Liam Lynch, the commander-in-chief of the IRA, was killed in action on 10 April and was succeeded by Frank Aiken. The Republican leaders now realised that they could not win the Civil War. Stocks of arms and ammunition were very low, and the sympathy of the general public was not with them. The IRA laid down their arms and went into hiding. The Civil War had ended.

Although the war was over, the bitterness and hatred caused by it were to last for many years to come. Some 600 people had died and there had been widespread damage to property and communications. The Free State government under W.T. Cosgrave had a difficult task ahead of them—to restore order and unity to a bitterly divided country.

Test your knowledge

1 Why did de Valera object to the Treaty?
2 How did Collins and Griffith defend the Treaty?
3 What was the view of the IRA on the Treaty?
4 What was the first incident in the Civil War?
5 What two Free State leaders died in 1922?
6 How did W.T. Cosgrave and his ministers deal with the threat to law and order posed by the Irregulars?
7 Why do you think the Irregulars lost the Civil War?
8 State two effects of the Civil War.

Chapter 68: Review

• The Sinn Féin MPs elected in December 1918 refused to take their seats at Westminster but met in the Mansion House in Dublin and set up the First Dáil on 21 January 1919.

• The War of Independence began on the same day that the first Dail met when the IRA attacked a group of policemen near Soloheadbeg in Co. Tipperary.

• In March 1920 the British government sent the Black and Tans to Ireland to combat the IRA. In August a smaller force known as the Auxiliaries was sent. Both these groups used widespread terror against the IRA and the civilian population.

• The IRA organised themselves into Flying Columns and carried out a guerrilla warfare against the British forces in the country.

• The year 1920 was the worst in the War of Independence. Two Lord Mayors of Cork, Tomás MacCurtain and Terence MacSwiney, died, Kevin Barry was executed; and on Bloody Sunday, 21 November, the Black and Tans opened fire on a crowd in Croke Park in retaliation for the assassination of British spies at the hands of Michael Collins' hit squad earlier that morning.

• The British parliament passed the Government of Ireland Act in 1920 which gave Northern Ireland its own parliament.

• By the summer of 1921 both sides in the War of Independence were anxious for peace. In July 1921, a truce was arranged and de Valera went to London for peace talks. These talks failed but further discussions were arranged for the following October.

• In October 1921, an Irish delegation, including Michael Collins and Arthur Griffith, travelled to London to draw up a treaty with Britain. Under pressure from the British prime minister, Lloyd George, the Irish signed a treaty on 6 December. The twenty-six counties of Ireland were given dominion status as a member of the British Commonwealth under the title the Irish Free State.

• The Anglo-Irish Treaty was debated in Dáil Éireann between 14 December 1921 and 7 January 1922. Michael Collins and Arthur Griffith defended the Treaty, while those against it included de Valera, Cathal Brugha and Erskine Childers. When the vote was taken on 7 January 1922, sixty-four voted for the Treaty while fifty-seven voted against.

• The Anti-Treaty IRA or Irregulars occupied the Four Courts in Dublin in April 1922. On 28 June the Free State army shelled the Four Courts—this was the beginning of the Civil War.

• In August 1922, two Free State leaders, Arthur Griffith and Michael Collins, died and W.T. Cosgrave became leader of the government.

• The Free State government set up military courts with the death penalty for those found carrying arms. Under this new law, many Republicans, including Erskine Childers and Rory O'Connor, were tried and executed.

• By the spring of 1923, the Free State government had gained firm control over the country. The Irregulars lacked the support which the IRA received from the local people during the War of Independence. As a result they laid down their arms and the Civil War came to an end in April 1923.

The Irish Free State: 1923–32

After the end of the Civil War in 1923, W.T. Cosgrave and his government faced many problems in building up the new state. In this chapter we will look at the main problems facing the government and the efforts made to deal with them.

The government of the Free State

W.T. Cosgrave, President of the Executive Council of the Irish Free State between 1922 and 1932.

A new set of laws, or *Constitution*, was drawn up in 1922 which outlined the structures of the new state. The following are the main points of the 1922 Constitution.

- The *Oireachtas* or parliament consisted of two assemblies: the *Dáil*, with TDs elected by the people, and the *Senate* which consisted of some members elected by the Dáil and others nominated by the leader of the government.
- Members of the Dáil and Senate were elected by a system of *proportional representation*.
- The head of the government was to be known as the *president*. He was leader of a cabinet of ministers known as the *executive council*.
- All members of the Oireachtas were required to take an oath of allegiance to the king of England as head of the Commonwealth. The king's representative in Ireland was to be known as the *Governor-General*.

Law and order

Ireland had not experienced peace and order for many years. The Civil War had left behind a deeply divided country. The restoration of law and order was, therefore, a high priority for the new government. This important task was in the hands of Kevin O'Higgins, the young and energetic Minister for Home Affairs. O'Higgins took the following measures to restore law and order.

Kevin O'Higgins, Minister for Home Affairs in Cosgrave's government.

The Garda Síochána, the police force which replaced the R.I.C. in 1923.

- In 1923, he set up an unarmed police force known as the *Gárda Síochána* which replaced the old Royal Irish Constabulary.
- He brought in the Courts of Justice Act (1924) which re-organised the system of law courts in the country.
- He introduced harsh laws to deal with the IRA. These included Public Safety Acts which gave wide powers of arrest to the police and provided for the death penalty in certain cases.

As a result of the steps taken by Kevin O'Higgins, order and stability gradually returned to the countryside. O'Higgins also played a key role in dealing effectively with another threat to the authority of the government. This threat took the form of the so-called *Army Mutiny*.

The Army Mutiny

At the end of the Civil War, the national army consisted of 60,000 men. The government decided to reduce the size of the army once peace was restored. This move was resented by some army officers who were also dissatisfied by the lack of progress towards a republic.

In March 1924, a number of these officers sent an ultimatum to the government insisting that their views be put into operation. O'Higgins acted swiftly to deal with the situation. He demanded the resignation of the senior officers involved. The Minister for Defence, Richard Mulcahy, also resigned. The national army was never again to question the authority of a government.

Test your knowledge

1 Who was the leader of the first government of the Irish Free State?
2 Name the two houses of the Oireachtas. How were their members elected?
3 Who was the Governor-General?
4 Who was the Minister for Home Affairs in the Free State government?
5 State two measures taken by O'Higgins to restore law and order after the Civil War.
6 Why were some army officers dissatisfied with the government?
7 How did the attempted army mutiny end? What was its long-term significance?

Ireland and the Commonwealth

Desmond FitzGerald, Minister for External Affairs in the Cumann na nGaedheal government.

The restoration of law and order was not the only achievement of the government of the Irish Free State. It was to play an important part in gaining more independence for Commonwealth countries by loosening the ties between them and Great Britain. In 1931, an important act was passed known as the *Statute of Westminster*. This stated that Britain and other members of the Commonwealth were now on an equal footing with Britain and that Commonwealth countries had the right to reject legislation passed by the Westminster parliament on their behalf.

However, for most ordinary people the most pressing concern was whether their living standards would improve under the new Free State government.

The economy

Despite all the hopes of a better world with the coming of independence, life for the ordinary citizen remained much as it had been under British rule. For most people, the standard of living remained low. There was a severe housing shortage, wages were low, and public health was a matter of some concern. For many people, emigration remained the only alternative to a life of poverty at home.

As Ireland was a rural country, agriculture was the biggest industry. Patrick Hogan was appointed Minister for Agriculture. He encouraged the export of Irish agricultural produce and took steps to improve the quality of Irish goods. As a result of these policies, Irish agricultural exports greatly increased during the 1920s. Hogan also set up the Agricultural Credit Corporation (ACC) in 1927. This gave loans to farmers who wished to improve their land.

Industry posed a different problem. With the exception of Belfast, Ireland did not have any large-scale industrial centre. In industry, as well as in agriculture, the government favoured the practice of free trade between countries. It was slow to protect Irish industries from outside competition by means of tariffs.

The greatest economic achievement of these years was the establishment of the Electricity Supply Board (ESB) in 1927 and the construction of a hydroelectric scheme at Ardnacrusha on the River Shannon. This was a giant project for the new state. It came into operation in

The construction of the Shannon Hydroelectric Scheme.

October 1929 at a cost of £5 million. It provided electricity for both Irish factories and homes.

Test your knowledge

1 What is meant by the Statute of Westminster?
2 What do you regard as the greatest economic achievement of the Irish Free State in the 1920s?
3 What do you understand by the term 'free trade'?
4 Name two organisations set up in 1927. State the purpose of each.
5 What problems remained for the ordinary citizen after independence?

Political developments

Within the Dáil, the Cumann na nGaedheal Party formed the government, and the Labour Party, together with a large number of independent TDs, became the opposition. Sinn Féin, under the leadership of Eamon de Valera, refused to enter the Dáil. They did not recognise the Irish Free State and would not take the oath of allegiance to the king as head of the Commonwealth.

As conditions in the country returned to normal, de Valera realised that he and his followers had little or no influence as long as they remained outside the Dáil. At the Sinn Féin Ard Fheis in March 1926, de Valera proposed that Sinn Féin TDs should enter the Dáil if the oath of allegiance was abolished. When this proposal was rejected, de Valera resigned from Sinn Féin, taking many followers with him. In May 1926 he founded a new party—Fianna Fáil. The new party had three main aims:

- To establish a 32-county Irish Republic.
- To restore the Irish language as the spoken language of the country.
- To make Ireland self-sufficient by protecting native agriculture and industry from outside competition.

1927: A dramatic year

A general election took place in June 1927. As a result, Cumann na nGaedheal won forty-six seats, Fianna Fáil forty-four, Labour twenty-two. The remaining seats went to small parties and independents. Cosgrave, however, had no difficulty in forming a government because Fianna Fáil would not enter the Dáil while the oath of allegiance remained.

De Valera leading a group of Fianna Fáil TDs from the Dáil after their refusal to take the oath of allegiance.

On Sunday, 10 July 1927, an event occurred which shocked the Irish Free State and led to important changes. On that day the Minister for Home Affairs, Kevin O'Higgins, was shot dead as he returned home from Mass. Although nobody was convicted, it was generally believed that the IRA was responsible.

As a result of O'Higgins' murder, the government immediately brought in two very important acts:

- *The Public Safety Act:* This was a very severe measure which gave large-scale powers of arrest to the Gardaí and set up special courts with the death penalty for those found illegally carrying arms.
- *The Electoral Amendment Act:* This stated that those standing for election to the Dáil or Senate must swear to take their seats if elected, and if they did not take their seats within three months of being elected, they would lose them.

A republican election poster in the elections of 1927.

This last act posed a major problem for Fianna Fáil. They were now forced to enter the Dáil even though they had to take the oath of allegiance. Fianna Fáil's entry into the Dáil was followed by another general election in September 1927.

While Cumann na nGaedheal still formed the government with sixty-one seats, Fianna Fáil became the official opposition with fifty-seven seats. The supporters and opposers of the Treaty now faced one another for the first time within Dáil Éireann. All was set for a stormy period in Irish politics.

The rise of Fianna Fáil (1927–32)

During these years, Fianna Fáil went from strength to strength while support for Cumann na nGaedheal was falling. This growth in support for Fianna Fáil was due to the following reasons.

- Fianna Fáil was a very well-organised party and carefully built up support throughout the country. Sean Lemass and Gerard Boland played important parts in this.
- The effects of the Great Depression were felt in Ireland after 1929 and made the Cumann na nGaedheal government very unpopular.
- In 1931, de Valera founded the *Irish Press* newspaper to spread Fianna Fáil ideas.
- The tough security measures taken by Cumann na nGaedhael made the government unpopular. This played into the hands of Fianna Fáil which was especially supported by those who favoured a republic.

All these factors would be of great importance in the run-up to the general election which was due in 1932.

The 1932 general election

The year 1932 opened with a general election in Ireland. The campaign aroused tremendous excitement among the people as the two main parties bitterly fought out the chief issues of the election.

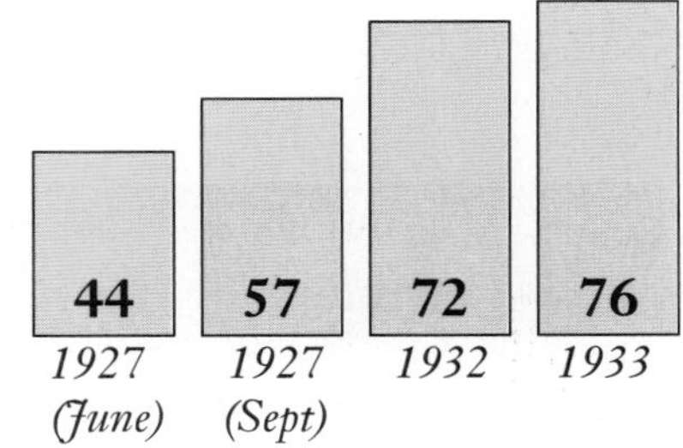

Seats won by Fianna Fáil 1927–1933

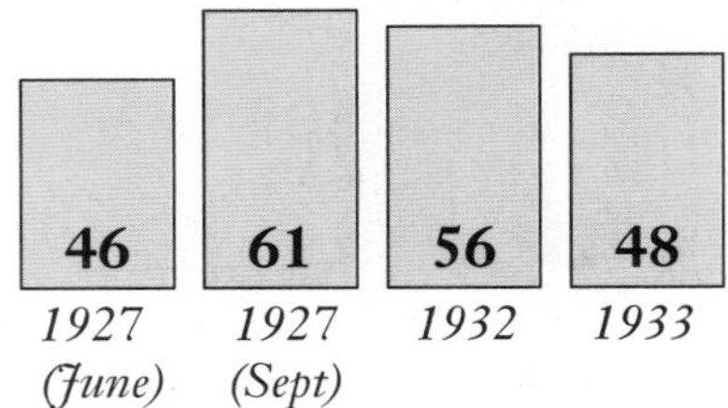

Seats won by Cumann na nGaedheal 1927–1933

The chart shows us the results of the general election. Although Fianna Fáil won seventy-two seats, the party did not have an overall majority and was only able to form a government with the support of the Labour Party. This was to mark the beginning of sixteen years of continuous Fianna Fáil government. In the following year de Valera called another election and secured an overall majority for Fianna Fáil. The party was to remain in power until 1948.

A Fianna Fáil election poster from 1932.

A Cumann na nGaedheal election poster in 1932.

Test your knowledge

1. What party formed the first government of the Irish Free State after 1922?
2. Who formed the opposition in the Dáil from 1922 to 1927?
3. Why did Sinn Féin TDs refuse to enter the Dáil?
4. What happened at the Sinn Féin Ard Fheis in March 1926?
5. Why did the government bring in a Public Safety Act in 1927?
6. Why did Fianna Fáil enter the Dáil in 1927?
7. State two reasons why Fianna Fáil grew in strength in the years 1927–32.
8. What was the outcome of the 1932 election?

Chapter 69: Review

• From 1922, W.T. Cosgrave and his new party, Cumann na nGaedheal, formed the government of the Irish Free State. A new Constitution was drawn up which stated that all members of the Dáil or parliament had to take an oath of allegiance to the king of England as head of the Commonwealth. Because of this, de Valera and Sinn Féin refused to enter the Dáil.

• The new Free State government was very concerned about law and order. The Minister for Home Affairs, Kevin O'Higgins, set up the Garda Síochána in 1923 and re-organised the system of law courts. He also dealt firmly with a group of army officers in 1924 when faced with an incident called the 'Army Mutiny'.

• During the 1920s, Ireland, together with other dominions, tried to achieve greater freedom for themselves within the British Commonwealth. In 1931, an act called the Statute of Westminster was passed. This made each dominion equal with Britain and gave each one the right to reject laws affecting them passed by the Westminster parliament.

• The Cumann na nGaedheal government supported the practice of free trade between countries—it did not favour the protection of Irish agriculture or industry. The great industrial achievement of the 1920s was the setting up of the ESB in 1927 and the construction of the Shannon Hydroelectric Scheme at Ardnacrusha.

• Between 1927 and 1932 Fianna Fáil was the main opposition in the Dáil and grew from strength to strength. They built up support throughout the country and set up their own newspaper—the *Irish Press*—in 1931.

• At the general election of 1932 Fianna Fáil won 72 seats, Cumann na nGaedheal 56. De Valera did not have an overall majority but was able to form a government with the support of the Labour Party.

CHAPTER 70 The Age of de Valera

A peaceful transfer of power

When the Dáil met on 9 March 1932, many people expected some trouble with the change of government. The wheel had turned full circle—those who had been on the losing side of the Civil War ten years before were now about to take over the government of the country. In fact, some Fianna Fáil TDs had guns hidden in their pockets as they went into the Dáil on the eventful day.

However, people's fears proved groundless as Cumann na nGaedheal peacefully handed over power to Fianna Fáil. This clearly showed that democracy was now firmly rooted in the Irish Free State.

The Fianna Fáil government which came to power in 1932.

De Valera dismantles the Treaty

De Valera addressing the League of Nations in Geneva. As well as leading the government, he also served as Minister for External Affairs. At Geneva he called for world peace, disarmament and respect for the rights of small nations like Ireland.

As soon as de Valera came to power, he set about dismantling the Anglo-Irish Treaty. He took the following steps to move Ireland towards a republic.

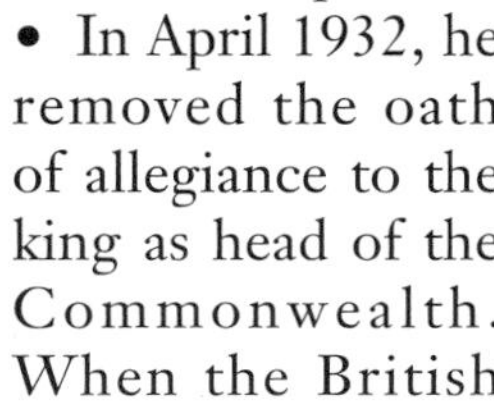

- In April 1932, he removed the oath of allegiance to the king as head of the Commonwealth. When the British government protested that the abolition of the oath broke the Treaty of 1921, de Valera ignored their protests.
- He set about downgrading the role of the Governor-General, the king's representative in Ireland. De Valera and his cabinet boycotted social functions at which the Governor-General was present and the office was eventually abolished in 1937.
- As the Senate of the Irish Free State opposed these measures, de Valera had it abolished in 1936.
- In the same year, a great opportunity arose for de Valera when King Edward VIII of England abdicated because of his proposed marriage to an American divorcee. De Valera used this crisis to bring in the External Relations Act of 1936, which had the effect of removing the influence of the king from the Irish Free State.

Test your knowledge

1 Why do you think many people expected trouble with the change of government in 1932?
2 How was it clear that democracy was firmly established in the Irish Free State?
3 What was the first step taken by de Valera in demolishing the Treaty?
4 How did de Valera treat the office of Governor-General?
5 Why did he abolish the Senate?
6 How did de Valera use the abdication of King Edward VIII for his own purposes?

A new constitution

By 1937, de Valera had succeeded in dismantling the Anglo-Irish Treaty and moving Ireland further towards a republic. The next step was taken when a new Constitution was drawn up in 1937. This was to replace the Constitution of 1922. The new Constitution *(Bunreacht na hÉireann)*, accepted by the people in a referendum in 1937, contained no references to the king of England and made Ireland a republic in everything but name.

Read the following extracts from the Constitution and then answer the questions which follow.

Working with evidence

Bunreacht na hÉireann
(The Irish Constitution), 1937

Article 2
The national territory consists of the whole island of Ireland, its islands and territorial seas.

Article 5
Ireland is a sovereign, independent, democratic state.

Article 8
1. *The Irish language as the national language is the first official language.*
2. *The English language is recognised as a second official language.*

Article 40
All citizens shall, as human persons, be held equal before the law...

Article 41
1. *The State recognises the family as the natural primary and fundamental unit group of society...*
2. *In particular, the State recognises that by her life within the home, woman gives to the State a support without which the common good cannot be achieved.*
3. *The State pledges itself to guard with special care the institution of marriage, on which the family is founded, and to protect it against attack.*
   No law shall be enacted providing for the grant of a dissolution of marriage.

1 What type of state did the Irish people accept in the 1937 Constitution?
2 What was the provision in the Constitution regarding the Irish language?
3 Which article of the Constitution guaranteed equality before the law for all citizens?

4 Would you agree that the family was singled out for special praise and protection in de Valera's Constitution? Support your answer with quotations.
5 Quote the extract from the Constitution which banned the granting of divorce.
6 What was contained in the Constitution concerning the role of women in the home?

The Blueshirts

Election meetings in Ireland at this time were stormy affairs which often ended in violence. The IRA constantly disrupted Cumann na nGaedheal meetings. In response to this, a group of ex-army officers set up an organisation known as the *Army Comrades Association* to protect these meetings from IRA interference. Because of the uniform they came to wear from March 1933, this group was known as the *Blueshirts*.

General Eoin O'Duffy addressing a Blueshirt rally.

The Blueshirt leader was Eoin O'Duffy who had been dismissed by de Valera from his post as commissioner of the Gardaí. The Blueshirts organised meetings and marches throughout the country. Because of their uniform and military-style parades, together with their strong opposition to Communism, many people at the time saw similarities between them and the Fascist movements which were then springing up in Europe.

A Blueshirt parade.

De Valera was determined, however, to clamp down on the Blueshirts. In August 1933, the government banned a big parade to Leinster House in Dublin which was planned by the Blueshirts to commemorate Michael Collins, Arthur Griffith and Kevin O'Higgins.

In September 1933, the Blueshirts joined Cumann na nGaedheal and a small party called the Centre Party to form a new political party—*Fine Gael*. Eoin O'Duffy became the first leader of Fine Gael.

O'Duffy's extreme views soon embarrassed many within Fine Gael and in September 1934 he was forced to give up the leadership of the party. The Blueshirts eventually declined as a movement and O'Duffy led a group of them to fight on the side of General Franco in the Spanish Civil War.

The Economic War (1932–38)

When Fianna Fáil came to power in 1932, they were committed to ending the *land annuities* to the British government. These were repayments made by Irish farmers of loans they received from previous British governments to purchase land. Britain responded to de Valera's refusal to pay the land annuities by placing a twenty per cent tariff on Irish agricultural exports. The Irish government responded by placing duties on British goods coming into Ireland. This dispute, which lasted until 1938, became known as the *Economic War*.

The Economic War had disastrous effects for Ireland. Farmers in particular suffered and many of them had to slaughter their cattle because they were unable to sell them. The value of Irish agricultural exports fell from over £38 million in 1929 to £14 million in 1935. The whole Irish economy suffered and unemployment soared.

By 1938, both governments agreed that the Economic War had gone on long enough. Discussions began in London in March 1938 which led to a settlement of the dispute. Under the terms of the Anglo-Irish Agreement, it was agreed that Ireland would pay a once-off payment of £10 million to cover the outstanding land annuity debts. The most important aspect of this agreement, however, was the return of the Treaty Ports (Spike Island,

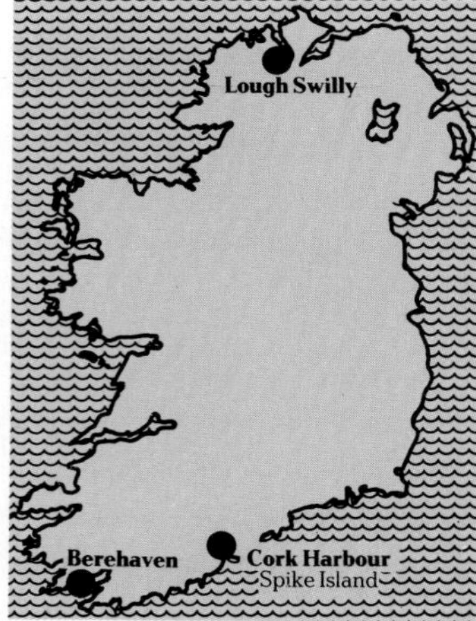

The Treaty Ports.

British troops leaving Spike Island.

Berehaven and Lough Swilly) to the control of the Irish Free State. Without these, Ireland could not have remained neutral in the war which was about to break out in Europe.

Test your knowledge

1. Why were the Blueshirts founded?
2. Who was the leader of the Blueshirts?
3. Why did many people see similarities between the Blueshirts and continental Fascist movements?
4. How did de Valera's government deal with the Blueshirts?
5. What were the land annuities?
6. What was the Economic War? How did it begin?
7. What effect had the Economic War on Irish agriculture?
8. What was the most important part of the Anglo-Irish Agreement? Why was this so?

A state of emergency (1939–45)

When World War II broke out in Europe in September 1939, the government of the Irish Free State declared that Southern Ireland would remain neutral. Two main reasons were put forward for this decision.

- As a small nation, the Irish Free State was open to attack by stronger powers.
- Partition: the continued division of the country ruled out any possibility that the de Valera government could enter the war on Britain's side.

The policy of *neutrality* was only made possible by the return of the Treaty Ports from Great Britain in 1938.

A *state of emergency* was declared giving the government extensive powers to ensure the maintenance of neutrality. Strict censorship of radio and newspapers was imposed. To meet any possible threat to neutrality from the pro-German IRA, internment was introduced under the terms of the Offences against the State Act (1941). The size of the national army was increased in preparation for a possible invasion and voluntary Local Defence Forces (LDFs) were established.

Life in Ireland during the Emergency

Rationing of essential items brought home the hardships of war to the ordinary people of Ireland. This was necessary because the disruption of shipping brought about shortages of food and fuel. A new Department of Supplies under the direction of Seán Lemass was established to organise the fair distribution of scarce commodities.

Stockpiling turf in the Phoenix Park, Dublin, during the Emergency.

NUGGET BOOT POLISH
Please use sparingly supplies are restricted
NUGGET
The Supreme Polish
★ We suggest its use on alternate days only and a brush up every day

Sparing the polish: a contemporary advertisement.

Ration books covering items such as tea, sugar and clothing were issued to each household in the country. Farmers were compelled by law to produce a certain amount of crops. In the cities, gas was strictly rationed and the gas inspector (known as the 'glimmer man') could be seen on his rounds.

Trains were largely run on turf, and private motor cars were rarely seen because of the scarcity of petrol.

People in Cork being told how to use gas masks in case of attack.

However inconvenient wartime shortages were, Ireland was spared the horrors of widespread bombing experienced by her European neighbours and Northern Ireland. Southern Ireland's worst experience of civilian casualties occurred when the Germans bombed Dublin in error on the night of 30 May 1941, with the biggest number of casualties occurring in the North Strand.

The scene of destruction following the German bombing of the North Strand.

The ending of the war

When World War II ended in the autumn of 1945, the Irish Free State had succeeded in maintaining its neutrality. At home, the Emergency produced greater unity and co-operation among people and helped to heal some of the Civil War divisions. To the world at large, neutrality proved Ireland's ability to stand alone as a small nation.

There were also some disadvantages attached to Irish neutrality. While other European countries were to take part in the move towards European unity after the war, Ireland was to remain aloof. Partition was further strengthened as Northern Ireland, which had taken part in the war, drew even closer to Great Britain.

However, through its policy of neutrality, Southern Ireland had avoided the horrors of war. This was its greatest advantage.

Test your knowledge

1 What made Irish neutrality in World War II possible?
2 State two reasons for Irish neutrality.
3 A state of emergency was declared in Ireland. What forms did this take?
4 What new department was set up during the war years? Who directed it?
5 Who was the 'glimmer man'?
6 State two effects which the policy of neutrality had on Ireland.

Chapter 70: Review

• Once de Valera came to power he set about demolishing the Anglo-Irish Treaty: he abolished the Oath of Allegiance; downgraded the role of Governor-General; and after the Abdication Crisis in Britain he removed the influence of the king from the Irish Free State.

• The Blueshirts grew out of the Army Comrades Association which was set up to protect Cumann na nGaedheal political meetings from IRA interference. Eoin O'Duffy took over the command of the Blueshirts. In September 1933, this group joined with Cumann na nGaedheal and Dillon's Centre Party to form Fine Gael.

• The Economic War was a tariff war between Britain and Ireland which began when de Valera refused to pay the land annuities to the British government. This disagreement had a terrible effect on Irish agriculture. It came to an end in 1938 when the Anglo-Irish Agreement was signed.

• A new constitution was drawn up by de Valera in 1937; this contained no references to the king of England and made Ireland a republic in everything but name.

• When war broke out in Europe in September 1939, the Irish Free State declared its neutrality. This policy was only made possible by the return of the Treaty Ports from Great Britain in 1938.

• A state of emergency was declared giving the government extensive powers to ensure the maintenance of neutrality.

• The wartime Emergency resulted in a shortage of essential goods. Ration books covering items such as tea, sugar and clothing were issued to each household in the country. This rationing was directed by Seán Lemass who became Minister for Supplies.

• While neutrality saved the Irish Free State from the horrors of war it also had disadvantages: the country was isolated internationally after the war, and it strengthened the partition of the island.

CHAPTER 71

From Depression to Prosperity: 1945–66

A new party is formed

The end of World War II in 1945 was not followed by an immediate ending of emergency conditions in Ireland. Food and fuel were in short supply and large numbers of people continued to emigrate. Many people were tired of Fianna Fáil which had been in government since 1932. The opposition parties—Fine Gael and Labour—were both weak at this time and did not appeal to the voters at large.

Seán MacBride, the leader of Clann na Poblachta.

A new political party was formed in 1946—*Clann na Poblachta*. This new party was very republican. It also supported social and economic changes such as a huge housing programme, improved health facilities and free education. Its leader was Seán MacBride, a former chief-of-staff of the IRA. Support for the new party rapidly increased as it promised to tackle many of the country's most pressing problems.

A general election was held in February 1948. Examine closely the table below showing the results of this election.

RESULTS OF 1948 GENERAL ELECTION	
Fianna Fáil	68
Fine Gael	31
Labour	14
Clann na Poblachta	10
Clann na Talmhan	7
National Labour	5
Independents	12

The first inter-party government (1948–51)

After the 1948 general election, the parties opposed to Fianna Fáil agreed to form an *inter-party* or *coalition government*. The main parties in the new government were Fine Gael, Labour, and Clann na Poblachta. John A. Costello of Fine Gael became Taoiseach; William Norton, the Labour leader, became Tánaiste or deputy prime minister; Seán MacBride, the leader of Clann na Poblachta, became Minister for External Affairs.

The first inter-party government is remembered for the following achievements.

John A. Costello, who became Taoiseach in the first inter-party government.

- In 1949, the *Republic of Ireland Act* was passed which officially declared the twenty-six counties of Ireland a republic and broke the last links with the British Commonwealth.
- Two important semi-state organisations were set up to promote Irish industry and trade—the *Industrial Development Authority (IDA)* and *Coras Trachtála*.
- The Anglo-Irish Trade Agreement of 1948 brought about higher prices for Irish agricultural exports to England.
- A national programme of building was begun. By 1950, 12,000 new houses were being built each year.
- Under the direction of Noel Browne, the Minister for Health, a programme for eliminating the killer disease, tuberculosis, was put into force. At the time, TB caused the deaths of 2,000–4,000 young people each year. Sanatoria were built throughout the country to help those with TB.

The fall of the government

Dr Noel Browne, a member of Clann na Poblachta and Minister for Health in the first inter-party government.

The Minister for Health, Noel Browne, proposed free hospital and health care for all mothers and their children. This was known as the *Mother and Child Scheme*. The doctors and the bishops strongly opposed this scheme of state medicine for everybody and put pressure on the government to drop it.

When the Taoiseach, John A. Costello, and a majority of the government agreed to abandon the scheme, Noel Browne resigned both from the government and from Clann na Poblachta. Other Clann na Poblachta TDs also resigned from the party. As a result of this, the government lost its majority in the Dáil and a general election was called in May 1951.

For many people, the Mother and Child Scheme crisis had shown the power and influence of the Catholic Church in Ireland.

Ireland in the 1950s

Fianna Fáil under de Valera were in power again from 1951 to 1954. Between 1954 and 1957, a second inter-party government under John A. Costello took over, and in 1957 Fianna Fáil again returned to power, this time with a large majority in the Dáil.

A march in protest against unemployment in Dublin in the 1950s.

Despite the frequent changes of government during the 1950s there was little change in the living conditions of ordinary people. Unemployment was widespread and the only option open to many young people was to leave Ireland in search of work. During the 1950s emigration reached huge levels not known since the nineteenth century. Some people wondered if independence was worth the struggle between 1916 and 1921 if, thirty years later, the country could not provide a living for its people.

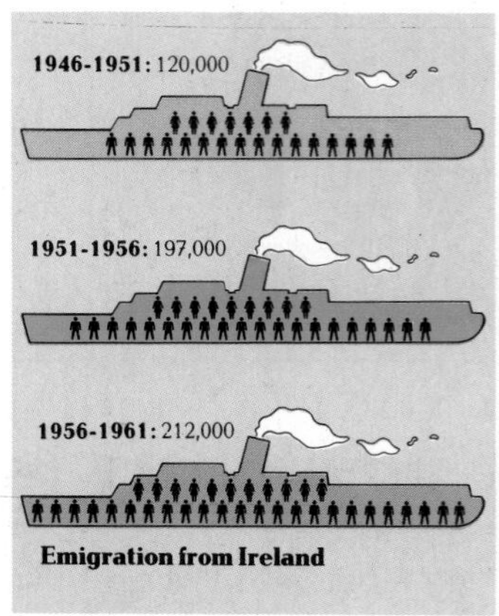

The number of emigrants from Ireland increased steadily during these years.

Eamon de Valera, President of Ireland 1959–73.

In 1959, de Valera, who at this time was seventy-seven years of age, resigned as Taoiseach and was elected President of Ireland. Under his successor, Seán Lemass, great changes came about. These changes were to result in a bright new future in the 1960s.

Test your knowledge

1. What new party was formed in 1946? Who was its leader?
2. Name the main parties which formed the first inter-party government.
3. What was the Republic of Ireland Act (1949)?
4. Why did the first inter-party government fall from power in 1951?
5. Why was emigration so high in the 1950s?
6. To what office was de Valera elected in 1959?
7. Who became Taoiseach in 1959?

The 1960s: A time for prosperity

Seán Lemass, Taoiseach 1959–66.

Seán Lemass, who was Taoiseach from 1959 to 1966, saw a great need for Ireland to industrialise in order to create jobs for her people. He believed that the government had a vital part to play in this.

In 1958, T.K. Whitaker, the secretary of the Department of Finance, drew up a plan known as the *First Programme for Economic Expansion*. Lemass put this plan for the economy into action.

T.K. Whitaker, whose First Programme for Economic Expansion brought about great changes in Ireland in the 1960s.

Under Whitaker's plan, grants were given to farmers and businessmen to help them produce more goods. Big foreign industries were attracted to Ireland by generous grants and tax concessions. A new town was built at Shannon, Co. Clare, where the first industrial estate was developed.

Due to government loans and generous tax-free concessions, many new factories were set up in Ireland during the 1960s.

POPULATION CHANGES IN THE REPUBLIC OF IRELAND

Year	Population	
1951	2,961,000	*During the 1950s the fall*
1956	2,898,000	*in population continued.*
1961	2,818,000	*This trend was reversed*
1966	2,884,000	*during the economic*
1971	2,978,000	*prosperity of the 1960s.*

During the 1950s the fall in population continued. This trend was reversed during the economic prosperity of the 1960s.

As a result of Lemass' efforts, many new jobs were created in the 1960s. Emigration was greatly reduced and, as the chart shows, the Irish population began to increase for the first time since the Famine. Two other economic plans followed, one in 1963 and another in 1969, but they were not as successful as the first.

Economic progress was not the only type of change experienced in the Lemass era. There were also significant changes in education and in society at large.

Great changes in education

Donogh O'Malley, the Fianna Fáil Minister for Education responsible for the introduction of free secondary education in the Republic of Ireland.

One of the main advances in the 1960s came in education. Donogh O'Malley, the Minister for Education, brought in free secondary schooling for all, and free transport for those who lived at a distance from schools. Grants were also provided for the building of new secondary schools.

All of these changes resulted in a huge increase in the numbers receiving a secondary education. By the late 1960s, 144,000 pupils were attending secondary schools—this was almost double the figure of ten years previously. Comprehensive schools and Regional Technical Colleges were also introduced at this time. These developments in education were to have far-reaching results.

School buses had a vital part to play in the greater availability of education throughout the Irish countryside from the 1960s onwards.

The 1960s: Great social change in Ireland

The 1960s were years of great social change throughout the Western world. There were new tastes in music and fashion, new attitudes among young people and massive changes in technology and communication. Ireland was part of this changing world.

In these years, the standard of living of most Irish people rose. This was made possible by greater job opportunities and higher wages. A returning emigrant who had left Ireland some years before would have seen great improvements in housing, sanitation, roads and in the diet and clothing of ordinary people.

On New Year's Eve 1961, Telefís Éireann, Ireland's first television station, began broadcasting. More than anything else, television brought Ireland into contact with the outside world and led people to question old attitudes. Travel opportunities increased for most people during these years. Aer Lingus, the national airline, expanded greatly, and more and more people came to own their own cars.

Telefís Éireann's 'Late Late Show', hosted by Gay Byrne, was a powerful influence in the 1960s.

The Catholic Church in Ireland also changed greatly in the 1960s. After the Second Vatican Council, lay people became more involved in Church affairs and many young people began to question the beliefs of the older generation.

Test your knowledge

1 What great need did Seán Lemass see?
2 Who was secretary of the Department of Finance? What plan did he draw up?
3 How was industry attracted to Ireland?
4 What were the results of Lemass' efforts?
5 Name two changes brought about in Irish education in the 1960s.
6 When did television come to Ireland? What effects did it have?

Chapter 71: Review

- Clann na Poblachta, a new political party under the leadership of Seán MacBride, was founded in July 1946. This party stood for great social and economic changes.
- In the general election of 1948, Clann na Poblachta won ten seats in the Dáil. It joined with Fine Gael and Labour to form the first inter-party government. John A. Costello of Fine Gael was the Taoiseach of the new government.
- In 1949, this government passed the Republic of Ireland Act which declared the twenty-six counties of Ireland a republic. A huge housing programme was launched by the government. Noel Browne, the Minister for Health, put a programme for eliminating the killer disease TB into operation.
- Noel Browne proposed a free medical scheme for mothers and their children known as 'The Mother and Child Scheme'. When the doctors and bishops brought pressure on the government to drop this scheme, Browne resigned and at the same time left Clann na Poblachta. As a result the government lost its majority and fell from power in May 1951.
- In the 1950s living standards in Ireland were very low. Unemployment was widespread and emigration reached levels which had not been known since the nineteenth century.
- In 1959, de Valera retired and was replaced as Taoiseach and as leader of Fianna Fáil by Seán Lemass.
- In 1958 T.K. Whitaker, secretary of the Department of Finance, drew up 'The First Programme for Economic Expansion'. Lemass put this plan of industrialisation into operation.
- Industry was attracted to Ireland through grants and tax-free concessions. The first industrial estate was set up at Shannon.
- As a result of Lemass' efforts, many new jobs were created in the 1960s. Emigration was greatly reduced and, for the first time since the Famine, the Irish population began to increase again.
- There were also important changes in education during the 1960s. Donogh O'Malley, Minister for Education, brought in free secondary schooling, and free transport was provided for students living at a distance from the schools.
- The sixties was a time of great social change in Ireland. Living standards rose. In 1961, television came to Ireland for the first time. Travel opportunities also increased greatly.

CHAPTER 72

Ireland: 1966–85

A new Taoiseach

In November 1966, Seán Lemass retired as Taoiseach and leader of Fianna Fáil. Although only Taoiseach since 1959, he had been involved in politics since the War of Independence. His successor as Taoiseach came from a younger generation of Irish politicians. A majority of Fianna Fáil TDs voted for the Minister for Finance, Jack Lynch, to succeed Lemass as leader of the party.

Jack Lynch, who succeeded Seán Lemass as leader of Fianna Fáil in 1966.

During his first two years in office, Jack Lynch's government continued to run a country enjoying economic prosperity. However, the rate of economic growth was slowing down and many critics of the government believed that more could have been done to help the under-privileged in society. Following the example of young people in Europe and America, Socialism became fashionable among Irish students. The Irish Labour Party gained many new recruits, including some prominent figures from universities and the world of broadcasting.

When Jack Lynch called a general election for June 1969 the Labour Party under its leader, Brendan Corish, fielded more candidates than usual and campaigned on a slogan 'The Seventies will be Socialist'. Fianna Fáil campaigned on their record, stressing improvements like Donogh O'Malley's Free Education Scheme. Since the main opposition parties, Fine Gael and Labour, failed to co-operate, Fianna Fáil gained an overall majority although the party vote had fallen since 1965. The position of Jack Lynch within Fianna Fáil was greatly strengthened by this victory and it appeared that he was now set for a secure term of office as Taoiseach. However, soon after the election, serious unrest broke out in Northern Ireland in August 1969.

For the previous year, members of the minority Catholic community were campaigning for equal rights with Protestants. This campaign was known as the *Civil Rights Movement*. Some extreme Protestants were prepared to use any methods to stop this campaign. In August 1969, widespread violence erupted in Belfast and Derry, resulting in many injuries and deaths.

This Northern crisis was to have a serious impact on the government and people of the Republic.

The Arms Crisis

In August 1969, in a famous speech, Jack Lynch hinted at help for Nationalists in Northern Ireland when he said that 'the government can no longer stand by' as Catholic communities were under attack. At the time there was widespread sympathy throughout the Republic for Catholics in Northern Ireland. Many people held simplistic views on Irish unification which took no account of the feelings of Northern Unionists. Within the ruling Fianna Fáil party there were many who held strong Republican views concerning the Northern problem. Some of these included members of the government. Despite his famous speech of August 1969, Lynch hoped to keep the Northern troubles from spreading into the Republic. Government ministers such as Neil Blaney and Kevin Boland believed that he was neglecting Fianna Fáil's aim of Irish unity.

Blaney, Boland, Haughey out of Cabinet

DEEP DIFFERENCES OVER NORTHERN POLICIES

Dramatic announcement by Lynch at 2.50 this morning

GENERAL ELECTION MUST FOLLOW

Most serious crisis since Costello's fall in 1951

Always the same at the Spring Show

NIXON PLEDGES–OUT AGAIN IN 7 WEEKS

Newspaper headlines announcing the dramatic departure of three ministers from Jack Lynch's cabinet on 6 May 1970.

On 6 May 1970, these divisions became public

Charles J. Haughey, one of the ministers dismissed from office by Jack Lynch in May 1970.

when Lynch dismissed two of his ministers, Neil Blaney and Charles Haughey, because they did not fully support government policy on Northern Ireland. Another minister, Kevin Boland, resigned in sympathy with his dismissed colleagues. On 28 May, both Haughey and Blaney were arrested and charged with attempting to import arms and ammunition for use by the IRA in Northern Ireland. The trial which followed became known as the *Arms Trial.* Both of the ex-ministers were found to be not guilty, Blaney in July and Haughey in the following October.

The Arms Crisis caused a sensation in the country and led to deep divisions within Fianna Fáil. Both Blaney and Boland left the party, but Haughey remained on and worked his way up to eventually succeed Lynch as leader in 1979. However, just after the Arms Crisis, Jack Lynch succeeded in remaining in control of Fianna Fáil. Over the following two years, against a background of increasing violence in Northern Ireland, Lynch and the Minister for External Affairs, Dr Patrick Hillery, prepared for an event which would shape the country's future destiny—Ireland's entry into the European Economic Community.

Test your knowledge

1. When did Jack Lynch succeed Seán Lemass as Taoiseach?
2. Name the political belief which became popular among Irish students in the 1960s.
3. What was the slogan of the Irish Labour Party for the general election of 1969?
4. What did the Taoiseach, Jack Lynch, hint at in his famous television speech of August 1969 concerning the Northern 'Troubles'?
5. Why were there divisions in Fianna Fáil in 1969 over Northern Ireland policy?
6. Name the two former government ministers involved in the Arms Trial of 1970.
7. What was the outcome of the trial?
8. Who was Minister for External Affairs in 1970?

Ireland joins the EEC

As far back as 1961, the Irish government of Seán Lemass had applied for full membership of the *European Economic Community* at the same time as Great Britain applied. However, when the French president, General de Gaulle, blocked British entry in January 1963, Ireland could no longer attempt to join because both British and Irish economies were so closely linked. However, in 1969, the new French president, Georges Pompidou, withdrew any objections to British entry and both Ireland and Great Britain re-applied for membership.

The Taoiseach, Jack Lynch, signing the Treaty of Accession to the EEC with the Minister for External Affairs, Patrick Hillery, at his side. Dr Hillery later became Ireland's first EEC Commissioner.

Farmers and businessmen were among those most in favour of Irish entry to the EEC. They argued that it would bring a better market for both agricultural and industrial exports and lead to a greater number of jobs in Ireland. Many trade union leaders were against entry because they believed jobs would be lost when cheaper goods from Europe replaced home-produced products in Irish shops. Although entry did not involve joining any military alliance, some people believed that Ireland's neutrality would be endangered as all of the other EEC states were members of the North Atlantic Treaty Organisation (NATO). When a referendum was held on the question in May 1972, Fianna Fáil and Fine Gael advised the people to vote 'Yes' while the Labour Party called for a 'No' vote.

The result of the referendum was a massive eighty-three per cent vote in favour of Irish entry to the Common Market. This decision confirmed the conditions of entry negotiated by Dr Hillery which had been signed as a Treaty of Accession in January

1972. All was now in place for Ireland to enter the EEC on 1 January 1973. Shortly after this historic occasion, Jack Lynch called a general election to be held the following month.

The coalition in power (1973–77)

Fianna Fáil entered the election campaign highly confident of victory. However, the fact that the party had been in power continuously since 1957 and the divisions during the Arms Trial encouraged the opposition parties to come to an agreement. Fine Gael under Liam Cosgrave and Labour under Brendan Corish produced a Fourteen-Point Manifesto and they agreed to form a coalition government if they had enough seats in the Dáil after the election.

Liam Cosgrave, Taoiseach 1973–77.

Although Fianna Fáil's share of the vote increased slightly since 1969, it lost six seats and fell from power. With a high level of vote transfers between them, Fine Gael and Labour together won an overall majority in the Dáil. The Fine Gael leader, Liam Cosgrave, became Taoiseach and Brendan Corish, the Labour Party leader, was appointed Tánaiste and Minister for Social Welfare. There were ten Fine Gael and five Labour ministers in the new government.

Dr Garret FitzGerald of Fine Gael was Minister for Foreign Affairs. Another important Fine Gael minister was Richard Ryan who was in charge of the Department of Finance at a time when the economy suffered because of a huge increase in oil prices in the Middle East.

The Minister for Posts and Telegraphs, Dr Conor Cruise O'Brien, was the most controversial member of the coalition. He frequently spoke out on the problem of Northern Ireland and condemned the attitudes of many Southern Irish people as being close to the beliefs of the IRA.

Throughout the four years that the coalition was in power, the 'Troubles' in Northern Ireland continued to influence people in the Republic. In 1973, Liam Cosgrave signed an agreement concerning Northern Ireland with the British prime minister, Edward Heath. Known as the *Sunningdale Agreement*, it was destroyed by extremists in Northern Ireland within a year. In May 1974, the violence spread to Dublin and Monaghan when several people were killed and injured in a number of horrific car bombings.

Bomb damage in Dublin in May 1974.

In response to the continuing violence, Cosgrave's government introduced a number of strict laws against members of the IRA and other illegal organisations. Members of these groups were banned from national television and radio channels run by Radio Telefís Éireann (RTE).

When Cosgrave called a general election for June 1977, the coalition parties, Fine Gael and Labour, believed that they would win. However, many people feared that the government was becoming too strict and they believed that the economy had disimproved.

Jack Lynch receiving his Seal of Office from President Hillery following Fianna Fáil's landslide election victory in 1977.

Fianna Fáil entered the election with a manifesto promising many improvements, including the abolition of rates on houses and of tax on private cars. The election resulted in a landslide victory for Fianna Fáil. They won an overall majority of twenty seats in the Dáil and Jack Lynch became Taoiseach once again.

GENERAL ELECTION RESULTS 1969–1977

	1969	1973	1977
Fianna Fáil	75	69	84
Fine Gael	50	54	43
Labour	18	19	17
Independents	1	2	4

Test your knowledge

1 When did the Irish government first apply for membership of the EEC?

2 What groups supported Irish entry into the EEC?

3 Which political party campaigned against Irish entry to the Common Market? Why?

4 What was the result of the referendum of May 1972 on Irish entry to the EEC?

5 Who became Taoiseach in 1973?

6 Name three ministers in the coalition government, 1973–77.

7 How did the government respond to the threat of violence from Northern Ireland?

8 Describe the results of the general election of 1977.

The rise of Charles J. Haughey

The first two years of the new government appeared prosperous. Many new jobs were created, especially in the public service in areas like teaching, nursing and the civil service. Included in the government were George Colley as Tánaiste and Minister for Finance, and Charles Haughey as Minister for Health.

Despite their huge majority, some Fianna Fáil TDs were afraid that they would lose their seats in the next general election. Fine Gael was becoming increasingly popular under its energetic new leader, Dr Garret FitzGerald, and in 1979 a new oil crisis in the Middle East damaged the Irish economy. After Fianna Fáil lost two by-elections in the summer of 1979, some of the party's TDs declared their dissatisfaction with Jack Lynch as leader. Therefore it came as no surprise to many people when he resigned suddenly in December 1979, hoping that his Tánaiste, George Colley, would succeed him in office. However, a majority of Fianna Fáil TDs chose the Minister for Health, Charles Haughey, as party leader. He was duly elected Taoiseach by the Dáil.

Charles J. Haughey giving a press conference following his election as the fourth leader of Fianna Fáil in 1979.

The new Taoiseach was fifty-four years of age and had a reputation for hard work and for making firm decisions. He appeared to have left the troubled times of the Arms Crisis behind him in the distant past. However, many people in his own Fianna Fáil party, including his former rival, George Colley, were suspicious of him and would have preferred another leader.

In January 1980, Charles Haughey went on television to warn the people that the government was borrowing too much money and that hard decisions would have to be made. However, few cutbacks in expenditure were made before the approaching general election which was held in June 1981.

Garret FitzGerald and the coalition

Dr Garret FitzGerald succeeded Liam Cosgrave as leader of Fine Gael in 1977. He served two terms as Taoiseach during the 1980s.

Fianna Fáil under Charles Haughey lost the election and were replaced by a Fine Gael–Labour coalition with Dr Garret FitzGerald (Fine Gael) as Taoiseach and Michael O'Leary (Labour) as Tánaiste. Soon after taking office, the Minister for Finance, John Bruton of Fine Gael, warned the public that the amount of money owed by the government was a very serious problem.

Throughout the 1980s, successive governments had to deal with this situation by increasing taxes and reducing government spending in areas like health and education. FitzGerald's first government was actually defeated in the Dáil when trying to raise a tax on children's shoes in January 1982.

In the general election which followed, Charles Haughey and Fianna Fáil were returned to power, but without an overall majority. They too faced the problem of reducing the massive public debt. Their attempts to do this partly by cutbacks in health care led to their defeat in the Dáil in October 1982.

The third general election within eighteen months resulted in the return to power of Garret FitzGerald at the head of a Fine Gael–Labour coalition. This time, the government had an overall majority and remained in power until the spring of 1987.

Former Fianna Fáil minister, Desmond O'Malley, launching a new political party - the Progressive Democrats - in 1985.

FitzGerald's government met with failures in some areas and successes in others. Because of disagreements between Fine Gael and Labour, it failed to take the harsh action needed to solve the debt problem by reducing government spending sufficiently. There was a global economic depression taking place at the same time which further damaged the Irish economy.

Soon after becoming Taoiseach, Dr FitzGerald expressed the hope that he could lead a 'Constitutional Crusade' to make the constitution of the Republic more acceptable to Northern Protestants. However, during his period as Taoiseach, a majority of the people voted against his advice in a referendum on the Right to Life of Unborn Children (1983) and on Divorce (1986). On the divorce issue, a majority of the voters decided to keep the ban on divorce contained in the Irish constitution.

Although largely unsuccessful in his treatment of the economy and in his 'Constitutional Crusade', Garret FitzGerald proved himself a statesman in his dealings with the government of Great Britain.

A meeting of the New Ireland Forum in 1984.

Test your knowledge

1 Who was Tánaiste in the Fianna Fáil government elected in 1977?
2 What position did Charles Haughey hold?
3 Why were some Fianna Fáil TDs worried about their future in 1979?
4 Who succeeded Jack Lynch as Fianna Fáil leader in December 1979?
5 What warning did Charles Haughey give on television in January 1980?
6 Explain the outcome of the general election of June 1981.
7 What was the main problem facing successive governments during the 1980s?
8 How did the coalition government of 1982–87 succeed in managing the economy?
9 What was Dr FitzGerald's 'Constitutional Crusade'? Did it succeed? Explain.

Northern Ireland

During 1983 and 1984, Irish Nationalists of all non-violent political parties from North and South met in Dublin to discuss possible solutions to the continuing crisis in Northern Ireland. They called their meetings the *New Ireland Forum*. Politicians, church leaders, professors and others from Ireland and Britain spoke at these meeting and over three hundred groups or persons sent in their views in written form. However, when the *Report of the New Ireland Forum* was published, the British prime

Garret FitzGerald and Margaret Thatcher signing the Anglo-Irish Agreement in November 1985.

The inauguration of Mary Robinson as President of Ireland in 1990. President Robinson, the Republic of Ireland's first woman Head of State, brought to her position a deep commitment to the reconciliation of members of the Nationalist and Unionist traditions on the island of Ireland.

minister, Mrs Margaret Thatcher, rejected all of the proposals. Dr FitzGerald continued to express his views to the British government and after long, patient negotiations, a historic agreement was reached in November 1985. Known as the *Anglo-Irish Agreement*, it gave the Irish government a say in British government action in Northern Ireland and a right to represent the views of the Nationalist minority there. Under its terms, closer links were set up between the Irish government and the British cabinet minister in charge of Northern Ireland so that they could work together to bring peace and prosperity to the whole island.

Chapter 72: Review

- In November 1966, Seán Lemass was replaced by Jack Lynch as Taoiseach. Fianna Fáil was returned to power under Jack Lynch in the general election of 1969.

- The outbreak of violence in Northern Ireland in 1969 had a serious impact on the government and people of the Republic. In May 1970, Lynch dismissed two to his ministers because they did not fully support government policy on Northern Ireland.

- On 28 May 1970 the two sacked ministers—Charles Haughey and Neil Blaney—were arrested and charged with attempting to import arms for use by the IRA in Northern Ireland. Later in the year, both were found not guilty.

- On 1 January 1973, Ireland became a member of the EEC. Dr Patrick Hillery became the country's first commissioner in Europe.

- An election in 1973 saw the end of sixteen years of Fianna Fáil power by bringing a coalition of Fine Gael and Labour into government. Liam Cosgrave, the leader of Fine Gael, became the Taoiseach.

- During the four years of coalition, the economy suffered because of the huge increases in oil prices in the Middle East. The general election of 1977 resulted in a landslide victory for Fianna Fáil and Jack Lynch once again became Taoiseach.

- In 1979, Jack Lynch resigned as Taoiseach and was replaced by Charles Haughey. By this time there was a huge national debt, but Haughey's government failed to tackle it. During the decade of the 1980s, successive governments tried to reduce this national debt by increasing taxes and reducing government spending.

- From 1983 to 1987, Garret FitzGerald was the leader of a Fine Gael–Labour coalition. This government is most remembered for negotiating with Britain the Anglo-Irish Agreement in relation to Northern Ireland.

CHAPTER 73

Northern Ireland: 1920–63

The foundation of Northern Ireland (1920)

King George V opening the first Northern Ireland Parliament on 21 June 1921.

The state of Northern Ireland consisting of the six north-eastern counties of Antrim, Armagh, Derry (or Londonderry), Down, Fermanagh and Tyrone was set up under the Government of Ireland Act which was passed by the British parliament in 1920. A Northern Ireland parliament and government were established in Belfast. Although the Six Counties remained part of the United Kingdom under the king of England, British governments did not interfere in the affairs of the province between 1922 and 1969.

Unionist workers in a Belfast shipyard demonstrating against Sinn Féin during the 1918 General Election.

From the start, the Unionist Party was in complete control of the government. You have seen already how Sir Edward Carson and Sir James Craig tried hard to prevent Home Rule coming to Ireland. Although they would have preferred to keep all of Ireland under the rule of the Westminster parliament, when this proved impossible they agreed to a divided or partitioned Ireland with the Protestant north-east forming a separate state. Although only four counties had Protestant majorities, the Unionists were influential with the British government and succeeded in having Fermanagh and Tyrone, with their slight Catholic majorities, included in Northern Ireland.

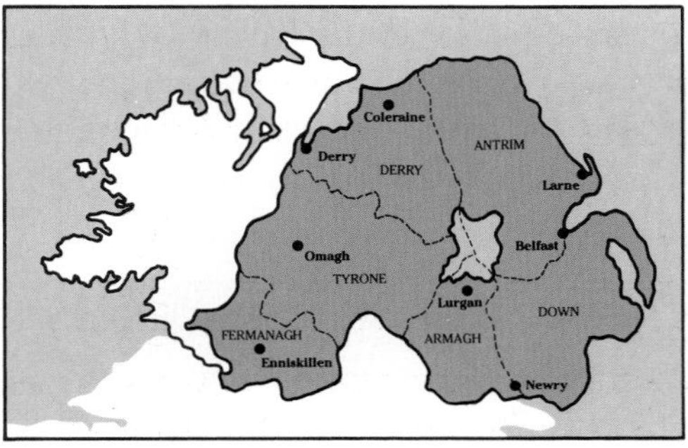

Northern Ireland.

The Ulster Unionist Party consisted almost completely of Protestants and had very close links with the Orange Order, an extreme Protestant organisation. James Craig, later Lord Craigavon, who was prime minister of Northern Ireland from 1921 until 1940, once remarked: 'All I boast is that we are a Protestant Parliament for a Protestant People'.

However, one-third of the population of Northern Ireland consisted of Catholics. Most of them were Nationalists who believed in a united Ireland. They were seriously distrusted by the Unionist majority and were never given a share in the running of the country.

Stormont Castle, the home of the Northern parliament from 1932.

Lord Craigavon, Prime Minister of Northern Ireland, 1921–40.

A one-party state

The state of Northern Ireland was designed so that the two-thirds Unionist majority would have a majority in parliament. Take a look at the chart of election results in Northern Ireland between 1921 and 1969.

GENERAL ELECTIONS IN NORTHERN IRELAND

	Unionists	Nationalists	Others	Total
1921	40	12	0	52
1925	36	12	4	52
1929	40	11	1	52
1933	39	11	2	52
1938	42	8	2	52
1945	35	10	7	52
1949	39	9	4	52
1953	39	9	4	52
1958	37	8	7	52
1962	34	9	9	52
1965	36	9	7	52
1969	39	6	7	52

You can clearly see how the Ulster Unionist Party always had a huge majority, unlike government parties in Great Britain or in the South of Ireland which were frequently turned out of office by the voters. As they had no fear of losing power, Unionist governments were not likely to listen carefully to criticism or to bring about badly needed improvements in the running of the country.

With no hope of gaining power, the large Catholic minority community was hostile to the new state of Northern Ireland. Unionists in turn saw Catholics as a threat to the state and were determined to secure their position by enforcing strict law and order.

Test your knowledge

1 What act of parliament established the state of Northern Ireland?
2 What party controlled the government there?
3 How many counties had Protestant majorities? Name them.
4 Who became the first prime minister of Northern Ireland?
5 Why were Catholics distrusted by the Unionist majority?
6 What was the response of Unionists to the threat to their position posed by the minority?

Law and order

The early years of the new state of Northern Ireland were marked by widespread violence and disorder. The IRA were active, especially in border areas. Thousands of Catholics were driven from their jobs and homes. After an inflammatory speech from Sir Edward Carson near Belfast on 12 July 1920, all of the Catholic workers in the city's shipyards were expelled from their jobs.

British troops manning the barricades in Belfast in 1921.

Against this background of violence and intimidation, the new government set up a police force, the *Royal Ulster Constabulary (RUC)* and a reserve force known as the *B Specials*. While Protestants regarded these forces as their protectors, they were never accepted by Catholics as fair upholders of law and order.

In 1922, the Northern Ireland parliament passed the *Special Powers Act* which gave the government extensive powers, including the use of the death penalty and internment without trial.

B Specials on patrol.

The most serious threat to the survival of Northern Ireland was removed when Sinn Féin and the IRA split over the Anglo-Irish Treaty of December 1921. The Civil War which followed in the South gave the Unionist government in the North a welcome opportunity to strengthen its control over the Six Counties without fear of intervention by Republicans from the South.

Riots in Belfast in the 1920s.

However, although law and order was restored in Northern Ireland by 1923, the government presided over a deeply divided society.

Discrimination in Northern Ireland

Joseph Devlin, leader of the Nationalist Party in Northern Ireland during the 1920s.

From the outset, the Unionists favoured their fellow Protestants and acted against the interests of Catholics. This policy was known as *discrimination* and was evident in the following areas:

- *In housing*: Catholics were frequently discriminated against by Unionist-controlled local authorities.
- *In employment*: Protestants tended to be favoured with jobs and more Protestants than Catholics were found in better-off jobs, in proportion to their numbers.
- *In the civil service*: the number of Catholics in the higher-up positions was very small indeed.
- *In elections*: the Ulster Unionist Party increased its control by two means;

1. The abolition of proportional representation (PR) in elections, as this had been fairer to minorities than the straight vote.
2. Gerrymandering—this was the rigging of constituencies and was most blatant in Derry where, despite a Catholic majority of voters, the corporation was controlled by Unionists.

As the years went by, Northern Ireland remained a divided society. Protestants and Catholics attended separate schools, separate churches, and for the most part did not mix socially. After boycotting the parliament for a number of years, the Nationalist Party under Joseph Devlin took their seats in 1926. However, they were always a small minority and their demands for change were ignored.

Test your knowledge

1 Who controlled the state of Northern Ireland after it was set up in 1920?
2 Who was its first prime minister?
3 What percentage of the total population was comprised of Catholics? What was their attitude to the new state?
4 What police force was set up in Northern Ireland?
5 Who were the B Specials?
6 State three forms of discrimination practised against Catholics in Northern Ireland.
7 In your opinion, why were Unionists suspicious of the Catholic minority?

A time of depression

In common with the rest of Europe, Northern Ireland was badly hit by the Great Depression of the 1930s. Many jobs were lost in the famous Belfast shipyard of Harland and Wolff, while the second shipyard in the city, Workman and Clark, closed down in 1934.

Unemployment levels were very high, reaching a peak of 100,000 in 1938. To make matters worse, there was very little assistance available from the state for the unemployed. In housing, medical services and public health there had been hardly any improvements since Northern Ireland was set up in

Children from the Belfast slums. There was widespread poverty in Northern Ireland during the 1920s and 1930s.

1920. Even the welfare payments which did exist were only about half the size of those available in the rest of the United Kingdom.

As a result of severe hardship, both Protestant and Catholic workers took to the streets of Belfast in 1932 to protest against their living conditions. However, Unionist leaders became alarmed at the solidarity of Protestant and Catholic workers and in various speeches they encouraged Protestant employers to employ Protestants in preference to Catholics. In March 1934 Basil Brooke, who later became prime minister of Northern Ireland, remarked:

> 'I recommend those people who are Loyalists not to employ Roman Catholics, 99% of whom are disloyal...If you don't act properly now, before we know where we are, we shall find ourselves in the minority instead of the majority.'

The protests of the poor against the government soon changed into sectarian riots between Protestants and Catholics, reaching a crisis point in July 1935. Fighting broke out during the Orange parade in Belfast of 12 July. This led to riots which lasted for three weeks and claimed the lives of eleven people, with nearly 600 injured. The British army was called in to restore order as the RUC could no longer control the situation.

Basil Brooke later Lord Brookeborough, Prime Minister of Northern Ireland 1943–63.

Tension between Protestants and Catholics remained high throughout the remainder of the 1930s. However, when Northern Ireland entered World War II along with Great Britain in September 1939, a period of economic prosperity was about to begin.

Test your knowledge

1. Why was there widespread poverty in Ireland during the 1930s?
2. What sort of assistance was available from the state?
3. Why did both Catholic and Protestant workers take to the streets of Belfast in 1932?
4. What advice did some Unionist leaders give to Protestant employers?

The war comes to Northern Ireland

The Unionist leaders immediately pledged their loyalty to the king of England and willingly entered the war. They believed, correctly, that with the Irish Free State remaining neutral, the war effort of Northern Ireland would lead to closer links with Great Britain.

Survivors examining the wreckage after the German blitz on Belfast.

The economy of the Six Counties improved steadily during the war years. The farmers got good prices for their produce in Britain, while in Belfast the shipyards and other heavy industries were busy producing materials needed in the war. When large numbers of British and American troops were stationed in Northern Ireland, local trade benefited as a result.

Belfast and other towns were to suffer from German bombing raids. In April 1941 when the worst raids took place, thirteen fire brigades were sent to the assistance of Belfast from the Irish Free State by the Taoiseach, Eamon de Valera.

As in England, the shared experience of wartime suffering brought all sections of the Northern community closer together. The widespread destruction of poorer areas of Belfast exposed the terrible living conditions in the slums and paved the way for improvements once the war was over.

The Welfare State

The Welfare State which was introduced in Britain after 1945 by the Labour government was also extended to Northern Ireland. It included the following improvements:

- A comprehensive scheme of insurance covering sickness and unemployment.
- A free health service for all and a serious campaign to wipe out the dreaded problem of tuberculosis (TB).
- A programme of house building.
- Far-reaching reforms in education, including free secondary education, a raising of the school-leaving age to fifteen, and grants for university students.

The reforms in education improved the position of the Catholic community by enabling future political leaders to receive higher education. In the years ahead, such well-educated men and women would not be willing to accept the status of second-class citizens in Northern Ireland.

Many new houses like these were built in Northern Ireland after 1945.

Although there were improvements in the economy during the 1950s, politics in Northern Ireland still remained linked to sectarian divisions between Protestants and Catholics. As long as Lord Brookeborough remained as prime minister, there was little hope of an easing of such tensions. However, on his retirement in 1963, he was replaced by a more moderate Unionist—Captain Terence O'Neill. It appeared at last that some healing of divisions between Protestants and Catholics might take place.

Test your knowledge

1 What was the attitude of the Unionist leaders to the outbreak of World War II?
2 Why did the economy of Northern Ireland improve during the war?
3 List two ways in which the war affected the people of Belfast.
4 What is meant by 'The Welfare State'?
5 Give three improvements which were introduced to Northern Ireland as part of the Welfare State.
6 How did education reform improve the position of the Catholic community?
7 Who succeeded Lord Brookeborough as Prime Minister of Northern Ireland in 1963?

Chapter 73: Review

- The state of Northern Ireland, consisting of six counties, was set up under the Government of Ireland Act in 1920.
- The Unionist Party, consisting almost completely of Protestants, remained in control of Northern Ireland between 1921 and the abolition of the parliament there by the British government in 1972.
- Catholics, although making up over one-third of the North's population, were not given a share in the running of the state.
- From the beginning, law and order was a problem in Northern Ireland. The government set up a new police force—the RUC—and a reserve police force—the B Specials.
- From the outset, Catholics were discriminated against in housing, employment and politics.
- In the 1930s, depression and unemployment hit Northern Ireland. However, its economy greatly improved during the war years.
- After World War II, a Welfare State was set up in Northern Ireland.
- In 1963, Captain Terence O'Neill became prime minister of Northern Ireland. He wanted to end discrimination against Catholics. Many Unionists were dissatisfied with his talk of reform.

CHAPTER 74 The Crisis Begins

Captain Terence O'Neill

Unlike his predecessors such as the Unionist leaders Craigavon and Brookeborough, Terence O'Neill believed in looking for the support of the minority Catholic community in Northern Ireland. He was to be seen visiting Catholic schools and hospitals and he hoped to end anti-Catholic discrimination. O'Neill realised that only by making Catholics contented citizens of Northern Ireland could the Union with Great Britain be made secure in the long term. Unfortunately for him, many of his Unionist colleagues did not share his generous approach.

Captain Terence O'Neill succeeded Lord Brookeborough as Prime Minister of Northern Ireland in 1963.

In 1965, two historic meetings took place, one in Belfast and the other in Dublin, between Terence O'Neill and the Taoiseach of the Irish Republic, Seán Lemass. This was the first time ever that the prime ministers of both states had met. Lemass realised at the time that he was taking a serious risk. The extreme Protestant leader, the Reverend Ian Paisley, organised a protest at the Belfast meeting of the two premiers. He was just becoming well known for his anti-Catholic protests in Northern Ireland, Britain and further afield.

The historic meeting between Lemass and O'Neill in Belfast in 1965.

As O'Neill moved slowly to persuade his own reluctant followers to introduce long overdue reforms, he was to encounter a mass peaceful movement among the Catholic community who took to the streets to demand their rights.

The Civil Rights Movement

During the 1960s, there were peaceful movements among black people in the United States of America to bring about full civil rights. At the same time, students in many parts of the world were protesting against injustice by taking to the streets in marches and demonstrations. These activities inspired the Catholic minority in Northern Ireland. As their demand for equal rights was ignored in the Unionist-dominated Northern Ireland parliament at Stormont, they too took to the streets to voice their grievances.

A Civil Rights protest in Derry in 1968.

In February 1967, the Northern Ireland Civil Rights Association was founded with the aim of securing full citizens' rights for all of the people of Northern Ireland. The first famous incident in the struggle took place at Caledon, Co. Tyrone, in the summer of 1968. Here the young Nationalist MP, Austin Currie, led a protest to a house which had been allocated to a single Protestant girl in an area where there were many large Catholic families on the housing waiting list.

In the following October, events in the city of Derry ensured that the civil rights struggle became

John Hume, one of the leaders of the Civil Rights Movement.

news all around the world. A peaceful march arranged for 5 October was banned by the Minister for Home Affairs, William Craig. When the march went ahead in Derry, the peaceful protestors, including a number of MPs, were brutally attacked by the RUC. Within hours the events were screened on televisions and described in newspapers around the world. Soon more and more marches were organised and Terence O'Neill's government promised to introduce reforms. However, while he promised too little to please Catholics, he had agreed to too many changes according to many of his own Unionist colleagues.

Ulster Unionists protesting against the reforms proposed by O'Neill's government.

Ian Paisley, an extreme Unionist, was a strong critic of O'Neill's policies.

At many civil rights marches, Ian Paisley and his followers organised counter-demonstrations and there was often fighting between both sets of protestors. When O'Neill called a general election in February 1969, Paisley campaigned strongly against him throughout Northern Ireland. Paisley also stood for election in O'Neill's own constituency where he came a close second to the prime minister. This humiliation of O'Neill, and the fact that his party was badly divided over its response to the Civil Rights Movement, led eventually to his resignation on 28 April.

Ultimately he had failed in his attempt to persuade his Unionist colleagues to offer the hand of friendship to the Catholic community. He was succeeded as Unionist leader by his cousin, Major James Chichester-Clark, a landowner from Co. Derry. The new prime minister attempted to restore Unionist unity and introduce gradual reforms. However, events soon got out of hand on the streets of Derry and Belfast and the British government had to intervene directly in Ireland for the first time since 1922.

Test your knowledge

1. How did Captain Terence O'Neill differ from earlier Unionist leaders?
2. What historic meetings took place in Ireland in 1965?
3. What movements inspired Catholics in Northern Ireland to struggle for civil rights?
4. Explain the Caledon protest conducted by Austin Currie in 1968.
5. What took place in Derry on 5 October 1968?
6. What was the reaction of Terence O'Neill to the Civil Rights Movement?
7. Who succeeded him as prime minister of Northern Ireland in May 1969?

The crisis of 1969

In August 1969, serious rioting broke out in Derry and Belfast. It began during the Apprentice Boys' Parade march in Derry on 12 August. This extreme Protestant organisation held a ceremony each year to commemorate the closing of the gates of the city against the attacking Catholic army in the siege of 1689. In the summer of 1969, despite a high level of tension between Catholics and Protestants, the Unionist government refused to ban the march through a city with a majority of Catholics. When the Apprentice Boys reached the Catholic Bogside area, missiles were thrown at them and large-scale fighting broke out. Later in the day, the RUC were prevented from entering the Bogside area by local people. For over two days a struggle known as 'The Battle of the Bogside' went on between the local people and the police. Bricks, pavement stones and petrol bombs were used against the RUC, whose

British troops arriving in Derry.

members replied with armoured cars and CS gas. One of the leaders of the people in the Bogside was a twenty-two-year-old girl from Tyrone, Bernadette Devlin, who had been elected an MP the previous April.

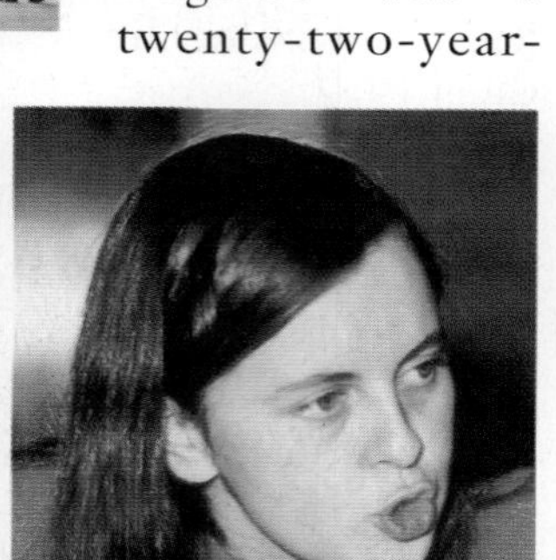

Bernadette Devlin was elected MP in April 1969.

The trouble soon spread to Belfast where some Catholic youths began rioting. Extreme Protestants, angered by the events in Derry, launched wholesale attacks on Catholic areas of Belfast. When the RUC and B Specials were seen to be openly in favour of the Protestants, the British army had to be called in to restore order. By the time they moved in on 16 August, the houses of over 150 Catholic families had been burnt out and six people were dead. Vastly outnumbered by Protestants, the Catholics in poorer areas of Belfast welcomed the British army on to their streets as protectors.

When the British home secretary, James Callaghan, visited Northern Ireland at the height of the crisis, he promised that the Labour government of Prime Minister Harold Wilson would ensure that all people in Northern Ireland, Catholics as well as Protestants, would be given full rights as British citizens. However, the hopes of many people for a brighter future were soon dashed when violent men on both sides of the divide began a campaign of shooting, bombing and destruction.

Republican versus Loyalist

Extreme Protestants were known as *Loyalists* because of their loyalty to the British monarch. Various British governments were to discover that these Loyalists would only follow instructions from London when it suited them. In particular, they were prepared to use violence to prevent the granting of civil rights to Catholics or the sharing of power between Protestants and Catholics. Various secret Loyalist paramilitary or violent organisations were set up. The most powerful was the illegal *Ulster Volunteer Force (UVF).*

Members of the UDA on patrol.

While extreme Loyalists were arming themselves secretly, they also set up a public organisation called the *Ulster Defence Association (UDA).* Many Unionist politicians encouraged Protestants to hold extreme anti-Catholic views. The most famous of these was the Reverend Ian Paisley who also ran his own religion, the Free Presbyterian Church. From 1969 onwards, Paisley went from strength to strength, winning seats at elections for himself and his followers and doing everything in his power to block concessions to Catholics such as 'One Man, One Vote' or 'Power-Sharing'.

On the Catholic or Nationalist side in 1969, the IRA was almost non-existent. However, in December of that year it split into two groups—the *Official IRA* and the *Provisional IRA*. Each had a supporting political movement, Official Sinn Féin and Provisional Sinn Féin. While the Officials had Socialist and Marxist views, the Provisionals wished to concentrate on removing Unionist and British control over Northern Ireland by means of violence.

Throughout 1970 and the first half of 1971, the level of violence increased greatly. In Catholic working-class areas in Belfast and Derry, people began to turn against the British army and to come under the influence of the Provisional IRA. The IRA shot soldiers and policemen and bombed Protestant-owned businesses. The Loyalist paramilitaries in turn shot Catholics and bombed Catholic-owned businesses.

Catholic youths join in an attack on British troops.

The Unionist prime minister, Brian Faulkner, who had succeeded Chichester-Clark in March 1971, decided on a new policy to reduce the level of violence. He persuaded the British government to allow him to introduce internment without trial in August 1971.

Test your knowledge

1 Why did rioting break out in Derry in August 1969?
2 What was 'The Battle of the Bogside'?
3 Why was the British army placed on the streets of Belfast in 1969?
4 What promise did the British home secretary, James Callaghan, make on visiting Northern Ireland?
5 Explain the meaning of the term 'Loyalist'.
6 What were paramilitary groups?
7 Name one Loyalist and one Republican paramilitary group.
8 Who became prime minister of Northern Ireland in March 1971?

Internment without trial

Around four o'clock on the morning of 9 August 1971, the British army arrested over 300 people. After careful examination, 240 of them were interned without trial. Although internment had helped to defeat earlier IRA campaigns, its use in 1971 proved a disastrous mistake for the Unionist government.

When it emerged that very few Loyalist suspects had been interned, Catholics of all shades of opinion united in anger. Many totally innocent men were interned and most of the IRA leaders escaped capture. In the months after internment, there were widespread protests throughout Nationalist areas of Northern Ireland and IRA violence increased dramatically. Already since internment, the IRA was receiving greater sympathy and support. Events in Derry in January 1972 were to increase this support further and to pave the way for the fall of the Unionist government at Stormont.

Bloody Sunday: Derry, 30 January 1972

On 30 January 1972, thirteen civilians were shot dead by the British army at the end of an illegal anti-internment march. While the army claimed that it was shot at first, the local people strongly denied this.

Father Edward Daly, the future Catholic Bishop of Derry, waving a handkerchief to escort an injured man to safety during Bloody Sunday.

The day soon became known as 'Bloody Sunday' and it caused deeply felt anger among Catholics in Northern Ireland. In the Republic, a huge wave of anti-British feeling spread over the country and protestors burned the British Embassy in Dublin to the ground. Relations between the Irish government under Jack Lynch and the British Conservative government of Edward Heath reached an all-time low.

It was clear that the Unionist government in the North could not control the situation and Edward Heath demanded that the London government should take over full control of law and order in Northern Ireland.

The fall of Stormont

When Brian Faulkner and his government refused to give up control of law and order, the British government was forced to act. On 30 March 1972, the British parliament suspended the parliament and government of Northern Ireland. Instead, the province would be ruled directly from London. A member of the British government known as the *Secretary of State* would be in charge. On 1 April 1972,

Edward Heath, the British Prime Minister whose government introduced direct rule to Northern Ireland from 1 April 1972.

William Whitelaw became the first such Northern Ireland secretary of state.

Protestants in Northern Ireland were shocked and horrified at the suspension of their Unionist-controlled parliament. On the other hand, most of the Catholic minority were pleased as they believed that they would receive fairer treatment from the British government.

The suspension of Stormont marked the end of an era in the history of Northern Ireland. It did not end the violence, however, as extreme Loyalists and Republicans continued their campaigns. Once the Stormont parliament was abolished, successive British governments made it clear that they would only return power to Northern Ireland if Protestants and Catholics agreed to a power-sharing arrangement.

Test your knowledge

1 When was internment without trial introduced in Northern Ireland?
2 Why were Catholics particularly angry concerning internment?
3 What effect did internment have on the IRA?
4 Explain the events of 'Bloody Sunday' in Derry on 30 January 1972.
5 What was the reaction to 'Bloody Sunday' in the Irish Republic?
6 What action was taken by the British government on 30 March 1972?
7 Name the first secretary of state appointed to Northern Ireland.

Chapter 74: Review

- In 1963, Captain Terence O'Neill became prime minister of Northern Ireland. He wanted to end discrimination against Catholics. He also had two historic meetings with Seán Lemass in 1965. Many Unionists such as the Reverend Ian Paisley were dissatisfied with his talk of reform.

- In 1968, Catholics began the Civil Rights Movement and took to the streets in an effort to draw attention to their grievances.

- In 1970, the IRA began operations again in Northern Ireland. In 1971, internment without trial was brought in to deal with the mounting violence. However, this only served to embitter many Catholics.

- On 30 January 1972, thirteen civilians were shot dead by the British army at the end of an illegal anti-internment march. This was known as 'Bloody Sunday' and caused great anger among Catholics in Northern Ireland.

- In March 1972, the British government abolished the Northern Ireland parliament and brought Northern Ireland under direct rule from Britain.

CHAPTER 75 A Divided People

The Sunningdale Agreement

In June 1973, a new assembly was elected in Northern Ireland. It included Unionists and members of two newer parties. One was the largely Catholic Social Democratic and Labour Party (SDLP) which had replaced the old Nationalist Party in 1970. The other was the small Alliance Party which drew support from both Protestants and Catholics. In November, these parties agreed to the British government's demand that they share power between them. As a result, a power-sharing executive or government was set up in Belfast with the Unionist leader, Brian Faulkner, as leader and the head of the SDLP, Gerry Fitt, as deputy leader. Both these parties, together with Alliance, had members in the executive.

The signing of the Sunningdale Agreement in December 1973.

In order to secure the agreement of the Catholic community to this arrangement, the British government under Edward Heath negotiated ties between North and South. This was known as the *Irish Dimension* and involved the setting up of an advisory Council of Ireland which would include politicians from both North and South of the border.

Brian Faulkner, Unionist prime minister when the Northern Ireland parliament was abolished in 1972, became the leader of the power-sharing executive under the Sunningdale Agreement.

These provisions were contained in an agreement signed at Sunningdale in England in December 1973 between the leaders of the Northern Ireland parties, Edward Heath, the prime minister, and Liam Cosgrave, the Taoiseach of the Fine Gael–Labour coalition government in power in Dublin.

The power-sharing executive began running Northern Ireland on 1 January 1974. Although the British government continued to take charge of law and order, the new executive had power in many areas of government. There were high hopes that it would mark the beginning of a solution to the conflict in Northern Ireland.

From the outset, however, extreme Protestants such as Ian Paisley and Loyalist paramilitary groups were determined to wreck the power-sharing arrangement. Indeed, many members of Brian Faulkner's own Unionist Party were opposed to sharing power with nationalists. In particular almost all Unionists regarded the proposed Council of Ireland as the first step on the road to a united Ireland.

Power-sharing received a serious setback in March 1974 when eleven out of the twelve Northern Ireland seats in the Westminster general election were won by Unionists who opposed the new executive.

Loyalists protesting at Stormont against the power-sharing executive in May 1974.

On 28 May, the power-sharing arrangement collapsed due to a general strike organised by Loyalist workers. The British Labour government of Harold Wilson had refused to use the army to keep essential services running. However, even without the strike it is difficult to see how power-sharing could have continued when most Unionist supporters were opposed to it.

With the fall of the power-sharing executive, Northern Ireland was placed under direct rule from London once again.

The violence continues

For the remainder of the 1970s, Northern Ireland experienced a continuation of violence resulting in many deaths and injuries. As one secretary of state was replaced by another, it appeared that the British government now hoped merely to keep the level of violence down and that they had no real hope of a better future for Northern Ireland.

Members of the IRA manning the barricades in Derry in 1976.

Both the IRA and Loyalist paramilitary groups continued to carry out shootings and bombings. In 1974, the IRA was responsible for a series of horrific bombings in England, including attacks on public houses in the city of Birmingham and the town of Guildford. Later on, it was shown that the wrong people had been imprisoned for these crimes. Such miscarriages of justice, added to the terrible loss of life and injury of ordinary English citizens, led to further misunderstanding and tension between the governments and peoples of Great Britain and Ireland.

The British army during a searching operation in Belfast, 1976.

In another terrorist incident, the IRA killed the British ambassador in Dublin, Sir Christopher Ewart Biggs, in 1976. During these years there were various attempts by the British government to set up another power-sharing arrangement in Belfast. However, they all failed as the Unionists refused to share power with the Nationalist minority.

The scene of the assassination of the British ambassador to Ireland, Sir Christopher Ewart Biggs, in 1976.

In May 1979, a new Conservative government was elected in Great Britain under Mrs Margaret Thatcher. A few months previously, her close friend and adviser, Airey Neave, the Conservative Party spokesman on Northern Ireland, had been killed in a car bomb attack near the House of Commons in Westminster. Mrs Thatcher was determined to do all in her power to defeat the IRA.

In the summer and autumn of 1979, it became clear that the IRA had no intention of ending their violent campaign. In August, they carried out an attack in which eighteen British soldiers died at Warrenpoint in Co. Down. On the same day, the IRA killed Lord Mountbatten, a close relative of the British royal family, by placing a bomb in his boat off the coast of Sligo.

A month later at the end of September 1979, Pope John Paul II made a strong appeal to the IRA to end the violence. He was speaking at Drogheda during his visit to Ireland. However, the IRA ignored the pope's plea and continued with their campaign.

They were now to enter into a bitter struggle with the Thatcher government over the conditions of Republican prisoners in Northern Ireland.

Mrs Margaret Thatcher. Her government was determined not to compromise with the IRA.

Test your knowledge

1 Name the three main parties elected to the Northern Ireland Assembly in 1973.
2 Who became leader of the new power-sharing executive?
3 What was the 'Irish Dimension' in the Sunningdale Agreement?
4 Who were the enemies of power-sharing in Northern Ireland?
5 How did the power-sharing arrangement come to an end?
6 Who became prime minister of Great Britain in May 1979?
7 What was the reaction of the IRA to appeals for peace by Pope John Paul II in September 1979?

The IRA hunger strikes

Some years earlier, Roy Mason, secretary of state for Northern Ireland in the Labour government, had put an end to special status for IRA prisoners. The British government claimed that shootings and bombings were criminal activities and that those responsible for them should be treated like other criminals and wear ordinary prison dress. The IRA, on the other hand, believed that their members were prisoners of war and entitled to wear their own clothes.

When the British government refused to meet these demands, IRA prisoners carried out various protests, including refusing to wear prison clothes and wearing only a blanket and dirtying their cells. When these measures failed, they turned to a form of protest with a long history in Ireland—the hunger strike.

The 'dirty protest' of IRA prisoners in the H-Block of Long Kesh prison in 1979.

Because the prisoners were housed in H-shaped compounds in Long Kesh prison, their campaign became known as the *H-Block Protests*. Mrs Thatcher's government was determined not to compromise with the IRA. The hunger strike proceeded during the spring and summer of 1981 and ten IRA prisoners died before it was called off.

The most famous of the hunger strikers to die was Bobby Sands who was elected as MP for Fermanagh-South Tyrone in a by-election while on hunger strike. Hunger strikers also took part in the general election in the Republic in June 1981 and two of them were elected as TDs. To many Nationalists in the North, the reaction of the British government was harsh and unyielding. As a result, the IRA and Sinn Féin gained increased support and sympathy in the years ahead.

Bobby Sands, who died on hunger strike in 1981.

During the early 1980s, further attempts were made to set up a power-sharing settlement in Northern Ireland. When these were unsuccessful, the British government moved towards an understanding with the government of the Irish Republic in order to bring peace to Northern Ireland.

The Anglo–Irish Agreement (1985)

The signing of the Anglo–Irish Agreement in November 1985 marked the greatest change in the government of Northern Ireland since the suspension of the Stormont parliament in 1972. This was an international agreement between the British and Irish governments. The British hoped for greater security co-operation with the Irish Republic, while the Irish government wanted to improve the conditions of the Nationalist minority in Northern Ireland.

Under the terms of the Anglo–Irish Agreement, two groups were set up:

- *The Inter-governmental Conference:* A meeting of ministers from both governments to discuss Northern Irish affairs;
- *The Anglo–Irish Secretariat:* A group of British and

Dr Ian Paisley addressing a protest rally against the Anglo–Irish Agreement.

Irish civil servants based near Belfast.

The Unionists bitterly opposed the Anglo–Irish Agreement. They objected to the role given to the Irish government in Northern Ireland affairs and felt that they had been betrayed by the British government. They organised huge protests against the agreement and refused to take part in any discussions as long as the agreement remained. Most Nationalists in Northern Ireland welcomed the agreement as an important advance. However, the IRA ignored the agreement and continued their campaign of violence.

This banner on Belfast City Hall summarised Unionist reaction to the Anglo–Irish Agreement.

For both governments, the Anglo–Irish Agreement was not seen as a final solution to the Northern Ireland problem. They hoped rather that it would provide a framework for peace and reconciliation in the future.

Test your knowledge

1 Why did the British government and the IRA come into conflict over prisoners in Northern Ireland?
2 List two forms of protest carried out by IRA prisoners.
3 What were the H-Blocks?
4 Who was the most famous of the hunger strikers to die in 1981?
5 How did the hunger-strike Campaign influence Nationalists in Northern Ireland?
6 Explain the functions of: (a) the Inter-governmental Conference; (b) the Secretariat set up under the Anglo–Irish Agreement of 1985.
7 How did the Unionists react to the signing of this agreement?

Northern Ireland 1968–1985

1968	Civil Rights Movement begins
1969	British army deployed on the streets
1971	Internment without trial
1972	'Bloody Sunday' in Derry
	Fall of Stormont government: direct rule from London
1973	Sunningdale Agreement
1974	End of Sunningdale Agreement
1981	IRA hunger strike campaign
1985	Anglo–Irish Agreement

Chapter 75: Review

- In 1970 a new party called the SDLP came into existence in Northern Ireland and represented nationalists.

- A power-sharing executive came into operation on 1 January 1974 as part of the Sunningdale Agreement. This had been negotiated between the Northern Ireland parties, the British government and the Irish government.

- From the beginning, extreme Protestants were determined to wreck this power-sharing arrangement and it eventually collapsed when Loyalist workers organised a general strike.

- For the remainder of the 1970s, Northern Ireland experienced a continuation of violence resulting in many deaths and injuries.

- In May 1979, a new Conservative government came to power in Britain under the leadership of Margaret Thatcher. Thatcher's government refused to give in to the demands of IRA prisoners for special status. A series of hunger strikes followed and ten IRA prisoners died before it was called off.

- The signing of the Anglo–Irish Agreement in 1985 marked an important change in the government of Northern Ireland. Most Nationalists welcomed the agreement while Unionists bitterly opposed it.

Ireland and the USA—Social Change in the Twentieth Century

Life in Town and Countryside

Ireland and the United States of America

In this section, we will look at the lives of ordinary people in both Ireland and the United States of America. From 1900 to the present, many changes took place in both countries in areas such as travel and transport, work and leisure, life in the countryside and the towns, and the role of women.

While there were often vast differences between developments in Ireland and in America, there were also close links between both countries. From around the time of the Great Famine onwards, millions of Irish people emigrated to America. They often left a life on the farm to begin a new life in the expanding cities of America.

Although most of the Irish emigrants struggled to survive in their new environment, many of them became rich and powerful. Some close links between Ireland and America have remained up to the present day.

In this chapter we will travel back in time and look at some of the important changes in towns and countryside in both Ireland and America from 1900 onwards.

The Irish countryside in 1900

In 1900, the great majority of the Irish people lived in the countryside where they worked on the land. Look carefully at the following pictures which tell us about the different groups of people living in rural Ireland.

The magnificent residence and estate of a wealthy landlord. A large number of servants and labourers were needed on vast estates such as this.

At this time, the population in the Irish countryside was falling. In fact, the number of people on farms in Ireland fell continuously from the time of the Great Famine onwards. Because only the eldest son could inherit the family farm, the younger sons usually emigrated. Often only the eldest daughter

A farmer's kitchen around 1900.

on a farm could get a dowry in order to marry. This left the other daughters with the choice of remaining on the farm as unpaid labourers or of boarding the emigrant ships.

POPULATION OF IRELAND 1851–1911	
1851	6,552,000
1861	5,798,000
1871	5,412,000
1881	5,174,000
1891	4,704,000
1901	4,458,000
1911	4,390,000

In 1900 there was very little machinery in use on Irish farms. Horses were still widely used and both men and women spent long hours toiling on the land.

Many labourers and small farmers lived in appalling conditions in cottages like this one in Donegal around 1900.

From around 1920 onwards, improvements came about slowly in living and working conditions in the Irish countryside.

Carrying turf in the West of Ireland.

A changing countryside

In general, Irish farmers were conservative and slow to change. Fathers were reluctant to hand over the land to the eldest son. By 1946, in fact, a third of all farmers were over sixty-five years of age.

Despite the fact that rural Ireland contained an ageing conservative population, important improvements took place from around 1922 onwards. The arrival of machinery marked an important change for the better. By 1960, over 40,000 tractors had been put into use on Irish farms. The arrival of electricity during the 1940s and 1950s improved living conditions on many an Irish farm. At around the same time, many rural homes got running water for the first time.

Despite various improvements, emigration from the Irish countryside continued. As you can see from the chart, emigration reached an all-time high during the 1950s, resulting in widespread rural depopulation.

EMIGRATION 1946–1966 *(average figures for each year)*	
1946–51	24,384
1951–56	39,353
1956–61	42,401
1961–66	16,121

As indicated in the chart over 400,000 people emigrated from the Irish Republic during the 1950s.

During the 1960s, some hope returned to the Irish countryside. Along with the rest of the population, farmers benefited from a general improvement in economic conditions. Bigger and better machines were in use and farmers received higher prices for their goods. However, the big breakthrough for Irish farmers came in 1973 when the country entered the European Economic Community (EEC).

The countryside today

Up to 1973, farmers had received grants and other assistance from the Irish government. From then on, they also received grants from the EEC. As well as this, farmers enjoyed guaranteed prices for their products under the *Common Agricultural Policy* (CAP). Many increased the size of their holdings and modernised them. As you can see from the picture, the most modern machinery increased production and efficiency on larger farms. However, a lot of small farmers, particularly in the West of Ireland, continued their

Modern machinery increased production and efficiency on Irish farms.

struggle to survive on uneconomic holdings.

Despite the fact that change was usually slow and undramatic, it is clear that life in rural Ireland today is very different from what it was in 1900.

Test your knowledge

1. Name the main groups of people living in the Irish countryside around 1900.
2. Why was the population in rural Ireland falling at this time?
3. Describe work on the farm around 1900.
4. Name two improvements in the Irish countryside between 1922 and 1960.
5. What changes came about during the 1960s?
6. How did Irish entry to the EEC in 1973 affect life in the countryside?

Irish towns in 1900

Dublin around 1900.

Today, most Irish people live and work in towns and cities and enjoy a standard of living far beyond the dreams of their grandparents' generation. In 1900, fewer Irish people lived in the larger towns and cities. At this time, Belfast was a booming industrial city which owed its prosperity to heavy industry such as shipbuilding and engineering.

Market day in an Irish town around 1900.

Dublin, unlike Belfast, had few large industries with the exception of Guinness and Jacobs. However, it was a centre of trade and commerce, banking and law, and the headquarters of the British government in the country.

Most of the other larger towns, such as Cork, Galway, Limerick and Waterford, owed their importance mainly to their functions as ports.

Work in the towns in 1900

Within the towns and cities there were great differences between rich and poor. People's standard of living depended largely on their occupation and particularly on whether they were skilled or unskilled. There were four main classes of occupation in the larger towns of Ireland around the year 1900.

Unskilled workers

A majority of urban workers were unskilled manual labourers, such as dockers, carriers and general labourers. Because of a surplus of these workers wages were low—about £1 per week—and steady employment was not guaranteed. Labourers were hired and fired at will. Dublin dockers, for example, were taken on every morning as casual labourers, but few were assured of continuous employment.

For women, domestic service in the houses of the well-to-do was the major source of unskilled work. This work was mostly done by country girls who earned about four shillings (20p) per week. However, they were better fed than their equals in other occupations.

Unskilled workers were not protected by trade unions at this time.

Skilled workers

These consisted of tradesmen or artisans such as plumbers or carpenters who had served their time in various trades. In Dublin, at the turn of the century, about one in every five workers was skilled. Protected by their trade unions, tradesmen earned about twice as much as unskilled workers.

Small traders and clerical workers

Around 1900, the number of small shopkeepers and publicans was increasing. In the towns, shopkeepers and publicans were richer than the population which they served. Clerical workers and teachers also occupied a middle place in society between rich and poor. Large numbers of clerical workers were employed in the civil service, the post office, the banks and in general offices. Such employment was regarded as respectable and secure.

Big business and the professions

The richest section of society earned its living either from big business or the professions, especially medicine and law. These groups had a high standard of living and many employed domestic servants in their large, comfortable homes.

Housing conditions in towns and cities in 1900

Working-Class housing

In Dublin around 1900, the typical unskilled worker and his family were housed in a tenement—that is, one or more rooms in a large house which was occupied by many families. Most of the tenements were located in the centre of the city. About one-third of Dublin's population lived in them. The situation was similar in other towns such as Cork, Galway and Limerick, although small cottages rather than tenements were more typical there. In Belfast, as a result of higher wages and more secure employment, housing conditions were better.

Tenements in Dublin around 1900.

The growth of suburbs

By 1900, the larger cities had expanded outwards to include suburbs. These suburbs were mainly inhabited by the better-off sections of society. A typical suburban house consisted of a front sitting room, dining room and kitchen downstairs, and three or more bedrooms upstairs—some even included a bathroom. The development of suburban housing was made possible by cheap and efficient transport to the city in the form of railways and trams. There was a great contrast between the terrible poverty of the inner city and the relative comfort of the suburbs.

Test your knowledge

1 What were the four main classes of occupation in the larger towns around the turn of the century?

2 What type of work was carried out by the unskilled workers?

3 What was the major source of female employment at this time?

4 Which groups occupied a 'middle place' between rich and poor?

5 How did the richest section of society earn its living?

6 Describe the housing of the typical unskilled worker.

7 Describe a typical suburban house of this time.

8 What development greatly helped the growth of suburbs?

Improvements in Irish towns

During the 1920s and 1930s, serious efforts were made to tackle the slum problem in Irish towns. Corporations began to build housing schemes for people who had been removed from the inner city. In Dublin, Cork and other towns, this led to the demolition of many tenements near the centre of town. The people were housed instead in new housing schemes such as Marino and Crumlin in Dublin or Gurranabraher and Ballyphehane in Cork.

The introduction of children's allowance payments and better medical facilities were intended to improve the lives of children living in poverty. In particular, the dreaded disease tuberculosis (TB), which attacked adults and children alike, was successfully eliminated during the 1940s and 1950s.

A street in Dublin's inner city around 1960.

The building of Corporation houses in Ballyfermot, Dublin, in the late 1940s.

As long as unemployment and emigration remained high, however, Irish towns, like the Irish countryside, could not hope to enjoy any real or lasting prosperity.

Towns and cities in modern Ireland

The economic prosperity of the 1960s had far-reaching influences on life in Irish towns. With more money in people's pockets, businesses responded accordingly. Supermarkets made their first appearance around this time. Local corner shops saw their trade decline as people were attracted by the cheaper prices in supermarkets.

Many publicans and shopkeepers began to modernise their premises during the 1960s. Lounge bars replaced traditional public houses and impressive hand-crafted shop fronts were often torn down and replaced by ugly plastic fittings and glaring neon lights.

Despite the growing prosperity of Irish towns from the 1960s onwards, not everyone fared equally well. Thousands continued to live in poverty in urban ghettoes. These were vast housing estates of working-class homes with very few leisure facilities in the area. Often they were built miles from the centre of town where the grandparents and other relations of their young families continued to live.

By the 1980s, crime had become a very serious problem in most Irish towns. Elderly people felt unsafe, even in their homes, and car theft had become a serious problem.

Unlike 1900, rich and poor people in towns in modern Ireland can rarely be precisely distinguished by their dress. However, deep divisions between rich and poor have continued. Despite various improvements, poverty and unemployment remain serious threats to the well-being of all who live in towns in Ireland at the close of the twentieth century.

Test your knowledge

1. What action was taken from the 1920s onwards to tackle the slum problem in Irish towns?
2. Name a disease which constantly threatened people in Irish towns up to the 1950s.
3. How did the economic changes of the 1960s affect Irish towns?
4. Show how the appearance of Irish streets changed around this time.
5. Did all town dwellers share equally in the prosperity of the 1960s? Explain.

The United States in 1900

Unlike Ireland, the United States of America in 1900 was a country with a rapidly expanding population. It was a vast continent containing huge farms or ranches on the one hand and growing industrial cities on the other. In Ireland, there was a serious unemployment problem leading to massive emigration at the time. The USA, on the other hand, needed many workers for its expanding industries. Consequently it encouraged the arrival of millions of immigrants from Europe. Many Irish people were among these immigrants.

The Statue of Liberty was the first sight seen by many immigrants on their arrival in New York.

Society in America in 1900 was far more mobile than in Ireland and other European countries. This means that, if people worked hard, they could rise up in society and others would admire them. It mattered little to people what type of work their parents or grandparents had carried out. This was definitely not the case in Ireland at the time, where most people continued to follow the occupations of their parents.

Unlike Ireland, where most people earned their living on the land, towns and cities were very important in the USA. But American agriculture still had an important part to play.

Agriculture in the United States

In some respects, agriculture in the USA was like that in Ireland. Farmers received uncertain and often fallings prices for their goods. At a time when industry was thriving, this led to a decline of the importance of agriculture in the economy as can be seen from the following table.

PERCENTAGE OF NATIONAL INCOME RECEIVED BY FARMERS IN THE USA		
1860	–	30%
1890	–	19%
1920	–	13%
1933	–	7%

If American farmers suffered like Irish farmers from uncertain prices, many of them also suffered from a backward standard of living. As a result, many sons and daughters of American farmers left the land to seek their fortunes in the city. Between 1870 and 1930 the rural population declined from eighty per cent to less than forty per cent of the total.

A cotton plantation in Mississippi around 1900.

As the population living in the countryside continued to decline, the political influence of farmers in the USA also declined. This was evident during the 1920s when the USA government did little to help them during a period of crisis. Between 1920 and 1932, total farm income declined from \$15½ billion to \$5½ billion. In 1933, as part of the *New Deal* of President Franklin D. Roosevelt, assistance was given to farmers to prevent them from going out of business.

During and after World War II, American farmers enjoyed widespread prosperity. However, after the establishment of the European Economic Community (EEC) in 1957, American farmers faced stiff competition from the products of their European counterparts on the world market.

Test your knowledge

1 List two ways in which the United States differed from Ireland around the year 1900.

2 What was the attitude of the USA government to immigration?

3 Would you agree that society was mobile in America at the time? Explain.

4 State two difficulties which faced farmers in both Ireland and America.

5 How did the falling numbers in the countryside affect the political influence of American farmers?

6 Show how the 1920s was a period of crisis in American agriculture.

7 What threat to American farmers began in 1957?

Towns and cities in 1900

Around 1900, a majority of Americans were living in towns and cities for the first time in the country's history. Huge businesses were run by very wealthy people. A study undertaken in 1896 calculated that one per cent of the national population owned nearly half of the country's wealth.

Between 1880 and 1900, the population of New York City, the country's largest city, had increased from 2 million to 3½ million. In the same period, Chicago's population had risen from ½ million to 1½ million, making it the second largest city in the land. Therefore the two largest USA cities in 1900 between them would have equalled the entire population of Ireland.

Tenements in New York in 1900. Many immigrant families first lived in this type of accommodation.

Life in the big cities of America was often tough

and difficult. People who arrived there from American farms or from foreign countries had to give up their old way of life and learn to adapt to the new situation. They faced a choice between hard work or poverty. There was no unemployment benefit or other welfare payments available at the time.

Very often, vast numbers of newcomers to American cities were exploited by corrupt politicians. Having got these people's votes, such politicians did little to improve living conditions; instead they used their power and influence to make themselves wealthy.

From expansion to depression (1920–40)

During the 1920s, the cities of America were at the forefront of the modern movement known as the 'Roaring Twenties'. Cities stood for excitement and adventure where the latest fashions in music, dress and behaviour could be found. Suburbs outside cities expanded rapidly as the motor car enable people to commute from home to work.

Describe this scene of Prohibition in America in the 1920s.

The 1920s was also the era of *Prohibition* in America. Alcoholic drink was banned by law. However, the law was openly flouted and many American cities witnessed violent feuds when the police raided illegal drinking places which were frequently run by criminal gangs.

This was also the era of gangsters and their mobs in the US. The most famous of these men was Al Capone whose gang terrorised the people of Chicago until he was shot in an encounter with the police in 1933.

The *Great Depression* followed the collapse of the American Stock Market on Wall Street, New York, in October 1929. This had a devastating impact on the lives of people in the towns and cities of the US. By 1933, the number of jobless people stood somewhere between 12 and 15 million. There were pathetic scenes witnessed in city streets as people who had lost vast fortunes threw themselves from high-rise buildings. Huge queues formed outside food depots where relief was handed out.

Panic spread as people lost their fortunes because of the Wall Street Crash in 1929.

Under the New Deal programme of President Roosevelt, the economy gradually recovered from the Depression. But not until after the end of World War II in 1945 did an air of hope for the future return to the towns and cities of America.

The modern city

From the 1950s onwards, American cities continued to expand. Much of the new space required for homes and businesses came in the form of high-rise skyscrapers. However, many of the city dwellers now chose to live in suburbs. As a result, the census of 1960 showed that in eight of the ten largest cities, the population had fallen since 1950 due to people moving out to the suburbs. At this stage between 40 and 50 million Americans were living in suburbs.

New York—a city of skyscrapers.

As a result of this movement, many central city areas became ghettoes where the poor lived. Not surprisingly, many ghetto areas had high levels of poverty, unemployment and crime. Crimes including murder, violent attacks, drug pushing and robbery have become part and parcel of everyday life in large American cities.

By 1970, nearly seventy per cent of the American population lived in or near big cities. At the same time, the total farm population was less than it had been in 1830.

At the end of the twentieth century, the USA clearly faces some of the same problems as Ireland.

In both countries there has been a continuous flight from the land. As Dublin has expanded, so too have American cities, with all the problems that the separation of people into wealthy and poor areas has brought about.

Test your knowledge

1 Show how wealth was unevenly distributed in the USA around 1900.
2 Name the two largest cities in the USA in 1900. Show that their populations were increasing rapidly.
3 Why was life often difficult for newcomers to American cities?
4 What were the 'Roaring Twenties'?
5 Explain what was meant by 'Prohibition'.
6 When did the Great Depression begin?
7 Show the impact of the Depression on life in American cities.
8 Why had the population of many American cities fallen by 1960?
9 List some of the problems found in modern cities in the USA.

Chapter 76: Review

• Historically there have been many close links between Ireland and America which have remained strong up to the present day.

• In 1900, most Irish people lived in the countryside where they worked on the land. Emigration remained very high from the time of the Great Famine onwards.

• Some important changes have taken place in the Irish countryside since 1922. The introduction of tractors and the arrival of both electricity and running water improved life and work on many Irish farms.

• The great change for Irish farmers came in 1973 when the country entered the EEC. As a result of grants and an increase in prices, many farmers modernised their holdings.

• Fewer Irish people lived in large towns and cities around 1900. Within the towns and cities there were great differences between rich and poor. The majority of workers were unskilled, while the richest section of society earned its living from big business and the professions.

• In Dublin around 1900, the typical unskilled worker and his family were housed in a tenement, while the better-off sections of society lived in the suburbs.

• During the 1920s and 1930s, many slums were cleared and people were housed instead in new housing schemes away from the city centres.

• From the 1960s onwards, city life in Ireland underwent many changes. Supermarkets and lounge bars became common. Thousands continued to live in poverty, and crime became a serious problem.

• Unlike Ireland, the USA in 1900 was a country with a rapidly expanding population. While most people at that time earned their living on the land in Ireland, towns and cities were very important in the USA.

• During the 1920s and 1930s, the population living in the USA countryside continued to decline, while big cities expanded.

• While cities stood for excitement and adventure, those living in them often experienced tough and difficult circumstances. The 1920s was the era of the gangsters in cities like Chicago, while the Great Depression had a devastating impact on people living in the towns and cities.

• From the 1950s onwards, American cities continued to expand so that by 1970, nearly seventy per cent of the American population lived in or near big cities.

CHAPTER 77

Leisure and Pastimes

Ireland around 1900

Unlike today, most people in Ireland around 1900 provided their own entertainment. In the absence of television, radio or videos, live home-based entertainment was the norm.

In both towns and countryside, people visited one another's homes in the evening to enjoy conversation, music and card playing. In many parts of the country, a local storyteller known as a *seanchaí* entertained his listeners with tales of long ago.

In Irish towns and cities, many people enjoyed musical evenings. Friends and neighbours would gather around the piano in the candlelight to entertain one another by singing and playing.

New Year's Eve party, around 1880.

There were many outdoor pastimes in Ireland around 1900. Hunting and horse racing were very popular among the rich. Sports such as rugby and soccer had grown in popularity. However, since the foundation of the Gaelic Athletic Association (GAA) in 1884, hurling and Gaelic football had become very popular throughout the country.

In both towns and cities, a visit to the theatre was a popular way of spending an evening. In 1904, the famous Abbey Theatre opened in Dublin. Here people came to see the work of great playwrights such as Yeats, Synge and O'Casey.

A scene from one of Seán O'Casey's plays, The Plough and the Stars, *which was first staged at the Abbey Theatre in 1926.*

The arrival of radio and cinema

Radio's first announcer in the studio of 2 RN in 1926.

The arrival of the cinema in Ireland was one of the greatest changes in the world of entertainment. Although some small cinemas had been set up before 1914, it was during the 1920s and 1930s that cinemas became extremely popular throughout the country. In the days before television, thousands of people flocked to the cinema each night to see their heroes and heroines on the big screen.

Another great breakthrough in entertainment in Ireland took place in 1926 when the country's first radio station, 2RN, was set up. This later became known as Radio Éireann. By 1940, not only news programmes and music but also Sunday matches were being broadcast throughout the country on radio.

Radio broadcasting for children in the 1940s.

The ballroom of romance

Dance halls were another popular form of entertainment in Ireland. Although some catered for Irish music and céilí dancing, jazz, swing and other forms of modern music were played in most dance halls.

During the 1950s, dance halls were at the centre

Dancing to the music of the 1950s and 1960s.

of the new Rock and Roll craze as Irish people enthusiastically took to the new dance forms popularised in Britain and America.

Many romances had their beginnings in the dance halls throughout the country. These centres of entertainment became even more popular during the 1960s.

Test your knowledge

1 What forms of entertainment were popular in Ireland around 1900?
2 Explain the role of the seanchaí.
3 Name the main outdoor pastimes in Ireland around 1900.
4 What theatre was opened in 1904?
5 When did cinema become popular in Ireland?
6 Name Ireland's first radio station and state when it was opened.
7 What type of dancing became popular in Ireland during the 1950s?

The age of television

On 31 December 1961, Ireland's first television station, Telefis Éireann, began transmitting for the first time. Within a short period, television became the most popular form of mass entertainment in the country. Television opened up Irish society to many outside influences. Programmes such as the Late Late Show started discussions on issues which had never been publicly debated before. Television also led to a decline in many traditional pastimes such as storytelling, card playing and music in the home.

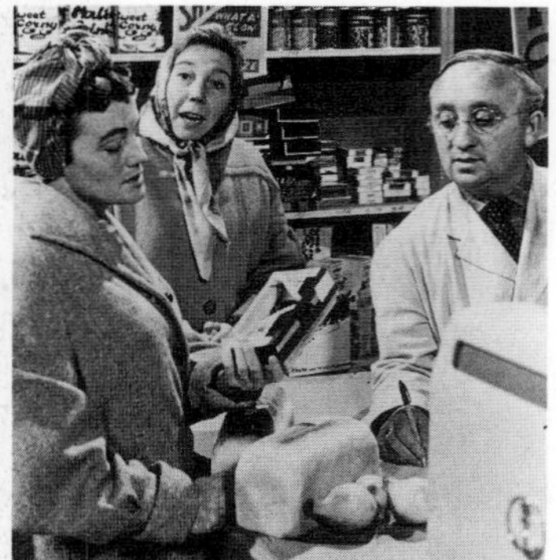
A scene from Tolka Row, a popular television soap opera of the 1960s, set in Dublin.

The 'Late Late Show', hosted by Gay Byrne, was first broadcast in the 1960s.

The cinema also declined in popularity in the 1960s and 1970s with many of the larger cinemas closing down as more and more people chose to stay at home watching television. During the 1980s, many families became owners of video recorders in addition to their televisions.

Popular music underwent great changes from the 1960s onwards. Young people everywhere danced to the music of the showbands during the 1960s. During the 1970s and 1980s, these were replaced by other forms of music, especially rock. The dance halls were largely replaced by the loud music and flashing lights of discotheques.

Irish traditional music experienced a revival from the 1960s onwards. Groups like the Chieftains, Planxty and Horslips made this form of music popular with the younger generation.

A different world

Leisure activities have changed dramatically in Ireland during the twentieth century. Today, people have more money to spend on entertainment, as well as much more free time than their ancestors a century ago. In 1900, most of the entertainment was centred around the home and provided by the people themselves. In today's Ireland, entertainment has become a multi-million-pound industry. There is now a great variety of entertainments to choose from. However, it is also true that some people regret the passing of many of the old forms of entertainment once provided by people in their own homes.

Test your knowledge

1 When was Ireland's first television station opened?
2 How did television affect traditional pastimes?
3 How did popular music change from the 1960s onwards?
4 State two ways in which entertainment in Ireland has changed between 1900 and 1990.

The United States around 1900

As can be expected in such a vast continent, a wide variety of leisure activities were open to Americans around 1900. Outdoor sports included hunting of all types, rodeo racing, horse racing and the two popular team games, American football and American baseball.

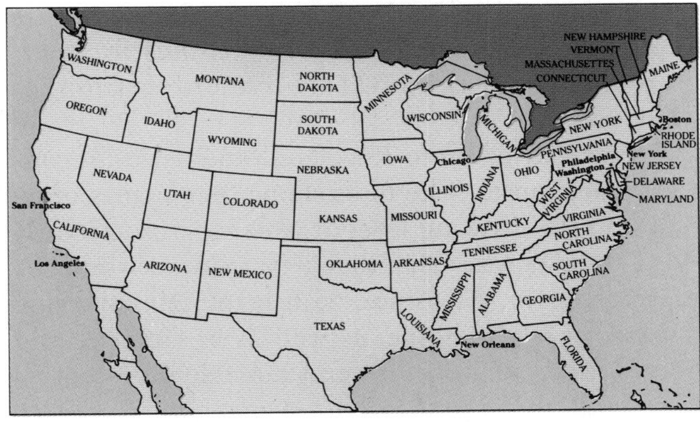

The United States of America.

Inventions were just beginning to have an impact in the world of entertainment. The earliest form of record, the phonograph, had arrived, as had the first silent movies. However, such novelties as yet posed no serious threat to the live theatre.

The most famous centre of live theatre in the USA was Broadway in New York City. There, shows of different types might be seen, ranging from opera and classical drama to the music hall style theatre known as *vaudeville*. It was still the era of the travelling theatre companies which moved from town to town throughout the country, bringing Shakespeare and the classics as well as more modern plays to local audiences.

Unknown to the wider world, a new type of music was becoming popular at this time in the Deep South of the United States. Centred on the city of New Orleans, this new type of music was known as *jazz*. It began among black musicians in that area. Within a short period, it became famous the world over.

The Roaring Twenties

After the sacrifices and difficulties of the war years, many Americans were determined to enjoy themselves during the 1920s. Fashions and general behaviour became more daring, and new and exciting dances such as the *Charleston* were the order of the day. Jazz became more popular and bands were formed to play the latest music.

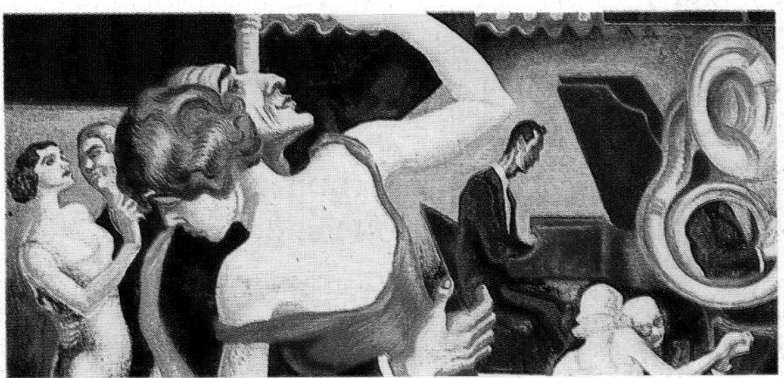

American women enjoying themselves in New York during the Roaring Twenties.

Unlike their parents, Americans in the 1920s did not have to play the music themselves or leave their homes in order to enjoy it. Gramophone records were becoming widely available and more and more families became owners of wireless or radio sets.

However, the most popular of all the new forms of entertainment was the cinema.

Test your knowledge

1 List some outdoor pursuits in America around 1900.
2 Name two inventions which became popular at the time.
3 What was the most famous centre of theatre in the USA at the time?
4 Where did jazz music originate?
5 What was the Charleston?
6 List two inventions which enabled people to hear the latest popular music in America during the 1920s.

The movies

From the 1920s onwards, the USA became the leading country in the world in the making of motion pictures, or *movies*, as they were popularly known. During World War I, a studio had been established at Hollywood in California for the making of silent movies where a huge film industry sprang up.

During the 1920s, the silent movies were the great form of entertainment. Stars like Charlie Chaplin, Mary Pickford and Rudolf Valentino entertained millions the world over.

Charlie Chaplin in the 'Great Dictator'.

From 1927 onwards, silent movies were replaced by the 'talkies' and in 1939 colour films made their first appearance. Film stars were hero worshipped by millions of loyal fans and different studios were in strong competition with one another.

From Swing to Rock and Roll

As well as in cinema, America led the world in the area of popular music. During the 1930s and 1940s, jazz and swing music were all the rage. It was the era of the big bands which played to vast live audiences or to millions over the radio.

Louis Armstrong, one of the great jazz musicians of his time.

When World War II broke out, many of these bands went on tours to entertain the troops. One of the greatest of all the big band leaders, Glenn Miller, joined the American air force and was killed on active service in 1944.

In the 1950s, a new craze hit popular music in America—Rock and Roll. Young people deserted the big bands in favour of new idols such as Buddy Holly or Bill Haley and the Comets. Rock and Roll also involved new forms of dancing. Many older people were shocked by the new fashions in music and dancing. However, the Rock and Roll craze went from strength to strength and paved the way for the emergence of 'pop music' during the 1960s.

Elvis Presley became a legendary Rock and Roll star.

Modern times

As in Ireland, entertainment in the United States from the 1960s onwards was greatly influenced by television and radio and by new inventions such as transistor radios and video recorders. People depended more and more on machines for their enjoyment and the level of live entertainment decreased.

Pop music led on to Rock and other types of contemporary music. The films shown in cinemas often reflected the growing level of violence in society. By the 1980s, it was clear that leisure time would be even longer in the future, with many labour-saving inventions in the home, as well as in factories and offices. As a result, more and more leisure centres were built and courses were set up to guide people in the use of their leisure time.

Test your knowledge

1. Name the main centre of the American film industry.
2. Name two stars of the silent movies.
3. What improvement took place in film-making in 1939?
4. Who was Glenn Miller?
5. Name a famous star of Rock and Roll.
6. What trends took place in entertainment in the USA from the 1960s onwards?

Chapter 77: Review

• Most people in Ireland around 1900 provided their own entertainment. Storytelling, music, card playing, sports and a visit to the theatre were widely enjoyed.

• The arrival of cinema and radio marked important advances in entertainment in Ireland.

• During the 1950s and the 1960s, dance halls were very popular places of entertainment in Ireland. During the 1970s and 1980s, the dance halls were largely replaced by discotheques.

• From the 1960s onwards, television became the most popular form of mass entertainment in Ireland. It also led to a decline in many traditional pastimes.

• A wide variety of leisure activities were available in the US around 1900. One of the most popular forms of entertainment was the live theatre. The most famous centre of live theatre was Broadway in New York City.

• During the 1920s, jazz became a very popular form of music. This was also the age of the cinema with stars like Charlie Chaplin and Rudolf Valentino.

• During the 1930s and 1940s, big bands like Glenn Miller's entertained huge audiences. During the 1950s, Rock and Roll became all the rage, while the 1960s saw the emergence of 'pop' music.

CHAPTER 78 The Role of Women in Society

Ireland in 1900

A hundred years ago, women played a much more restricted role in public life in Ireland than they do today. Whether rich or poor, they were frequently dependent on their fathers or husbands. The wives and daughters in rich or middle-income families did not go out to work. Instead, they remained at home, waited on by servants. Better-off women often visited one another's houses or became involved in local charities. They were also expected to be accomplished in skills such as drawing or playing a musical instrument. In dress, they followed the latest fashions from London or Paris.

Women's fashions in Ireland around 1900.

Most Irish women in 1900 did not enjoy lives of luxury and ease. In the countryside, the wives and daughters of all but the richest farmers were expected to work hard on the land. The farmer's wife had particular responsibility for the care of poultry. Very often, the money earned from selling eggs was the only income handled by the women on the farm.

Working-class women in towns and cities frequently had to go out to work as well as take care of the home. In the North of Ireland, such women found steady work in mills and factories. In Derry, they were often the only breadwinners as their husbands were unemployed. In Dublin and the rest of Southern Ireland, working-class women had to rely on very badly paid work such as house-cleaning or street-selling. Even when women did get steady work, their wages were always much lower than men's.

Many single working-class girls were domestic servants in the homes of the better-off. Here they worked long hours with little time off and earned very low pay.

Despite the disadvantages facing women in Ireland around 1900, there were signs of improvements for the future. The number of girls in secondary schools and colleges was steadily increasing. As well as this, the type of education available to them was improving, thanks to the existence of many excellent Catholic convent secondary schools and Protestant girls' secondary schools.

Some Irish women who protested against unequal treatment in the workplace.

At the same time, a small group of Irish women was organising to fight for a basic civil right which was still denied to women—the right to vote.

The Suffragette movement in Ireland

Irish suffragettes march to demand the vote for women.

By 1900, although women who owned property were allowed to vote in elections for corporations and county councils, no woman was allowed to vote in parliamentary elections. At the time, Irish MPs sat in the British parliament at Westminster. In Britain, a powerful women's movement was being organised to fight for the right to vote, or *suffrage* as it was called. The more militant members of this movement were known as the *Suffragettes*. Although some working-class women joined the movement, it consisted mainly of middle-class, well-educated women who resented this denial of equality with men.

Although a much smaller organisation than its British counterpart, the Irish Suffragette Movement shared the same ideals. The first group with this aim, the Dublin Women's Suffrage Society, had been founded as far back as 1876 by Anna Haslam. In 1908, a much more militant group, the Irish Women's Franchise League, was founded by Hanna Sheehy-Skeffington. It was modelled on the British Suffragette Movement and did not hesitate to use violent methods of protest when the British government continued to deny women the right to vote or to sit in parliament.

Like their fellow suffragettes in Britain, Irish suffragettes broke windows, went on hunger strike in prison and attacked members of the government. The prime minister himself, H.H. Asquith, had a hatchet thrown at him by a suffragette during a visit to Dublin in July 1912.

Working with Evidence

Read the following contemporary comments on the Suffragette Movement in Ireland and answer the questions which follow.

Extract A The Reason for Joining

'I was then an undergraduate and was amazed and disgusted to learn that I was classed among criminals, infants and lunatics—in fact, that my status as a woman was worse than any of these.'

Hanna Sheehy-Skeffington

Extract B

'The police should use whips on the shoulders of those unsexed viragoes.'

A letter writer in the Evening Telegraph, *9 July 1912*

Extract C

'That strange tribe, small in number, that has arisen on the horizon in Ireland in quite recent times. They are not men, they are not women. Woman: the idea comprises dignity, self-respect, refinement, reserve. I don't find any of these qualities among the Suffragettes.'

Monsignor Keller of Youghal

Extract D

'Take up your responsibilities and be prepared to go your own way depending for your safety on your own courage, your own truth, and your own commonsense, and not on the problematic chivalry of the men you may meet on the way.'

Countess Markievicz, speaking to Suffragettes in 1915

1. What political disability did women share with 'criminals, infants and lunatics' according to Hanna Sheehy-Skeffington?
2. Describe the violent response to the Irish Suffragettes displayed by the letter writer in the Evening Telegraph.
3. How did Monsignor Keller try to blacken the name of the Suffragettes?

4 Would his view of the role of women be widely accepted today?
5 What was the main theme of Countess Markievicz's message to women?

The divisions between Nationalists and Unionists which were so deep at the time also affected women's groups. Some gifted women, although fully supporting women's rights, believed that the struggle for independence from Great Britain should come first. By the time women in Ireland got the vote in parliamentary elections in 1918, the country was in the throes of a violent struggle between the British government and Irish Nationalists. Many women took a very prominent part in that movement.

Test your knowledge

1 Describe the lifestyle of better-off women in Ireland around 1900.
2 List two groups of women who frequently had to work outside the home.
3 What signs of improvement in the conditions of women were there around 1900?
4 What was the main political disability suffered by women at this time?
5 When was the first women's suffrage group set up in Ireland and by whom?
6 What society did Hanna Sheehy-Skeffington found in 1908?
7 List some of the tactics used by Irish suffragettes.
8 When were women in Ireland given the right to vote in parliamentary elections?

Irish women in the independence movement

From 1900 onwards, women were to play an important role in the movement for Irish independence. Maud Gonne established a special society *Inghinidhe na hÉireann* for women with Republican views. Jennie Wyse Power, a supporter of the suffrage movement, was also a vice-president of Sinn Féin, the Nationalist organisation founded by Arthur Griffith in 1905.

Republican women helping to smuggle weapons to Ireland for the Irish Volunteers.

The most prominent of all women in the independence movement was Constance Gore-Booth, who later became Countess Markievicz. Born into a rich Anglo–Irish landowning family in Co. Sligo, she devoted much of her life to working for the poor. She was closely involved with James Larkin and James Connolly on the workers' side during the strike and lockout in Dublin in 1913. She was also a leading member of the Citizen Army. Countess Markievicz was involved as well as an organiser of the Fianna Éireann, a Republican boy scout movement.

Countess Constance Markievicz and her children.

Countess Markievicz was sentenced to death for her prominent part in the 1916 Rising, but this was commuted to a term of imprisonment. In December 1918, she became the first woman to be elected to the British parliament but she refused to take her seat there as she was a member of Sinn Féin. She became Minister for Labour in the first government set up by Dáil Éireann in 1919.

During the 1916 Rising, the War of Independence and the Civil War, women were very active in caring for the sick, carrying messages and providing other back-up services. They had their own organisation known as *Cumann na mBan* which was banned by the British government.

Independent Ireland (1922–60)

Between 1922 and 1960, women in Ireland were part of a fairly conservative society. Most people continued to believe that a woman's place was in the home and women's pay continued to lag behind that of men. On getting married, women nearly always gave up their jobs and in some areas such as teaching and the civil service, they had no choice but to do this.

In the new constitution adopted by the Irish people in 1937, the importance of the role of the woman in the home was recognised.

'In particular, the State recognises that by her life within the home, woman gives to the State a support without which the common good cannot be achieved.

The State, shall, therefore, endeavour to ensure that mothers shall not be obliged by economic necessity to engage in labour to the neglect of their duties in the home.'

Bunreacht na hÉireann, Article 41.

Despite the assurances in the constitution, many Irish women continued to live in poverty which forced them to go out to work.

Despite the existence of poverty and unemployment, the position of women was improving gradually up to 1960. As in earlier times, their increasing access to education was one of the keys to an understanding of this trend. When the economy improved in the 1960s, Irish women, along with women in many parts of the world, made their voices heard in a demand for full equality with men.

The modern women's movement in Ireland

From 1960 onwards, women in Ireland have been concerned with bringing about improvements in a number of key areas:

- More equal educational opportunities.
- Equal pay for equal work.
- Greater involvement by women in politics and public life generally.
- Higher participation by women in the top positions in various careers.

Continuous efforts have been made since 1960 to improve educational opportunities for women and to enable them to enter courses traditionally dominated by men such as honours mathematics and engineering. In 1974, a law was passed making equal pay for equal work compulsory. Three years later, the *Employment Equality Act* (1977) was passed. This made discrimination on the ground of sex or marital status illegal. It also set up the *Employment Equality Agency* to act as a watchdog in this area.

From the 1960s onwards, women in Ireland took a more active role in politics and public life. The number of female TDs and senators increased slowly but steadily and women became government ministers.

Gemma Hussey, a government minister between 1982 and 1987.

Mary Robinson was elected President of Ireland in 1990.

The number of women in the top jobs in the country remains extremely small, however. The fact that women are often expected to run a home as well as a career has been blamed for this situation.

Despite the various inequalities between men and women which remained in Ireland, by 1990 no one can deny that Irish women have come a long way since the time of the struggle for the vote at the start of the century.

Test your knowledge

1. Name the women's Republican group founded by Maud Gonne.
2. Where was Countess Markievicz born?
3. What was her role during the 1913 strike and lockout in Dublin?
4. Name the Republican boy scout movement which she organised.
5. List two important 'firsts' recorded by Countess Markievicz in 1918–19.
6. What did the Irish constitution (1937) state about the role of women in the home?
7. List three aims of the women's movement in Ireland since the 1960s.
8. Explain the Employment Equality Act (1977).

Women in America around 1900

Around 1900 women in the United States of America had one great advantage over women in Ireland—they were needed as workers by an expanding economy. Ever since the foundation of the United States, women had been scarce, especially in the west. Because of this they gained a status still unknown in Europe. Visitors to America from Europe often remarked on the greater freedom enjoyed by American women.

Industrialisation also helped their position. The mass production of cheaper clothes and other goods lessened the load of a woman in running a home. More importantly, there were far more jobs becoming available for women. Telephone operators, typists and clerical workers now took their place alongside traditional women's jobs such as seamstresses, mill workers and teachers. However, although the number of jobs available to women was increasing, wages lagged significantly behind those of men. In 1900, one study in the United States found that, on average, women's wages were only fifty-three per cent of those of men. The main reason for this was that most women worked in the poorer-paid areas of the economy.

A girl working in an American factory around 1900. Women and girls played a vital part in America's industrial expansion. However, most of them were found in lower-paid jobs.

Learning and voting

The United States had a very good reputation in the area of higher education for women. From the end of the Civil War in 1865, many women's colleges had been founded and some older universities like Cornell and Michigan had become co-educational. It is not surprising that there was this demand because, by 1900, girls outnumbered boys among those who completed second level education.

It was to be expected that well-educated women would demand full civil and political rights. In line with the good record on women's education, some parts of the United States had taken the lead in granting women the vote.

In 1869, the territory of Wyoming granted women the right to vote and the neighbouring territory of Utah followed suit in 1870. However, it was not until 1920 that the right to vote was extended to women throughout the United States by the nineteenth amendment of the US constitution.

American women campaigning for the right to vote in 1905.

Changing lifestyles in America (1920–60)

During the 1920s, the role of women in the United States was changing rapidly. Many women had worked outside the home during World War I (1914–18). After that war, a new wave of greater freedom in personal lifestyles swept America and greatly influenced the lives of women. Over twice as many women entered the labour force between 1920 and 1930 as had done so between 1910 and 1920. By 1930, the number of women typists had increased tenfold since 1900.

During the 1920s, women's fashions changed with shorter dresses and lighter clothes. At the same time they could be seen drinking and smoking in public, something which 'respectable' ladies would not have done before 1914.

Throughout the 1920s, the divorce rate increased by fifty per cent. This was in marked contrast to Ireland where divorce was not permitted.

Marilyn Monroe, the famous American actress. Acting was one of the few occupations in which women were as successful as men.

In the USA during the 1920s, over two-thirds of the divorce proceedings were started by women. This was a sign that they were seeking an escape from marriages if they could not secure equality. Even during the Depression decade of the 1930s, the numbers of women entering the workforce continued to rise.

During World War II, almost 4 million more American women entered the country's offices and factories. Despite the advances made by 1960, women's wages were still a long way behind those of men and many American women believed that vast inequalities between men and women still existed.

Test your knowledge

1 Why was there a greater degree of freedom for women in America than in Europe around 1900?
2 How did industrial expansion assist women?
3 What was the result of a survey on women's wages in the USA in 1900?
4 When were women first granted the right to vote in part of America?
5 Give an example of the increased participation of women in the American workforce during the 1920s.

Women's liberation

From the 1960s onwards, a powerful Women's Liberation Movement existed in the United States of America. Men and women who were involved in or supporters of this movement were known as *feminists*. Most American feminists agreed on the need for equal pay, better educational opportunities and a shared workload in the home.

However, there were also deep divisions in the Women's Liberation Movement. Some feminists campaigned for the right of abortion and opposed any attempts to restrict abortion facilities by those who wanted to protect the right to life of the unborn child.

Throughout the 1960s, 1970s and 1980s, greater numbers of American women became involved in public life. In 1984, for the first time ever, one of the candidates for vice-president of the United States of America was a woman, Ms Geraldine Ferraro.

The fact that the United States is the richest country in the world explains the strength of the women's movement there. More women than in other countries had the wealth, education and leisure to engage in a campaign for women's liberation.

Chapter 78: Review

• In Ireland around 1900, the wives and daughters of rich people did not go out to work but remained at home where they were waited upon by servants. In contrast, working-class women in towns and cities often had to go out to work as well as taking care of the home.

• In the early 1900s the Suffragette Movement in Ireland led by Hanna Sheehy-Skeffington campaigned for the right to vote.

• Women also played an important part in the movement for Irish independence, most notably Countess Markievicz.

• Between 1922 and 1960, many people continued to believe that a woman's place was in the home. There were many inequalities between men and women, especially in the area of pay.

• During the 1960s, the modern women's movement emerged. Over the years, many of its aims—such as equal pay for equal work and more equal educational opportunities—were achieved.

• In the US, women around 1900 had far greater freedom than their European counterparts. While many more women worked, their wages lagged significantly behind those of men.

• The US had a very good reputation in the area of higher education for women. By 1900, girls outnumbered boys among those who completed second level education.

• Between 1920 and 1960, many changes came about in the lifestyles of American women. However, as in Ireland, the great change came about in the 1960s with the establishment of a powerful Women's Liberation Movement.

CHAPTER 79

The Changing World of Transport

On the move

From around 1900 onwards, there have been vast and exciting changes in travel and transport. These have greatly influenced the lives of ordinary people in both Ireland and America. Photographs taken through the years provide us with vivid sources concerning these changes. Throughout this chapter we will see for ourselves how transport has progressed from the era of the horse and cart to the modern day Space Age.

A slower age

A 'long car' in Co. Wexford around 1900 used for carrying passengers.

Unlike today in Ireland, in 1900 many ordinary people depended completely on walking in order to travel. There were many people indeed who rarely travelled outside their native parish, village or town. Other people thought little about going on walks of many miles' distance.

At the time a new invention was becoming popular in Ireland—the bicycle.

Many poorer people living in the Irish countryside travelled by donkey and cart.

In both towns and countryside horse-drawn transport was still widely used for work and leisure. Look at the pictures to see horses at work on the farm and drawing goods through the streets of towns. In the early years of the century, horse-drawn transport was widely used, ranging from the carriages of the rich to the pony and trap used by ordinary people.

From 1900 onwards, electric trams were beginning to replace horse-drawn vehicles in the main cities.

An electric tram in Dublin around 1914.

At the same time, Ireland had an extensive network of railways. These trains had luxurious first-class carriages for the rich. However, poorer people were also able to use this relatively cheap and comfortable form of transport. Cheap excursions to the seaside by rail helped the growth of seaside resorts such as Bundoran, Bray and Youghal.

Test your knowledge

1. What was the main means of transport for most ordinary people in Ireland around 1900?
2. What new form of transport was becoming popular at the time?
3. How were horses used in the countryside and the towns around 1900?
4. What form of transport was replacing horse-drawn transport in the cities?
5. State two ways in which railways affected the lives of ordinary people in Ireland around 1900.

The age of the motor car

Around 1900, motor cars made their first appearance on Irish roads. At first, only very rich people could afford this new form of transport. By 1914,

A parade of new cars on the road around 1920.

motor cars were common sights on Irish roads. After World War I, petrol-driven lorries and buses were seen in towns all over Ireland.

During the 1920s and 1930s, road transport competed successfully with the railways and more and more railway lines were closed.

In 1944, a semi-state company known as *Coras Iompair Éireann (CIE)* was set up to take charge of the railways and buses throughout the country. This company controls public transport in Ireland up to the present day.

Modern times

We have seen already how Ireland experienced major industrial expansion during the 1960s. Travel and transport were a central part of this rapidly changing scene. As people became more affluent, there was a great increase in the number of family cars. At the same time, better roads were being provided throughout the country.

Railway transport also changed as steam engines were replaced by diesels.

Passengers leaving an Aer Lingus flight around 1950.

One of the great successes of modern Ireland was the national airline company, *Aer Lingus,* which had been founded in 1936. During the 1960s, air passenger transport increased and business expanded at the three main airports of Dublin, Shannon and Cork. By the 1980s the country had come a long way indeed from the days of the steam engine and the pony and trap.

Test your knowledge

1 What form of transport had become popular in Ireland by 1914?

2 Name the company set up in 1944 to take charge of public transport in Ireland.

3 Name two important developments in transport during the 1960s.

4 What is the national airline company called?

5 Write down two ways in which transport in Ireland in the 1980s had improved since 1900.

The United States of America in 1900

The transport needs of people in the US around 1900 were vastly different from those of people in Ireland. Whereas Ireland was a small country with a declining population, the US was a vast land with a rapidly increasing population, partly caused by a high level of immigration.

Construction workers on the American transcontinental railroad around 1870.

A huge railway network criss-crossed the continent from the Atlantic in the east to the Pacific in the west. Many people alive in the US at the time could recall the Pony Express bringing the mail. Indeed, trains had arrived in remote western areas only twenty years previously.

Because of the vast populations in American cities, satisfactory systems of transport were required. The Americans were fortunate that many inventors of genius lived in the US at the time. These inventors put their minds to work on transport needs and came up with some impressive results. One of the earliest of these inventions was the cable car developed by Charles Harvey, a New York inventor. By 1900 cable cars were in use in twenty-three American cities where they carried 370 million passengers a year.

In 1880 the famous inventor, Thomas Edison, experimented with a form of electrified railway. This was the forerunner of the streetcar, the American name for a tram. By 1900, many American cities had streetcar systems. Streetcars were faster and cleaner then horse-drawn trams or cable cars. As a result, by 1903, America's 48,000 kilometres of street railways were ninety-eight per cent electrified.

As in Ireland, however, great changes took placed with the arrival of the motor car.

The arrival of the motor car

In the USA, the development of the motor car will always be associated with the name of Henry Ford whose ancestors had emigrated from Co. Cork. Little did people in 1900 realise the revolution which was in store! In October 1899 an American magazine, the *Literary Digest*, contained the following prophecy:

> 'The ordinary "horseless carriage" is at present a luxury for the wealthy; and although its price will probably fall in the future, it will never, of course, come into as common use as the bicycle.'

Cars being assembled at the Ford Motor Company in Detroit, Michigan.

Thanks largely to the initiative of Henry Ford in his Detroit Motor Company, the 'horseless carriage', or motor car, did come into 'as common use as the bicycle'. In 1908, Ford produced his famous 'Model T' motor car, popularly known as the 'Tin Lizzie'. Its design remained the same for the next twenty years. However, the price continued to drop due to increased efficiency in production. By 1925, Ford was turning out 9,000 cars a day or one every ten seconds. Led by Ford, the number of automobiles in the US rose from one million in 1913 to 10 million in 1923.

These developments in turn led to the construction of lorries and trucks and the building of larger and better roads throughout America. The finances to improve these roads came from taxation on petrol.

As America led the way in road transport in the 1920s and 1930s, it was also to be in the forefront of a transport revolution of a very different kind after 1945—travel by air and space.

Proud owners of a Ford car.

Test your knowledge

1 How were the transport needs of America different from those of Ireland in 1900?
2 Who invented the cable car?
3 Were cable cars widely used in 1900? Explain your answer.
4 What was a streetcar?
5 Why were streetcars often preferred to horse trams or cable cars?
6 Name Henry Ford's most successful type of car.
7 Explain how the car industry in the US was expanding rapidly by the mid 1920s.

Air and space travel

America had been a pioneer in terms of air travel. In 1903, two American brothers, Orville and Wilbur Wright, had made the first flight in the world in an aeroplane.

During the 1920s and 1930s, the American airline industry expanded rapidly. In 1929, the large American company Trans World Airlines (TWA) was established, seven years before Ireland followed suit with the setting up of Aer Lingus. As well as organising international passenger flights, American airline companies built up a huge network of internal flights. By the 1960s, many people in America travelled from city to city by air instead of by road or rail.

It was also during the 1960s that the Space

programme came into its own. This was a decade of intense competition with the Russians who had been the first to launch a man into space. In 1969, American efforts paid off when the United States became the first country to land a man on the moon. In July of that year, American astronauts Neil Armstrong and Edwin ('Buzz') Aldrin, members of a three-man expedition on the spaceship *Apollo 11*, became the first people to set foot on the moon. All around the world, people watched the event on their television screens. By enabling astronauts to travel to the moon, the Americans had shown how incredible had been their progress in transport and travel since the days of the invention of cable cars and streetcars around the beginning of the century.

The first flight by the Wright brothers.

Charles Lindberg, the first person to fly solo across the Atlantic in his plane, The Spirit of St Louis. The journey, which took place in May 1927, lasted 33 hours.

Chapter 79: Review

- In Ireland around 1900, people largely travelled on foot or by using horse-drawn transport, electric trams and trains.
- During the 1920s and 1930s, motor transport was becoming popular, and in 1944 CIE was set up.
- There were major changes in the area of transport from the 1960s on. In particular, air passenger travel greatly expanded.
- By 1900, the USA had a vast railway network. Cable cars and streetcars were also widely used.
- In 1908, Henry Ford produced his famous Model T motor car. By the 1920s the number of cars in the USA had greatly increased.
- The USA had also been the pioneer in terms of air travel. During the 1920s and 1930s, the American airline industry expanded rapidly.
- During the 1960s, the USA was to the forefront in the Space Age. In 1969, the USA became the first country to land men on the moon.